**WITHDRAWN
UTSA Libraries**

RENEWALS 458-4574
DATE DUE

ECONOMICS OF INTANGIBLES

ECONOMICS OF INTANGIBLES

GARY ZATZMAN
AND
RAFIQUL ISLAM

Nova Science Publishers, Inc.
New York

Copyright © 2007 by Nova Science Publishers, Inc.

All rights reserved. No part of this book may be reproduced, stored in a retrieval system or transmitted in any form or by any means: electronic, electrostatic, magnetic, tape, mechanical photocopying, recording or otherwise without the written permission of the Publisher.

For permission to use material from this book please contact us:
Telephone 631-231-7269; Fax 631-231-8175
Web Site: http://www.novapublishers.com

NOTICE TO THE READER

The Publisher has taken reasonable care in the preparation of this book, but makes no expressed or implied warranty of any kind and assumes no responsibility for any errors or omissions. No liability is assumed for incidental or consequential damages in connection with or arising out of information contained in this book. The Publisher shall not be liable for any special, consequential, or exemplary damages resulting, in whole or in part, from the readers' use of, or reliance upon, this material.

This publication is designed to provide accurate and authoritative information with regard to the subject matter covered herein. It is sold with the clear understanding that the Publisher is not engaged in rendering legal or any other professional services. If legal or any other expert assistance is required, the services of a competent person should be sought. FROM A DECLARATION OF PARTICIPANTS JOINTLY ADOPTED BY A COMMITTEE OF THE AMERICAN BAR ASSOCIATION AND A COMMITTEE OF PUBLISHERS.

LIBRARY OF CONGRESS CATALOGING-IN-PUBLICATION DATA

Islam, Rafiqul, 1959-
 Economics of intangibles / Rafiqul Islam and Gary Zatzman, editor.
    p. cm.
 Includes index.
 ISBN 13 978-1-60021-316-8
 ISBN 10 1-60021-316-2
 1. Intangible property--Economic aspects. I. Zatzman, Gary. II. Title.
 HF5681.I55.I85
 338.5--dc22

2006
2006019801

Published by Nova Science Publishers, Inc. ✣ *New York*

CONTENTS

Preface		vii
Introduction		1
Chapter 1	The Tangible-Intangible Nexus	9
Chapter 2	Intangibles in the Big Picture: The Delinearised History of Time	39
Chapter 3	Intangibles in the Big Picture, Continued: Information Technology and the Global System	101
Chapter 4	Tangibles in the Big Picture	158
Chapter 5	The Aphenomenal Model	235
Chapter 6	The New Synthesis	291
Chapter 7	Conclusion	355
References and Bibliography		357
Index		385

PREFACE

Up to now, economics as a branch of social science has been concerned mainly to map the commercial and financial relations of Humanity, including a wide variety of institutions spawned to sustain livelihoods within these relations. Although these relationships, *qua* relations, are by definition intangible, the forms by which these relations are expressed – and in which they may even be quantified, predicted and managed – are all tangible. Thus we arrive at the tantalising paradox wherein, for economists, tangibles seem to occupy the entire space of interest, even though that which has given rise to their very field in the first place are actually social relations that remain utterly intangible.

Always and everywhere, the tangible is also quantifiable. However, lifting this veil uncovers something very strange. To the extent that tangible economic activity takes quantifiable form, it is possible to generalise about the forms themselves and-or to verify them, without reference to any further information as to the intent, conscience or consciousness of those who gave rise to these activities in the first place. This elimination of "subjective factors", such as intention, was long trumpeted as the economists' greatest success (as social "scientists") – but is it?

We live today in what is commonly called the Information Age. One of its outstanding features is the extremely powerful extension that the rapid spread of digital information technology has given to an already lengthy historic process of ever-increasing socialisation of material production. Today there remains no populated area on earth where modern industrial production, low-tech or medium-tech or high-tech, cannot be introduced and undertaken. There are two important corollaries to this rather astonishing fact.

First, it challenges a particularly long-held assumption among many disposed to defend the status-quo, that industrialised commodity production could expand and coexist eternally with a global condition in which there would always be highly advanced and extremely backward countries and peoples, so long as the latter forever remain subjects of and chained to the former.

Secondly, it also challenges an equally long-held assumption among many working to overturn the status-quo, that such an acceleration would not occur without first putting an end to what were viewed as essentially master-slave arrangements. Such has been the cunning of history that, precisely in order to save itself from the fate of the former Soviet Union and its bloc, the U.S.-led bloc embraced the Information Age. Thus has it come to pass that our world's highly globalised system, in what might be described as its post-bipolar phase, has either – depending on one's point of view – released the genie from its bottle, or unlocked Pandora's box...

Although modernisation of the scale of industrial production began just before the First World War and raced ahead for a time, particularly in Russia following the Bolshevik Revolution, subsequent developments proved halting and incomplete, and in some parts of the globe, most recently in the Soviet bloc, there was even utter collapse. At the same time, however, wars on a genocidal scale and other social injustices that used to embrace small countries and perhaps limited regions now envelop entire continents. This suggests the arrival of the Information Age has not in itself been sufficient to reform, correct or end ongoing social and economic injustices. Instead, the current world stage is characterized by a welter of ideological confusion.

In the middle of the 1800s, the British Empire stood literally on top of the world. With the exception of Antarctica, British industry and commerce backed by the Foreign Office and Colonial Office controlled territories on all continents. Its banking, shipping and mercantile systems dominated transoceanic and world trade. Its industrial products dominated markets globally. However, it was not maintaining this position on the basis of fostering innovation. Rather, it found ways and means to turn scientific discoveries into products and to leverage its superior means of projecting its presence across oceans and continents to connect these products to markets far beyond the British Isles. This vending and re-vending of more of the same old wine in new bottles reinforced an appearance that Great Britain, with its parliamentary system, apparent social stability and vigorous and global industry and commerce, represented a new developmental stage in the evolution of human civilization. Within this environment, there appeared two profound challenges to the established order of thought, led by Karl Marx in the field of economic and social science and Charles Darwin in the field of natural science. They shared in common a line of thinking which had emerged sharply yet entirely naturally in response to the vast changes being wrought across the European continent since the mid-1700s by both the industrial revolution and, later, the French Revolution. This was thinking to the effect that the unchanging stasis of the old pre-industrial and pre-republican order was doomed. It was an atmosphere in which the idea of the necessity and inevitability of change had become as natural as breathing. Marx as a social scientist and Darwin as a natural scientist worked without reference to one another, in unrelated fields, and held very different views as to the desirability of the contemporary *status quo* to boot. Nevertheless, with each of them, the notion that meaningful innovation and understanding of the world required taking change into account as something consequential, rather than assuming it to be aberrational or an exception to the natural order, was practically instinctual. In this, they were not unique. Throughout the 19th century, the ranks of scientists, researchers, writers, industrialists and politicians were driven by a huge divide that opened among all their ranks over this question of the necessity and inevitability of change. However, Marx and Darwin in particular drew the wrath of the established social and religious orders respectively when they asserted that change had come and would continue to come regardless of anything the established order could do or might say about it.

Through this fog, there has run a common thread, the thread concerned with the increasingly urgent role for conscience and consciousness in daily life, in economic activity, and in the affairs of Humanity-at-large. This book uncovers and explores this thread and its role throughout the contemporary social fabric, focusing particularly on the role of social conscience and of something we call "human factor / social consciousness" in economic life and economic forms. In this work, it is adduced that further acceleration of the socialisation of production in the specific conditions of the Information Age, unaccompanied by requisite transformations away from the currently highly-privileged manner in which Humanity's wealth is appropriated by a tiny few, may be guaranteeing only something so one-sided as to become inherently unsustainable. Humanity is left with its conscience being rankled by two very large questions: first, if matters indeed are continuing on this path, are we in danger of witnessing, sooner rather than later, social and economic disasters on a quasi-planetary scale directly endangering entire continents; and second, if the means are indeed at hand for Humanity itself to save the situation, can any conscious, sentient member of our species seriously contemplate such a prospect with equanimity?

Halifax, Canada
18 November 2005

INTRODUCTION

It seems absurd on its face: "economics" and "intangibles" yoked together in the same title. Do such things exist in daily life, and if so, how do such matters pose themselves?

One view, widely popularised in recent years through the works of popular writers like Naomi Klein (2002) and by many economists inspired by the classic work of the late John Kenneth Galbraith (1967), sees actual costs, including ongoing costs, of great economic disasters – especially those involving great pollution burdens added to the waters, the ground or the atmosphere, as well as bankruptcies of major projects important to social development – as an important uncounted, and in that sense intangible, cost of unregulated, uncontained and purely profit-driven "development". Conventional economics refers rather moralistically to these costs as "externalities", meaning unintended or unplanned costs, and – being unplanned – not fair to assign responsibility for to the corporate or commercial interests that gave them rise (Friedman 196?). Mysteriously, conventional economics expresses no moral qualms whatsoever about any of the privately-appropriated profits, surpluses or revenues occasioned by society's responses to such events as pirated booty that – following this same logic – ought to be disgorged from the control of those who usurped it and placed under social control for societal purposes. One recent documentary, *The Corporation* (2004), makes a case for revisiting the legal person-hood enjoyed by modern corporate entities with a view to limiting their freedom to continue foisting the costs of all these "externalities" onto the rest of society. At the same time, countering even this extremely limited prospect for optimism, an entire body of writings largely inspired by Paul A. Baran and Paul Sweezy's *Monopoly Capital* (1965) suggests rather more darkly that the portion of the surplus generated especially as so-called "waste" revenues utterly incidental to productive`e investment, and arising precisely from costs that are shunted aside as "externalities", has come to bulk so large that the economic system cannot do without it. In effect, according to this view, the corporate sector has hijacked the rest of society and rendered it complicit in finding ways to continue to sustain the inherently unsustainable.

The standpoint of the present work is that the matter is important enough to command a major research effort on a far greater scale than has been mounted to date, but in the end human social problems have human social solutions. In order to open the path on which such research can accomplish fruitful discoveries, the starting point adopted here is to chart what would be a useful and meaningful "economics of intangibles", a social science of those wellsprings and pathways of phenomena operating beyond our immediate view or ability to detect directly. Of course every kind of crackpot conspiracy theorist will offer something sounding similar, but this work diverges from the method of conspiracy theorising in at least one overwhelmingly crucial respect: regardless of whether the intentions of the various economic actors are long-term or short-term, the consequences of their actions are both long-term and short-term and the time-scale on which such analysis therefore needs to be conducted and solutions proposed must take the long-term into account, both historically to the present and from the present looking to the future.

The matter of path is important. It is often the case when disasters or serious reversals befall that people start looking for any intangible factors at work, but a science of "economics of intangibles" cannot confine itself to documenting the consequences of "externalities" or to taking stands within the above-mentioned spectrum of limited-optimism to darkest-pessimism. If the new departure being proposed here is indeed scientific, its analytical and predictive methods should produce useful, objective output regardless of whether one is proceeding from the inside of a corporation planning the response to some disaster and the post-disaster course of policy, or from the outside as a student, observer or researcher of these phenomena. Consider in this connection the catastrophic sinking of the Ocean Ranger offshore oil drilling rig in the stormy waters of the northwest Atlantic Ocean off the island of Newfoundland in February 1982, and the resultant loss of scores of lives.[1]

The government of the Canadian province of Newfoundland conducted a judicial inquiry chaired by the Chief Justice of the province's Supreme Court, Alex Hickman, a former Justice minister in the provincial government and long-time politician. His report eventually recommended offshore oil exploration companies take legal responsibility for outfitting their rig personnel with personal-flotation-device wetsuits and seeing that this and other safety measures were strictly followed. Even though the inquiry itself cleared the onboard safety committee and onboard safety arrangements and drill procedures of any responsibility in the *Ocean Ranger*'s sinking, the intangible message sent by this recommendation was that the rig workers would hereafter share some potential liability alongside their employer. Once the rig was deemed to have been demolished by a rogue wave, neither this inquiry nor the companies involved with the drilling project ever proceeded subsequently to model either its actual physical failure or the "how and why" of the particular conditions of the storm in which the rig and its crew perished. The lack of such failure modeling and of any legal compulsion to do so sent a further intangible message to the effect that operators would continue to enjoy a certain impunity to maintain an undeclared "reign of terror" over rig workers' lives, and this not on the high seas but within the 200-mile exclusive economic zone maintained under Canadian federal government jurisdiction. In addition to the incalculable but intangible human losses to the families and communities affected by these deaths, the extreme narrowing of operators' liability to a very specific safety question bolstered the impunity that these operators would continue to enjoy with respect to the entire body of safety and labour regulations administered by the provincial government – yet another intangible.

---

[1] The horrific details are dispassionately recounted in full in (Hickman 1984). Here this event will serve as the metaphor and template for many other disasters including the December 2004 tsunami in the eastern Indian Ocean, the earthquake disasters of recent years along the central Asian plate from Georgia to Turkey to Iran and Pakistan, the sinking of New Orleans into the Gulf of Mexico in the wake of Hurricane Katrina in August 2005, the bombing of the King David Hotel in Jerusalem by the 'Irgun' terror gang in 1948, the destruction of the World Trade Centre on 11 September 2001, the London bus and tube bombings of 7 July 2005, the hotel "suicide" bombings in Amman, Jordan of 9 November 2005, etc.

Along with these intangibles come a range of "hidden" or "unaccounted" costs, and at least four questions into which this inquiry chose not to inquire and which no one has since inquired:

1) what was foreseen and acted on in advance;
2) what was foreseen and not acted upon, perhaps even suppressed;
3) what emerged after-the-fact that was not foreseen but might conceivably have been foreseen; and
4) what emerged that was unforeseen and contributed new knowledge.

As a first-level summary, then, it emerges that there exists a great deal, in connection with major economic, financial decisions, processes which are sloughed off as "managerial problems" but that are, or were, inherent in original decision(s) to proceed and the implementation of said decision(s), or that is incorporated after-the-fact as a cost-determining or profit-targeting factor in future projects and decisions. All these together form one part of what may be called "economic intangibles" as seen from a cost-accounting standpoint. The nature of the "intangibility" of these four elements consists in the fact that they are in fact each highly tangible-in-themselves, but elude one's grasp when it comes time to comprehend their role and where they fit in the larger picture.

Many financial operations, and the particulars of their pathways, have become particularly murky and intangible in this sense. Most notoriously within this category are the operations of so-called mutual funds. These are supposed to redistribute investment risks such that investors can still come out ahead even if certain stocks and bonds at certain times undergo reversals. This notion in itself stands unremarked, perhaps so as not to draw attention to a scam of the kind that a more openly racist Eurocentric world routinely used to blame on "Persian rug merchants" and "Arab traders" but taking place on a far more lucrative scale. Exacerbating the problem is disinformation purveyed both from government and the corporate sector concerning the secrecy/confidentiality rules supposedly designed to insulate certain client investors' information from being misused against other client investors by funds managers operating as middlemen. Repeatedly, experience discloses how these confidentiality rules are manipulated mainly to protect from regulatory scrutiny the ongoing operation of a game of chance offered to outsiders but entirely rigged by insiders, like any casino. Mutual funds' operations are now annually investigated by the Ontario Securities Commission (OSC). In 2003 the OSC found things wrong and contacted various mutual funds but kept the identities secret and unpublished. In 2004 again it found things and proceeded in the same manner. Noting the OSC's express wish that maintaining this confidentiality would encourage wrongdoers to "improve" next year, one financial columnist commented sarcastically: "Just like last year" ("Feed The Goat" 2004). The columnist dared not wield Occam's Razor – perhaps out of fear of whose throat might be slit – and state the obvious conclusion: that the entire sector remains murky and suspect as long as the OSC proceeds in this manner. Nor did he dare suggest that perhaps serious investors should consider pulling the plug on such investments unless either the newspaper column, or the fund in question, or both, come clean as to the OSC's findings. The disinformation surrounding all the official secrecy should not distract a dispassionate rational investigator from asking the obvious question: how is a mutual fund's sales pitch offering a "no lose" proposition to be believed as true or even possible in the first place? Rendering the pathway to achieving "something for nothing" more intangible does not erase the intention to acquire something for nothing. On the other hand, exposing this intention from the outset would have brought into the open all the questions that need to be asked before money is tossed down a sinkhole for the benefit of people who do not wish you well.

The above examples are adduced to illustrate how the intangible element is ever present regardless of the elaborate efforts undertaken to "disappear" it like some unwelcome protestor in the main square of the capital of some seedy dictatorship. Apart from disastrous, catastrophic or otherwise-fraught outcomes, meanwhile, in daily life there is another entire class of economic intangibles that are truly intangible.

If the sledding already seems tough for an "economics of intangibles" at the level of the relatively straightforward daily-life examples just discussed, consider what becomes involved when the central, prime problem of intangibility in economics at the level of theory is addressed, *viz.*, the explanation of use-value, or utility.

"In the literature" (of formal academic economics), notions of use-value and utility have long been linked with – and, we will argue, improperly and unjustifiably reduced and restricted to – the question of the so-called "theory of marginal utility". This theory underpins what is known as "neoclassical economics", microeconomic theory, theories of "consumer sovereignty" and some other areas.

Historically, this theory of marginal utility was actually linked with and became embedded in the industrialisation of the colonial system by the British manufacturing class in the middle of the nineteenth century (Zatzman *et al.* 2003; Islam and Zatzman 2004, 2005a and 2005b). With this, there arose an attendant necessity to ensure, as well as justify, the monopolisation of all profitable and potentially profitable energy sources and resources in the hands of this class.

This process is marked by three (3) important features:

1) coal sources / resources and technologies defined all prospects and possiblilities for development, as these were all or largely in British hands; other energy forms were dismissed (Jevons 1865)
2) development / maintenance / expansion of the energy source base was defined as a function of the trading system and associated infrastructure for moving goods to markets (Jevons: ibid; Zatzman and Islam 2005); and
3) markets were defined according to an intangible yet "mathematisable" criterion of so-called "marginal utility" (Mosselmans 1999)

Thus, at a second level of summation, the following can be stated: while concealing (in and at the marketplace) the links of finished-goods sellers to capitalisation of the production of these same goods in the first place, this approach inherently disenfranchises buyers of commodities (in and at the marketplace) of any role other than that of "consumer". This process marginalises and even makes disappear the other economic role to which this system had already consigned the vast majority of society. That role is one of mere sellers of their labouring power as a commodity, in the form of "labour-time". The terms of sale are dictated by owners of capital acting as a class. This social fragment can be said to constitute a class in two senses. First, it is the collective owner of the society's means of production which alone can unleash the value-addable as the result of application of the living labour of this social, collective labour-power at the capitalists' disposal. Second, as a class of individual enterprises/entrepreneurs, it is their mutual competition which establishes the socially-necessary quantities of labour-time to be capitalised and requisitioned – as an outlay advanced against future production, and not as some cost merely incidental to the production process – in order to realize (and capture, and pocket) surplus-value. This surplus itself is the sole object of the entire organisation of this social mode of production in the first place.

Thus, the market as the temple of this economic system is not where buyer and seller actually encounter one another as equals. It is the place rather where highly unequal relations, relations that were actually established before they confront one another in the marketplace for the exchange of money against finished goods, become entrenched, cinched, rendered irreversible between "workers" and "capitalists" – meaning, generally, those who are in the market to sell their own labour power on the one hand and those who are in the market to advance some capital in their possession for the purpose of purchasing others' labour power on the other. On the one hand, workers must sell their creative labouring power, that special commodity unleashed as living labour which is uniquely capable of self-expansion of its value once harnessed to the dead labour of the capitalists' factory machinery. On the other hand, the capitalists are in the market not only as the principal purchasers of this commodity but also as sole appropriator of the surplus-value created entirely as a result of the application of this living labour to dead labour, *i.e.*, past labour accumulated in the form of machines and factories. (Zatzman *et al.*: *ibid.*).

Thus we arrive at what is actually the key moment of intangibles-transition, disguised as the act of exchange between "equals" in which a "demand" is satisfied by the "supply" of some desired use-value in the form of commodities. Supply and demand operate to regulate swings in one direction or the other within a certain range while certain conditions obtain. However, neither supply of labour-power and-or commodities, nor demand for labour-power or commodities, brings the marketplace into existence in the first place. Furthermore, contrary to the claims of the theory of marginal utility and all its illegitimate spawn, supply and demand do not and cannot mutually regulate one another. Acts of exchange, which appear the most tangible and definable – mathematically and every other way – are in fact the most mysterious, their systematic features hidden or misrepresented as individual "quirks" and the actual *modus operandi* of assigning, or mapping, value to these commodities in the form of a money-price is concealed behind the "averaging" of discrete individual acts of exchange into what appears to be a behavioural continuum of endlessly-repeated acts of consumption.

Not all acts of commodity exchange, then, are equal: there is a fundamental transaction that trumps subsequent related acts of exchange. When labouring power is sold, its buyer controls all the conditions in which that labouring power is to be employed. First: this labouring power is useful in very different ways to the individual with labouring power to sell on the one hand and the individual or company with capital to purchase it on the other. The labourer could produce purely for himself or his family or extended relations, or in cooperation with other labourers provide all their various needs collectively as the result of combined labours. Such collective approaches could also settle the matter of the conditions in which the combined creative labouring powers of the entire society are employed. In principle, the functions inserted by the Gentlemen of Capital need not be considered unique or exclusive to those possessing money for their employment. The problem is in the pathway: once this first act of exchange takes place, it is irreversible. Its effect cannot be cancelled by some subsequent counter-transaction, like entering a credit in an accounting ledger to balance a debit. This transaction has, completely intangibly, handed over and subjugated the labour-power (sold as undifferentiated labour-time, rather than as such-and-such a specialised skill) to the forces that command not only capital with which to purchase that labouring power but also all the conditions in which that labouring power will be employed. Considered as a phenomenon of economic behaviour, the essence of intangibility is whether human individual and social needs, or some other force, end up directing the combination of tangible means and sources of value, on the one hand, with residual powers over the conditions in which, and by which, these means and these sources give rise to value, on the other. (These "residual powers" include many of the items consigned to the "externalities" category but misleadingly labeled "non-economic" because of their intangibility.)

Restarting investigation of economic theory from such a vantage point makes it possible to renovate some badly run-down parts of this edifice. Classical and neoclassical theory were obsessed with the problem of accounting for economic profit and the societal surplus generated as a result of the production of commodities by means of labour bought and sold as the special commodity labour-time. From the standpoint of elaborating an economics of intangibles, the most meaningful understanding to have concerning profits or surpluses is that of waste. Waste can be converted – with knowledge based on research, and rationally managing time with the intention of achieving results that are sustainable for the long-term – into production that ensures that basic needs are looked after on a society-wide scale rather than as some chaotic scramble by individuals to beggar their neighbours. Spending profits and surpluses on non-productive outlets, on the other hand, will both make the waste pile grow and induce a huge parasitism on the entire economic mechanism. This has already been seen in the massive diversion of the economic surplus into stock markets, where the prospect of consuming without producing takes precedence in the short term and a dangerous kind of amnesia fogs the brain of even the most knowledgeable about the fact that in the longer term, that which has not been produced cannot be distributed and, therefore, continuing to consume without producing must lead to a massive crash. The other devastating outlet for this waste spending, of course, has been the machineries of war and aggression imposed by Great Powers on the weakest and most vulnerable countries. Thus, for example, the increase alone in the 2004-05 budget for the U.S. Department of Defence was more than the combined military budgets of all its NATO partners, and the total budget before allowing for expenditures in Iraq and Afghanistan war theatres was more than the entire military spending of all other countries in the world combined (Bilmes and Stiglitz 2006).

Why has this introduction been designated "Chapter Zero"? On the east coast of Canada, at the city of Halifax, one of the main highways has an off-ramp which has been designated Exit 0. Exit 1 and all subsequent junctions of this highway have both an on-ramp and an off-ramp; uniquely, Exit 0 however has only an off-ramp. It was added decades after the highway's original construction at a point about half a kilometer from starting-ending point of the highway to provide a convenient exit directly into the regular city street system separately from the highway's highly congested and extremely busy exit-entrance. Doubtless the exit was numbered "0" because "1" was already taken; but the absence of an on-ramp that would normally have complemented the off-ramp unexpectedly disclosed an interesting metaphor for so labeling this exit.

All other numbers in the "Real" numbers are positive or negative, as all integers exist in complementary pairs; 0 uniquely is neither. However, it is when 0 and 1 together are examined and compared that some truly peculiar behaviours manifest themselves. The product of multiplication by zero is defined always to be 0, no matter the multiplicand; the product of multiplication by 1 is the multiplicand itself. However, the moment one attempts to map the purely theoretical notion of a binary operation called multiplication on some member-numbers of the Real-number field to actual physical quantities, the contradictions scream out. Multiplying any physical quantity by one is not, physically, an act of multiplication. Physically speaking, multiplying some quantity by zero also means no multiplication was performed, but instead of the multiplicand remaining unchanged, as it did when "multiplying by 1", it becomes zero! Similarly, by the rules of the algebraic structure known as the real field, the addition of 0 to or its subtraction from any other real number leaves the original number unchanged; 0 is therefore called the "identity operator" for addition and subtraction just as 1 is called the identity operator for multiplication of member-numbers of this field. Physically, however, addition or subtraction with zero means no addition or subtraction took place. Finally, there is the anomaly of the quotient resulting from division by 0, which as a matter of theoretical definition of the rules of this binary operation in this algebraic structure (and all others), is "undefined". Again, mapping this to physical reality, division by zero is oxymoronic: it is division by that which does not divide, that which forms no part of any physical number and represents, physically speaking, the absence of number. The thesis from which the present work proceeds is that contradictions of this type are symptomatic of the existence of intangibles; that is why the obvious absence of number can be assigned a number, 0, with special rules of operation that govern no other number, and why – similarly – the number that signifies absence of any presence of something in quantity (beyond the mere fact of its existence) can also be assigned its special number, *viz.*, 1, with its special rules as well. Far from being merely "constructed" merely as the result of apparently attempting to compare apples with oranges, these contradictions indicate that whatever it is that links apples to oranges, or that could be said to be shared in common by them, is intangible in the sense of inaccessible to us.[2]

The foremost set of questions addressed in the present work concern the nature and roles of time and of knowledge as key intangibles in all fields of science, economics included.

In the first chapter, the mutual inter-penetration of tangible and intangible factors and elements is examined in order to establish a basic guideline, which is that while each set of factors conditions the other, knowledge of the intangible factors and the roles they play is decisive for mastering economic and related social and political phenomena and putting both the tangible and intangible factors to the socially most beneficial use.

---

[2] This is where we leave Cantor's infinitely-denumerable sets behind. Thanks to Cantor's elaboration of "transfinite sets", it is not a source of inconsistency to treat the Real numbers as an infinitely dense continuum of numbers, so long as we can map each such number, one after the other, into another number. The issue raised here, however, is different: in some special cases of operations with certain numbers, the intentions and requirements of these operations cannot be transferred willy-nilly from the theoretical realms of mathematics to practical applications without redefining their intention in the practical application. To assert the existence of a result and the legitimacy of the operation that produced it on the basis of assuring membership in some transfinite set does not bridge this gap. An exciting discussion of some other gaps that Cantor's theory bridged or failed to bridge runs between the covers of (Wallace 2003).

Within mathematics, this is very much in the arena of what has become known as "non-standard analysis" based on the so-called "set of the hyper-real numbers" (Robinson 1966; Goldblatt 1998; Dales and Woodin 1996; Gilman and Jerison 1960). The "hyperreal set" is a generalisation of the values on the Real line lying between 0 and 1, somewhere in the interval $[0+\varepsilon, 1-\varepsilon]$ which excludes both 0 and 1, according to the understanding of 0 representing absolute certainty that something cannot be, and 1 representing absolute certainty that it can, and is (Keisler 1976). Its practical applications in the theory of mathematical probability would seem to represent a kind of shame-faced acknowledgment of the intangibility with which the authors are wrestling throughout the present work.

In the second, third and fourth chapters, the "big picture" – first, of intangibles in Chapters Two and Three and then of tangibles in Chapter Four – is examined with reference to important, but buried and misinterpreted, pieces of significant economic history as well as of the development and application of various leading-edge technologies. One long-buried piece is the disastrous destruction, wrought overwhelmingly in a 40-year span following the end of the Second World War, of the vast fish resources of the northwest Atlantic. This resource had been developed originally to feed the transatlantic slave trade, laying the foundations for European colonisation of the New World (Innis 1954). It was sustained as both an international and coastal fishery throughout that 300-year saga and for more than another century following President Lincoln's Emancipation Proclamation. Excavating in detail a serious misrepresentation of this tragedy and the defects in the theory underlying the misrepresentation, a textbook lesson is drawn of the consequences that flow from failing to provide a proper appreciation of the role of historical time as a key intangible. Chapter Two deconstructs certain large deficiencies in a widely-touted "radical alternative" body of economic theory in order to show that, when it comes to analysing / modeling system failure and pointing the way to pro-Nature alternatives that could enable humanisation of the environment in which fisheries of comparable scale are conducted, it is as incapable as the theory it would replace. Continuing on the theme of intangibles in the "big picture", Chapter Three examines the technologies of our current "information age" which promised liberation from drudgery but forged new chains by taking knowledge gathered in the search for truth and shattering it into information bits and bytes available under one or another regime of controlled release, *i.e.*, dictate. Just how precious human knowledge itself has become as a key intangible of economic development is seen in the titanic struggle over humanising the environment in which the further development of the Internet/World Wide Web has become embroiled. Chapter Four discusses the historical evolution of the "energy crisis" showing how those positioned to dominate development and exploitation of non-renewable sources moved mountains to obstruct development of renewable or other sources of energy outside their control

In the fifth and sixth chapters, the aphenomenal model in the realm of economic development is elaborated with an emphasis on the grave dangers posed for Humanity by its inherently anti-Nature and thus unsustainable essence, offering nothing but the deadliest of toxic dead ends, and then some potentially fruitful avenues of research and investigation countering this trend are discussed. While Chapter Five goes into the details of the aphenomenal model that implements the anti-Nature program and shackles Humanity in its train, Chapter Six discusses new possibilities from the field of energy pricing for shifting and rearranging the processing, refining and supply of energy sources to a pro-Nature basis that holds out the twin promise of technological breakthroughs favouring adoption of inherently sustainable practices as well as the prospect of preserving the natural environment by further humanising it.

Some conclusions are drawn in the final chapter. The appendices go into some detail on certain important subjects that are raised only in passing earlier in the book. The central position is that humanising the environment constitutes the liberation economics of intangibles for a modern world in which the human factor/social consciousness can, at last, exercise its leading role: going with Nature, rather than against, and empowering people immediately and first and foremost in their actual, living social collectives.

Chapter 1

THE TANGIBLE-INTANGIBLE NEXUS

ABSTRACT

The central animating idea of this chapter is that all tangibles have intangible components. This fact, as well as any of the relationships between a tangible and its intangibles, encounters continual attack from all-sided disinformation. Even if the fact of the existence of some intangible within some tangible phenomenon is acknowledged, one may be unable to make any sense or use of this fact. This latter phenomenon of powerlessness is the symptomatic indicator that disinformation is alive and well, and that people are being or becoming "disinformed".

From this starting-point, certain fundamental notions of economics in their tangible and intangible aspects are recapitulated. This brings out some of the ways in which disinformation does its work of stopping people from being able to use this knowledge positively for the benefit of society and Humanity. In particular, for this purpose, the misrepresentation of the category of "value" is revisited.

Uniquely and for the first time, this examination:

1. elaborates the disinformational quality inherent in the theory of supply and demand, pointing out its silence about the environmental and social underpinnings of wealth in Nature and Labour;
2. puts into proper historical context its reduction of the value category to the subjective whim of individuals averaged over countless random transactions; and, finally,
3. brings out – from the example of the life and work of William Stanley Jevons – how an implicitly subjective theory of value distorted the nature of Britain's coal supply crisis in the middle third of the 19th century for the purpose of generating a self-serving conclusion. The patent absurdity of the conclusion – that there was no alternative to dependence on coal as the primary energy source – would become exposed only much later. Meanwhile, the logical process that gave rise ot the conclusion was being reapplied in numerous other contexts as "accepted" and "authoritative" "economic theory".

In this manner, both the fundamental disinformation which underpins the entire gamut of generally-accepted definitions, as well as notions said to constitute the proper concern and field of economic study which have this misrepresentation of the value category as their starting-point, are exposed. The decrepit state of public transport in southeast England after years of Thatcherite privatization is adduced as a simple concluding example of where this ends up. This reference is deliberately inserted in order to introduce the Thatcherite notion that "there is no alternative" to the status-quo. This so-called "TINA syndrome" provides the fundament, the actual rock, on which the political, economic, military and other elites and establishments of the Anglo-American world and European bloc have built their church, inscribed with its motto that "there is no god but monopoly and maximum is his profit". From this base, continuous attacks are launched on the very concept of intangibles, which forms the subject matter of Chapter 2.

1.0. INTRODUCTION

Economics as a science in the "Western", *i.e.*, European, canons of knowledge originates in the Greek word and conception of *οικονομεια*, or "household". It had to do with organisation of the highest and best uses of the resources available to the household for meeting the needs of its members. This sense is retained most fully today in the Russian term *хозяиство* ("khozyaistvo"), which means "economics" and "household" (depending on context), and such Soviet-era neologisms as *колхоз* ("kolkhoz"), short for *коллективное хозяиство* ("kollektivnoye khozyaistvo" or "collective farm", *i.e.*, collective household economic unit) (Chernenko and Smirtyukov 1967).

Where any U.S.-type economic system – the model touted globally in our day – stands in relation to this concept is disclosed by the terminology pioneered for the post-Soviet period by President Clinton, his Secretary of Labour Robert Reich and his Secretary of the Treasury Robert Rubin. Each of them transformed the grammar and meaning of the word "economy" in the English language with their discourse about "growing the economy". For a modern U.S.-type economic system, "economy" is cinched to growth, and anything less than some continuous level of growth is deemed unsustainable. Implicit in this viewpoint is the idea that economics is all about tangible goods or services. Growth is the measure of society's progress in making more goods and services more available, and moreover in all the forms people expect.

Regardless of Soviet Russia's abandonment decades earlier of the achievements of a collectively-based and collectively-developed economic existence, for as long as the Soviet Union existed, its originating model continued to hold out promise to many countries and peoples around the globe. When the Soviet bloc imploded during 1989-1991, many of the forces that routinely used to defend this stance abandoned the battlefield of ideas. This was the moment that opened the way for the current "all private economy all the time" discourse to monopolise the strongest positions. This discourse, regenerated by Ronald Reagan and Margaret ("there is no such thing as 'Society'...") Thatcher, reached its acme of refinement during the Clinton administration.

Clearly this did not and could not take place on the basis of any process of rational argument and persuasion. Rather, it was stampeded into public social discourse using every manner of means in media, political advertising and you-name-it to overwhelm all those maintaining any other viewpoints. However, mere external imposition of force would not have won the day if the forces available to defend what had previously been widely accepted had not been caught off guard and their reactions either paralysed or rendered totally ineffective. These ideas about how to construct and maintain collective societal livelihood had not been hatched on the fly but developed both in theory and practice through the preceding six and half decades.

If the ideas themselves were not refuted, and the defenders fled and abandoned the field before there was any threat of physical extermination, what else could account for the result? These symptoms point to massive disinformation being at work. The entire section of society interested in defending these ideas had become disinformed, like the reaction of a body paralysed by a stun-weapon or any other external force capable of rendering the limbs unable to articulate properly.

What is most correct and necessary about the collective economic forms of what has been called "the social economy"? It is to be found in the relationship between what is intangible within and about any tangible economic product or category. By rendering conscious and explicit all information about the connections of the intangible to the tangible, society's members acquire the means to assess rationally what to keep and what to junk in their collective best interest. Every other approach has proven and continues to prove itself unsustainable. Every other approach that selects the short-term over the long term, instead of developing for the long-term in order to secure both the short-term and long-term interests of Humanity, is bound to fail. In this chapter, the links, or "nexus", of the tangible and intangible are discussed, and much that is murky clarified, by exposing disinformation and how it has been spread.

1.1. THE PROBLEM OF DISINFORMATION[3] AND PEOPLE'S KNOWLEDGE OF SOCIAL EXISTENCE

Awareness of intangibility and its link to what is tangible has become one of the main targets of disinformation in our day. Knowledge of the intangible is a matter of science and research. Making use of this knowledge, on the other hand, is another matter. Consider the matter of interest rates. For some time it has been evident that the developing countries are falling further and further behind the developed world. They can't pay their debts, which continue to mount at compound rates of interest. Now it has come out in John Perkins' book appropriately entitled *Confessions of an Economic Hit-Man* (2004) that this situation has been deliberately engineered by the CIA and others to tie many of these countries very closely to the U.S. and its system.

Many observers involved in researching and writing about these matters have long known or strongly suspected what this book spells out in detail. So have considerable numbers of people from these countries. But where the revelations of this book were "news" – in North America – there was hardly a peep of reaction. How could this be?

---

[3] This topic and its contemporary historical conjuncture were thoroughly discussed at the *Halifax International Symposium on Media Disinformation* – the subject of a forthcoming book and ongoing project of which one of the present authors is organising secretary – convened at Dalhousie University 1-4 July 2004. Out of this event there emerged a working definition that provides a starting point for the modern theory of disinformation (Website 6). Some implications of modern disinformation for sustainability of engineered interventions in the natural environment are discussed in (M.I. Khan *et al.* 2005b).

This is the effect of disinformation. Even though the truth and reality is available and accessible, one must first be in a position to set aside the considerable number of lies and planted stories that are circulated alongside. Disinformation is recognisable not only by its content – in which planted stories predominate, followed by artful distortions of key parts of otherwise truthfully-reported news stories – but more especially by its effect, which is to render people incapable of taking action in their own best interests where such action would bring them into conflict with the leading imperial power and any of its friends. At this level, an attack is taking place on one's very cognition and understanding. One of the key targets of this assault is the connection between the intangible and the tangible and how people understand and use it.

The following figure summarises how disinformation is calibrated to operate on human memory and experience in very definite ways:

	Memory	Experience
Dependent on mediation?	Long-term or Historical: YES Short-term or Cognitive: NO	Cognitive or Individual: YES Collective: NO
Dependent on consciousness?	Visual or Cognitive: YES Non-Visual Perception: NO	YES

Figure 1-1. Fundamentals of the Memory-Experience Nexus – The representation of the memory-experience nexus formulated here is intended to facilitate discussion and analysis of how ***disinformation*** operates actually to disinform the individual. The table-matrix therefore specifies certain distinctions between "memory" and "experience" which are significant for evaluating, or taking into account, the potential or actual effects of, any source(s) of external mediation or any alteration of the individual's conscious state. In order better to distinguish *memory* (as both a form of knowledge retention, and a mechanism for its retrieval) from *experience* (as both the content of this knowledge, as well as the mode of its acquisition as data by the individual), here we treat as part of "memory" that which pragmatic and idealist philosophers and social psychologists often label "sense experience". "Mediated" experiences include experiences whose actual content is received and already-processed information. From this matrix, the specific forms and-or states of memory and-or experience that disinformation can affect are:
- long-term or historical memory that is externally mediated, *e.g.*, what we learn about historical or contemporary events from books or the media;
- visual or cognitive memories initially dependent on what the state of the individual's consciousness was when the memories were formed but subsequently externally processed;
- anything consciously experienced but subsequently unconsciously externally processed; and
- cognitive or individual experiences that are mediated.

Note that collective experience which is not mediated, *e.g.*, working life or participation in social or political affairs, as well as mediated short-term or cognitive memories and non-visual forms of perceptual memory, *e.g.*, data or findings received from others but not subjected to any other "processing" as well as similarly-unprocessed sounds, smells etc., appear relatively resilient. It is widely assumed that the rich and powerful have all the means at their disposal to have their way with people anywhere and at any time, whereas the people are utterly powerless to end or reverse their subordination to external forces. The standpoint developed from the matrix attacks the anti-scientific essence of that approach, and suggests forms and modes that people should strengthen and broaden in order to defeat disinformation attacks or hold them at bay.

1.2. TANGIBLE-INTANGIBLE NEXUS

The links of the intangible to the tangible can be very generally presented. A "topological space" of the tangible and the intangible can be said to have a certain defining condition: on the one hand, there are as many intangibles as there are abstract conceptions, or "abstractions". On the other hand, the number of tangibles is finite: it may be a very, very large number, even (seemingly) "infinite", but it is some (finite) number. However – most important – *there is no tangible without some, at least one, intangible element* attached to, or compounded within it. The following tangibility / measurability / quantifiability spectrum can be set forth:

	Physically incommensurable	Quantifiable
Tangible	to some degree NO	to large degree YES
Intangible	to large degree YES	to some degree NO

Figure 1-2. Tangibility / Measurability Matrix.

Reflecting the fact that there is a range, or spectrum, of possibilities involved, the above matrix incorporates two important corollary conditions:

1. the mere fact that an entity is *tangible* does not assure in or of itself that it can or will be quantified fully or properly, for example: elements of energy prices having nothing whatever to do with supply or demand; and
2. similarly, the fact that an entity as a function of its being *intangible* is physically incommensurable does not in or of itself foreclose whether it may nevertheless be quantified, for example: the "value-in-use", *i.e.*, for each of us, of some commodity.

A major pressure of disinformation in our own time is aimed at sowing confusion about these fundamental yet not obvious considerations by which all of us routinely link intangible components to the tangible that is immediately observed. A particularly rich example in economics concerns deciding what is a "value" and how people act on such a judgment or decision.

1.3. VALUE AS AN EXAMPLE OF AN ECONOMIC TANGIBLE-INTANGIBLE NEXUS

Economics as practical matter of living is always and everywhere about value: comparative value, value in terms of costs of production, value in terms of price. What could be more tangible? Value always has a number associated with it. However, a moment's reflection discloses a hole in this bucket. What is an item's value to its user or its purchasor? Can it always be quantified? And why is oil three to four cents a litre in Caracas but more than one dollar a litre in Calgary, the oil industry capital of Canada in the western province of Alberta and political base of the country's current Prime Minister Stephen Harper, a region no less central to massive oil and gas production than Caracas is in Venezuela? Of course it is easy to supply the usual explanations – a subsidy by the government here, so-called "free market" forces at work there, etc. But the problem remains in the sense that a definition of value has not been pinned down. There is the problem of value: it has both tangible and intangible form. It is no good to say it is all one or the other: it is both. Nor is it sometimes one and sometimes the other: on the contrary, their tangible and intangible forms are cinched, often indissolubly. It is not at all a trivial question, but rather one that goes profoundly to the heart of how Humanity earns its livelihood. It is indeed of such importance that, literally whether millions of people around the globe wake up the next morning or gather enough food and other material necessities to get to the next day depends on a correct understanding of the value nexus.

Modern economies are formed as a network of activities dominated by large-scale industry producing commodities by means of commodities. This includes the commodification of creative human labouring power as socially-averaged labour-time. These historically new and specific features of the social mode of production brought about by the factory system were first summarised in the mid-19th century on the basis not of an ideological prejudice but almost entirely from the relentless facts in the so-called "Blue Books" on working and living conditions in the new industrial towns, compiled by the English factory inspectors. Others, such as Piero Sraffa and the neo-Ricardians in our own time, continue to elaborate their implications.

From this perspective come two key points:

1. the inputs as well as the outputs of the production process are equally commodities; and
2. the decisive creative force and source of all value is human labouring power, but in order to capture that value in a profitable, i.e. surplus-accumulating, form, this labouring power must itself first be commodified.

Not all production is commodity production. Commodity production is a stage of production by society of goods more, and other, than those needed immediately for household use that gives rise to exchangeable or tradable products. Thus all commodities are tradable products. However, not all tradable products are commodities. Trade itself preceded the emergence of commodity production by several millennia. Commodity exchange gives rise to features that did not previously exist in the trade/exchange of mere products, such as the modern system of credit. The emergence of products trade, whether as barter or involving money exchange, indicates a level of social development in which some kind of surplus had begun to emerge episodically but not yet generally. The rise of commodity production was an indicator that society was now continually accumulating surplus products including surplus monies needed to facilitate their exchange. For anyone participating in the economy as a provider of Capital (rather than selling their labour-power), "Accumulate! Accumulate! That is Moses and the Prophets," one student of the pohenomenon pointed out (Marx 1867). The subtle distinction between a commodity and a product is that the former presupposes the existence of society and social needs whereas the latter does not.

Commodities contain, and as objects of exchange serve also as vessels of, "value". This is no longer "value" principally for individuals, however. Rather, it is social, it is averaged, and conceals in its material form, in its physicality and in its utility a social relation, *viz.*, a contradiction between the interests of the capitalist as employer of labour and owner of means of production on the one hand and the interests of the worker on the other hand with no commodity to sell but his labouring power. At the level of "value", this contradiction within the commodity appears as an antinomy between value-in-use and value-in-exchange. This is the first and central intangible of all modern economic existence.

1.3.1. Value in Use and Value in Exchange

Marx (*ibid.*) observed and investigated how this latter pair of value-concepts, use-value and exchange-value, form a dialectical unity, that is to say: a "unity" of opposites. They are united by virtue of the plain and simple, obvious physical and economic fact that they cannot be separated: they are bound up in each and every commodity. They are opposites in the sense that, during that period in which a commodity is off the assembly-line or out of the production facility, either being warehoused for delivery to market or in the market awaiting purchase, in its period of quasi-independent "existence" as a potential object of commercial exchange, its value-in-exchange will determine whether it ever acquires any actual value-in-use. Its value-in-use, its "utility" to any individual, is in fact non-existent and pointless to discuss until the commodity has been exchanged in the market for money (or by bartering some other acceptable equivalent in goods and-or services). Note the vectorial character – use and exchange. Note also the irreversible arrangement of the components of these vectors: there must be exchange before we can talk of utility. Whether the utility has any material economic consequence is contingent on money, a socially-accepted universal equivalent, changing hands as distinct from a privately-accepted bartered equivalent. Although widely eschewed by academic economists, again perhaps mostly as an outgrowth of opposition to the individual's politics, Marx's elaboration of the two kinds of value locked inside one and the same commodity remains unique in having captured a snapshot of the intangible essence lurking beneath the surface of the most commonplace physically tangible commodity.

Marx went even further to assert that revolutionary overturning of the established order by those at the bottom of society's heap was no terrorist conspiracy of social undesirables. Rather, his conclusion was that such a thing was a social expression of the necessity and inevitability of change. By contrast: nothing in Darwin's theory threatened the existing social, political or economic order. Darwin's theory of evolution was very extensively documented to establish how the emergence of different species of flora and fauna had most likely taken place. It stood much of the traditional understanding and interpretation of Christian scripture and religious belief on its head. Darwin's *Origin of Species* (1859) found no reason to believe that further evolutionary speciation was impossible, but a later work, *The Descent of Man*, did not render any opinion as to whether further development of the human species might not also take place. This opened the door for an entire trend in social science to emerge proclaiming that humans are the species fittest to survive in the animal kingdom because certain groups within the species, – not characteristic features, but entire groups – must have become better fitted for survival than others. This notion itself never formed any part of Charles Darwin's plan or intentions. However, it was to have huge consequences for commerce and industry in the United States and even more profoundly destructive consequences for European politics before and especially following the First World War. In social science, it gave rise to the theory of what is known as "social Darwinism." Darwin's theory never had anything to do with classifying peoples by the aphenomenal category of "race", or even by something authentic like ethnic origin. However, claiming through Darwin some connection with biology, another related theory emerged falsely as the basis for what became known as "scientific racism" and later by the name "eugenics". This theory became the basis for many schemes in North America involving the warehousing or segregation of poor and oppressed people, especially African Americans. The Nazi movement adapted eugenics for its own purpose, to justify physical extermination of gypsies, homosexuals, persons suffering mental illness, political opponents and members of the Jewish religion. As for social Darwinism: in commerce and industry, especially in the United States following the Civil War, gigantic industrial conglomerates seized control of large parts of the economy by ruthless undercutting of weaker competitors in the name of "survival of the fittest". In academic social theory this notion of "survival of the fittest" was already widely propagated in the works of Herbert Spencer (1857), a contemporary of Darwin's. Darwin's theory was converted by man into "scientific" evidence for Spencerian social views. This counterfeiting made it possible to spread public opinion that would justify the most brutal exploitation and plunder of colonies in Asia, Africa and Latin America as simply "Nature's way" of "improving the species". There was no interest whatsoever here in Darwin's extraordinarily careful use of scientific method and induction from evidence.[4]

1.3.2. Privatisation Demystified: Making Money Go 'Round and 'Round So it Comes Out... Here

Money is that universal equivalent which makes possible in the first place exchange as well as some value-in-use for the purchasor. One of the buzzwords spread in the 1980s by British Prime Minister Margaret Thatcher and U.S. President Ronald Reagan was "privatisation". This was a programmatic notion envisioning the selloff of profitable government-run operations (especially in the transport sector), as well as the abandonment of expensive bits of health care and education services, to private companies. Except for her most fanatical supporters, Thatcher's dismantling of British Rail has subsequently come to be acknowledged by all as an act of wanton destruction of public transport. While in opposition, the British Labour party described the Thatcherite reforms in health and education as "wrecking". The "new Labour" cabinets of Tony Blair, however, have not lifted a finger to undo or repair any of the wrecking, and have added a number of "anti-terrorist" excuses to criminalise any public resistance. In contrast to the rarified atmosphere surrounding much of the discussion about the principle of public versus private ownership, all this has taken place at the public's expense. The entire ideological "debate" over "public *versus* private" has served no practical purpose other than to paralyse the organising of any serviceable alternative. What happened with British privatisation clearly establishes, first, that the private sector maintains only those formerly public services that turn a profit and slough them off as soon as they lose money, and second, that the government only maintains public service

---

[4] Similarly, before Karl Marx died, there were no lack of schemes initiated by individuals claiming to be his followers that attempted to suppress the political-revolutionary content of his views – to such an extent that he was compelled to write his close collaborator Frederick Engels and point out frequently to others that "I am no 'Marxist'!" While the caricature of Darwin's theory remained useful to the established order, nothing of Marx's was. Meanwhile, at the start of the 21st century, the greatest irony has emerged today in the United States – the very birthplace of "social Darwinism" – whereby Darwin's scientific method itself is now targeted by many forces supporting the established order.

responsibilities where it has yet to figure out how to avoid or how to crush potential public resistance to further service cutbacks, whether under government or private management.

In the U.S., privatisation has been most extensively applied to turn the prison system of many states into profit centres for private corporations who broker the labour of inmates at absurdly cheap rates: brokers typically collect eight to 10 dollars for every 50 cents-an-hour of pay allotted the inmate worker.[5] The real issue obscured by this phoney "public-private debate" is whether the people who will need these services should control their management and availability, or some ruthless, self-interested private or public syndicate of gangsters. This gangsterism has been notably overt in post-Soviet Russia, where the oligarchs' takeover of large portions of the former Soviet state holdings in industry and agriculture has been stigmatised by Joseph Stiglitz, among others, as an exceptional case of "piratisation". Parodying the popular song about music traveling through the passageways of an instrument, in all; theses privatisation schemes, the money goes 'round and 'round 'til it comes out in the pocket of someone, somewhere in the private sector.

However, any distinction between good "privatisation" and bad "piratisation" seems moot. Before August 1991, when it was all still formally considered "state", *i.e.*, public, property, most of today's Russian oligarchs were Soviet state officials managing these same properties theoretically as state assets but in fact only for themselves and their friends. Again this brings out that the real issue is not whether the ownership and management takes the form of a government department or a private company, but rather whether the services themselves are actually controlled by those who use and need them. The careers of a number of former bright lights from Harvard University have been especially emblematic of the degree of corruption enmeshed in these problems and their real-world manifestations – especially U.S. involvements in "privatising" the former Soviet bloc. Thus for example, Harvard economist Jeffrey Sachs, who today sings loud public dirges alongside international pop-star celebrity Bono bemoaning the beggaring of the most impoverished states in Africa by Western aid-donor countries, organised the piratisation of the post-Soviet economy of Poland into the lap of a cabal of international banks close to the Clinton Administration. According to one account, the Harvard Institute for International Development (HIID) "eventually collapsed in scandal, when it was revealed that the principals of its Russian project, [including] Andrei Shleifer .. had been buying Russian stocks and dickering for the privilege of getting the country's first mutual fund license, while dispensing advice to the Russian government. ..Shleifer was one of the trinity of so-called Harvard *Wunderkinder* .. the other two were Lawrence Summers - and Sachs.." (Henwood 2005). At the end of February 2006, Summers was removed from the presidency of Harvard reportedly, in part, because of his shielding Schleifer from a U.S. government lawsuit seeking repayment of the estimated $30.0-million that these machinations had looted from the American taxpayer and HIID in the name of "accelerating privatisation of post-Soviet Russia."

The public-private "debate" thus has absolutely nothing to do, either, with the superiority or inferiority of public or private ownership or management and solely to do with increasing

---

[5] One of the biggest companies in this field was hardly a stranger to the method of inflicting a crushing level of exploitation by messing with people's rights Its former main line of business during the 1960s and 1970s was the supply of "replacement workers", or scab labour, during legal strikes by unionised workers. Before that, it was prominently involved in the "labour spy" racket: entrapping union organisers in compromising positions, occasionally arranging untimely disappearances or death of political and labour activists uncovering the truth about corporate criminal actions.

the profitable exploitation of vulnerable inmates, consumers and even entire countries. When these goods and services circulate purely in the public sphere, their exchange – even for money – retains the character of barter. Mere exchange by itself – such the effective barter of money wages and other operating expenses to those provisioning government-mandated social services, from public transport to prisons – does not create value-in-use of the kind that could be equated with what the economists call "effective demand". Exchange of *commodities* for money creates, or enables realisation of, value-in-use in a manner that further stimulates effective demand, whereas barter merely enables distribution of a wanted good to a willing or interested consumer. Public goods and-or services may have been produced and brought to the market as commodities, but their subsequent distribution and-or consumption by means of barter actually extinguishes their commodity character. They have only value-in-use. They therefore cease to represent value-in-exchange of the kind that is of interest to Capital, *viz.*, as a generator, or repository, of "effective demand" (meaning: the extension of further production of the said goods or services for the market).

There is a view, expressed widely in the media and academia, that disdains "government" while applauding "private enterprise". Government is excoriated as a parasitic drain on society's resources as well as an overbearing and interfering overlord in people's lives, while corporate enterprise on the other hand is lauded as everything government is not: the model of nimbleness, of timely response to real problems and a source of real, earned, just reward for actual work done. In reality, the modern corporation and modern government are indistinguishable in how they process a workflow from input to output. Each relies on committee structures to distribute responsibility for decisions taken, not to mention countless elaborate mechanisms for assembling the resources necessary for implementing them. Aversion to actual or potential liability or personal responsibility are endemic to both. All leadership in the end comes from the top down, and regardless of all the trappings of collegiality surrounding the highest executive levels of both, the job of leader in each is the loneliest of all. The absence of any accountability of higher levels to lower levels, combined with extreme concentration of all effective authority at the top of the pyramid, are surefire guarantees that the negative consequences of any dysfunctionality are massively multiplied throughout the organisation, paralysing some or most of the decision-taking organism before any fix can be effected. In government this situation is justified on the basis that only the elected politician has to render account; in business corporations, the upward-only direction of accountability is justified on the basis that whatever takes place is ultimately ruled in order or out of order by the company's shareholders. The former is the justification based on the notion that the affairs of government are public property. The latter is the justification based on the notion that the affairs of business are private property. However, the end result is the same: the public is and can be cheated, left without recourses or remedies or means to put them forward in either kind of corporate body. The ideological labels "private" associated with business and "public" associated with government have become poisoned with prejudices that no longer match or reflect the reality, which is that all such corporatised approaches which serve or operate to insulate participants from taking responsibility and learning from and correcting mistakes are utterly self-interested and self-serving, doing whatever is best for themselves before even considering what might be good for all.

Quite apart from anyone's political opinion as to the desirability or undesirability of privatisaion of social services in general, the following must be acknowledged regarding the privatisation of those services originating in the public sector:

1. the services are widely available because governments "grew" them that way,
2. the scale of circulation of money-capital of and from these services is correspondingly vast and
3. the rate of profit and of surplus-accumulation enjoyed by the private-sector corporate interests acquiring control of these operations is far higher than any comparable transaction to acquire similar goods or services on the same scale purely within the private sector. Why? Because the market for ongoing generation of revenue from these formerly publicly-owned and -operated capital goods is guaranteed and practically monopolised, whereas the public sector operator has already largely paid off the originating capital costs associated with being able to provide these goods or services in a manner widely accessible to the general public in the first place. This means, at the level of principle, that all such privatisations of social goods and services in the Western countries are indistinguishable from the "piratisations" so bemoaned by Stiglitz and others when it comes to activities of so-called oligarchs from the former Soviet Union.

1.3.3. Money as a Value-store: Why Consumption Can't Regulate Production or *Vice-versa*

Money at the same time is also the storehouse / benchmark of all "value". This serves to influence from several directions decisions at all levels, from the production cycle of the given commodity to decisions affecting fundamental and far-reaching aspects of the entire chain of processes known as "extended social reproduction" (Sraffa 1960) or "the business cycle" (Schumpeter 1939).

Examples of how value-in-exchange and value-in-use form a unity of opposites are legion. Some obvious and well-known ones include: the value-in-use compared to the value-in-exchange of water (including bottled waters), of domestic housework, ore-bearing rock, unrefined mineral ores, etc. On the other hand, goods and services that enjoy the highest value-in-exchange, such as armaments and war preparations, represent for individuals and society as a whole either zero or infinitely negative "value-in-use."

As events such as the Great Depression and the persistence of high levels of mass unemployment in quite a number of developed and developing countries has proven repeatedly, demand and supply do not match and cancel out one another. Neither value-in-use nor value-in-exchange serve in principle to regulate the other: an increase or decrease in one frequently (and usually) has little or no bearing on the other. Value-in-use is associated with "consumption", while value-in-exchange is associated both with "consumption" as well as "production". However, the outstanding feature of production of commodities by means of commodities remains that, just as value-in-use and value-in-exchange cannot mutually regulate one another, neither can or do production and consumption mutually regulate one another. In other words every single one of those supply-demand curves in the Economics 101 textbooks are a description only of what might be under theoretically perfect conditions. Such conditions, asserted in economics theory everywhere, are actually approximated nowhere in economic practice. Behind their reasonable-seeming account of how the selling or market-clearing price is formed at the point where the supply and demand curves intersect lurks a crucial assumption, *viz.*, that supply and demand always mutually regulate one and another. As discussed more thoroughly in Chapter Two, the real-world economic system operates according to precisely opposite premises, and indeed crisis is its fellow-traveller.

The English economics writer William Petty, who was researching and writing after the English Civil War, grounded the discussion of value in something highly tangible when he pointed to Nature as the mother and Labour as the father of all wealth (Petty 1662). Only human labouring power could add value, and value in exchange was based ultimately on the amount of labour-time expended in producing the item being exchanged, regardless of the differing subjective opinions about an object's "value" held by buyer and seller. We add to this theory the role of inflation, another intangible of prime importance. A product on which a great deal of labour has been spent but with the motivation of self-interest in the short term cannot gain in value. The only way this product can be sold is by imposing disinformation, most commonly in the form of advertisement. This concept of value addition through labour and good intention is as old as human civilisation itself. The rest of the present work can be taken as something of a gloss on the incredible range and variety of efforts expended from various directions to obliterate Petty's fundamental insight and its significance for solving economic problems of our own time or, for that matter, any time. This line of attack, on Nature as the mother and Labour as the father of all wealth, characterises the central content of the widespread disinformation about economic matters identified in this and subsequent chapters.

Reflecting the emergence of multifarious possibilities in the contemporary world for expanding and extending knowledge without need any longer for, or recourse to, the Eurocentric gatekeepers of "Science" ensconced in all the great academies and research centres of the world, it is entirely possible to begin to think and to work in terms of what is essentially knowledge-based development – starting, paradoxically enough, in some of the most allegedly "underdeveloped" parts of the world. What is being mooted is nothing less than transcending Petty's notion of Nature as the mother of wealth and Labour as its father with the notion of socially-necessary production as the child of Knowledge, produced by the marriage of Nature and Labour guided by a positive human social intention. This is development in which socially necessary production can be planned and achieved not only without resorting to the involuntary servitude of physically-enslaved labour but also without having to rely on the voluntary servitude of waged labour hitched to the dead labour of machinery producing only what can be sold as commodities in the market.

1.4. THE SPREAD OF A BLOOD-STAIN: A HISTORY OF MONEY

Money comes into the world with a congenital blood-stain on one cheek.
Marie Augier (1842)

The history of the development and use of money is actually a history, in three acts, of the displacement of natural with unnatural forms and treatment of labour, in the sense of "human creative labouring power". In the conventional discussion of money and the history of its use, this reality has unfortunately become heavily obscured by the narrow instrumental focus on money as a medium of economic exchange used as a measure of the value and price of goods and services, without reference to any of the underlying intentions driving how money emerged and how its forms and uses have changed.

In the first act there arises what may be considered *the pre-industrial view*. This is marked by the emergence of *two* kinds of "money" that converged on the same quality of impermanence as a store-of-value, but that diverged in their respective capacities as media-of-exchange. The conventional histories disclose how, as early as 5000 BCE, cowries were used as money in Egypt and in 1500 BCE in China, where the ideographic representation for money originally was a cowry shell. Cowries have been used as money in other places at different periods. For example, in America they were used by Native Americans for this purpose, as well as in parts of Africa such as Tanzania and Togo. In this era, wealth is a hoard. Money in its earliest forms emerged in Asia-Middle East, Graeco-Roman Europe, Africa, Oceania etc. as a subdivided representation of the ruling family's hoard. It was circulated only as either a sign of approval for, or inducement of participation by, individuals outside the ruling family or circle. This gave rise to notions of money-of-account and the associated notion of storing precious metals as the payment medium for this very special money in central vaults controlled by the ruling family. Thus after *ca.* 3100 BCE, with the invention of writing in Mesopotamia mainly to keep accounts, banking for the ruling family and slaveowners closely associated with it emerged *ca.* 3000 BCE, using temples and palaces as centres both for ingot storage and for collecting the taxes in the form of grain deposits and other goods. These latter were used to pay state officials directly or exchange for metallic coinage to pay soldiers or the nobility for services rendered. In the Fertile Crescent these relations became sufficiently complex over the next millennium that a centrally regulated banking system is required: in the reign of Hammurabi (1792-1750 BCE), laws to govern it were promulgated in his famous Code.

Meanwhile, a parallel but unrelated "money" started to circulate as a facilitator of the exchange of equivalents in trade. When one ruling group displaced another, new official money was frequently struck rendering the previous money worthless. Similarly, when changing circumstances brought trade relationships to an end, the value of money exchanged and accumulated also came into question. Value was seen as originating in both labour and use, but labour-time at this stage of human development was neither bought nor sold. To this extent, labour remained natural, even though at the same time the labouring power of slaves was not differentiated from those who were not. That condition was an unnatural one for, and a threat to the livelihood of, the ordinary labourer. Its monetary expression could be seen in the proliferation of metallic coinage throughout the 700 BCE-300 CE millennium of the Persian, Greek and Roman Empires. Herodotus dated the invention in Lydia (Asia Minor) at 687 BCE of coinage made from electrum, a naturally occurring amalgam of the precious metals gold and silver. Spreading to Greece, in 595 BCE Aegina, in 575 BCE Athens, and in 570 BCE Corinth started to mint their own coins. After the capture of Croesus King of Lydia by the Persians in 546 BCE, the use of coins as money spread to Persia. With this proliferation, however, there also emerged money-lending: by 350 BCE it was already recorded, by Demosthenes, that the normal rate of interest in Greece was 10% except for "risky" businesses such as shipping, where interest rates of between 20% and 30% prevailed. With the reign of Alexander the Great (336-323 BCE), the conquest of Asia Minor entailed an expenditure for maintaining his armies of about 20 talents or half a ton of silver a day. Initially this was covered by the capture of huge quantities of Persian bullion, but the most significant impact emerged as soldiers were demobilised and settled in the new towns and settlements of the Alexandrian empire, hugely stimulating trade and compelling Alexander to fix an exchange rate between silver and gold of 10:1 By 269 BCE, silver coins were being minted by the Romans and used as money.

It is from this same contradiction revolving around the freedom or indenture of labour (as slaves, as imperial soldiers, as craftsmen) that there originated money as we would understand and recognise it, including all its possible functions and purposes as a store of value, medium of exchange and eventually even a means of making more money (not just insuring risk). In the pre-modern period of European civilisation, during the millennium extending from the fall of the Roman Empire until the Renaissance, money came to be used interchangeably for functions of government as well as for trade. The overwhelmingly dominant Christian religion of the time bans the charging and collection of interest, *i.e.*, the making of money from money, as the sin of "usury" – and then assigns this function exclusively to Jewish moneylenders, so that, whenever these societies go hungry, or some foreign power invades, such governments can secure and maintain their position by directing the public's anger at... the Jews. Meanwhile, this moneylending bankrolled European crusaders' invasions of the Muslim world, European monarchs' wars with one another, and European merchants' slave and other trading with Africa, the New World of the Americas, Asia, China etc. This globalised the circulation of money, creating with it at first the possibility and then the actuality of money accumulating not only as hoarded wealth, but as capital, to be advanced in all manner of adventures in order to make yet more money. As one writer would scathingly summarise: "Capital comes dripping from head to foot, from every pore, with blood and dirt." (Marx *ibid.*)

All these developments globalised the circulation of money – *but* all without any control being exercised over the issue of currency. Only after 1689, starting with the victory of the alliance between anti-feudal aristocrats and the rising commercial middle classes assuming, in the name of the entire population a sovereign power, through their control of Parliament, over spending by government over the other powers of the monarch, was this matter resolved by establishing the Bank of England as the sole and central authority backing the currency with its central hoard of gold. While there had been little that was systematic about money, its introduction or use in pre-industrial conditions, everything changed with the emergence of a section of the social division of labour specialising in the management of trade in goods and hence in the handling and exchange of money in a wide range of forms including commodity monies-of-account, metal coinage and paper bills, and a fundamental misconception justifying the necessity and indispensability of such a subdivision of social labour arose. This was the notion that linked money as a material established as a standard of value and used legally in settling debts with some notion of alleged "intrinsic value" or backing from natural resources, including agricultural, marine, and mineral commodities. By installing money with its own power above everything and everyone else, the instituting of a central bank like the Bank of England was a highly significant landmark of the new stage of social development in which labour was stripped of its last remaining original natural feature, *viz.*, the option of avoiding servitude, voluntary or otherwise, to anyone possessing money. This power of money-possession, legalised and backed by banking institutions, is sharply satirised in the German playwright Bertholt Brecht's mordant verse:

"It is an open question / Who the greater crime has done: / The man who went and robbed a bank / Or the men who opened one?"[6]

In any event, by thus paving the way for uprooting of labourers from the countryside and their arrival in the urban centres destitute and desperate for employment, the next act in the history of money opened with the new *industrial view*. Wealth from now on would be accumulated mainly or entirely from *exchangeable* value. All value originated in labouring effort, but exchangeable value depended in particular on the purchase and sale of labouring-power / working-time, thus giving rise to the division of labour in industrial production. There was also value purely in use, giving rise to an entire disinformational, so-called "neoclassical", economic theory, alongside classical theory, in which the industrial division of labour disappears. With it there also disappeared any acknowledgment of the inherently unnatural character of the industrial division of labour. Exchangeable value means money, and its history begins to be written in this same period. In these histories, labour disappears entirely, replaced by fables and folklore about the various forms of money. This kind of writing about money continues into our own time, where any quick search on the Internet will dredge up endless repetitions of the same stories about "commodity money", "credit money", "fiat money", the "backing" of currencies by "gold and other precious metals" etc.

During the 19th century, industry's rise subordinates trade, commerce and all other finance; however, such extreme subordination of exchange to availability of money increasingly repositions all functions in the economy involving the self-expansion of value into the hands of those engaged in monetary exchange, eventually creating finance and its management, credit, etc. as an additional arena in the social division of labour that emerges as a parasitic drain on the already unnatural industrial division of labour. This transformation sets in at the start of the 20th century. Credit in its various forms – and the power to withhold it, which is really the point – increasingly displaces people's cash, money, savings, etc. as the preferred instrument of exchange. By thus prioritising exchanges using plastic cards, the convenience enjoyed by the individual consumer becomes nothing compared to that enjoyed by the machineries of interest-collection and debt management.

This development also brings increasingly to the fore the increasing aphenomenality of monetary currency and credit-based exchange (described in Chapter 5 as "consumption without production"). A most outstanding example was seen on 15 August 1971, when the U.S. government officially breaks any link between the U.S. dollar and gold by rendering it illegal to redeem gold held in the U.S. Federal Reserve for what is still called "legal tender" but henceforth actually is stripped of part of that function. The post-1971 U.S. dollar is called "fiat money" and thereby placed on the same plane as official currencies issued in many Third World countries without any backing by gold, precious metals or stores of resource riches, but this comparison is only superficially true, confined to the coincidence that all such currencies are backed by government order. None of these others can be used as a global reserve currency. Nor is any part of the world's fossil-fuel energy supply is denominated in their currencies. Nor are any but token quantities of their currencies held anywhere outside

---

[6] In the German original, from *Der Dreigroschenoper* [The Threepenny Opera] (Brecht and Weill 1928):
Es ist ein offene Frage
Wer schlechteres hat getan:
Die eine Bank geöffnet haben
Oder ein Raubermann

their own countries. If their central bank prints more of the currency it only accelerates inflation and eventual bankruptcy of workers and institutions in their own countries, whereas, when the US Federal Reserve does the same, it lowers the amount of U.S.-dollar-denominated debts expressed in current dollars that will actually have to be repaid 10, 15, 20 and 30 years hence, thereby enriching all holdings of current U.S. dollars while paradoxically and simultaneously inflating those dollars and reducing their purchasing power. The vulnerability of the U.S. dollar is not that it is a fiat currency but rather that it is backed principally by a system of fossil-fuel energy production and pricing which had up to now kept far more dollars outside that country than inside in circulation and valuable but which can only take advantage of increasing opportunities for growth outside the U.S. sphere of economic exchange by abandoning use of, or reliance upon, the dollar as a world reserve currency in favour of the Euro, or some combination of dollars and euros.

Had the computer not provided such an incredible speedup, at several orders of magnitude, for the circulation of capital and its collection of interest, it is debatable how far computers would have spread into so many areas of people's lives giving rise to our own so-called "information age", and its *post-industrial view*. This period – our own – is marked by the ready availability, on a global scale, of knowledge, information and evidence of many different approaches to the question of how labour is disposed of and how time and effort may be accounted, all coexisting with one another as well as with one particular model that senses a mortal threat from the existence of any others and acts to preserve itself by striving to dominate all others and displace them. While the dominant model moves towards utter aphenomenality – evidenced in the notion of "electronic funds transfer", which is nothing but a transmission of information about debit-credit accounting entries, enjoying priority and preference over any material exchange of currency for some actual purchase of goods or services that has taken place, *i.e.*, not merely promised or "credited" to take place and-or to be compensated somehow, somewhere in future – other modes of exchange are even criminalised. This has been the fate, for example, suffered by the "hawala" remittance system, which is managed entirely on the basis of relationships of personal trust with no involvement of banks and used extensively by persons from Muslim countries working in western countries to send money home. Here in this case the logic justifying this suppression, *viz.*, that any money transfer outside a monitorable banking channel must carry some potentially terrorist intention, is as absurd as the commercial banking system's forcible imposition of its monopoly over such transfers is, in fact, the real – and likely the only – terrorism. At a stroke, all notions of a just price are dissolved, as there is now no longer any way left to muster some good intention or its equivalent for, say, my neighbour's cow. All notions of "natural price" are adjusted on the basis of declaring the new dominant mode of exchange the most, or even the only, "natural" one.

1.5. DISINFORMATION ABOUT THE INTANGIBLE-TANGIBLE NEXUS STANDS AT THE HEART OF CONVENTIONAL ECONOMIC THEORIES

The theories of modern economics taught today all start from something called "the theory of marginal utility". This was first developed in the 1870s by the English economics writer William Stanley Jevons (1870) and furthered in the works of Austrian economist Carl

Menger (1871), Leon Walras (1874) and by 1890 Alfred Marshall back in England. Its underlying thesis, which became the basis of an elaborate theory known as neoclassical economics, is that endogenous "choices" about price operate entirely according to personal choice or desire for access to, and use of, some good or service, with the last unit of demand determining the price "at the margin". All of this takes place without reference to any exogenous conditions such as the monopolised character of production, the cartelised character of international trade, or the role of imperial dictate, rivalries and-or wars in suppressing or further distorting the operation of supply and demand. Consumption takes place without reference to how commodities were produced in the first place. How, indeed, could that which was not yet produced supposedly be distributed and consumed? "At the margin!" reply the neoclassical economists. But one has merely to ask the obvious question: "whence the originating intention to consume, or to produce?" – and the curtain suddenly rises on a bigger picture, one resembling that of the fable about the child pointing out that the emperor has no clothes while everyone else in the picture behaves as though the emperor is not only dressed but present among them in full imperial regalia.

The specific role asserted for the theory of marginal utility in this arrangement reduces the domain of concern to "The Margin" so as to simplify the handling of the relevant variables. It is precisely in this process, however, that the counterfeiting job is carried out, as all exogenous conditions beyond "The Margin" are simply removed from the domain of consideration, including any – such as intention – that may themselves be playing some role in defining the boundary of, and-or the conditions at, "The Margin".

The mathematical assumptions fundamental to the basic theory of marginal utility are another source of serious misdirection, in which the still unaddressed question of intention becomes layered in further opacity. In order to model the individual's "choice"-behaviours in economic reality, an untestable assumption that is completely subjective and individual, *viz.*, that individuals' behaviour consists of maximizing personal pleasure and minimizing personal pain, is used to measure what happens on a societal scale. To proceed in such a manner is to assume society is just the individual multiplied uniformly and homogeneously over and over. This procedure also transfers the short-term perspective of the individual to society as a whole. However, since the death of any individual or individuals obviously cancels their personal term without shortening the term of society's existence, such a procedure is inherently and patently absurd. Jevons in particular declared economic behaviour to be nothing more nor less than the materialisation in social form of this allegedly universal and thoroughly selfish principle. What the worker does to avoid starvation is thereby equated with what the business owner does to screw another few pennies of profit out of the powerless public. Jevons even suggested a mathematical model justifying his standpoint, arguing that the discrete choices of millions of economic actors may be approximated meaningfully or usefully by continuous-type mathematical functions. He combined this with the notion of processes that would eventually reach steady-state conditions, adapting to economics a mode of analysis that researches in thermodynamics especially in England and France had pioneered widely by the middle third of the 19th century.

Like the vast majority of educated Europeans of his time, Jevons believed human actions were ultimately to be accounted for as some variant of animal instincts to eat, procreate etc., that the most civilized arrangement for people would be one in which the instinct to self-preservation were molded or made to gravitate towards pursuit of self-interest while the same pursuit by all individual would be commonly protected by a state that would intervene only to prevent or reverse gross injustice. The factory system was already almost a century old, but – apart from Marx, a few of the followers of David Ricardo and an even smaller number of the followers of Adam Smith – neither Jevons nor any other economists acknowledged that this system had already given rise to an entirely unprecedented social order, one in which labour and its output were increasingly socialized, and not just a vast accumulation of products and opportunities for enrichment.

Economic theories are often announced or explained as final finished products. In reality, however, they are anything but. They express ideological and political priorities of the ruling forces of the establishment in the short term at various times in response to various pressures. Thus for example the long-standing current defence of conventional establishment economic theory takes the form of an argument to the effect that, so long as all economic players act according to their self-interest in the marketplace either as a buyer or seller of commodities, they will each maximise their own satisfaction. The general welfare is also supposed to be improved to whatever extent the sale compensated the seller's outlays and the purchase enabled the buyer to satisfy a need in the most cost-effective manner possible in given conditions of production and availability of the commodity or commodities of interest. The solution to each short-term problem is cast as one more step towards, and something that clears the horizon for, the longer term. Achieving the long term is recast as a succession of solutions to short-term conditions.

From such a standpoint, the solving of problems in the short-term entails no additional responsibility for the longer term. Each solution-step is already at the same time a further discharge of the individual's responsibility for the long term. The underlying logic of the position is that greed is just another form of need. The economy itself exists in the first place mainly or only to allocate scarce resources for production – either into finished goods or necessary services – as rationally as possible. Therefore, overproduction can be at most a passing and temporary aberration. On the other hand, underconsumption – because of its potential to disorganise or destabilise the aforementioned allocation of resources that were scarce to begin with – is a most dangerous threat.

This version of conventional theory replaced an earlier version which had declared that the marketplace was guided by an "invisible hand". This supposedly maximised the satisfactions of both buyer and seller, so long as neither buyers nor sellers combined to restrain the freedom of the other in the marketplace and so long as well that government resisted all importunings ever to interfere in the operations of the marketplace. If all these conditions were met, all markets would clear, and there would be no danger from overproduction or underconsumption. Subsequently in the Great Depression of the 1930s, the emergence of vast concentrations of ownership and of production confirmed, disastrously, the validity of all the earlier warnings against combination by sellers of finished goods in the marketplace. It also demonstrated conclusively that, once such monopolies emerged, overproduction had become endemic to the short term and the long term of the economy. This in turn greatly strengthened arguments in favour of reorganising production for the long term, on a very different basis. The new basis proposed increasingly widely envisioned the elimination of the capture of surpluses and profits as the main and sole driver of economic development and investment, either in the short term or the long term.

To combat the possible outbreak of high levels of social struggle, even revolution, implicit in such a position, a compromise was developed, based on the theories of Lord John Maynard Keynes. This was premised on the idea that deficit spending by governments could temporarily subsidise the maintenance of employment until the next upswing in the economy. This proved highly effective during the Second World War and for the next 35 years afterward in America, western Europe and Japan. It began to lose steam in the 1970s and crashed to the ground in the 1981 recession. That downturn was created by regulatory bodies following all the standard Keynesian policy prescriptions to the letter. Central banks raised interest rates, in the name of combating inflation, to levels considered stratospheric in these countries – only to end up eliminating millions of jobs concentrated in the heavy-industrial bases and heartlands of these economies. The present economic establishment theory focuses far more narrowly on maintaining high levels of consumption of goods and services regardless of what havoc is done to the environment in the course of creating and meeting so many new "needs". It emerged to "correct" the Keynesians' "failure".

As this brief history reveals, for some time, the aim of economic theory has not been to figure out what serves society best. The aim has been rather to buttress the ability and capacities of the establishment to overcome massive resistance to its activities in the short term. As numerous commentators in U.S. media from the "left" and the "right" of the political spectrum have noted: in order – and in the course of taking the appropriate steps – to finance various wars, to establish and maintain questionable trade deals and sometimes to shield key allies from application of the Rule of Law, the U.S. has gone into debt to the tune of $40 trillion, an amount far beyond the ability of the present generation, or even the next two generations thereafter, to repay. In addition to the damage they can inflict in the long term, which is extensively discussed among scholars, there is growing evidence for the conclusion that conventional economic theories are highly dysfunctional in the short term in the short term as well.

Only after Jevons' death, as it became crystal clear that this new kind of social order was not moving in the direction that its main beneficiaries in Victorian England might have preferred, was a concerted effort mounted to convert what Jevons had offered the public as a mixture of scientifically researched conclusions mixed with much questioning and speculation into a dogma, *i.e.*, into the basis of what is today taught as "neoclassical economic theory".

Students of Jevons' career seem to have fallen into one of two ditches off the main path. Some of these writers present on one side of the boundary the kingdom of Jevons the Cassandra of coal, propounding his paradox with the aim of alerting the overseers of empire to wake up before the coals that fuel Great Britain's global supremacy are burning down to their last embers. Others portray the world on the other side of that imaginary boundary in which Jevons the Mahatma of marginal utility – apparently no relation to the phenomenon on the other side of the boundary – holds forth. What brings the two realms into any kind of connection is an assertion to the effect that the net increased production of goods and services (and hence the net overall increase in energy use) uncovered by "Jevons' paradox" somehow demonstrates the supremacy of "consumer choice" over the entire economic system. This is the central doctrine of neoclassical economics: Jevons raised to the power 'dogma'.

Although a number of his speculations turned out to be wrong – for example, his linkage of a correct insight that business seemed in the 19th century to move in approximately 11-year cycles to a guess (thoroughly refuted decades after his death) that this might be correlated with the sunspot cycle notion; or his dogmatic insistence that coal was the last word in industrially useful energy whereas petroleum was an overpriced substitute and electricity about as practicable as a perpetual-motion machine – in no contemporary sense today can

Jevons be considered to have written or worked in his own day as some kind of flack for ideas that were already dubious or failed. For one thing, likely as a result of the experience of his own family's circumstances in which during his own childhood his father suffered financial ruin in the iron business, Jevons was well aware of the limitations imposed by received historical conditions on the capacities of the economic system of his time to meet the needs of those who stumbled in the great individualistic and cutthroat economic competition that capitalism generates, and nowhere did he advocate that the ability to acquire wealth was in itself any proof either of an individual's virtuousness, sterling character or even entrepreneurial skill. Any of these linkages – none of which withstands serious evidentiary scrutiny – may in our time be found frequently throughout the writings of American academic economists. For another, Jevons nowhere assumes that the production of wealth in itself guarantees future plenty. On the contrary, the guideline implicitly framing his entire body of economic theory was that of an ineluctable and irremovable scarcity of necessary and vital energy supply. Again, however, discussion in general of problems of long-term scarcity in the American economy is a minoritarian trend in the academic literature. However, quite specific discussion of shortages and gaps in U.S. energy supply has become something of a growth industry since the 1970s, with entire journals dedicated to aspects of that subject. Almost everything dealing with depleting reserves of oil and gas, in fact, relies heavily on a dogmatic rendering of Jevons' views about depleting supplies of coal in his day and on a misreading of Jevons' famous "paradox" that is pure disinformation. In Chapter Three, where the contemporary "energy crisis" is discussed at length as the tangible problem of our time, the authors examine how Jevons' theories about coal depletion and about marginal utility as the most efficient pricing mechanism have been recycled in a form that blocks progress to the self-evident solution to this entirely removable "crisis". More immediately, the current discussion takes up "Jevons' Paradox".

1.5.1. Jevons' Paradox

"Jevons' Paradox" is the notion that a lowering of unit costs of production, on the basis of technological changes that lower the rate of energy consumption by using the same fuel source more efficiently than before, tends to bring about an increase in the production of commodities across all sectors using or relying on that same energy source, thus tending to increase the net consumption of energy.

This "paradox" was first formulated in Jevons' *The Coal Question* published in 1865. A typical modern-day restatement by University of Houston [Texas] engineering professor John H. Lienhard, follows below from a piece entitled "No. 984 – Failed conservation?" on his "Engines of Our Ingenuity" website that continues arguments elaborated in his book *The Engines of Our Ingenuity: An Engineer Looks at Technology and Culture* (2000). This particular installment discusses a recent review (Inhaber and Saunders 1994) of Jevons' classic:

> Herbert Inhaber and Harry Saunders take a disturbing look at energy conservation. They begin in 1865. An English mathematician, William Stanley Jevons, had just written a book titled *The Coal Question*. Watt's new engines were eating up English coal. Once it was gone, England was in trouble. And Jevons wrote:

".. some day our coal seams [may] be found emptied to the bottom, and swept clean like a coal-cellar. Our fires and furnaces .. suddenly extinguished, and cold and darkness .. left to reign over a depopulated country."

The answer seemed to lie in creating more efficient steam engines. Jevons may not have realized that steam engines were already closing in on thermodynamic limits of efficiency. But he did see that increased efficiency wouldn't save us in any case.

Look at the Watt engine, he said. It was invented because the older Newcomen engine was so inefficient. Did Watt cut coal consumption by quadrupling efficiency? Quite the contrary. By making steam power more efficient, he spread the use of steam throughout the land. Coal consumption was skyrocketing.

A few years later, Henry Bessemer invented a new highly energy-efficient scheme for smelting steel. Jevons's argument played out once more. Now that we could have cheap steel, we began making everything from it – plows, toys, even store fronts. Energy-efficiency had again driven coal consumption upward.

We saw Jevons's script replaying yet again after the Arab oil embargo in the 1970s. Our response was to create more energy-efficient cars. Since then, Americans have increased the number of miles they've driven to 162 percent of what it was.

… Inhaber and Saunders offer hope. Sure, they trash any hope of creating a decent world with laissez-faire mechanisms. But they also remind us that we will conserve energy when we, as individuals, want to conserve energy. We'll conserve energy when we choose to turn off the lights as we leave the room – when we choose to recycle bottles and ride the bus. It is you and I who'll save ourselves. It's never been anyone else – not our government, not the collective.
…

The existence of unoccupied economic space under free competition is a precondition for any further specialisation within the industrial division of labour to give rise to a net addition to the stock of industrial productive forces (even as productive forces at the margin were being destroyed or otherwise rendered economically redundant). That is what actually accounts for the possibility of technological changes that increase the efficiency of utilisation of an energy source to become linked with, and eventually bring about, the net increase in overall consumption of the said energy source observed by Jevons.

Lienhard's "fuel-efficient cars" comparison, on the other hand, is completely inappropriate, if only because the consumption of refined petroleum is a very different problem than the consumption of a coal resource for which there appeared to be no satisfactory replacement available in the ground. Furthermore, his notion that conservation cannot be organized on a collective basis is profoundly irresponsible.

Fundamentally, the accounting trick involved in making this "paradox" seem more real than it actually is an arithmetic sleight-of-hand. The lowering of unit costs of production is associated mainly with technological change, but the conditions in which the technological change took place – in Jevons' time: during a crash of the business cycle – are nowhere referenced, giving the affair quite a mystical quality of one "thing" giving rise to another "thing", in a veritable orgy of tangibles. The introduction of new technologies of this order is invariably undertaken at the upturn of the next cycle by the enterprise or enterprises that wiped out many rivals during the preceding slump. In other words, a mass of productive forces were destroyed which new technology will render superfluous or displace, and so any associated lowering of unit costs of production, an increase in economic efficiency, will be manifested only in specific industries or sectors where production became more concentrated as a result of the previous crisis clearing weaker economic players away or severely marginalizing them in the market. Energy consumption per employed worker will therefore go up as production becomes more concentrated in fewer more highly capitalised enterprises probably employing fewer workers than the entire sector employed before the crisis. Reality is that the capitalization of certain sectors in any given crisis are strengthened through such processes while weakened in others; Jevons' method, however, proceeds according to a fallacious assumption that what is true for any one sector will be true for all, just as whatever is true for the individual consumer will be true for consumption in general in society as a whole.

If the losses to the whole of the economic system occasioned by the bankruptcies and other epiphenomena of the crisis were added back in, but in the post-crisis phase, as deductions from overall energy consumption, what would the net energy consumption picture look like? It might well have changed little if at all. In effect, the increased production of commodities, and accompanying increase in energy consumption, referenced by this so-called "paradox" can also be seen as "over-compensating" the losses represented by sidelining or destroying other productive forces. In this respect, the "paradox" is only the outward appearance of an undamped oscillator.

Another feature, of which Jevons was not (and, indeed, could not be) conscious, was that economic space would become completely occupied as oligopolies and cartels consolidated their overall role throughout the economy. The space in which free competition once predominated would thus be eliminated. Already, in Jevons' day – although this was not understood at the time for what it actually was – this space was being pushed to the margins.[7] The English economist J.A. Hobson writing about the British Empire as an economic proposition wrestled with certain parts of the problem as early as 1902 (Hobson 1902). The Austrian economist Hilferding glimpsed some implications in 1910 of the rise and role of finance capital, which he defined as the merger of banking and industrial capital (Hilferding 1910).[8]

The crucial fact about an economic space that has already been divided up and can only be redivided is that an increase or decrease in energy consumption loses any clear-cut linkage to or dependence upon changes in "productivity." These cease to regulate each other in any predictable way. In effect, as oligopoly, cartels and monopoly displace free competition while appropriation of the fruits, and ownership of the means, of production remain private, the impossibility of production and consumption mutually regulating one another spreads to encompass all other relationships engendered earlier when free competition reigned supreme. Thus, Jevons' paradox disappears because the relationship it proposed in order to account for phenomena that appeared sequentially related no longer exists – even though the phenomena themselves persist.

---

[7] Mud slung in retaliation against the political challenge hurled by Marx and Engels at the industrial foundations of European colonial expansion to all the other continents of the planet has long since buried in obscurity Volumes II and III of Marx's *Capital*, prepared after Marx's death for publication between 1884 and 1892 by Friedrich Engels, but these marked the first analyses to focus on any of the implications of the displacement of relatively free competition by the tendency towards monopoly.

[8] Although widely shunned by economists because of his political role, V.I. Lenin's *Imperialism the Highest Stage of Capitalism* (1916) delivered a further theoretical treatment that continues to challenge conventional wisdom at many levels.

1.5.2. The "Marginal Revolution" as a Legacy of Utilitarian Philosophy

During economic crises under modern oligopolised and cartelised commodity production, most of the price of technological advance – especially advances in the efficient utilization of energy sources – has been paid by those productive forces caught on the margins of the economic system at the moment of crash and-or crisis. As will be discussed in some detail in the next chapter, this was vividly illustrated in the east coast fisheries of Canada before and after the five collapses (1971, 1974, 1981, 1984 and 1990) experienced in this sector between 1968 and 1992. In each of these moments, more small-boat fishermen lost or suffered serious contractions to their livelihood. Many were confronted with the stark option to quit the fishery or do deeply in debt to finance acquisition of more advanced means of production to enable them to stay competitive with the fleets of the leading processors Canadian and foreign. In net terms, over this period, the numbers of small-boat fishermen in the four Atlantic provinces fell by half while overall catches offshore and inshore rose approximately four times. Essentially the seasonal fish plant, small processor and independent fisherman were displaced by foreign factory trawler fleets and by local trawler fleets owned and operated by a much smaller group of giant processing interests.

In Jevons' lifetime, although free competition still predominated, there nevertheless arose, with the further consolidation of railways especially after the inauguration of Free Trade, examples increasingly of tendencies to what would later be identified as "vertical integration", the resort to the stock markets to float so-called joint-stock companies, and there were also increasing examples of leading companies in various fields colluding to fix prices as a means of excluding other competitors from markets. Yet the centrality of the role of free competition in giving rise in the first place to the very relationship spotlighted in "Jevons' paradox" was invisible at the time to those living through it. At the same time its very invisibility – like the gravitational effects of black holes and so-called "dark matter" in outer space – served to "distort the optic" of those theorising about the significance of contemporary developments. This recognition is of profound importance, as it points to a major potential source of error unleashed by paying insufficient attention to the role of intangible factors when summarizing the historical line of a social phenomenon's development.

Jevons and others following on the same line believed overproduction crises were aberrations that the further evolution of civilisation would eliminate. By thus refusing to acknowledge the destruction of productive forces at the margins of the factory system as a consequence of overproduction crises in general, they were utterly unable and unfitted to see, let alone acknowledge, the so-called "paradox" as something resulting from tendencies peculiar to the mechanics of such crises under conditions of free competition in particular. Viewed in this light, Jevons' failure actually to penetrate the veil of the apparent "paradox" is symptomatic.

Theorists of Jevons' time – the Victorian era – were saddled with philosophical baggage that rendered them incapable of accounting theoretically for Jevons' paradox in anything resembling a scientifically convincing fashion with anything resembling a sound argument. They were still operating according to certain assumptions about the nature of interrelationships between the individual, society and Nature that were only beginning to be challenged at the time and would not be supplanted until years after the First World War.

As far as Jevons' own ideological predispositions are concerned, the "form" seems well-known: a devotee of the original utilitarian doctrines of Jeremy Bentham, when it came to defining the source of value he dissented from the modified translation of Benthamite principles into economic theory proposed by fellow utilitarians James Mill and his son John Stuart Mill. Although this heritage is most widely remarked as though it were the most significant feature, however, it is actually the least useful for grasping anything fundamental in Jevons' outlook.

The central issue which would sharply differentiate Jevons from most educated people living since the middle of the 20th century would be the understanding of the role of Nature and the role of society (or more precisely: the forces of social class and social strata).

For Jevons and many of his fellow Victorians, scarcities arose from, or were embedded in, Nature; inequality was not necessarily synonymous with injustice; mutual pursuit of self-interest among people would harmonise, rather than divide, society; and the pursuit of self-interest was the anteroom to exacerbation of inequalities. Society was the product of individuals, whereas the individual was not the product of society and had no claims to entitlements of any kind from society. Like many mainstream utilitarians, Jevons rejected any notion of natural rights, or "rights of man", as a dangerous incitement to revolution, anarchy and Jacobinism.

Flowing from the assumption that the effects of pursuing self-interest would be harmonising, self-correcting and generally equilibrating, it then becomes apparent that Jevons could not assign responsibility for the deteriorating state of Great Britain's coal resources to individuals. Ultimate responsibility could derive only from the fact that coal was a finite, non-renewable natural resource.

Objects of exchange, on the other hand, were a different matter, insofar as the process of exchange repeated many times over connected all such objects to some definite individual. These objects were thus deemed to have acquired their value from their "utility" (and relative scarcity) for the individuals seeking their purchase. The relative stability in the price of many common items of daily consumption reflected the equilibrating effect of countless independent acts of exchange pursued by individuals with differing degrees of need for an item proffering approximately the same "utility".

In Jevons' view, as a utilitarian, the notion that value could inhere in objects without, or independently of, a potential utility for some potential purchaser was the height of theoretical inconsistency. Hence his vehement rejection of the position taken by James Mill and John Stuart Mill, as leading utilitarians, which accepted the views of Adam Smith and David Ricardo that the value of a commodity-object in the marketplace was imparted, prior to its purchase, by the human labouring power applied to give rise to these commodities in the first place.

In this, of course, Smith, Ricardo, the Mills (father James and son John Stuart) and others had extrapolated the Aristotelian conception of "natural price". Jevons, on the other hand, was insisting that, for the sake of consistency in the application of fundamental philosophical principles, the actual content of all such concepts as value or price would have to be redefined and expressed in terms of the utilitarian pleasure-pain calculus. It was an obvious truth of daily life that value in the marketplace, as reflected in an item's price, was one kind of value – value-in-exchange – whereas value in use for the individual was of a different order, not necessarily quantifiable and even where quantifiable not necessarily equal to the value assigned by the marketplace. Yet, instead of acknowledging let alone confronting this problem, Jevons one-sidedly made it disappear by an act of purest solipsism. He asserted: (a) that all value is essentially value-in-use as determined by and for the individual purchaser, and (b) price is the material quantification of that use-value.

For a consistent utilitarian, value in exchange is only a quantified form of "real" value – which is value-in-use, for some individual. The problem is that in practice, it is extremely effective to deal with commodities and what happens to them precisely as so many units of exchange-value. Meanwhile, at the level of theory, the utilitarian approach denies the existence of commodities as exchange-values by simply asserting that a commodity's price is the quantification of its use-value. Hence, for the utilitarian, only use-value exists.

A similar problem emerges when utilitarian doctrine attempts to comprehend and elaborate the character of labour and its economic form: the social is collapsed into the individual, or assumed to be but the multiplication of the individual. For Jevons and company, the social character of modern, *i.e.*, factory-based, commodity production was and remains irrelevant and actually oxymoronic. Indeed, Jevons theorised that production was induced as the result of the workers' "pleasure" from / desire for continuing to eat and reproduce outstripping the "pain" of labouring effort. In effect, in yet another solipsistic leap, labour that is effectively and for all practical purposes social in character is re-cast as purely individual.

1.5.3. By Deriving the Social from the Individual and Merging the Tangible into the Intangible, the "Marginal Revolution" Actually Marginalises Any Role Whatsoever for Intentions

In economic life, tangible goods and services and their circulation provide the vehicles whereby intentions become, and define, actions. Locked inside those tangible goods and services, inaccessible to direct observation or measurement, are intangible relations – among the producers of the goods and services and between the producer and Nature – whose extent, cooperativeness, antagonism and other characteristic features are also framed and bounded by intentions at another level, in which the differing interests of producers and their employers are mutually engaged.

Two very important sources of distortion may be identified immediately. First of all, for theorists, and theories, of marginal utility (MU), this societal complex, rife with non-linear dependencies, seems superfluous and its existence irrelevant, driving a tendency to linearise by chopping out the difficult bits which may be loaded with all kinds of crucial information but are ill-posed and thus intractable.

Secondly, lines in the plane intersect as long as they are not parallel, *i.e.*, as long as the equation-relationships they are supposed to represent are not redundant. This enables use of the "=" sign, where everything to its left is equated to everything to its right. Equated quantities cannot only be manipulated, but – especially – interchanged, according to the impeccable logic, as sound as Aristotle (who first propounded it), which says: two quantities each equal to a third quantity must themselves be equal to one another or, symbolically, that 'A = C' and 'B = C' implies that 'A = B'. As seductive as this indeed is, in leading the analyst towards "a solution", it masks a very profound problem similar in its potential impact – a loss of possibly critically important information – to that unleashed by deliberately removing some dimensionality at the outset in the interests of simplification. That "=" sign is conventionally employed in the discussion and analysis of conditions of "economic equilibrium". The *terms on the left and right-hand sides of the mathematical function-statement* employed to describe that equilibrium state may indeed be interchangeable around the "=" sign. However, the *actual conditions giving rise to that equilibrium* may not be anywhere near so interchangeable – for example, if the "equilibrium" is only temporary and otherwise highly dynamic, or if the equilibrium is the outcome of some struggle between conflicting intentions and interests. This can thus be a very effective method for eliminating any information or suggestion of the actual role of intention in an economic process.

To simplify the dimensions of consideration introduces another irrecoverable kind of error. To begin with, the economic actors of MU-land are as oblivious to the existence and operation of this societal complex as any resident of Flatland would be to the existence of the third dimension (Abbott 1884). Their production functions – representing the supply of some tangible goods or services – and their consumption functions – representing the effective demand for those goods or services – may be represented by curves extending across the flatness of planar space. The point of intersection of these curves, called the equilibrium price, marks the selling-price point at which the entire product of said goods or services will be consumed. The aggregation of all such market-clearing activities comprises... the economy. According to the authority of the mediaeval Catholic Church, folk were doomed to fall off the edge of the earth if they dared to venture more than a few hundred miles west of the edge of the European continent. Guided by the neoclassical economists, inhabitants of MU-land come to learn that beyond the point, or points, at which markets clear lies... nothingness.

To aid in attaining a systematic comprehension of the subject matter of any science, it helps to apply relevant or appropriate mathematical concepts. Residents of MU-land, unfortunately, have a strong affinity for graphs, points and lines that can be expressed in the ultimately linearising space of the flat plane. Meanwhile, however, the life and times of points and lines in planar space stand in relation to the life and times of points and lines in non-planar, three-dimensional space as earthlings stand in relation to extraterrestrials in another galaxy.

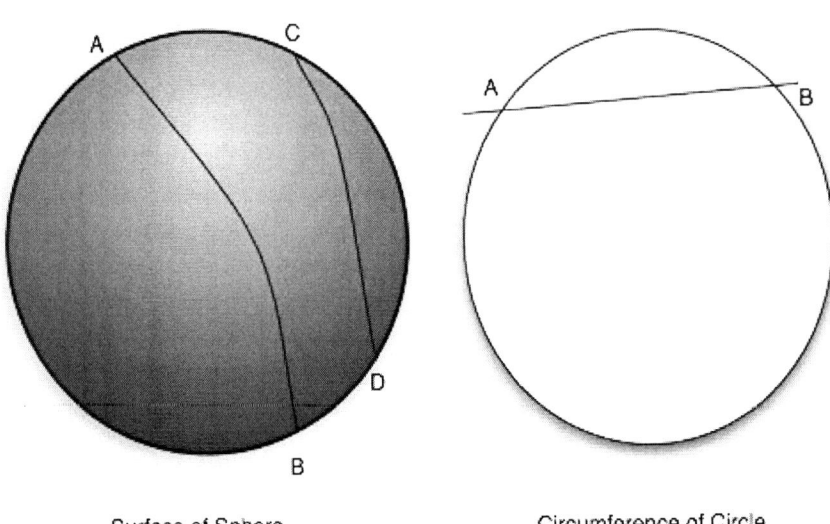

Figure 1-3. Sphere and Circle Compared.

This state of affairs is rife with consequences. Compare the circle to the sphere, in Figure 1-3 above. The shortest distance between two points A and B on the circle's circumference is a straight (secant) line joining them, whereas the curved arc of the circumference between the two points A and B is always longer than the secant. (Indeed, it is even longer than quite a few curves that could be drawn between the points.) The shortest distance between two points on the surface of a sphere, on the other hand, is always a curve and can never be a straight line. Furthermore, between two points A and B lying on any great-circle of the sphere (*i.e.*, lying along any of an infinite number of circles that may be drawn around the surface of the sphere whose diameter is identical to that of the sphere itself) and between any other two points, say C and D, a curved line of the same length joining each pair of points will subtend a different amount of arc. For the points not on the great-circle, the same length-distance will subtend a greater arc than for points on a great-circle; curvature k in each case is uniform but different. On the other hand, what makes a circle circular rather than, say, elliptical, is precisely the condition whereby equal distances along its circumference subtend equal arcs, because curvature k anywhere along the circumference of a circle is the same.

Is anyone whose comprehension remains confined to cases of the circle in flat planar space likely to infer or extrapolate from such knowledge whatever they would need in order to grasp and use such differences found on the curved surface of the sphere? Of course not: indeed, any solution or solutions obtained for a problem formulated in two-dimensional space can often appear utterly aphenomenal when transferred or translated to three-dimensional space. In terms of the originating example of the fundamental metrics of the two kinds of surfaces: to those working in the environment of spherical surface-space, it becomes quickly obvious the shortest distance between two points that stand really close to one another on the surface of a sphere will approximate a straight line. In fact, of course, it is actually a curve and the idea that "the shortest distance between two points is a straight line" remains something that only approximates the situation in an extremely restricted subspace on the surface of a sphere. All this suggests that any attempt to simplify a model used to account for complex phenomena by chopping dimensions away at the outset (with the idea of adding them back in at the end) is about as practicable as trying to make water run uphill.

The relevance of this for the present case is that, by deriving the social from the individual and merging the tangible notion of "value-in-exchange" into the intangible notion of "value-in-use" as its quantification, the theories, and theorists, of the "marginal revolution" end up denying intentions any role whatsoever in economic affairs.

1.5.4. In the Market-Space of MU-Land, See the Tail Wag the Dog, Making Anything Available if the Price is Right...

Truly scientific efforts in economics may be characterised as those aimed at quantifying economic activity on a social scale, rather than just on the scale of some individual enterprise, or within an abstract model of a market comprising, say, a single seller confronting a single buyer (like those developed from the mid-to-late 19th century). Socially-based models of such quantification emerge, for example, from William Petty's work in 17th century England quantifying the amounts of labour, currency, seamen, etc. actually needed to sustain the commercial activity of a nation (Petty 1678); or in the *Tableau économique* of the *Physiocrates* in 18th century France (Quesnay 1766); or in the charts of "extended social reproduction" produced in Volume Two of Karl Marx's *Capital* (as completed by Frederick Engels) in the 1880s (Marx [Engels ed.] 1884); or in the voluminously detailed works produced from 1925 onwards by Госплан (*Gosplan*), the body which drew up the Five Year Plans of the former Soviet Union (Chernenko and Smirtyukov 1967) . On the one hand, intentions could be deduced from the societal consequences of actions; charting efforts of this kind, each in its own way, served to map these rather explicitly. On the other hand definite, although intangible, social relations between and among participating economic groups were also implicit to such mappings.

In the second half of the 20th century, a renovation of economic science was undertaken. A key assumption of the abstract single-buyer single-seller market model on which it had been based turned out to be seriously deficient – specifically, the assumption that whatever was theoretically "true" at the microscopic level would be replicated at all other scales. This assumption broke down when it came to predicting either persistent unemployment of the 1950s (for which the market-clearing principle of the theory denied almost any possibility), or the persistent inflation of the 1960s due to military spending (which conventional theory modeled with the government as buyer and weapons manufacturers as sellers), or persistent stagflation of the 1970s (which conventional theory asserted to be impossible). By insisting on some level of verification from actual microeconomic and macroeconomic data, an abstract model of economic equilibrium had by the 1980s been partially rescued from the obscurity into which much of the work of the early theorists of marginal utility had fallen. What happened, however, to the existence of intangible factors, or to any acknowledgment, implicit or explicit, of their role?

Partly to answer this question, and partly to facilitate examination of the scientific method involved, the "information problematic" below labelled "Algorithm #1" has been prepared. In this figure, a generalised market-space is elaborated according to the assumptions of the renovated equilibrium model. However, the bevy of supply-demand equations at the margin normally used to illustrate conventional economic analysis has been suppressed. As becomes clear at first glance from this skeleton outline of a renovated equilibrium model (in which, by the way, both intentions and intangibles are already subsumed), the actual scientific method of such an approach to economics shares something in common with botany, anatomy or zoology: classification and typology are crucial for defining the market-space itself. What is missing, however, is anything resembling either a systemic conservation principle or law of motion. This absence – which would be much harder to spot if the conventional equations-based presentation had not been suppressed – is indeed quite glaring. There may be some kind of law of motion based on incentive connected with this model, but such incentives as exist in practice comes only from individual economic agents: they are not built into the economic system as such. In the market space proper, acts of exchange are paramount. However, the entire giving rise in the first place to objects of exchange, and to mechanisms for distributing them in the second place, must all be derived from whatever happens in the market. In effect, the tail wags the dog. This arrangement itself obscures the fundamental absurdity of the assumption that the buyer-seller nexus is the primary economic relationship in the first place: how can that which has not yet been produced be consumed?

Step 1 – **Define the elements that occupy market space as:**
- agents of exchange
- acts " "
- objects " "

Step 2 – **Classify by:**
- type of *Exchange-agent*
- " " *Exchange-act*
- " " *Exchange-object*

Step 3 – **Group by broadly similar features** ($_3C_2+_3C_3 = 4$ possible combinations):
- certain types of *Exchange-agents* and *Exchange-acts*
- " " " " " " *Exchange-objects*
- " " " " " " *Exchange-acts* and *Exchange-objects*
- " " " " *Exchange-acts* and *Exchange-objects*

Σ - This algorithm generates a case-typology of all possible elements, classifications and groupings occupying the market-space, in all categories of combination or isolation

STRENGTHS OF THIS ALGORITHM:
~ the data themselves are *objective*: others observing the same space at the same time (or at the same point in the economic cycle) would see data of the same kind, even though the number of elements or the number of classifications might have changed from one time of observation to another.
~ without loss of generality, by removing Exchange-agents' data and adding a defined timespan for a production-distribution cycle, this market-space description acquires flesh and blood as a "Leontieff table" of all inputs and outputs in the economy

IMPLICIT (unstated) ASSUMPTIONS OF THIS ALGORITHM:
~ *relative size or strength* of participating exchange-agents is a matter of indifference to the operation of the market-mechanism itself;
~ *dependencies* developed among exchange-agents are a matter of indifference to the operation of the market-mechanism itself;
~ *constraints on the range or number of exchange-acts and-or of exchange-objects*, including any induced by the above-mentioned dependencies, are also a matter of indifference to the operation of the market-mechanism itself.

Figure 1-4. ALGORITHM #1 – In the above model, the only relevant intention of any exchange-agent derives entirely from his/her position in the market, as buyer or seller for the purpose of completing some transaction or set of transactions. At the point of transaction, *i.e.*, of clearing the market of the good or service being sold, all intangible social relations are reset, transaction time *t* resets back to 0, and any other intangibles incorporated in the commodity being exchanged have now been transferred to their new owner. Hence, whatever significance or role such intangibles acquire subsequent to the transaction cannot bear any relationship whatsoever to whatever significance or role they possessed before. Since, as a matter of economic fact and social reality, intentions and intangibles continue and persist – for example, the claim of workers on the social product, part of which has been produced without their being paid for it – it is to say the least extremely convenient to model the primary economic relationship such that intentions and intangibles are cancelled or reset at the point of transaction. As can be inferred from the list of the model's implicit assumptions, only the market-mechanism itself is modeled. Presence in the market is assumed, with no theoretical consideration being given, nor practical weight assigned, to the possibility of various actual or potential barriers to market access, such as stronger exchange-agents squeezing weaker ones through marketing or production "agreements" of various kinds.

In the post-Soviet epoch, when British Prime Minister Thatcher intoned that "there is no such thing as 'Society'", not a jot or tittle of any neoclassical or marginalist economics textbook produced over the preceding 100-plus years had to be adjusted. However, as anyone knows or has experienced after using the London tube (starved of maintenance resources by her privatisation crusades), or British Rail services between the capital and the suburban reaches of East Anglia, Oxfordshire, Buckinghamshire, Hampshire, Sussex or Kent (which her governments also extensively privatised), there is now, today, no almost such thing as reliable public transport serving the nearly 30 million people living and working in the southeastern corner of the British Isles. According to Baroness Thatcher, her governments' privatisation and similar wrecking measures saved Britons from coming under the thrall of "the nanny state", *i.e.*, a condition in which the needs of individuals are provided and regulated according to the needs and capacities of Society as a whole. Placing the individual above and outside society in this way, meanwhile, has also made it extremely difficult to sort the dimensions of any actual tangible problem properly, let alone grasp its intangible elements and begin to fix the mess left behind. That is the nub of the issue the authors take up in this work. The asserted absence of alternatives could be due just as much to the resistance put up by the gatekeepers of the intellectual and scholarly commanding heights of the status quo to acknowledging this state of affairs. The following two chapters, examining what has happened with intangibles in the Big Picture, explore the consequences of this approach taken up at the same time in Thatcher's Britain and Ronald Reagan's United States, which Prime Minister Thatcher defended on the grounds that "*t*here *is no a*lterrnative" but which the rest of the world has come to recognize and brand as "the TINA syndrome".

Chapter 2

INTANGIBLES IN THE BIG PICTURE: THE DELINEARISED HISTORY OF TIME

INTRODUCTION

The so-called "TINA syndrome" provides the fundament, the actual rock, on which the political, economic, military and other elites and establishments of the Anglo-American world and European bloc have built their church. Inscribed over its entrance stands the motto: "there is no god but monopoly and maximum is his profit". On this basis, continuous attacks on the very concept of intangibles are launched, most prominently against time-consciousness. Especially singled out is time-consciousness based on appreciating and-or priorising the long term over the short term, as well as placing the interests of the social collective over the interests of any individual member of the collective. In this portion of the chapter, it is argued that Humanity has been on the wrong track since Sir Isaac Newton published his Principia Mathematica at the end of the 17th century, and that the scientific research enterprise developed since then has taken the world on a merry chase to nowhere.

Without exception, the assaults on time-consciousness, and on cognition of what happens in and through the passage of time, take the form of a denial of the principle of Nature as the Mother of all wealth. The denial of this principle has always encountered resistance. Some resist by breaking the attacks down and responding to selected cases. For example, the contributors to the book Underdevelopment and Social Movements in Atlantic Canada (Toronto 1979), following precisely this tact, act according to the principle that "the movement is everything…" This places the struggle of the people for livelihood where it belongs, viz., at the centre of economic theory and practice. However, these writers' version of this approach is silent about long-term or final aims. Their work actually priorises t = "right now" over longer-term views of the role of time in social-historical processes. People's deepest desires to see Justice prevail and Injustice sent packing are generally aroused, positively, by their apparent stand on the side of "labour" against "capital"; a great deal of hope might well be vested in these stands. Has this hope, however, been misplaced? Analysis of these authors' collective work from 1979 (as the Soviet Union began its final slide to oblivion by invading Afghanistan), and its source in theories of "regional underdevelopment" (formulated at the Cold War's height in the late 1950s), suggests this may be the case. Especially disturbing is the outlook underlying that theory, and specifically its extreme pragmatism and welter of contradictions and inconsistencies. These disclose a position entirely at odds with the proclaimed mission to establish the truth of matters under investigation.

In order to maintain a position in what they see as the mainstream today, some of these writers have taken matters further, adapting to fit the cut of current discourse in the early 2000s some of the concerns raised in the earlier work. En route, however, they make a major concession to the disinformation of the Canadian fisheries department that "there are too many fishermen chasing too few fish". Disguising the concession as an appeal for "ecological sanity" in the face of a pending environmental crisis of raw material food supplies during a period of still-excessive capitalization in the coastal fishing industry, those putting forward this argument decline to challenge the claims by the government and the largest fish processors that the problem at bottom is a shortage of raw material, a defect in Nature. As, however, the problem is actually one of how Humanity has arranged its affairs when it comes to extremely fundamental matters like food-gathering, this concession, no less than any of the other more direct attacks on time consciousness and on cognition as a source of reliable information, forms part of a far more general and sweeping assault on the very concept of human agency. This assault challenges the fundamental notion that no human social problem is without some human social solution. The fact of the matter is that the essence of human social agency lies on the path of pursuing knowledge. Whosoever would increase knowledge is bound to disturb the status quo, but even so, a person must increase his knowledge of the truth.

2.1. NEWTON'S "LAWS OF MOTION" – *VERSUS* NATURE'S

As an enterprise entailing apprehension and comprehension of the material world existing external to consciousness, science – meaning the scientific approach to investigating phenomena – requires examining both things-in-themselves and things in their relations to other things.

One of the most fundamental nuts to be cracked in this exercise involves mastering and understanding laws of motion as they apply to the matter under investigation. The importance is simply that motion is the mode of existence all matter. Whether it is energy, or matter that has become transformed into energy, or energy that became transformed into matter, there is no form of material existence that is not in motion.

There are two variables that have become especially critical for modelling and tackling the actual laws of motion of modern economic life: time and information. Both are utterly intangible. Up to now, however, they have been incorporated into economic analysis on the basis of rendering them tangible. This has created more problems than it solved.

2.1.1. The Continuity Conundrum

On the front of scientific work undertaken to investigate and determine laws of motion, Isaac Newton represents the watershed. His elaboration of the general laws of motion of all matter was a huge advance over the incoherent and conflicting notions that prevailed hitherto.

Of course, various limitations appeared at certain physically measurable/detectable boundaries – at speeds approaching the speed of light, for example, or within space approaching the measurable minimum limit of (approximately) 10^{-32} m, etc. This led researchers to make important corrections and amendments to Newton's formulae. The fact remains, nevertheless, that Newton's fundamental breakthrough lay in the very idea of summarising the laws of motion itself, common to all discrete forms of matter understood and observed to that time, *i.e.*, not atomic, molecular or sub-atomic. Equally remarkably, in order to take account of the temporal component attending all matter in motion, Newton invented an entirely new departure in mathematics. A new departure was required because existing mathematics were useless for describing any aspect of change of place while matter was undergoing such change.

Apart from their long standing despite some amendment, this mathematical apparatus used to describe and apply Newton's laws is worth re-examining to get a better understanding of some of the basic tools used throughout scientific work in all fields, including fields far removed from having to deal with laws of motion. Here we have in mind the fundamentals of integral and differential calculus.

Newton's mathematics made it possible to treat time as though it were as infinitely divisible as space – something no one had ever conceived of doing before. This worked extremely well for purposes involving the relative motion of masses acting under the influence of the same external forces, especially force due to gravity and acceleration due to gravity. Extended to the discussion of the planets and other celestial bodies, it appeared that Time throughout nature – Time with a capital "T" – was indeed highly linear. For Newton and for all those applying the tools of his calculus to problems of time and space comprehensible to ordinary human perception, t_{LINEAR} and $t_{NATURAL}$ were one and the same.

Newton's was an extremely bold and utterly unprecedented maneuver. It arrived as the fruit of an unpredicted turn in the profound revolution in human thought already under way since the start of the Renaissance during the century and a half predating Newton. Launched from the leading centres of the Bourbon and Hapsburg Empires, to reverse the correct verdicts of the new science of Copernicus, Kepler, Galileo and others that emerged during the European Renaissance in increasingly open revolt against the authority of Church dogma, the Catholic counter-reformation had failed, and failed utterly. Throughout the continent of Europe, Catholic monarchs and the authority of the Holy Roman Catholic Church were placed entirely on the defensive. In England, the "Catholic forces" were entirely routed, and among that country's scientific and philosophical circles, Newton, along with many of his colleagues in the Royal Society, were standard-bearers of the newly-victorious forces.

Newton's mathematical labour was nothing like the mystical, quasi-religious revelation that his fellow eighteenth-century Englishman, Alexander Pope, captured in the line "God said: 'Let Newton be', and all was light." To elaborate his method into what he called, in the *Principia Mathematica*, a "theory of fluents and fluxions", Newton built on and refined the implications and tentative conclusions of a number of contemporaries and near-contemporaries who, although lacking an overarching theoretical framework, were already working with processes of infinite summation that converged to some finite value. He proposed differentiation as a method for deriving rates of change at any instant within a process, but his famous definition of the derivative as the limit of a difference quotient involving changes in space or in time as small as anyone might like, but not zero, *viz.*:

$$\frac{d}{dt}f(t) = \lim_{\Delta t \to 0} \frac{f(t+\Delta t) - f(t)}{\Delta t}$$

Figure 2-1. Formulation of Newton's breakthrough idea (expressing Leibniz' derivative notation in Cauchy's "limits" notation)

set the cat among the pigeons. It became apparent that, without further conditions being defined as to when and where differentiation would produce a meaningful result, it was entirely possible to arrive at "derivatives" that would generate values in the range of a function at points of the domain where the function was not defined or did not exist. Indeed: it took another century following Newton's death before mathematicians would work out the conditions – especially the requirements for continuity of the function to be differentiated within the domain of values – in which its derivative (the name given to the ratio-quotient generated by the limit formula) could be applied and yield reliable results.

Only seven years after Newton's death, the main arguments hoisted against his mathematics and especially some of its underlying, implicit notions came not from scientists but from Christian theologians, led by Church of England bishop George Berkeley. He was the most prestigious among those who considered inherently blasphemous the very idea that mental apparatus of the human could aspire to manipulate and control any infinite process. Although such an idea would be unlikely to occur to modern reader, not all the Bishop's remarks were without merit. Deriding Newton's differentials as "ghosts of vanishing quantities", Berkeley (1734) encapsulated the actual problem in terms that would echo among mathematicians for another century. Others on the same line all but accused Newton of poaching on The Infinite as a supposedly exclusive turf of the Almighty. Newton's public posture was that men could know a Divine plan for Nature through grasping the physical laws, but he declined to publish his own views more fully. From his private papers it is now known that he saw knowledge of these laws mainly as a potential source for individuals to enrich themselves. His motive in uncovering natural laws was also in part linked to the desire he shared with many other English men of science of his day to discredit those doctrines – especially concerning the nature of matter, motion, and planetary bodies – whose sole support rested on the authority of the Catholic Church and its papal index.

2.1.2. Continuity and Linearity: Confusion Twice Confounded

It was in the period 1740-1820 that the basic theory of differential equations also came to be elaborated. Newton's notation was almost universally replaced by that of calculus' cofounder Leibniz, facilitatiing the achievement of several further breakthroughs in the theory of analysis for the Swiss mathematician Euler among others. Many notable techniques were developed using the techniques of superposition (Kline 1972).

The notion of superposition was an ingenious solution to a very uncomfortable problem implicit in (and left over from) Newton's original schema. Under certain limiting conditions, his derivative would be useful for dealing with what today are called vectors – entities requiring at least two numerical quantities to fully describe them. All the important and fundamental real-world entities of motion – velocity, acceleration, momentum etc – are vectorial insofar as, if they are to usefully manipulated mathematically, not only their magnitude but also their direction must be specified.

Here there inheres an limiting condition for applying Newton's calculus. So long as magnitude and direction change independently of one another, no problems arise in having separate derivatives for each component of the vector or in superimposing their effects separately and regardless of order. That is what mathematicians mean when they describe or discuss Newton's derivative being used as a "linear operator". The moment it is not possible to say whether these elements are changing independently, however, a linear operation will no longer hold. Because modelling is always an approximation, this for a long time provided many researchers a licence to simplify and relax requirements, to some degree or other, as to just how precisely some part of natural reality had to fit the chosen or suggested model. Naturally, one could generate some sort of model, and results, provided the assumptions – boundary conditions or initial conditions – were then retrofitted more or less so as to exclude unwanted dependencies. The interior psychology of this act of choice seems to have been that the linearised option would reach a result, therefore it could and should be used. The implication of this choice has been rather more mischievous: everything non-linear has been marginalised either as exceptional, excessively intractable in its "native" non-linear state, or usable only insofar as it may be linearised.

In the actual evolution and development of what became the field of real analysis, of course, every step was taken incrementally. Newton's discoveries were taken up and re-used as tools. Meanwhile, however, the theoretical work needed to explain the conditions under which analytic methods in general, and the derivative in particular, were applicable had not reached the stage of explicit elaboration. Thus, the notion of the derivative as a linear operator, and even aspects of a more generalised theory of linear operators, began to develop and be utilised before the continuity criteria underpinning the entire field of real analysis were made explicit. This led to associating linearity principally with superposition techniques and the possibility of superposition. By the time Cauchy published his work elaborating the importance of continuity, no one would connect continuity with linearisation. In real analysis, as Kline (1972) and most other modern historians of mathematics have observed, discontinuity became correlated mainly and even exclusively with undifferentiability.

With the rigourising of real analysis by Cauchy and Gauss, applied mathematics in the middle third of the nineteenth century developed a powerful impetus and greatly broadened its field of action throughout all the natural sciences, especially deeply in all areas of mechanical engineering. There arose a preponderating interest in steady and-or equilibrium states, as well as in the interrelations between static and dynamic states.

While this was not at all unexpected, it is crucial at this point to make what was actually going on more explicit. Some initial analysis of a deliberately simplified example (see Figure 2-2) will help illuminate something that often becomes obscured:

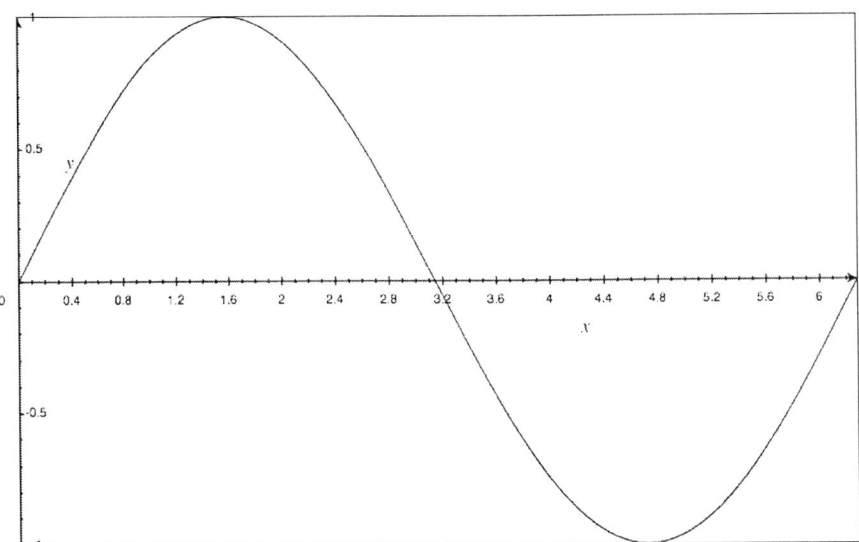

Figure 2-2. Graphic representation, in Cartesian coordinates, of the classic simple function $f(t) = \sin t$.

Assume some process described by the simple sine function illustrated above. As may be recalled from introductory calculus, using Newton's difference-quotient formula (from Figure 1), the instantaneous rate of change anywhere along the graph-line of this function, which will be continuous anywhere within the interval $(-\infty, +\infty)$, i.e., $-\infty \leq t \leq +\infty$, can be computed stepwise as follows:

$$\frac{d}{dt} f(t) = \lim_{\Delta t \to 0} \frac{\sin(t + \Delta t) - \sin t}{\Delta t} = \lim_{\Delta t \to 0} \frac{\sin t \cos \Delta t + \sin \Delta t \cos t - \sin t}{\Delta t}$$

As Δt approaches 0, $\cos \Delta t$ approaches $\cos 0$, which is 1. Meanwhile, because $\sin x$ approaches x for decreasingly small values of x, the term $\dfrac{\sin \Delta t}{\Delta t}$, also becomes unity. So:

$$\frac{d}{dt} f(t) = \lim_{\Delta t \to 0} \frac{\sin(t + \Delta t) - \sin t}{\Delta t} = \lim_{\Delta t \to 0} \frac{\sin t \cos \Delta t + \sin \Delta t \cos t - \sin t}{\Delta t} =$$

$$\lim_{\Delta t \to 0} \frac{\sin t + \sin \Delta t \cos t - \sin t}{\Delta t} =$$

$$\lim_{\Delta t \to 0} \frac{\sin \Delta t \cos t}{\Delta t} = \lim_{\Delta t \to 0} \frac{\sin \Delta t}{\Delta t} \cos t = \lim_{\Delta t \to 0} \cos t = \cos t$$

$$\lim_{\Delta t \to 0} \frac{\sin \Delta t \cos t}{\Delta t} = \lim_{\Delta t \to 0} \frac{\sin \Delta t}{\Delta t} \cos t = \lim_{\Delta t \to 0} \cos t = \cos t$$

Figure 2-3. Generating the first derivative $f'(t)$ for the function $f(t) = \sin t$ using Newton's difference-quotient formula.

This means that, as one moves continuously along the domain t, the *instantaneous rate of change* along the curve represented by the graph for f(t) can be computed by evaluating the cosine of *t* at that value on the horizontal axis. What is being described is change *within* the function; *the function itself, of course, has not changed.* As this particular function happens to be periodic, it will cycle through the same values as the operational output described by this graph proceeds through subsequent cycles. This makes it quite easy to see that the function itself describes a steady-state condition. In fact, however, even if the function were some polynomial, anything lying on the path of its graph would represent the steady-state operation of that function: steadiness of state is not reducible to some trait peculiar to periodic functions.

Newton's method itself, long described as "Newton's method of tangents" because it could be illustrated geometrically by picturing the derivative as the slope of a straight-line segment tangent to the curve of any function's graph, relies implicitly on the notion of approximating instantaneous moments of curvature, or infinitely small segments, by means of straight lines. This alone should have tipped everyone off that his derivative is a linear operator precisely because, and to the extent that, it examines change over time (or distance) *within an already established function, i.e.,* within a process that has reached its steady state.

The drive to linearise covers a multitude of sins. Thus for example, as bold and utterly unprecedented Newton's approach, it also contains a trap for the unwary: going backward or forward in space or in time is a matter of indifference. If natural reality is to be modelled as it actually unfolds, however, the requisite mathematics has to close the door on, and not permit the possibility of, treating time as reversible. What use can be made, then, of such mathematics for describing anything happening in nature according to naturally-conditioned temporal factors? To engineer anything in Nature, applying Newton's calculus requires suppressing or otherwise sidelining such considerations, and indeed: it has long been accepted, as a pragmatic matter, that fudge factors and ingenious work-arounds are needed to linearise the non-linear. What has not been clarified, or discussed much if at all up to now, is that this is *inherently* what they must be about. If this nub of the issue is inherent, then it follows that merely backing up a few steps on the path that brought matters to this stage, back to the point where everything still looked more or less linear and the non-linearities had not yet taken over, is not going to overcome the fundamental difficulty. The starting-point itself contains the core of the problem, which is that Newton's calculus edifice, in its very foundation, is truly anti-Nature. Starting anywhere on this path, one will diverge ever further from Nature.

One starting point for a new path might go somewhat as follows: consider as the starting point for modeling such natural processes some series of observations of an ongoing phenomenon for which there is no "analytic" function that fits perfectly or even fits over an extended run of results. Results are needed that are grouped reasonably closely in time (the assumption of continuity must be more-or-less likely or possible to validate). Instead, however, of computing a difference quotient based on evaluating the limit at some arbitrary common value like 0, consider what happens if some positive finite constant real value c were used instead. A new derivative may be defined thus:

$$f'(t) = \frac{d_c}{dt} f(t) = \lim_{\Delta t \to c} \frac{\sin(t+\Delta t) - \sin t}{\Delta t} = \lim_{\Delta t \to c} \frac{\sin t \cos \Delta t + \sin \Delta t \cos t - \sin t}{\Delta t}$$

Now, as Δt approaches c, $\cos \Delta t$ approaches $\cos c$, which is anywhere in the interval [-1,+1]. Meanwhile, the term $\frac{\sin \Delta t}{\Delta t}$ may fall anywhere in the interval $[-\frac{\sqrt{3}}{2}, +\frac{1}{c}]$. Applying these maxima and minima generates the open interval $-(2\sin t + \frac{1}{c}\cos t) \leq \frac{d_c}{dt}f(t) \leq \frac{1}{c}\cos t$, in which:

- at $t = 0$ (+2kπ), $\frac{d_c}{dt}f(t)$ converges to a single value, viz., $\frac{1}{c}$, which is positive (> 0);

- at $t = \frac{\pi}{6}$: $-(2 + \frac{\sqrt{3}}{2c}) \leq \frac{d_c}{dt}f(t) \leq \frac{\sqrt{3}}{2c}$, which straddles 0;

- at $t = \frac{\pi}{4}$: $-\sqrt{2}(1 + \frac{1}{2c}) \leq \frac{d_c}{dt}f(t) \leq \frac{\sqrt{2}}{2c}$, which straddles 0;

- at $t = \frac{\pi}{3}$: $-(\sqrt{3} + \frac{1}{2c}) \leq \frac{d_c}{dt}f(t) \leq \frac{1}{2c}$, which straddles 0;

- at $t = \frac{\pi}{2}$: $-2 \leq \frac{d_c}{dt}f(t) \leq 0$, which is mainly negative (≤0);

- at $t = \frac{2\pi}{3}$: $-(\sqrt{3} - \frac{1}{c}) \leq \frac{d_c}{dt}f(t) \leq -\frac{1}{2c}$, which is entirely negative (<0);

- at $t = \frac{3\pi}{4}$: $-\sqrt{2}(1 - \frac{1}{2c}) \leq \frac{d_c}{dt}f(t) \leq -\frac{\sqrt{2}}{2c}$, which is entirely negative (<0) and reduces,

- at $c = 1$, to $-\frac{\sqrt{2}}{2}$.

From here, heading towards $t = \pi$, other features emerge:

- At $t = \frac{5\pi}{6}$, $\frac{d_c}{dt}f(t)$ lies somewhere between $-(1 - \frac{\sqrt{3}}{2c})$ and $-\frac{\sqrt{3}}{2c}$, in which:

- for $c = \frac{\sqrt{3}}{2}$, $-1 \leq f'(t)|_{\Delta t \to c} \leq 0$;

- for $\frac{\sqrt{3}}{2} < c < \sqrt{3}$, while for $c > \sqrt{3}$, $f'(t)|_{\Delta t \to c} < 0$; and

- for $c = \sqrt{3}$, $f'(t)|_{\Delta t \to c} = -0.5$;

- At $t = \pi$: $-\frac{1}{c} \leq \frac{d_c}{dt}f(t) \leq \frac{1}{c}$

Figure 2-4. Generating family of first derivatives, $\{f'(t)|_{\Delta t \to c} = \frac{d_c}{dt}f(t)\}$, for $f(t) = \sin t$ using modified difference-quotient.

Here we are dealing with multiple, in fact: infinite, solutions, as should be expected when modeling problems in Nature. The impossibility until relatively recently, *i.e.*, the last third of the 20th century, of computing such representations efficiently, or at all "within anyone's lifetime" for that matter, and their inherently inelegant appearance as represented by the system of notation available, doubtless drove many away from even considering these phenomena as worthwhile subjects of investigation. Many researchers applying mathematics to modelling real-world phenomena would likely reject, as an extremist position, the militant insistence of the British mathematician G.H. Hardy (1940), briefly the mentor of the Indian mathematical genius Ramanujan, that one should approach and present mathematics as some kind of pure thought-experiment continuous in time, untainted by (and having nothing to do with) any possible application. Nevertheless, Eurocentric conceptions, stemming from ancient Greek philosophy, of beauty as a function of two-dimensional symmetry, "balance", etc. remain very much part of the expectation of most mathematicians alive and working today on current problems of both pure and applied mathematics. This has served to reinforce a tendency to discard or dismiss as unlikely an "inelegant-looking" result.

2.2. FROM ILLUSIONS OF PRECISION AND REPRODUCIBILITY IN NATURAL SCIENCE TO DELUSIONS OF NORMALCY IN SOCIAL SCIENCE

Newtonian calculus had become cluttered with refinements and special recipes of all kinds by the 19th century. The precision and especially the reproducibility of results achieved using it were nevertheless remarkable. The physical sciences were written about and spoken of as "exact sciences". There were not a few who understood very well the price of such progress. Appropriate initial and-or boundary conditions had to be established in which a given differential equation could be applied. An inappropriate selection would render any results from using the equation meaningless. There were probably rather fewer who also understood that preparatory research would be required: *before* selecting and applying any existing linearising model equation to the task of extracting possible solutions, exactly how invariant any actual initial and-or boundary conditions might be, with time, for a process taking place in nature has to be established. Against this overwhelming current, however, who was going to look back and question the applicability to the reality of nature of methods and models emerging from the linearising assumptions of real analysis? Unfortunately, this set the context in which researchers in social science also became concerned with rigourising their methods in the middle of the nineteenth century. The rigourisers were feeling increasingly pressured from two directions.

Dynamism is inherent in all social or individual development. The idea that equilibrium is normal and anything other than the steady state is a disturbance and disruption is a notion that has served every Establishment in all times and places. However, it is not a true description of social, economic or political reality. Such striving for the steady state emerged clearly at the time of Sir Isaac Newton. It invaded and permeated his scientific work. From his time to date it seems hardly accidental that "success" in a scientific career is correlated strongly with supporting the *status quo* of the day. Is this an accident, or a position based on prejudice rather than science? Certainly the historical argument can be made that, in Europe during the Inquisition and earlier, scientific integrity pitted many researchers openly against the authority asserted over scientific matters by the Church, with Galileo representing only the most dramatic and highest profile in a long line of similar cases that preceded him.

The argument can be advanced even more compellingly on scientific grounds. If such a thing as steady-state equilibrium is possible, and actual, anywhere in Nature, how is it *also* possible that matter and energy can be neither be created nor destroyed, but only change form, sometimes even changing one into the other? One or the other: *either* steady state, in which case neither matter nor energy can be changing form, *or* motion is the mode of existence of matter. This is fudged in various ways. For example, repetitive forms like reciprocal or cyclical motion are often represented as a kind of pseudo-steady state within a delimited range. However, the maintenance of real-life reciprocal motion, like that of pistons in an internal combustion engine, requires a directed expenditure of energy in a bounded chamber that ceases once the supply of combustible fuel is cut (by running out of fuel or turning the engine off). This is a human-engineered phenomenon, normally not found anywhere in Nature. Cyclical repetition in Nature does not repeat the exact same path in each circuit, any more than the Earth repeats the identical path in its orbit around the sun. Even the repetitive cycles of "chaotic attractors" (like Julia or Mandelbrot sets) generate an infinite number of "self-similar" but unique, non-identical cycles.

The reality – that, regardless of what can be engineered to happen for some finite period, there exists no such thing anywhere in Nature as a steady state – has been masked. Instead Newton's First Law of Motion is widely accepted as the first and last word on the inertial properties of *matter*. This provides that "an *object* at rest tends to stay at rest and an *object* in motion tends to stay in motion with the same speed and in the same direction unless acted upon by an unbalanced force." On its face, this law does indeed appear to provide definitive criteria for the analysis of inertia in all possible cases – at rest, or already in motion. However, in fact, it is at the very least a potential source of disinformation because 1. *resistance to* motion is identified, at the empirical level of "objects", with *absence of* motion, and 2. even at apparent equilibrium, *i.e.*, at a point between a previous completed state of motion and a pending resumption of motion at some subsequent stage, something at the microscopic level of matter remains in motion, *e.g.*, at the molecular level. If Newton's First Law is loosely applied to all forms of matter in general, however, motion ceases to be an inherent property of matter. Once this separation is effected, all kinds of mischief comes in its wake.

A great paradox and howling contradiction is widely accepted without further thought. is that, on the one hand, we cannot have motion without equilibrium moments, whereas the disinformation is that all motion tends towards equilibrium in the presence of an appropriate balance of forces. In the unceasingly dynamic environment that continues to exist outside and around a stationary observer, how matters may appear to such an observer can hardly be accepted as the final word or definitive description of what is actually taking place. In other academic realms apparently far beyond or unrelated to natural science, such as politics and social science, the same lure of the steady state is undeniable, but once again its aphenomenality inevitably leaps out. Consider Georg Wilhelm Friedrich Hegel (1833), the philosopher of the modern era credited with doing more that anyone since the ancient Greeks to restore respectability to the notion popularised by Heraclitus that "all is in flux". Hegel wrote that the autocratic, militarily powerful, small German-speaking state of Prussia in the 1830s represented the apex of human achievement in statecraft, and a balanced polity which could not and would not be further improved upon, *i.e.*, nothing in Prussia was any longer in flux!⁹

The first challenge posed in the modern era to the staeady-state paradigm came in the works of Karl Marx (1867). It was widely followed up in many others' work by the start of the twentieth century. According to this new paradigm, the entire social order currently and historically never represented any such thing as true equilibrium or steady state. The bourgeois order of 19th century Europe was dominated by the societal model of France and the industrial model of Great Britain. Many viewed this order as the epitome of "Progress"-in-general with a capital "P". For them, this message of incessant societal flux was anathema. Influenced by the positivist trend pioneered in French philosophy and social science by Auguste Comte (1848), many researchers in social science saw development in their own time as a struggle between "forces of progress" and forces opposing progress. The present moment in western European social development was identified as "progress." All opposition was portrayed as potentially or actually opposed to progress. All tendencies reinforcing the current line of development within the status quo, especially everything tending towards equilibrium, were presented as a support for progress (Butterfield 1968). In this way, time based on the steady state, *viz.*, an inherently linearised conception of time, was confounded with the notion of time as a measure of "progress." Subsumed by the achievement of equilibrium, the irreversibility of actual time was made to disappear.

INTANGIBLE	**TANGIBLE**
Value *(Value-in-Use)*	**Price** *(Value-in-Exchange)*
Surplus	**Profit**
TIME (Historical)	**TIME (Linear, i.e., t2 – t1)**

Figure 2-5. Tabular comparison of some tangible and intangible categories of economics.
The Marxian categories of "value" and "surplus" included the more familiar notions of "price" and "profit, respectively, as tangible subcategories. The concepts of time associated with the intangible and the tangible sets of categories were $t_{HISTORICAL}$ and t_{LINEAR} respectively. See further discussion at *2.3.2* below.

---

⁹ Following the implosion of the Soviet Union, the former U.S. State Department official Francis Fukuyama (1992) famously declared "the end of history", meaning the U.S. system had now demonstrated its superiority forever to the end of what remained of recorded time. In 2003 Fukuyama declared it was the destiny of the United States as the premier upholder of the banner of freedom and democracy on earth to invade Iraq and topple Saddam Hussein, but in early 2006 recanted by declaring the entire affair a great "mistake". These prognostications reflected something other than a scientific investigation of historical developments and their direction or meaning: the Prussian government paid Hegel's salary as a university lecturer, while the network of opinion-makers and government officials for whom Fukuyama was an occasional mouthpiece went from riding high in the opinion polls and counsels of the executive branch to losing the public's trust. If dynamism is

Thus was the notion of $t_{NATURAL}$ extended now to include social phenomena – but t_{LINEAR} and $t_{NATURAL}$ still remained one and the same.

Furthermore, according to this logic, any disturbance of this equilibrium was illegitimate. Such disturbances were to be accounted as the work of deranged, deviant, alien sources and forces. The French sociologist Emil Durkheim acknowledged at the end of the 19th century that the society itself could be the seeds of many of these disturbing phenomena, but the individual was ultimately responsible in any particular case since deviance itself manifested itself individually. (Durkheim 1897)

Long-term thinking empowers people and enables people to empower themselves. (The moment one becomes hooked on long-term thinking as a habit, it becomes blindingly clear that all true empowerment derivesa from oneself and one's relations with other people, not from any externally-imposed or externally-induced condition.) Long-term thinking means thinking about the consequences of one's own actions. It also means re-examining everything reported from the standpoint of extracting its longer-term significance, beyond what is being immediately reported. Within the very process of daily living, it ought to be well within everyone's interest to apply long-term thinking in all times and places. Yet, this has not happened. There are what are called "pressures of daily life" – which actually means pressure to produce some outcome in the short term – which are usually blamed for this shortfall. But the fact remains, and it cannot be made to disappear by being glossed over, that it is actually in the *interest* of the vast majority of individuals, viewed either in the short term or for the long term, to apply long-term thinking as a habit in all times and places. Human conscience exists in all times and places and it will always assert its claims in the field of human action. Just because individuals can and do frequently suspend listening to their conscience does not make it go away or disappear. The key to maintaining long-term thinking is to suspend listening to, or being pressured by, anyone and anything that places the interests and needs of the short-term ahead of the long term. If the long term is not continually attended to, there will be not only no long term but the short term will become far shorter. There is nothing at all mysterious about long-term thinking. Start with clarifying *where* whatever it is you are thinking about fits or exists with respect to the Past, the Present and-or the Future, and with *why* it is of any significance or importance to you. That already takes care of two profoundly significant intangibles: time and intention. Just as there cannot be such thing as matter without motion (*i.e.*, energy), there is no such thing as understanding, *i.e.*, meaningful knowledge, without the individual taking action to "find out". A positive, *i.e.*, pro-social and long-term, intention ensures that the seeker will find something useful. Finding out something for oneself is the most empowering thing there is. "Learning" something on the say-so of some "authority" is the most disempowering and enslaving thing there is. What is so especially empowering about long-term thinking is not whether this-or-that piece of knowledge was already known or even previously thought about, but rather the journey on which it takes the seeker.

An associated concern expressed by many of the "rigourisers" about Marxist approaches had to do with the Marxians' foundation in historical scholarship. The data of history disclose patterns that could be explained in terms of the actual social and economic structures in place at the time. However, Alfred Marshall, the founder of neoclassical economics as an academic

---

Nature's reality, denial of it in any form or to any degree is always part of the agenda of some force or other from the Establishment be it in government or academia.

discipline, argued that such historical consideration and analysis were useless and irrelevant anywhere in the social sciences. In his view, Darwin's theory of evolution demonstrated that the only factors decisive in any process of change would be found among those most recently-generated, not among those historically handed down (Marshall 1890). Here lies the source of two unwarranted assumptions: 1. the closer time t is to "right now", the less-qualified and more precise will be the mathematical rendering of whatever the social condition being studied, and 2. the justification for resorting to steady-state, equilibrium-based models. Although Marshall may have believed his theories were objective to the extent that they hewed to this notion of the relative indifference of temporal factors, his prejudice itself had little to do with the correctness or incorrectness of his own theory in particular. The late John Maynard Lord Keynes was probably the greatest refuter among 20th century economists of much of the *corpus* of Marshall's neo-classical assumptions and analysis. He also believed that historical time had nothing to do with establishing the truth or falsehood of economic doctrine. "In the long run, we are all dead," he wrote. He tied this to a stance that attacked all easy acceptance without question of any of the underlying assumptions propping up all forms of orthodoxy. Accordingly, this retort was taken as the sign of a fresh and rebellious spirit. However, in his own theoretical work he was frequently at pains to differentiate what happens to individuals who are driven by short-term considerations from what happens at the societal level at which he was theorising about broad historically sweeping movements of economic cause and effect (Keynes 1936).

Although not alone in this interpretation – many of his peers in both the social and natural sciences shared it – Marshall for his own purposes seriously misconstrued the thrust of Darwin's argument. Darwin said only that the emergence of a species distinct in definite ways from its immediate predecessor and new to the surrounding natural environment generally marked the final change in the sequence of steps in an evolutionary process. The essence of his argument concerned the non-linearity of the final step, the leap from what was formerly one species to distinctly another species. What Marshall had in mind *viz.*, the proximity of that last step to the vantage-point of the observer – which might be centuries or millennia or longer – was *not* the relevant temporal factor. Rather the length of time that may have passed between the last observed change in a species-line and the point in time at which its immediate predecessor emerged – the characteristic time of the predecessor species – was the time period in which all the changes so significant for later on were prepared. This latter could be eons, spanning perhaps several geological eras. This idea of $t_{NATURAL}$ as characteristic time was the one which Marshall's misappropriation of Darwin's idea obscured. Even though Keynes was prepared to suspend obsessions with the short-term for the purposes of establishing his analysis of the broad historical sweep, he stood side by side with Marshall in marginalising any role for or consideration of $t_{NATURAL}$ in the setting of actual policy, especially where economic gain could be enhanced in the short term by disregarding it.

A second, but equally telling source of pressure on social scientists to mathematise their research methodology was a sense that their work would not be taken seriously as scientific without some such mathematical rigour. As the models and mathematics from the so-called "exact" sciences would hardly be appropriate or seem credible in any field of study focusing on human beings and their incredible variety of needs, wants and impulses, another kind of mathematics would have to do. Questions of history and historical phenomena were also a convenient target because of the lack of any means to describe them with any meaningful, non-trivial mathematical model.

The solution to both the Marxian-influenced challenge concerning incorporation of historical time-scales and the "rigourising" challenge was to come from ... statistical science, based on theories of mathematical probability and its probability measures of "uncertainty". The disinformational role of statistical and probabilistic models in the social sciences was discussed earlier in the section on "laws of motion", "natural law" and questions of mutability. A particular area of interest in connection with the concerns about "rigour", however, was that part of mathematical statistics based on the theories of probability in which the discrete is analysed on a scale in which it could be said to approximate the continuous. This maneuvering around the discreteness of social events finessed the entire question of discontinuities in general, including the discontinuity that marks the onset of some new turbulence. (There will be frequent occasions throughout the present volume to comment on and mark some of the most egregious cases of this maneuver). The underlying probability distributions for these "continuous approximations of the discrete" were exponential mathematical functions, thereby furthering the tendency to linearise.

The current state of affairs has made it very difficult to remember, and appreciate the consequences of, a quite fundamental fact: the mathematical models used and applied to "get a handle" on engineered and-or natural phenomena are, first and foremost, *images* of an ideal form. Today, when it comes to appreciating scientifically and correctly the intangible aspects of temporal factors of any phenomenon, scientific workers – having been put through the ringer of quantum mechanics, etc. – know that t_{LINEAR} and $t_{NATURAL}$ cannot possibly remain one and the same. Although a linear model applied to linearly-engineered phenomena is known to work well under circumstances where some operating limits have been experimentally verified, a linear model applied to phenomena that are themselves not linear is another matter.

Nothing in nature is linear. Linear independence cannot be a feature of any model purporting to reflect the reality of a situation where everything affects everything else and there are literally dependencies upon dependencies; the notion of any system operating in isolation, or of modeling the solution of any problem presented in Nature by assuming the condition of some isolated system or sequence of such systems, is aphenomenal. Changes of state occur, appear or disappear both continuously as well as discontinuously. There is no such thing as "steady state". Problems as found in their natural setting always appear "ill-posed" but up to now there seems to have been a concerted effort not to attempt solutions to problems in this state. Instead a problem that looks like the actual problem but which can be posed in more or less linear form is solved instead and this result is declared to be something approximating the solution of the actual problem... given the addition of certain conditions and boundaries to the original problem's definition. This distorting technique starts very early, with high-school/first-year university instruction in how to solve problems associated with simple harmonic motion of a pendulum using Newton's Second Law of Motion in a linearised approximation as the governing equation. As mentioned above, one convention widely adopted up to now involves artificially and arbitrarily hedging the reality to be observed in nature with various time-constraints so that some relatively tractable mathematical model may be applied. This is not unrelated to the fact that the solution schema developed for such models have become ever more elaborate. These linearised images have served to sustain an illusion that nature's secrets are being discovered at a rate that is in lock-step with the advances taking place in the technology of electronic computation. Somewhere, somehow, no matter how general and even non-linear the governing partial differential equation to be modeled and solved, linearisation continues – a truth reflected either in the ongoing production of unique solutions, or small sets of multiple solutions, from these models (Islam 2005).

This is a final and total abandonment of any last shred of scientific integrity. To seriously propose such solutions and models is to proceed utterly deaf to the ancient injunction that "Nature cannot be fooled" (Feynman 1988). Over the past more than 300 years going down Newton's road, these are the typical consequences that flowed from the more-or-less uncritical assumption of the difference-quotient formula for the derivative, premised on evaluating "in the limit", *i.e.*, as $\Delta t \rightarrow 0$.

Time rendered tangible by Newtonian linearisation proceeds at a pace whose uniformity or otherwise is a matter of indifference. For many real-life situations, such a misrepresentation of an intangible of such importance has frequently produced meaningless results, sometimes leading to results so ludicrous that "interpolation" was required. Is the Newtonian linearisation all there is? One meaningful and non-trivial mathematisable conception of "historical time" might be to consider the passages of time in terms of cycles whose periodic features change at specific branch-points. This would entail a complete and final break with any notion time linearised by Newtonian methods. "Well-behaved" functions whose initial and-or boundary conditions permit extraction of a solution or solutions would be subordinated to the reality of mathematical chaos, where extreme sensitivity to initial conditions carries "stability" implications about the meaning or existence of a function over one or more sub-intervals nested within the function's overall domain of interest. In addition to restoring a modicum of humility as well as integrity to the scientific enterprise by solidly repositioning the non-linear as the general case and the linear as the exception, such an approach should make it possible to disclose and elaborate the "characteristic time" of many real-life processes in nature (Islam: *ibid*). In this connection, Chapter Six addresses the possible rationales for encouraging investment for periods exceeding the expected human lifespan, as well as for recalculating "return on investment" in terms of what would be a meaningful characteristic time of project's actual service to Humanity. An important consideration is that the timespan adopted for purposes of analysis exceed whatever the characteristic lifespan.

2.3. MUTABILITY

2.3.1. "Laws of Motion", "Natural Law" and Questions of Mutability

In science, not all laws are equal – some may describe an empirical relationship, others define fundamental features common to an entire category of processes. Newton's calculus held out a seductive promise of all relationships becoming in principle quantifiable, even computable. However like all "law", this promise was actually a double-edged sword. Would such laws as those that Newton's calculus might describe be relationships that captured the reality of change in the natural world, or would they be mere snapshots freezing some relationship in an artificial bubble of permanence?

It is entirely possible for quite fundamental laws to operate even as their very existence remains vehemently denied. Take, for example, the basic law of operation of capitalist political economy, which is that the rich get richer and the poor get poorer. On the other hand the basic law of operation for the development of theoretical models of this political economy is to stop at nothing to deny or obfuscate this basic law of operation of that actual economy.

A recent interview by the London *Independent* (Vallely 2006) cast 2001 Nobel Economics Laureate Joseph E. Stiglitz as an Old Testament prophet. The tradition of religious prophets was that they pinpointed defects in the current course of their societies on the basis of disclosing the truth, measured against an unvarying moral standard, about the society's past, present and future as they had come to understand from observing contemporary events unfold around them. Stiglitz's own words as relayed by this interviewer seem, however, to disqualify him from membership in such an exalted category. For example, he is quoted in the following context saying global warming shifted within a decade from being a theoretical possibility to a serious threat today (all emphases added):

> A decade ago Mr Stiglitz was a member of the Intergovernmental Panel on Climate Change. Today his concern about global warming has been turned into alarm. *"Ten years back the theory was clear, as was the evidence of the increasing concentrations. But no one thought it would manifest itself as quickly, and in such a dramatic way."* (Vallely: *ibid.*)

What has accumulated in the last decade is a massive amount of data that could be evidence of... just about anything, from climate change on a cycle as long as several human lifetimes to planetary warming whose reversibility is unknown (because the only projections that have been investigated are cascades of consequences, rather than any set of indicators of a temporary equilibrium in the future that will differ from whatever temporary equilibrium has been put behind us by developments of the last two generations). While the increased presence of CO_2, an essential component of the atmosphere that makes human and other life possible on this planet, has been identified, no differentiation has been made between fresh and extremely old CO_2, and little has been elaborated concerning the pathways of the vast number of toxic byproducts of petroleum refining and other chemical processing borne aloft with the CO_2. To suggest that his "concern... has been turned into alarm" by what has happened over the last decade is to engage in disinformation. If someone tells me: "I am more scared today by what I don't know than by what I dismissed 10 years as relatively unimportant in the near term", my instinct is to reply: "Then stop playing 'Chicken Little' waiting for the sky to fall and go find out!" But without addressing the business of actually finding out the science of climate change, Humanity is indeed paralysed. According to the interview, however, without doing anything to establish the science of anything, the problems that now loom so large in the short-term that we can no longer even discuss the possibility of a future can be solved by a couple of quick fixes:

> Mr Stiglitz offers two solutions *[to managing global warming - Ed.]*. The first is to increase incentives for developing countries to get involved in global warming reductions. Carbon-trading initiatives offer a market-based solution. But there is need for more. "Kyoto offered financial rewards to Third World countries for planting new forests, but not for maintaining existing ones. So Papua New Guinea can get money if it chops down its forest and replants it but not if it just keeps its forest. *That's silly.*" (Vallely: *ibid.*)

What the interview report leaves out is that developed countries with large forest cover, including the U.S., Canada and post-Soviet Russia, are indeed permitted not only to count such forests but to trade them with developing countries for emission credits – that's not silly, that's dead serious – but neither Brazil nor countries to its north and west that share any portion of the Amazon basin are permitted to count much less trade for emission credits any part of the Amazon rain forest under the pretext that the Amazon rain forest forms part of the common heritage of Mankind and is not for sale! The disinforming, paralysing part is that, by insinuating that independent development in developing countries outside the Kyoto framework would at least compromise if not threaten outright the ability of Humanity to breathe clean air and drink fresh water, this position also simultaneously pre-empts and forecloses such an alternative. This report creates that disinformation by failing to point out that emission-trading schemes are premised on developed countries being able to buy or to sell these credits, while developing countries are permitted only to buy credits, and even then only from countries in the developed-country group. What Stiglitz accurately describes as a "market-based solution" is taking place, but for the purpose of preserving an economic environment in which developed countries continue to call the tune in developing countries. However, when it comes to establishing the real test of prophecy these days, one's positions on global warming and Kyoto have been completely displaced by the matter of where people stood at the time the U.S. government began publicly declaring that Saddam Hussein was so dangerous that only a full-scale invasion could save Mankind from the fate his continued presidency in Iraq held in store. Tens of millions of people participated in protest marches in almost 3,000 cities and localities around the globe in the four months preceding the invasion: clear, one would think. But the *Independent* interview quotes Stiglitz on this question as follows:

> "..It's hard to rebuild infrastructure *[in Iraq - Ed.]* because of the insurgency. It's hard to deal with the insurgency because of lack of jobs. And it's hard to provide jobs because of lack of infrastructure.
> "Those, like me, who warned they were walking into a quagmire were more right than even we supposed. The lack of analysis and preparedness of the Bush administration - and of Tony Blair by association - was astounding, particularly since this was a war of choice .." (Vallely: *ibid.*)

If this indeed be the test or proof of prophecy, or of qualifications to be considered an "Old Testament prophet," perhaps it is time to re-examine that very notion and the ancient traditions associated therewith. Parodying Groucho Marx: the others might no longer wish to be associated with a club that could accept Joseph Stiglitz as a member.

This is an all-sided continuous campaign. It began long before Marx and the publication of *Capital*. Since then it has become far broader and more desperate. Its aim, however, remains the same: to ensure survival of the status quo by stifling any consciousness or source of consciousness about any alternatives. As one of the recent leaders of this campaign, former British prime minister (now Baroness) Thatcher, used to intone: "There *Is No A*lternative."

Using the initial letter of each word in the phrase to form an acronym, critics have labelled this ongoing campaign the "TINA syndrome". Over the 25 years or so, this campaign has emerged in a wide range of manifestations, throughout all fields of study in politics, economics and policy. Throughout the social sciences and even in the natural sciences, assertion of the TINA syndrome and the struggle against its assertion have together spurred an intense and renewed interest in the meaning of "law" in general, and of how particular processes may be considered to be governed by some sort of law, or pattern, or set of relationships. It is difficult enough to conceive anything more intangible than a "relate" or relationship, let alone one such as the TINA syndrome that has produced such wide and highly tangible impacts. There is indeed no alternative at this point but to take the plunge and examine what the brouhaha is all about.

The industrial revolution was already under way for a generation in Britain when Adam Smith famously put forward his theory of the so-called "invisible hand":

> ..every individual necessarily labours to render the annual revenue of the society as great as he can. He generally, indeed, neither intends to promote the public interest, nor knows how much he is promoting it. By preferring the support of domestic to that of foreign industry, he intends only his own security; and by directing that industry in such a manner as its produce may be of the greatest value, he intends only his own gain, *and he is in this, as in many other cases, led by an invisible hand to promote an end which was no part of his intention.* Nor is it always the worse for the society that it was no part of it. By pursuing his own interest he frequently promotes that of the society more effectually than when he really intends to promote it. I have never known much good done by those who affected to trade for the public good.
> Adam Smith, *An Inquiry into the Nature and Causes of the Wealth of Nations* (1776)
> [Emphasis added – Ed.]

Implicit in Smith's invocation of the superiority of the individual pursuing his self-interest over the interests of society or the public lies a notion of the shortest conceivable time-span, one in which $\Delta t \to 0$: "he intends only his own gain". Chapter Five discusses this aspect of the aphenomenal model – it is actually a defining feature – by considering what happens to "self-interest" transplanted to a context in which $\Delta t \to \infty$: clearly, self-interest in the long-term becomes the pursuit of gain or benefit for society as a whole. Otherwise, it would be akin to dividing by zero, something that would cause the model to "blow up".

All the defenders of, and apologists for, the status quo have pointed to Adam Smith's argument as their theoretical justification for opposing in principle any state intervention in the economy. Chanting their mantra of the invisible hand, policy-makers on the same wavelength have been confining and restricting such intervention to those parts of economic space in which there operates no profitable production of goods or services with which such intervention would be competing. At the practical level, the only question remaining about this "invisible hand" is whether its invisibility arises from absence, *i.e.*, non-existence, or from darkness, *i.e.*, a sinister existence like the Black Hand.[10]

One rather profound and deeply disturbing truth about the TINA syndrome that has begun to dawn far more widely than ever before since the disappearance of the old Soviet bloc is that neither the State as bogeyman nor the State as employer-substitute is a viable option for Humanity. There is in fact no alternative but something other than either of these options. This is a subversive consciousness very much resisted by both proponents of TINA and their detractors. Once $\Delta t >$ some characteristic time, and a measure of the change in

---

[10] The Black Hand was the Serbian secret society, likely modelled on a much older secret society of the same name founded in Sicily in the 1400s and said to be the origin of the Mafia, which carried out the assassination of the Austrian Archduke Ferdinand in June 1914, precipitating the outbreak of WW1. The Serbian Black Hand's history remains so tangled that to this day no authority is absolutely certain what combination of European intelligence services actually financed the crime. Ever since, the Black Hand has become a metaphor for the murkiest of murderous mayhem (Tuchman 1962).

economic space, s, exceeds the lone individual, *i.e.*, as $\Delta s \gg 1$, then the role of the human factor – social consciousness can indeed become decisive. It increasingly must displace the need for a State to play all or any of its previously accustomed roles in the economic life of society. At that point, intentions that serve the society as a whole no longer require the application of some power previously delegated to an external force (the State) in order to prevail as a norm. That is the stage in which the intangible – good intentions – can finally command the tangible.

At the theoretical level, the significance of Smith's observation of the so-called "invisible hand" is that the outcome of normal operations of commodity production are achieved independently of the will of any individual participant or group, *viz.*, "an end which was no part of his intention".

Significantly, Smith does not say that money-capital wedded to the short-term immediate intentions of some individual (or grouping of common interests) will not achieve its aims. Rather he confines himself to observing that objectives which formed no part of the originating set of immediate short-term intentions, *viz.*, "an end which was no part of his intention", may also come to be realised thanks to the intervention of the "invisible hand". Chapter 6 will discuss what can happen with intentions in our own day by applying the economic theory of intangibles advanced in this book, so that intentions are translated and expressed in a socially positive manner, for long-term aims.

Smith believed that "an end which was no part of his intention" came about as a byproduct of how competition operates to "regulate", in a rough and overall manner, both the supply of and demand for socially necessary goods and services. The will of any consumer(s) or producer(s) by itself would never suffice. The secret to the "law of motion" of an industrial commodity economy lay in how the marketplace under conditions of free competition allocated economic resources.

Underlying Smith's view was a broader 18th-century Deist philosophical outlook already prevalent among a broad section of the European intelligentsia of his day. Anything could be examined as the outcome of a process comprising observable, definable stages and steps, and linked ultimately to some Prime Mover (or initiating force). The scientific model for such narratives was provided by Sir Isaac Newton's *Principia Mathematica*, crowned by his discovery and elaboration of the laws of motion and the principle of universal gravitation. (Newton 1687)

For most scientists of the 17th and 18th centuries, an analysis ascribing a process to some Prime Mover manifesting itself as Newtonian "mechanism" was the best of all possible worlds. On the one hand, a natural occurrence could be accounted for on its own terms, without having to invoke any mystical forces, divine interventions or anything else not actually observed or observable. On the other hand, the divinity of Creation need not be dispensed with or challenged. On the contrary: this divinity was being reaffirmed, albeit indirectly "at a certain remove" insofar as whatever was required to sustain or reproduce the process in question could now be attributed to some even more fundamental "law of motion".

The revolution occasioned in scientific outlook since the publication of Charles Darwin's *Origin of Species* (1859) has become so complete and all-encompassing that, from the vantage point of the start of the 21st century, it is hard to remember that much of the support for, and embrace of, Newtonian mechanism (and the attendant penchant in many fields for "laws of motion") derived from the belief that it could be reconciled with a Creationist assumption, not just about Man *within* Nature, but about the very existence of Nature itself.

Re-examined in this light, the impact of Smith's assertions about the "invisible hand" among his contemporaries can be better understood. In essence, he was declaring that economic life comprised phenomena that could be analysed and comprehended as scientifically and as objectively as Newton had analysed and disclosed the laws of physical motion of all forms of matter in Nature and even the universe. Furthermore, such investigations would provide yet another proof of the divinity of Man's existence within that natural universe.

Between the time of Sir Isaac Newton in the early 1700s and that of Charles Darwin in the middle third of the 1800s, these considerations were framed and understood by scientific investigators within a larger context, *viz.*, the conception of "natural law". Using scientific method, Man could come to know, understand and make use of natural laws – laws operating within observable processes in Nature itself, and discoverable from systematic observation of these processes. However: *these natural laws in themselves were immutable.* This was the same as with any mathematical function whose "Newtonian" derivative yielded an instantaneous rate of change between points on its graph but which itself did not change. In fact, it was precisely this notion of the immutability of natural law that was assumed and implicit within the general and more widely-accepted view that some law of motion, eventually connectible back to a Prime Mover, must account for any and every process observed in Nature.

The conundrum was simply this: if natural law were not immutable, science would be compelled to account for innumerable random divine interventions in any natural process, at any time. Such a course could drag science back into the swamp of the metaphysical idealism of Bishop Berkeley – Newton's great antagonist – who famously explained that objects in physical nature continued to exist beyond out perception because God exists to cognise them while and whenever human beings are not available to cognise them (Berkeley 1734). In the words of a limerick popularised widely in the 19th century specifically satirising Berkeley:

There was a young man who said "God
Must think it exceedingly odd
If he finds that this tree
Continues to be
When there's no one about in the Quad."

"Dear Sir, your astonishment's odd;
I am always about in the Quad
And that's why this tree
Will continue to be
Since observed by Yours faithfully, God."

No one would accept something so contrary to common sense; science and scientists would be come laughing-stocks. If natural laws were not held to be immutable, how could logical reasoning guarantee that error could be detected and rejected?

The actual solution of this conundrum in practice came in the course of further, deeper-going research into actual phenomena. Since the middle of the 19th century, starting with Marx in social science and Darwin in natural science, and extending early in the 20th century to physics and chemistry with the elaboration of theories of quantum mechanics, it has become increasingly clear that the mutability or immutability of any natural law is actually a function of, and dependent on, the time-scale selected for observation and study. The problem here in general is one of method. The particular source of the problem lies how the methods of scientific investigation that are applied to comprehend the material deal with temporal factors, the passage of time, the role of time.

In social science, the appropriate time-scale is the historical period of a given social mode of production. Before the epoch of a given mode of production, for example, there might be a certain law of population growth/decline, but with the emergence of the new epoch this law would change its form and-or manifestation. Thus Rev. Thomas Malthus' notorious extrapolation of population growth overwhelming increases in food production depended on a failure to distinguish, on the one hand, the disappearance – in less than two generations, as people left to find work in the new industrial centres – of a rural population that had been stationary for the preceding five and one-half centuries from the rapid increase, on the other hand, of population in the industrial centres during the same period. The law of population growth/decline governing the latter was bound to be entirely different from the law of population growth/decline governing the former because the manner in which the society procured its food supply and other needs had been completely transformed. By ignoring this distinction, however, Malthus' *Essay on Population* (1798) perpetrated a misunderstanding that persists to this day with periodic predictions reappearing from time to time of global collapse due to overpopulation, regardless of the fact – thoroughly and repeatedly exposed by Boyd-Orr *et al.* (1937; 1940; 1943) – that not a single one of any of the hundreds of similar such predictions in earlier periods has ever been validated by events.

In the geological record, entire species appear in one epoch only to disappear in a later one; ludicrously, this has been adduced by so-called "Creationists" as evidence that Darwin's theory of evolution – which used such leaps and gaps precisely to explain speciation – must be untrue! Of course, evidence of this kind proved only that the notion that evolution should take place as a smooth process uninterrupted by quantum leaps – the very view that Darwin's analysis and evidence definitively refuted – was devoid of reality. The same issue of time-scale is now just beginning to be understood regarding some of the earliest states of matter in the first few picoseconds of the Big Bang.

With the exposure of these absurdities, it has become possible to start hammering the final nails into the coffin of the "TINA syndrome". All phenomena or effects duly observed in any natural or social process arise from some verifiable cause, but in accordance with the operation of some body of law that remains constant and consistent, and always within some definite spatio-temporal boundaries. To argue immutability outside such boundaries is open to serious question, while to deny or ignore the existence, and the role or consequences, of such boundaries is a source of scientific disinformation.

"Scientific disinformation" is a most apt description of the condition in which provision of scientific theory and researched data nevertheless leave the social order incapacitated when it comes to framing and-or selecting a course of action to carry out consciously programmed changes in the status quo. It explains very well why, for example, literally millions of people in our own time have become perfectly well aware that the existing social and economic system itself reproduces a condition alluded to at the start of this section – in which the rich get richer and the poor get poorer – but nevertheless no agency of the social order is capable of intervening to turn the situation around.

Assume for the moment that this societal condition is recognised as a scientific and verifiable fact. For the moral philosopher, the matter of responsibility is immediately posed. For the more dispassionate scientific observer, it would be important to establish causes and effects in order to sort out the dynamics of this condition. How to alleviate the negative consequences of such a condition in various areas – the health of the population, the education of the upcoming generation, etc. – would accordingly preoccupy specialists in the relevant respective fields of social science and policy. However, there is indeed a way to present the evidence of this condition in its various aspects, and of the extremely negative consequences flowing from this condition, so that everything is to blame for the condition, and hence no one thing is to blame for any part within the overall. One approach that fills this bill very nicely is the resort to statistical methods in social science – especially those involving correlation.

One of the most important consequences of resorting to statistical methods was the finessing of the need to establish and distinguish cause from effect. To be able to assert that A and B are related by some correlation coefficient χ appears highly suggestive of underlying reality even as it skirts at the same time the entire issue of whether $A \rightarrow B$, $B \rightarrow A$, or actually $Q \rightarrow A$ and $R \rightarrow B$ while in fact no causal relationship whatever exists between A and B. Correlation is very useful where causal relations are already known and established. In the social sciences, however, in the absence of – or inability to gather – any other evidence from more direct or more thorough experimental observation, it has become *de rigeur* to employ correlation to imply or suggest a causal relationship. Is the publication of caveats about the distinction between demonstrating a correlation and suggesting some relationship of cause-and-effect sufficient to shield such activity from merited condemnation as a serious abuse of the requirements of scientific integrity?

One of the most fundamental requirements of science properly conducted is that one's work at the end of the day draws some line of demarcation between what is known to be false and what may not yet be fully understood to be the truth. Detection of error and elimination of falsehood are absolutely fundamental to scientific enterprise at any level. In this respect, the "Correlation" bucket has holes in it big enough for a veritable spotlight to coruscate. Consider the following example. If one were to correlate "intensity of religious faith", "presence of exact bus fare" and "frequency of arrival at a preset destination on public transit", any number of clearly nonsensical, as well as a number of apparently reasonable, correlations might be elaborated, *e.g.*, "faith and a two-dollar coin gets you downtown on the bus." However, regardless of how anyone might go about weighing the various possible renderings of the available evidence, the results would always be insufficient to rule out possibilities lying on the farthest margins and perhaps bordering on nonsense, *e.g.*, what happens if you have the two-dollar coin but lack faith? This converts the likely acceptance of the apparently more reasonable-seeming possibility (or possibilities) into a matter of purely personal prejudice. It is no longer guided by a procedure that meets the fundamental requirement of any scientific method, *viz.*, that a clearly erroneous result will be excluded by the weight of the evidence and not by the prejudice of the investigator.

Statistical modes of reasoning carefully employed, in a context where there exists some actual knowledge of definite causes and definite effects, can be subtly powerful. But it is an entirely different story when reasoning proceeds from the grouping of data according to statistical procedures derived from the norms of some abstract probability distribution. No groupings of data, however well-fitted to some known probability distribution, can ever be the substitute for establishing actual causes and actual effects. Substitution of the "statistically likely" or "probable" in the absence of knowledge of what is actually the case is a truly inexcusable breach of scientific integrity. For one thing, speaking purely in terms of how the logic of an explanation for a phenomenon comes to be constructed when inputs are "probable" or "likely" but not actually known, if any of the steps on the path of reasoning toward an actually correct conclusion are themselves false, neither Bayesian methods of inferring conditional probabilities (Jevons 1870) nor Pearsonian methods of statistical correlation (Pearson 1892) will assist the investigator to reason to the particular conclusion that will be demonstrably most consistent with known fact. Consider this syllogism:

- All Americans speak French [major premise]
- Jacques Chirac is an American [minor premise]
- Therefore Jacques Chirac speaks French [conclusion-deduction]

If the information relayed above in either the major or minor premise is derived from a scenario of what is merely probable (as distinct from what is actually known), the conclusion, which happens to be correct, would be not only acceptable as something independently knowable, but reinforced as something also statistically likely. This then finesses determining the truth or falsehood of any of the premises… and, eventually, someone is bound to "reason backwards" to deduce the statistical likelihood of the premises from the conclusion. Indeed this latter version, in which eventually all the premises are falsified as a result of starting out with a false assumption asserted as a conclusion, is exactly what has been identified and labelled elsewhere as the aphenomenal model (Khan, Zatzman and Islam 2005)

An extreme example of the utterly specious procedure that is generated by such degenerate reasoning, and the layers of opacity that it can be used to generate, made it recently to the front page of the October 24th, 2005 editions of the *Wall Street Journal*, in an article by reporter by Jon E. Hilsenrath about how a "Novel Way to Assess School Competition Stirs Academic Row" (excerpted below). The major premise in this case goes: "public schools located in different parts of the same district produce different student outcomes". The minor premise goes: "a common geographic factor associated with the neighbourhood of schools with the best outcomes is the presence of water-streams". The conclusion-deduction is: "public schools located near water streams produce better outcomes than public schools that are not". Empirical evidence for the conclusion actually exists, and was compiled by the up-and-coming researcher-star at Harvard University's economics department whose work stands at the centre of the aforementioned "academic row." The major premise, which posits physical location as a determining factor *irrespective of the demographics of either the student population or the teaching staff*, is either meaningless or demonstrably false. The minor premise holds syllogistic value if and only if either the major premise is non-trivial or if no other geographic factor is found to be common to schools with the best outcomes. This research actually argues that, since previous research (much of it premised on linking student or staff demographics to outcomes) produced conflicting results, an allegedly "random" correlation should be sought instead which would avoid the biases that ensured the previous research approach would produce such an indecisive wash:

> Five years ago Harvard's Caroline Hoxby, a rising star in economics, wrote a paper that reached an unusual conclusion: Cities with more streams tended to have schools with higher test scores.
>
> Today her work is a widely cited landmark in the fierce national debate over free-market competition in public schools. And it's at the center of a bitter dispute with another economist that is riveting social scientists across the country.
>
> Her adversary is Jesse Rothstein, a young professor at Princeton, who says her study is full of flaws. In a rebuttal to her critic, Dr. Hoxby wrote of his work: "Every claim is wrong." She has also accused him of ideological bias. Dr. Rothstein, in turn, says she resorts to "name-calling" and "*ad hominem* attacks" on him.
>
> The unusual spat has put a prominent economist in the awkward position of having to defend one of her most influential studies. Along the way, it has spotlighted the challenges economists face as they study possible solutions to one of the nation's most pressing problems: the poor performance of some public schools. Despite a vast array of statistical tools, economists have had a very hard time coming up with clear answers.
>
> "They're fighting over streams," marvels John Witte, a University of Wisconsin-Madison professor of political science and veteran of a brawl over school vouchers in Milwaukee in the 1990s. "It's almost to the point where you can't really determine what's going on." (Hilsenrath 2005b)

In fact, as the article more or less brings out, the real *casus belli* over this research is that the role of school vouchers for parents to choose the best school for their child is treated as a neutral and non-biasing factor, whereas the opponents of the "streams" research and its conclusions are damned by the pro-"streams" faction as an elitist coterie of anti-voucher, anti-choice fanatics. Thus indeed it turns out that the research design of the "streams"-camp has its own agenda, *viz.*, to occupy the education outcomes research space by ousting the anti-voucher elements that prevailed a long time there. At the same time, the initiator of school-voucher economics of parental choice, the authority and reputation of Milton Friedman – practically a demi-god of the Wall Street Journal famous for restoring monetary theory, dethroning Keynesian "orthodoxy" and capturing the Nobel Prize in Economics for his trouble (Friedman 1976b)– is involved, and so the reporter is compelled to turn himself into a human pretzel and couch his findings about this "academic row", which are actually quite damning for the voucher-choice camp, in terms that are as uncondemning as possible:

> Milton Friedman, the Nobel Prize-winning economist known for his free-market views, proposed 50 years ago that to improve schools, parents could be given vouchers – tickets they could spend to shop for a better education for their kids. He theorised that the resulting competition among schools would spark improvements in the system. Free-market advocates loved the idea. Teachers' unions hated it, arguing that it could drain resources from some public schools and direct resources to religious institutions.
>
> Research on these programs turns up evidence of benefits from school choice. But it hasn't proved strongly convincing, and testing the hypothesis is anything but simple. In the mid-1990s, researchers battled over how to interpret studies of voucher use in Milwaukee. In 2003, they tried to evaluate voucher experiments in New York and ended up squabbling over the right way to decide if a child was African-American. Last year, in assessing charter schools – institutions that are publicly funded but not bound by traditional rules – they argued over how to take into account differing backgrounds of the children who attend.

Analysts have searched as far away as New Zealand for evidence about the effects of competition in education – and disagreed about what was found there, too. Now there is Hoxby vs. Rothstein.

Up to now, the ace-in-the-hole argument for relying on statistical procedures and processes to rigourise social science has been that, apart from investigations of extremely limited phenomena, and since results cannot be reliably duplicated where input conditions cannot be fully or faithfully replicated, lab-controlled experimental reproducibility of the kind routinely utilised in the natural sciences is really not an option in the social sciences. Does it follow from this, however, that phenomena observed in society, its politics and its economics cannot be ascribed accurately to definite causes? Instead of addressing this meat of the matter, advocates of statistical methodology as the heart and soul of rigorous social science raise their diversion that, without a probability measure, there is too much room for subjective opinion and judgment. What has either not occurred to some of them, or already been dismissed by others among them, is the idea that, instead of blithely and unquestioningly assuming that the status quo is all there is, all there has ever been and all there will ever be, such arbitrariness is precisely what could be reined in by properly and duly incorporating characteristic historical time-dependent conditions attending the emergence or disappearance of societal phenomena.

The "properly and duly" caveat is important in this connection, as it is entirely possible to arrange historical data so that one arrives at no single determinable cause or clearly-defined pathway of causation. As Gilbert and Sullivan parodied in their operetta *Trial By Jury*, the English judiciary strutting about like truly feudal nobility could assert their eternal right to control the status quo by noting that "if everybody's somebody, then no-one's anybody". In the social sciences, modern-day academic nobility – actual or aspiring – behave exactly the same when they assert that a phenomenon that they have studied to the point of practically converting it into their personal property has so many causes that no one cause or pathway can be sorted out. How do those who commit such felonies against scientific integrity and the authority of authentic knowledge get away with it? By improperly and unduly manipulating the intangible aspect of temporal factors.

2.3.2. Essential and Intangible Role of Temporal Factors – A Detailed Example

2.3.2.1. Detaching Canada's East Coast Fishery from its History: Causes and Consequences

Coming mostly from large institutions based in the United States and others around the world following their lead, there is a trend that has come to predominate in current social-science writing which generally avoids historical dynamics altogether and resorts to mining history mainly or only as a source of factual documentation of past events. The period immediately preceding that *coup* was rich with examples of exactly this kind of felonious assault upon scientific integrity, and works from that period provide some of the richest teaching material by negative example.

This section discusses one particular example at length. Of course there is much to elaborate about the particular subject matter – the east coast fisheries of Canada – which in itself is hardly a commonplace everyday subject. But the central error in its methodology is common to a very broad range of writings especially in the fields of economics, development and theories of social and economic systems and their interrelationships.

The work in question is a collection of monographs by then-young and upcoming economists, historians, political scientists and sociologists dealing with the fishery of the Atlantic provinces of Canada. Published in 1979 by "New Hogtown Press", a special imprint of the University of Toronto Press, the collection was entitled *Underdevelopment and Social Movements in Atlantic Canada* (hereafter: *U and SM*) and edited by Canadian sociology professors Robert J. Brym and R. James Sacouman (Brym and Sacouman 1979). As recently as October 2001, more than two decades after the appearance of this book, at a conference on "regional underdevelopment" convened at Saint Mary's University in Halifax, Canada. Several of the work's contributors were still actively defending the lines of interpretation advanced earlier in *U and SM*.

Veltmeyer and Petras have further developed certain aspects of the line of thought in Veltmeyer's piece in *U and SM* into a thesis concerning the purported ecological disaster of the Canadian east coast fishery as an example of what they call a "system in crisis" (Veltmeyer and Petras 2004). Veltmeyer and Petras (hereafter *V and P*) repeat the claim popularised by many observers that the shutdown of the commercial fisheries of eastern Canada by the federal government since July 1992 had to do mostly with overfishing of the resource base in the sense of causing the resource base to be reduced below a level that could sustain a similar level of fishing effort, and then they argue from this what a blight on Nature and the ecosystem such excessive plundering represents.

Is there evidence that these fish stocks were being harvested beyond their capacity to sustain such effort? Yes. Is this, however, evidence also at the same time of too many fishermen? *V and P* duck this question, by stressing the devastation of the resource base. But economics being about human livelihood, it is for our purpose an absolutely crucial question. It is not enough to consider the relation of persons to Nature when it comes to pursuing a livelihood; the relations of persons to one another in the pursuit of livelihood is equally important because, as will be discussed below, our starting point is that Nature is the mother and labour is the father of all wealth. Failure to take this properly into account has led and seems always to lead researchers away from accepting, acknowledging and reckoning the most important corollary flowing from this observation, *viz.*, that politics cannot be separated from economics and, indeed, commands it.

Behind the use of the overfishing thesis to explain or justify the government's "groundfish moratorium" of July 1992, is the doctrine repeatedly put forward by the Canadian federal Department of Fisheries and Oceans: that there were too many fishermen chasing too few fish. The scale of the event alone, however, renders that explanation immediately suspect. This was the single largest lay-off in Canadian history, in which 40,000 livelihoods were eliminated overnight almost entirely in the outports of the south, west and northeast coasts of the island of Newfoundland (as well as to a much lesser extent in parts of eastern New Brunswick, Prince Edward Island and eastern and southwest Nova Scotia). Government-collected data on fish catches inside Newfoundland and Nova Scotia territorial waters (within 12 miles of shore) disclosed a pattern of overfishing in all the principal commercial species by the early 1980s. The peak catch by Canadian fishermen on the east coast had been recorded in 1968 and this overall total had been in decline ever since (Harris 1998).

V and P mention the role of the expansion of the 200-mile offshore economic zone as a factor stimulating excessive fishing effort by Canadian as well as foreign fleets in the northwest Atlantic. However, they do not analyze or explain how the corporate sector used its connections in the Canadian government to multiply the effect of its domination of the processing and harvesting sectors of the fishery to drive the small independent fishermen to the wall, out of fishing altogether. This is significant as the contributors to the earlier *U and SM* volume had produced their papers mostly at the time, or just before, the 200-mile limit was introduced in 1977. In any event, their treatment of the general impoverishment and social-economic stagnation of the great mass of fishermen in the coastal communities over a lengthy historical period, pays no attention to the specific impact of the vertically-integrated corporate sector on how so many coastal fishermen continued to harvest most species. They manage this independently of any relationship with these processors, certainly at increased cost to themselves and hence also at the cost of continued marginalization of their incomes from fishing. None of the papers reflect any consciousness of its imminence even though the Canadian government had made clear as early as 1975 that it would proceed with such a policy once it negotiated and signed bilateral fishing agreements with the largest of the 18 foreign fishing fleets, led at that time by the Soviet Union, harvesting catches within 200 miles of the Atlantic coastline. The bilateral agreement reached between Canada and the Soviet Union in 1976, three years before the appearance of *U and SM*, actually provided its fleets could take up to 88.4 per cent of the fish stocks inside the 200-mile limit on the east coast, according to the principle that Canada treat all fish stocks not being commercially harvested or developed at the time of the agreement as "surplus to Canadian needs". Such vending of offshore sovereignty registers nowhere in *U and SM*, a circumstance that seriously blighted any possible value of their analysis. At the same time, this is hardly surprising as the body of economic theory underpinning that work nowhere acknowledged even the possibility of rival imperial interests – in this case, the U.S., and then-Soviet Union – contending for supremacy and privileges in one and the same zone, *e.g.*, Canada's northwest Atlantic littoral, lying beyond the formal territorial control of either Washington or Moscow.

The table of contents of *U and SM* discloses its general drift:

1. The Capitalist Underdevelopment of Atlantic Canada, by Henry Veltmeyer;
2. The Differing Origins, Organisation and Impact of Maritime and Prairie Cooperative Movements to 1940, by R James Sacouman;
3. Political Conservatism in Atlantic Canada, by Robert J Brym;
4. The Emergence of the Socialist Movement in the Maritimes 1899-1916, by David Frank and Nolan Reilly;
5. Underdevelopment and the Structural Origins of Antigonish Movement Cooperatives in Eastern Nova Scotia, by R James Sacouman;
6. Underdevelopment and Social Movements in the Nova Scotia Fishing Iindustry to 1938, by L Gene Barrett;
7. Inshore Fishermen, Unionisation and the Struggle against Underdevelopment Today, by Rick Williams;
8. The Capitalist Underdevelopment of Nineteenth-Century Newfoundland, by Steven Antler;
9. Regional Factors in the Formation of the Fishermen's Protective Union of Newfoundland, by Robert J Brym and Barbara Neis; and
10. Towards a Critical Analysis of Neo-Nationalism in Newfoundland, by James Overton.

In addition to the broad topic of Canada's east coast fishery, these essays share two other links in common. First, they share an acknowledgement of the need to incorporate historical reality. Second, but unfortunately coupled with the first, they also each fail to think through the impact such a procedure must have on the manner in which the more conventional tools of their particular discipline are handled and applied. As this failure forms the starting point of the discussion rather than its conclusion, it is appropriate to set out the starting point adopted for the purposes of the present critique.

As a social political and economic fragment, observed from the vantage point of the present, Canada's east-coast fishery can neither be separated from national and international politics nor reduced to a riot of spontaneous parochial conflicts. Looking back into the past from the vantage-point of the present, it can be seen that, from its inception during the dawn of colonial expansion into the northwest Atlantic approaches of the North American continent at the end of the fifteenth century by Europeans, politics has always commanded economics in Canada's east-coast fisheries.

The "conventional" approach taken by government and industry economists, however, assumes the vantage-point of the present mainly in order to focus on the future understood in the most immediate short-term. As a result, this approach tends to separate the politics of the fishery from economics. Struggles, contradictions and other disturbances are viewed as aberrations from the norm, rather than as natural products of the politics and economics of the fishery. The contributors to *U and SM* write critically about the politics, economics and history of the east coast fishery – and at this point in their careers mostly independently of the policy-setting apparatuses of government or industry – taking a "critical" approach. They concentrate on the struggles, contradictions and disturbances of this sector, but narrow their focus to the immediate, current, contemporary social and economic conditions giving rise to such struggles.

Here, however, in the narrowness of this focus lies a most serious problem. Such an apparently analytical and even "critical" approach loses sight of the big picture in which politics and economics are acting in combination. In fact, it reduces the fishery to a riot of spontaneous parochial conflicts, in the sense that these points mark the contours of its development path. Wittingly, or unwittingly, however, such a procedure incidentally also jettisons information – historical data – about both the persisting continuities from the past into the present as well as about whatever phenomena discontinued during the passage from the past into the present. By making so many pertinent facts disappear, this jettisoning has created large gaps in understanding and provoked researchers to suggest dubious explanations and conclusions.

Consider the fishery in the present-day provinces of New Brunswick, Nova Scotia, Prince Edward Island and Newfoundland and Labrador, taking one snapshot in the last third of the 19th century and another in the last third of the 20th. In the late 19th century, nearly all labour in these fisheries was part-time and-or seasonal, the vast majority of it unwaged. The workforce of than 1.2 million persons comprised more than 80 per cent of the total population of these provinces/colonies. In the late 20th century: all labour, full time or part time, had become waged. The total population living off the fishery was cut in half. The fishery labour force itself had been reduced to one-tenth of the population resident in the coastal fishing communities. The value of primary and processed output had increased more than 100 times. Some 90 per cent of that value was being produced by about one-fourteenth of the entire labour force directly employed in the fishery. The rate of profit generated by the exploitation placed on the shoulders of this fourteenth part had become extremely high compared to the rate and level of profit generated from the same level and intensity of exploitation applied in various other ways to the other 13/14-ths of the labouring population. Over this entire period, regardless of the dramatic transformation in productivity represented by these data, the standard of living and working conditions for more than half the population of the fishing communities continued to fall behind the Canadian standard.

All these differences in income and huge differential in rates of exploitation between the fishery and sectors of other economic activity in Canada are symptomatic of an economic order in which overall development is characteristically highly uneven. This unevenness reflects both the degree to which, as well as the manner in which, material production and its ownership have become intensively concentrated in fewer and fewer hands. The same can be said of the large disparities in income and living conditions that persist and continue into the 21st century to grow both between the best-off parts of the fishery and the worst, as well as between the best-off parts of the fishery and the Canadian standard.

For all this transformation, much of it quite marked, certain invariant features persisted to this day. What remained more or less the same was the proportion of Canadian-generated output from these fisheries that went to markets outside the country. Furthermore, the fish harvesting effort initiated from coastal communities in these provinces/colonies in the northwest Atlantic fisheries always remained less than the effort mounted by the foreign fleets catching fish in these same waters. These invariants are not discussed or mentioned by any of the contributors to *U and SM*. Something somehow inaccessible to their methods of evidence-gathering or detection seems to be going on. How else can one account for these invariants on the one hand and their non-observance on the other? This was a fishery whose very discovery by European capital in the 15th century contributed to creating a world market in foodstuffs in the first place and whose existence and operation continued on the basis of participating first and foremost in this same world market even more than 100 years after its occupation by Canadian fishery enterprises and workers. Apart from a stale reference to (and dismissal of) the work of the Canadian social scientist who pioneered some initial investigation of this global aspect in the 1920s (Innis 1954), in the work of *U and SM*'s contributors there is no consciousness whatever reflected anywhere of how highly remarkable such an economic fragment is – either for the part of Canada in which it operates, or for the international standing and role as a whole of Canada itself. The fact that some sea-change took place since that time is obvious only from the vantage-point of the present looking back. On the other hand, any attempt to account for either the fact or scale of this evidently intangible transformation by methods that rely upon or use t_{LINEAR} – a linearised conception of time moving forward through some interval starting at $t_{initial}$ and ending at t_{final} – would completely miss this transformation.

What constitutes historical perspective and how can it be incorporated as objective historical data in social science research? There are various ways to look back into history. One might look back on the basis of meeting what is found in the past "organically", so to speak, on its own terms, *i.e.*, suspending one's own contemporary understanding of what was unknown, misunderstood or not recognised back in the period or at the time of interest. Alternatively, one might look back in a linearised way, taking the present as t_{final}. Historians and economists in the main have been systematically trained to follow, almost unconsciously, the latter path. The mindset and assumptions that accompany the conventional presentations prove it: the historical orthodoxy is that this fishery itself arose spontaneously as an accident of European discovery, while the economists' orthodoxy is that its commerce and industry developed as an epiphenomenon of Adam Smith's "invisible hand".

Taking the "naturalised" historical viewpoint, however, a different picture emerges. From the end of the 15th century to the middle of the 18th, this activity emerged as the conscious, not particularly well-planned, and highly contradictory outgrowth of competing Great Power schemes of colonisation. There was the global Roman Catholic missionary agenda of the "united crown" of Ferdinand and Isabella of Spain. There was the struggle of the English crown to free its merchants' activities in the "Western ocean", *i.e.*, the Atlantic, from the control or interference of the Spanish navy. There was also the struggle of the French monarchy to colonise the "New World" as a means of bolstering its absolute rule over an increasingly fractious feudal nobility.

As a result of the aforementioned information loss generated by the so-called "critical" approach, however, and irrespective moreover of the differences between the approach-path of the "critical" analysts and that of the "policy wonks" in government and industry, the window in which to observe and note the big picture as it actually plays out becomes shattered into countless fragments. In that shattering, politics once again becomes separated from economics. In that separation, yet more information is also lost about the meanings and intentions of the various actors at different times and places in the east coast fishery. Some of this editing is deliberate, based in a confusion about the supposed need to restrain or prevent excessively subjective modes of interpretation being imposed on the "bare facts" of "history". Obviously, however, at the time these actors acted, history was neither yet history nor "bare facts" but a set of problems being taken up for solution.

2.3.2.2. Mishandling Temporal Factors: A Problem of Method

The actual development of Canada's east coast fishery cannot be reconstructed without analysing and re-synthesising, **in real time**, the interaction and consequences of the human labour of fishing on the social as well as the natural environment which surrounded it and which supplied and enabled this activity in the first place. "Real time" means not necessarily the present, but as things actually happened: starting with the origins in its actual history and peculiar conditions. The unfolding of the key moments of human history surrounding its development must be faithfully reflected. Thus, for example, in the beginning there was the colonial expansion and ambition of states, as public entities, to increase their power relative to rivals and competitors. There were the ambitions of various individuals and groups (in a capacity or station distinct from the state) to acquire enormous private wealth by joining the trend. This combination encountered the Grand Banks fisheries off Newfoundland at a time of Great Power contention over who would control the riches of the New World (which included maintaining a vast international traffic in slave labourers). Our main concern, however, in the present work – which is neither the time nor the place for accomplishing such reconstruction – is to illuminate the failure of the *U and SM* contributors' analysis of the transformation of the socio-economic organisation of the Canadian east coast fisheries **in order to disclose how that failure is linked to mishandling intangible temporal factors**. This mishandling leads to glossing over, mis-stating, misinterpreting or missing altogether the causes and consequences of these transformations and thereby holds out larger lessons and warnings for contemporary social science research in general and as a whole. This task is essential for clearing the path to elaborate on a scientific basis the promise of the present volume, *viz.*, an "economics of intangibles".

Consider what would be involved if one were to re-till the ground ploughed up by the contributors to *U and SM* with the aim of re-doing the work. In order to eliminate misleading, unwarranted or demonstrably false conclusions and inferences developed in the essays of the present work, two tasks would urgently present themselves:

1. to review the *U and SM* contributors' selection of dynamically important criteria that influenced the actual development of the conditions of the past towards what emerged as the conditions in the present, re-examining them from the standpoint of determining their correctness or incorrectness relative to how faithfully and especially how non-anachronistically their use of historical materials and dynamics actually reconstructs the past; and
2. to review the contributors' selection of dynamically important criteria influencing development in the present whose origins are to be specifically located in the past.

The difficulty is that these errors and sources of error are bound up with the banner of "radical critique" which the editors of the *U and SM* project planted throughout. If one were trying to re-do this work on a consistent and scientifically sounder basis, it would not do to become become bogged down in refutation of details. Nor, however, would it do to simply wave an opposing flag. The issue here would become: how to show one's colours through the deed of taking a clear-cut stand restoring scientific integrity in social science. In reference to this specific work and its scope, it is here we encounter the nub of the problem, *viz.*, how does one tackle, *i.e.*, break down, the notion that "critical" = "Marxist"? That is, setting aside any urge either to purify the Marxism of the contributions to *U and SM* or eliminate it, how does one overcome the syndrome according to which donning the mantle of "critic" also confers a licence to recycle assumptions in the name of scientific method or of "Marx's method" – assumptions and methods that, upon further scrutiny, turn out to be indistinguishable from the assumptions and methods of those who were being attacked for the conventionality of their approach or the narrowness of their service to the interests of industry and the state?

There are two issues involved with these "critical" essays. On the one hand, as far as existing approaches are concerned that purport to explain the status-quo by affirming it, critique has a positive role to play. On the other hand, no amount of wielding of the categories of some method (in this case, Marx's actual method) at one's opponents is going to penetrate social reality to its roots and faithfully represent its actual processes of change, development and motion in their all-sided profundity. Given our concern here with what happens to scientific method in general and the optimal use of historical dynamics along with historical facts as temporal factors in particular, this is a matter of some moment. What is needed is both time as it is experienced in living reality, and time conceived historically, *i.e.*, over periods that may exceed many lifetimes. The former without the latter eliminates all perspective. Going down that road, we may as well all proceed to join the Flat Earth Society as to conduct serious further research in economics or any other field of social science. The latter without the former, on the other hand, renders the experience of economic reality inaccessible and unreal and disconnects the long-term from the short-term or "immediate reality." That leads to "science" that is useless. The only path on which scientific integrity can be maintained for this task is to revisit some fundamental definitions.

Throughout scholarly discussions of economics, the conventional metric adopted for the concept of wealth and its quantification actually marginalises the role of Nature in the extreme. Neither the conventional nor the avowedly "critical" approaches to Canada's east coast fisheries, for example, uphold the principle that Nature is the mother and labour the father of wealth. This rejection is implicit in their mode of presenting value-in-exchange of fishery products in the marketplace as the prime concern at the business, commercial end of the fishery which drives all other concerns and thereby leapfrogs having to examine the value-in-use both of fishing as an activity as well as of fish as food. The idea itself, of the complementarity of Nature and Labour, other versions of which appear in ancient Greek philosophy, only came to be formulated this way in the late 17th century by the English writer William Petty (1678). Yet it encapsulates a truly time-tested principle – *viz.*, that wealth itself is something not to be hoarded but first and foremost to be "created", *i.e.*, fashioned, from raw materials worked upon by human labour. This principle takes into consideration that economic activity which produces what can properly be considered "wealth" comprises relationships not only between between people and Nature, but between a person or persons and another person or persons. What, however, happens the moment both the conventional and critical factions of the fisheries discussion shunt this old-fashioned idea aside? This is precisely the point at which politics gets separated from economics, with Nature (in the form of waters and the fish) and Labour (the fishermen) banished to the periphery. Although the "critics" dispute many of the conclusions of the conventional economists, they never challenge the conventional economists' basic method. As a result of the fact that they share a common approach with the conventional economists, the critics in every one of their contributions to *U and SM* end up conciliating the separation of politics from economics. The problem with such separation is that, once politics – the matter of interests and especially of intentions – is removed, economics is reduced to considerations of time t = "right now".

Conventional economic science remains insistent that such separation ensures an economics that is stands above, and remains untainted by, the crass conflict of competing political interests and intentions. Is this now, or has this ever been, the case? On the contrary: it actually politicises scientific inquiry in the worst possible way, by weaving together scenarios and explanations that enshrine the TINA syndrome. As economic existence – the winning of mankind's bread and livelihood from participation in social labour – is an arena in which constant turmoil, and not the steady state, is the norm, the absurdity of TINA-type analysis and conclusions based thereon is self-evident. At the heart of this lofty pose of objectivity and standing above the political fray there is nothing but a rabidly fanatical ideological commitment to the status quo, no matter how much "science" is mustered in justification. The approach taken by conventional economists to the fisheries universe is the same as the approach taken by Ptolemy and the mediaeval Vatican to the physical universe. According to Ptolemy, using crude instruments and guesswork, the Earth was at the centre of the universe and the sun and the rest of the heavens revolved around it. With better instruments and more precise guesswork, Ptolemy might have junked his erroneous initial guess and hypothesised otherwise. We will never know for certain, but at least he advanced his hypothesis on the basis of what he thought were sound and verifiable observations. According to the Vatican, however, everyone had to accept Ptolemy's conclusions without question — regardless of the findings of science and observation to the contrary centuries later. This approach to matters of science can be faulted on two counts. First, a key assertion is accepted as fundamental without further testing. Second, the assertion of a preference is permitted, encouraged and upheld regardless of the evidence of objective, material reality. The starting point of serious scientific enquiry, however, cannot be the wishes of any individual or group, however just or unjust. Objective phenomena have material causes and effects that have to be observed and accounted for as they actually are, not as anyone might wish them to be.

Not interested to deal with actual historical development, however, proponents of both the conventional and "critical" approaches choose instead to place the enterprise and initiative of individuals or corporations at the centre of their fisheries universe. In effect, this is an implicit declaration that whatever is true for individuals counts for more than whatever the truth of the overall picture discloses. This removes the problem from the frying pan, however, only to toss it onto the open fire. As a scientific matter, the political economy of the fishery has to be explained in terms of the relations of cause and effect as they develop in the actual material conditions. These conditions are something in which the will of individuals or companies plays some role, but only in the context of the objective laws of motion guiding that system in a certain direction at a given time, regardless of what those exercising or chronicling that role may choose to believe. This cannot be an overall determining role. Even if one starts from enterprise structures and-or functions, this must be done non-anachronistically. It must be done in a manner that that will remain faithful to how the reality unfolded in historical time. Developments must be traced from their emergence on the margins of the European commercial and slave systems to the present day, out of conditions in which the merchant was the factor outfitting and equipping the producers who organised all the actual production functions, to conditions where vertically-integrated units of finance capital emerged in dominant roles.

Men make their own history: for the conventional approach this is enough. A confusion arises on this point, however, when it comes to the work of proponents of the "critical" approach. Karl Marx himself issued a famous caveat about men making their own history, *viz.*, that this takes place in circumstances already shaped by actions of others in the past and thus not in circumstances entirely the choosing of those acting in the present (Marx 1859). What is missing from the contributions to *U and SM* is any consciousness about what it means or how to apply this criterion to the material in question. When it comes to making due and proper use of intangible temporal factors, what becomes crucial is the implication of Marx's caveat, *viz.*, that material systems of relations of cause and effect have their own laws whose structure as a system then shapes how contending interests form their will as well as how they may implement that will.

In the process marginalising the role of both Nature and Labour, the conventional economists' approach seeks categories of discourse that are as bloodless as possible. Instead of explicitly differentiating causes from effects, they revert to eclecticism. Frequently some effect is blamed on a multiplicity of causes of different kinds and qualities. If no single cause can be found to account for all facets of a phenomenon, then — according to this line of reasoning — there cannot even be some single cause that would account for just the principal features or essence of the phenomenon. Here is the point at which Science is grabbed by the lapels, beaten up and hurled into a dark alley to be left for dead as its positions are simply usurped... by Solipsism. Instead of zeroing in on intentions – on correlating the negative consequences with ill intentions and positive consequences with good intentions – matters are reduced to the supreme Solomon-like judgment of the omniscient individual. The individual as ultimate arbiter in charge of assigning Causes and Effects is a scenario that has put in its appearance in many a "study" of the problems of the Canadian east coast fisheries, but here one example will suffice. In 1982, the Kirby task force on the Atlantic fisheries produced a report entitled *Navigating Troubled Waters* which declared that, when it came to differentiating actual causes from effects in the real world fishery, "where you stand depends on where you sit." (Kirby 1982) In other words, everyone had an axe to grind or special interest which would colour their analysis. That is likely true, but the unwarranted further conclusion extracted from this is that nothing could be sorted out objectively. This sets up a scenario in which Canadian fisheries expertise, backed by the government, plays Solomon in resolving the contradictory claims of livelihood from the fishery in the coastal fishing communities on the one hand, and profits from the processing and sale of fish products in the boardrooms of the corporations involved on the other. This unwarranted conclusion is based on assuming precisely what was yet to be proven or disproven after an objective weighing of the evidence. Such an approach yields a variant of what has been identified elsewhere as the aphenomenal model (Khan, Zatzman and Islam 2005). It ensures that no problem will be analysed to its root and solved by sorting out actual causes and effects.

The situation with the economic theory and analysis of the "critics" contributing to *U and SM*, however, is still more complicated. Explicitly they affirm and start by placing the situation facing the people at the centre. They do not hesitate to criticise openly the conventional wisdom that consigns these concerns to the periphery. Appearances, however, are deceptive. The problem starts when they posit the situation in the fishery in terms of something they call "regional (capitalist) underdevelopment" (hereafter: RCU), blaming everything that doesn't fit the norm of the conventional experts on, or ascribing it to, this "underdevelopment." As will be shown, this recapitulates the error of conventional economists' eclecticism. Once again, it blames something on "everything" and thereby on nothing, while at the same time also denying any role of intention, and it does this no less systematically than the conventional economists. Its implicit utopian and unwarranted assumption is that an ideal world would provide full economic planning including some rational restraints on freedom of movement for Capital. Although RCU is put forward as a reinterpretation and refocusing of the historical background, and the present and future of the east coast fishery, it is not advanced on the basis of any actual or thoroughgoing deconstruction-and-reconstruction of that history. Rather it is based on a much more limited approach of arranging and rearranging key developments. Notwithstanding the burden of responsibility and quasi-magical powers with which these critics have invested RCU, however, this makes these essays just as instrumentalist as any conventional economist insisting on working within an unmodified status quo. No less than any conventional economist, these critical essays are just as unconcerned to get to the bottom of matters, to establish and distinguish actual causes from their effects. Not surprisingly, therefore, do they end up eventually affirming the TINA syndrome albeit in modified form.

2.3.2.3. Social Science and the Problem of Linearised Time

All this poses the question: how could such loudly proclaimed progressive social commitment end up affirming the status quo? Here there is plenty for historians of political ideology to mine. In the present work, a little further on, the historical context in which RCU theory emerged is set out. Of more immediate concern, however, is the evident problem such a state of affairs suggests regarding the methods of these "critics" as social scientists. The immanent cause of the difficulties and contradictions rending *U and SM* is a notion that one becomes the most radical critic of everything existing merely by donning the mask of The Most Radical Critic Of Everything Existing. However, neither dismissing this caricature of

"Marxism" for being a caricature, nor pointing this out and condemning its immaturity, gets to the bottom of matters. That there is more than enough Marxism in these critics' madness cannot overcome serious deficiencies in their method. The essence of the problem that will Inow be examined lies with that method. In its attempts to attack and expose ongoing effects of European colonial expansion in newly independent countries, this critique has borrowed some terminology from Marx, but otherwise it has nothing to do with Marxism. Most tellingly of all in the context of the present work, this critique fails to identify the core of the anti-Nature, Eurocentric outlook responsible for the full-scale assault unleashed by that process of expansion against, and at the expense of, Humanity's prospects. For these critics, the times are literally out of joint. What is required here is to tackle precisely whatever is responsible for the improper and undue manipulation of the intangible aspect of temporal factors on display in this collection of essays, and use such deconstruction to construct or point to a proper method.

To accomplish this entails:

1. an examination of the intangible aspects of temporal factors involved in the introduction and expansion of the colonial system to the "New World", *i.e.*, the Americas, which serve to particularise the emergence of full-blown industrial capitalism as a world system while at the same time differentiating its actual development in specific sectors and regions;
2. an examination of how and where, in the context of the contradictions that emerge in Canada's east coast fishery, the intangible aspects of temporal factors operate to universalise some elements of the operation over the passage of time of the industrial capitalist system as a whole, but not others; and
3. an uncovering of the source of much mischief-making lying at the heart of efforts to rationalise and-or justify the TINA syndrome, in the massive confusion surrounding the intangible aspects of temporal factors and their significance in general. This includes in particular the significance of the differences of t_{LINEAR} in all its various forms from all forms of $t_{NATURAL}$, including $t_{HISTORICAL}$ which is the form that $t_{NATURAL}$ takes in social science.

Establishing points (1) and (2) is straightforward. A limited amount of historical exegesis is sufficient to compel a broadening of consideration, even a partial reconsideration, of the manner in which the expansion of the North Atlantic fishery played its role in the expansion of European capitalism during the early modern period. The third point, on the other hand, raises directly the question of the context and applicability of t_{LINEAR} to historical phenomena. This is indeed a problem that is profound and complex at the same time. Later this analysis will go into some detail as to how far this distorts the entire fisheries problematic. At this point, it is possible and perhaps necessary first to introduce what is at stake as far as scientific method is concerned.

Consider the category "accumulation of Capital". Whether as a mass of exchangeable value or as a collection of exchangeable values, accumulation of Capital may be investigated and summarised objectively (in the sense of "independently of anyone's will") as a function (or set of functions) of some independent variable that will assume one or another form of t_{LINEAR}. By its very nature, the important things to know when attempting to measure accumulation of Capital are the starting and ending points of whatever the selected time interval. It would be entirely expected of anyone investigating this scientifically to wield the tools of Newtonian calculus, utilising an independent temporal variable in t_{LINEAR} form.

Within this, however, there lies an interesting, and remarkably unremarked, paradox. In capitalist societies, there is only the aim of maximising individual wealth and no overall *societal* aim. Overall economic development proceeds through cycles of time in which there are innumerable branch-points. Such an inherently non-uniform time span cannot be classed as a form of t_{LINEAR}. Nevertheless it is considered entirely reasonable to examine certain specific epiphenomena within such cycles, such as "accumulation of Capital", still utilising one or another form of t_{LINEAR}. This approach may even be extended to define the total capital of such a society as the sum of all the individual capitals thus accumulated.

When it comes, however, to comprehending *changes of state*, as it were, what justification remains for continuing to rely on any form of t_{LINEAR}? (By "changes of state, we have in mind" what takes place, for example, in the overall cycle of investment boom, overproduction and crash, or in the movement from one cycle to the next, or in the emergence of innumerable unintended consequences, especially the rising impoverishment and related degradation of the general population that arise during and as part of these cycles.) What basis is there to assume a similar applicability for a linear scale of time in which only the starting-point, ending point and duration in between are of interest? While the recurrence of the cycle ensures that these phenomena will also recur, the mere fact of such recurrence in itself neither predicts the onset of these manifestations of the anarchy of production, nor the exact position in the cycle of the branch-point associated with such onset (Kondratieff 1935).

This pattern for the category "accumulation of Capital", which is a category that is central to any and every part of the capitalist system, can be repeated for any other individual category. This suggests that t_{LINEAR} works adequately when it comes to looking at rates of change for any element of individual capital. However, it cannot provide a significant source of non-trivial information about the larger societal picture. Under modern capitalism, how do prominent individuals continue to play leading roles? They do so no longer in and of themselves, or – speaking more objectively – in or according to the amount of capital they personally represent, but rather as agents of a grouped, collectivised corporate capital, a capital that has been assembled by expropriating large dollops of social capital through government connections, membership in interlocked directorates of corporate and bank boards (Mills 1956). The relatively more prominent role traditionally assigned, from an earlier stage of capitalist society, to the individual (over and as opposed to social collectives) cannot account, however, for this difference in the viability of basing serious analysis on forms of t_{LINEAR}. Applying the principle of "Occam's Razor" – the principle of reasoning according to which conclusions which would follow from the available evidence (as opposed to wherever anyone might wish the evidence to point) provide at least a first approximation of the truth – we find a more compelling reason. No form of t_{LINEAR} can provide useful information about developments or categories that are functions of such collectives.

Above all, however, the question "why accumulate?" is not posed, nor are the intentions of those who would accumulate explored. The essays in *U and SM* typify an opposing standpoint – that the temporal metric, linearised or historical, is a matter of indifference. The arguments of its contributing authors are all based on the assumption that political-economic *function* is entirely a matter of socio-economic *structure*, with time simply passing along like some classic Newtonian independent variable. According to this viewpoint, it would make no difference whatsoever, analytically speaking, if "the price of widgets in Slovenia" were substituted for historical periods incorporating the profoundest social transitions. The question of intention being neither asked nor answered, there is no way to satisfy any of the fundamental demands of the polity for accountability in the sense of the taking of social responsibility by individuals for the consequences of their actions in the fisheries sector.

The "accumulation of capital" category itself provides no information whatsoever about the actual development of any of the new resources generated by and available to a society in collective forms as the result of expanded investment in material production as such, *i.e.*, in the production of the use-values humans needed for societies to sustain themselves as human societies. Such socialisation of produced wealth completely transforms the temporal metrics needed for measuring progress and detecting leading or lagging indicators of where the society as a whole is headed. In particular, t_{LINEAR} becomes useless and meaningless as the length of the cycle required to reproduce and replace needs is itself shortened many times over and transformed by the new forms of social organisation made possible as the result of such collectivisation of the entire social product. The secret of this difference – one which is seen everywhere these days in Cuba, for example, and widely recognised and commented outside that country – lies in the conscious decision that is taken whether to prioritise on the one hand the accumulation of wealth in the form of exchangeable value, either (in the case of developing countries) ahead of all other considerations or (in so-called more "developed" economies) to the exclusion of all other considerations, or whether to prioritise instead the capture and achievement of the intangible social, long-term benefits lurking potentially within any socially-organised form of material production.

The development of objective descriptions of relationships in social science was profoundly affected by the fact that t_{LINEAR} *à la* Newton had been monopolising European scientific discourse from the early 18th century onwards. Even $t_{NATURAL}$ was partially fitted by resorting to periodically predictable regularly-spaced cycles, while exponential time was readily fitted by means of Euler's famous discovery that $e^{i\pi} = -1$. Other timescales or models of time were adapted to fit these parameters. Those that did not or could not fit, like $t_{HISTORICAL}$, were by and large dismissed. Such a marginalisation of reference-frame scrapped a potentially huge source of information of a kind obtainable in no other form.

This loss is not a purely passive one. Marginalising the reference-frame is also a tremendous weapon to wield against the challenge that a new discovery might pose to established knowledge. The struggles waged in European intellectual circles throughout the 17th, 18th and 19th centuries may no longer have involved stakes as high as they had been during the Catholic inquisition of previous centuries, but the struggle to establish scientific method and differentiate scientific investigation from self-interested assertions by persons said to speak with "authority" was no less intense just because it now stood at a certain remove from life-and-death. Instead of the immortal soul of the individual, what was now at stake was the sovereign claims of a social order based on private property and the right, and especially the untrammeled freedom, of those possessing private property to exploit those lacking in private property. There was now to be no freedom higher than this freedom, and this included freedom to research and establish the truth. Here was laid the foundation of all subsequent aphenomenal modeling in the social sciences (Khan, Zatzman and Islam: *ibid*).

Accordingly, by the middle of the 19th century, the challenges posed to established notions in particular by the works of Karl Marx and Charles Darwin were not small. Darwin's explanation of speciation was particularly subversive. The emergence of new species only made sense as the non-linear outcome of a lengthy series of processes that must precede and prepare the way for the emergence of a new species. At the same time, knowledge about these earlier processes, no matter how complete, still would not enable a specific and absolutely reliable prediction of all the features expressed in the new species. The story of how upsetting this was to a few religious figures concerned about the authority of the Biblical story of Creation is an old and well-told one (Irvine 1955). The upset actually went much further, however. One of Darwin's closest collaborators was the geologist Sir Charles Lyell. For the first 10 years after Darwin published his landmark work, Lyell would not publicly defend the theory of evolution. Fear of unknown consequences outweighed any other consideration, including even the fact that Lyell's own work established the notions of the fossil record and geological time the fact that Lyell encouraged Darwin through the more than two decades that would elapse between the completion of the voyages of the *Beagle* to the Galapagos and readying his *Origin of Species* for publication. Until he openly defended his friend, he officially retained public doubts about Darwin's assertion of the mechanism of "natural selection", even as Darwin was corresponding with him about these ideas (Darwin 1892).

Marx's approach to social science was even more problematic: the New would come out of the struggle between contradictory tendencies in the situation that preceded its emergence. However, the necessary precondition for such a struggle to develop in the first place was the entire historical development preceding the outbreak of that struggle. Thus the New must inevitably include some aspects of the Old, while the struggle to get there jettisoned other aspects of the Old (Marx 1859). There was one and the same message, being delivered from two very different fields. It was a message fundamentally challenging the very foundations of t_{LINEAR}: the New, or the Future, far from being mainly or only an incremental superposition on the past or the present, is a quantum break away from both.

In the natural sciences during the 20th century, work continued in many fields using t_{LINEAR} *à la* Newton. Some theoretical work on the frontiers such as Einstein's theory of relativity seriously tackled, at the level of the universe, the need to correct, at least in part, Newton's assumptions and implications about temporal factors and to render time's irreversibility explicit. Other theoretical and applied work such as quantum mechanics took the path of applying probability measures of uncertainty to the coordinates of elemental matter at the inter-atomic and sub-atomic levels. In general, the response in the natural and engineering sciences to this exposure of the inadequacy of existing temporal reference frames was neither uniform nor coherent.

In social sciences, there were also consequences, but the script ran somewhat differently. By the end of the First World War, the urgency of the scientific challenge represented by Marx's work as a student of economics and history was greatly increased by the emergence of actual political revolutionary movements. These challengied the established order based on private ownership of the means of production and even overthrowing longstanding regimes such as that of Tsarist Russia, the country that had become the bulwark of world reaction following the defeat of Napoleon and the settlement of European diplomatic arrangements at the Congress of Vienna in 1815. Anything considered serviceable to any part of the revolutionary agenda was thereafter branded either "communist" or outside the proper sphere of concern of economists (Böhm-Bawerk 1898). Attempts thereafter to update Marx's analysis of capitalism in conditions of free competition in order to account for changes introduced as a result of the subsequent suppression of free competition and its replacement by oligopolistic and monopoly-like "competition" waged an uphill and indecisive battle for academic acceptance (Hilferding 1910). In contrast to the general incoherence spread throughout natural and engineering science, this resulted in what might best be described as a reactionary coherence.

This reactionary coherence, meanwhile, did little for the reputation or image of work in these fields as science. Since the Great Depression of the 1930s, an endless volume of policy-related number-crunching and bean-counting took place in these fields. However, during the 1960s and 1970s, rebellion against this condition came into full flower in universities across the Americas and Europe. A parallel condition emerged, during the Cold War just before this rebellion, with the rise to power of the Khrushchev group in Moscow and their acolytes in the member-states of the Council for Mutual Economic Assistance (COMECON). Among social science academics in Soviet bloc countries in this period, as well as in developing countries sympathetic to the Soviet side, the reduction of western social science to policy-related number-crunching and bean-counting was reproduced as policy-related number-crunching and bean-counting for "market socialism" schemes along the lines opened up earlier by Oskar Lange (1938). This was very much promoted as an advance out of the alleged straightjacket of official Soviet ideology (Stalin 1952).

The result was a "renovation" and revival of Marxian thinking in social science in the West – but on the basis of t_{LINEAR}–based models. A new common ground was discovered for "Western" post-Soviet and eastern-bloc post-Stalin Marxian social science researchers. Henceforth, they would both proceed from the idea that socio-economic structure discloses everything needed to understand political-economic function. In effect, the lifetime of t_{LINEAR} would be extended in order to rationalise these changes of direction in the socialist camp with theories about a "third way." This "third way", still alive in our own time as the favourite doctrine of "new Labour" under governments led by Tony Blair in Britain, an economic course was to be plotted and followed outside capitalism or socialism, one that might be open as well to former colonies and semi-colonies of the Great Powers. Such was the setting in which theories about "underdevelopment" emerged (Baran 1957).

2.3.2.4. The Dialectic of Nature and its Usefulness for the Social Sciences

Nature is a dynamic environment in which changes are continual, but as a result of a strong Establishment bias against looking at processes by taking change as primary and stasis as exceptional, models that have attempted to account for the process of change have been ignored and dismissed in favour of models that attempt to account instead for tendencies towards equilibrium and the steady state. Even if claims for the primacy of change are acknowledged over those for the steady state, however, the continual changes found in natural processes are not necessarily continuous in the specialised mathematical sense. Smoothwise continuity in any natural process may be an appearance, *i.e.*, an illusion, or it may provide an approximation of a certain limited usefulness, but it seems highly unlikely as an accurate or useful description of what is taking place inside or within any moderately complex natural process overall. Relative to the particular phenomenon or phenomena under observation, Nature is observed generally from a stationary or quasi-stationary position "outside". Various hypotheses can be tested to account for the pathways that took a process or phenomenon from input to output, or from starting point to end point, but – because of this often largely unbridgeable barrier of outsidedness – complete information in many cases is unlikely to be attainable from direct observation alone.

Even when the modeler has the integrity and humility to admit that this in itself is in fact only approximating even observable phenomena, and not describing them fully or precisely, continuity-based mathematical modeling can still mislead to the extent that it sustains an unwarranted reassurance that it is of little or no moment whether the point of change within any natural phenomenon is more often like a non-linear switch or cusp-point rather than monotonically increasing or decreasing in some smoothwise continuous way. Clearly, however, if the observed pathway of a phenomenon actually looks more like

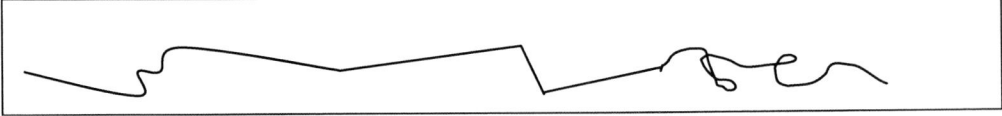

than like

it would seem a safe bet that whatever is causing the dips and changes in the first pattern is not what has given or could give rise to the second pattern. At the same time, it is also evident that the first pattern could be stretched and smoothed to produce something akin to the second, which could subsequently prove entirely misleading – especially if such mathematical tractability became installed as a criterion for deciding between equally aphenomenal "explanations" of the process being modelled.

On the other hand, if this drive to linearise is replaced from the outset by a recognition that change within a process is continual, then the basis, or cause, of change has to be clearly differentiated from the conditions in which the particular change is enabled, blocked or cancelled out. This is hard work; numerous trials may be necessary, and all this before there is any mathematical model in sight! These conditions are never internal to a process, however, and the basis of a change is never external. The conditions that enable a change to go through are external, but what could impel change in the first place is not. Thus, any conceivably applicable mathematical model is going to be inherently non-linear and must be capable of generating some discrete a number of degrees of freedom, guaranteeing a multiplicity of solutions, if those solutions can indeed be found. This is where a new axiom of choice is needed that will not automatically reduce the possible solutions to some unique set. On this score, the dialectical principle nicely fits the bill. It simply posits that the state of a process after some change is to some degree, or in some sense, "opposite" to – in the sense of different from – the state of the process before the change, and that change was impelled internally by the emergence of some contradiction. If the progress of the process is reconstructed and represented as the sequence of contours appearing at each and every change-of-state in the process, what has then been mapped may be considered as the stage-by-stage unfolding of each of the contradictions to which the progress of the process itself gives rise and their resolution. From this one assembles a sequence of testable hypotheses, and careful experiment can then establish what is likely by eliminating what is false or unlikely.

Since ancient times many phenomena of social as well as natural development have been presented in this light, as a "struggle" of opposites. The great knock against this approach always was that it seemed to displace any concern for the long-term, which in some respects exists in the present only in some idealized form, with immediate or short term concerns of the "here and now". In formulating the groundwork for our "economics of intangibles", however, we have found this approach reopens important questions that the evidence of events have proven were in fact not settled or explained satisfactorily by existing theory, and in a manner that does not allow the loop to be closed before all accumulated relevant elements of knowledge have been examined and applied to explaining and accounting for the development of whatever the phenomenon of interest. In and of itself, the dialectical method may be applied to explaining phenomena of the external material world to satisfy a hankering for the short-term solution or to reposition what is happening in the present in terms of what is best for the long term. Which direction is something that depends on the intentions of the investigator / researcher.

2.3.2.5. Placing t_{LINEAR} on Life Support

At the level of consciousness and thinking about these large social questions, persistent efforts to extend the lifetime and lifeline of t_{LINEAR}-based methods and lines of research in the social sciences continue to pose a major obstacle. The distorted view perpetrated by the contributions to the *U and SM* volume would not have been possible to engender otherwise, let alone continue to recapitulate itself a generation later into a new century (Petras and Veltmeyer 2004).

The cribwork for the theoretical foundations of the work of the contributors to *U and SM* came from three distinct but related sources, each of them a variant on the common theme of how to describe and realistically render, using modeling based on t_{LINEAR} conceptions, the *dynamics* of economic growth based on private accumulation, *i.e.*, how the conventional capitalist model moves through space and time. The first variant of this one, common t_{LINEAR}-based dynamics was elaborated in the work of the Stanford University economist Paul A. Baran entitled *The Political Economy of Growth* (Baran 1957); the second by a German-born scholar who was one of the earliest U.S.-educated "Sovietologists", Andre Gunder Frank, in his classic work *Capitalism and Underdevelopment in Latin America* (Frank 1967) which acknowledged an academic debt to Baran; and the third in the work of the African-born and French-trained economist Samir Amin beginning with his *Accumulation on a World Scale* (Amin 1970) which acknowledged a debt to the work of Baran, his long-time associate Paul Sweezy and Gunder Frank.

Baran himself marks the starting point of this work on the dynamics of capital accumulation explicitly in the Introduction to the Second Edition of his book released in 1962 by pointing to the influence of various developments in world politics on his decision to carry out this project. The key developments he mentions are the Bandung [Indonesia] Conference of 1955 in which the foundations of the present-day Non-Aligned Movement were laid (see *infra*), and the Twentieth Congress of the Communist Party of the Soviet Union in February 1956. In other words, this was a theory that acquired legs to the extent that it engaged some of the causes and consequences of changing directions in the socialist camp and stimulated theorisings about a "third way" outside capitalism or socialism.

On the latter occasion, the Khrushchev group ascended to full power throughout the Soviet party and state. When Khrushchev used the occasion to declare a great deal of the previous thirty years' political development null and void or a distortion due to excessive promotion by the former leadership of a so-called "cult of personality" around the person of Joseph Stalin, the former General Secretary of the party as well as Premier and head-of-state, he scandalised public opinion throughout the Soviet bloc, unleashing dangerous genies from various bottles which compelled Soviet military intervention against Hungary, a fellow socialist country and Warsaw Pact ally, in November 1956. Simultaneously and however indirectly, Khrushchev also gave encouragement to a variety of interventionist schemes of the U.S. and former European colonial powers, including most notably the Suez debacle of October 1956 initiated jointly by Britain, France and Israel (which ended with Israel becoming a client-state of the United States), the collapse of the Fourth Republic in France and of the Eden government in London, the Anglo-American plots to assassinate the leaders of Syria and Iraq during 1957 and the subsequent US invasion of Lebanon in 1958.

Implicitly accepting Khrushchev's critique of Soviet economic and political development from 1924 to 1952 as definitive, Baran repudiates the entire politics and economics of socialist construction in the Soviet Union and asserts that the socialism of the Soviet experiment shares many of the deficiencies and marks of backwardness notable in many newly-independent or decolonising countries of Africa, Asia and Latin America but blames the massive and continuous external pressures applied by former European colonial empires and current imperial powers like the United States for causing such "underdevelopment" to persist in countries both socialist and capitalist (Baran: *ibid*).

The essential thesis put forward by those contributors to *U and SM* who were concerned to elaborate RCU theory is that entrapment in a state of permanent inequality as a consequence of "regional underdevelopment" gives rise to social movements seeking economic and political changes. According to their thesis, the role assigned to the construct described generally as "capitalism" is two-fold. First, in its modern form as both a generalised as well as global system of economic colonisation that is no longer confined, or available only, to this or that so-called Great Power, this "capitalism" comprises a set of relations that may entrap economic regions (which may include sectors of economies or the economy of entire countries or even groups of countries) in systems marked by more or less permanent social, economic and political inequalities. Second, it is in the nature of these inequalities that they are common to the capitalist social and economic system prevailing in the "metropolis", *i.e.*, in the region whence originated the investments in production in the underdeveloped region.

To what part, if any, however, of the real-world history of the notion of "underdevelopment" does this abstracted conception actually apply? As one looks around, in the present, at many regions of the globe, there are numerous struggles in which demands for economic and social equality, or an end to specific inequalities, are being raised. Does this tell us anything other than that we are living presently in a period that undergoes continual change, development and motion as societies and regions at different levels and stages of development sort out all manner of contradictions? It has the merit of demonstrating from actual facts on the ground the absurdity of the kind of steady-state equilibrium posited in more strictly conventional economic theories. As a description of present-day development, however, this conception of "regional underdevelopment", or even "regional capitalist underdevelopment" is not only unexceptional and uninformative, but it is also actually a starting-point for a great deal of disinformation.

The relevant modern real-world history of the notion of "underdevelopment" begins indeed with the conference referenced by Paul Baran. This was hosted by then-president Sukarno of Indonesia at Bandung, Indonesia in 1955 of 22 countries from Asia and 7 from Africa. The roster notably included one very large, and at that time anti-capitalist, regime, the

People's Republic of China. Bandung's deliberations were also watched with interest from then-Soviet Russia, Central and Latin America and even France, a Western country with an extremely negative colonial past in Africa and Asia which had just suffered a serious military defeat in Vietnam, at Dienbienphu, the year before. It was very consciously snubbed and boycotted, on the other hand, by the United States and the other member states of the NATO alliance as being "pro-communist". The conference formulated the Bandung Principles, which would become the basis for establishing the Non-Aligned Movement in 1961 (the label of the grouping was supposed to define non-alignment of any member with either the United States or the Soviet Union, although in many cases this was more military-diplomatic fiction than economic reality).

The main thrust at the time, however, while not in fact "pro-communist", was clearly opposed to any continuation, either as "aid" or in any other form, of schemes for further plundering the natural resources of these countries on the basis introduced by European and North American colonising powers. These methods were blamed for preventing the economies of these countries from ever catching up with and fully providing for the full range of needs of their own populations. "Underdevelopment" was thus intended to describe both the current economic level of these countries and the future they faced if their current course did not change. There was no confusion whatsoever among the participants that a future hewing wood and drawing water for former colonial exploiters was no improvement whatever on their previous condition of direct colonial enslavement, and that economic development based on extracting and exporting raw materials without further processing and without using these raw materials to develop home industry offered a future without hope, *i.e.*, no future at all worthy of the name.

With the inauguration of the Kennedy Administration in 1961, the United States changed course in the policy area of foreign aid. This was widely justified and rationalised as a "liberal" swing of the pendulum back from the conservative extremes of the Eisenhower administration. However, as was clearly exposed by the American adventure at the Bay of Pigs, which militia-level people's forces of the Castro regime repelled and smashed with little need of heavier artillery support from the regular armed forces, the political essence of the Kennedy administration remained no less reactionary than its predecessor. Similarly, the aims of its foreign aid programs also remained the same. However, the effort became invested with a new justification in the theories of "economic takeoff" (Rostow, 1960).

The presentation of this theory married a discredited notion from the Victorian industrial era – that of the "deserving" and "undeserving" poor – to a strikingly modern idea, borrowed from atomic physics, of the so-called "critical mass". Proposing that U.S. foreign aid should be increased to many areas of the world up to then ignored – but mainly for purposes that would stimulate private investment and markets for U.S. goods ("deserving poor") as opposed to subsidising governments' ability to subsidise non-profit, not-yet-profitable or unprofitable necessary social services ("undeserving poor") – the Rostow model contended that such selectively targeted "aid" would assist those countries already enjoying a certain "critical mass" of private-sector-based economic development in the private sector to reach "economic take-off" and grow their way to a "modern" economy (and high-consumption "Western" way of life) for their citizens.

For the U.S. economist Andre Gunder Frank and his co-workers, it was increasingly apparent that this "aid" bolstered Latin American dictatorships in power against, and at the expense of, their own people. Even disseminating aid to "the deserving poor", so to speak, *i.e.*, on the basis of "takeoff" criteria being fulfilled, could only benefit a tiny elite at the top while continuing to condemn the vast majority to severe impoverishment and "underdevelopment". Hence, these analysts concluded, there was a deeper structural problem, or set of problems, which would have to be addressed in those societies and that could not be solved in principle by outside aid – no matter how free of strings. (Gunder Frank 2000)

Here, then, originated the theory of *regional* underdevelopment taken up by the contributors to *U and SM*, which will be tackled *infra*, as well as the debate among a number of variants, *e.g.*, "development of underdevelopment" and "uneven and combined development".

The concept of "underdevelopment" presented by Baran, Gunder Frank and Amin is derived from a peculiar theory about the nature of economic development. It is a theory based on recasting the rise of the Soviet economic model as an alternative variant of one and the same paradigm of Western economic development since the Renaissance. They achieve this identification by taking one feature of the Soviet economy and absolutising it. The feature they absolutise is the orderly intervention of the State in regulating the sphere of operation of the Law of Value, by, for example, subsidising the supply on the one hand of necessary goods or services while surtaxing revenues generated from the sale of luxury goods or services.

This absolutisation does two things. First and foremost, it dismisses or ignores any role for revolutionary struggle. The Bolshevik Revolution uniquely and alone provided the energy to eliminate the old Tsarist state, bureaucracy and army and expropriate the entire property of the foreign and big-Russian owners of heavy industry. Yet, obviously, without such an intention, no such category as "Soviet economy" was possible or conceivable. Such marginalising and narrowing of focus simultaneously set aside any discussion of the revolutionary aim of the Soviet system on the economic front – which was not "development" in the sense of accumulation of capital but transformation of the very relations of production and social life based on eliminating private ownership over the means of production.

Second, such absolutising the planning and interventionist features of the Soviet system created the impression that the only important difference between Soviet and non-Soviet economic systems was the lack of state planning in the non-Soviet systems (Baran: *ibid.*). That argument runs something like this: because their governments do not step in and regulate, wealth and poverty in non-Soviet economies accumulate at opposite social poles, thus piling injustice atop social inequality. So, although Soviet-type societies on the other hand cannot overcome inequalities due to natural differences in talent, etc., their state intervention attenuates any tendency towards injustice. The problem here is that the lack of state intervention in the economy of a non-Soviet system predicts absolutely nothing whatsoever about the level of societal justice or injustice. Hence, the conclusion that, if the state is looking after the people's economic needs, its intervention also becomes a force for increasing social justice is unwarranted.

This was the period of the politics of the Cold War. In that era, who was going to show public contempt towards such avowed well-wishers even when their proffered "help" was really unwelcome? In any event, no one at the time in the Soviet Union said such things about their own system. Its implication was demonstrably false and the reasoning that produced it deeply flawed. If what these writers had absolutised indeed constituted the *principal* difference between Soviet and non-Soviet economic systems, then the difference between the two systems would reduce merely to one of policy objectives. Since each member of every policy-making community wants only what is best for their own people, the exercise degenerates into a stale argument about matters that can never be decided. In actual fact, this so-called "socialist-capitalist convergence", as it was then called, was converted into so-called "peaceful competition." This was the context in which Khrushchev's group absurdly promised the Soviet people would catch up to and surpass the United States by 1970. (At the time, the following bitter joke circulated widely against this commitment to forget about any further revolutionary or qualitative transformation of Soviet life: "under capitalism Man exploits Man but under 'socialism' it's the other way round.") The aim, meanwhile, of these theoretical acrobatics in the model-building exercises of Baran, Gunder Frank and others following them was to create a typology of human progress. This typology would anchor comparisons of human social progress in general, including level of meaningful economic development, or relative underdevelopment, across different societies. It would rank societies according to how large or fast-growing the accumulation of poverty and other negative phenomena might be. From this typology and ranking, information could then be assembled into a realistic picture of the true relations between the exploited and the leading social classes of each society.

One consequence of this evolution in the field of economic theory, the promotion of a so-called "third way" between capitalism and socialism, has been widely discussed elsewhere (Blair 1998). Our interest here, however, is to deconstruct the "development-underdevelopment" continuum on which the entire subsequent evolution in international economic theory and practice came to be based. All kinds of societies could now be ranked and compared on one and the same "development-underdevelopment" continuum – Soviet-bloc countries, developing countries and developed countries. What Baran, Gunder Frank *et al.* called "underdevelopment" and defined as development's polar opposite was in fact, however, *not* just the *negation* of development as they were suggesting, *i.e.*, not just the accumulation of excessive poverty at one pole. Furthermore, despite the appearance of a potentially universal range of application to Soviet and non-Soviet, developed and underdeveloped, this apparent broadening of the field-of-vision was actually a narrowing achieved as a result of chopping the role of revolutionary, transforming struggle out of the picture. What they called "underdevelopment" was actually a subcategory of a much broader, but partially intangible, idea of interconnections and disconnections between the growth of tangible material forces of production and immaterial or intangible relations of production (Wallerstein 1974).

The very different effects of narrowing or widening a field of definition can be quite dramatic. Compare what is involved in mathematics, for example, when the derivation of formulas for "sin $n\theta$" or "cos $n\theta$" is attempted *without* any knowledge of the complex-number field, to what is involved *after* such knowledge is acquired. In the former case, restricted to the real-number field, quite elaborate plane-geometric or Cartesian-coordinate figures are required, considerable symbolic computation is involved for each different positive integer value of n, and the sin $n\theta$ and cos $n\theta$ formulae have to derived separately each time. In the latter case, simply by broadening the view-plane to the complex-number field, in which a number of the general form "cos θ +$j$sin θ" can be represented by the exponential $e^{j\theta}$, it becomes a matter of raising such a number to the *n*-th power, or $(e^{j\theta})^n = (\cos\theta + j\sin\theta)^n$; rearranging as $e^{j(n\theta)}$; re-stating $(\cos\theta + j\sin\theta)^n = \cos n\theta + j\sin n\theta$ as a binomial expansion of $(\cos\theta + j\sin\theta)^n$; and, finally, collecting all the real-valued terms as the equivalent of cos $n\theta$ and the imaginary-valued terms as the equivalent of sin $n\theta$. Instead of struggling asystematically with geometric figures, an algebraic expression expanded, for any chosen value of n, according to a known formula in order to provide the necessary sequence of coefficients gives the result simultaneously for cos $n\theta$ and sin $n\theta$.

Proceeding from its safely narrowed field-of-vision, shorn of dangerous "revolutionary baggage" and "rhetoric", the notion and theory of "development" in its original most pristine form – that laid out in Baran's *Political Economy of Growth* (1957) – comes asymptotically close to the underlying truth that would expose just how alien from nature and history the temporal notions embedded in conventional capitalist development model are... only to diverge at the last possible moment. Thus, Baran correctly distinguished the concept of surplus from the notion of profits. However, he completely missed the serious and essential, even defining, difference of temporal dimension involved: "profits" are associated with t_{LINEAR} whereas "surplus" is associated with $t_{HISTORICAL}$. What does this mean? What is its significance?

In order to grasp the economics of intangibles, it is necessary first to appreciate that fact that t_{LINEAR} is not the same as $t_{HISTORICAL}$. With the latter, cycles reappear, but nothing can exactly repeat because context was changed by development during the previous cycle or since: this is exactly what happens with the social surplus, which cannot and is never intended to be consumed in a single cycle or accumulated to some final value after some finite passage of time. With t_{LINEAR}, on the other hand, differences arising from mere temporal displacement of subsequent cycle(s) of similar development(s) are less consequential than structural similarities – sometimes even much less. Thus t_{LINEAR} is an essential instrument for measuring and-or predicting the profits generated by a particular but cyclically-repeated production arrangement – a structural similarity recurring in each cycle – involving some given quantum of capital advanced as wages and some given quantum of capital being exhausted in the wear and tear of equipment and consumption of raw materials by the production process of that cycle.

From the standpoint of t_{LINEAR}, it seems logical and possible to argue thus. A European cultural, economic and political setting framed the emergence and development of industrial capitalism and its mode of capital accumulation in a European setting. A similar pattern and degree of development was not achieved when industrial capitalism came to parts of the world outside western and central Europe. It would seem to follow that, in attempting to account for one and the same "development / underdevelopment" nexus throughout the capitalist system anywhere on the face of the globe, the required categorisations and narrative are incomplete and require supplementation. What made sense of, and sustained, a coherent critique of industrial capitalism and its mode of capital accumulation in a European setting cannot provide a common meaningful narrative for all examples of development / underdevelopment throughout the capitalist system on world scale. For this purpose, t_{LINEAR} is neither the correct nor applicable temporal factor. The appropriate temporal factor to employ in all such cases is $t_{HISTORICAL}$: once development of industrial capital accumulation starts to take place, the context changes in both the hinterland and the metropolis, and the next locale in which development / underdevelopment appears will now operate somewhat differently.

(Of course: the data of contemporary and historical events and development could be more readily handled if everything were reducible to t_{LINEAR} . The problem is that such reduction, however precise and seemingly complete and closed within the terms of its own scale, also entails a loss of information at other scales. Could this information be preserved from loss by incorporating a $t_{HISTORICAL}$ metric? The following line of argument is certainly suggestive. Obviously: $_2t_{LINEAR} - {_1}t_{LINEAR} = \Delta t$, at some scalar value, whereas it is difficult to define what computing "$2t_{HISTORICAL} - 1t_{HISTORICAL}$" might mean, and at the same time $t_{HISTORICAL}$ is a far less trivial notion than t_{LINEAR}. One approach might be to define a quantifiable entity called $\tau_{HISTORICAL}$, comprising a "real" t_{LINEAR} component and an "imaginary" component labeled "β" which is a composite index incorporating some quantifier of how long the current historical cycle-of-interest has lasted, some qualifier of the historical sub-period, and quantifiers of the number of characteristic features of the sub-period that have persisted and that have disappeared respectively. Thus $\tau_{HISTORICAL} = t_{LINEAR} + j\beta$, which could be expressed (and more readily manipulated) as $\tau_{HISTORICAL} = \exp[j*\arcsin \beta /(\sqrt{t^2 + \beta^2})] = \exp[j*\arccos t /(\sqrt{t^2 + \beta^2})])$

Outside those countries actually wrestling with constructing and sustaining a socialist social economy with the fullest participation at all levels of society in the tasks confronting the entire society – Cuba today, for example – the line of march on which Marx set out has been ignored by academic economists. Marxian social science was deemed value-loaded, biased against private property and consumed with pursuing a single-minded political agenda (any of which is true for those who consider the *status quo* all-important). Most academic economists abandoned further efforts either to refute Marx's method or otherwise deal seriously with it. Others, however, like the theorists of "underdevelopment", have wrestled with reconciling Marx's uncompromisingly $t_{HISTORICAL}$ approach with the t_{LINEAR} approach drummed into their consciousness and practice from formal training in academic social science. The contributions to *U and SM* by their acolytes typify the eclectic upshot of such attempts to reconcile the irreconcilable. This became yet another direction from which efforts would be launched to maintain t_{LINEAR} and its legacies on life-support.

From a $t_{HISTORICAL}$ standpoint, the increasing replacement within the conventional capitalist economic system of living labour by dead labour, *i.e.*, automation and the microcomputer, must outstrip the generation and origination of surplus from the exploitation of living labour. From this, Marx elaborated his theory of the falling rate of profit as the basic tendency of this economic system. However, examining the capitalist order headed by the United States in the late 1950s and early 1960s, following an extended period of economic growth in that country without major recessions or depression, Baran and his co-author Paul Sweezy (Baran and Sweezy 1966), who would outlive him to see their joint work, *Monopoly Capital*, into print, noted a continuing high level of profit alongside a rising surplus. From this he concluded that Marx's prediction of a basic tendency of the rate of profit to fall was a double-barrelled mistake. First, while this tendency was observable in the industrial system of mid-19th century Britain, it engendered an over-enthusiasm about revolutionary prospects left unfulfilled by subsequent events. Second, the industrial and financial structures of capitalism that emerged after Marx' and Engels' time eliminated the tendency, negating the entire line of theory developed around it.

The flaw in this line of reasoning, however, lies in its basis, which is the t_{LINEAR} approach. What actually happened was that the organisation of new wars, especially world wars between rival imperialist groupings and cartels, greatly supplemented the generation and origination of surplus from the exploitation of living labour sufficiently to override for entire periods the increasing replacement of living labour by dead labour. Hence the contradiction and its basic tendency persisted even if punctuated by periods during which the expanded sources of surplus through extra-economic means overwhelmed the normal operation of the economic law. However, Baran and Sweezy, fanatically and ideologically predisposed to push $t_{HISTORICAL}$ firmly and finally off a cliff and proclaim "the Way, the Truth and the Light" of the t_{LINEAR} approach, concluded instead that the rising surplus in and of itself had become the dominant tendency. As for pooh-poohing predictions of revolution, has it turned out anywhere that this economic system changed gears and started producing greater satisfaction and less want? On the contrary: as long as the exploited class, which is this system's special and essential product, did not rise up, this system would and did develop into one that "eats its young", a system of monopolies and cartels that fleece the peoples at many levels and on a world scale. Again: the t_{LINEAR} – minded, who hoist the telescope to look through the wrong end, cannot account for such an evolution.

One implicit thesis of the development/underdevelopment eclectics is that if there is not a non-linear branch-point event supplied by something like revolutionary overthrow, then there will no other further branch-point. From a $t_{HISTORICAL}$ standpoint, on the contrary: if there is not one non-linear event, *e.g.*, revolutionary overthow, there will be another non-linear event *viz.*, displacement of free competition by monopoly. Thus, *e.g.*, the predictions, by English Fabian socialist economists – starting before World War I with Wicksteed (1910), a fan of Jevons' work on marginal utility, and going all the way up to the Webbs (1920) and G.D.H. Cole (1944; 1956) after World War II – of smooth gradual transformation being averted by the peaceful reformist path is only possible by assuming a t_{LINEAR} path. Looking through the wrong end of the telescope, the devotee of the t_{LINEAR} view sees that there is a rising surplus alongside rising profits, but – lacking the depth of view available to those who assess these matters from a $t_{HISTORICAL}$ standpoint, does not grasp that these can only be consumed by some destroying the capital of others. Baran saw in the ever-rising surplus the signs of waste and parasitism, *e.g.*, the entire military-industrial complex, but the necessity of U.S. subordination of capitalist competitors in order to keep that surplus rising seems to have escaped his ken. Neither he nor Sweezy would ever connect the dots. This could have clarified that only the surplus in the dominating imperial centre rises without limit and only for so as long as it is "on top".

2.3.2.6. Merchant's Capital – Key Historic Intangible of the East Coast Fishery

It is undeniable that there has been great social and economic backwardness in the Canadian Atlantic provinces, largely as a legacy of British colonial rule and its articulation of an economy that engaged not merely in primary production but in producing outputs for end-markets tailored to requirements set by the British colonial system, controlled entirely from outside. Many backward-looking social relations and conditions were retained especially tenaciously in the fishing outports even for centuries. The problem is not with the accuracy of describing such phenomena as examples of "underdevelopment," but rather with using this concept to explain away everything. This tendency emerges directly from the reduction of all phenomena, especially in the work of Gunder Frank (1969), to some location on the all-embracing "development / underdevelopment" continuum. The concept becomes so broad as to end up explaining precisely.. nothing.

The Baran-Sweezy conception of monopoly capital which supplements and informs the theory of the "development / underdevelopment" continuum is riddled with many unstated, unwarranted and highly contradictory assumptions. Some are more fundamentally erroneous than others. For example, Baran and Sweezy certainly seem to subscribe to the notion that causes and effects in social-economic systems are objective processes taking place independent of any individual's will. However, they also posit that such a social-economic system of nominally material cause and effect may be driven by arbitrary and-or random intersections of the will of the Giant Corporation with the operation of these laws. In other words, some of the driving forces of this system lie outside its own laws. This is very much like the theological view which affirms the universality of Newton's laws of motion while also affirming that a Deity must exist outside time and space capable of intervening in and possibly altering these laws or their operation. Making this special allowance for corporate deity, the "critics" published in *U and SM* end up espousing the same metaphysics as the conventional economists they oppose. They differ with the conventional economists' assertion that the Sun must revolve about the Earth, *i.e.*, that the laws of economic science are the creature of the will of Giant Corporations, by trying to accommodate this alongside the alternative possibility that how corporations work is a function of economic laws, *i.e.*, that the Earth revolves about the Sun.

This concession is critical. It amounts to asserting there can be phenomena within a system supposedly governed by objective laws that cannot be accounted for by the normal operation of these laws. Either analysis of phenomena is carried out on the understanding that the phenomena under study are accountable in terms of objective laws outside anyone's will, or else the effort reduces to just another exercise in stating an opinion dressed up as analysis but corresponding to nothing objective. The philosophical position underlying the idea that a system is entirely explainable in terms of the objective operation of its laws of motion independent of anyone's will is materialism. The idea that, on the other hand, within this system, there can also be unknowable things-in-themselves is Kantian idealism. The idea that both concepts can fit together within one and the same system is pragmatism. Pragmatic approaches are very appealing for quick fixes often beloved by engineers and economists alike, but they are deadly for the kind of theoretical understanding required for serious science.

The Great Corporation of fishing enterprise, as a thoroughly tangible object, was the embodiment of a number of significant intangibles that provided the driving force. From the time the Europeans arrived at the end of the 15th century, the east coast fisheries were constructed and prosecuted directly and specifically in accordance with the requirements of colonial policy and imperial ambitions. Innis, the key source for the much criticised "staples theory," was hitting the nail on the head and proceeding from the correct starting-point for investigating the development of the east-coast fisheries when he observed that "the fishing industry of the North Atlantic has been exogenous in its development." (Innis 1954). Linked crucially to this was the overweening role exercised by merchant over the actual fishery producers, a condition that would introduce habits of subordination tending to render the producers unfitted to defend their own interests effectively when outside interests directly threatened their livelihood. Merchant's capital was the most powerful intangible factor guiding the fate of the fishing communities of the region well into the 20th century – long after its former highly tangible economic role had become thoroughly marginal.

Starting in the middle of the nineteenth century, railway expansion greatly expanded the base of and investment in agriculture, forestry and other resource extraction industries. The industrial capitalist system of the time seized dominant positions throughout these sectors of the economy, as well as to others linked to them in Canada before and after Confederation. This largely wiped out the retarding effects of merchant's capital. In the east-coast fisheries, however, merchant's capital persisted in its distorting and destructive role well into this century because of features peculiar to the historical development of the fishery. The coastal fisheries and offshore fisheries originated with the rise of the capitalist mode of production during European colonial expansion to the New World, India and China. The creation of a world market vastly expanded the basis for commodity exchange. The rise of the capitalist mode of production stimulated manufactures and further development of the division of labour as the feudal system was increasingly breached.

During this phase of capitalism's ascendancy, the leading role was played by merchant's capital, the specialist in exchange. Capital in this form opened up the complex traffic and exchange of various raw and finished products as well as slave labour between Europe and its colonies and among the colonies proper — for example providing food for slaves from salt fish in Newfoundland, the rum-running of merchants from colonial New England between the West Indies and the Thirteen Colonies, etc. At Chapter XX of Volume III of *Capital*, Karl Marx explains that:

"Merchant's capital, when it holds a position of dominance, stands everywhere for a system of robbery, so that its development among the trading nations of old and modern times is always directly connected with plundering, piracy, kidnapping slaves and colonial conquest." (Marx 1892)

The capitalist mode of production arrived in the region of the New World colonised by England with the development of seasonal fishing enterprises by European fleets off Newfoundland at the end of the 15th century. However, as Marx explains:

"Merchant's capital does no more than carry on the process of circulation. Originally commerce was the precondition for the transformation of the crafts, the rural domestic industries and feudal agriculture into capitalist enterprises. It develops the product into a commodity, partly by creating a market for it and partly by producing new commodity equivalents and providing production with new raw and auxiliary materials, thereby opening new branches of production based from the first upon commerce, both as concerns production for the home and world market." (Marx: *ibid*.)

From the start of the 16th to the middle of the 18th century, merchant's capital played an important role in opening up the New World by virtue of its dominating the rise and development of the east-coast fishery:

"The merchant establishes direct sway over production. However much this serves as a stepping-stone.., it cannot by itself contribute to the overthrow of the old mode of production, but tends rather to preserve and retain it as its precondition." (Marx: *ibid*.)

In other words, this activity at its outset was propping up the Old World as much as it was opening up the New. Aspects of relations of production from the decline of the feudal system were transferred into the east-coast fishery from the outset. The methods for drying and salting fish catches, such as the so-called green cure which came out of the feudal system in Brittany. The methods for paying and hiring fishermen on the basis of so-called "catch shares" and "boat shares" similarly came out of late-feudal Europe. These methods were not yet fully capitalist. Unlike the proletarian, the fisherman was not without some means of production. The merchant, unlike the factory owner, "shared" the means of production because he could not fully own them. However, just as it was the merchant's dictate that set these relations in motion, it was also the merchant who was in the position to bind fishermen to him by advancing credit against future production. Marx points out that:

"This system everywhere presents an obstacle to the real capitalist mode of production and goes under with its development. Without revolutionising the mode of production, it only worsens the condition of the direct producers, turns them into mere wage workers and proletarians under conditions worse than those under the immediate control of capital." (Marx: *ibid*.)

On the world scale, "as soon as manufacture gains sufficient strength and especially large-scale industry, it creates in its turn a market for itself, by capturing it through its commodities. At this point commerce becomes the servant of industrial production, for which continued expansion of the market becomes a vital necessity." (Marx: *ibid*.)

The mercantile system and merchants dominated the east-coast fishery from the end of the 15th century to the middle of the 18th, before commerce would "become the servant of industrial production." In this period, the settlement of the fishing areas along the eastern seaboard was severely restricted, and outrightly forbidden in Newfoundland, by merchant's capital. As large-scale manufacture arose in England, converting merchant's capital into its servant, the population of North America proceeded to expand. This provided the market that would be captured by English manufactures in America during the earlier part of the nineteenth century.

In the fishery of its remaining North American colonies, however, after the Anglo-American colonists won their independence and with the rise of industrial capitalism in England, the yoke of merchant's capital over the east-coast fisheries was intensified. This form of capital was uniquely positioned to link the colonial territories as a market for finished commodities from industry in England. This was encouraged insofar as it helped to keep British North America out of the clutches of competing interests from the United States. Commerce conducted by merchant's capital under these conditions "will have more or less of a counter-effect on the communities between which it is carried on. It will subordinate production more and more to exchange value by making luxuries and subsistence more dependent on sale than on the immediate use of the products. Thereby it dissolves the old relationships. It multiplies money circulation. It encompasses no longer merely the surplus of production, but bites deeper and deeper into the latter, and makes entire branches of production dependent upon it." (Marx: *ibid*.)

However, precisely what this "disintegrating effect" would be, and the forms it would take, depended "very much upon the nature of the producing community," according to Marx. That was why in the Thirteen Colonies, where capital was accumulated independent of the British, certain typical features of social disintegration did not appear which would on the other hand become rife throughout British North America in the early decades of the 19th century. In the fisheries of Newfoundland and the Maritimes, whenever an industrial or commercial crisis broke out, there were outbreaks of famine, disease, riotous and spontaneous uprisings of producers against the material conditions and - above all - massive emigration to the New England states in search of work.

The ruinous consequences of merchant's capital retaining its yoke long after it had exhausted any remotely progressive social role can be illustrated by comparing what happened to the popular impulse towards independence in the United States, in the British North American colonies outside Newfoundland, and in Newfoundland. The impulse towards domestic manufacturing grew like an incubus within the Thirteen Colonies, fuelling the anti-colonial independence war that would eventually give birth to the United States and making the social class interested in furthering this development its principal social beneficiary. In what would eventually become Canada, on the other hand, that same social class furthered its interests by signing away any and all rights or notions of genuine independence and national sovereignty in exchange for a protected position as a British Dominion, *i.e.*, as the world's first modern neocolony. In Newfoundland, however, the yoke of the merchant classes remained unchallenged by any local manufacturing interest. They retained their position and wealth by liquidating and diverting the slightest tendency among the people towards independence.

What the merchant did to the small fisherman in Newfoundland for about 300 years was done to small fishermen in the Canadian Maritimes on a less brutalising basis but with certain important similarities. In all four Atlantic Canadian provinces, the dependence of coastal communities on commercial fishing grew as a function of the entrepreneurial classes' freedom to compel relatively excessive numbers of people to remain involved and connected to the fishery as a source of income, especially part-time, and tied to the middleman either as the holder of the mortgage on some fishermen's boats, or as a supplier of gear or as the factor for getting the catch somewhere somehow into the market. By maintaining the coastal fisheries as a pool of cheap surplus-labour offering itself under terms of voluntary servitude, without overt external compulsion, the commercial operators in these fisheries tied up almost no capital of their own in equipment or wages for any extended length of time.

The salt fish trade was the mainstay of Canada's and Newfoundland's Atlantic fisheries. Whem it collapsed after the First World War, new products had to be produced by modern fish-processing factories for markets in the United States. The mercantile interests of the previous period and its arrangements weathered the transition largely intact by interposing themselves between the working fishermen from the Canadian coastal communities and the foreign investors, mostly from large U.S. food-processing corporations. (The latter, starting in the 1920s, were establishing processing plants along Nova Scotia's South Shore.) Thus, for example, local fisheries middlemen claiming to speak in the name of the coastal fishermen opposed the entry into the Canadian east coast fishery of large scale fishing trawlers from New England. Naturally the Canadian coastal fishermen were indeed concerned but few if any could know the extent to which a number of these self-appointed saviours were already either themselves fronting for, or working with the locally-organised corporate combine fronting for, the U.S. fish processing interests in the province some of whom were already heavily invested in the New England trawling fleets coming to Nova Scotia waters.

Up until the groundfish moratorium of the early 1990s, all the Canadian-owned but vertically-integrated fishing companies, *i.e.*, owning their own trawler fleets supplying their fish plants, entirely based and fishing along the Atlantic coastline, as well as the smaller processors relying on independently-operating fishermen to supply them, were keen to maintain a large pool of surplus-labour in the fishing communities. By this time, unlike industry in the interior of Canada, the fishery received absolutely no new entrants from foreign worker immigration to Canada while its immediate workforce continued to age and the young generation in these communities, increasingly able to access the large cities, drifted away from following their father's or grandfather's career in the most unsafe labouring occupation in the country after coal mining.

To the contributors of *U and SM*, armed with their RCU theory, these cheap surplus-labour pools in the outports symbolised "underdevelopment." In later writings, some of them explicitly linked its persistence to the excessive fishing effort for which subsequent fish stock depletion was blamed and the eventual groundfish moratorium even justified. We now know, however, that while overfishing may have provoked officials to take a moratorium option seriously, the readiness of the corporate sector to acquiesce in this measure had nothing at all to do with enabling regional fish stocks to rebuild. On the contrary, when the Soviet Union collapsed in 1991, its fishing fleet – then the largest in the world – was largely liquidated by the Yeltsin government. Enormous surplus inventories of fish catches from the Russian fleet piled up on landing wharves literally around the globe ready to sell at distress prices. The Canadian moratorium enabled the largest fish companies, saddled with expensive fleets catching diminishing quantities of raw material per unit effort, to dump their groundfish fleets and supply all their own customers and markets by purchasing very considerable lots of these Russian inventories. The largest vertically-integrated Canadian fishing companies, who had depended heavily on their own fleets' catches, reduced their scale of operations by shedding much of their fleet operations but did not not lose money in net terms after the moratorium was introduced.

As part of the rules under which the Uruguay Round of the General Agreement on Tariffs and Trade restructured itself into the World Trade Organisation in the 1990s, the Canadian government was compelled to end many programs of direct subsidies to industry, including the construction of new fishing trawler fleets. Thus once the moratorium was in place, the leading vertically integrated processors had a strategy in place whereby they would return to their pre-1960s form as merchandisers of others' catches, only now the catches could be from anywhere around the globe and the foreign fishing fleet might land their catches in a Canadian port for processing. In fact this sparked a spontaneous rebellion by southwest Nova Scotia fishermen in July 1993. For more than a week, they blockaded a Russian fisheries vessel as it attempted to unload catches at a plant in Shelburne, NS. As there would be no further subsidy for constructing a new fleet, these companies also needed the moratorium to remain in place indefinitely as an argument against acquiring new vessels or rehiring fishermen. Thus the companies became invested in maintaining the moratorium not out of concern that the stocks off the east coast ever rebuild, but so that that their monopoly as globalised fish merchants would develop undisturbed.

The contributors to *U and SM* seeking evidences mainly and only of "underdevelopment", by and large completely bypass or miss any of these significances of merchant's capital in the east coast fishery. Given their approach as already described, and the blinders on their vision, where would they find it? In the 18th century Newfoundland outport, the merchant resided in St. John's or more likely in England. His agent might put in an appearance when the ship came at the end of the season to collect the dried product and settle up the accounts for the year. No cash whatever changed hands. Supplies of food, clothing and other things not producible in a settlement on barren rock devoid of resources plunked down in the middle a sparsely settled wilderness were issued "on account". The merchant and his "factor" controlled the accounting. In the Newfoundland fishery, the English cod merchant aristocracy managed to impose a state of degradation that, absent only the acts of open racist oppression, outdid the plantation slavery system of the American colonies in one significant respect: whereas the slaveowner still had the inconvenience of having to supply out of his own revenue his slaves' dietary needs, the English cod merchant told his indentured servants in the outports once a year that this was the state of the account, you owe me this much for food and supplies out of your labour which I have tallied, like it or leave town never to return. How much more tangible can the economics of an intangible become? (Morgan 1992)

The history of east coast fisheries both in Newfoundland and the Canadian Maritimes thus richly demonstrate how tangible and intangible *roles* cannot be confused with an economic category's tangible or intangible *appearance*. Exactly the same is true of commodity economy in general, as the next section discusses at some length.

2.3.2.7. The 800-Pound Gorilla

Is the enterprise or the commodity the basic unit of economic life? It sounds like an invitation to discuss how many angels could dance on the head of a pin, but in fact on the outcome hinges a great deal of misunderstanding and even disinformation about modern economic life. A correct understanding of all the phenomena of modern economic life, from how planes fly to how oil and gas are gotten out of the ground to refineries and residences and everything in between, depends on how this question is answered.

A principled analysis must uphold the commodity as the basic cell life-form of the capitalist economic system. That is where all the key intangibles reside. In that sense, the commodity plays the role of the proverbial 800-pound gorilla in the room: everyone knows it is there, none dare acknowledge it. This goes completely against the lines of analysis of both the conventional economists and that of their so-called "critics" contributing to *U and SM*. They each take as their starting point the operations and transactions of enterprise (firm or individual).

Chief among these "critics" is the Baran-Sweezy school and those such as the theorists of regional underdevelopment who derive their analyses from its positions. They see the capitalist system as an "immense accumulation of commodities" instead of penetrating the veil of the commodity-form. As a consequence they end up capitulating to commodity-fetishism, the religious reflex of the capitalist system, and baking their "theory of regional underdevelopment" as yet another version of the "theory of productive forces", *i.e.*, the idea that what people can do economically and politically is already pre-conditioned by, *and locked into*, the level of technologies and production already achieved.

The issue of the commodity as the basic cell-form of the prevailing economic system is a matter of considerable theoretical importance. Why take the commodity as starting-point of investigation? Firstly, commodity economy existed before there was industrial capitalism. It arose as the physical form in which exchange of goods can take place. Exchange arose to overcome the gaps and defects of division of labour in assuring adequate production and reproduction of socially necessary goods. Secondly, commodity economy can operate regardless of whether production is private or social. Our capitalist systems, however, are historically and structurally a special stage of development in the history of commodity economy, in two key respects:

a) the issue and special circumstance surrounding commodities and capitalism is that only under the capitalist mode of production is labour-power bought and sold as a commodity and able to generate surplus-value only if bought and sold as a commodity; and

b) labour-power can only be bought and sold as a commodity if ownership is private and production is social.

Marx wrote in the first two sentences of the first chapter of the first volume of Capital:

> "The wealth of those societies in which the capitalist mode of production prevails presents itself as an immense accumulation of commodities, its unit being a single commodity. Our investigation must therefore begin with the analysis of a single commodity." (Marx 1867)

This is an extremely interesting choice for a starting point. It is right under everyone's nose. No college degree is required to grasp a commodity, and you certainly don't have to be a rocket scientist to notice commodities everywhere, forming that "immense accumulation." But what is most interesting about this starting point is that the bland and unremarkable surface appearance of commodities, taken individually or as an "immense accumulation," veils an extremely complex history and development of relations between exploiters and exploited.

In fact, the most deceptive feature of commodities, regardless how physically different or variable they are, is their very "thing"-ness. No matter how variegated the physical form, every commodity veils one and the same basic social relation — a civil war between Labour and Capital.

The commodity is the materialisation of value in society. Put another way – it is the tangible vessel for an entire array of intangible relationships between producers and Nature, the mother of all wealth, as well as among the producers themselves, whose collective labour constitutes the fatherhood of all wealth. This value can only be captured, extracted through exchanging commodities against each other. Furthermore - and this is peculiar to capitalist societies - every commodity contains unpaid surplus-labour which is also exchanged as commodities are exchanged. So: commodity-exchange means that, on average, value is exchanged for equivalent value, this value can only be realised through exchange - but, at some point en route, as the commodity was coming into existence, some surplus-value was appropriated by someone somewhere in this process.

The physical appearance of the commodity as a tangible object masks not only an entire array of intangible relationships: it also masks intention. The surface appearance is that there is no systematic or socially-organised compulsion for anyone to buy or sell commodities. In fact, one section - the workers engaged in actual material production - have, through prior appropriation by others of their means of production, nothing left but their labour-power to sell in exchange for the commodities necessary for sustaining their lives. They must exchange their labour-power as a commodity with the other section that owns the means of production. The surface appearance is that this exchange takes place freely, but in fact the means of production are privately owned by the same social interest that is uniquely positioned to purchase the workers' labour-power and dispose of it as a commodity. So the seller of the commodity of labour-power has first to submit to this law of private property. This dictates all the terms and conditions of the purchase and sale of labour-power as a commodity and commands all the fruits of the workers' labour. Unlike every other commodity, labour-power has no value in itself apart from its cost of reproduction. Yet it is the source of all other commodity values which accumulate in the hands of Capital as wealth.

Commodities have value in use as well as value in exchange. These use-values can only be realised when the commodity is consumed (purchased). However, such consumption presupposes production aimed not at producing use-values for their own sake but, on the contrary, solely at realising their value in exchange. Hidden in this exchange-value is surplus-labour appropriated by Capital at the point of production and realised (turned into money) as surplus-value at the point of exchange (through sale). So: under the capitalist mode of production and its labour-process, there has to be production in order to have consumption – otherwise, labour-power cannot be reproduced and sustained for resale. But, likewise, there must also be further consumption in order to have further production - otherwise, goods pile up unsold, and Capital ceases to realise surplus-value and ceases to accumulate.

Virtually by definition, however, the capitalist system separates, and indeed has to separate, the exchange-value of a commodity from its use-value. Otherwise, surplus-value could never be realised, and Capital could then not expand. This produces the conundrum whereby not only are production and consumption separated, but they are unable mutually to regulate each other, and instead of production developing smoothly, there are crises of overproduction from which Capital can recover only by liquidating an entire mass of productive forces (through layoffs, shutdowns, unemployment, the bankrupting and-or takeover of weaker competitors, rationalisation, downsizing, etc.). Crises are built in, not accidental.

The importance of identifying surplus-value is that it connects the added value to its source in living labour. The more common term for this surplus is "profit", but it is important to recognise that profit – meaning industrial profit, profits garnered from the organization of industrial commodity production – is but one branch of the entire social surplus. Rent and interest are also forms of surplus-value but they pre-date the rise of industrial commodity production and the generating of profits from the exploitation of waged, *i.e.*, living, labour. As a result, in general, economists and others fail to connect these forms of the social surplus with living labour. (In this sense, by the way, although profits are quite tangible, surplus seems somewhat more intangible.) The fact of the matter is that once industrial production became the main source of generating surplus in society, the rates of interest and of rent were adjusted to compete with industry in attracting capital for investment. Thus the rate of exploitation of living labour in industry becomes the trendsetter for the overall average rate at which rent is charged or money is loaned, and these rates move up or down with the industrial profit rate; the latter is a leading indicator of where the former will likely end up.

Thus, the operations and transactions of enterprise (firm or individual) cannot be taken as the starting point by anyone investigating how any section of an economy based on industrial commodity production and lead them to correct conclusions. The preceding is sufficient to establish that what happens in a sector such as the fishery in Atlantic Canada cannot be meaningfully understood mainly or purely as a function of arbitrary actions by either Big Government or Big Business (the Giant Corporation). A systematic process is at work, in which particular features of this or that company or government policy may provide specific content but cannot alter the basic form of the relations involved, or the essential result. Only by penetrating the commodity-veil can serious understanding of the theoretical issued be attained.

As part of yet another deeply intangible set of relations, the commodity-form veils how and why the social labour of individuals for others takes place under capitalism by representing "labour" as value, on the one hand, and labour-time by the magnitude of that value on the other. In the production and exchange of commodities, the real social relations of life and labour become disguised in the fantastic form of social relations between things, material objects, commodities. This is the signal that production under such a system has taken command over man. People no longer command their own productive activity or any aspect of how their labour-time is used. Indeed this is what renders "time" such a crucial intangible underlying all the categories of social-scientific investigation in general and economic science in particular.

On the one hand, the capitalist mode of production sets in motion a mechanism that compulsively socialises labour: people are compelled to produce for society and modern society lives at the expense of the actual producers, as opposed to the era of outright slavery when toilers lived at the expense of society.

Personal labour for others, which was clearly delineated in feudal society, disappears with the rise of capitalist commodity production. It renders all qualitative differences between different kinds of labour superfluous. It reduces all labour to an undifferentiated mass of social labour-time, and reduces the differences between kinds of labour to quantitative relations between this or that amount of labour-time – congealed in the form of the commodity and disguised in the value-form of the commodity.

The value of commodities, especially the surplus-value congealed as surplus-labour in the commodity is realisable only through exchange. Consciousness of how the capitalist system actually operates in this regard, however, cannot be gleaned without penetrating the commodity-veil. Left on its own, the real social relations of commodity economy and their potential remain wrapped in mystery. In such a society, commodities as such, in spontaneous consciousness, become society's central holy fetish or "religious reflex." This fetishising of commodities is peculiar to capitalism. To the extent that the producers themselves are not freely associated or conscious of the possibilities of becoming freely associated, they remain subject to apparently mysterious, apparently "unknowable," unconquered forces of Nature and society.

Consciousness is thus a function not of the level of development of the productive forces, or of whether a region or its people are "underdeveloped," but rather of the struggle the producers wage to free themselves from the social and economic fetters imposed by the interests of others on the lives they want to lead. The Baran-Sweezy school was only the latest in a long line to pay lip service to this definition of social consciousness and its source while proceeding along blithely to define the enterprise, such as the Giant Corporation, as the basic cell of the capitalist economy, rather than the commodity.

This spawns many irresolvable contradictions. For example, as previously mentioned, there is the case of the so-called "staples theory" of how Canada came into existence. This theory has been used to argue that the east-west character of Canadian national geography, the tradition of state involvement in the economic life of the country and thus the "essential" characteristics of the Canadians as a people arise out of how the fur trade enterprise or the cod fishing enterprise or the timber cutting enterprise or the wheat-growing enterprise opened up the northern half of North America.

The "Giant Corporation" approach leads to or is connected with many other dilemmas that paralyse real movement.

First of all, the target of any serious popular movement has been financial oligarchy. But the whole thrust of positing the Giant Corporation as the basic unit and engine of the system is to deny the existence and role of the financial oligarchy.

By the end of the nineteenth century, competitive capitalism had given way to monopoly in all fields. This monopoly capitalism became the basis of modern imperialism. Imperialism means not simply land-grabbing, or colonial policy or other processes identified only with particular countries and particular historical periods. Imperialism actually means a system and purpose for the entire social-economic order structured on a very definite basis, possessing a global reach and operating in all countries. It multiplies all the contradictions in various directions and adding to the basic contradiction between the bourgeoisie and proletariat other major contradictions such as that between nations oppressed by imperialism and the imperialists, and sharpening contradictions among the monopoly groups and between rival imperial interests.

Its economic base is monopoly, its political content is reaction all down the line, and it proceeds and spreads by way of local and world wars with war preparations as its most profitable business. However, Baran and Sweezy posit "something quite different." They locate the base of "monopoly capitalism" in "the giant corporation."

Initially they argue this does not negate the notion of the financial oligarchy, only the notion of its power and authority:

> "There is no implication .. that great wealth, or family connections, or large personal or family stockholdings are unimportant in the recruiting and promoting of management personnel. .. It may indeed be taken for granted that they are normally decisive. What we are implying is something quite different: that stock ownership, wealth, connections, etc. do not as a rule enable a man to control or exercise great influence on a giant corporation from the outside. They are rather tickets of admission to the inside, where real corporate power is wielded. Mills put the essential point in a nut shell:
>> Not great fortunes, but great corporations are the important units of wealth, to which individuals of property are variously attached
>
> "What needs to be emphasised is that the location of power inside rather than outside the typical giant corporation renders obsolete the concept of the 'interest group' as a fundamental unit in the structure of capitalist society. ..
>
> "A whole series of developments have loosened or broken the ties that formerly bound the great interest groups together." (Baran and Sweezy 1966)

In other words, financial oligarchy ('interest groups') where necessary, but not necessarily financial oligarchs: the 'giant corporation' is posited explicitly in opposition to the concept of finance capital as the deepest economic basis of monopoly.

Monopoly capital is an economic form. The giant corporation is another economic form. According to the logic of Baran and Sweezy, the latter is the innermost basis for the former. But, in reality, can one economic form be the basis of another economic form? The basis of an economic form cannot be some other economic form. What happens is straightforward enough: human animals, socialised independent of anyone's will, enter into definite relations for the purpose of reproducing existence — which is also independent of anyone's will. The sum-total of such relations form a social mode of production that characterises an entire epoch of social development. These social relations become crystallised in the form of definite social classes defined by their status within the given mode of production, especially as regards ownership or control over the forces of production. The activity of the members of these social classes according to definite relations of production give rise to an economic form. Nothing else can give rise to an economic form.

The giant corporation is a form of monopoly capital. As such it is an instrument of the system and rule of the financial oligarchy. The fact that a corporation may follow a course opposed to the desire of this or that financial oligarch or group does not mean that it is independent of the financial oligarchy. It means only that there are different competing interests within this oligarchy and one may have bested another. If there were no financial oligarchy there would be no giant corporations.

What is the significance of Baran and Sweezy's substitution of the giant corporation for the financial oligarchy? It is utterly pragmatic, *viz.*, "the location of power inside rather than outside the typical giant corporation." But what basis is there for asserting that the locating of power centres inside a corporation negates the possibility of power centres outside it?

The claim that the old industrial trusts ("interest groups") have been broken up is dishonest sleight-of-hand. For example, in the 1980s the American Telephone and Telegraph (ATT) trust, controlling the tens of thousands of electrical, electronic and telephone patents of the Bell group of companies, was broken up by court order into 13 "regional operating Bell companies" (RBOCs).[11] By 2005-6, the wheel was coming full circle, with major RBOC spinoffs seeking or being sought for mergers with long-distance service providers, on the one hand, and unprecedented activities to merge entire telecommunications monopolies (combining control of wireless, land-line and Internet services) on transcontinental scale, in order to remain competitive in global market terms with individual telecommunication monopolies from India and China that service, within only one or two jurisdictions, hundreds of millions and even billions of customers. (Kermisch and Smith 2005; Silver, Young and Abboud 2006)

Baran and Sweezy's "whole series of developments" that "have loosened or broken the ties that formerly bound the great interests groups together" are evidence only for the limited proposition that alignments in the financial oligarchy can shift, not of some qualitative change whereby the power and role of the financial oligarchy has been terminated or displaced. According to the logic of Baran and Sweezy, the monopoly capitalist system suffers from incidental difficulties (some problem here or there), but there is no problem with this pragmatic method. The grand attack on the "power centres" of the "giant corporations" reduces to little more than an appeal to the corporations to reform themselves.

Is government intervention and involvement in the fishery incidental or fundamental? If it is fundamental, then the state machine must be understood as having been integrated under the sway of the monopolies. That is called "state monopoly capital." Another major defect in the concept of monopoly capital put forward by Baran and Sweezy, however, stems precisely from their repudiating the emergence, role and significance of state monopoly capital.

They write:

> "Lenin spoke of the 'epoch of the development of monopoly capitalism into state monopoly capitalism'..
>
> "We have chosen not to follow this precedent but rather to use the terms 'monopoly capital' and 'monopoly capitalism' without qualification for two reasons. In the first place, the state has always played a crucial role in the development of capitalism, and while this role has certainly increased quantitatively, we find the evidence of a qualitative change in recent decades unconvincing. Under the circumstances, to lay special emphasis on the role of the state in the present stage of monopoly capitalism may only mislead people into assuming that it was of negligible importance in the earlier history of capitalism. Even more important is the fact that terms like 'state capitalism' and 'state monopoly capitalism' almost inevitably carry

---

[11] These companies, operated separately, nevertheless sent a single spokesman, from one of the companies that is now almost as large by itself as the entire AT and T system was at the time of the court-ordered breakup, to harangue the American president-elect Clinton in front of live gavel-to-gavel television coverage at his two-day economic summit in Little Rock, Arkansas on 15-16 December 1992. This industrialist's message was that the so-called "Baby Bells," as they are known, should be allowed to cooperate more openly precisely in the areas of computer telecommunications that provided the rationale for applying anti-trust restraints on AT and T in the first place a decade earlier. This "proposal" went on to be implemented as actual policy under a series of special committees directed by the then U.S. vice-president, Al Gore, advised by the former chairman of Apple Computers, John Sculley, one of the leading unofficial economic policy advisors to the Clinton administration.

the connotation that the state is somehow an independent social force, coordinate with private business, and that the functioning of the system is determined not only by the cooperation of these two forces but also by their antagonisms and conflicts.. In reality, what appear to be conflicts between business and government are reflections of conflict within the ruling class." (Baran and Sweezy: *ibid.*)

State monopoly capitalism means precisely that the state power has been subordinated to the interests of monopoly. State power is not independent of the power of the monopolies. Nor is it co-ordinate with, let alone competitive against, such private power. Furthermore, although the state has always played a role, even a "crucial role," in the development of capitalism, what is different under state monopoly capitalism is that the involvement of the state machinery becomes a norm. No longer is it just a particular intervention at a particular time.

What is qualitatively new about this state compared to the state under competitive capitalism is the narrowing of its social base of support and the narrowing of its perspective. After substituting "the giant corporation" for the financial oligarchy so as to make the crucial political role of the financial oligarchy disappear, however, it is hardly surprising that Baran and Sweezy should "find the evidence of a qualitative change..unconvincing."

Baran and Sweezy's repudiation of the notion of "state monopoly capital" is also based on an unsupported claim that the rise of monopoly may have altered the "laws of motion" of capitalism.

According to Baran and Sweezy, "the Marxian analysis of capitalism still rests .. on the assumption of a competitive economy" because, although Lenin pointed out that "imperialism is the monopoly stage of capitalism," apparently "neither Lenin nor any of his followers attempted to explore the consequences of the predominance of monopoly for the working principles and 'laws of motion' of the underlying capitalist economy" in which "Marx's Capital continued to reign supreme." (Baran and Sweezy: *ibid.*)

The evolution from competition to monopoly, however, takes place within one and the same capitalist mode of production. The laws of motion and working principles do not change for a given mode of production. Rather, if different working principles and laws of motion apply, the mode of production must have changed. The shift from competition to monopoly represents a shift not in the working principles or laws of motion, but in the motive for production under capitalism. It is a shift away from being satisfied with average profit to requiring and insisting on nothing less than maximum profit.

Baran and Sweezy misrepresent the effect of this change on the motive for production (from average profit to the maximum profit) as a change in the central tendency from the tendency of the rate of profit to fall into some alleged tendency for the surplus to rise forever.

This is the most outstanding and notorious distortion of their work. The cogent argument of Karl Marx was that the class aim of the capitalist system – to extract the socially average rate of profit in a given branch of material production on the basis of maximising the rate of extraction of surplus-value, which means simply to maximise the exploitation of the workers of a given enterprise or enterprises of a given capitalist – was at loggerheads with its central tendency for the rate of profit to fall. Contradictorily and inexorably, even while tending to push the system forward, this could trigger devastating crises. But Baran and Sweezy eschew the notion that the monopoly capitalist system has a class aim. By thus disregarding or disclaiming any class aim for their system, the contradiction between class aim and the central tendency has been suppressed.

Baran and Sweezy's central tendency amounts to declaring that monopoly capital has an infinite capacity to regenerate and eternally reproduce itself. Evidence of counter-tendencies such as revolutions and overthrow are considered aberrations. According to this logic, the problem is in the sphere of consumption, as opposed to the sphere of production, which begs the question of how the social relation of Capital (and monopoly capital) was created in the first place. Everyone knows the chicken cannot be separated from the egg, and as a practical matter the egg cannot be placed before the chicken. Similarly, there could not be consumption separate from production, and, as a practical matter, something — the commodity — must first be produced before we can speak about consumption. This illustrates how positing the analysis of the entire social-economic order of monopoly capitalism on the asserted central tendency of the surplus to rise without limit leads to various positions that are rife with other contradictions and errors. This leads to the idea, for example, that crises arise from and reflect not overproduction, but only underconsumption. Hence what needs attention is only the system of circulation and distribution (to ensure the "immense accumulation of commodities" is distributed and consumed).

By thus reducing the world to bite-sized digestible bits and eliminating the big picture, intangibles are reduced to something ghostly and evanescent, if not the stuff of conspiracy buffs, and the "reconciliation" thus obtained between t_{LINEAR} and $t_{HISTORICAL}$ appears little different in principle from the "reconciliation" achieved in the fairy tale between the lion and the lamb.

Chapter 3

INTANGIBLES IN THE BIG PICTURE, CONTINUED: INFORMATION TECHNOLOGY AND THE GLOBAL SYSTEM

INTRODUCTION

There is much disinformation widely purveyed about our current "Information Age" as a "post-industrial" era, as though "information" had now displaced Nature as the mother of all wealth. Upon further investigation and analysis of various theories advanced regarding these purported "post-industrial" qualities, however, some disturbing evidence emerges concerning the current roles of information in the modern economy as the intangible that is supposed to control how both the tangible and intangible components of time itself are managed and reconciled. This evidence suggests that Humanity now stands poised on a dangerous perch from which it is as likely to re-enslave, as it is to liberate, itself. Everything ultimately depends on how active a role is allowed for the human factor-social consciousness.

3.1. THE INFORMATION-INTANGIBLE

3.1.1. Perception ... and the Truth

For some time, economists and others had observed how markets are frequently not what economists call "Pareto-efficient". That is: suppliers of goods and services of the best quality, at the price that sets the market equilibrium among all possible and likely purchasers, may not always be the most successful against competitors supplying goods of inferior quality or at prices above or below the equilibrium price. Prof. Stiglitz, and those who have further developed the line of work he opened, propose to overcome the drag effects and other inefficiencies and sources of dysfunction in the market arising from the failure to achieve Pareto-efficiency by overcoming imperfections in the supply of information available to buyers and sellers.

The market mechanism and space of the information economics theory and conventional economics are both indifferent as to the passage of time and its effects. However important time factors are in actual commercial practice, they are usually considered an unnecessarily complicating encumbrance on the immediate tasks facing the theorist. At this theoretical level, the only time factor of interest is, usually, time as the quantifiable and relatively constant duration of a transaction, or as the frequency of a transaction or sequence of transactions. In light of such assumptions, however, should it be expected that the perfecting of information would really redirect markets to function closer to Pareto-efficient optimality?

Visualize an electric fan rotating clockwise. This is actuality: the truth, not a matter of perception or blind faith. Any model that predicts contrary to the truth is a model based on ignorance; thus, for example, to predict something based on the earth being flat cannot pass. This is the aphenomenal model – aphenomenal as in non-existent (Khan *et al.*, 2005), which is examined in some depth in Chapter 5. As opposed to the aphenomenal model, the knowledge-based model should predict the truth.

A knowledge-based model is dynamic: knowledge is infinite it cannot be asserted at any time that all information is available and the description of a process complete. Every phenomenon will have room for more investigation. As long as the direction of the investigation is correct (something that can only be ascertained by the intention of the investigator), further facts of about the truth will continue to reveal themselves. Because everything is in an unsteady state (Islam 2004), such investigation in time takes on a different meaning as the observed phenomenon is constantly changing.

Returning to the electric fan: any model that would proclaim that the fan is rotating counter-clockwise would do nothing to the truth. It would simply falsify perception. For instance, if observation with the naked eye is assumed to be complete, and no other information is necessary to describe the motion of the electric fan, an aphenomenal result will be validated. Using a strobe light, the motion of the electric fan can be shown to have reversed, depending on the applied frequency of the strobe. If the information that the observation of the electric fan was carried out under a strobe light is omitted, knowledge about the actual, true motion of the fan would be obscured (to say the least): simply by changing the frequency, perception has been rendered the opposite of reality.

How can it be ensured that any prediction of counter-clockwise fan rotation is discarded? If mention of the frequency of the light under which the observation was being made is included, it becomes obvious that the frequency of the strobe is responsible for perceiving the fan as rotating counter-clockwise. Even the frequency of the light would be insufficient to re-create the correct image, since only sunlight can guarantee an image closest to the truth and any other light distorts what the human brain will process as the image. Frequency is the inverse of time, but as this example serves to make more than clear: time is the single most important parameter in revealing the truth.

All steady-state models, models based on a central equilibrium, are aphenomenal. Their most important features are their tangibility and the confinement of their operating range to time t = 'right now'. While steady-state, and therefore all tangible, models are thus inherently aphenomenal, intangible models are inherently knowledge-based. Such is the aim of the intangible model being developed through this work in science, economics, and engineering. How does this apply to the electric fan example? Two things have been observed that directly conflict, but by knowing the time-dependence (frequency), what is true may be readily differentiated from what is false. Similarly, when it comes to economic analysis, the path that some species of wealth (tangible or intangible) has traveled, and the path that it has set out to travel, must be known or at least considered before knowledge-based analysis is applied.

Whatever seems to happen, or not, within the buyer-seller nexus of the market seems hardly different in principle from what has just been described regarding the appearance, as distinct from the reality, of the fan's rotation after a strobing pulse of light reached a certain frequency. If certain information from the outset is suppressed or concealed, no amount of perfecting of information will alter the result in any sustainable direction. If real-world time passage is cut out of the picture from the outset — and, with it, the different intentions of economic participants and the intangible elements of their relations and dependencies – what useful application can be found for whatever theory is eventually elaborated? Surely, information that conceals intention or other intangibles amounts to disinformation.

If it is taken as an advertising slogan, or as one of a number of possible techniques or "policy objectives", the concept of a "knowledge-based" approach, which has been advanced in this work (as well as in a companion work [Islam 2003]), will be grasped only incompletely and incorrectly. For one thing, all advertising must necessarily propagate some lie somewhere, by its selective emphasis, suppression of this or that fact, etc. For another – even more important in this case – the "knowledge" component itself does not yet exist: the researcher has to undertake the acquisition of the relevant knowledge and find the appropriate ways of developing its basis and elaboration. This is not a question of teaching techniques. Rather, an educational process is required of a sort that is not necessarily conventionally supplied, in which, instead of recycling of knowledge already previously compiled by others, both the necessary confidence and the intellectual means are developed for attaining authentic knowledge of one's own on one's own. The fact that the world exists, and is no mere personal mental phantasm of sense-experiences, guarantees nothing whatsoever about any individual's ability to acquire useful knowledge about any piece of it. It is impossible to speak of knowledge without sense-experience, without sorting these experiences against the findings of systematic observation, or without the individual exercising powers of rational thought to assemble some meaning from the riot of such facts and data that will approach the truth. Knowledge cannot be equated with any database of choices. It does not come from a machine and does not exist before the human brain has processed some information. Everything that reduces, demeans, marginalises or otherwise displaces this human factor in the knowledge-building process is anti-conscious and, because humans must live in, through and for society, also anti-conscience.

In social and economic affairs no less than in matters involving physical nature, it is necessary, as well as logical and just, to pursue and aim to achieve that which is sustainable. Sustainable development is characterised by certain criteria. The time criterion is one of the main factors in achieving sustainability in technological development; much of the discussion of Chapter Two concerned the consequences of misapprehending this criterion. Even when we cannot determine the characteristic rate for any process, including the time factor in the calculation and observing the impact when time goes to infinity can be a definite basis for the selection of technologies. This "time tested" technology will be good for Nature and good for Humanity. All natural ecological functions are truly sustainable. That is how the world sustains its fertility and nurtures all flora and fauna. Taking a simple example of ecosystem technology (natural ecological function) to understand how it is time-tested: in nature, all plants produces glucose (organic energy) through utilizing sunlight, CO_2 and soil nutrients. This organic energy then is transferred to the next higher level of organism, which is a small animal (zooplankton). The next higher (tropical) level organism (higher predators) utilizes that energy. After the death of any organism, the body mass decomposes to soil nutrients, which plants again take up in order to keep the organic energy loop alive. This natural production technique does not degrade on its own into dysfunction, and can be sustained for an infinite time: this is what is meant by a "time-tested technique". Although the overall process is clearly sustainable, however, could we have reached this conclusion if we had focused instead on, say, one single animal – and that for a time frame shorter than even the lifecycle of that animal? Put more broadly is, the fundamental epistemological question is: could we have detected the full pathway – and eventually inferred useful and correct information therefrom about intentions – if our perception had not been so massaged and biased before undertaking to observe and record our observations? This question frames the deconstruction of the concepts and social-economic uses made of "information" in the present chapter.

This chapter proceeds to tackle this question by first tackling the material, tangible foundations of the "Information Age" in the development of microporcessor technology. Standing at the centre of what is commonly referred to in our day as the "information age" and the so-called "information revolution" is the almost iconic symbol of our time – the digital computer, including all its related offspring (cellular telephones, laptop computers, CD, DVD and MP3 players, iPod devices, etc.). Among electrical and electronic engineers and technologists, there is a tendency to view this development as the natural evolution of the technology of the digital microprocessor. While this is the centerpiece of the technological history, a closer examination of the historical context of the development of this technology suggests that the "information age" and "information revolution" are only peripherally about information and even more peripherally, *i.e.*, even less centrally, about the underlying technological developments. When it comes to the social-economic context for either information or the technologies that harness its gathering, storage and transmission, there is both a great deal less than fills the ear and a great deal more than meets the eye. The "information age" and "information revolution" are in fact emblematic of an entirely globalised social and economic order struggling to escape the circumstances of chronic economic crisis and devastating wars of aggression which seem now to dog its every step.

Information itself has become a most highly-prized commodity in our time. Some aspects of this are utterly aphenomenal, but that does not alter the reality which is that information is the intangible that transforms how the intangibility of time is made tangible and practically utilised. The economics of information has become something prepossessing the work and thought of researchers from the Nobel Prize level (Prof. Joseph E. Stiglitz of Columbia University was awarded the Nobel Prize for Economics in 2002 for his work in this area) to all areas of business management and many areas of scientific endeavour. Like time itself, information has its tangible as well as its intangible element. However, just as the tangible links and history of the conception of time are not to be found in the work of even a professional theoretical physicist such as Stephen Hawking, the tangible links and history of the modern concept of information have to excavated independently of the path hewn by theoreticians like Prof. Stiglitz who approach the concept hermetically on its own terms before considering the origins of its current form in modern-day social reality. In that light, therefore, this chapter takes up an objective critique of Prof. Stiglitz' own perception of the nature and meaning of "information economics". This helps bring to the fore some important insights into the role and nature of intention and the challenges and opportunities which this "Information Age" poses for humanising the economy.

3.2. Origins of the "Information Age" in the Political Economy of Globalisation

3.2.1. From the Vietnam War to the OPEC Oil Embargo

From 1965 to 1973, the United States deployed more than half a million troops in Indochina. Approximately 57,000 were killed there. Another more than 150,000 were wounded. This force also propped up and equipped the so-called "Army of the Republic of South Vietnam". These forces combined slaughtered almost 3 million Vietnamese men, women and children. In this eight-year period, the United States alone dropped more bombs on North Vietnam and Cambodia than the combined airforces of Nazi Germany, Imperial Japan, Great Britain and the United States used throughout six years of the Second World War. The sheer scale of such parasitic spending on military end-uses had consequences for the entire American economy. As the engine responsible for enabling and producing such destructive displays, that economy had become seriously challenged by the massive inflation such spending unleashed, and on 15 August 1971, U.S. president Richard Nixon was compelled to devalue the U.S. dollar currency, declaring it would no longer be "backed by gold". Technically, this meant one would no longer be permitted to redeem gold in exchange for U.S. dollars or *vice-versa* (the rate at the time was US$ 35.00 per troy ounce, or about 10.3 cents U.S. per gram). Practically, it meant the only thing now supporting the dollar's value was fear of the far less predictable consequences of ceasing to believe in it.

The Vietnamese drove the U.S. invaders out at the end of April 1973. Immediately following, however, in October, another shock was delivered to the American economy as the State of Israel moved from threatening to invade to actually invading some of its neighbours and oil-exporting countries in the Arab world retaliated by embargoing shipments and sales to the U.S. and other key allies of "the Jewish State". Effectively, this tripled the world price of oil, and to finance the anticipated expansion of the federal budget deficit that could be expected as a colnsequence, the U.S. Treasury now proceeded to borrow heavily. The Treasury Department's view was that, once the shock of the increased oil price worked its way through to consumers, an economy supposedly shifting back to "peacetime" mode should restabilise normally with improvements in productivity. On the one hand, this policy escalated bond sales, taking advantage of the prospect of using increasingly inflated, *i.e.*, devalued, dollars to repay those lending money to the government on 20- and 30-year terms. However, on the other hand, this same policy accelerated the currency's devaluation, engendering serious worries in some quarters of a collapse of the dollar.

At the same time, to contain any tendency for this unilaterally-imposed course of devaluation to descend out of control, the circulation of capital in U.S. dollars was enhanced and encouraged from every direction, both inside and even more especially outside the United States. Assisting this process was the extraordinary step taken by the Shah of Iran, a leading power in the Organisation of Petroleum-Exporting Countries (OPEC). He prevailed on OPEC members

1. to drop the embargo but cut production to maintain the tripled world price for oil; and

2. to continue to conduct all oil transactions in U.S. dollars. In effect, as a result, the U.S. dollar now acquired a new kind of backing – by "black gold", rather than the traditional yellow, metallic kind.

For the purpose of maintaining this globally expanded circulation of U.S. dollar capital, banking systems in the United States and western Europe introduced information-transfer technology in depth and in breadth. Financial information coded and stored electronically in minicomputers and on large mainframe computers would now be fed in large quantities to central banks and government treasury departments at all hours around the clock by telephonic data-transferring systems. By the end of the 1970s, the effects could be seen at head-office level in all the major financial hubs of America and Europe. Marking the maturity of information technology as a principal facilitator of this seemingly infinite expansion of opportunities to speed up the circulation of capital, computerised information systems, comprising a central database networked to countless "dumb terminals", had become their most commonplace feature.

3.2.2. Control of the Supply of the World's Principal Reserve Currency Has its Privileges

In recent years, the internationally recognised credit institution, American Express, ran a series of advertisements in magazines and on television under the slogan: "Membership has its privileges". As just described, occasioned by its wars of aggression in Southeast Asia and their deteriorating impacts on a number of key present and future economic indicators, the U.S. executed a major shift of macro-economic gears in the 1970s. The secret of how this morphed into the "information age", affecting the world economy in its every pulse and pore, was simply this: exclusive control of the supply of the world's principal reserve currency has its privileges.

One event in particular was responsible for precipitating the subsequent course of the most significant developments, beginning less than six years after withdrawing from Southeast Asia: in 1979, the people of Iran overthrew the regime of the Shah. Overnight, this unstuck many crucial fundamental elements of U.S. global strategic planning that had unfolded over the previous 26 years, from the time the U.S. Central Intelligence Agency overthrew the Mossadegh government in order to install the Shah. Under the Shah, Iran had become both a major oil-exporting state in the U.S. camp located adjacent to U.S. petroleum interests in countries of the Arab world that were much less friendly to the United States, as well as a major purchasor of the most advanced U.S. weapons systems – amounting to some U.S. $6-billion per annum or more than three times the quantity being sold at the time by Washington to the State of Israel – to be positioned near Iran's border with the then-Soviet Union, then the main hostile global rival to the United States.

Under the Shah, Iran became an extremely critical chess-piece in U.S. systems of global security:

1. Teheran was the single largest base of operations for the CIA outside the United States;

2. the U.S. Sixth Fleet commanded the Persian Gulf from Iranian-based port facilities, giving it a huge policing presence over oil tanker traffic from around the globe into the member-states of the United Arab Emirates as well as the eastern tidewater termini of the oil pipeline systems in the Saudi peninsula; and
3. because of the scale of Iran's oil production and exporting operations, as well as the special position the Shah enjoyed with the U.S., Iran competed with Saudi Arabia for dominant influence in OPEC, enabling the U.S. to obstruct efforts by the Arab oil-producing states to establish any systematic or permanent method to raise the price of oil so as to protect their interests as raw material producers of a declining resource.

Achieved against the massive, but unarmed, opposition of every section of Iranian society, the Shah's domestic policy, developed in service of American interests, was defended by the most draconian domestic police, torture and spying network developed anywhere on the planet since the fall of Hitler.

With the Shah gone, the new regime in Iran established itself as a bulwark against any resumption of U.S. dictate or subversion. It used its position as the third largest producer in OPEC to triple the price of oil for the second time since the 1973 Arab oil embargo as well as to obstruct U.S. allies within OPEC from intervening to moderate the impact of the increase. This renewed pressure on a federal budget deficit now clearly gone out of control. The intensified borrowing that ensued provoked the largest increase in interest rates in the recorded economic history of Europe and America, from around 8% at the time of the OPEC increase to more than 21% in the next eighteen months. The result was a crippling recession and massively increased unemployment throughout all parts of the world economy tied to the financial and trade machinery of the United States.

Hoping to eliminate Iran and its independent course, the U.S. armed Saddam Hussein's government in Iraq to drag its neighbour into an inconclusive slaughter for the next eight years, killing more than one million men on both sides but failing in its basic mission. Preparing a major naval showdown to seize control of Iran's economic lifelines in the Persian Gulf, the Pentagon commissioned an unprecedented expansion of naval vessels for what the Reagan administration touted as a "600-ship navy" (Holland 2000).

This and more was paid for by converting the United States from the world's richest creditor state into its biggest debtor state in less than eight years. As the world economy absorbed the increased oil price, the Arab and other oil exporting states (excluding Iran) were awash in "petrodollars" – US currency and credit in US dollars in use outside the United States by petroleum-exporting countries – with the U.S. economy as the best place to spend and invest the windfall. With the Soviet invasion of Afghanistan in December 1979, the U.S. nudged the Arab states in the neighbourhood, starting prominently with Saudi Arabia, to spend some of their windfall on more and more advanced weaponry to "combat the communist threat on the doorstep".

The financial impact of the Pentagon spending programs of the Reagan years amounted to a kind of remilitarization of the economy insofar as they restimulated all the inflationary pressures of the Vietnam War years. Key among these spending programs was a greatly increased demand for new generations of weaponry incorporating computerised command and control systems.[12]

International trade, a major thrust of U.S. government policy during the 1980s, was an area in which the Reagan administration acted like an old-fashioned protectionist, all the while browbeating other countries in almost every other sector of production to open their markets to cheaper U.S. exports. Inspiring the revived U.S. interest in selectively freer trade were the new prospects created by its expanding global military and commercial reach along with the steady inflation of the U.S. dollar. Behind its protectionist insistence on both special "intellectual property" rights for computer software produced in the U.S. as well as on the rigid controls of the Paris CoCom agreements against transferring any software to Soviet-bloc countries or any countries deemed "friendly" to the Soviet bloc, the U.S. aim was to ensure that its software command and control systems commanded the majority of computer platforms in use among its allies and remained out of bounds to its enemies as a matter of international law, prosecutable in the courts of all countries party to the relevant international agreements (Lipson 1999).

The course of development triggered by the Iranian revolution thus drove the United States to resume massive military spending based on hugely accelerated foreign borrowing and an unprecedented worldwide expansion of not only the electronic hardware but especially the software – the programs and networks of centralised command and control – required for managing and directing all these development in the interests of the United States. Thus the command and control over the systems of the U.S. Federal Reserve as the principal printer of new U.S. currency, and over the systems of the U.S. Treasury as the principal issuer of new debt – the credit extension of the money supply – were entirely controlled in and from the United States using computers and software specially protected by the United States within the international trading system.

This insight is important in helping to account for why the October 1987 crash of stock markets in the U.S., which also shook and crashed currency trading and other business activity in major stock exchanges elsewhere around the globe, wiped out literally trillions of dollars in paper values – more than ten times the financial destructiveness of the 1929 stock market crash which produced the Great Depression of the 1930s – all without bringing any part of the working economy even remotely near to a halt anywhere throughout the U.S.-dominated system of markets around the world. Shortfalls and credit exhaustion in one market were met by electronically-dispatched cash or credit from another corner of the world separated by many time zones, in order to "cover the gap" before the market reopened the next morning. In the case of amounts that could not be covered in the timespan of a single after-hours period, a special electronically-signalled "circuit breaker" took effect, postponing resumption of transactions in the affected stock or debenture or currency until some further source of covering cash or credit could be tapped. For the time being (this first-ever circuit-breaking tactic was an improvisation that formed as yet no part of any systematic plan), the

---

[12] Thus for example, in close coordination with the Reagan program for a 600-ship navy, many NATO member states including Canada also became involved in revived naval shipbuilding. The Canadian Patrol Frigate Program, officially described as "the largest single defence procurement ever undertaken by Canada" which called for construction of 12 naval frigates represented a negligible proportion of spending by all NATO participants. Nevertheless, as a result of the proprietary and specially-patented character of some of the computerised systems involved, between 1983 and 1992, the frigate project budget rose 170 per cent from CAD$ 5.43 billions to more than $9.31-billions (Canada 1999).

experience of surviving the 1987 crash revealed that the U.S. system as a global regulator had proven itself too important and crucial for its creditors to let sink. Exclusive control indeed has its privileges.[13]

3.2.3. Infrastructures of Globalisation

Bailing the U.S.-dominated world financial system out of the 1987 crash had a number of important impacts for the future in the short- and medium-term. First, it readjusted the position of all countries already participating in that system by actually burdening every one of them with new tributary responsibilities to the U.S. financial system to a greater or lesser degree. Second, it fully and finally slammed the door against any possibility of a country or people attaining full economic and financial independence unless it was prepared to wage a protracted and tenacious struggle to protect its formal political independence. Third, and perhaps most ominous, it set the stage for economies that would be set adrift following the collapse of the Soviet-bloc market mechanism, the Council for Mutual Economic Assistance (COMECON), to capitulate to U.S.-dictated demands for the restoration of full free-market capitalism as a condition of being allowed even to purchase the necessities that they could no longer themselves produce.

The conventional assumption touted everywhere between the fall of the Berlin in 1989 and the collapse of the Soviet Union in 1991 was that restoration of a free-market capitalist system was the voluntary will of the peoples of each of the former socialist states. The reality was that, in order to eat, the peoples of these countries were left with no alternatives but to either develop full independence – which there were no forces positioned to organise – or accept western capitalist tutelage within the globalised financial system that cemented its yoke following the 1987 crash. That is how and why the entire world economy became globalised at a stroke when these countries capitulated.

To appreciate what happened to those countries that could not "make the grade" set out by the G-7 powers under this new system, one need only look at the situation besetting most of the countries on the African continent. To appreciate that this globalization was also very much about punishing peoples most cruelly for not having been capitalist before the fall of the Soviet bloc, one need only look at the grim social statistics of the Russian portion of the former Soviet Union by the mid-1990s, where destruction of the state-owned sectors of the economy led directly to sharp drops in life expectancy, the destruction of the public health system etc. in addition to massive impoverishment as the social programs supported by the previous system were now taken away from people who had been getting along with relatively modest personal incomes.

In the context of what amounted to a unipolar, or more precisely a post-bipolar, globalization of the economy, the interests of the United States which had been controlling the infrastructures of existing global institutions such as the International Monetary Fund, the World Bank and the successor to the GATT which was renamed the World Trade Organization, became the interests controlling the main flows of capital throughout the whole

---

[13] Critical to the restabilisation that followed the 1987 crash was the development by New York Stock Exchange authorities of Rule 80B, dealing with "Trading Halts Due to Extraordinary Market Volatility" (Hasbrouck, Sofianos and Sosebee 1993).

system. This provoked a response among the largest concentrations of capital and production in Europe, where they reformed and expanded the former European Economic Community and its executive body the European Commission as the European Union and issued the Euro as a common currency in order to keep the U.S. dollar at bay. At the same time, large individual countries with some significant level of development of information-management technology – especially India, China and, following a currency crisis in 1998, a somewhat recovered Russia – also began to carve out a semi-independent course in the global economy, dealing with both the U.S. and Euro blocs. Yet a third course involving the use of information-management technologies to enhance regional economic integration without any single power or currency playing a dominant role was launched by developed by Cuba and Venezuela since 2002 and has been taken up increasingly as well by Argentina, Brazil, Bolivia and Ecuador.

Such have become the infrastructures of globalization: a single marketplace, riven by the divergent ambitions of regional groupings, with one dominant player striving to maintain control over the information technologies that formerly gave it an edge over all rivals but which today serve mainly to accelerate the circulation of capital and thereby threaten the overall stability of the world system. Thus has the chronic crisis of the capitalist system become globalised, along with all its supposed efficiencies – regardless of the disappearance of the old Soviet bloc. Such is the true legacy of the technological revolution labelled the "Information Age" once it was overtaken by the operation of the law of uneven political and economic development. Information – the most intangible thing imaginable – has thus become far more potent than yellow or black gold.

3.3. THE MICROCOMPUTER "REVOLUTION"

As a computing device the microcomputer, in this context a computer system that occupies a desktop area of space or less (*e.g.*, the laptop), emerges from a previous more energy-intensive and much bulkier computer system known as the minicomputer. The minicomputer for its part was developed as a less energy-consuming but more compact version of the original commercial computer known as the (IBM) mainframe.

The memory of the mainframe was based on a technology employing magnetic fields on iron cores. As the electronic engineering of semi-conducting materials (transistors) matured through the 1950s into the 1960s, a technique was perfected for using transistor combinations as memory devices. Electrical power requirements for operating a computing device could be greatly reduced. It became feasible to replace the vacuum elements of the earlier mainframe with transistorised circuitry as well. The net effect was to reduce the average production cost of a mainframe computer by several times. This opened up the possibility of producing another kind of computer less powerful than the mainframe design, but more affordable by a wider spectrum of potential users in business and industry. This was the origin of the minicomputer.

In 1958 Jack Kilby and co-workers demonstrated the first integrated circuit (IC) (Kilby 2000). This was only a decade since Shockley, Bardeen and co-workers at Bell Laboratories successfully demonstrated a commercially feasible transistor (Shockley 1956; Brattain 1956). The integrated circuit incorporated a number of transistor-equivalent elements into a single device, electronically and electrically related as though they were discrete transistors in a circuit: hence the idea of integrated circuit. But American industry and finance, which held a hammerlock on the transistor and semi-conductor technology associated with and supporting it, was not interested to press ahead as vigorously with perfecting and fully commercialising integrated circuitry. It had neither the incentive of rising foreign competition nor the incentive of significantly greater profits to do so in the late 1950s, so transistorisation pressed ahead, while integrated circuitry stayed in the laboratory.

The US wars of aggression in Southeast Asia turned the situation around in the mid-1960s by generating a tremendous demand for new weapons systems, avionics, etc. While the transistor retained and extended its predominance in civilian and consumer electronics, the integrated circuit and systems based on it were widely developed and applied throughout military electronics. As the Vietnamese people threw the American invaders out in the early 1970s, the American electronics sector geared itself for peacetime conversion. Transistor-based devices in the civilian arena were targeted for eventual replacement by systems based on the electronics of integrated circuitry.

The research arm for perfecting and applying the integrated circuit for military electronics was developed out of these companies and projects linked to the U.S. space program. Thus Texas Instruments of Lubbock and Houston (the locale of the Houston Space Center) was positioned in the early 1970s to monopolise this peacetime conversion. It produced the first the first generation of cheap, readily available integrated-circuit chips for a wide variety of applications in civilian electronics. All the designs had already been proven in military applications. All the chips for civilian applications used one series of identification numbers; the same ICs for military applications were engineered to withstand a greater range of extreme conditions but were otherwise electronically identical to civilian-destined counterparts. The chips designed to military specifications were identified by numbers differing only in one digit from the civilian version: the 7402 was for civilian use, the 5401 for military, etc. (Texas Instruments 1974)

The microprocessor was developed as a kind of Large Scale Integrated Circuit (LSIC). Such chips are sufficiently sophisticated in their design and capabilities to serve as the central processing unit of a computing device. In mainframe and minicomputers, the central processing functions were implemented by special groups of circuits of discrete transistors: the microprocessor could emulate entire such groups of circuits.

LSIC technology was a byproduct of the scramble to find profitable "spinoffs" in the consumer/civilian/commercial market for the same integrated circuit technology that had just transformed military electronics. The military demand for this technology, along with the military's general demand of new weapons systems, had contracted rapidly with the winding down of the Vietnam-Cambodian wars. The business interests that had come into existence to meet this demand had come into existence to meet the demand had to stimulate new markets into existence in order to survive.

Technical and economic factors combined further to favour the orienting of IC technological development specifically towards microprocessors. An alternative line of development which would have seemed more "natural" at the time was the development of linear integrated circuits, which emulate analog electronic processes: an increased input or output is reflected as an increase or decrease at the output. At that time ($ca.1974$), a major stumbling block in the path of such a line of development was the lack of any means of emulating the circuit functions of either a capacitor (a device for storing circuit energy in an electric field) or an inductor (a device that stores circuit energy in a magnetic field) on an IC chip.

The most outstanding political-economic fact of the time was the onset of the worst recession since the end of the Second World War. Among other consequences, this precluded any major effort to research and develop a profitable solution to this problem. In these conditions the engineering art of the integrated circuit developed in another direction. The IC would be further developed, but as a digital device, rather than as a linear-analog device.

There are two distinct approaches to making an electrical/electronic circuit function as though it were "intelligent" to an external process or user. In analog circuits using linear components this is achieved by way of a negative feedback path from the output to the input: present output conditions future input such that the circuit appears to an external observer or process to have "a mind of its own", which changes in accordance with changes in conditions at the input or output.

A digital circuit is based on a non-linear principle: the principle of a switch from one machine state to some other discrete, distinct state. One change of state can trigger some other change of state. These triggers can be sequenced; such a sequence constitutes a program. The "intelligence" of the microprocessor derives precisely from this addition of programmability onto a non-linear switching device that operates at electronic speeds.

Digital ICs cannot handle heavy current loads. In the recession of the mid-1970s, resources were not made available for the R and D needed to safely and effectively combine such low-power (and heat-sensitive) devices with analog components.

In these conditions, the only application that could be developed for this technology was one in which the IC would itself be the central and principal active component. This technical state of affairs also tended to favour development of microprocessors over any other type of digital IC as the central component for such applications. In fact, the first mass consumer marketed product based on a microprocessor as central component was the hand-held "pocket" electronic calculator (pioneered by Hewlett-Packard, a major benefactor of Pentagon contracts during the Vietnam War).

The key political-economic condition that determined the emergence of IC semiconductor technology over transistor semiconductor technology was the defeat of American aggression in Southeast Asia and the sharp inter-monopolistic competition over market share that resulted among leading U.S. engineering conglomerates which had become so dependent on Pentagon contracts. The key political economic condition determining the priority that digital IC technology would enjoy over analog-linear technology was the outbreak of the energy crisis and global recession of 1974, the worst economic crisis since the end of the Second World War. The crisis wiped out hundreds, if not thousands, of smaller, more innovative electronics engineering enterprises. This further concentrated the hegemony over the newly emerging IC technology, its digitisation etc., into the hands of the very largest corporate monopolies of this sector. This further determined that the subsequent engineering and perfecting of this technology would be dictated by the drive for maximum profit in minimum time. This drive for maximum profit determined the selection of technical priorities, of the microprocessor over any other line of development of IC technology, as well as digital components over linear-analog components.

For years an incessant propaganda has been shouted about everywhere that microcomputers and small systems are part of a leading edge towards decentralization of the advanced industrial economy, of an "information revolution", "post industrial man", the

"Third Wave", etc. But the facts of industrial life are as follows: at the point of production, the digital technology presupposed by this conception of small-scale cottage-industry-type production itself presupposes the most extreme concentration of ownership of the means of production. The digital IC is a highly engineered commodity, the end-result of a process requiring enormous capital investment in highly specialised technical means. At the same time, this process can produce countless billions of components: only other monopolies can compete against such infinitesimal unit costs of production, the result of vast economies of scale.

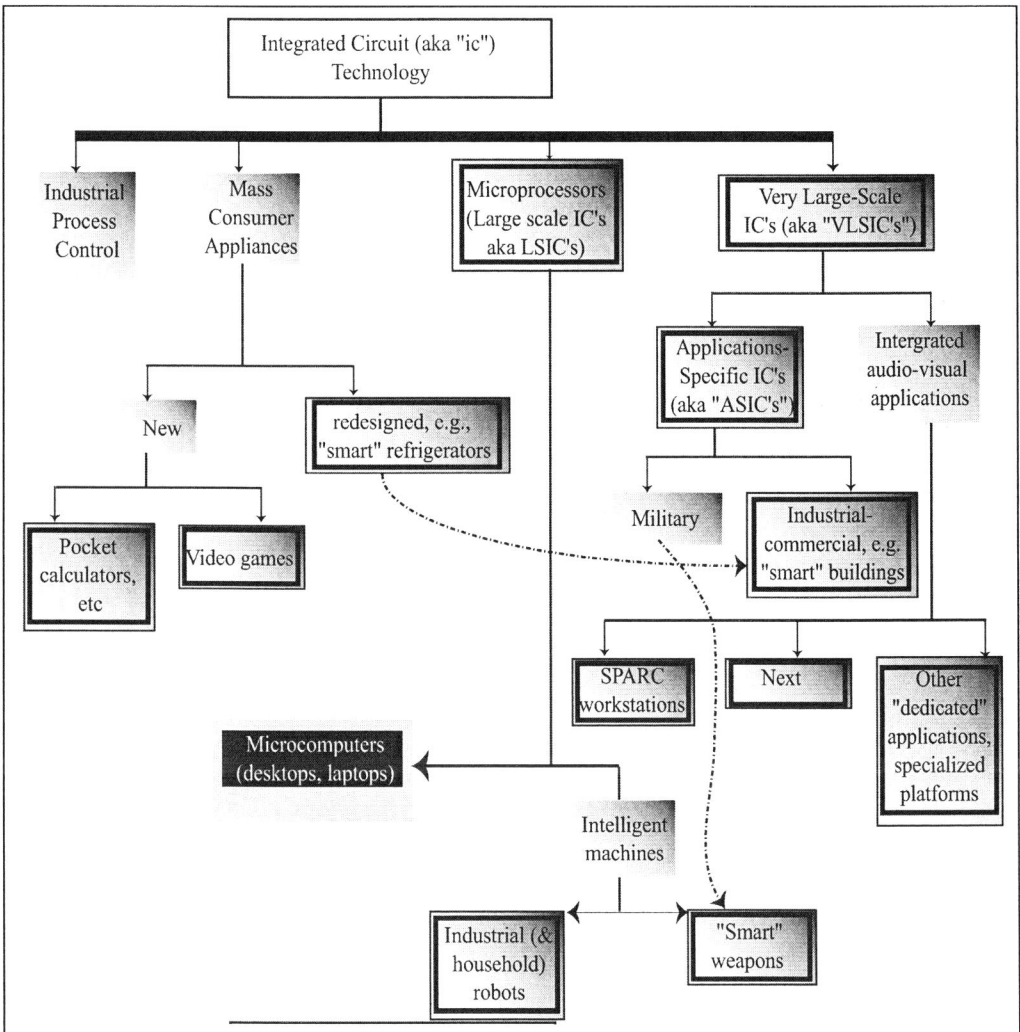

Figure 3-1. Charting the evolution of integrated-circuit technologies and applications.

Figure 3-1 illustrates some of how the integrated circuit (IC), as the central technology that made possible the transition from what looked originally like an "age of information technologies" into what is widely called the "Information Age", came to be applied in political-economic reality. All items with a diagonally-shaded background are technologies, not necessarily, or confined to, specific products; the double-bordered items indicate actual commodities and technologies in the marketplace, the former displayed in a horizontal shading pattern; arrowheads point to actual applications of the technology; diamond-heads indicate seminal ideas for an entire genus of applications of the technology; the "military" as a branch-point to start a further, entirely separate chart is marked with a circular dot. A point in common among the technical applications charted above is that, at the point where a user engages the technology, a programmable interface had been inserted in which either a human user would select from a range of preset options and combinations, or – in a more industrialised context – an operator could select another program that does this selecting.

This chart documents where and how IC technologies were applied to provide programmable switching capabilities across a wide spectrum of applications, starting with industrial process control, certain consumer appliances, microprocessors (the central processing units, or CPUs, of "thinking", "intelligent" or otherwise "smart" machines), and very-large-scale ICs. The latter was crucial for the development of "smart" weapons. Microprocessors, as CPUs for computing devices, enabled the production and marketing of entire computers as portable units.

Thus, from the chart, it emerges that the essence of this technological development and its evolution was not that machines in general became "smart", but that, as workers creating all this technology and its applications, people's economic relations to one another became more social. The significance of this chart is therefore manifold. It immediately smashes two very widespread myths to smithereens: first, nothing inherently "post-industrial" is taking place, and second, production of goods is not being displaced by provision, or provisioning, of services. Behind the notion that the spread of digital information technologies marks the dawn of a "post-industrial" era in which production of services prevails over production of goods, is something else. The underlying idea is that the nature of this era in history has changed such that

1. none of the well-known economic consequences of expanding industrialization – as a form private property of whose ownership and-or control is-are highly concentrated – continue anywhere any longer; and that
2. neither a policy of extreme reaction in the home countries of the biggest most powerful combines, nor a policy of repression in other countries where these combines have imposed their interests, nor a policy of aggression to redivide markets and access to natural resources on the world scale with rival combines exists any longer or is anything like the factor it was up until the Second World War.

What has actually taken place is a massive globally-distributed redivision of the "division of labour", in the new conditions of a globalised marketplace in which the formerly separate and protected international marketplace of the old Soviet bloc was wiped out. As a consequence of the operation of the law of uneven political and economic development, some portions of an earlier arrangement of the division of labour – under which, for example, many activities commanded by heavy industry were situated in and monopolised by the home bases of vertically-integrated corporate entities in the developed countries – have been redistributed to the economies of developing countries.

Most of this transition is still controlled from the head offices of these entities in developed countries. Some of the transition is being effected in partnership with powerful industrial-commercial groups in certain developing countries, *e.g.*, with the Tata and Birla industrial clans in the Asian subcontinent. Yet other phases are being coordinated with government-run franchises in other developing countries and especially in former member-states of the old Soviet bloc, where entire industrial sectors formerly operated as government ministries. This has "modernised" the external appearance and operation of these societies to resemble life and replicate the aspirations of "consumers" in western Europe and North America. This has, however, by no means eliminated resistance to the homogenising or other enslaving consequences of such "development". What is really new here is neither this "modernization" nor yet the resistance to how this is externally and repressively imposed, but rather that this resistance itself has developed in the absence of any Great Power being available, even if only rhetorically, as any kind of prop or support. What remains the same is that those needing to crush all such resistance never hesitate to condemn it outright as Luddite or terrorist, even as they impose destructive force and wars in order to impose and control these economic redivisions and rearrangements.

In what way, then, can it be asserted that the nature of this era in history has changed? The "information age" has opened possibilities and prospects for people to rediscover the power of their own agency, their collective power to say "No!" and prevent imposition of that which goes against the interests of a society as a whole, the long-term interests of everyone living today on this planet and that of future generations.

A related techno-utopian set of arguments presents the emergence of microprocessor technology as a natural evolution of a particular engineering art to ever-higher stages of perfection. This is the basis for speculations concerning the potential replacement of human intelligence by artificial machine intelligence. The facts, however, show that the emergence of the microprocessor was the result of a desperate inter-monopoly struggle for survival and continued maximum profits, in which definite choices were made, in the early 1970s, affecting the course of developments in this sector for decades into the future. These choices generated definite consequences as specific courses of future technical development were priorised, on the one hand, while certain other lines of development were rejected.[14]

Even more elaborate theories have attended the articulation since the 1990s of globe-girdling electronic networks – governmental, private and everything in between – over the "Internet" system known as the "World Wide Web". These have become quite remarkable tools but the mind-set of monopoly is inexorable and its appetite seems to grow with the eating. After tolerating with little overt interference the global spread of networks for the last decade over the ARPANET system (which was originally designed by the Pentagon for the purpose of maintaining command and control of whatever might survive a thermonuclear war), the U.S. government in November 2005 put its foot down at the United Nations, with almost 200 other countries ranged against them, and declared an exclusive jurisdiction to

---

[14] In his 1989 work *Behind the Silicon Curtain: The Seductions of Work in a Lonely Era* (Boston: South End Press), Dennis Hayes documents extensively how the techniques of so-called "structured programming", married to the doctrine of "national security" which enforced the strictest compartmentalisation of the software development environment throughout Silicon Valley, facilitated both a military-quality, top-down, unquestioning discipline in the workforce alongside a more or less total incoherence as the members of the workforce in this sector became less and less able to talk to one another. Such is the workplace reality of the Aphenomenal Model, discussed in Chapter 5, of many so-called "information age" corporations. Hayes may well also have hit upon the insidious secret of the financial success enjoyed, for a time, by many high-tech startups of the 1980s and 1990s, especially in the United States, up until the so-called "tech wreck" of March 2000, when the bottom fell out of the high-technology sector of stock markets there.

manage this entire global network. This stage of the struggle promises either utterly to transform the Internet, or sink it.

The rise of the Internet itself to its present state of global ubiquity shares something fundamental in common with the rise of the microcomputer. The technologies of the microcomputer emerged from a fierce inter-monopoly competition in the mid-1970s among manufacturers of electronic systems in the wake of an unanticipated contraction in the military end market for what was then the latest generation of electronic devices. It so happened, as part of the economic fallout of the collapse of the Soviet bloc after 1989-1991 and the precipitous end it brought to the Pentagon Cold War gravy train of endless development of newer, more competitive weapons systems to pit against the other superpower, the electronic high-technology sector would give rise by the mid-1990s to the globalised, and globalising, networked reality of the Internet.

3.4. ECONOMICS OF INFORMATION:
INTENTIONS AND THE MYOPIA OF JOSEPH STIGLITZ

Globalisation has gone down unhelpful paths and taken wrong turns. Such has been the result of the fact that so many of the most intractable elements of globalisation are themselves symptoms of how information technologies are being applied in finance and commerce. This has unfolded in such a way that monopoly right has become utterly insulated from serious challenges, whereas considerations of public right on the other hand have been utterly marginalised. This usurpation of public right by monopoly right is registered nowhere explicitly as such anywhere, either in current microeconomic or macroeconomic theory or practice. Nevertheless, it has become highly manifest in the realm of policy, and especially so since 11 September 2001, when the U.S. government responded to the attack on the World Trade Centre by unfolding its global "war on terrorism" as the common infrastructure to frame and optic in which to view its macroeconomic policy as well as its diplomacy.

As elaborated with some cogency during the 6th International Conference of Economists and Accountants on Globalisation in Havana in February 2004, the philosophy and ideology of pragmatism originating in the work of John Dewey at the University of Chicago, and its intimate connections with the notion of globalisation based on "free market solutions" which was pushed with greatly renewed vigour in the Reagan years, codified at the institutional level in the form of the Washington Consensus, and then spread with a vengeance in former COMECON member-states following the collapse of the Soviet bloc after 1991, lie at the root and have played a critical role of this entire line of policy and its development (Zatzman et al. 2003). One of the world's leading economists tackling the role of information in economic decision-taking has been Prof. Joseph E. Stiglitz of Columbia University. For his work of the preceding 40 years in this area, he was awarded the Nobel Prize in Economics in December 2001. According to his presentation to the 4th International Conference of Economists and Accountants on Globalisation in Havana in February 2002, however, globalisation is basically a good idea threatened by poor quality information reaching the key decision-takers in major international economic institutions such as the World Bank, the International Monetary Fund and the World Trade Organisation.

In his Nobel Prize lecture at Stockholm on 8 December 2001, Stiglitz argues that this problem, as a technical matter, is eminently fixable thanks to modern conditions available for perfecting the information available to decision-takers, but that there has for some time been a more fundamental problem of incorporating a role for information within conventional economic theory in the first place – establishing the necessary rationales for this at the level of the fundamental theoretical principles of economic science has been the main theme of his career – and there is also the unavoidable practical reality to contend with that policy is implemented according to political imperatives confronting the government of the day (Stiglitz 2002).

As he demonstrates with reference to certain aspects of the history of plantation slavery, Stiglitz's work on the consequences of imperfect information makes it possible to reformulate why certain economic outcomes failed to conform to the predictions of conventional theoretical analysis. In more contemporary contexts, his approach also serves to reformulate certain elements and aspects of well-known problems. However, when it comes to policy recommendations for the World Bank or the International Monetary Fund, he not only accepts without question these institutions' proclaimed aims, but also their capacity to accomplish these aims. Thus, even as he acknowledges the tremendous difficulties encountered by less-developed countries in an environment of increasingly globalised markets and marketing, he applies his theories of information and its economic role only to the relatively narrow arena of equalising the information in the hands of these institutions and their clientele, without even pausing to question whether any policies reformed in line with such an approach can possibly make a difference. This deeper question is not a trivial one. The role that these institutions themselves have developed, in purveying certain information to the finance officials of these governments while reserving other crucial information for private sector corporate interests planning possible investments in such countries, has itself come under increasing fire. Potentially, a fully transparent economics of information might well serve to clarify and shine light on many dark or unjust pathways that are costing governments and peoples dear in the developing countries, but it might also raise deeper questions as well about the applicability of many other areas of existing conventional economic theory and practice. If information and the theoretical appreciation of its role were significant in the way that he has suggested, how is it that inclusion of its roles leaves the processes addressed by economic theory, and especially how those processes are viewed and handled at the level of theory, intact and largely unchanged, such that although defects in accounting for certain features of past economic performance appear to be explained, not one of the institutional foundations of contemporary macroeconomic policy or practice needs to be even reconsidered much less thrown out? Stiglitz's version of the economic theory of information and its role is singularly remarkable in its failure to question any of the institutional foundations, and specifically the ongoing hegemony of the United States, characterising the current globalising order of post-bipolar economics – foundations whose very staying power observers openly and increasingly question.

3.4.1. Taking Economics Backward as Science

From the discussion that follows of some of the more provocative themes from that lecture, it becomes apparent that, although some of the practical implementation of his ideas in the policies adopted or modified by the World Bank under Stiglitz's own stewardship may indeed have assisted the United States and certain global financial institutions to stickhandle some difficult situations which emerged at the end of the 1990s, his actual accomplishment on the theoretical front probably took economics as a science further backward. One reason could be his penchant to deliver an examination of the consistency of proposed innovations in economic theory in terms of the paradigm of neoclassical economic theory. Such an exercise, which feels increasingly more like the exhumation of a corpse than an examination of a paradigm, conventionally presents parties to a transaction, *e.g.*, buyer and seller, confronting one another in the market as the essential micro-foundation of all economic theorising. With this encrusted standpoint comes a great deal of baggage that has to be "examined" and then retained or cast aside:

> The standard theory assumed that technology and preferences were fixed. But changes in technology, R and D, are at the heart of capitalism. The new information economics — extended to incorporate changes in knowledge — at last began to address systematically these foundations of a market economy. As I thought about the problems of development, I similarly became increasingly convinced of the inappropriateness of the assumption of fixed preferences ... I have criticized the Washington consensus development strategies partly on the grounds that they perceived of development as nothing more than increasing the stock of capital and reducing economic distortions. But development represents a far more fundamental transformation of society, including a change in preferences and attitudes, an acceptance of change and an abandonment of many traditional ways of thinking... (Stiglitz *ibid.*:520)

Stiglitz says the problem with neoclassical theory was "the assumption of fixed preferences", but what he goes on to describe as lacking, *viz.*, any notion of development as "a far more fundamental transformation of society, including a change in preferences and attitudes, an acceptance of change and an abandonment of many traditional ways of thinking", are intangible elements that no part of conventional economic theory is prepared to embrace. Similarly, he ascribes to market inefficiency the lack of any consideration of the intangible psychological factors that form part of whether a workforce is motivated or not:

> In some ways, as I pursued perspectives, I was returning to a theme I had raised thirty years ago, during my work on the efficiency wage theory in Kenya..., where I had suggested how psychological factors — morale, reflecting a sense that one is receiving a fair wage — could affect efforts, an alternative, and in some cases more persuasive reason for the efficiency wage theory, that has subsequently been developed further... It is curious how economists have almost studiously ignored factors, which are not only the center of day to day life, but even of business school education. Surely, if markets were efficient, such attention would not be given to such matters, to issues of corporate culture and extrinsic rewards, unless they were of some considerable importance... (Stiglitz *ibid.*:521)

How could such matters not have been "studiously ignored" by economists trained in conventional models and schema that subsume or otherwise bury intangible and intentional elements involved in economics?

3.4.2. Developing a Theory of "Marginal Information Utility" Based on "the Alternative Approach of Beginning with Highly Simplified, Quite Concrete Models"

Discussing what he describes as "asymmetries of information", Stiglitz describes the problematic in what he calls a "decentralized market economy" thus:

> Information imperfections are pervasive in the economy: indeed, it is hard to imagine what a world with perfect information would be like. Much of the research I will describe below focuses on asymmetries of information, that fact that different people know different things: workers know more about their ability than does the firm; the person buying insurance knows more about his health, whether he smokes and drinks immoderately, than the insurance firm; the owner of a car knows more about the car than potential buyers; the owner of a firm knows more about the firm that a potential investor; the borrower knows more about his risk and risk taking than the lender. The essential feature of a decentralized market economy is that different people know different things; in this sense, economists had long been thinking of markets with information asymmetries. But the earlier literature had neither thought about how they were created, or what their consequences might be... (Stiglitz *ibid.*: 488-a)

What has he actually described here? It is nothing less than the foundation for a theory of the "utility" of information "at the margin", a *theory of marginal information utility*. The reference to a "decentralized market economy" is a smokescreen. Actually, all the assumptions of a free competition have been smuggled back in, painlessly without anyone noticing, when the reality is that such freedom of competition in the 19th century is long dead. The notion itself of a "decentralized market economy", invented in the first place to be counterposed to the so-called "command economies" of the former Soviet Union and east-European member states of the Council for Mutual Economic Assistance (COMECON) – all of which disappeared after 1991! – is a completely aphenomenal idea, thus reinforcing the suspicion that it is planted as a stand-in for the free-competition models of the original theorists of marginal utility.

Amazingly, Stiglitz insists that no, he has not gone "back to the future", but rather opened a brand new path:

> Some earlier work, especially in general equilibrium theory, by Radner..., Hurwicz..., and Marschak..., among others had recognized the importance of problems of information, and had even identified some of the ways that limited information affected the nature of the market equilibrium (e.g. one could only have contracts that were contingent on states of nature that were observable by both sides to the contract.) But the attempt to modify the abstract theory of general equilibrium to incorporate problems of information imperfects proved, in the end, less fruitful than *the alternative approach of beginning with highly simplified, quite concrete models.* (Stiglitz *ibid.*: note 50, 488. Emphasis added)

However, is this indeed "the alternative approach"? And, what does one do if both sides are wrong? *Equilibrium itself* is the dubious assumption. Remodelling neoclassical equilibrium to take into account the consequences of imperfect information at the disposal of buyer and seller confronting one another, and-or competing with other buyers and-or sellers, at the point of transacting their business in the market, presupposes the existence of equilibrium as a norm. For the "economics of intangibles", this assumption is relaxed to the point of dispensing with it altogether. The grounds for such dismissal are obvious: how can the analysis of a *mathematical function*, or even of a simultaneous layering of any number of mathematical functions, *e.g.*, the scenarios to which Fast Fourier Transform methods are conventionally applied, be equated with – or applied to – analysing *the consequences of an intention* or of some struggle among competing intentions? Information is not neutral. One of the problems with the entire buyer-seller nexus at the foundation of the market model of neoclassical microeconomic theory is precisely that it assumes a relative or rough equality of buyer and seller precisely at the level of intention: they are each in the market to find the other, transact their business and then go on their way. No other intention matters here, and according to this assumption, nor do the 1,001 other ways in which they are not at all the other's equal matter either. Clearly, however, these are precisely the intangible aspects that inevitably colour the receptivity of either party to whatever additional information becomes available.

In order to delineate the field in which one is most likely to find solutions to problems, those working with applied natural science, like engineers, and those working with applied social science, like economists, both work extensively with models. Consider the following engineering problem: the process of producing synthetic plastic starts with very old vegetation, *e.g.*, crude oil, which is broken down into monomers that are converted into polymers. On this path, however, is the original living plant reconstituted? This is by no means as trivial as the simplicity of the description suggests. In the work engineers routinely do with mathematical modelling, a process known from the outset to be non-linear is rendered tractable by some kind of linearisation (either of the equations, or of the conception of the overall process, or both). Then at a later stage – in the name of a requirement to obtain multiple solutions, for example – non-linear components are added back in. However, applying the resulting "solutions" never succeeds in reconstituting the authentic original non-linear process. In general, when it comes to modeling processes from the natural-physical environment, a linearised rendering of anything originating in a non-linear state denatures the original. This holds profound implications for engineering solutions to technical problems in general, and for engineering solutions based on modelling the etiology of processes from the natural-physical environment in particular. Before anyone comes along striving to solve some problem(s) that arise within it, the story is the same for the societal environment in which any economic problem or problems emerged and posed themselves. For the economic theory that is supposed to enable choosing a most appropriate policy of development, or the highest or best use of technologies, this same obstacle must be addressed.

It must be asked: what problems from the real world does "the alternative approach of beginning with highly simplified, quite concrete models" actually address, let alone solve? As demonstrated over the last several decades through discussions and examples of "cellular automata" in the "Mathematical Recreations" columns of Martin Gardiner in *Scientific American* since the 1980s, the numerous contributions there on this topic by Kee Dewdney, among others, and the serious attempt by Stephen Wolfram to rigourise work in this field (Wolfram 2002), with his commercially highly successful *Mathematica* software a landmark in this respect, a completely consistent body of mathematically functional theory can be built utilising a large number of theorems that have only contingent, non-universal validity with hardly any weighty universal axioms. Many real-life situations have been simulated on this basis, obviously without any reference to historical developments that led to the real-world analog that these cellular automata are supposedly emulating. That is: one can reproduce the effect or sequence of effects without any knowledge of real-world causes. As ingenious as it sounds, it is the ultimately useless achievement: what is required of a truly innovative theory is surely not mere instrumentalism, but the forging of a new path that averts repetition of past error on the basis of understanding what caused the errors. "Beginning with highly simplified, quite concrete models" might very well produce an alternative – but it is unlikely to be an alternative that innovates on such a sound basis.

Not a little of what passes for "sustainable development" is generated from precisely such instrumental thinking, taking pragmatic shortcuts around the more difficult procedure of first ascertaining the truth of a situation. The following scenario illustrates precisely how such things happen:

If the addition of 2 to the square root of 3 is attempted, an answer that will fall within the set of the natural numbers (the "numbers like 2") cannot be expected. An answer can only exist if, and after, a set of numbers has been defined that includes both numbers like 2 and numbers like the square root of 3. The problem is simply this: it so happens that while, on the one hand, the set of numbers like 2 will always be a subset of the collection that includes both these numbers, there is, on the other hand, no number like the square root of three to be found anywhere, at any time, among the set of numbers like 2.

Now consider what happens when the addition of "sustainable" *components* to management practices applied to some production or exploration process in the natural-physical environment is attempted – as distinct from, and as opposed to, designing an entire sustainable process based on researched, investigated knowledge of the overall problematic. If the components of the natural-physical environment that are indeed sustainable are not taken into account from the outset, it will not matter how many ways the management plan for the noble objective of sustainable development is configured or reconfigured. To fantasise that this or that modification of management practice will render the engineering intervention sustainable, without first assessing and identifying what is sustainable in the natural-physical environment when such engineering interventions are undertaken, always leaves the manager in the position of the fellow who could add 2 to the square root of 3 ... but only in the natural numbers. On the good days, he would overshoot and announce the result to be 4, on the bad days he would undershoot and announce the result to be 3, but he would never come close to 3.732... Indeed: such a number could not and would not exist for him, any more than the third dimension could exist for the novelised residents of Flatland discussed earlier in Chapter 1. It would utterly elude his consciousness or understanding, but this in itself would in no way deter him from proposing ways in which the overshooting days might be "balanced" by the undershooting days so that, "on the average", everything would balance out and the process thus prove itself "sustainable".

Shortcuts, however seductive, can never be seriously advocated or accepted as a substitute for an actual solution – in economics, in economic theorising or in anything else. In this regard, the equilibrium hypothesis itself is one of the worst culprits. Frankly unsatisfied with the rather limited usefulness achieved in practice with equilibrium-based models, Stiglitz bravely proceeds on the assumption nevertheless that, with enough information, a better form of equilibrium theory is possible:

> Perhaps the hardest problem was modeling equilibrium. It was important to think about both sides of the market — employers and employees, insurance company and the insured,

lender and borrower. Each had to be modeled as rational, in some sense, making inferences on the basis of available information. Each side's behavior too had to be rational, based on beliefs about the consequences of their actions; and those consequences in turn depended on what inferences others would draw from those actions. (Stiglitz *ibid.*:487-a)

Here we see the real problem with equilibrium-based modeling: its grouping of data-cases in complementary divergent pairs (*i.e.*, "employers and employees, insurance company and the insured, lender and borrower") is neither the only possible grouping, nor the best one. Stiglitz seems to sense this as part of the problem. At the end of the lecture, he approvingly cites he following passage from Charles Darwin's *Origin of Species by the Principle of Natural Selection* (1859), on the matter of dependencies and influences outside such artificial pairings:

"The plants and animals of the Galapagos differ radically among islands that have the same geological nature, the same height, climate, etc.... This long appeared to me a great difficulty, but it arises in chief part from the deeply seated error of considering the physical conditions of a country as the most important for its inhabitants; *whereas it cannot, I think be disputed that the nature of the other inhabitants, with which each has to compete, is at least as important, and generally a far more important element of success.*" (Darwin 1859 – emphasis added)

Neither the criterion of "rationality" nor that of "available information" can effectively predict actual choices in any given case. What, then, is equilibrium modeling beyond some form of probability curve? Prof. Stiglitz' real problem seems to be: how far can a theory be "patched" before none of its original material remains? His reliance on "enough" perfection of information recalls to mind the remark of a Reagan Administration official to journalist Robert Scheer, intended to reassure people that the principles of "civil defence" propounded in the 1950s at the start of the so-called "balance of terror", or thermonuclear standoff, between the US and the former USSR still held true: "with enough shovels", he told Scheer, Americans could build enough bomb shelters to survive an attack (Scheer 1982).

Far from seeing the incorporation of the "information"-intangible as something that could, or even ought, to challenge the conventional market model in any fundamental way, Prof. Stiglitz wants to reconcile it with another intangible, that of "incentives", for which a metric, a system of quantifying, already exists within the market model. He broaches this matter thusly:

There is another important consequence: if markets were fully informationally efficient — that is, if information disseminated instantaneously and perfectly throughout the economy — then no one would have any incentive to gather information, so long as there was any cost of doing so. That is why markets cannot be fully informationally efficient (Stiglitz *ibid.*: 491-b).

Stiglitz is inferring that, while the failure of markets to clear in the manner predicted by theories based on the neoclassical paradigm may indeed reflect a failure of production and consumption to mutually regulate one another, this result itself is rooted, *not* in the intentions of the supplier-manager of capital, but rather in the imperfections of information available to buyer or seller. The issue here, however, is how he arrives at that point: he gets there by assuming, implicitly, a structural role for incentives. The notion of incentive to be inferred from his use of the term throughout this Nobel Prize lecture is a pseudo-Newtonian First Law of Notion for economic theory, which might be roughly framed as follows: "an economic process proposed without incentive will remain dormant unless provided with incentive, and any economic process already in train will continue unless deprived of incentive".

In addition, however, to providing unexpected confirmation of the thesis advanced earlier in Chapter 2 concerning the deleterious influence, across many areas of research having nothing to do with physical nature, of exogenous Newtonian "prime movers", such "incentivising" of an economic role for information that would remain consistent with the rest of the market model has broader negative consequences. An extraordinarily striking example is disclosed in Stiglitz' stickhandling of considerations about potential consequences stemming from a *relative* lack of information between opposite parties to a transaction in the market:

> This is but one of many examples of the interplay between market imperfections. Earlier... we discussed the incentive problems associated with sharecropping, which arise when workers do not own the land that they till. This problem could be overcome if individuals could borrow money, to buy their land. But capital market imperfections — limitations on the ability to borrow, which themselves arise from information imperfections — explain why this solution☐ does not work. (Stiglitz *ibid.*: 491-a)

The "problem" could also be "overcome" if families could secure their needs without having to sell their labouring power to someone else on terms dictated by conditions outside their control. Stiglitz is blinded to this possibility, however, by the dogma of incentivisation. According to this dogma, capital needs incentives to invest and workers equally need incentives to work. Since the freedom of capital to pick and choose how, where and when to invest is premised in the first place not on the availability of incentives or otherwise, but solely on the worker not enjoying comparable or equivalent freedom to choose how, where and for whom to work, this is a bogus equality. Furthermore – and this seems to be the most negative consequence – the act of propounding this dogma actually spreads disinformation that shields this aforementioned socially-organised compulsion from criticism.

Stiglitz' formulation of the key issues and problems of an "economics of information" is even more important than anything he has written specifically about these issues and problems. After all, it is in the formulation of the theory, in its "big picture", that the broad tendency of the overall approach can best be detected. In this connection, three passages from his Nobel Prize lecture stand out in particular in revealing the method and direction of his approach.

Stiglitz says:

> The fact that information was imperfect was, of course, well recognized by all economists. While they may have hoped that economies with imperfect information behaved much like economies with perfect information, they real reason that models with imperfect information were not developed was that it was not obvious how do to so. There were several problems that had to be overcome: while there was a single way in which information is perfect, there are an infinite number of ways in which information can be imperfect. (Stiglitz *ibid.*: 486-b)

This suggests *either* that the relative perfection, or imperfection, of information is a non-linear condition (*e.g.*, "*infinite number*" of ways in which information can be imperfect"), *or* that the relative perfection, or imperfection, of information is an eclectic's catch-all broth of all manner of things that remain unspecifiable any further. It is difficult to doubt Stiglitz' general point that there are far more ways for information to be imperfect than perfect; but how can anyone say there is only way information can be perfect? A standard is being imposed implicitly that "perfect"= complete, but although there is assuredly only one way to have complete information, such a condition is in fact aphenomenal, *i.e.*, impossible. One way or another, non-linearity is almost certainly the case, but Stiglitz provides no mathematical or other conceptual apparatus for handling such a notion; instead, he has handed his reader an exclusive either-or condition. Thus what remains is eclecticism, when what is needed is the delineation of specifics about pathways, *e.g.*, A → B, C → D, etc. When it comes to cause-and-effect, the eclectic argument is that effects that have multiple causes cannot be assigned any single cause, or major precipitating event.

3.4.3. Imperfections of Information, or Oligopoly and Monopoly?

The kind of eclecticism that Stiglitz is propagating is hinted at thus, in a passage that precedes the one just quoted:

> Perhaps most importantly, under the standard paradigm, markets are Pareto efficient, except when ... one of a limited number of market failures occurs. Under the imperfect information paradigm, markets are almost never Pareto efficient. While information economics thus undermined these long standing principles of economics, it also provided explanations for many phenomena that had long been unexplained. (Stiglitz *ibid.*: 486-a)

and

> Market clearing was not a constraint on firms. If all firms were paying the market-clearing wage, it might pay a firm to offer a higher wage, to attract more able workers. The efficiency wage theory meant that there could exist unemployment in equilibrium. It was thus clear that the notion that had underlay much of traditional competitive equilibrium analysis — that markets had to clear — was simply not true if information were imperfect. (Stiglitz *ibid.*: 480)

This begs the question of why information might be imperfect. No evidence is adduced to establish whether imperfect information is or is not a transitory, transient symptom, within a pathway of symptoms, of something more fundamental. When Stiglitz gets around to discussing the role of his theoretical innovation with respect to the "standard adverse selection model", however, exactly what it is that his eclecticism aims either to cover up or take the edge off emerges much more clearly:

> For instance, the standard adverse selection model had the quality of the good offered in the market (say of used cars, or riskiness [*sic*] of the insured) depending on price. The car buyer (the seller of insurance) knows the statistical relationship between price and quality, and this affects his demand. The market equilibrium is the price at which demand equals supply.

But that is an equilibrium if and only if there is no way by which the seller of a good car can convey that information to the buyer — so that he can earn a quality premium — and if there is no way by which the buyer can sort out good cars from bad cars. Typically, there are such ways, and it is the attempt to elicit that information which has profound effects on how markets function. To develop a new paradigm, we had to break out from long established premises, to ask what should be taken as assumptions and what should be derived from the analysis. Market clearing could not be taken as an assumption; neither could the premise that a firm sells a good at a particular price to all comers. One could not begin the analysis even by assuming that in competitive equilibrium there would be zero profits. In the standard theory, if there were positive profits, a firm might enter, bidding away existing customers. In the new theory, the attempt to bid away new customers by slightly lowering prices might lead to marked changes in their behavior or in the mix of customers, in such a way that the profits of the new entrant actually became negative. (Stiglitz *ibid.*: 487-b)

One of the key things that Stiglitz has not addressed is the availability to corporate and non-corporate consuming entities alike – and the significance of such availability – of information that was previously the almost exclusive preserve of the corporate oligopolies-monopolies. Such information "leakages" across the buyer-seller divide indicate the increasing porosity in that wall, suggesting that, even in areas of the economy where the appearance of a modicum of free competition persists, it is nevertheless in decay. Perfecting information available to participants in the market may overcome dysfunction in some specific aspect or other – but it cannot reverse social-economic decay, or erase these signs of its spread.

Instead, there remains for Stiglitz an implicit assumption that buyer and seller enjoy more or less equal chances to acquire the information they seek. Although this is an absurdity that Stiglitz would likely reject, nothing in this formulation excludes it. If it is acknowledged that asymmetry is a non-trivial consideration at the level of theory, then it follows that it must be taken into account. Markets fail to clear, *and* there are asymmetries of information; however, *both* are symptoms of something else, possible/likely a common "something-else".

What could that "something-else" be? Stiglitz himself cruises within extremely close striking distance of a possible answer – before veering away like a cruise missile failing to reach its target:

> There were other aspects of the standard paradigm which seemed hard to accept. It argued that institutions did not matter — markets could see through them, and equilibrium was simply determined by the laws of supply and demand. It said that the distribution of wealth did not matter. ... And it said that (by and large) history did not matter — knowing preferences and technology and initial endowments, one could describe the time path of the economy.[40] ...
>
> Note 40. Strictly speaking, this was not an inevitable consequence of the neo-classical assumptions (e.g. it would not hold with irreversible investments)... (Stiglitz *ibid.*: 483)

In fact, Stiglitz has substituted "imperfections of information" for *deviations from conditions of idealised freedom of competition*. The discovery before the First World War, by Rudolf Hilferding (1910), of oligopoly-monopoly as the outward expression of the merger of banking and industrial capital had already accounted for the emergence of many of the "information asymmetries" that Stiglitz proposes to address. One of the key things that Stiglitz is not addressing, *e.g.*, in the car-purchasing example *infra*, is the availability to corporate and non-corporate consuming entities alike – and the significance of such availability – of information that was previously the almost exclusive preserve of the corporate oligopolies-monopolies. As already noted: such information "leakages" across the buyer-seller divide indicate not some advance in the sophistication of the operation of the market model, but only the increasing porosity in that wall. In other words: even in areas of the economy where the appearance of a modicum of free competition persists, it is nevertheless in decay.

Stiglitz credits his theory of imperfect information with enabling economists at last to account for the failure of the neoclassical paradigm to deliver the goods on its claim that, "knowing preferences and technology and initial endowments, one could describe the time path of the economy". However, this claim also fails to withstand closer scrutiny. Alfred Marshall's first [1890] edition of the *Principles of Economics* rushed with indecent haste to bury from the outset any role for historical factors in "the time path of the economy" on the strength of a claim that Charles Darwin's theory of evolution had demonstrated, as a general principle of Nature herself, no less, that only the final transformation of a predecessor to a new species was of decisive moment:

> …We meet at starting with the difficulty that those propositions which are the most important in one stage of economic development, are not unlikely to be among the least important in another, if indeed they apply at all.
>
> In this matter economists have much to learn from the recent experiences of biology: and Darwin's profound discussion of the question(2*) throws a strong light on the difficulties before us. He points out that those parts of the structure which determine the habits of life and the general place of each being in the economy of nature, are as a rule not those which throw most light on its origin, but those which throw least. The qualities which a breeder or a gardener notices as eminently adapted to enable an animal or a plant to thrive in its environment, are for that very reason likely to have been developed in comparatively recent times. And in like manner those properties of an economic institution which play the most important part in fitting it for the work which it has to do now, are for that very reason likely to be in a great measure of recent growth. (Alfred Marshall, *Principles of Economics*. Vol 2 section 2. London, 1890)

The most serious limitations inherent in Stiglitz' approach of refusing to abandon the market economy model and start fresh become palpable when the discussion turns to the role of political factors. While not dismissing political factors as being non-economic and outside the purview of economics, he nevertheless still seeks to reconcile the imperatives of government policy with the "laws of motion" of the market model. Here he sets out to attribute to imperfect information the limited success of government intervention in the economy to fulfill the Keynesians' fantasy of eternal equilibrium. To get there, however, he has first to re-explain the failure of Adam Smith's "invisible hand" in terms of the new paradigm of the economics of information. Thus:

> Perhaps the most important single idea in economics is that competitive economies lead, as if by an invisible hand, to a Pareto efficient allocation of resources, and that every Pareto efficient resource allocation can be achieved through a competitive mechanism, provided only that the appropriate lump sum redistributions are undertaken. It is these fundamental theorems of welfare economics which provide both the rationale for the reliance on free markets, and the belief that issues of distribution can be separated from issues of efficiency, allowing the

economist the freedom to push for reforms which increase efficiency, regardless of their seeming impact on distribution; if society does not like the distributional consequences, it should simply redistribute income. The economics of information showed that neither of these results was, in general, true. To be sure, economists over the preceding three decades had identified important market failures — such as the externalities associated with pollution — which required government intervention. But the scope for market failures was limited, and thus the arenas in which government intervention was required were limited. (Stiglitz *ibid.*: 503)

But the linkage of competition, efficiency and distribution is once again the weak link of the entire argument advanced here. Confusion of value with its magnitude as represented by price disguises the fact that its source lies in the application of living labour to raw material – using equipment, and in conditions, supplied by a party prepared to engage the labourer's service for wages. This disguise then effects the separation of the magnitude of the value as represented by price from its source. Hence, as a theoretical proposition, it cannot possibly be competition – again, one of the conditions attending production and sale of labour-power and one not under the control of the labourers – which is responsible either for allocating resources, efficiently or otherwise, such that resources are rendered scarce for some and sufficient for others. Competition affects the assignment of magnitudes for the exchange-values at which markets for these resources will clear to the satisfaction of those positioned to pay the most or buy the most. Again, however, the value of these resources is first and foremost a function of the living labour worked up in them – the least refined being cheapest and the most refined dearest. It is thus no accident that entire countries can become impoverished if they position themselves mainly as purveyors of raw material – like the oil-producing states – whereas the oil-consuming countries can enrich themselves at their suppliers' expense by virtue of their control of *all* the present and future value-added to be generated from their virtual monopoly over petroleum refining. Thus arise some of the economic bases for subsequent policy.

Instead of resolving or overcoming any of the inherent contradictions of the market model, Stiglitz' conception of an economics of information creates new shells under which to place things. Instead of addressing the impacts of the disappearance of free competition on both economic theory and practice, he substitutes a spectrum of perfection of information. When it comes to major politically-engineered economic events of our time, such as the disappearance of the Soviet bloc, he confounds the essential meaning of the concept of "privatisation" once again to deny the effects of the emergence of monopoly and oligopoly based on finance capital, with its norm of monopolistic competition through cartels, etc., on the formerly mainly industrial economy operating by and large according to the norms of free competition:

> The transition from communism to a market economy represents one of the most important economic experiments of all time, and the failure (so far) in Russia, and the successes in China, shed considerable light on many of the issues which I have been discussing. The full dimension of Russia's failure is hard to fathom. Communism, with its central planning (requiring more information gathering, processing, and dissemination capacity than could be managed with any technology), its lack of incentives, and its system rife with distortions, was viewed as highly inefficient. The movement to a market, it was assumed, would bring enormous increases in incomes. Instead, incomes plummeted, a decline

confirmed not only by GDP statistics and household surveys, but also by social indicators. The numbers in poverty soared, from 2% to upwards of 50% (depending on the measure used.) While there were many dimensions to these failures, one stands out: the privatization strategy, which paid little attention to the issues of corporate governance which we stressed earlier. Empirical work confirms that countries that privatized rapidly but lacked good corporate governance did not grow more rapidly. As Sappington and my paper warned, privatization might not lead to an increase in social welfare, rather than providing a basis for wealth creation, it led to asset stripping and wealth destruction. (Stiglitz *ibid.*: 519)

Yes: the privatization strategy adopted in the former Soviet Union played a large role – but why such a major role, dramatically affecting important social indices?

Surely the answer is not "informational asymmetries" in general but rather the particular exploitation of the privileged positions of "insiders". Social state assets were usurped and stripped by those who were already thoroughly familiar with the internal workings of these assets. Thus, no process of due diligence was necessary. The norms of third-party or arm's-length intervention, intended or designed to prevent the overwhelming of principles of fair corporate governance for all shareholders by conflicts of interests among insiders, were never applied. This suggests a class aim or intention at work and that the process lauded as "privatisation" (and branded "briberisation" by Stiglitz elsewhere) was in fact the conversion of what had been state-monopoly property in practice (disguised as socialist social property in theory) into private monopoly property by the forces who had effectively controlled these assets when they were operated as state-monopoly property. Thus, it was not "privatisation" in the sense of any kind of conversion of assets from ownership or control by the State (representing the public interest of the citizenry) to ownership or control by private interests outside the State: the status of the assets underwent no material or actual *shift* out of the realm of public right to the realm of monopoly right, only a rhetorical "shift". The only strategy that could have stopped it would have to have been organised to seize back control of state and industrial finance in a post-Soviet order operating independently of these oligarchical forces; no section of the peoples of the former Soviet Union was prepared to wage this struggle or organise its waging.

In the end, Stiglitz' "informational asymmetries" approach is not only unable to settle accounts with the thoroughgoing inadequacies of the conventional market model, but it also leads to serious capitulation before the authority of the conventional policy-setting institutions of the new globalised economic order. As serious as the implications of his failure are for economic theory, the implications of this capitulation in the field of policy are even more profound. He writes:

> The United States and the IMF argued strongly that lack of transparency was at the root of the 1997 financial crisis, and said that the East Asian countries had to become more transparent. The recognition that quantitative data concerning capital flows (outstanding loans) by the IMF and the US Treasury could have been taken as a concession of the inappropriateness of the competitive paradigm (in which prices convey all the relevant information); but the more appropriate way of viewing the debate was political, a point which became clear when it was noted that partial disclosures could be of only limited value, and could possibly be counterproductive, as capital would be induced to move through channels involving less disclosure, channels like off shore banking centers which were also less well regulated. When demands for transparency thus went beyond East Asia to Western hedge

funds and off shore banking centers, suddenly the advocates of more transparency became less enthralled, and began praising the advantages of partial secrecy in enhancing incentives to gather information. The United States and US Treasury then opposed the OECD initiative to combat money laundering through greater transparency of off shore banking centers — these institutions served particular political and economic interests — until it became clear that terrorists might be using them to help finance their operations; at that point, the balance of American interests changed, and the US Treasury changed its position. (Stiglitz *ibid.*: 522)

Stiglitz implicitly assumes and-or imposes a spectrum of transparency of governance ranging from well-regulated through less well-regulated (and, presumably, unregulated), and a related spectrum of transparency of information, from full disclosure to Swiss-bank secrecy. This approach, however, finesses the evidence of actual observation, to the point of vitiating it entirely. This evidence discloses that there are those who compete, and sort winners from losers, on the basis of "playing", *i.e.*, participating, according to mutually-accepted rules; there are those who operate outside those rules; and there are those who themselves play by the rules but summon and make use of those who operate outside those rules. This is how Rule by Exception is achieved within the context of the drug the Rule of Law.

Even admitting – after all this – that global politics is a most uncertain arena in which to hold out overly optimistic expectations, Stiglitz nevertheless argues in the end for improving economic planning, intervention and policy by increasing the quantity and quality of information available to buyers and sellers in any and every marketplace:

Without unbiased information, the effectiveness of the check that can be provided by the citizenry is limited; without good information, the contestability of the political processes can be undermined. One of the lessons of the economics of information is that these problems cannot be fully resolved, but there are laws and institutions which can decidedly improve matters. Right-to-know laws, demanding transparency, have been part of governance in Sweden for two hundred years; they have become an important if imperfect check on government abuses in the United States over the past quarter century. In the last five years, there has become a growing international movement, with some countries, such as Thailand, going so far as to include them in their new Constitution. Regrettably, these principles have yet to be endorsed by the international economic institutions. ...(Stiglitz *ibid.*:524)

Apart from the reputation of the individual speaking these words, is this credible, or does it not rather reflect a serious case of myopia concerning the nature and role of the intentions of economic actors and actions?[15]

---

[15] According to Aumann (2005), cooperation among those whose positions place them in competition with one another is not possible, to the extent that it cannot provide a rational game strategy; while according to Stiglitz, cooperation would appear conceivable only if there is first some kind of narrowing of any inherent inequalities of information available to both parties of a transaction. Research, however, into "the evolution of cooperation on graphs and social networks" published recently by Ohtsuki *et al.* (2006) suggests both views are limited and seriously deficient, and that, on the contrary, potential cooperation is built into all transactional "games" from the outset.

3.5. "HUMAN FACTOR – SOCIAL CONSCIOUSNESS"

The rotating fan example discussed at the opening of this chapter pointed to a very deep problem for the new departure into the "economics of intangibles" being proposed in this book, *viz.*, the connections between perception, intention, and the reliability of our knowledge including access to the information needed to arrive at useful, knowledge-based conclusions. In this section the matter of the role of intention is discussed, and a necessity to develop the human factor-social consciousness is adduced. (Chapter Five discusses how the distortion of perception to disguise intention is modulated to entrench and energise the Aphenomenal Model.)

3.5.1. Intentions

If we follow the path of human intentions in social form, we uncover the important but often overlooked fact that Intention is not a wish or an aspiration. Rather, it is a plan, a way to create a pathway.

The overwhelmingly predominant Intention governing contemporary economic existence is the corporate plan to control, contain, and sell off the whole world, again and again, obliterating Nature and the natural world by transforming everything in it to products.

In the 19th century, in the period immediately preceding the emergence of history writing and analysis as an academic profession with certain standards regarding the handling and interpretation of documents, British writers of historical works popularised what became known as the "Whig interpretation of history" (Butterfield 1931). According to this paradigm, the entire panorama of human history consisted of the unfolding of ever-greater "freedom" and "democracy" on the British model, *i.e.*, towards some form of popular representation such as the House of Commons, complete with constitutional monarchy. While this specifically British-imperial "Whig interpretation" came increasingly under challenge as a result of the development of more refined research methods and specialisation among academically-trained historians, there remains a strong lingering bias, quite prominent in the Anglo-American world of popular journalistic as well as more scholarly writing, that all social political development of Humanity has broadly followed this story-line arc of Progress (with a capital-P) away from monarchy and absolute rule towards popular control of the rulers. The problem with this assumption emerges the moment the world beyond the Eurocentric reference frame of the originating Whig interpretation is brought into view. When the non-European civilisations of the ancient world in Egypt and the Middle East along with other Muslim regions of southern, central and western Asia and ancient China and Japan are considered, a range of tendencies becomes apparent.

Absolute monarchy of the Eurocentric type is associated entirely with the emergence of the Roman Catholic Church as a "body corporate" spanning "Christendom". In these other cases, centralised systems of administration prevailed – sometimes headed by military rulers, sometimes by individuals claiming divine descent, and sometimes by individuals claiming descent in an established "royal" line – in which the uniformity of conscience and belief characterising mediaeval western Christianity was neither sought nor imposed. In the Eurocentric world, on the other hand, the contradictions that such prearranged ideological uniformity inevitably set in motion were answered by the methods of "power-sharing" – between Church and State, and later between monarch and Parliament. In reality, however, these rearrangements went ahead not so much as episodes in the gradual devolution of power, as the Whig and Progress interpretations would lead one to believe, but rather of in the service of ensuring that actual sovereign power to rule never passed into the hands of anyone, or any force, standing outside these ruling circles or their central apparatuses of administration. By comparison, in the period of the Prophet Muhammad and his family (620-660 CE), as well as during Mughal, *i.e.*, Muslim, rule in the Indian subcontinent and for most of the period of Ottoman rule in eastern Europe and western and central Asia, issues and forms of Eurocentrically-styled "power sharing" did not arise because the particular kind of contradictions such power-sharing schemes were intended to finesse could not develop in conditions where ideological uniformity was generally neither imposed nor demanded.

In Europe, the way out that the peoples themselves discovered for expressing their own sovereign will was in revolutionary movements like that which seized France in 1789 and many other parts of the continent in, or by, 1848. The feature of these movements was the rallying of the people as the Nation declaring their national collective will to be the source of all sovereignty. The victories scored by these movements sharply curtailed the role and influence of the Church and of hereditary aristocracy, but could not dislodge the Money-power that had already overtaken the governing apparatuses of every country western Europe. In the northern part of the Americas, a parallel but separate line of development saw the smashing of the colonial dictate of a foreign monarch by a popularly-supported movement of non-indigenous European settlers in support of a federal republic. This new model upheld equal rights for all men of property from the ranks of the European settlers, a state of civil death for women and black slaves possessed by these settlers, and a constitutional order that, by making the guarantee of the currency an exclusively federal responsibility, ensconced the money-power, rather than a king, at the centre of the national level of government and that also, by barring Congress from funding the establishment of any religion over or above any other, subordinated all religious impulse to this money-power as well. Furthermore, as an affair confined to, and defined by, those whose very presence was premised in the first place on stealing the lands of the indigenous population, this system of a "government of laws, not men" guaranteed nothing but genocide for the indigenous populations.

The negative consequences of ensconcing the money-power above all religious, aristocratic hereditary, popularly-based or even land-stealing settler-based claims have continued to date. However, such has become the urgency to establish once and for all who and what is really sovereign in a modern society that the terrible consequences of this money-power itself stirred and fomented and even more powerful revolutionary wave in the 20th century, starting with the Bolshevik Revolution of 1917. This renewed process has repeated and amplified the demand from below by the entire working people – regardless of ethnic, religious, indigenous or other background – to constitute the Nation in order to vest all effective sovereignty in themselves.

Throughout the 20th century to date, the intention of corporate capitalism (the amalgamation of entities that come together by law for the purposes of doing business) has been to try to sell everything on this planet: not only manufactured products and the food we must buy to eat, but also the very bodies of humans through our labor, our body parts as consumer items (breast modification for women, penile implants for men, internal organs as replacement parts, etc.), animals as pets, health, transportation, education, culture, war, and even the very air we breathe and the water we drink, all natural resources – all *for a price*, all for sale only. Nothing is sold that does not profit the seller all the way down the extraction and production chain.

The commercial business corporation is the most recent – and, as some argue, likely the last – of the great "bodies corporate" spawned within what is commonly called "Western civilization." (That term itself refers originally to western Europe, even though it came to include phenomena adapted in the European context but originating elsewhere). But it is quite unlike previous bodies corporate in one key respect. The first such body corporate was the Vatican – the administrative centre of the Roman Catholic faith. Closely aligned in time with its emergence as an entity enjoying what its own leaders described as "temporal" power (not just spiritual or doctrinal religious authority) was the institution of monarchy, which in Europe was that of one land-owning family enjoying some greater prominence, status or authority on some basis over other land-owning families of otherwise roughly equivalent social standing or rank. During and especially after the Crusades, in the High Middle Ages, various monarchies in Europe increasingly aligned themselves with those who could raise or loan them money. This rearrangement liberated them from a formerly prepossessing reliance on the professed loyalty of surrounding nobility. Such monarchs subsequently became more and more absolute, like Louis XIV the so-called "Sun King" of late 17th century and early 18th century France. Some, like the early 17th century British ruler James I, uttered doctrines such as the Divine Right of Kings. These royal courts were products of their own circumstances but nevertheless all looked as though they were modelling themselves on those of the ancient Egyptian Pharaohs and other Eastern potentates.

Their corporate essence emerged in how the matter of royal succession – the inheritance of royal authority by the eldest son upon the death of the father – was settled. Instead of succession being contested, as was frequently formerly the case – for example, in what is known to history as "the Wars of the Roses", two families claimed the British monarchy for more than a generation in the middle third of the 15th century, succession became increasingly accepted and eventually even constitutionally required. However, the key point is this: although religious and monarchical corporations did not define their right to exist in terms of whom they served, they clearly did serve actual human social constituencies. The Church acted in the name of its "flock" of believers. Monarchs acted in the name of all the other noble families swearing their allegiance. Today, modern governments, in which singularly-privileged individuals enjoying the absolute privileges and immunities of a mediaeval monarch are now very rare, inherited much of the old monarchies' corporate principle of immortality of function, but also claim their authority rests on the constituency they purport to serve, *viz.*, the citizenship of the country they govern.

However, one searches in vain to locate exactly what human constituency is served by the commercial business corporation. It employs its employees, but cannot be said to serve them. It generates profits for its shareholders and even richly rewards its senior executives. Essentially, however, the commercial business corporation puts money to work in the service of making more money. It is considered more efficient the more it subordinates serving any human need or constituency to this central mission. On this path, the commercial business corporation has done to the concept of civilisation what money has done to Humanity.

The drive to privatize started in Britain in the 16th century. Systematically, most of the world's land was converted into 'property' 'owned' by individuals, and later by corporate entities (which enjoy the rights and personality of individuals under the law). The first act of the Bolshevik Revolution of 1917 was to eliminate such private property in land. The entire social system elaborated from and on the basis of that act, on one-sixth of the earth's surface, threw into a chronic crisis the economy in the rest of the world. In the United States and Europe in particular the regime of private property – not only in land, but in means of production in general, including factories, distribution networks, etc. – still held sway. However, increasingly in these countries, the State was interposed

1. as guarantor of all parts of socially necessary services that were of minimal profit to private capital;
2. as guarantor of all high-risk energy development projects; and
3. as financier of parasitic spending on, and the endless and guaranteed market for, weapons systems of every description. In these and other ways, the self-interest of private property and its unquenchable appetite for gain could still carry on – only disguised as government-approved and, therefore, somehow pro-social.

The focus on "the bottom line", on money and on money making money – the very things that make the business corporate model such a potent force in eroding, liquidating or entirely dismissing the relations, loyalties, commitments or concerns of actual human persons – is frequently viewed through the other end of the telescope and transmuted into the well-known claims about the modernity and efficiency of business-like approaches and methods. When the modern business corporation encounters the economic field of a developing country, of course, there soon emerges a potential to unleash an enormous power never before seen or experienced in that society, with many possibilities to do tremendous damage – especially insofar as the modern business corporation literally "takes no hostages" and operates utterly indifferent to, and without the slightest concern for, the fate or feelings of any particular population.

Reflecting the scale on which finance and other forms of capital can be assembled in its systems of circulation and marketing, the most comprehensive corporate models have emerged in the United States. The success of the business corporate model has thus become associated with the prominence of the United States in all fields – business, technology, culture, military affairs and much else. As a result, emulation of the modernity and efficiency that provides the external surface appearance of the operations of the business-corporate model frequently takes the form of emulating the United States. Viewed from the perspective either of countries that seem to have been left far behind in material prosperity, or in which the leaders have become obsessed to match in material prosperity, the light that seems to shine from the United States can be blinding. However, once a knowledge-based approach such as now becomes possible in our Information Age is grasped and taken up that comprehends and masters the nature and role of intangible factors in economic development, it is no longer necessary to remain blinded by that light.

Once sight is lost of one's intention, no amount of alternative development or alternative ideological disposition can save the victim. Thus, for example, at the XXIst Congress of the Communist Party of the Soviet Union in 1959, the leadership commanded by Nikita Khrushchev pronounced the new mission of the society was no longer to revolutionise anything, but rather to move Heaven and Earth in order "to catch up and surpass the United States by 1970" (Chernenko and Smirtyukov1967). Even the justification they offered for their new course of avoiding struggle to establish the truth and giving up building a world fit for humanity for the time being Khrushchev and his successors all the way to Gorbachev imposed the corporate criterion everywhere in the service of improving the Soviet Union's ability to compete with the U.S. However, not only was the neo-corporate state he and his successors built unable to attain this goal, but the Soviet Union itself, having – like Icarus of the ancient Greek myth – flown too close to the sun on this mission, despite everything it had learned from hundreds of space missions more advanced than those of NASA, nevertheless crashed and burned, imploding and disappearing in 1991. In 1998, before he went on to become President of India, Abdul Khallan proclaimed that India should strive catch up with the U.S. In today's Information Age, given what can already be seen looming on Humanity's horizon, should the peoples of the Indian subcontinent put their shoulder to the wheel and nose to the grindstone so that, in 50 years' time, they too can send troops to Iraq?

With the disappearance after 1989-1991 of the regime of socialist social property in the Soviet Union and eastern Europe, meanwhile, the chronic crisis of the established capitalist world order did not come to an end. On the contrary, the crisis itself has deepened by becoming more chronic, with serious decay in social indices from alcoholism to infant mortality and premature death throughout the former socialist countries as well as a change in some of the forms of this crisis. In addition to certain individual countries such as the Republic of Cuba and the Democratic People's Republic of Korea which still maintain a socialist system as a barrier against the revival of private property in general, there are today a number of economic blocs that have formed – most dramatically and recently ASEAN in China and southeast Asia, and the ALBA project led by Cuba and Venezuela in Latin America and envisioned eventually to incorporate Argentina, Brazil, Chile, Ecuador and Bolivia as well – on the basis of reining in previously absolute freedom for private property, especially in the form of foreign credits or foreign direct investment from U.S. or European sources, to overrule the needs of individual member-states.

Early civilizations considered themselves the guardians and caretakers of all living things on the lands they inhabited and responsible for future generations. Indigenous American Nations considered themselves one with all around them. There was no special word for Nature, no separation: plants, animals, and humans were considered interdependent. In this world it was the coming of the European invader, funded by their own rulers at home, that led to the eventual privatizing of the earth which all living things share in common, into a commodity to be broken up at will, through wars and theft. The advent of property laws made the thievery 'legal', a concept derived to protect corporate property.

The deepening of this crisis is marked by a simultaneous extension of corporate abuse of Humanity's rights of access to fresh air, clean water and other absolute necessities alongside a growing rebellion by the human productive forces sustaining these corporations, as their market, against government accommodation of the abusers and their abuses. There was a time in the history of the world, not that long ago, where water and air were unindustrialized, free to breathe and to drink and by today's standards, uncontaminated. Today, all this has changed. Water and air have become commodities. Governments and corporations now own access to water. Overuse by industry and agriculture have made it into a scarce commodity over which future wars will be waged. Contaminated by industrial and agricultural runoff, the sale of bottled water, or home filters to the public who can afford it, is promoted as uncontaminated. Pollution itself, created by chemical poisons released into the air by industry and agriculture, and the automobile, has become a money-making commodity – with the sale of pollution credits from one polluter to another. Home filters to clean the air in homes and public buildings, promote clean air, again for those who can afford it, autos in many places are required to have catalytic converters to filter out poisons emitted from the burning of fuel, to keep down air pollution. At the same time corporate impunity, with its virtual immunity from prosecution, legal sanctions or legal responsibility in its home bases and main markets, is purchased and maintained by trying to dump unwanted wastes in various parts of Africa and Asia. This is arousing more and more people in the rest of the world against corporate fiat and dictate, energizing in its wake a rapidly widening discussion of alternative arrangements for Humanity's continued existence on this planet. Accordingly, the intention to control nature has become the last remaining pathway by which corporations hope to ensure a constant, never-ending stream of profit – and a battleground on which the fate of Humanity for generations to come may be decided.

Both the intentions of any corporate entity exercising power over others, and the pathways by which those intentions are realised, are conventionally understood as instruments or aspects of whatever its mission. While the mission is often analysed and discussed, however, how these corporate structures actually address the human factor, which is highly intangible and difficult to reduce in advance to set rules and procedures, is another matter. The modern business corporation directly serves no actual human purpose, individual or social – or, equivalently, it serves all purposes but only indirectly through the medium of money. During the 1950s in the United States, this "soullessness" and the depersonalising anonymity of the corporate business culture in general was widely commented and documented in works by social scientists, such as David Riesman's *The Lonely Crowd* (1950) and C. Wright Mills' *White Collar* (1951). Reducing and streamlining many relationships to interactions defined entirely by set rules and procedures is a normal development in any bureaucracy or hierarchy. However, within those corporate structures that either cease to serve a human constituency in any meaningfully direct way, or that were designed in the first place to serve people only indirectly through money relations, these processes are particularly fraught with a consequence that is rarely if ever discussed in this light. What happens when such organisational forms encounter challenges to some program in the process of its execution? The organisational form itself musters a response, delivered through the agency of an individual acting as its representative, which always takes the form of "exercising The Prerogative" in order to demonstrate "who's the boss." Far from reasoning with the individual who is disagreeing or raising a question, it sets out to crush the individual, isolating the person in order to render them as vulnerable as possible, and then attacks them. What masks the exposure of this process is that the attack is delivered by some individual against another individual. Thus, if the tables turn and questions come to be raised about the attacker, the response is that it was an overzealous individual or – as is frequently the case with young men abused by Catholic priests in private Christian religious schools in North America – a large portion of the priesthood is blamed for being sexually perverted. Of course, if everyone is guilty, then no one is, but if "the problem" can be reduced to a few "rotten apples," larger and more difficult matters concerning the corporate modus operandi can be ignored. In human terms, it is hard to conceive anything more evil than ganging up to attack the weakest and most vulnerable, yet precisely this response is quintessential to the modus operandi of any and every corporate structure that demeans, dismisses or otherwise marginalises the human person or recognition of the worth of every human being.

The most efficacious route by which humans can begin to restore the earth to some kind of balance is through education. By "education" here, however, is meant the ability to look at the world unencumbered by preconceived notions. Thus, it is neither job skills training, nor the ability to earn more money, nor what takes place in institutions calling themselves universities but operating in a bubble, separated from real life around them as the captives of corporate intentions. Education as it has been up to now – the instrument by which capitalist society prepares the next generation of workers according to the needs of capital in the short term – is utterly inadequate for the demands of the Information Age.

3.5.2. The Myth of Emulating Nature

Nature appears to man as perfect, especially in the sense of complete. In fact, nature is so fully-formed and comprehensive that emulating nature has formed the basis for virtually all branches of knowledge, ranging from natural justice and dialectics of the social system to technology development. Notwithstandiung the vaunted intelligence of mankind, however, no modern technology truly as yet emulates the *science* of nature. It has been quite the opposite: observations of nature have rarely been translated into pro-nature process development.

Even though it is widely accepted in the social framework that pro-Nature arrangements such as would ensure natural justice and social equity, are absent – and not by accident but by design, few paid attention to the problem in so-called natural science. Today, some of the most important technological breakthroughs have been mere manifestations of the *linearization* of nature science: nature linearized by focusing only on its external features. Linearization forms the basis for the first line of lies involved.

Nature is non-linear and the claim of emulating nature with linear formulae is inherently untrue. Today, computers process information exactly opposite to how the human brain does. Turbines produce electrical energy while polluting the environment beyond repair even as electric eels produce much higher-intensity electricity while cleaning the environment. Batteries store very little electricity while producing very toxic spent materials. Synthetic plastic materials look like natural plastic, yet their syntheses follow an exactly opposite path. Furthermore, synthetic plastics do not have a single positive impact on the environment, whereas natural plastic materials do not have a single negative impact. In medical science, every promise made at the onset of commercialization proven to be opposite what actually happened: witness the growing number of cases implicating the drug Prozac™ in suicides, the pain-killer Vioxx™ in heart attacks and Viagra™, the pill for erectile dysfunction, in eventual male impotence.

Nature does not allow a single product to impact the long-term negatively. Even the deadliest venom (*e.g.*, cobra, poisoned arrow, tree frog) has numerous beneficial effects in the long-term. This catalogue carries on in all directions: microwave cooking, fluorescent lighting, nuclear energy, cellular phones, refrigeration cycles to combustion cycles. In essence, nature continues to improve matters in its quality, as modern technologies continue to degrade the same into baser qualities.

Whereas the quest for homogeneity seems to motivate much of modern engineering, Nature thrives on diversity and flexibility, gaining strength from heterogeneity. While modern applied science continues to define problems as linearly as possible, promoting "single"-ness of solution and particularly avoiding non-linear problems, Nature in its non-linearity inherently promotes multiplicity of solutions. Whereas engineered solutions today start with a "safety factor", promoting an obsession with excess (hence, waste), Nature is inherently sustainable and promotes zero-waste, both in mass and energy. While engineering is obsessed with standards and replicability, always seeking "steady-state" solutions, Nature is truly transient, never showing any exact repeatability or steady state.

Of course, in social development, such obsession with linear models is reflected in the promotion of homogeneity, uniformity, and symmetry. The essential common feature is the institution of an absurd model (for instance, there is no such entity as uniform, homogenous, or symmetric), followed by a false promise. Consider Table 3-1, listing various technologies that had a promise attached to each commercial product. With today's knowledge, we know that each promise was a deliberate lie. In every case, researchers were aware of the long-term implication of the product but were not allowed to publish their work.

How could this happen? Our research shows that none of these technologies emerged from any good intention. "Good" here implies long-term good, for the general public. The promoters of these products are not incapable of developing good products. Rather, they are incapable of seeing that "doing good is good business". In conventional business development, self-interest in the short-term reigns supreme and promoters of these models are so blinded in their short-term focus that they cannot even fathom the thought of seeing beyond the quarterly profit. They are quite aware that their motive of amassing profit at the expense of natural justice would offend any consumer, so they resort to lying about their motive right from the beginning. In this, the consumer can also be faulted – but only with lack of research. Every effort is expended in marketing the short-term and external gains themselves such that few, if any, consumers can read between the lines to notice that the overwhelming corporate message: "Shut up and buy!". Often, they even forget what was the reason behind buying a product other than the fact that it was on sale, was seen on TV, or so on.

From the vantage point of today's Information Age, how could we have averted the following disasters?

1. Until some 120 years ago, wearing more clothes was synonymous with civilization. In fact, with the exception of Islamic era, covering more with more expensive clothing was the symbol of aristocracy. Even though France tried to 'break free' from this trend of thinking, the culture of 'wearing less means you are civilized' was started by the introduction of the Playboy magazine in the United States. This 'pioneer' work would explode into all aspects of commercialization (including journalism) soon after the sex revolution in the sixties. Today, nudity is synonymous with civilization.

2. In 1960, when birth control pills were first introduced, each pill contained 10 times more male hormone than necessary to abort the egg. What was the promise behind? Liberation of women. Soon after, the anti-nausea drug thalidomide was introduced for pregnant women. What was the promise? Women would have easy pregnancy by removing nausea. In reality, 20% of babies who mothers were on the drug became severely deformed. This drug was banned in 1962 but now it is making a comeback. Today, even a 12 year old can get prescribed for birth control pills (at least in Canada) and the same industry is busy producing 'correction pills' that would 'eliminate' inherent injustice of woman's biology by stopping menstruation altogether (*Maclean's*, December 2005).

3. In 1940's, baby disposable diapers were introduced. The inventor, Marion Donovan noticed that her babies would 'nearly instantaneously' wet their cloth diapers as soon as they were changed. In 1946, she introduced the 'breakthrough' technology of disposable waterproof diaper. Did the habit of nearly instantaneously wetting the diaper go away? Of course not. In fact, the first name of these diapers was 'the boat', indicating it was meant to keep babies afloat on their own urine. Our survey today indicates, disposable diapers are synonymous with keeping the babies dry and civilized. Only the rich ones in the western old can afford to use all-cotton nappies (something that was commonly used in the third world) while remaining 'civilized'.

Could you open a plastic surgery, introduce the birth control pill, or non-stick plastic in cookware, or formaldehyde in lipstick, or white lead in cosmetics, or bleach in detergent and body soap, or toxic agents (butane, etc.) in body mist, or toxic chemicals in the name of "preservatives", or freon in refrigerators, glycols and DEAs in the gas stream, microwave – all of them transitions from good to bad – devoid of some purposeful motive?

Overall, modern development and social progress can be characterized by its driver, which is greed. Nature, on the other hand, operates on the basis of need. There arises no need to make false promises or to institute opacity if one wishes to introduces pro-Nature development. The result of greed-driven social development has been what Nobel laureate Gordon Curd calls "our technological disaster". Marginalizing the concerns and participation of that part of the population interested to care for Nature has produced a result not unlike Ptolemy's famous error – which the Vatican for almost two millennia enforced as "Truth" – that pictured the Sun revolving about the Earth: it has placed those focused on self-interest and short-term gain at the centre of all development. In this period, the quality of human health has suffered tremendously: over the last 50 years: a 50-times increase per capita in the use of sugar (refined, externally processed, carbohydrate), plastics (wrinkle-free™, leather or fabric, durable™ wood), fertilizer ('refined' biomass), spirits (refined alcohol), cigarettes (refined tobacco), chemicals (preservatives, pasteurization, antibiotics), and remediative surgery, while life expectancy has increased hardly at all. As Figures 3-2 and 3-3 illustrate, this life is being promoted as the only life human beings should live for.

In any research work undertaken in the natural or social sciences, although accurate observation and recording of what has been observed poses its own non-trivial set of issues, the problem of data (content) is usually not reducible to the matter of its accuracy or any other quality (including quantity) of the data *per se*. Two other crucial elements enter the picture.

For one thing, the observer must be prepared to consciously acknowledge any role that his/her frame of reference may be playing in framing what may be observed of what is actually taking place. In many cases, errors that arise from ignoring or misunderstanding this role can be corrected without having to undertake the observation anew; sometimes, the effect may be so serious as to mandate another set of observations being taken. In this context, because of its asserted promise (not always realised) of shortcuts and efficiencies in completing the research process, the notion of what constitutes "experimental error" becomes very important to nail down quite specifically. If standard error is assumed to exist, it is entirely possible to group in the "experimental error" category precisely those anomalies in output data or results that point to something previously unreported, unacknowledged or unknown. As we now know from James Watson's recollections in *The Double Helix*, if anomalous-looking data from Rosemary Franklin's X-ray crystallography slides had been so dismissed, the helical conformation of the DNA molecule would never even have been guessed; no amount of playing with three-dimensional molecular models would even have suggested such a conformation as the basic starting-point. All this forms one point of tangible-intangible bifurcation. To ignore the intangible component means selecting the path that leads to falsehood.

For another, there is the question of the observer's own intention in undertaking the observation: is the aim one of finding out, or verifying an existing previous prejudice? This is yet another point of tangible-intangible bifurcation in which, again, ignoring the intangible component means selecting the path that leads to falsehood. In this case, the distorting effects of an observer's intention – and these run the gamut from intentionally deceiving others to merely fooling oneself – cannot be corrected without undertaking the observations anew, if necessary by another observer or observation team.

Thus far we have mentioned only with the truth-falsehood bifurcation associated with the data content of what is observed. Another set of issues arises when it comes to the forms of this data – especially the forms in or by which it is transmitted to, or published for, others. A key intangible feature, connected with the form in which knowledge or data or information might be transmitted, is the extent to which whatever is transmitted appears to the receiver to be complete, with all the loose ends tied, and all open loops closed.

This points once again to a profound contradiction alluded to in other contexts elsewhere in the present work. In economic affairs, a good or service bought or sold as a commodity, which itself may actually veil a struggle waged between the massed forces of Capital and Labour in order to give rise to it, appears to the buyer as the midpoint of a loop that begins with coming to the marketplace with money for transacting an exchange or exchanges and ends with the satisfied customer leaving the market place as proprietor of the commodity s/he sought. The same commodity appears to the seller as the midpoint of a loop in which s/he brought his good or service to the market to sell and, after transacting some sale or sales, departed with a money-equivalent that covers the costs of producing the commodity and bringing it to market. (If middlemen that specialise in assembling the conditions of production and distribution of commodities happen to predominate in that particular system of commodity exchange, part of what the seller takes as payment is a profit margin over and above the costs already mentioned.) Not only do selling and buying the commodity each form closed loops for seller and buyer, but the processes impelling each to enter the market to transact the exchange – what the seller had to do to get the product to market, and what the buyer needs the product for – also form their own separate closed loops. At the level of the society as a whole, meanwhile, the production process giving rise to these commodities and their exchange is not a closed loop at all, but more like an undeclared civil war.

Human knowledge is never complete. Any suggestion otherwise is immediately false. Nevertheless it is a fact that, in the short-term, the sale of an idea or the reception given a concept can superficially be boosted by resorting to the techniques of advertising. Advertising is widely deemed a kind of "commercial speech" and granted as much freedom as, or even more freedom than, any other form of speech – political, scientific etc. – because of its economic function of boosting sales, or what economists call "assisting markets to clear." Everyone knows very well what happens if the truth about the larger picture insinuates itself into advertising. If I am advertising that you should subscribe to The New York Times, it may close your loop [and make your mind up] to know that it is delivered to your door before 6 a.m. If, however, my advertising went on to mention how much of the woodlands of the

Canadian provinces of Quebec and New Brunswick are felled to accomplish this feat, and the consequences this visits on the natural wildlife of those zones or on the livelihoods of the human communities there, your decision might well be different.

After knowledge gathering and knowledge dissemination comes the entire realm of human governance and how policy is made – and also the level at which any contradiction not detected or sorted in any earlier stage will stand out screaming and howling its absurdities, with no possibility remaining of confusing what is true with what is false. Thus in the recent Canadian elections of 23 January 2006, the party asked to form the government, which formed the official Opposition during the previous Parliament, rules as what is called a "minority government", possessing insufficient seats in the House of Commons to impose its will – as was the case for the preceding party in power, now the official Opposition, over the previous 19 months. It is dependent on the goodwill of the opposition parties, or on their financial exhaustion in the last election contest, to fend off possible defeat of its legislative program in the House. In the year preceding the calling of the last election, the party now governing which was then in opposition, spent time researching and proposing its "accountability" agenda. It insisted that it would not repeat the paths into corrupt practices of the government of the day (these were becoming ever more embarrassingly public as the result of a formal inquiry being conducted by a retired senior judge). Its first legislative act, it promised in the election campaign, would be a new Federal Accountability Act. This would set out the way the truth and the light to government conducting the people's business according to the merits of serious proposals and not as so many favours for cronies of the governing party. Upon its successful election on the basis of this program, its leader (and now Canada's Prime Minister) found his government lacking a powerful voice from the Montreal business community. Accordingly the Prime Minister exercised his legal discretion, appointing to the Senate just such a representative whom he then named to the Cabinet. (Canadian parliamentary practice does not allow naming unelected persons to Cabinet but does allow appointing of Senators and including Senators in the Cabinet. Another of the policy planks of the new governing party has been that the Senate should all be elected.) In the spring of 2005, the previous government saved itself from calling an election by inducing a prominent member of the Opposition front bench to join the Cabinet. Not to be outdone, when the "new" government – all the while talking "accountability" – no sooner found itself lacking a senior voice from the business community in Vancouver, it induced precisely such a representative who had been a Cabinet member in the former government to cross the floor and enter the new Cabinet. Days before tabling its vaunted Federal Accountability Act, the new government issued an untendered contract to a company with government-friendly connections to study and recommend reforms to the government's tendering processes. (This was one of the sorest of sore spots largely responsible in the first place for the entire almost two-years-long scandal that led to the previous government's defeat.)

Once again, the role of intention poses itself. As we have seen with the Aphenomenal Model in general, and once again in these recent Canadian political developments, closing the loop entrenches an actor's self-interested, anti-social, anti-natural intention that not only damages other people's short term but also cancels his/her own long term. On the other hand, taking every decision-point, every point at which another choice has to be made, as a point of potential bifurcation, a well-intended choice benefits everyone in the short term – at least to the next point of decision – and saves the actor's long term and short term. Those who organise their own knowledge-gathering and do their own research can prevail in any circumstance, and not become waylaid by errors or deliberate lies whether in the gathering of knowledge or its transmission to others, provided they continue to gather knowledge themselves and conduct their own research without a short-term aim of closing any particular loop.

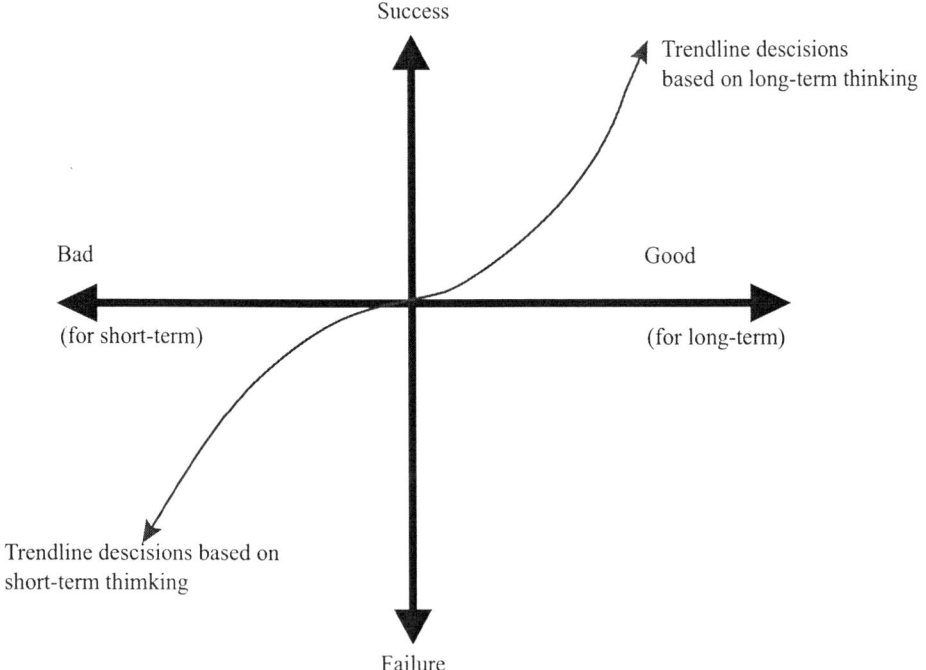

Figure 3-2. The human brain takes something like 500,000 decisions a day. The trend in a line of these decisions comprises discrete points. At any one of these points, a bifurcation can begin when a well-intended choice is taken based on appreciating the role of intangibles. The overall trends of long-term and short-term thinking are nevertheless quite distinct.

3.5.3. Origins of Intention

Every action is preceded by intention. Every civilization, ranging from ancient Indian to European culture has recognized the role of intention. For instance, the relationship between 'Chetna' (inspiration) and 'Karma' (deed) was outlined in Mahabharat and in the scripts of Buddha. In Europe, the ancient criminal justice system was based on 'guilty mind' (*mens rea*). The most famous saying of the Prophet and the first one cited in the collection of Bokhari is indeed the one that characterizes any deed based on the intention. A review of human history reveals that the perpetual conflict between good and evil has always been because of the diametrically opposed intentions. The good has always been characterized by the intention to serve a bigger mass while evil has been characterized by the intention to serve self-interest.

Table 3-1. Some "breakthrough" technologies

Product	Promise	Truth
Microwave oven	Instant cooking (bursting with nutrition)	97% of the nutrients destroyed; produces dioxin from baby bottles
Fluorescent light (white light)	Simulates the sunlight and can eliminate 'cabin fever'	Used for torturing people, causes severe depression
Prozac (the wonder drug)	80% effective in reducing depression	Increases suicidal behavior
Anti-oxidants	Reduces aging symptoms	Gives lung cancer
Vioxx	Best drug for arthritis pain, no side effect	Increases the chance of cancer
Coke	Refreshing, revitalizing	Dehydrates; used as a pesticide in India
Transfat	Should replace saturated fats, incl. high-fiber diets	Primary source of obesity and asthma
Simulated wood, plastic gloss	Improve the appearance of wood	Contains formaldehyde that causes Alzheimer
Cell phone	Empowers, keep connected	Gives brain cancer, decreases sperm count among men.
Chemical hair colors	Keeps young, gives appeal	Gives skin cancer
Chemical fertilizer	Increases crop yield, makes soil fertile	Harmful crop; soil damaged
Chocolate and 'refined' sweets	Increases human body volume, increasing appeal	Increases obesity epidemic and related diseases
Pesticides, MTBE	Improves performance	Damages the ecosystem
Desalination	Purifies water	Necessary minerals removed
Wood paint/varnish	Improves durability	Numerous toxic chemicals released
Leather technology		
Freon, aerosol, etc.	Replaced ammonia that was 'corrosive'	Global harms immeasurable and should be discarded

Because Nature itself is such that any act of serving others leads to serving self in the long term, it is conceivable that some acts of self-interest in the long-term are also acceptable. Unfortunately, history also tells us that the perpetrators of evil have always covered up their intentions. From ancient Pharaohs to modern Czars have invariably maintained 'it is all about setting things straight'. Fortunately, the onset of the Information Age has made it difficult to cover up intentions for long. Recent events already unfolding in this new millennium show clearly that covering up intentions is bound to be very costly and will have short-term consequences. In this, the Information Age has accelerated the role of *karma* and practically made the aphenomenal model (based on covering up followed by justification) irrelevant. Ironically, the role of intention has been either ignored or carefully put aside in practically all scientific analyses in the last 200 years.

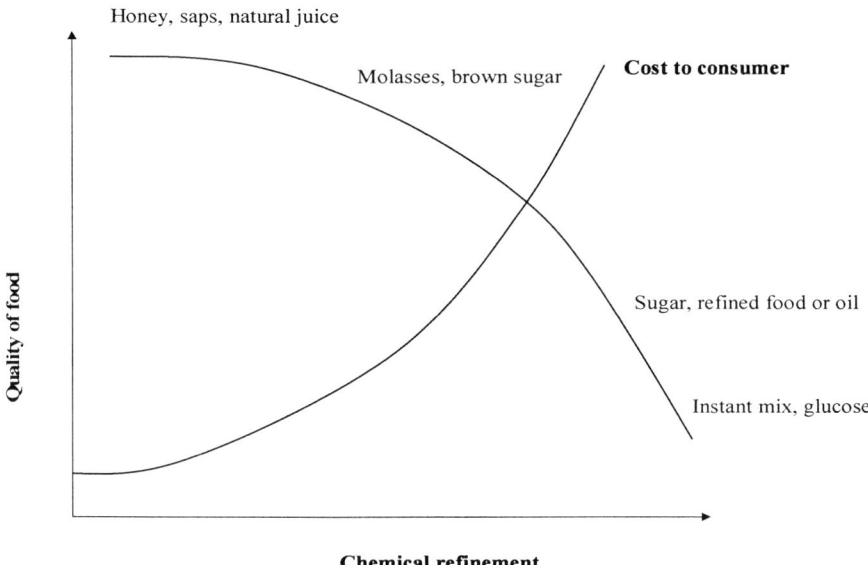

Figure 3-3. The outcome of greed-driven technology. The same applies to quality of human beings that have been 'refined' with the greed-driven education system or to the quality of human health of people who adopted this anti-Nature culture.

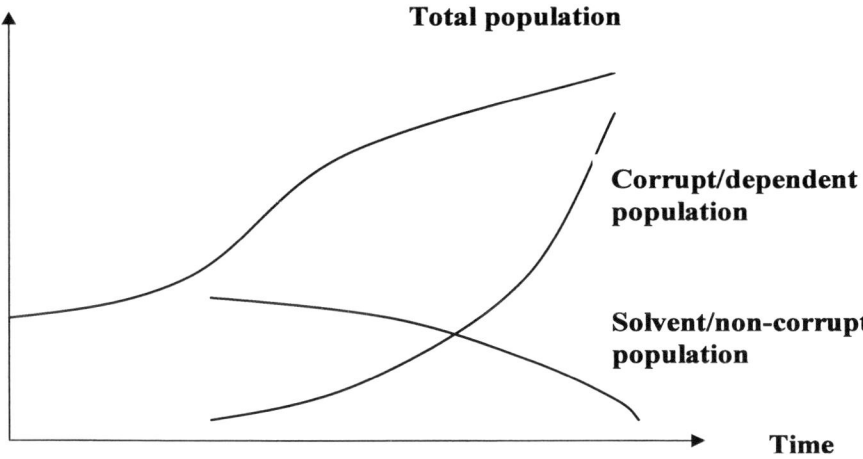

Figure 3-4. With the greed-driven social progress, we are seeing increasing rate of decline in good people. In the west, all but USA shows any population growth. In the third world countries, the top 1% of the society succumbed to "family planning" propaganda while the dependent group has grown exponentially. This imbalance in the third world is rarely talked about.

This chronology coincides with commercialisation of practically everything (including socially necessary services such as education). The moment any action is judged against a commercial value, it is inherently assumed that the intention of the action does not have any bearing on the action. This detachment from intention, which is actually the driver of all human action, is so embedded that our research found no model that considers this factor in any model of the modern age. Absurd as it may sound when spoken aloud, people have grown used to believing that intentions don't matter. Even though in medical science there is some recognition of how a positive outlook boosts and a negative outlook impairs the immune system, discussion of this aspect emerges rarely mentioned in other fields, particularly commerce or finance. Today, there is an all- pervasive perception that intentions don't count. The work of Linus Pauling in structural chemistry – for which he was awarded the Nobel Prize in 1954 – was transmuted by some of his followers into the notion that Humanity generally could live better with itself and with Nature through the widest possible use and-or ingestion of chemicals, and that "chemicals are chemicals", *i.e.*, that knowledge of chemical structure discloses everything we need to know about physical matter and all chemicals of the same structure are identical regardless of how differently they may actually have been generated or have existed in their current form. Paralleling this idea that "chemicals are destiny", as discussed earlier in this chapter, Prof. Stiglitz, would appear in effect to have redefined the entire field and science of economics along the line of the notion that "information is destiny".

Such dogmas have proven especially harmful for health and quality of life in the West and for basic economic welfare in the developing countries of Africa, Asia and Latin America. If the "chemicals are chemicals" mantra were true, why should we see signs in every health store, "organic fertilizers only"? When then every nation that fell in the trap of chemical fertilizer now is trying to get out of it in utter desperation? If money, or investment, is "destiny" – which would mean you can become rich with the money loaned from your enemy – why do we see repeated economic collapse in developing countries proportional to the money invested from developed 'donor' countries? Figure 3-4 illustrates this point. Ironically, following his term of service at the head of the World Bank, it was Prof. Stiglitz, in an August 2003 speech in Bangladesh, who stated that "the World Bank and IMF only serve the interest of developed countries". From the time these institutions overhauled their basic posture during the Kennedy Administration and, guided by the theories of "economic takeoff " propounded by Prof. WW Rostow (1960) reoriented and realigned their policies in the closest possible collaboration with the United States' Agency for International Development (AID) programs, could such an outcome ever have been in doubt?

Conventionally, it is understood that we live in four dimensions – three spatial dimensions, plus time (designated hereafter as 1D, 2D, 3D and 4D). Consider the following:

- 2D has 1D as subset, but this subset must always be less than the full 2D set, else the 2D set reduces to 1D;
- 3D has 1D and 2D as subsets, but these subsets combined must also be less than the full 3D set, else the 3D set reduces to 2D; and
- 4D has 1D, 2D and 3D as subsets, but these subsets combined must also be less than the full 4D set, else the 4D set reduces to 3D

As discussed in Chapter 3, with reference to the example of observing a rotating fan before and after applying a strobe light in the observation chamber, our actual knowledge of, or about, time and its effects "right now" occurs in a frequency domain. Thus another dimension must be posited in which we may have time, *i.e.*, the 4th dimension, as a subset. As explained above, in order to have 4D as a subset, we must posit 5D with 1D, 2D, 3D and 4D as subsets. This fifth dimension is the Knowledge dimension.

Various factors are operating actively to obscure this. A leading one is the notion of "time" as conventionally presented in the physics and mathematics and incorporated in the educational curriculum everywhere. This is the notion whereby time exists either as a point in "time", or as a duration of some length – full stop. This reduces any other sense of time, for example: any sense of *time as a characteristic feature of each phenomenon* and process occurring either in Nature or in Society, to merely an interpretation imposed on the phenomenon or process by this or that individual. *Just because the individual's tangible sense of time is not fixed, and indeed changes with a change of the frame of reference, does not mean that time is not a characteristic feature. It means only that the individual's tangible sense of it varies with any change in the individual's frame of reference.* Regardless of one's frame of reference, and at least until some other circumstance intervenes to cause this orbit to precess towards the centre of our solar system, the actual amount of time it takes the Earth to traverse its orbit around the Sun remains roughly, plus or minus some moments, what we call "one year".

In all the sciences, natural and social, every mathematical approach to rendering the inner meaning and relations of phenomena assumes "time" to be "the independent variable." As discussed earlier in Chapter 2, this notion was central and quintessential to the calculus first elaborated by Newton. However:

- if time is treated as *the* independent variable, in which no point in time is more remarkable than any other save for its position further to the left or the right along the positive portion of R_1 (the Real number-line), then any given time t becomes "right now." All the possible values that any function of time can take – resulting from selecting any particular point in, or interval of, time – are entirely accounted for by that function;
- if, on the other hand, time and everything else about a phenomenon are all changing, which is the situation actually found in any natural phenomenon, we can no longer say that time is varying independently and hence it is no longer acceptable to treat time as the independent variable.

Mathematical analysis applied to the first frame of reference just described must produce unique solutions, either singly or in sets of unique solutions; mathematical analysis applied to the second frame will produce multiple non-unique solutions. This second frame is clearly more in tune with phenomena in Nature or Society as they are experienced. The first frame, which is valid only for abstractions from that reality, for a long time provided the only practical and mathematically tractable route to sorting out the inner relations. Given the computational capabilities now available to us in the Information Age, need we any longer feel so constrained?

Multiple solutions means multiple pathways, and the following simple graph suggests how the bifurcation principle developed in chaos theory might be applied to uncover / discover those pathways applying the "dimensional" approach suggested at the onset (so to speak…) of this discussion:

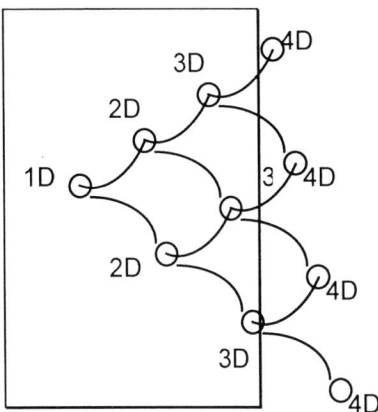

Figure 3-5. Bifurcation – a familiar pattern from chaos theory – is useful for illustrating the engendering of more and more degrees of freedom in which solutions may be found as the "order" of the "phase space" – in this case, dimensions – increases from one to two to three to four.

The whole point of operating in the Knowledge dimension is that it becomes possible there to uncover / discover the intangible factors and elements at work that normally remain hidden or obscured from our view. In this dimension, no one would seriously consider or undertake the experimental regime described at the start of Chapter 4, in which Galileo's insight into what really makes objects accelerate towards earth at the same rate would not only never be regained but a mass of experimental evidence might well be compiled to prevent anyone from ever thinking of "going there." More generally, the method that plagues a great deal of investigation in the natural and social sciences today – the method of advancing a hypothesis to test only within the operating range of existing available measuring devices and criteria, then declaring one's theory has been validated when the "results" obtained as measured by these devices and criteria correspond to predictions – would be replaced by a Knowledge-based approach that would ask the relevant and necessary questions about the available measuring devices and criteria before proceeding further.

This is the theoretical framework in which we raise the notion of a Knowledge-driven economics that would be based truly on economising rather than wasting. The Knowledge dimension is where the intangibles that Humanity has not dealt with up to now can be discovered and used. Consider the following pair of figures. The first displays all possible pathways for quarterly income in some timespan – examined and visible within the Knowledge dimension. The second displays a truncation of the same information to two dimensions – a truncation of the kind conventionally presented in business and economics texts, with time as the independent variable.

It is a classic case of what U.S. Defence Secretary Donald Rumsfeld in another context famously called "your 'unknown unknowns'". Of crucial importance here, however – in contrast to the atmosphere of fear and loathing about the future suffusing the United States in the days and months following the terrorist attacks of 11 September 2001 on the World Trade Centre, in which Secretary Rumsfeld was listing this category alongside "your 'known knowns', 'unknown knowns', 'known unknowns'" – is the fact that the information in the first figure of this pair exists and is accessible to anyone applying the Knowledge-based approach discussed throughout this work:

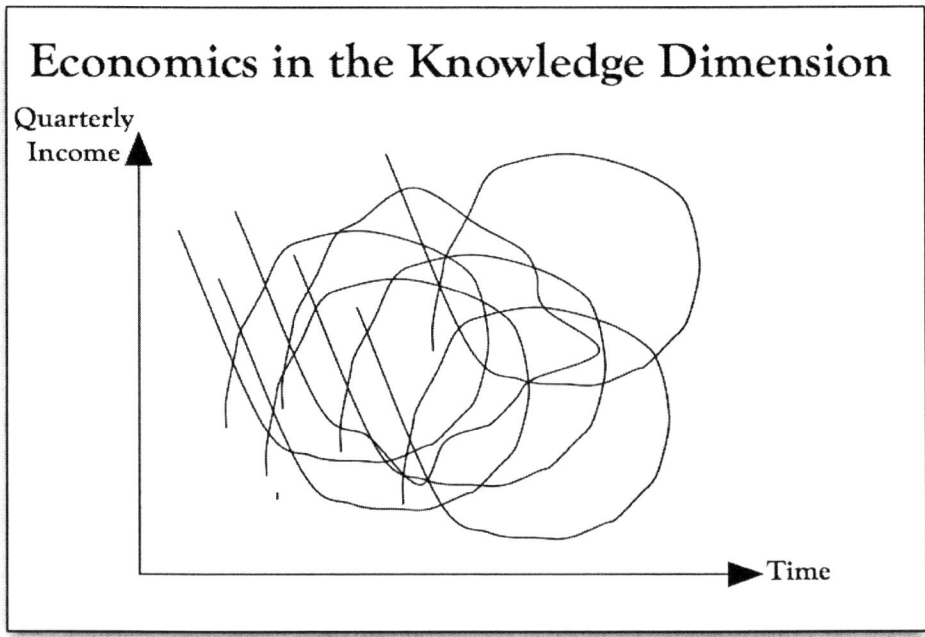

Figure 3-6a. In the Knowledge dimension, data about quarterly income over some selected timespan displays all the possibilities – negative, positive, short-term, long-term, cyclical, in hystereses, etc.

However, the information in the second, while abstractly suggesting a positive trend, actually achieves this effect by leaving out an enormous amount of information about other concurrent possibilities:

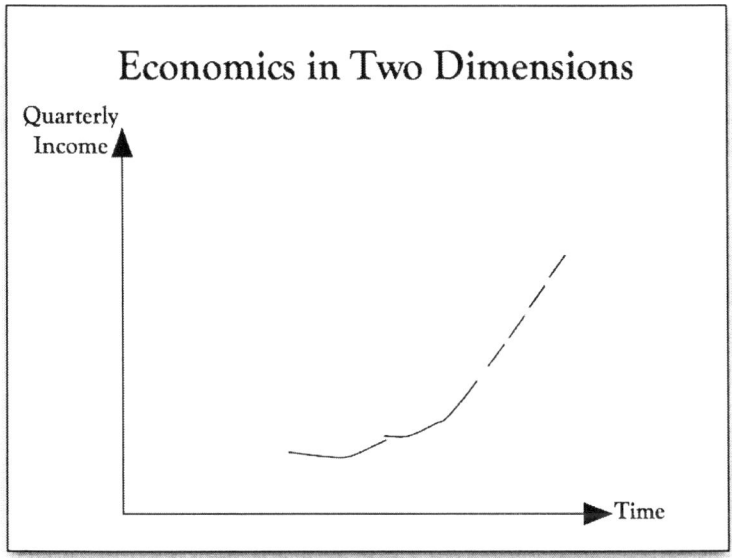

Figure 3-6b. Presenting the same data in two dimensions, taking time as the independent variable, only a single upward trend might still be visible.

3.5.4. What Is Anti-nature about Current Modes of Economic Development?

As already discussed earlier in this article, the current process is driven by greed, which comes from ignorance (because if you knew what greed will lead to, you'd realize it isn't something that helps you, even in the short term). Nature is an infinite source of wisdom, and therefore, in this sense, actually anti-greed. Nature operates at zero-waste, hence waste-based technology is anti-nature. Where Nature turns things from good – in the sense of functional for our purposes – to better (in the sense of even more functional), anti-Nature approaches turn good to bad to worse (even in the short-term). By taking the short-term approach, we create mechanisms that make things continuously worse. What Figure 3-6 elaborates below about this with respect to technology development may readily be extrapolated to other aspects of social development, including politics and education. The absence of good intention can only bring long-term disaster.

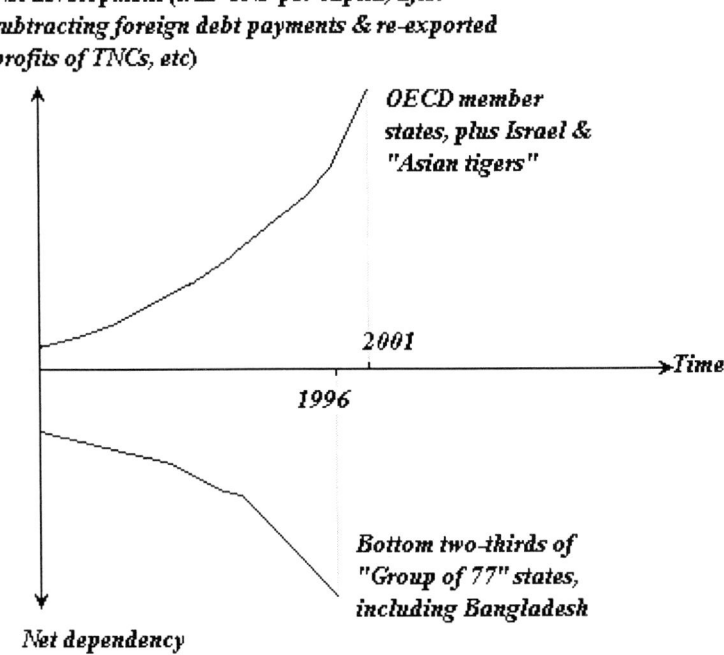

Figure 3-7. As a result of the overextension of credit and subsequent manipulation (by the creditors: Paris Club etc) of the increasingly desperate condition of those placed in their debt, nostrums about "development" remain a chimaera and cruel illusion in the lives of literally billions of people in many parts of Africa, Asia and Latin America. (Here the curves are developed from the year 1960.).

3.5.5. The Science of Intention

Consider the transition highlighted in Table 3-2 below. We always started off with natural products. Any alteration in these natural products ended up making these products toxic in the long term. The question becomes, why did we allow this transition? For the perpetrators, it is clearly greed. For the victims (consumers), it is ignorance. In a way, both of them suffer from the same focus on tangibles. None of these products would have a chance, if people were consciously making decisions before any of their actions. This consciousness can come only with the awareness of intentions. In the past, this important intangible has been ignored.

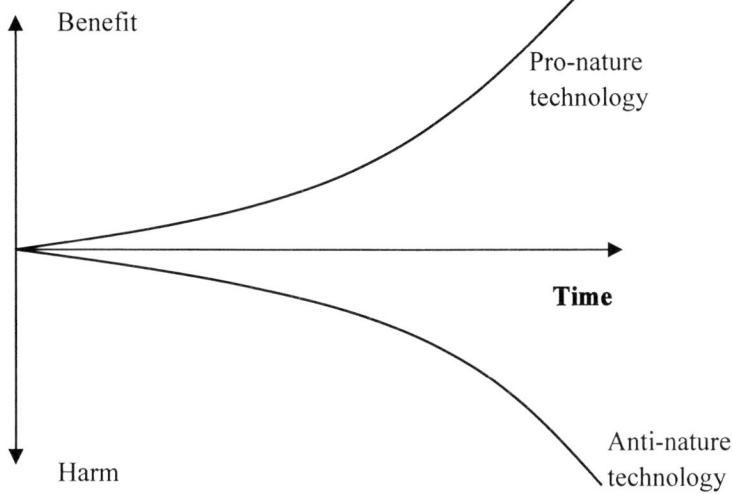

Figure 3-8. Pro-nature and anti-nature development schema diverge in beneficial impacts. Only intention can account for this failure of greed-driven initiatives in bringing long-term good.

Table 3-2. Various transitions as a product of the greed-based development

Wood → plastic
Glass → PVC, fiberglass
Cotton → polyester
Natural fiber → synthetic fiber
Clay and limestone → cement
Molasses → Sugar → NutraSweet
Fermented flower extract → perfume
Water filter (Hubble bubble) → cigarette filter
Graphite, clay → chalk → marker
Vegetable paint → plastic paint
Natural marble → artificial marble
Clay tile → ceramic tile → vinyl and plastic
Wool → polyester
Silk → synthetic
Bone → hard plastic
Vegetable glue → plastic glue
Organic fertilizer → chemical fertilizer
Adaptation → bioengineering

Intention should essentially mean good intention and has to be guided by the conscience, which is unique to human beings and is the core of what sets humans apart from other animals. Other animals, fortunately, act uniquely on instinct and hence do not risk violating their natural traits. This is also true of every other entity, including, one could argue, the inanimate objects. Only human beings have the ability to intervene in order to alter the natural course of nature. If this intervention is motivated by greed or self interest in the short-term, this intervention will invariably lead to disasters.

If no human being succeeds in reversing this pattern, Nature will make adjustments in order to alleviate the long-term harm of greed-driven initiatives. Here, we include effects that result from man-made activities. For instance, the used of refined oil in combustion engines has led to global warming that has destabilized the entire climate system. The reaction of Nature has not been the "wrath of God". Rather, we have watched Nature's noble effort gather steam to reverse the current trend. The emergence of numerous diseases among humans is not "God's revenge", but the manifestation of human bodies (a very natural system) trying to resist the ill effects of viruses – biomolecular, but non-living, elements of matter that are highly reactive in the presence of living matter but which themselves are the product of anti-nature processes and lack any of the developed microstructures – cells, etc. – characteristic of complete life-forms.

3.5.6. Nailing One's Intentions to the Mast, *Aka* "Belling the Cat"

The economic transformation advocated in the present work is based, broadly speaking, on correcting the use and relationship of intangible components relative to tangible ones in all economic settings – be it the garnering of a livelihood, the organisation of some wealth-generating activity, the settling of contractual and other arrangements for the production and-or distribution of goods and services, etc.

The long-term sustainability of the proposed approach will depend on a certain political as well as social and economic transformation of contemporary society – the subject of another book, not this one. But the achievement of the goal is a function first and foremost of the re-setting of intention. First it must be acknowledged that all economic activities are indeed intentional with implications for collectives and not just individuals, and development must then be consciously planned around that acknowledgment.

The participating humans is the decisive factor in economic (or any other social) activity. It is therefore necessary to restrain or eliminate obstacles created by institutional forces that continue to claim primacy for themselves over human individuals. The guideline for economic participation and all other social participation must be explicitly set out as follows, that *understanding requires conscious participation of the individual in acts of finding out*.

With this approach, what we call the human factor-social consciousness can begin to play its full role and displace all claims from other agencies of anti-conscious behaviour and outlook. All aphenomenal models are anti-conscious. All activities carried out in a mechanical and uninvestigated manner "because we always did it this way" must be exposed and criticised, in this principled manner and not as a weapon to undermine the status of one in order to usurp authority for another.

Like the new mathematical tools hinted at and envisioned back in Chapter Two, the arrangements needed to enable and sustain an economics of intangibles are not, and cannot be, fixed in advance by some formula. That which does not serve the collective need will be jettisoned, while that which serves self-interest only, and that only in the short-term, will not attain priority. Guides to action that enable a range of appropriate solutions will be operative, while formulae that promise a uniform, homogenized outcome will for that very reason be suspect. The test will be not practice, in the narrow pragmatic sense that prevails today, but knowledge and research. There is, however, no single arrangement that guarantees the goal. The main guideline must come from human individual and social conscience as well as consciousness.

This does not do away with a need for organisation. Rather, it entails developing a new science of organisation that will at last give intangible factors and elements the recognition they have long been due. The consciousness that would guide that new science of organisation would be of the same kind that has guided the research and writing of this book, viz., *recasting conventional approaches to economic theory onto a new philosophical foundation erected at the point where dialectics and a theory of knowledge based on intention converge*. What is meant here by organisation is not some mechanical process or formula that gives rise to uniformity or homogenisation of thought or action, but rather a continuous process of accumulating knowledge on the basis of the conscious participation of individuals in acts of finding out, a process that prepares conditions for unity in thinking as well as unity in action.

Accordingly, we may sum up the investigation into the history of economic thought that was undertaken for this book as an act of finding out that maggots are not born out of meat: there are causes, there are effects, and we have to work to create what we want according to the actual laws of motion, the conditions and the objective and subjective tasks which history has imposed on society as we find it in our own time. The beginning of true freedom – freedom from the inevitable consequences of ignorance, of failure to participate in acts of finding out – is not the mere assertion of subjective whims and desires, but the recognition of such necessity. It is as the product of definite conditions, and in order to free ourselves of any of the forces in Nature or society that operate to enslave or limit us as human beings, that we must recognise the necessities of the times and circumstances.

What then does it mean to call for "recasting conventional approaches to economic theory onto a new philosophical foundation erected at the point where dialectics and a theory of knowledge based on intention converge"? The advance does not lie in merely proclaiming the task, although such proclamation is a necessary first step. The necessity is to create conditions for realising and completing this task, such that, once the conditions are prepared, the task proceeds forward and cannot be reversed. What can thrive in such conditions are research, and technologies arising from the research, that develop entirely in the hands, not of corporate or other self-interested parties, but of individuals and their social collectives. Grasping the living connection between their intangible social relations and the tangible resources and products they need – like fresh fruiot and vegetables – the approximately two-million people of the city of Havana, Cuba today grow more than 90 per cent of their fruit and vegetable requirements on the rooftops of their residential and commercial buildings. With almost no open space available at ground level for conventional crop-raising, the Havana district is one of the leading agricultural production zones in a country that was supposed by now to have been brought to its knees by its former extreme dependence on imported fruits and vegetables. Havana itself has become the highest per capita consumer of organically-grown produce in the world. Reversal – in this case, back to large-scale dependence on food imports, coupled to cropping based on costly imported chemical fertilisers – has become impossible because the conditions that could have sustained such a reversal have been removed. To develop that outlook and put it on a par with science as a necessity in the work of unfolding that which is truly innovative, truly new in technology, research and related areas of economic development: this is an achievement that lies within the reach of the present generation.

3.5.7. When Theoretical and Practical Intentions Collide…

Government taxation policy has emerged as one of the premiere examples of fields in which the linearising "logic" of the Aphenomenal Model (discussed more thoroughly later, in Chapter 5) reigns supreme. "Tax incentives" instituted by government as the public sector supposedly drive major investment decisions by corporations in the private sector. In reality, shielding actual intentions behind loud grousing about unfair taxation, the shrewd corporate investor holds the public up for ransom to extract the most profitable deal. This is where theoretical and practical intentions frequently collide. The life and livelihoods of hundreds of rural communities in Canada and the United States are balanced on the knife-edge of such government decisions, and held hostage by public-private "negotiations" of new arrangements. If people themselves were paying less tribute to the state and making more decisions of their own, then decisions about development might actually be moderated by the input of the communities affected. The key is to switch to taxing economic inactivity rather than taxing economic activity. In modern societies, so great and prepossessing has become the power of those who have hoarded great wealth in the form of stockholdings, investment certificates and other claims on exchangeable value created by others that the principle of taxing income progressively no longer has much if any effect, because so many of these forms of wealth can be sheltered from tax under categories counted as "capital" or "investments" rather than as "income". Taxes on consumption that target necessary goods like food and clothing clobber the incomes of those compelled by circumstances actually to spend the bulk of their earnings on necessities. Figure 3-8 stacks up what happens in practice against what was promised in theory:

What would comprise a correct appreciation of the intangible character of Knowledge? In line with a bias developed from training in engineering, and because so much about Knowledge is not immediately accessible to our view or to any of our other senses – the very condition that defines its intangibility – let us consider for the moment the Knowledge intangible as a kind of "black box". In this setting, a correct appreciation of the intangible character of Knowledge should discourage tendencies either to "sample without replacement" from the black box, or to accepting someone else's description of the contents of the black box on trust or as a matter of blind faith. The first condition being discouraged is the idea that any of this Knowledge is some private affair or magic talisman just for you: every individual is born into Society and is accountable to Society for whatever Knowledge is gained and-or applied. Intangibility of knowledge cannot mean available for you but actually unavailable to others: such a position is fundamentally unbalanced from every viewpoint, not to mention anti-social. The second condition being discouraged is the idea that Knowledge is being transferred or acquired when one "learns" without applying (because someone or some book told one "the truth"), or when one memorises some information without thinking about or reflecting on its meaning. The intangibility of Knowledge does not mean you cannot know it for yourself; rather, it means you must seek it in order to find it out for yourself.

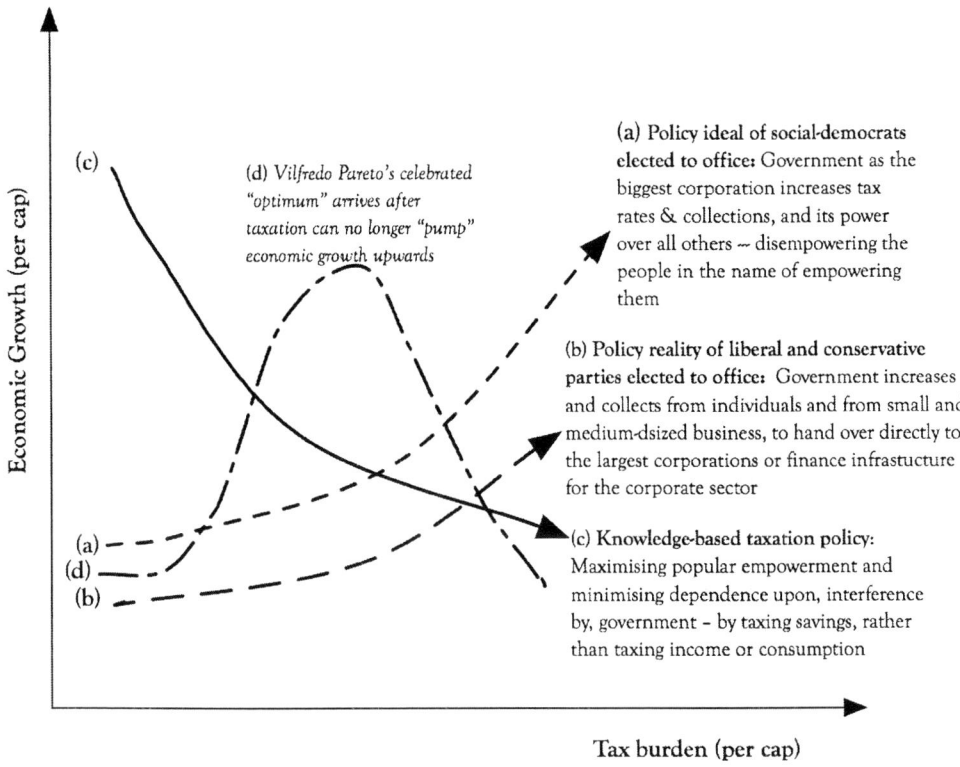

Figure 3-9. Theory versus practice of modern taxation policy – Vilfredo Pareto's celebrated "optimum", which arrives after taxation can no longer "pump" economic growth upwards, was "disproved" following the end of the Second World War by Keynesian programs of governments spending beyond their normal budgetary means, into long-running deficits. Although Lord Keynes cautioned this was only to carry on while growth continued to be recorded, it became useful for private corporate interests to encourage continuation of such deficit spending in ways that would cushion or eliminate risks incurred by their own investment activities. Social-democratic governments in certain Canadian provinces and west European countries have taken this still further, with a questionable ideological justification that identified replacing private corporate capital with state corporate capital with "empowering the public." Once the private sector was able to ride to the rescue of the over-extended, debt-ridden state sector, starting in the time of Thatcher and Reagan, this taxation policy continued, spreading from taxing income to taxing spending and taxing the income of people without capital. From the early 1990s to date, people were so "empowered" by this expansion of government taxation that they have been unable to defend a single social program, from health to education, from being gutted in order to ensure the creditors were paid their pound of flesh. Note that a knowledge-based policy of taxing savings instead of income or consumption breaks the cycle of disempowerment, paying the price of a certain reduction in the rate of GDP growth by continuing to lower the tax burden.

The individual's acquisition of Knowledge cannot be marked by comparative scoring of an examination given to members of some class or group that have been investigating or learning about the same subject matter. To go from not knowing to knowing something marks the most fundamental non-linear transformation available to human beings. In young children undergoing the transition from no schooling to being schooled, a most remarkable transformation that takes place – without anyone remarking upon it – occurs when a youth first learns to read.[16] In seemingly no time, knowledge of the world acquired before one could read is rapidly swamped by the new galaxy one now enters, as the unbounded character of available Knowledge opened up as a result of acquiring the tools of literacy takes over before the individual has even become conscious of any boundary existing before. In adult literacy students, the identical process takes place, only much more consciously. Of course, here the Knowledge to which the thesis of non-linear transformation applies is knowledge of the kind that changes one's path or choices of path. It is the same thing experienced in the researcher's thrill at making some breakthrough scientific discovery.

No less important than Knowledge itself is the manner in which one goes about acquiring it. Knowledge and one's confidence in it really grows exponentially as a result of how many other dots it connects to related areas that were previously unknown, unobserved or not reflected upon. Of course, these are the dots the knowledge-gatherer connects, not the picture received from someone else. Very importantly in this respect, by the way, the black box mentioned at the start of this discussion about the Knowledge intangible stands in no way isolated or disconnected its surrounding environment. The knowledge gatherer has the responsibility of discovering those otherwise intangible connections to the rest of what is often called "The Big Picture."

This interconnectedness is brought out well in many pieces of contemporary fiction. For example, in Ray Bradbury's science-fantasy short story, "A Sound of Thunder" (1952), some time-travelling "tourists" purchase a "tour" by time-machine back to a prehistoric era, which the time-machine operator has carefully striven to preserve by requiring customers to use an anti-gravity pathway that hovers above the surface of prehistoric Earth. Inevitably, one member of a touring party momentarily loses his balance, the toe of his shoe touching the earth's surface for but a fraction of a second. Nevertheless, by the time they have returned to their own time and step out of the time machine, their entire world lies in ruins. The power of the reception accompanying the appearance of such literature may be taken as something of a gauge of broad, even inchoate, societal concerns of the time. The arc of this story addresses a broad spectrum of the anxieties, which ran particularly high in those early years of the so-called Cold War, about how responsibly advanced technologies might come to be applied, by any advanced industrial technological power (not just the U.S. or then-Soviet Russia). The Cold War is gone but, as everyone living today well knows, this anxiety is not. In any event, the message still resonates loud and clear: the interconnectedness of Knowledge imposes a huge social responsibility on knowledge gatherers, even as this awareness liberates the knowledge gatherer from the consequences of labouring too long amid the narrowest confines of excessive specialisation. This interconnectedness means that we are each of us accountable for every action, recognising that every action affects everyone else (including us); logic says if your intention were self-serving, you should end up the worst off. There are yet other

---

[16] One of the authors learned to read from his grandfather. He was an autodidact who left school after second grade. Noticing the young boy's curiosity, he sat his grandson down with the local daily newspaper. What had piqued the grandson's interest? Watching his grandfather pick up one paper, the local daily, and read it from left to right, then pick up the other paper (the *Jewish Daily Forward*, at that time printed in Yiddish, *i.e.*, in Hebrew script, running right to left). What did a three-year-old know from reading? Absolutely nothing. But one and the same act being conducted both left-to-right and right-to-left: how mysterious could it be, this thing the adults called "reading"?

consequences of the intangible character of Knowledge and the importance of handling this intangible "interconnectedness" aspect properly for research of any type aimed at gathering Knowledge of the truth. To achieve this aim, Nature, or Society, has to be observed as it is – without forgetting that the observer is him/herself always part of Nature or Society, but also without additional intentional further interventions by the observer. Since all the phenomena that will be observed are somehow inter-related, including the time things are taking to occur – over which individuals exercise little or no power – it becomes important in this phase to pay close attention to the sequence(s) of events, rather than attempting to draw any conclusions before the entire chain of observations has been recorded and reviewed. Indeed the path along which Knowledge comes to be acquired is decisive. Figure 3-9 illustrates the problem.

The non-intervention just mentioned does not mean, of course, non-participation, but rather a carefully prepared participation. It is critically important not to permit this stage of knowledge gathering to be "efficiency"-driven. In practice that means one should not entertain notions of designing experiments controlling for particular variables until *after* one has some idea of the big picture, *not before* one has one's own idea of the larger terrain, *or without* one's own idea of the surrounding terrain. That is what is so crucial about intial observation of the overall terrain. It does not advance matters or provide a shortcut to take someone else's word – for example, to take experimental results found or reported by others but never re-investigated by you as the starting point for designing your experiments. This amounts to starting by at least partially assuming one's conclusion: it is an aphenomenal mode of proceeding. It is not achieving understanding on the basis of personal participation of the individual in acts of finding out.

This approach to knowledge means not linearising the subject-matter of investigation, be it Nature or Society. Because the entire training of the educational system has equipped us precisely to seek such linearisations – falsely promoted as "Knowledge" in a superior, abstract form of the most general application – there is considerable struggle involved in avoiding the pitfalls that our conventional training would lead us into if we were not paying attention and on the lookout. All the methods developed in formal mathematics that produce unique solutions or unique solution sets are especially seductive in this regard. Phenomena that are being observed in a state or condition that no one is yet engineering cannot be assumed to operate the same as phenomena that that are engineered to produce an explicit outcome or set of outcomes. To abstract them onto the same plane, ripped out of their very different natural *versus* artificial contexts and historical *versus* structural-functional modes of development, and then deal with them as though they were the same is absurd. If, for example, one were designing an analog electric circuit to work in its linear operating range, mathematical methods that allow superposition of results as one designs for the effects of one variable after the next are necessary and valuable. But to apply the same methods to analysing unengineered phenomena, such as circuitry in the human body, would be truly aphenomenal. In the first we are engineering to achieve an effect; in the second we are striving to attain actually scientific knowledge.

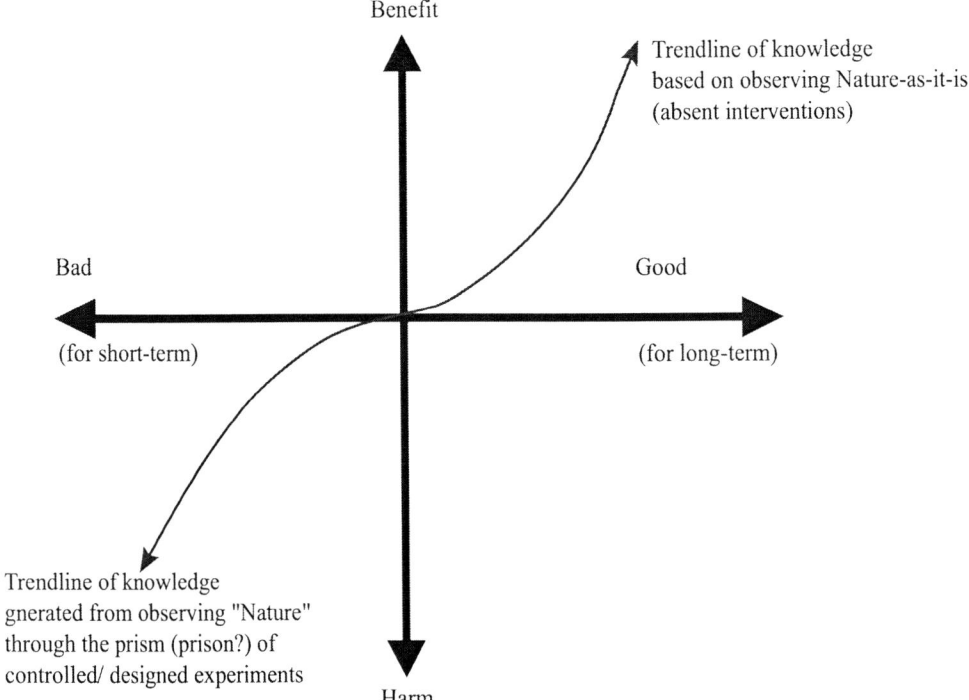

Figure 3-10. The Knowledge Trendline – The path along which Knowledge is acquired is decisive. Knowledge acquired as unquestioned received opinion, or as someone else's experimental result not further checked or verified, is simply not on the same path as Knowledge that could accomplish long-term good. Regardless of whether it is more or less precise, Knowledge based on one's own observations and thinking is more reliable. In natural sciences, this is the Knowledge acquired by observing Nature as it is; in the social sciences its equivalent would be Knowledge acquired by documenting social, political, cultural or economic reality.

With full-blown emergence of the Aphenomenal Model, unfortunately, the notion has gained ground that "Nature has to be fixed when it fails to conform to theory." Theory here means "theory" constructed upon some result that could be engineered without, or before, fully establishing the science of the principles underlying the natural phenomenon. The absurdity of this notion was never clearer, or more bitter, than during the period of the devastation of New Orleans and nearby areas on the coast of the Gulf of Mexico following Hurricane Katrina in August 2005. The basic story line has been that the hurricane was responsible for the destruction and chaos. Could this be true? It has come out ever more glaringly that the final preparations before the annual hurricane season of the refurbishments needed in the city's system of dikes and levees were, criminally, neglected. These fixes had been awaiting completion for more than two decades. Without them, it was only a matter time before sufficient wind and water in combination would bring Lake Pontchartrain to the north of the city to burst its banks and find the shortest, lowest-lying path to the Mississippi River delta west and south of the city. The neglect began from the office of the President of the United States. It carried on down through the relevant segments of the Federal Emergency Management Agency of the Department of Homeland Security. The Louisiana state and local City of New Orleans levels themselves lacked any reserve financial means or reserve means of emergency temporary shelter sufficient for the numbers of people bound to be affected. In addition, there has been the role of the U.S. Army Corps of Engineers over the preceding decades: its re-engineering of the flow and "straightening" of the banks of the Mississippi, carried out in the name of controlling overflow of the river's banks in populated, mostly urban, centres has gravely intensified destructive effects of any episode of excessive flow either as the result of heavy rains, tornadoes or winter and spring floods on the river's flood plain in the rural areas. In the wake of the additional stresses visited by the hurricane, the slogan of the State of Louisiana Tourism Board, "come as you are – leave different", thus came to be implemented in the most horrific manner. The hurricane came as it was, but the failure and breakdown of the human social factor - whether managing the humanitarian emergency or realigning the Mississippi's flow – ensured it would leave everything "different."

The intangible dimensions of Knowledge are of no less moment than any of its most tangible aspects, and suggest the following paradigm:

- *Law of Conservation of Matter and Energy*: Neither matter nor energy can be created or destroyed. They can only change form, one into the other, either direction
- *Law of Conservation of Momentum*: Momenta of matter or energy, regardless of form, can be neither created nor destroyed
- *Law of Knowledge Discovery and Preservation*: Knowledge may be either lost or found, but neither created nor destroyed

Chapter 4

TANGIBLES IN THE BIG PICTURE

INTRODUCTION

Continuing the theme opened in the previous two chapters concerning intangibles, the examination of where tangibles fit in the big picture now proceeds. The discussion of intangibles pointed to the areas in which new tools of analysis need to be forged to account not only for intangibles but where tangible economic phenomena now fit, much in the same way as, in mathematics, advanced analysis – the theory of functions of complex variables – repositioned how to look at so-called "real" numbers, which up to that point everyone had been brought up to think of as the only numbers. Furthermore, there is the assumption closely bound up with the production, distribution and exchange of tangible goods and services that all growth is ipso facto good, which the new theory does not presume. Discussion at this stage proceeds in the context of elaborating the modern economics, and nexus, of energy and food supplies. In this arena, affecting all Humanity, a global struggle is raging between the interests of preserving imperial sway and privileges and the interests of Humanity to be fully and finally free of all external forces of domination and dictate. Rather than assume all growth is good, it seems more prudent first to consider whether an economic actor's intention is pro-Humanity.

Having indicated the need in the earlier two chapters for new tools suited to the new approach of an "economics of intangibles", this chapter takes up some initial tool-building. In contemporary economic life, notions of social responsibility have been corporatised and stripped of human content as world-grabbing concentrations of capital and economic power have become concentrated in very few hands. The tools of conventional economic theory have been further refined to produce ever more elaborate and absurd justifications for the resulting state of affairs. In this chapter, some of the principles and approach developed in the earlier deconstruction of intangibles and their role are applied for the first time to approach the "true costs" of continuing on this course. This starts with reckoning where some of these hidden costs have accumulated up to now. Of particular importance are the costs accruing from the consumption of natural resources that are not directly replaced for the next cycle of production. This includes cases where truly irreplaceable human resources were expended without any real enhancement of human social prospects ensuing as a result.

The question will inevitably arise: is this not mere "bitching" about the bad old days, what The Wall Street Journal frequently dismisses as a doleful wail of impotence from history's losers?

In certain fields of applied science, such as petroleum engineering, a major intervention in the natural-physical realm is required, and serious research entails considerations of mass-balance and energy-balance. In social sciences such as economics, some intervention in particular societies and their material conditions and capacities as they exist at some definite stage of historical development is similarly either necessary, involved or implied. Why then should we not develop theories based on a consideration a "social capacity balance"? Sustainability criteria are certainly a starting-point in this direction. Unfortunately, up to now in the social sciences, such application has been confined to sustaining the present indefinitely into the future; consideration of pathways for achieving pro-social goals that find little or no purchase in the present is not even on the radar. To point out that societies have paid a huge intangible toll historically for the plundering inflicted on them by colonising interests is not history's losers seeking revenge, but a sober acknowledgment of the need to restore the "social capacity balance". How can something which was consumed but not actually, i.e., physically, replaced, viz., a society's fish resources, or its oil or gas, be considered to have been "compensated" merely by covering the cost, meaning only the magnitude of monetary value, of its replacement by some equivalent from elsewhere? The current chapter tackles this question from the standpoint of elaborating approaches, expressed as a function of time considered historically, that place a tangible magnitude of monetary value on the intangible toll.

To get there from here, however, a leap of imagination is required. It won't do just to go off and measure some externally visible manifestation without first establishing what manifestations are relevant, and why. Speaking methodologically as to the process involved, it is necessary to "abstract absence", to ask: what is the goal, then ask: what is missing between here and the goal, and finally consider approaches and instruments that could supply what is missing. In practice, this is not as simple as was just represented. The conceiving of the goal, in the most pro-social form of the greatest use to Humanity as a whole, has itself been rendered extremely difficult as a result of the aforementioned corporatisation of social responsibility and the stripping of the human content of such an idea by world-grabbing concentrations of capital and economic power. Wherever it collides with special, highly-concentrated interests, the idea that all growth is economically positive acquires the form of pure disinformation. This is reflected in claims throughout the fishing industry that there are "too many fishermen chasing too few fish", for example, or that there has been "too much consumption and not enough production" in the energy field. The process of abstracting absence and conceiving the goal in pro-social terms, along with an approach that makes it attainable, requires uncovering in some detail how this disinformation is constructed and spread as well as at whose cost.

These claims constitute disinformation from two standpoints:

1. those who purvey these claims harbour no pro-social aim; and
2. if and when those who have to tackle actual problems besetting these activities adopt or accept these claims, the effectiveness of their intervention is degraded, undermined or even paralysed.

The resort to wide-scale disinformation in this form has three aims.

The first aim is *to reverse certain standards and paradigms in which the sources of creative labouring power had previously established some stake*. Such alterations follow in the wake of any re-integration process that resets the scale on which some wealth-generating activity was conducted, as "new" standards are arbitrarily promulgated and monopolistically imposed. In the case of energy extraction and production, it was precisely the need to justify such an activity being accepted as the natural monopoly of a single global industrial power that led to W.S. Jevons' rewriting of classical economics – in which living labour as the source of value had been recognised – such that, as already discussed back in Chapter 1, value was reduced to a matter of personal subjective utility and the objective claims of labour to the full social share of its product dismissed. On the scale that emerged in the 20th century, an ever-more-dictatorial approach flowed from the very structures common to the entities that undertook these activities. Formed as a merger of industrial capital and banking capital or connections, the early modern corporation conducted business as a form of warfare in which competitors were targeted not only to be defeated but destroyed. In the U.S., the Standard Oil Company as established by the Rockefellers was probably its best-known expression. Even after the U.S. government broke up the Standard Oil trust before WW1, the separate parts emulated the original parent. The leading European oil companies, such as British Petroleum and the Elf-Aquitaine group from France followed a similar organizational pattern and manner of conducting their business affairs.

At the start of the 1920s, British oil interests grabbed the oil fields of northern Iraq for themselves by slaughtering the Kurds and favouring the Arabs there. By the mid-1920s, as US oil companies tried to enter the zone, the British and French oil companies struck their Red Line agreements defining the effective borders of Syria, Iraq and Iran according to the nature and extent of the major oil and gas finds that they planned to develop, and on the basis of keeping US oil companies out and favouring Shi'a over Sunni Arabs. At the close of World War Two, positioning itself as the ally of the mainly Sunni Arab world against any revival of British power in the region, the US government colluded with the House of Saud to carve out the Arabian Peninsula as the exclusive bailiwick of US oil companies, largely excluding European oil majors. After 1971, when oil production within the United States was no longer sufficient for its domestic needs, oil was deemed to be "running out" around the globe and, accordingly, since 1973, any claims by the long-beggared oil-producing countries for a more just price on their product could be painted as a blackmail operation staged by inferior tribes against the very citadels of civilisation, culture and enlightenment. The all-or-nothing, "take no prisoners" approach of Big Oil – Dick Cheney as CEO of Halliburton once declared: "we do War and Peace" – was developed in the context of redividing economic space and resource zones that had already been divided under different pre-existing arrangements. Such redivision was carried out not only in terms of the financial strength of the contending entities but often enforced by resort to the military means of the governments they patronised. This feature, which lent any reversal of standards or re-integration an aura of irreversibility, if not permanence, was intended to discourage any challenge, however just. But, as has also become the case in our own day – in Iran, Venezuela, Bolivia and some other locales – such methods can also unite the general population against any further permission for any powerful foreign-based oil company or syndicate to maintain operations in their jurisdiction.

A second aim is *to tie extraction/harvesting, refining/processing and sale of tangible products to the short term, the* t = *"right now" reference frame*. Implicit in this process is a major effort to reject any notion that Labour could be the father of wealth and especially the notion that it should retain on that basis any claim on what becomes of its product after it has been produced. Imposition of this separation-rejection often follows the apparently fortuitous revelation of some hitherto undetected gap, inequality, mismatch or "disequation". Announcement of such a "discovery" frequently takes the form of "everything was going along tickety-boo when out of the blue – a catastrophe".

A third aim connected with this is *to deny the producers of Humanity's collective goods and services any further agency* as producers or consumers. Either in the form of corporations or through the State, private powers assert instead a priority for accumulating tangible wealth over and ahead of ensuring sustainability for collective, public Humanity. This attacks all the social relations to which these production and consumption activities have given rise. However, the very intangibility of these relations conceals the attack from view. As a result, people frequently encounter this negation of their agency in the form of a fait accompli masking some previous act of stealth. Thus, in 1992, the Canadian government banned coastal communities in eastern Canada from catching groundfish (cod, etc), and inaugurated The Atlantic Groundfish Strategy. This scheme, known by its initials as TAGS, was widely hailed as an income support program for the fishery equivalent to paying farmers not to plant new crops. After entire communities throughout coastal Newfoundland, Nova Scotia and New Brunswick were rendered dependent on these payments, the government disclosed that fishermen would not be allowed to resume catching groundfish species, even if the codfish stocks revived, because ... there had allegedly been "too many fishermen chasing too few fish"(sic) all along.

The guiding line of thought always takes the form of the "devil theory of history" – the idea that everything was going just right... until the Devil intervened. A dangerous form of ignorance cultivated by those who believe they have nothing to learn from unfolding events, such "devil theories" began their life in formal philosophical discourse during the European Middle Ages, when scholars enjoying the favour of the Pope in Rome would routinely dismiss anyone challenging their conclusions as "agents of the devil", thereby ensuring their target was tortured by the Inquisition. Modern-day "devil theories" aim not to drown serious challengers in boiling vats, but – perhaps more ruthlessly – to marginalise them forever in the deepest possible obscurity.

Thus, with regard to the world's food supply: in the 1980s, at the very moment the fishing fleets of the former Soviet Union exceeded those of Japan and other large long-time global plunderers, "overfishing" was suddenly discovered in 15 of the world's 18 leading commercial fishing basins and deemed a "crisis". Certain circles were keen immediately to attribute all responsibility for the situation to the Devil in Moscow. By this time, many people were somewhat suspicious of the devil theories of the Cold War. Accordingly, another kind of ideological goods had to be kept in stock to overcome such skepticism. This took the form of disinformation framed as neo-Malthusian theory to justify itself a soberly scientific analysis of the "crisis". According to this analysis, the coastal fishermen as the catchers with their individual vessels were to be condemned as equal in guilt and responsibility to the fish processing companies with their fleets of far more elaborate and extensive means of fish harvesting.

Similarly, with regard to the world's energy supply: today, no approach to supplying Humanity's energy needs is to be countenanced, or treated with anything but the greatest contempt, that does not genuflect in full obedience before those who insist that fossil fuels shall rule the supply picture forever. Instead of even considering proceeding on the basis of escaping that path, conventional energy economics treats with the greatest contempt all plans or proposals for large-scale long-term replacement of oil with natural gas, or long-term replacement of oil- or gas-fired power generation with solar or wind sources, or using renewable energy sources directly rather than first converting them to electricity. Underlying this Devil theory – which like all other forms of the Devil theory declares "there is no alternative" to the status quo – is the notion that nothing moves without money first. Either one begins by acknowledging that there is no god but Monopoly Capital and maximum is its profit, or one is headed straight for the fires of eternal damnation, a land without research grants or any other form of recognition.

Disguising itself as a concern for sustainability, the "peak oil" theory is yet another variant of the same old refrain: the Present that it wants to sustain into the Future is directed by a superpower. The emergence of post-Soviet Russia as an oil and gas power especially in Europe has provided both a living refutation to these homogenising ambitions of the sole remaining superpower of a post-bipolar era, as well as a reminder that the U.S. intervention in the affairs of Arab oil states may have settled its imperial competition with Great Britain and France as metropolitan Great Powers only to open up a much broader multi-level struggle with regional oil and gas powers in Iran and Russia as well as new rising industrial powers in China and India

As a starting point, in order to discuss these pre-determined and disinforming objectives from a transparent position, it is necessary to isolate some indexation methods that have been developed, within the conventional discourse in economics, for summarising and "averaging" large quantities of data about tangible, measurable economic activity. Throughout the rest of the chapter, and always keeping in mind that such a procedure throws down the gauntlet at one level or other at one or another such index, the contrast between the reality of actual conditions and the supposedly disinterested claims asserted by conventional theory (or the less disinterested claims of policy-makers) is repeatedly highlighted,. This sets up the presentation of the material in Chapter 5, in which the struggle around the Aphenomenal Model is fully elaborated and documented.

4.0. INTRODUCING THE ROLE AND MISSION OF "ECONOMIC INDICES"

The idea of an "index", widely employed throughout discussions in econmics, is based on comparing similar elements from different sets of circumstances – either to one another, or against some idealised "norm". Indexation in the form of "normalisation" of data according to some common standard is routine in all fields of engineering as well as the social sciences. The premise of normalisation and all other forms of indexation – by which elements of context that would tend to particularise the data and its meaning are stripped away, in the name of ensuring that "apples are not being compared with oranges" – yields a result that is, and indeed must be, inherently aphenomenal.[17]

The above triptych of data, collected by a group formed to omitor the political involvements of this particular corporation, about the progress of the stock price of Halliburton, its revenues from operations in Iraq and the deaths of U.S. soldiers in Iraq – all reported over the identical time period of the current war and occupation carried out by U.S.-led forces there – clearly illustrates the glaring absurdities involved. The only logical connection one could invent to connect what these three graphs report is that Halliburton's shareholders need more U.S. soldiers to die in order to justify their continued investment in the company and its involvement in Iraq. Otherwise [continuing the logic to its end]: if casualty rates fall Halliburton's stock price and revenues from operations in Iraq should fall! The tangible external connection is a visual one: the trend lines in all three graphs is upward from the lower-left towards the upper-right. This in itself, however, actually says nothing about whether these phenomena are connected or how they might be connected. Apart from that, the only other connection is the fact that Halliburton has business in Iraq (among other places) and U.S. troops are fighting and dying in Iraq (among other places).

Many indices that are widely taken for granted operate just as aphenomenally as this example, by reason of their abstracting for comparison "facts" that have been "normalised" by being ripped out of the very contexts that give them their meaning in the first place. Thus, for example, there is a United Nations Food and Agricultural Organisation (FAO) standard of malnutrition: daily intake of less than 2,500 calories correlates globally with reported occurrences of malnutrition. While this is likely valid for industrial societies in Europe and America, no one has bothered to find out what the norm would be in predominantly rural societies whose economic activity is mainly primary resource extraction destined primarily for meeting everyday subsistence needs, and only secondarily as feedstock sources for manufacturing. Regardless: on the basis of the FAO standard, the people of Bangladesh were subjected to the novelty of "zinc-fortified" rice to ensure maintenance of a basic level of nutrition as far as the national staple food was concerned. In the event, it turned out that the fortification process applied to their rice diet rendered many Bangladeshis ill for various periods. To suggest doing anything about such processing, however, let alone that there might be something doubtful about the underlying standard, risked inviting the sharp retort that such criticism undermined the noble effort of the government to stave off malnutrition.

One of the best examples of an aphenomenal usage of a falsely abstracted "standard" is provided by so-called "intelligence testing", or the IQ test, applied widely throughout school systems in many countries around the world. The premise of IQ-scoring is that, in the absence of any specific knowledge as to how intelligence, creativity, knowledge or access to information are actually distributed among any population, the assumption of randomness – that these are as likely to be normally distributed, with most outcomes tending to fall around

---

[17] The concept of "aphenomenality" introduced in this book is defined fully at Chapter 5.

some central value, as they are to be distributed in any other way – is taken as the starting point. The "test" consists of a single set of questions asked to all members of a sample group, without regard to differences of individual background and otherwise known to have gone through a more-or-less common schooling regimen. This testing approach produces results that nicely fit the "bell" curve of the normal distribution – but of course individual capabilities are in no way being directly examined because the premise of the entire process negates from the outset any significance for individual differences. As this procedure tells us nothing about the individuals taken separately, the serious question must be posed: what is it telling us about any individual ranked in comparison to other individuals? Just because one has no information that "intelligence" (as measured by response to a set of standardised test questions, a dubious enough notion in its own right) is not normally distributed seems hardly acceptable as the basis for assuming that it is or could be so distributed.

All the economic growth indices and related indices of efficient use of capital and resources – Consumer Price Index, Gross Domestic Product, Gross National Product, etc. – have been developed and applied in similarly aphenomenal ways. The more abstract and the more detached from the reality of the conditions of distinct areas of the planet, the more authoritative the index standard is deemed to be. In principle, standards are an excellent idea; but they must be knowledge-based and reflect the truth of matters as they actually stand, not as someone might like that truth to be. Otherwise their application turns into enforced ignorance and further backwardness and enslavement of the South by the North. For countries, governments and peoples of the global South, there is no hope on the path of competing to come up the standards imposed by the global North. Hope lies on the path of the Knowledge-based approach of evolving standards and criteria based on one's own actual reality. Just because the global North devalues the global South's vast labour-intensive sources of human capital relative to the capital-intensive heavy equipment, computers and credit systems of American and European banking and industry does not mean the governments or peoples of the global South should follow suit.

4.1. THE ROLE AND MISSION OF SCIENCE IN THE ECONOMIC AFFAIRS OF HUMANITY

The first chapter brought out how the foundations of conventional economic theory have been converted into disinformation, by misrepresenting and suppressing any role for intangible factors. Chapters 2 and 3 discussed the consequences of failing to take proper account of three of the leading intangibles of profoundest consequence for economic theory, *viz.*, Time, Information and Intentions, and the attendant confusion and difficulty this created for correcting the deficiencies, failures and shortcomings of conventional theory. In the process of deconstructing conventional theory, some sketches, hints and suggestions have been elaborated of what a model or theoretical foundation suitable for overcoming these deficiencies, failures and shortcomings would require. However, the proof of the pudding is in the eating. With this chapter, which discusses the tangible components that comprise the ordinary, everyday, conventionally accepted "meat and potatoes" of economics both in theory and practice, the time has come to apply the elements of the new theory elaborated thus far and test how completely the new theory accounts for actual conditions.

According to conventional economics, one set of tangibles may be said to "cause", or bring about, another set of tangible effects. By attributing economic causes and effects to the "invisible hand", any role generally for the conscious intervention of human actors is denied. Such intervention is only considered when looking only at how and where some pre-existing, already established interest was rationally calculated and then served. Societal nature external to the individual is otherwise treated pseudo-scientifically as something that operates "like" physical nature external to the human being. This method of accounting for tangible causes and effects eliminates any consideration of subjective causes and intentions especially for apparently complementary phenomena, *e.g.*, supply and demand, production and consumption, inflation and unemployment. These are presented instead as outward expressions of appetites and other drivers that would exist regardless of anyone's will or intention. These complementary phenomena are deemed to operate entirely in terms of one another, each determining the other independently of anyone's intentions. For example, no distinctions connected with any change of conditions over time are made between gluttony, hunger, want and a living organism's nutritional requirements for survival: they are just different locations across a single timeless spectrum.

At the same time, by dismissing or marginalising consideration of the role of context – wherein many intangible factors lurk, including subjective judgments and human interventions – this approach reinforces the appearance of social change, development and motion as a relatively arbitrary sequence of tangible causes and effects. Conventional theory therefore disclaims any responsibility to have to account for historic changes, such as changes of context and fundamental conditions. Indeed, it rejects such responsibility with a clear conscience, precisely because it assumes that any connections between the present, past and future are entirely arbitrary. Within this limited sphere, it claims for itself an authoritative role in accounting for economic behaviour under conditions of varying degrees of perfection of competition, it dismisses military spending as an externality of no great significance for the economy as a whole, it builds models that assume available technologies to be either more or less constant, or responsible for changes at a level that has little or no knock-on effects on consumer choice or product pricing.

Extensive data series can be and have been generated and analysed according to the criteria of conventional economic theory. Many of these phenomena have been studied to exhaustion in absolutely microscopic form. Although few macroscopic conclusions have been drawn, endless policy prescriptions are written detailing the consequences of this or that infinitesimal adjustment to this or that utterly inconsequential fine detail. As long as matters carry on in this vein, can it be said that science is advancing? For example, in a world that lacked the findings of Galileo and Newton, someone could observe and write up everything about an experiment involving dropping a weighty lead ball from the top of the Tower of Pisa. On another occasion the same could be done for an experiment entailing dropping a feather from the top of the Tower. Comparing the two, the key observation might well be that the lead ball fell to the ground faster and, from that fact, it might even be speculated that the difference in the time taken to reach the ground was a function of the difference in the weight of the feather and the lead ball. Indeed: no matter how much more precise the measuring of the two experiments became, in the absence of any other knowledge or discovery it would be difficult to overthrow or reject this line of reasoning. Now, let's say the measuring devices available for subsequent repetition of this pair of experiments over the next 10, 20 or 30 years develop digital readouts, to three or four decimal places of accuracy. From a certain standpoint, it might be argued on these grounds that science has undergone a measurable advance: the experiment can be conducted with greater precision and this enhanced precision strengthens our confidence in the conclusion. The tiny, niggling difficulty remains, of course, that the conclusion is absolutely hair-raisingly and howlingly wrong. Confirming it, however, to ever-greater degrees of precision strengthens confidence in a conclusion that is utterly anti-scientific as well as wrong; and going solely on the basis of the existing (external) tools of reasoning and-or experimental measuring equipment would not be enough to escape or overcome the seductiveness of a conclusion first suggested more than two millennia ago by Aristotle, an authority not to be cavalierly dismissed.

Of course, what is missing in this exercise is, precisely, science. The question that was not asked (and therefore not answered) was: could there be one and the same force attracting all objects to fall towards the earth? As long as that question is not tackled, the inference that the different weights of the lead ball and the feather account for the difference in the time each took to reach the ground cannot be rejected. In fact, the only basis for adducing this inference proceeds from Aristotle's famous "Law of the Excluded Middle", which says (in modern parlance) that in a Universe that has been completely defined, everything is either A or not-A. In this case, what is *missing* from the Universe (comprising "all objects falling towards the earth" and "objects not falling towards the earth") is "objects of a weight that cannot overcome air resistance". It was because that class of objects was implicitly excluded from this Universe that the inference about the different weights being material could not be excluded.

There is a psychology, both individual and social, to both the notion and the actual habit of "saving". It reinforces the idea that, in general, saving of any kind is a Good Thing. This idea actually begins before the emergence of human communities as the next stage following the emergence of humanoid species living in extended kinship groupings, possibly as recently as twenty to thirty thousand years ago. This process of beginning to live in communities extending one's immediate kinship grouping continued well into the earliest appearance of village life based on some level of animal husbandry and crop-raising supplementing a diet based on hunting and an associated seasonally nomadic lifestyle. Within this evolution, the habit emerged of setting aside reserves of food against unanticipated reversals of weather, climate or other contingencies affecting hunting and foraging prospects.

This notion of saving for a rainy day remains possibly the most elemental notion of saving that many still harbour. The earliest "religious" reflex of humanity, in which sacramental significance was invested in various natural phenomena such as the arrival of the equinoxes, the Sun, the Moon etc., seems similarly to have entrenched itself precisely as a response to such adversity. Of course the practical necessity for individuals to save in that way was largely overcome as society emerged and found ways to look after more and more of these contingencies. With the end of the isolation of tribes from the jungles of New Guinea, the interior of central Africa and Amazonia, as well as the Arctic regions of Russia and North America, any further justification for this psychology of "saving" also came to an end. Today the beginning of human life and its end remain the two contingencies operating largely outside individuals' control, over which no amount of "saving" can give individuals more control. At the same time, with these as with any other contingent events some features of which cannot be controlled in advance, this very old "psychology" of saving still intervenes, still pushing its line that, if only something has been set aside in advance, our powerlessness in the face of the unknown would be lessened.

In conventional economic theory, "savings" occupy a space somewhere between "dark matter" and fallow, inactive / inert matter. The problem has become ever more ill-defined as a result of the divergence between the claims made in favour of the "savings" habit and the forced regime that "saving" has actually become in the modern economy, especially since the end of the Second World War. Observing the conditions that hit the global economy during the Great Depression of the 1930s, John Maynard Keynes theorised (1936) that aggregate demand could be maintained by government intervention to maintain investment by maintaining employment, thereby overcoming at least temporarily the consequences of the credit drought and subsequent disappearance of savings occasioned by the liquidity crisis that the crash of the stock market in 1929. Following the war, amid the trauma seizing policy-making in those parts of the world economy where people had not risen up to throw out political and economic system that had sustained Italian, Nazi or Japanese fascist occupation along with local agents of such occupation, Keynes' temporarily-intended, highly conditional insight into the specific conjuncture of conditions of the 1930s became dogmatised into Keynesian-guided permanent government intervention in the economy, including deficit budgeting as a creator of new economic demand. The financial sector exploited the newfound family economic security of the so-called "social safety net" by developing and offering new "products" befitting the new circumstances. Should the children of the baby-boom generation grow up without the security of knowing they can afford to go onto a college career? Have the parents set aside some monthly sum for the next 18+ years, per child (this could start to add up...). That would bring an end to worries, especially an end to the worry in the financial sector about the petering out of the pent-up demand of wartime savings once everyone had a new car, new house, new fridge, new stove .. It was increasingly evident that the profits to be garnered in this way off children before they even enter the economy as contributing producers could be redoubled. How? As part of the evolution of the modern consumption-oriented economy, family systems as support networks operating simultaneously across multiple generations were increasingly shattered. As the baby boomers aged towards retirement, even "early retirement", with grandchildren who could not afford college education, the financial industry realised that their parents – the children of the baby boomers – could now be turned into a profitable market for the point at which they retire from the labour market, and another new generation of products effloresced. Since the late 1980s, pension responsibilities of governments and, since the late 1990s, of large-scale industrial employers as well, are increasingly sloughed off or abandoned. The ruthless consequence of this combined assault has been yet another regime of forced saving imposed on many people to look after themselves in retirement. The "Investment Retirement Account", a popular U.S. tax-shelter commonly known as the IRA, and similar Canadian investment vehicles such as the "Registered Retirement Savings Plan" (RRSP), the more corporate-oriented "income trust" and the rest of it are nothing but schemes of the leading powers of finance to make capital bleed from every pore of social being, even when people are no longer in a position to participate in full-time employment. The "rainy day" justification is trotted out, but it is a purely aphenomenal sort of justification: saving of this kind has become necessary only to the extent that all other props and social supports have been smashed. Anyone who is unable to "save" by paying tribute to the financial sector in one or another of these ways faces even greater uncertainty.

It seems to shock people when someone points out that the way to conquer anxieties about what is unknown is to go forth and gather some knowledge, develop a plan of action and execute it. No amount of "saving" is going to save anyone from the consequences of their own ignorance. To be rendered powerless or otherwise vulnerable by circumstances beyond one's control is one thing; to be so reduced as a result of one's own ignorance, on the other hand, is entirely avoidable: go find out what you need to know, and solutions will emerge. Saving "in itself", so to speak, remains of no positive value whatsoever in itself, economic or otherwise. Investing what has been saved can be very valuable for the long-term and the short-term. Piling savings up – hoarding – just serves to stimulate waste. Saving in the sense of withholding from socially-useful or long-term-oriented spending is a source of imbalance, and hence anti-Nature – in the sense, here, of anti-societal.

Keeping this in mind, certain guiding criteria may be elaborated for how theory can be usefully developed and applied to real-world economic phenomena:

1. The first requirement of the theory being developed in the present work is to be able to account for conditions as they actually occur in economic reality. All methods and approaches based on comparing "structures" of economic phenomena according to some presupposed idealised abstract standard are rejected from the outset. In fact, economic phenomena that do not share at least a common historical context should not even be considered for comparison; anything elaborated on the basis of such comparisons will be nonsense.

2. Quantitative equality may provide another red herring, and the greatest skepticism and wariness on this front is highly recommended. Just because two tangible economic phenomena carry around the same price and-or cost-of-production data does not make them equivalent. They may indeed exist in some relationship to one another, but for purposes of inferring anything further about either phenomenon, or about the two phenomena in combination, mere quantitative equality in itself is either unnecessary, insufficient, irrelevant, highly misleading or any combination of the foregoing. The problem is that the usual quantitative measuring-stick is monetary value, but the source of value exists independently of and has nothing to do with money. Furthermore, money itself for that matter is not a neutral measuring stick but a political as well as economic instrument for dominating others, including falsifying the scale according to which values are being measured or applied.

4.2. REVERSALS OF FORTUNE: A HISTORY LESSON

A number of the largest corporations dominating world oil and gas business originated in the latter part of the nineteenth century, but the world as a whole may be said to have entered, or – more precisely, been dragged into – the era of Big Oil only since the end of the First World War.

Today, as the following chart indicates, this energy producing effort spans the entire globe and continues ceaselessly to grow.

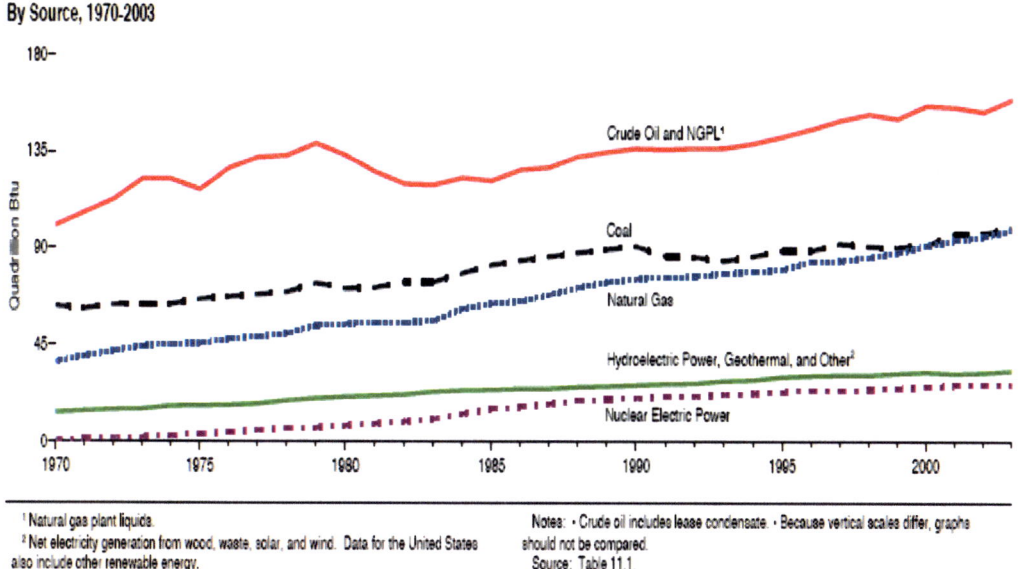

Figure 4-1. World energy supply – Although the shift in energy-market growth prospects away from North America and Europe towards China and India, as well as the increasingly global character of the continuous expansion of energy production, are both masked by this presentation, it does disclose that the main change over time has been the rising production, distribution and sale of natural gas on the global scale. (Source: U.S. Department of Energy, *Annual Energy Review 2004*, p 98).

It is a curious fact that natural gas prices continue not to head towards a single world price, whereas the oil price continues to be a single price no matter the very different conditions, and local energy needs and demands, attending its production. Conventionally, the tendency towards a single world oil price has been explained as the outcome of the overwhelming concentration of refining capacity in the leading consuming countries. However, the tendency to maintaining a single price in global export and import markets has in now way been attenuated by the rise of refining capacity in a number of the leading OPEC countries, including – in the cases of Venezuela and Iran – an increasing export trade in refined products, and no longer just crude oil.

Examination of the history of the main forces impelling oil and gas exploitation and market development since the First World War helps clarify this anomaly and illuminate much else about this commodity and its marketing besides. What is the connection, if any, between the increasing resort to natural gas and the continuing absence of a single world price? Even as the rates of increase in certain periods especially since "9-11" have tracked upwards or downwards mostly in conjunction with what was happening with the world oil price, and sometimes even remarkably closely although not generally so, it is important to grasp that, in general, no such convergence emerges from examining any current contracts, future contracts or spot markets.

The temporary tripling of the Henry Hub spot price for natural gas disclosed in Figure 4-2 demonstrates the extreme potential effect of a short-term event – in this case, Hurricane Katrina which, in the end, was found to have caused little consequential damage to the gas pipeline network along the Louisiana coast, whose throughput at Henry LA forms the basis for the so-called "hub price". This single event and speculation before, during and after it about the potentially disastrous consequences of the 2005 hurricane season in the Gulf of Mexico nevertheless enabled sellers into markets basing themselves on the Henry Hub to double the price from the US$ 5.00-7.50/Mcf band in which gas had traded from 1 September 2004 until the third week of August 2005. Such a jump would not be possible if there was a world price for this commodity. By contrast, there was in the same time period an even shorter-lived "speculative premium" that bumped the price of oil from US$65 to US$70 / bbl; it lasted les than 72 hours precisely because a world price exists that dampens the impact of such events.

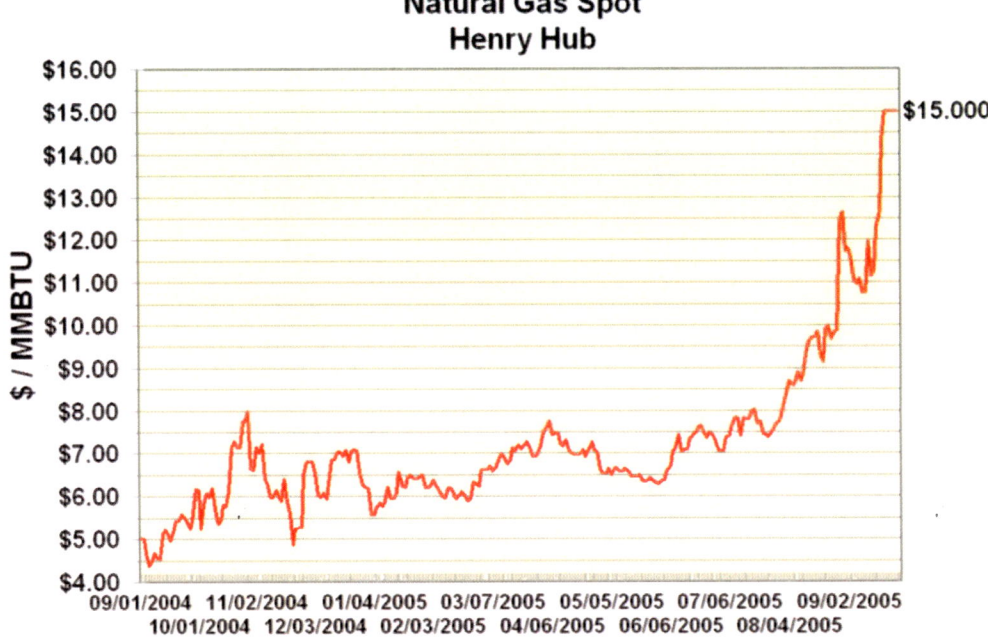

Figure 4-2. Henry Hub Natural Gas Spot Market Price 1 Sep 2004-1 Sep 2005 *(Source: WTRG Economics)*.

The secret of the divergence between the tendencies of oil and natural gas prices is buried in the historical foundations of modern fossil fuel exploration and production. Such examination discloses unexpected and surprising features of the true relations governing the exploration, production and processing of fossil fuels in general as well as of natural gas in particular.

4.2.1. Foundations

Modern-day prospecting for natural gas mimics procedures applied in Arab/Middle Eastern countries was developed by vertically-integrated European and American concerns as they commanded major prospecting efforts in search of crude oil reserves. The application of these techniques to natural gas unfolded most extensively and intensively since the end of the Second World War, within a political and economic context quite different from the one attending the earlier development of modern oil exploration and production. However, this earlier development nevertheless framed many of the conditions that would attend how natural gas was developed later. This point and its implications are often overlooked when energy pricing aspects of natural gas are considered. The key to the overall picture is to be found beginning with the history of how oil exploration and production came to be conducted in the first place across such vast territorial tracts in what was still called Persia (today: Iran), what used to be called Mesopotamia (today: Iraq), and within the Arabian Peninsula (today: Saudi Arabia, Yemen and parts of the United Arab Emirates) beginning in the 1920s (Sampson 1976).

Conventionally, the expansion of oil prospecting and production originating from Western companies in the Middle East has been attributed to varying combinations of engineering expertise, entrepreneurial drive and some additional happily serendipitous intersection of means with opportunity. While this rosy view makes undoubtedly heartwarming reading for engineers and entrepreneurs, certain historical facts can hardly be ignored, much less dismissed — as the late American industrialist Henry Ford used to do — as "the bunk". As their reward for combining to cripple the imperial ambitions of the Kaiser by starving Germany of oil in the last year of the First World War — and thereby salvaging some future for the British and French empires — the leading British and French oil companies of the day, as an adjunct to the terms of the Versailles Peace Treaty formally ending the war, were granted enormous, unprecedented and exclusive oil prospecting and production concessions in these regions.

These concessions became a seriously destabilizing element in the re-ordering of global priorities that the postwar peacemaking process at Versailles was supposed to regulate. Essentially, the private determination by the leaders of Great Britain and France to use the Peace Conference as the means for carving up the Middle East and its resources as their own joint but exclusive sphere of influence stimulated a particularly vigorous challenge from the commanding heights of industry and finance in the United States. In the early1920s, the biggest U.S. financial houses, led by J.P. Morgan and the First National City Bank interests of the Rockefellers, subverted the punitive reparations clauses of the Versailles Treaty imposed against Germany by establishing the Dawes Plan. Proposed for the immediate purpose of restabilising the German currency, which had become less than worthless during the disastrous inflation of 1923, this Plan also enabled financing of industrial reconstruction in the Weimar Republic, led by German branches of U.S. industrial concerns such as Ford Motors (Sayers and Kahn 1947).

As part of the same broad movement towards heightened export of capital, U.S. oil companies joined the campaign to break the Anglo-French yoke over Middle Eastern oil resources, attempting to insert themselves into the already-divided pie. Assisted by Calouste Gulbenkian, an Armenian/Turkish entrepreneur acting as a neutral third party, the British and French oil giants of the time responded by drawing up a so-called Red Line Agreement to protect their duopoly and exclude other oil companies from the region. Eventually the Standard Oil of New Jersey group, the grandfather of present-day Exxon Corporation (Sampson 1975) asserted and inserted itself (Tarbell 1904). At the end of the Second World War, the U.S. President, Franklin Delano Roosevelt, captured Ibn Saud, the king of Saudi Arabia, as a U.S. ally. U.S. oil interests soon moved into the Arabian Peninsula as their own exclusive turf and turned it into a base from which to marginalise in stepwise fashion British and French oil company concessions and prospecting and production activity elsewhere in the region. This struggle developing within the processes of Western companies in general expanding their oil prospecting and production in the Middle East formed another of the main stages within a larger and all-sided commercial struggle among the leading Western imperial powers. This was a political-economic struggle to redivide the spoils of two of the most destructive wars and associated diplomacy recorded in world history to that time (Higham 1983).

Many commentators ascribe a major role to technical and-or entrepreneurial innovation in expanding this tendency. Such innovations, however, fail to explain anything concrete about how or why an ancient region of the world with its own systems of property-holding going back millennia came to be carved up as more or less the exclusive private property of a handful of giant, foreign, privately-held corporations. The larger political-economic framework that was being shaped by these historical currents needs to be elaborated in order to make sense of that crucial development.

From the time British and French companies entered the region, they dismissed any legal standing or authority for the traditional arrangements. These arrangements, established centuries previously and maintained to that time by the tribes and clans of these regions, provided usufructuary rights of access to these lands. The companies acted with the support of their home governments. The British government went to the extent of introducing a novel measure that, when implemented by the Soviet government to protect its own industrial development, was being condemned everywhere at the time as "Bolshevik nationalization" and "communistic interference with the rights of private property" (Chester, Faye and *Young* 1967): on the advice of Cabinet member Winston Churchill, the government purchased the assets of Anglo-Iranian Oil Company, converting it into what later became British Petroleum (Simons 1994).

When the local Kurdish population protested British moves to seize the large oil and gas fields of northern Iraq around Mosul for British Petroleum, Churchill as "Minister of Air" dispatched the Royal Air Force to bomb the unarmed civilian population with poison gas, thereby incidentally also setting the dubious precedent of introducing chemical warfare to the Middle East (Simons, 1994). As for either ideological objections about "Bolshevik nationalization" and "communistic interference with the rights of private property" – or, conversely, the claim that there might be something useful after all in such measures: this was neatly countered by asserting that oil prospecting and extraction formed something called a "natural monopoly". Anyone taking issue with this unilateral and unrequested appropriation of other countries' resources would first have to reckon with Nature and with God.

The companies presented their deed-registry-based systems as a special form of private property required merely for arranging matters only among the corporate entities. This approach was intended to ensure that the companies encountered few if any obstacles. Even as they worked out how to ensure that these forms of private property would enjoy precedence over even outright ownership of a land surface, the companies were careful to reassure local inhabitants that these matters were little or no concern of theirs. Cooperative members of the local elites were accommodated with substantial "commissions".

With the American companies' arrival, very particular and consequential "legal" innovations were added. First, U.S. commercial law backed by a number of Supreme Court decisions treated as "costs of doing business" any commission payments to non-U.S. citizens for services rendered in furtherance of a transaction but not necessarily forming a direct or essential part of the transaction. That is, in U.S. law, such activity carried no imputation whatsoever of corruption. This particular legal exception authorizing the deliberate corrupting of foreign government officials (so long as they were careful enough not to possess U.S. citizenship) remained undisturbed and part and parcel of American law until the 1970s. Second, in the technical area of international law known as extraterritorial rights, the United States developed a lengthy and peculiar history all its own. This became evident as early as the so-called "policy of the 'Open Door'". Promulgated in 1899-1902, at the time of the Boxer Rebellion, the "Open Door" became the United States' pretext for invading and penetrating China as the equal of Japan and the European powers already there. At the same time, having opened the door to China under the pretext of the "Open Door", the U.S. took the unprecedented step of extending the traditional "public international law" of what was in those days called "the comity of nations" to radically broaden application of the principle of extraterritoriality. Until that moment, invocation of this right — defined as the right of a physical person to enjoy legal protection from the application of the laws of a foreign jurisdiction while resident in that jurisdiction—had been restricted to apply only to formally designated representatives of foreign governments while resident in the country to which their government assigned them (Hunt 1983). Once it gained entry to China, however, the U.S. redefined extraterritoriality to include a right for the U.S. government to intervene to protect the rights of any U.S. citizen living or working in a foreign country to the same degree as s/he would enjoy if s/he were still living in the United States.

4.2.2. Origins of Oil's Pre-eminence and Satellite Status for Natural Gas

This aspect of the U.S. Open Door policy did not affect other foreign interests carving China up at the time. Furthermore, for its own interests, Great Britain alone among the European Great Powers supported the U.S. Open Door, even as Whitehall chafed privately over Washington's "going too far" regarding the rules of extraterritoriality (Young, 1968). Thus, the European colonial powers and the Japanese authorities took no action to assist the tottering Chinese regime to resist this self-serving U.S. innovation. Its unilateral application, however, created an important precedent for expanding the bases on which later U.S. interventions would be conducted in other countries. Accordingly, entering the oil-bearing regions of the Middle East in a major way after the Second World War, the U.S. now added a further innovation. It deemed extraterritoriality applicable to all those deemed "legal persons" under U.S. law (Higham 1983).

The implications of this move were truly profound, because not only U.S. statute law but extensive judicial practice in the federal and Supreme Courts includes corporations in all definitions of what constitutes a "legal person". Thus, corporations were now empowered to claim extraterritorial rights. This would include any corporation's rights under U.S. law to buy, sell and enjoy the use of property in a foreign jurisdiction as though it were conducting its affairs in the United States. According to John J. McCloy (1976), a prominent U.S. oil magnate who led in establishing these arrangements and long-time close associate of the U.S. Central Intelligence Agency, in order to anchor this entirely novel and unilaterally-asserted right of extraterritoriality for its corporate entities, the U.S. conceded the authorities in Saudi Arabia — its primary foreign oil source — full jurisdiction for Saudi laws over the conduct of U.S. nationals while working or residing in, or visiting, Saudi territory. This included banning alcohol consumption in public and the appearance of women uncovered in public (Sampson:

ibid.). Another similar concession to Saudi "national dignity" emerging from these arrangements was the acceptance by the U.S. Navy of the norm — one followed everywhere else in the world by every other navy, yet consciously and to date still not observed by the U.S. Navy when its vessels visit the ports of any other country — of flying the host country's national flag astern while in port. Interestingly, a search among the frequent outbreaks of media hysteria over Saudi "immorality police" enforcing the alcohol ban and female covering injunction has uncovered total silence about the hugely valuable and enriching quid-pro-quo responsible in the first place for such exercising of Saudi policing powers. As for the U.S. Navy's exceptional respect for Saudi sovereignty, port management officials in Canada are well briefed on these matters internally by their superiors (Zatzman, 1975), but at this time of writing, no formal, *i.e.*, official, documentation of this arrangement or its link to overall U.S.-Saudi arrangements has become publicly available.

In order both to regulate their mutual interactions and exclude the possibility of any significant interference from local authorities, the corporate sector imposed their own systems and notions of subsurface rights as a special form of private property. This form took precedence over even outright ownership of a land surface. Meanwhile, in the public mind there had already developed a widespread and well-established association of Big Oil with command and control over the disposition of resources across vast territorial basins in oil-producing states. Thus did this regime of corporatised and exceptionalised private property also came to be adduced as evidence in support of such notions of command and control. Note that there was no formal cession of sovereignty; no treaties were either negotiated or signed to that effect between the U.S. government and any of the oil-producing states in which its oil majors conducted their activities.

This notion of corporate command and control remains silent about corporate command and control in general over the power, *viz.*, that of the U.S. government, "under" whose authority Big Oil purports to be conducting its business. This is one of the areas in which a confusion was crfeated about oil and natural gas. The failure to particularise the exceptional role of Big Oil, and especially the path on which it was attained, has served to bias, however subtly, a proper understanding of what happened with the development of natural gas. Command or control of natural gas resources and their development came with the exercise of governmental authority. However, in themselves, they were neither a key nor otherwise essential to how state power in general was exercised for the purposes of commanding and controlling strategic resource-bearing territory. The basis of how natural gas came to be developed and priced in the market can therefore *not* be adequately accounted for by relying mainly or solely on notions of "monopoly" versus "competition".

Seemingly in tandem with the extension of that command and control in the Middle East oil basins, a great deal of natural gas development later followed. At the same time, unlike crude oil, most of the natural gas produced from these basins was not shipped abroad. Indeed: it was not extensively developed until pipeline networks were constructed and positioned to take gas to markets. These were located usually in land-wise relatively contiguous territories elsewhere in the same country, or in a neighbouring country. The key to expanded exploitation of these sources of natural gas lay with the pipeline rights-of-way developed in connection with the oil companies' original assertion of command and control over oil prospecting and extraction and delivery to tidewater for shipping. Exploitation of the former piggy-backed on the development of the latter. Once again: contrary to the impression created as a result of the extremely narrow focus of conventional theory and research on the microeconomic level, such a line of development had less than nothing to do with deregulation of market and price-determining mechanisms.

This is another example where a causal relationship is ascribed to the mere presence of something in some result or effect that played no actual causal role in producing the said effect. An increasingly prominent feature to be found in many areas of social science, this kind of thinking entails an almost obtusely deliberate misreading of cause and effect that some researchers have recently been dubbing "Osama-isation". An earlier generation working in the natural sciences heaped similar contempt on this same kind of shoddiness of logic and disrespect for scientific method especially in experimental work, dubbing it "cargo cult" science (Feynman, 1985). It has played a huge, even if up to now unacknowledged, negative role in confounding the entire discussion of energy pricing in general and natural gas pricing in particular.

4.2.3. The Unnatural History of a "Natural Monopoly"

Since the 1980s, it has been taken practically as holy writ that natural gas is yet another "natural monopoly". It is true that this industry indeed fits the economists' conventional definition. It is indeed an industry with investment costs so high that, if more than one firm tries to supply the same market, all except one (the one with the deepest pockets) is likely to be bankrupted as no others would be able to achieve a profit. A product as standardized as natural gas does indeed invite competition, as also anticipated by the very definition of "natural monopoly". Moreover, as the absence or irrelevance of any differences in its quality leaves no room for developing or serving niche markets at differing price levels, and as it is also unlikely or impossible that the industry's high costs could be covered in a competitive environment, there eventually emerges a condition in which only one enterprise literally in a position to monopolize the entire available market can charge and obtain high enough prices to sustain the industry.

The only thing is: there is nothing in the least "natural" — in the sense of characteristic to how any industry in particular is organised — about the process just described or how it takes place. What is being called "natural" is a struggle for survival as one pole of capital always tries to consume any weaker pole of capital. The "high investment cost" is the cost of pipeline, processing and storage infrastructure. The possibility of such infrastructure presupposes access to, control over, or possession of pipeline rights-of-way. The places where the gas industry was indeed developed as a natural monopoly are precisely where such an enterprise was in a position to piggy-back on rights of way established earlier by a parent corporate entity in the course of the parent developing a major oil find. These rights of way were virtually free, *i.e.*, without cost: the abovementioned example of Anglo-Iranian was indeed typical.

Table 4-1. Initial Development and Regulation of Natural Gas in the U.S. — A Timeline (Compiled from Fleay [1998])

Development and Regulation of Natural Gas
1859 – Col. Drake, US Army, drills first commercial oil well at Spindletop, Pennsylvania. Ambient shows of natural gas are "flared off". This technique comes to be applied generally in oil fields until the start of World War II.
1900s – Starting in New York and Wisconsin, municipalities enable articulation of gas pipeline networks into urban neighbourhoods to provide an alternative to coal for domestic cooking and heating.
1935 – U.S. Federal Trade Commission (FTC) report notes with concern the increasing merger of financial interests from the electric and gas utility industries and recommends intervention to regulate in the interests of consumers.
1938 – U.S. Congress passes Natural Gas Act (NGA) in response to the FTC recommendations and continuing widespread public agitation over cartelization of utilities raising the cost of delivering an essential service on an uncompetitive basis at a time of widespread impoverishment and want. Drawing on the model of the Interstate Commerce Commission Act of 1913, the NGA proposes to arfrest their negative consequences of excessive concentration by empowering the Federal Power Commission to regulate interstate development of pipeline networks and sale of gas.
1941/45 – The U.S. enters the war against Japan. Within a year, as it becomes clear that domestically produced oil will be needed for the war, especially for the fleet, the U.S. government mandates widespread development of natural gas in the domestic market as a wartime substitute for refined petroleum wherever possible. In the U.S., a Supreme Court ruling regulates the wellhead price of gas where the utility and the pipeline are part of the same financial entity.
1954 – Supreme Court renders its decision in *Phillips Petroleum Co. v. Wisconsin* (347 U.S. 672 [1954]). In this decision, the Supreme Court ruled that any natural gas producer selling natural gas into interstate pipelines fell under the classification of 'natural gas companies' in the NGA, and were subject to regulatory oversight by the FPC, simultaneously streamlining regulation of both the rates at which producers sold natural gas into the interstate market and the rates at which natural gas that was sold by interstate pipelines to local distribution utilities. This sets the stage for the issue on which the deregulation melodrama unfolds, as a liberation of the producers from the tributary yoke of the pipeline companies backed by the FPC.
1970 – U.S. domestic oil production reaches a peak from which it has declined without interruption to date. Energy industry planning of domestic supply centers hereafter around natural gas.
1998 – The role of oil in supplying the commercial energy of the entire globe had fallen to about 40 percent; natural gas had risen to about 22 percent. Some 60 percent of the consumption of oil is been taken up by transport systems – rail, sea and air.

Furthermore, the fact that a single enterprise can readily dominate a particular natural gas market does not in itself ensure any sort of equilibrium. Indeed it has become almost universally the case throughout the United States that the most intense competition for market share characterises the activities of the various monopoly groups each attempting to eliminate the control any rival or rivals may exercise in any adjacent or contiguous market areas. This asymmetric competition was the predictable outcome of how natural gas was developed in the U.S. The sole regulatory mechanism provided by the Roosevelt Administration in the middle of the Great Depression under the formal aegis of the Federal Power Commission was actually as an extension of the kind of powers vested a generation earlier in the Interstate

Commerce Commission (ICC). The ICC was a tool created by the railway trusts in 1913 to eliminate the massive Populist protest movement of small farmers, small-town businessmen and urban progressives against the railways price-gouging on transportation rates.

What constitutes either a monopoly or natural monopoly depends on historical context as well as structure and function. As Map 4-1 later in this chapter clearly serves to demonstrate, it will not do to limit matters to counterposing notions of competition or the operation of a "free" market.

As Table 4-1 illustrates, from the outset, the rising importance of gas within the U.S. energy supply picture could not long be separated from issues of regulation. The first 30 years of this process developed from the supply of gas as a customer service being regulated as a residential utility, like electrical service, to its delivery being regulated across state lines, on the basis of preventing the emergence and dictate of oligopolistic firms operating as a restraint upon free competition. The exigencies of wartime sequestering of petroleum, to meet the demands of modern motorized forms of warfare on land, sea and in the air, opened the prospect of gas being substituted for oil in the supply of electric power to industry and local utilities. By the 1950s, the bias of regulatory effort shifted towards attenuating tendencies among producer oligopolies, pipeline oligopolies and supplier oligopolies to poach one another's turf.

As the point of market saturation and the peak in the increase of the rate of return on investment in natural gas production, processing/transport and delivery was passed, the pressure grew to consider deregulation. This pressure greatly intensified as it became apparent after 1970 that the U.S could no longer profitably increase its domestic production of petroleum. Table 4-2 documents the manner in which, since 1978-85, deregulation has been introduced to enable the most powerful natural gas suppliers in the U.S. market to shape the fate of to weaker rivals. Over the last 20 years, this has often taken the form of subcontracting arrangements in which the smaller partner carries all the actual costs including the cost of paying the stronger partner a "tribute" for the privilege of being permitted to convey natural gas over the right-of-way controlled by the stronger partner. The result was the generation of a double jackpot: first, the attraction of massive amounts of new investment out of domestic oil production and into the gas sector, and then – in tandem with the deregulation of electricity rates more than 80 years after both electricity and gas rates were first regulated in the U.S. – a bonanza from the prospect of utilizing natural gas to fire new electrical power plants.

4.2.4. "Natural" Monopoly's True Nature: Why the U.S. "Deregulated" Gas Only after Phasing out the Oil Depletion Allowance

The notion of gas as a natural monopoly is an extension of a similarly unsubstantiated claim advanced since the 1920s that the prospecting and exploitation of the oil resources of the Middle East was a natural monopoly. Indeed, what at first appears to be entirely a coincidence, however neat, is anything but. The widespread promulgation of the notion of natural gas as a natural monopoly followed exposure by unfolding events of claims that oil prospecting and extraction formed a natural monopoly. The two are intimately connected.

**Table 4-2. Timeline of Natural Gas Deregulation in the United States
Compiled from LIHEAP Clearinghouse**

A CONDENSED DEREGULATION TIMELINE

1978 – Natural Gas Policy Act ends federal control over the wellhead price of "new" gas as of January 1, 1985, but keeps in place wellhead price controls for older vintages of gas. According to the American Gas Association, the leading natural gas producers' cartel in the U.S., with this administrative change of everything except the wellhead price for existing supplies, "the laws of supply and demand begin to work again in the natural gas industry." [This logic brings to mind the old American one-liner: "But apart from that, Mrs. Lincoln — how was the play?" – Edd.]

1985 – Order 436, issued by the Federal Energy Regulatory Commission (FERC), establishes a voluntary program that encourages natural gas pipelines to be "open access" carriers of natural gas bought directly by users from producers. This order brings the separation of pipelines' merchant and transportation functions, and it initiates a restructuring of the natural gas industry's regulatory structure.

1989 – Natural Gas Wellhead Decontrol Act lifts the remaining wellhead price controls on natural gas.

1992 – FERC Order 636 orders interstate natural gas pipelines to "unbundle," or offer separately, their gas sales, transportation and storage services. The goal of this order is to ensure that all natural gas suppliers compete for gas purchasers on equal footing.

1996 – The first residential natural gas customer choice programs are implemented. By 1997, local natural gas utilities in 17 states and the District of Columbia had proposed and/or implemented such residential customer choice policies or pilot programs.

– On 31 August and 1 September, the Legislature in Sacramento, California, the most populous state in the United States, authorizes deregulation of electric power rates to begin 1 January 1998

1999-2000 – During one of the hottest summers on record in the State of California, a private corporation in Houston, Texas set up under the name Enron to purchase electric power from deregulated utilities and re-sell it to customers in other deregulated jurisdictions, corners the California market and people's air conditioning bills skyrocket. Mustering the facts of the brownouts and related power cuts and outages caused by the unprecedented demand in conditions of such artificially restricted supply as evidence of the need for massive increases in power supplies generally, lobbyists for the power engineering cartel in Washington DC put the case for expanded federal subsidies and incentives to construct new power plants across the United States. As an unexpectedly long cold snap hits the populous regions of the US eastern seaboard and southeast in late 2000, the Federal Energy Regulatory Commission permits a fourfold increase in the wellhead price (Henry Hub) of natural gas — the main proposed feedstock for the proposed future plants. (United States [LIHEAP] 1999)

During the Arab oil boycott following the 1973 Arab-Israeli War, OPEC as a cartel of oil-producing states emerged onto the world stage. In exposing the fallacy of the notion of "oil as natural monopoly", this single development achieved more than 1000 textbooks or learned disquisitions could ever hope. A scant five years later, the actual plan of deregulation of natural gas pricing in the U.S. was produced, touted of course as something that would lead to "greater competition". The year in which deregulation of natural gas began first to be mooted — in 1975 — was precisely that the U.S. Congress began the official retirement the so-called "oil depletion allowance" system.

This had been one of the most notorious decades-long scams of the "oil patch". The oil depletion allowance developed as a U.S. federal government incentive that provided a fabulous labyrinth of opportunities to write all costs incurred by oil exploration activity within U.S. territory (including any indirect costs linked as a consequence of an involvement in exploration) off the corporate income tax return as kind of discounted resource rent. The lucrative attraction lay in the provisions for how the allowance was to be accounted on a company's books: in annual installments and often for decades into the future — long after the corporate entity might either no longer exist, or a resource basin from which it was still claiming a depletion exemption had ceased to show any new potential. The admission of indirect costs, and the amortization feature, meant in practice that costs amounting to as much as 200 percent of a company's expenditure on actual exploration would be written off. Instead of a tax incentive arranged as a legitimate temporary deferral of liability to pay until there is actual revenue generated from an investment, under the oil depletion allowance system the U.S. taxpayer was simply paying the companies to drill, sometimes even doubling private investors' money.

The idea of incentivising oil exploration within the U.S. in this particular form of a resource rent discounted over time back to the risk-taker originated in the late 1920s following the so-called Teapot Dome scandal. It was designed specifically to address how to encourage oil exploration on unexplored federal government land while discouraging at the same time any further swaps and sales of these lands without first obtaining some independent determination of their resource potential (the condition that had been corruptly exploited by former US Secretary of the Interior Albert B. Fall and his cronies, exploding into scandal).[18]

After 1973, with exploration investment in the Middle East now confronting the enormously powerful attractor of a tripled oil price, if the oil depletion allowance system were not reformed, further serious oil exploration on U.S. territory might well have disappeared. This was a major national security nightmare of the Nixon administration that would be inherited by, and actually fixed under, the administrations of Presidents Ford and Carter.

These political-economic realities attending the timing of the phasing-out of oil depletion allowances further suggest that the timing of the launch of natural gas price deregulation was hardly a coincidence. In effect, after 1975, the U.S. shifted from subsidising production (on the basis of the oil depletion allowance system) to subsidizing consumption after 1990-91 and the First Gulf War. Before the 1973 embargo and tripling of oil price, subsidising production in the U.S. had produced large additional profits based on maximising a spread between the actual costs of bringing oil to the surface in the Middle East and the actual costs of bringing

---

[18] In the early 1960s, the Kennedy administration was looking into reforming the arrangement (to one where liability to pay was deferred until an investment started to produce revenue) when the president was assassinated in Dallas. Some of the largest corporate players of the oil patch were involved at the time in East Texas, where new oil exploration had tapered off sharply since the early 1950s. For the duration of the presidency of Lyndon Johnson, a career politician with his base in East Texas who would attain supreme executive authority as a byproduct of the assassination, Congress declined to tamper with the basic standard oil depletion allowance, which was held steady at 27.5 percent.

oil to the surface on the territory of the United States. With the increase in the cost of bringing oil out of the ground in the Middle East, this spread narrowed. It would thus become more profitable to leave oil on US territory in the ground. Some of that energy production would have to be replaced. Hence the interest to attract investment into exploring and producing natural gas.

4.2.5. Rigid Separation of "Upstream" from "Downstream": The Secret, and Consequences, of a Single World Oil Price

Starting with the oil producing regions of the Middle East after the First World War, and again after the Second, the companies were able to have their way from the outset without impediment. From this fact, however, a most fundamental yet simple historical scenario unfolded that would turn out to be freighted with the profoundest implications. First and foremost, when it came to establishing a world system for producing and marketing petroleum and its refined byproducts, the producing states themselves played no role whatsoever. Oil explorations conducted on the scale introduced by American and European corporations in the Middle East presupposed that any crude oil actually brought to the surface was to be piped to the nearest tidewater port facility for removal by ship — actually by an entire global network of ocean-going oil tankers, either owned by or available for lease to the oil companies — entirely away from the territory in which it was "discovered", off to refineries and markets on distant continents. The actual costs of extracting the raw material and bringing it to tidewater, however, were many times less than the shipping-transport cost per unit of the raw material, while the latter cost itself tended for extended periods of time towards some equilibrium value. This essential pre-condition for setting a world price was greatly bolstered by the deliberate separation of consuming regions from producing regions which the vertically-integrated corporate "producers" had effected.

With the discovery of significant shows of gas in the same reservoirs as these crude oil discoveries, exploration and drilling for natural gas in recent decades was revived on a large scale in tandem with such crude oil exploration and drilling, taking advantage of the potential "economies of scale" that could be tapped when it came to developing pipeline rights-of-way. However, although the markets for much of this gas were also no longer primarily local, they were not yet transoceanic. As the "refining" value-added derivable from refining natural gas was negligible compared to the value-added derivable from refined petroleum and its byproducts, there was for a long time little or no inherent incentive to cartelize the marketing of this product by establishing even a standard for a world natural-gas price.

There has emerged a very definite — and peculiar — pricing mechanism for oil that is intimately bound up with this upstream-downstream separation. However, the story that is told about as to what factors of this mechanism are supposedly most important in determining this price diverges in many crucial particulars from "facts on the ground". In this divergence there lies the single most critical element of the entire mix — the systematic underdevelopment of livelihoods and economic prospects for dozens of countries and peoples across a wide swath of Asia, Africa and Latin America.

The separation of "upstream" from "downstream" activity which – outside of Russia and China – has been effected in the oil industry worldwide, meanwhile, has become a fact of life widely taken for granted or not even thought about. In the story of how this actually came to pass, however, it is possible to begin to glimpse the profound and potentially subversive challenge posed within the global energy production picture to the extremely monopolized positions of Big Oil by the further development of natural gas sources and resources on the world scale and the elaboration, in the context of such development, of marketing and pricing regimes based on criteria advanced independently of the kind pushed by the oil cartel.

It is widely known that oil pricing does not conform to the conventional supply and demand theory. In theory, energy price is set based on projected world demand. Because this projection is determined by a small group of economic conglomerates, the flexibility in projection techniques demonstrates the most acute shortcoming of the energy pricing models. In conventional pricing, the role of point-sources of supply (any particular country, set of fields) is marginalized, despite the provision of a grading system that is based on sulfur content, etc. Furthermore, it is customary to discuss in terms of world price that differs little from various locally-cited prices. This is regarded as a price "brought to equilibrium" by the forces of competition. The competition is a monopolistic one, not free competition, and thus the alleged "equilibrium" is essentially contingent and unstable, subject to changes in the prevailing balance of forces among globally-operating, vertically-integrated suppliers, spot-market availabilities, and the cartel of principal producing states. Meanwhile, there has emerged an increasingly broad-based discussion emerging around how to eliminate the demand-based model, and move to setting price based principally on known, actual supply. Advances in technology (especially in reservoir characterization, the development of "virtual reservoir" production models, novel refining capability, as well as certain trends in EOR, etc.) make this increasingly possible, and there is certainly growing pressure from newer producers who have no interest to remain eternally bound by the existing cartel and its various deals with the so-called "majors". In short: as monopolized and cartelized as the oil pricing mechanism has become, resistance and opposition to its consequences continues to grow, while the rationales offered in defense of the status-quo become increasingly incoherent. There is in particular a growing consensus around the realization that uneven development is built into demand management, not its accidental byproduct. Although, at the consumer end of the chain, the price of oil seems to remain unjustifiably high, this matter is quite separate from the actual cost of its production. Here the historic and ongoing reality is that the cost of producing oil is and remains low. Indeed it is low enough such that the producers can never recover a reasonable share of the value of the wealth they are exporting (invariably as raw crude), while the oil majors from the consuming countries retain maximum freedom not only to trap the producer-states in ever-rising mountains of debt, but also to extract superprofits — using the tax regime throughout the developed countries — while spreading the tale far and wide among the people of these countries that the producer-states are to blame for having erected a cartel, *viz.*, OPEC.

The demand for oil has steadily increased over the last 50 years, as the growth of the world economy cannot be sustained without fuel and oil plays a particularly vital role. Data on world energy consumption show a steady increase in recent years in oil's share of the total, a trend likely to continue. Indeed: as Figure 4-1 showed *supra*, during 1989-1999, world energy consumption increased for every type of energy source except coal, and in gross amount – reflecting the explosive growth of all motorized forms of transport – that from oil more than from any other source. The increase in consumption due to renewable sources such as geothermal, solar, wind and hydro was small in comparison, and oil is thus likely to continue to predominate in the years to come. In response to widespread pollution concerns about coal burning, coal consumption declined slightly, but more coal energy was used in 1998 than natural gas, even though natural gas produces far less pollution, such that, on balance, it appears that environmental policies aimed at cutting pollution and greenhouse gases by reducing coal consumption have had little effect. The supply of oil remains constrained by its non-renewable character, associated costs of production, and — maybe most of all — by the extraordinary extra-economic power enjoyed by the leading oil majors, from the U.S. and a few other leading countries of the Organization of Economic Cooperation and Development (OECD), over everything downstream from production-as-such of crude oil. In the U.S. and other OECD countries, demand for oil is many times higher than the domestic supply, giving rise to a chronic excess demand for oil (EDO).

As Figure 4-3 establishes, although upstream and downstream activity in the oil industry has been rigidly separated to facilitate the efforts by those controlling the downstream sources of value-added to maintain a single world price, it has also created a permanently unbreachable EDO which has served to insulate the profits of those controlling the downstream end from the vicissitudes of supply and demand. Effectively, supply and demand play little or no role in setting the long-term price of oil in the world market.

The supply of oil remains constrained by its non-renewable character, associated costs of production, and — maybe most of all — by the extraordinary extra-economic power enjoyed by the leading oil majors, from the U.S. and a few other leading countries of the Organization of Economic Cooperation and Development (OECD), over everything downstream from production-as-such of crude oil. In the U.S. and other OECD countries, demand for oil is many times higher than the domestic supply, giving rise to a chronic excess demand for oil (EDO) shown in Figure 4-3. Shortage or excess demand trend for the oil in OECD countries — the difference between trends of demand and supply — has never ceased to increase. Between 1985 and 1999, a shortfall of about 17.4 million barrels per day (MMBPD) increased to 26.2 MMBPD, or 50.6 percent, while supply remained more or less stagnant: 20.1 MMBPD in 1985, 21.4 MMBPD in 1999. Actual demand for oil in the OECD countries increased from 37.7 MMBPD in 1985 to 47.6 MMBPD in 1999, an increase of 9.9 MMBPD.

Meanwhile the effective increase in available supplies grew only 1.3 MMBPD. OPEC supply patterns are closely linked to this OECD shortfall: indeed, the shortage or excess demand for oil trend and OPEC's oil supply trend have become important indicators of the actual elasticities affecting oil price. In 1985, OPEC supplied 0.2 million b/d less than the shortage of oil of the OECD countries; the price stood around $27.50 per barrel (bbl). Since 1985, as OPEC's oil supply trend surpassed the OECD shortfall, the price dipped, lower and lower. EDO requirements are imported as crude, then usually refined, processed and marketed in the oil-importing countries. The persistence of EDO often sparks price hikes, and recent oil price hikes are no exception. If EDO = 0, current prices remain the same; if EDO < 0, prices fall, and vice-versa.

As a result of relying in this manner on consuming countries' shortfall to keep crude prices downwardly inelastic, the producing states have actually been absorbing an enormous and actually increasing (although absolutely unaccounted) additional burden. These arrangements enable the oil majors, based in the consuming countries but commanding most of the refining and marketing, effectively to nullify or render irrelevant actual or effective conditions of oil supply. Essentially, in exchange for preventing an oil price collapse, the producing states remain the hostage of the developed countries.

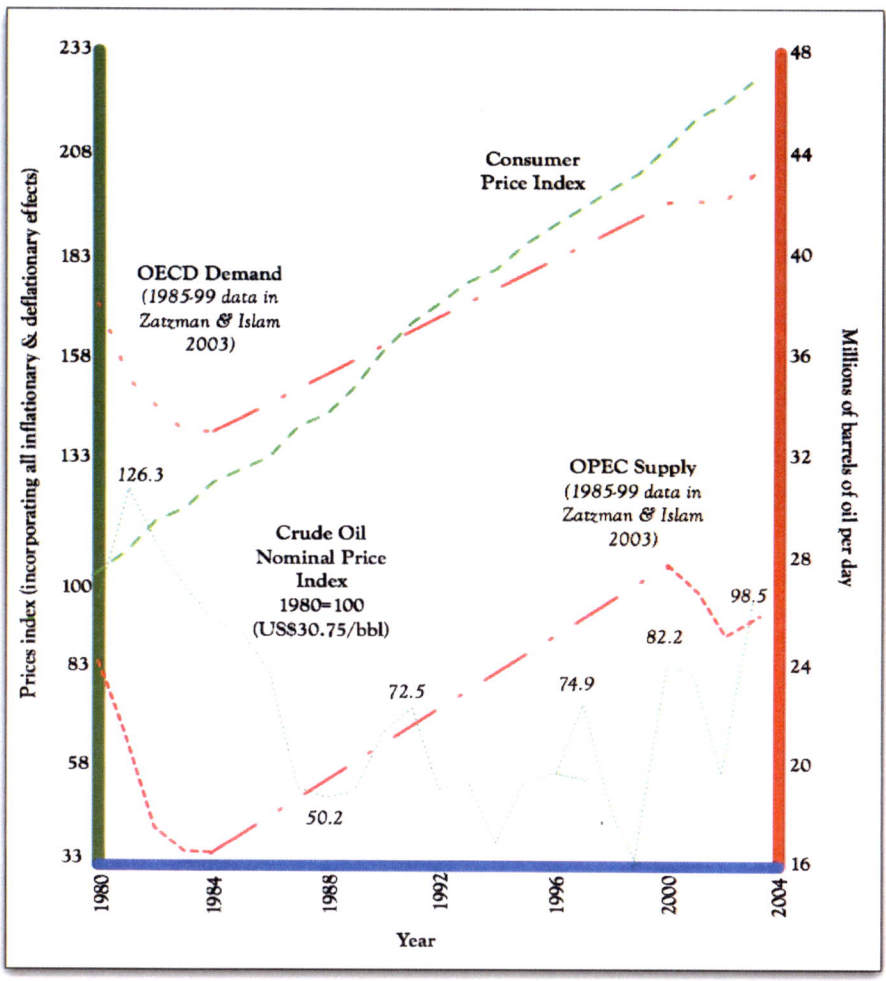

Figure 4-3. Crude Oil Nominal Price Index (CONPI) *vs* CPI, and the permanent excess OECD demand compared to OPEC supply (EDO) – The green lines show the price of oil as indexed by its nominal price (Crude Oil Nominal Price index) fluctuates without reference to, and far below, the Consumer Price Index. The red lines hows that the supply shortfall is permanent. The CONPI trendline relative to the demonstrated EDO shows neither oil supply nor demand regulate one another. This line of investigation based on CONPI is further elaborated at Islam and Zatzman 2004a. (Sources: U.S. Bureau of Labour Statistics, *Consumer Price Index* [Washington DC: 18 January 2006]; Tables 1.2, 2.2 and 7.1, Energy Information Administration, *International Energy Annual 2003* [Washington DC: U.S. Department of Energy, 2005]).

For some time, for example, among those concerned about post-sanctions scenarios, anxiety surrounded the vexed question of re-introducing Iraqi crude in the world market. Adelman (2001) wrote: "When the sanctions regime finally erodes, Iraq will behave like an 800-pound gorilla: it will bring in foreign companies to invest and expand while leaving other members out". Instead, Iraq was marginalized by Russia's record oil output (1.5 MMBPD more than Saudi output, while oil prices remained higher than what was believed to be a "fair" $25/bbl world price). Even with 140,000 troops on Iraq's territory since toppling the regime of Saddam Hussein in April 2003, in the absence of any agreement with the Paris Club of long-term creditors of the former regime (Russia, France, etc.), the current regime remains unable to secure even pipeline transport of Iraqi oil out of the territory let alone bulk transportation contracts with international shippers. Meanwhile, the meter keeps ticking on the coalition's billion-dollar-a-day war and occupation, which was to be paid for from exports of Iraqi oil. Nevertheless, after dipping below US$24/bbl at the moment Saddam was toppled, the world oil price crept back up, but only to the US$27-US$30/bbl range typical of the period of the winter heating season in the northern hemisphere, where the largest per-capita energy consumption markets are located. By the summer of 2005, the price had escalated to US$65-70/bbl.

Cheap crude oil was in fact fundamental to the economic growth enjoyed by the OECD consuming countries — but ready or steady supply of crude oil, obviously a matter of considerable importance for the producing states, was irrelevant to the concerns of the oil majors calling the policy shots for the consuming countries. Indeed, the suppression of oil prices below the market price would cause oil production to fall in the long run, and as average variable costs (AVC) of oil exploration from high-cost wells surpass the ceiling or suppressed price, the short-run tendency would be (and has been) for such wells to shut down. As this condition spread, oil production fell worldwide in the short-term, inducing a condition of chronic shortages and outages which has appeared alongside a global picture of apparently excessive supplies of still-easily-accessible oil. In this way, the oil majors, as proprietors of most of the refining capacity and downstream marketing and distribution system, have been able further to shift the burdens of business risk onto the consumers of petroleum products in the developed countries, while simultaneously increasing insecurity among the producing countries and increasing those countries' dependence in the short term on the entire externally-controlled downstream network.

As a constant-dollar analysis makes immediately clear, crude oil has remained historically cheap. Actual costs of production of goods and services (net taxes) thus also remained low — with significant impacts on overall international trade flows far beyond the oil and gas sector. After the Second World War until 1973, the oil price index was much lower than the consumer price index (CPI). Figure 4-3 shows these trends. When crude oil producers realized the gap between CPI and Oil Price Index was widening, they attempted to narrow it and set as a target that the oil price index should catch up to the CPI. However, except for a few short-lived periods, the oil price index had remained below the CPI during the previous 50 years. As a result, most of the OECD consuming countries retained a comparative advantage at the level of international trade in petroleum and petroleum products: as the lowest-cost producers of goods and services in greatest demand, they could retain dominant or otherwise significant positions as exporters of such goods and services to the producing countries. Already large-scale exporters of capital goods, these countries in this way could also enhance the policy of trade expansion they were already pursuing with both members and non-members of the OECD. Conversely, however, this meant that, apart from their obviously highly-specialized position in the export of crude oil, the oil-producing countries' positions in international trade generally weakened at some cost to these countries effective economic independence.

By cartelizing their petroleum production, OPEC producers could for a time reduce the impact of the international oil companies on their sovereignty and even expand some of that sovereign space. However, as only a production cartel, and commanding none of the forward linkages in the consumer countries, OPEC member-states could not obtain any restitution from, or reversal of, what amounted in effect to a massive permanent outflow of wealth. Blamed for the ballooning in price of refined products in the consumer countries, the indeed bitter irony for OPEC countries was and remains that the revenue-hunger of governments in the consuming states, not the alleged "greed" of OPEC producing states, led to a massive expansion of taxation on petroleum and petroleum products regimes that actually garnered super-profits for the major oil companies from these countries.

With increased production of oil and its revenues, demand in oil-exporting countries for food, luxury consumer goods, equipment for oil industry and light capital goods increased exponentially. Paying those bills of course has made most of their oil revenue flow back into OECD consuming countries. The petrodollar has become the very symbol of this pattern. OECD countries significantly increased their exports to OPEC countries over the years and the ready availability of petrodollars especially during the 1970s and 1980s, seemingly as endless as the very sands of the deserts of the OPEC countries themselves, stimulated excesses reflected today in debts exceeding hundreds of billions of US dollars in the producing states — an extremely burdensome and potentially ruinous legacy for the long term.

"Value-added" from refining, processing and marketing enjoys overwhelmingly greater economic weight than primary production of crude, the source raw material. This mode of "value addition" cannot be sustained in the Information Age as the opacity is removed and general public gets to see the big picture.

Some 90 percent of the petroleum imported by OECD countries is crude oil; finished or refined products account for the remaining less-than-10 percent. In this way, the richest oil-importing countries monopolize the entire arena of value addition: oil exploration, oil refining, processing, marketing, shipping, wholesaling, retailing and distribution are all major industries in OECD countries, and most of the oil majors come from these countries. Some of these oil companies' final sales exceed the annual GDP of major crude oil producers from OPEC. These majors are also involved in oil exploration and marketing of petroleum products between third countries, thus enhancing for them most of the forward and backward linkage effects from vertical (or upstream plus downstream) concentration and integration. Of these benefits, the crude oil producing countries garner virtually zero.

Since no other energy sources have been, or under present economic conditions can be, developed to challenge the extraordinarily dominant position of petroleum and its byproducts in the energy supply profile of any modern country, the ongoing cycle of ever deepening impoverishment of the producing states coupled to ever more excessive wealth accumulating among the super-rich of the consuming states appears to be the fault somehow of oil, or its producers, or its consumers. But in fact, as we have already seen, energy pricing policy can never be just about oil. This problem is the result of the way an entire economic system goes about distributing the production of all manner of goods and services, not just energy and not just oil.

Oil is an important input in every conceivable production function. Crude oil is even used to produce other energy sources such as electricity, aviation fuel, etc. In times of economic expansion throughout the 1960s, 1970s and 1980s, demand for energy increased as OECD countries enjoyed access to the cheapest energy sources from the oil exporting countries. However, mainly as a byproduct of the tendency of governments in oil-importing countries to add taxes to petroleum products at all levels (crude importation, refining, wholesaling and retailing), overall prices of energy sources in general also surged significantly. As the option of not consuming petroleum and any of its byproducts simply doesn't exist anywhere in a modern economy, this development has created its own further burden. Since the rates of growth in gross sales revenues of enterprises that add tax upon tax to each level of production and distribution are not likely to be matched by many, if any, other enterprises, this additional power to attract investment out of other sectors into oil and gas becomes a kind of tribute exacted out of the rest of the economy by the oil majors.

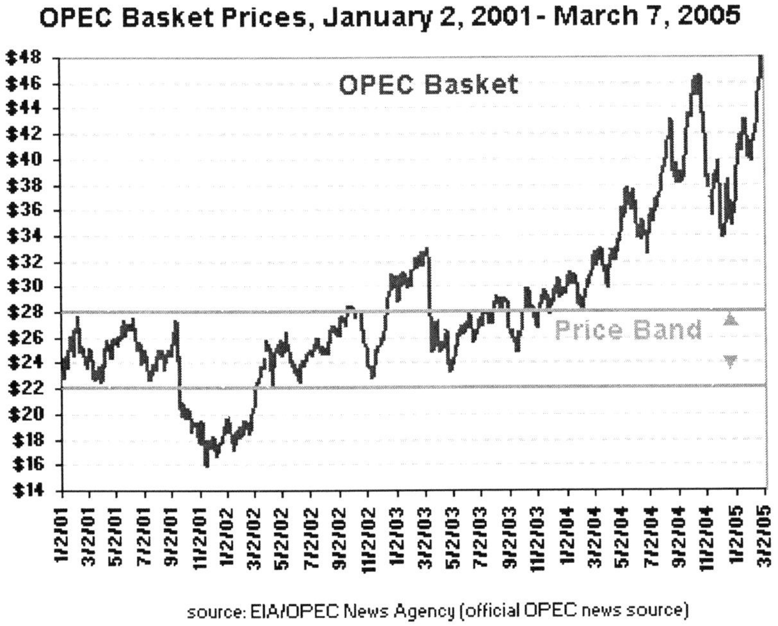

OPEC Basket Prices, January 2, 2001 - March 7, 2005

source: EIA/OPEC News Agency (official OPEC news source)

Figure 4-4. OPEC "Basket" Prices for Crude Oil, January 2001 – March 2005 (Data from United States Energy Information Administration and OPEC). At its March 2000 meeting, OPEC set up a price band mechanism triggered by the OPEC basket price, to respond to changes in world oil market conditions. According to the price band mechanism, OPEC basket prices above $28 per barrel for 20 consecutive trading days or below $22 per barrel for 10 consecutive trading days would result in production adjustments. This adjustment was originally automatic, but OPEC members changed this so that they could fine-tune production adjustments at their discretion. Since its inception, the informal price band mechanism has been activated only once. On October 31, 2000, OPEC activated the mechanism to increase aggregate OPEC production quotas by 500,000 barrels per day. On March 4, 2005, the OPEC basket price rose to $48.37 per barrel, its highest price since the price band mechanism was established. Since December 2, 2003, when the basket price last crossed the $28 per barrel threshold, the OPEC basket price has traded above the $28 per barrel level for 325 consecutive trading days through March 7, 2005 without triggering the price band mechanism. At its January 30, 2005 meeting, OPEC decided that market changes had rendered the band unrealistic, and decided to temporarily suspend the price band mechanism, pending completion of further studies on the subject.

Exacting such tribute at the downstream end undermines the relative position and clout of the producers at the upstream end. For a certain period, starting in 2000 when the world oil price was slumping and OPEC members were pumping at much lower rates than today, the

Saudi kingdom prevailed oin the rest of OPEC to introduce a floor price but this would be disguised as a price band so it could be argued that it would also protect consumers from excessive price increases beyond a certain level. External political developments connected with U.S. preparations against Iraq, meanwhile, gradually rendered the price-band idea increasingly unworkable. This is illustrated in Figure 4-4.

As Iraqi resistance grew, Iraqi fossil fuel exports plummeted to somewhere between 15 and 35 per cent of pre-invasion levels, compelling other members to increase their pumping levels both to cover the Iraqi shortfall in the market and at the same time maintain their relative positions in OPEC itself. Until the January 30, 2005 elections in Iraq, it briefly appeared that production in the northern fields around Mosul would be largely restored, but this never happened. Eventually, with George W Bush's re-election in November 2004, OPEC abandoned the "price band".

One of the most difficult situations emerging during 2004-5 was what appeared to be an acute drawing-down of unused production capacity in the hands of the national oil companies of the OPEC countries. While some commentators have tried to suggest this circumstance is connected with attempts to avert the consequences of the "peak oil" scenario, facts suggest such claims are disinformation aimed at hiding how the powers concentrated in downstream activity such as refining, instead of investing their increased profits from increased prices in additional refining capacity, have chosen instead to make the members of OPEC pit themselves against one another in a "race to the bottom" to see who can be forced to pump the last barrel of oil before any other member.

According to data compiled from Inernational agency reports by Hiromi Kato, managing director of the Institute of Energy Economics Japan (IEEJ) in an article for the Journal of the IEEJ entitled "Effects of the Oil Price Upsurge on the World Economy" (December 2005), as OPEC abandoned its price-band strategy following the re-election of George W. Bush at the end of 2004, the speculative game of bidding up the future delivered price of oil is starting to play havoc with production plans and pumping regimes within OPEC.

Even if something could be done to alleviate the deleterious impacts and burdens shifted by Big Oil and government taxations regimes on the public in the developed countries, there remains the unresolved consequences of the extreme exacerbation of uneven development inflicted by the North on the South largely abetted by Big Oil.

As already mentioned, at the start of the 1920s, British oil interests grabbed the oil fields of northern Iraq for themselves by slaughtering the Kurds and favouring the Arabs there. By the mid-1920s, as US oil companies tried to enter the zone, the British and French oil companies struck their Red Line agreements defining the effective borders of Syria, Iraq and Iran according to the nature and extent of the major oil and gas finds that they planned to develop, and on the basis of keeping US oil companies out and favouring Shi'a over Sunni Arabs. At the close of World War Two, positioning itself as the premier ally of the mainly Sunni Arab world against any revival of British power in the region, the US government colluded with the House of Saud to carve out the Arabian Peninsula as the exclusive bailiwick of US oil companies, largely excluding European oil majors. After 1971, when oil production within the United States was no longer sufficient for its domestic needs, oil was deemed to be "running out" around the globe and, accordingly, since 1973, any claims by the long-beggared oil-producing countries for a more just price on their product could be painted as a blackmail operation staged by inferior tribes against the very citadels of civilisation, culture and enlightenment. The all-or-nothing, "take no prisoners" approach of Big Oil[19] was developed in the context of redividing economic space and resource zones that had already been divided under different pre-existing arrangements. Such redivision was carried out not only in terms of the financial strength of the contending entities but often enforced by resort to the military means of the governments they patronised. This feature, which lent any reversal of standards or re-integration an aura of irreversibility, if not permanence, was intended to discourage any challenge, however just. But, as has also become the case in our own day – in Iran, Venezuela, Bolivia and some other locales – such methods can also unite the general population against any further permission for any powerful foreign-based oil company or syndicate to maintain operations in their jurisdiction.

4.3. PRESERVATION OF EMPIRE *VERSUS* FREEDOM OF PEOPLES: MODERN ECONOMICS OF ENERGY AND FOOD

Energy supplies and food supplies are each essential for continued progress and life on this planet. Technologically speaking, there already exist many links connecting the development of each in terms of the other. Potentially there are even more connections that could be considered and developed for the betterment of Humanity's condition as a whole and not on the basis of one being drained at the expense of the other, or on the basis of one region of the world – for example, the global "South" – being drained and exploited for the ever greater rise of and domination by the countries and peoples of the "North" over everyone.

Although many economists and other social scientists have been delving into these problems, for almost two generations, their success has been limited by the intentions informing their intervention as well as by the tools they bring to the task. Conventional economics, for example, has not really addressed this problem at the level of theory. The authors' view is that this theory is unable to address these problems properly not for lack of trying but because it is utterly unfitted for the job. Furthermore, for a number of ideological, political and historical reasons, conventional economic theory cannot be fitted to accomplish this task any more than a bicycle wrench designed to unscrew nuts of a single size can be either used to repair a car engine or refitted for such use. Nor will the problem at the theoretical level achieve correction by endless practical experimentation, any more than the theory of gravitation would be discovered by repeating the lead ball-feather dropping experiments on the basis of refining measurement of their different rates of fall.

4.3.1. The Energy-food Nexus of the Canadian Atlantic Provinces

The starting point is some set of actual conditions, as given by some definite historical development. Although the particulars of a given development path are specific, the path

---

[19] Current U.S. vice president Dick Cheney, when he was CEO of Halliburton, was heard by several score of witnesses declaring from the rostrum of an offshore oil and gas seminary in Halifax, Canada in May 1999 that "we do War and Peace." See "Eastern Canadian Natural Gas Conference Report" from the June 1999 edition of *Atlantic Progress* magazine.

itself is generic to a certain set of political and economic arrangements that prevail across a broad range of different local, regional, national and sometimes even continental conditions.

In this chapter, the reference set of conditions are those of the coastal fisheries and offshore oil and gas development of the four Atlantic provinces of Canada: Newfoundland and Labrador, Nova Scotia, Prince Edward Island and New Brunswick. These provinces form the country's northwest Atlantic littoral, and the inland sea known as the Gulf of St. Lawrence. The fishery of the region is 500 years old. Offshore oil and gas development in the area is 35 years old. The rise of the latter from occasional exploratory drilling to full-time exploration and actual production was greatly facilitated during the 1990s by destroying a large mass of the productive forces of the former.

The regulating force governing both activities is the Canadian federal (national) government. As far as constitutional legality goes, developments on the regulatory front since the 1990s in both fields have entered a zone in which exceptions become the rule by top-down decree. The Canadian constitution in theory provides that resources like fish and fossil fuels should normally be the exclusive jurisdiction of the provincial territory in which they occur. However, during as well as since the Cold War, Canada's Atlantic ocean access has become strategically very important to the United States and the conduct of its foreign policy. In response the Canadian government, as a U.S.-dependent ally, has subordinated the affected provinces' interests in, and concerns for, these resources to those of imperial and superpower politics. The capital staked by the Canadian business community at the table of the Great Powers, entitling it to join their game, is the 200-mile limit or "exclusive economic zone". On the Atlantic side of the Canadian land-mass, this zone represents almost one third of the land area of the rest of Canada, the world's third-largest national territory. Here lies the secret of what has actually rendered provincial powers, constitutional law, and the democratic rights of the Canadian people to participate in decision-making entirely and truly irrelevant: alongside the Canadian government's asserted exclusive authority within the country over matters pertaining to this vastly unexplored treasure trove of resources and raw materials, the control over hundreds of billions of dollars' worth of financial capital is concentrated in the hands of the tiny elite who get to represent "Canada" on these matters at the international level.

Local or Canadian markets are only incidentally served, if at all, by the material production in either of these sectors. The fishery production of the region has always served and been oriented to world markets of whatever the leading Great Power in the Canadian state. When Britain was the leading Great Power, the fish landed in Newfoundland (then a separate British colony) and the other three provinces was destined for markets of the British Empire. As the United States displaced Britain's role in the Canadian state, these fish products went to U.S.-dominated markets. Quantitatively, the Canadian domestic market for these fish products never exceeded ten percent of the landed or processed value.

When it comes to oil and gas, the Canadian role is even more skewed towards serving a single foreign master. The oil from the Hibernia field off Newfoundland is produced entirely for the U.S. market. Some of it is feedstock for the refinery at Come by Chance, at the head of Placentia Bay in southeastern Newfoundland, and the refined product then goes to U.S. markets. The gas piped ashore from the Sable Island fields near the coast of Nova Scotia is sent by a pipeline directly to the New England states with only insignificant quantities reserved for less than half a dozen small urban markets along the pipeline's route on the Canadian side of the border, in Nova Scotia and New Brunswick. This is no longer just production for the world market of a dominant Great Power, but a compensation for Canada accepting a present and future *de facto* annexation to the United States. When it comes to modeling an "economics of intangibles" rooted in historical and contemporary reality, it suggests consideration should be given to an annexation factor, A^+ ("big-A plus"), when calculating effective values and amounts gained or lost in this sector.

4.3.2. Canada's Role as an Energy Corridor for the United States

The actual conditions of offshore oil and gas production along Canada's east coast disclose much that stands 180 degrees opposite to the assumptions informing the economic models employed in planning their development – all of which make no allowance whatever for A^+. First and foremost, this production is a byproduct and servant of the needs of the United States. In natural gas production, marketing and pricing, the United States has developed a cartelising model that has successfully presented itself as a model and high point of deregulated competition. However, it is also a model for annexing neighbouring countries like Canada and Mexico. The U.S. supplies its market in amanner that facilitates pressures to annex, in the form of integration of these countries' energy production.

According to EIA data, From 1949 to 1973, annual market consumption of natural gas in the United States increased from about 5 trillion cubic feet to a peak of more than 22 trillion cubic feet. Throughout most of the 1980s and 1990s, it fell back, but resumed a second steady upward climb to its next peak in 1998, at about 23.1 trillion cubic feet. Two factors account for most of this post-war expansion: the explosion of the housing market throughout the United States, especially during the main years of the "baby boom" (1945-1960), and the expansion of medium and heavy industry beyond the coal-and-steel belts of the US northeast and Great Lakes to new urban growth centers of the West Coast, the "right-to-work" states in the South and the tremendous expansion of population and industry in Texas and Florida. By the mid-1990s, with some 70 percent of new homes in the U.S. being heated with natural gas, the residential services market was saturated. The only way towards further growth was to raise the price of gas, but this was a commodity extensively locally regulated throughout the country. Accordingly, between 1978 and 1985, the United States instituted "deregulation" of natural gas pricing. To obtain official certification from all the relevant government bodies that they were no longer in a cartelising situation actually or potentially, the natural gas producers divested themselves of any significant further financial involvement pipeline and-or other distribution networks and infrastructure (Udall and Andrews 2001).

Arguing that they would now need to be able to compensate their operations for losses in future revenue to be anticipated from declining demand for residential service, the gas producers were now free to re-combine in setting the wellhead price. This so-called "Henry Hub" price, based on delivery at the main hub on the US Gulf Coast (whence comes some 60 percent of US-produced natural gas) quadrupled in 2000. Far from ensuring themselves against future losses of revenue, the producers were actually harvesting the windfall created by deregulation of electricity prices, a phenomenon whose consequences would prove most dramatic in California with the Enron scandal. It was in order to keep electric power generation profitable in a deregulated market that natural gas was increasingly substituted for oil and coal, thereafter to be produced increasingly as a feedstock commodity for the electricity-generating market, amid an ongoing decline in the portion of overall revenue from home heating markets concentrated in the Boston-to-Washington corridor, where population continues to fall. (Udall and Andrews: *ibid.*).

In 2000-2001, the collapse of Enron – headquartered in Houston at the centre of the natural gas boom, but doing most of its business in California in the form of Ponzi-type "contracts for future supplies of electric power" – ended this boom. With its collapse, natural gas prices fell back 50 percent from their historic highs. Superprofits were garnered in any event, however, as a result of the confluence that winter of an extremely cold and extended heating season in the US northeast alongside the Enron-induced brownouts and blackouts suffered by residents of California. The United States' "long-standing glut of natural gas and electrical capacity, along with the world's spare oil capacity, vanished simultaneously in spring 2000. .. Fueled by cheap energy, the U.S. economy grew 60 percent since 1986, an astounding five percent in 2000 alone. Gas consumption grew 36 percent over that period. But it was the demand for electricity … up 5.4 percent in 1998, an astounding rate for such a large economy … that has had the biggest impact on gas prices. To meet .. growing electricity needs, utilities have ordered 180,000 Megawatts of gas-fired power plants to be installed by 2005. It was a logical thing to do: gas is the cheapest, cleanest way to convert fossil fuel to electricity. But if ordering one gas turbine makes perfect sense, ordering 1,000 is a recipe for disaster. No one in the utility industry asked the key question: can we produce enough gas to run all those plants? Many experts think the answer is no."

Reproducing a previously published 20-year projection of natural gas consumption in the U.S. for the period 1997-2017 estimating relatively moderate increases in annual industrial consumption (from about 8.7 to slightly more than 9 trillion cubic feet), residential use (from 5 to 5.5 trillion cubic feet), and commercial applications (from 3.2 to 3.5 trillion cubic feet), Udall and Andrews (*ibid.*) also point out that gas for electricity generation was predicted to nearly triple over the same period, from about 3.2 to more than 9.1 trillion cubic feet per annum, at a time when pipeline infrastructure is also in need of major overhaul throughout the United States. "Most date to post-World II, when Gulf Coast supplies were tied to markets in the Midwest and New England. Since pipelines are prone to corrosion, beer keg-sized diagnostic tools called 'pigs' are pushed through the lines to search for weak spots, not always in time. In August, 2000, a pipeline exploded in New Mexico, killing 10 people, and crimping gas deliveries to California. Many aging pipelines need to be rebuilt, replaced, or expanded to deliver more gas to urban areas, where the new fleet of gas-fired power plants will be moored. In December 2000, gas delivered to L.A. briefly fetched $69, equivalent to $400 for a barrel of oil." (Udall and Andrews *ibid.*).

By stepping up the tapping of Canadian supplies, the U.S. natural gas industry averts many of the additional costs, especially legal and regulatory, associated with pipeline replacement on existing U.S. rights of way. This holds the profoundest implications for the American interest in such relatively marginal frontier projects as that undertaken in The Gully zone of the Sable Island field along the Atlantic coast of the Canadian province of Nova Scotia. This gas find was developed entirely with US markets in mind. Its estimated life is only about 20 years. In late 2005, after six years' production, the total recoverable reserve estimate was reduced to about 1.3 trillion cu ft (from more than 3.6 trillion cu ft during the exploration phase of the mid-to-late 1990s). The principal enduring longer-term asset developed along with the extraction of this reservoir seems to be the Maritimes and Northeast pipeline. This runs from Goldboro, Guysborough County, NS where Sable Island gas is brought ashore, west-northwestwards across central and northern Nova Scotia through the neighbouring province of New Brunswick, then across the international border with the State of Maine southwest-wards as far as the Boston-area suburb of Everett MA, the nearest U.S. gas pipeline distribution point.

Map 4-1. (left). How the U.S. gas pipeline industry originally aimed to annex part of Canada's 200-mile limit is disclosed by the Canadian Dept. of Energy & Natural Resources (NRCan Report, 2004). This scheme was abandoned in late 2005.

All this suggests yet another hitherto unexamined reason for the intense rise of U.S. interest in liquefied natural gas (LNG). On several occasions from the mid- to late-1990s, local authorities were trying to arrange such development directly at portside storage facilities in existing large U.S. urban centers on the Eastern Seaboard. When efforts to obtain public financing for such developments failed to obtain support, local referenda were arranged in rural locales on the southern Maine coast that went down to defeat as well. With the bringing of Sable gas and its pipeline delivery system on time and within budget, Canada as an LNG corridor became the next most attractive option, the fact that the Maritimes and Northeast pipeline was already built and paid for, but its unused capacity was increasing as Sable gas production declined, proving most attractive of all. Another highly important factor was and remains to date the fact that the bottom-up democratic traditions of the New England town meeting, which the gas producers could not defeat, are utterly alien to both the law and custom in Canada, which inherited both from an essentially colonial top-down system created by the British and therefore makes no provision for a local referendum process to bind a spending or investment decision by a public governmental body in any way whatsoever.

On this point, a survey of the Canadian energy industry vetted and published in the winter of 2005 by the U.S. Energy Information Administration noted, in a highly misleading way, that "while not without controversy, the Canadian LNG terminals have not met with the same level of resistance from local residents and environmentalists that similar facilities in the U.S. have faced" (United States 2005) – the reality of the "resistance from local residents and environmentalists that similar facilities in the U.S. have faced" being those local referenda that defeated these schemes, and the lack of "the same level of resistance from local residents and environmentalists" in Canada being the fact that such tendencies enjoy no comparable bottom-up, democratic outlet, a fact left unmentioned anywhere in the EIA's online review or other such reviews.

Earlier in 2005, in connection with the Maritimes and Northeast pipeline, two proposals won approval in principle (*i.e.*, approval pending a formal environmental impact assessment) from Canada's National Energy Board:

- A facility that would connect to this pipeline to be owned and operated by Irving Oil Ltd. This company is Canada's largest privately-held vertically-integrated oil refiner and marketer and operator of the country's largest refinery (250,000 bbl/day). It is based at Saint John, NB, where Irving already maintains its own ocean tanker loading and unloading facility known as "Canaport". The estimated throughput is 500 million cubic feet per day (United States: *ibid.*).
- A facility capable of delivering twice as much as the Irving project – one billion cubic feet per day – is proposed for at Bear Point, NS outside Point Tupper/Port Hawkesbury, Richmond County NS – near the pipeline's Goldboro terminus – to be owned and operated by Anadarko Petroleum. This is a U.S. company which is already involved extensively in the Alberta oil patch in the Western Canada Sedimentary Basin, on the other side of the continent from Nova Scotia (Website 2).

Both proposals combined would effectively add 1.5 billion cubic feet per day (bcfd) to the 1.0 bcfd from the Sable gas field: the additional portion from LNG would increase while that from the Sable project tailed off, and as the Canadian Atlantic ports are ice-free, deliveries could continue year round. In total, including schemes for bringing LNG to Quebec during the seven or eight-month shipping season in the St Lawrence River, there are plans to build over 4.0 bcfd of LNG receiving capacity by 2008 in eastern Canada alone. (At this writing in September 2005, there are still several further LNG-terminal proposals on the Pacific and Atlantic coasts waiting to go before the National Energy Board.) Even before the latest Maritimes-based projects mentioned above, a $1.3 billion, 0.5 bcfd LNG terminal at Gros Cacouna, Quebec, along the St. Lawrence River to be built by Petro-Canada and TransCanada Pipelines was approved, apparently in connection with the signing of a deal between Petro-Canada and Russia's Gazprom to feed the Gros Cacouna terminal from Gazprom's Shtokman field (United States: *ibid.*) This and other proposals are documented in Table 4-3.

Table 4-3. Proposed LNG terminals in Canada (NRCan Report, 2004)

Operator (Name)	Location	Send-Out Capacity (Bcf/d)	Earliest Start Date	Status
Projects Under Review				
Anadarko Petroleum Corporation (Bear Head)	Canso Strait, NS	1.00	2007	Received federal-provincial environmental assessment approval in August 2004.
Irving Oil Limited (Canaport)	Saint John, NB	1.00	2007	Received federal-provincial environmental assessment approval in August 2004.
Enbridge/Gaz Métro/ Gaz de France (Rabaska)	Beaumont, QC	0.50	2008	Undergoing federal-provincial environmental assessment. Process commenced June 2004.
Keltic Petrochemicals	Goldboro, NS	0.50	2008	Undergoing federal-provincial environmental assessment. Process commenced August 2004.
Galveston LNG	Kitimat, BC	0.61	2008	Undergoing federal-provincial environmental assessment. Process commenced August 2004.
TransCanada/Petro-Canada (Cacouna Energy Project)	Gros Cacouna, QC	0.50	2009	Undergoing federal-provincial environmental assessment. Process commenced September 2004.
Other Announced Projects				
Westpac Terminals	Prince Rupert, BC	0.3	2009	Conceptual. Project not yet under review.
Statia Terminals	Canso Strait, NS	0.50	2009	Conceptual. Project not yet under review.
TOTAL CANADA		4.91		

Sources: Industry press and company websites.

Canada currently supplies about 16 percent of natural gas consumed in the U.S. (US Department of Energy, 2005), which represents 57-60 percent of all the natural gas produced in Canada in 2000-2003 (Canada 2004).[20] Clearly Canada is not producing gas for itself and exporting what it cannot consume. Rather it is producing gas for export while domestic consumption develops only incidentally. With the 400-km Maritimes and Northeast pipeline, the story is the same: more than 99 per cent of current throughput goes straight to the U.S. Some has been promised but nothing actually reserved for limited local markets, mostly industrial, in suburban Halifax-Dartmouth in Nova Scotia, and Moncton and Saint John in New Brunswick, comprising a total population of about 600,000. The question arises as to whether the world to become witness to a new and rather disturbing feature of the increasing embroilment of Canadian resources and territory for this latest phase of U.S. industrial expansion. Table 4-4 documents the pattern of the evidence.

These developments follow a period in which, from about 2001 until late 2005, Canadian Superior Energy Inc., in collaboration with a U.S. pipeline developer El Paso, aspired to develop the pipeline pictured in Map 4-1, along the Atlantic coast between the Sable gas field, Shelburne (Nova Scotia), and then again following the coast down to the U.S. state of Connecticut. This line would have annexed the entire offshore zone – the Canadian 200 mile limit – off the coast of Nova Scotia to the United States. The evidence of this claim is the landing point of the line in Shelburne NS. No Canadian authority could interrupt the flow of gas in that pipeline without triggering a claim by the pipeline operators against the Canadian

---

[20] Popular Canadian standup comedian Dave Broadfoot joked some years ago that Canadians may actually be "evolving [from] being mere 'hewers of wood and drawers of water' to 'passers of gas' as well."

government under the terms of Chapter 11 of the North American Free Trade Agreement (NAFTA).

Table 4-4. Comparative data on Canadian natural gas production for export and domestic markets (NRCan Report, 2005)

	2003 (Bcf)	2002 (Bcf)	Change (Bcf)	Change (%)
US Residential	5,085	4,890	195	4%
US Commercial	3,127	3,103	24	1%
US Industrial	6,966	7,557	-591	-8%
US Electrc Power	4,929	5,672	-742	-13%
US Other[1]	1,769	1,796	-27	-2%
Total US Demand	*21,877*	*23,018*	*-1,141*	*-5%*
US LNG Exports	64	63	1	2%
US Exports to Mexico	333	263	70	27%
Total US Gas Disposition	*22,274*	*23,344*	*-1,070*	*-5%*
Canada Residential	675	620	55	9%
Canada Commercial	518	486	32	7%
Canada Industrial	1,029	970	59	6%
Canada Electric Power	282	261	21	8%
Canada Other[2]	410	399	11	3%
Total Canadian Demand	*2,914*	*2,736*	*178*	*7%*
Total N.A. Demand	24,791	25,754	-963	-4%
Total N.A. Disposition	25,188	26,080	-892	-3%

Sources: EIA, StatCan Notes: [1]Other includes pipeline and distribution use, lease and plant fuel and vehicle fuel. [2]Other includes pipeline compressor fuel, processing fuel and line losses.

This chapter of the NAFTA specifies an unconditional and unqualified, absolute right of private property over and above any policy changes of a government party to NAFTA that might affect the enjoyment of its property by any corporation engaged in legally allowed commerce under NAFTA. All producers sending gas down this pipeline would enjoy equal protection from any alternative plans of the Canadian government, serving effectively to annex the entire production zone offshore to the United States. The only way out would be either for Canada to renounce adherence to the NAFTA, with all manner of potential and unforeseeable consequences for bilateral trade and investment, or – as happened in this case – for the private sector proponent to abandon the pipeline scheme.[21]

Like the situation with east coast offshore oil and gas, the overall Canada-U.S. energy nexus is unidirectional but nevertheless attended by serious internal contradictions. Canada as a source of natural gas for the United States will become increasingly problematic to the extent that synthetic crude oil exports from Canada become a larger part of projected U.S. "energy security" and security of supply. The fact is the key to expanding production to meet such enhanced demand for synthetic crude will involve diverting more and more of Alberta's natural gas reserves to processing tar sand bitumen, the raw material source of synthetic crude. "Canada's proven natural gas reserves, 56.1 [trillion cubic feet] as of January 2005, only rank 19th in the world. These reserves have decreased by 13.3 percent since 1996, and at

---

[21] At the end of 2005, as the other schemes to convert Canadian territory onshore into an LNG corridor for the U.S. began to materialise, El Paso folded its tent, closing for good its last office in southwest Nova Scotia.

current rates, production will completely deplete reserves in 8.6 years." What could cause such a drastic depletion? "The oil sands industry is heavily reliant upon water and natural gas, which is necessary in both the extraction of bitumen from oil sands and the upgrading of bitumen to synthetic oil" (United States: *ibid.*). The vulnerability of existing marketing mechanisms of the entire "downstream" sector of the North American oil and gas sector to increases in natural gas prices or sharp reductions in natural gas supply would be extremely unevenly distributed, with the oil sands industry likely to experience the most critical repercussions.

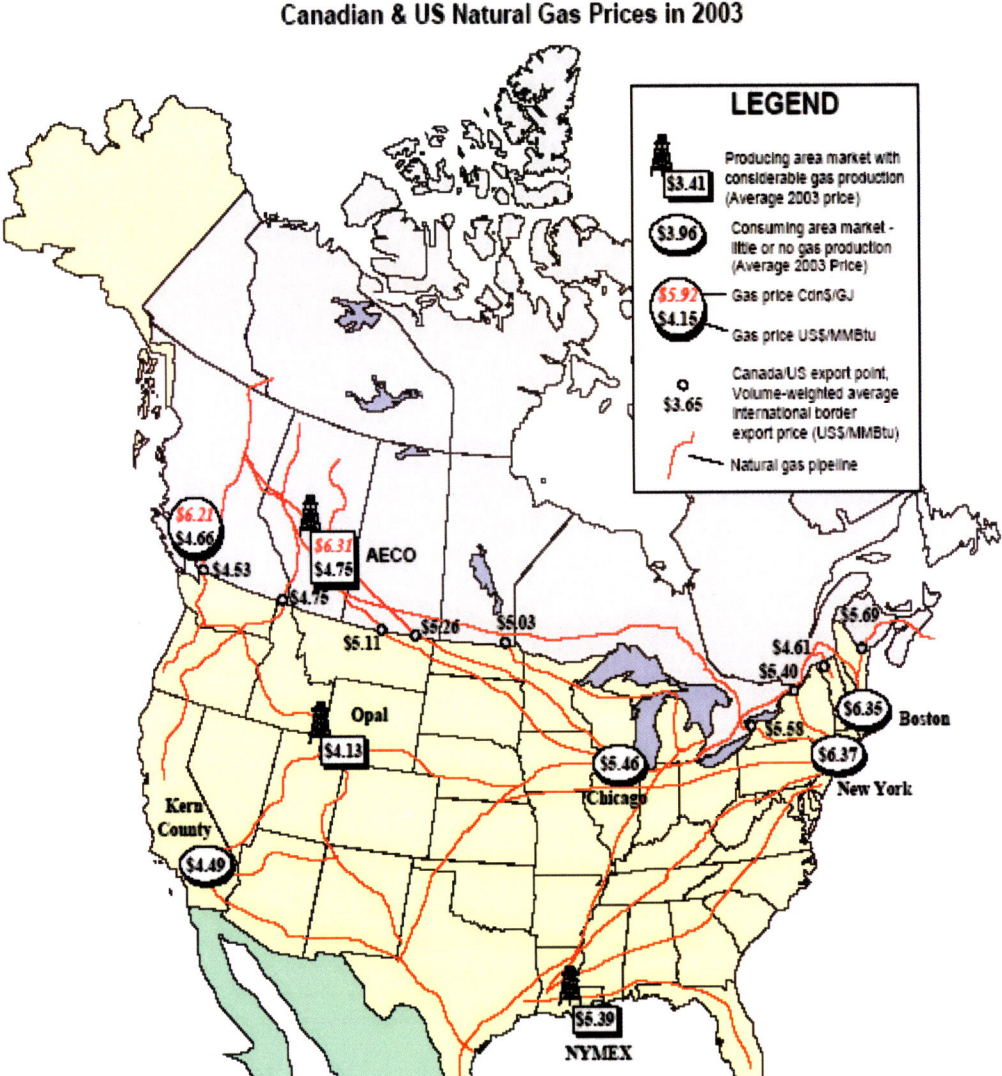

Map 4-2. The important price-points of the Canadian side of this integrated market are not cities, but only the toll-gates where the gas crosses the border into the U.S. (Canada 2004).

This information strengthens the case for the interpolation the authors believe to be most consistent with the known facts, *viz.*, that, short of new discoveries of natural gas in Canada, the main use of Canadian territory by the U.S. gas market in coming years will be for transiting LNG from its ports and pipelines to U.S. markets. Adding further credibility to that scenario is a published projection of LNG's share of the U.S. gas market rising five times over the next 15 years to 2020 (Canada: *ibid.*). The profitability of such arrangements is clearly premised on utilising new / future supplies gas increasingly and mainly for electrical power generation and related industrial use, and less and less for residential or other commercial uses (*e.g.*, as an alternative to gasoline).

It would seem clear, then, that one major premise built into meeting expanded U.S. market demands for natural gas by supplying LNG is indeed an increasing overall integration and annexation of Canadian territory, resources and resource-delivery infrastructure by and for U.S. interests, not confined to oil and gas. Map 4-2 illustrates the considerable degree to which Canadian natural gas marketing arrangements have already become integrated into the U.S.

This is a remarkable annexationist feature built into the evolution of U.S. energy policy. It is something not seen at all in the long-term natural gas delivery contracts negotiated earlier in 2005 between the Islamic Republic of Iran and the People's Republic of China or between the gigantic Russian gas syndicate led by Gazprom and its various governmental and corporate customers in the European Union or Japan.

The relative underdevelopment of resource extraction infrastructure in general in Canada beyond the existing populated areas is driving this trend. Map 4-3 clearly indicates how focused the interest in Canadian gas actually is upon the current state of relative underdevelopment compared to the U.S. The proportion of gas resources in Canada that are undiscovered or not yet in production is far ahead of the same proportions on the U.S. side of the picture.

4.3.3. Separating the Short-term to Reject the Long-term

The outstanding overall feature of the case of eastern Canada, and of this nexus around which its productive economic activities have formed, is that primary raw material extraction takes place without reference to the needs of the people of the area or even the country. Whatever limited secondary processing has arisen alongside, in the fishery for example, is increasingly dependent on foreign-supplied raw material. The end market for the vast bulk of either the primary raw material or any finished product is not the population of the country in which the raw materials are being extracted or refined. Instead of producing locally for local as well as global needs, the economic model in place produces entirely for selected high-end-value segments of the global market in order to obtain revenue from which to purchase whatever is needed from elsewhere to meet local needs.[22]

---

[22] The absence of any consciousness among the corporate and policy elites about this problem and what it portends for the long-term as well as the short term of Canadians' existence as a people, or Canada as a country, is profound and disturbing. The following blocks of references comprise a sublist, from an almost comprehensive list, of the most informative and complete newspaper articles covering current-affairs developments in, and analysis of, Canada's oil and gas development and markets, covering the period 6 Apr 2005 through 27 Apr 2006. They were compiled from *The Globe and Mail,* Canada's leading national newspaper of record based in the country's financial hub, Toronto, incorporating a daily "Report on Business" and indexed and accessible through libraries as well as online from the newspaper's website. The single outstanding feature of the collection as a whole is an almost total lack of any reflection about the fact of the existence of the planet beyond Canada

This orientation is an inherently unsustainable one, no different in principle than turning all energy sources into electricity, regardless of the real costs in terms of unnecessary waste and accumulating inefficiencies, in order to maximise the revenue stream that the biggest, or best-connected, player(s) may capture. This unsustainability itself can and should be tangibly accounted; for purposes of modeling a reality-based "economics of intangibles", the unnecessary waste and accumulated inefficiency inflicted on the region as a result of not applying any of these resources to strengthen self-reliant development can be counted as a B^- ("big-B minus") factor.

The reference frame described earlier in Chapter 2 as t = "right now" is the reference frame to which extraction/harvesting, refining/processing and sale of tangible products in the short term has become restricted. Here this aspect of model-building is treated as a "separation-rejection" process: the *separation* of the needs of the short-term from those of the longer term, coupled with subsequent *rejection* of any weight or significance for the long-term. For the moment, in the real world economy, the resource base of the northwest Atlantic has become tied to arrangements in which large-scale extraction of crude oil and natural gas has entirely marginalised the formerly most profitable segments of the commercial fishery.

In the worlds of social and economic analysis and commentary as well as model-building, this marginalisation has been ascribed generally to Nature, *i.e.*, the fish stocks "disappeared". In 1992, the Canadian government banned coastal communities in eastern Canada from catching groundfish (cod, etc), and inaugurated The Atlantic Groundfish Strategy. This scheme, known by its initials as TAGS, was widely hailed as an income support program for the fishery equivalent to paying farmers not to plant new crops. After entire communities throughout coastal Newfoundland, Nova Scotia and New Brunswick were rendered dependent on these payments, the government disclosed that fishermen would not be allowed to resume catching groundfish species, even if the codfish stocks revived, because ... there had allegedly been "too many fishermen chasing too few fish"(*sic*) all along.

In the coastal communities, it felt as though the last props were being kicked out from underneath their livelihood, way of life and right-to-be. At the same time their catches had been in long-term decline. Perhaps the biological stock itself was gone? In the circumstances, most kept their heads down. Very few (a number that included one of the authors) dared openly to question the equating of commercial collapse with biological desrtruction of the fish stocks.

---

and the United States, as though the rest of the world exists only in relation to Canada-U.S. concerns: (Brethour *et al.* 2005a-u; 2006a-g), (Chase *et al.* 2005a-d; 2006a-b), and (Ebner *et al.* 2005a-hh; 2006a-l).

Nothing could be starker than the contrast with coverage of oil and gas questions by the elite business press of the United States, in this case *The Wall Street Journal* of New York, in which every other part of the world is assumed to stand, today or in the future, in a dependent or otherwise subordinate relationship to the leading U.S. corporate entities of this economic sector. The following collections of references are replete with, and remarkable for, their copious and rich examples of these calculations. Nevertheless, they are as one with the Canadian elites' prioritising the short-term over the long term: (Bahree *et al.* 2005a-g; 2006a-g), (Ball *et al.* 2005a-g; 2006a-g), (Berman *et al.* 2005a-e), (Carlyle 2005a-c; 2006a-b), (Cummins *et al.* 2005a-d; 2006), (Fialka *et al.* 2005a-f; 2006a-h), (Gold *et al.* 2005a-g), and (Luhnow *et al.* 2006a-e). Again, these form a sublist of a more comprehensive collection from 2005-2006.

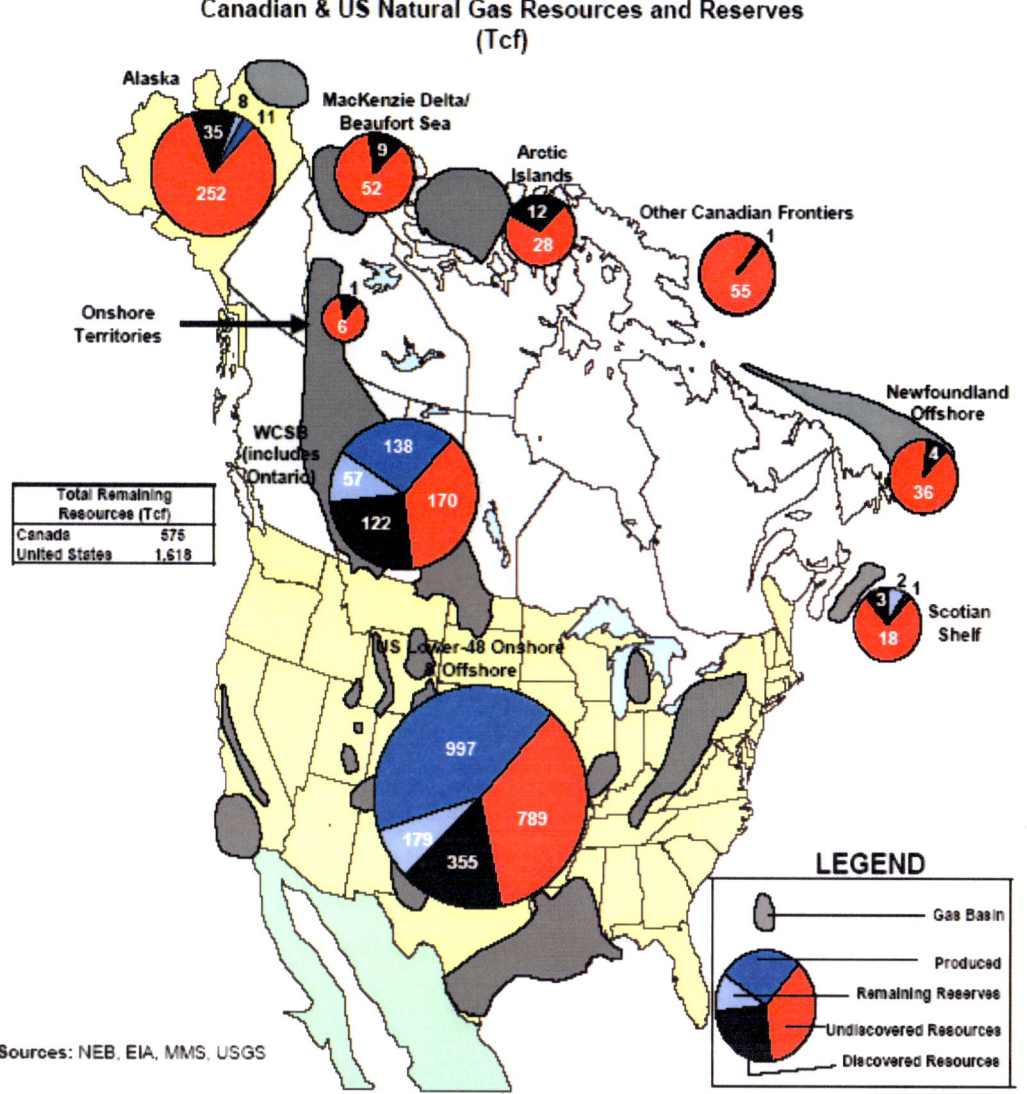

Map 4-3. Deregulated free market – or integration and subordination? (NRCan Report, 2004).

Recently, in the internationally-acknowledged work of Myers and Worm (2003), the evidence has now emerged to at least strongly suggest that such ascribing of catch declines to biological decline itself was probably just another planted story. This story has proven remarkably easy to plant and even more difficult to uproot despite the ocean of doubts that are emerging about its veracity. In the face of repeated demands, beginning in the 1970s, to authorise any investigation of the facts, the relevant authorities in Canada, the U.S. and Europe failed to establish even whether the collapse of fish stocks was biological or not. Myers and his coworkers were focusing on establishing the pathway to the disappearance of shark, tuna and other populations of large sea mammals when they stumbled unintentionally upon evidence that depths and regions of the Atlantic basin long assumed either not to be, or incapable of, supporting marine life on any significant scale turned out to be teeming with marine life. New data are capable of overthrowing not only the conclusions drawn from earlier quantities and runs of less complete data, but possibly also any of the assumptions which informed the gathering of that earlier data. Thus, as a result of leaving open – in the sense of ambiguous and uninvestigated – the question as to whether the increasingly evident shortfalls in northwest Atlantic catches of commercially valuable species reflected the physical destruction of the biological stock and its basis, or reflected instead only the departure of these species (and-or some portion of their food supplies) to survivable habitats within the ocean in which harvesting activity was absent or present only on a scale whose impacts could be much reduced, assumptions about the relationship between whatever is inherently sustainable in an ecosystem and whatever is only relatively sustainable about the technologies harnessed to harvest certain selected resources within that ecosystem have yet to be revisited.

This became, in effect, a matter of systematically maintained ignorance. One of its results was that, as a matter of how developments unfolded in the real world economy, the actual specifics of the failure of an almost 500-year old fishery to sustain itself commercially were never modeled in terms of the overall mass of knowledge that had accumulated over the centuries about the various fish stocks of the northwest Atlantic and their inter-relationships both with one another and with near-shore and offshore harvesting operations in various seasons. Hence, instead, the supplanting of the groundfish sector of the fishery by Big Oil became ascribed to the operations of mere, and sheer, Chance. This has subsequently been spun into a tale of not just Chance as blind happenstance, but as positively Good Fortune, perhaps even the economic salvation, for a hard-pressed region with limited prospects. Such setting of context prepares the planting of yet another story at some point in the future. (What has limited those prospects is precisely what is left unexplained, opening the door for the entire disinformation about "regional underdevelopment" which is discussed exhaustively in Chapter 2 *supra*.). For purposes of modeling a reality-based "economics of intangibles", the tangible measurable consequences stemming from the cultivation of such ignorance could be represented by some I_C ('big-I sub-C") factor, and the future economic losses projected and ascribed – through planted stories – to continuing with whatever was already working instead of handing over everything to the new carpetbaggers by a P_L ("big-P sub-L") factor.

Was offshore gas developed near the coast of eastern Nova Scotia, and oil off southeastern Newfoundland, simply in response to the discovery of "commercially feasible" deposits? The evidence of the context in which this development actually unfolded refutes the idea from several directions.

The commercial scale of the Sable oil and gas find off Nova Scotia was confirmed in 1970; that of Hibernia in 1979. Yet almost no development towards production ensued until the mid-1990s. At the time these discoveries were announced during the early and late 1970s, vertically-integrated fish harvesting-processing corporations backed by the federal government were crushing the last sources of localised community resistance to their monopolistic dictate, while striving both to contain the rising labour militancy of the trawler workforce in the main fishing towns and also work out a common front with the Canadian and US governments to drive the Soviet-bloc long-distance fleet out of the fishing grounds beyond the 12-mile territorial limit.

These discoveries were brought into production only after the groundfish moratorium of 1992 became general and permanent, that is: after the fishing grounds within the 200-mile limit were cleared of foreign, domestic corporate and individual fishing vessels, the communities' former implicit control over the supply of labour power for ocean-based activities had been demolished, and the United States sought to ensure and advance its role as the world's sole remaining superpower by annexing as much economic territory as possible. The financial participation of the Canadian government in raising PetroCan's participation from a five per cent to a 25 per cent stake in the Hibernia project as the Reichmann family pulled its Gulf Canada Resources investment out of Hibernia was arranged despite an official Canadian policy at the time to desist from investing in the private corporate sector in general and in oil and gas development in particular. The PetroCan investment was made public in early 1993, six months after the groundfish moratorium had been extended throughout all Atlantic Canada suggests by its very deliberateness some considerable premeditation on the part of both government and the corporate interests affected, in both in the fishery and the petroleum exploration sector. In the fishery sector, fishing fleets were retired from further fish-harvesting in this zone only for their corporate owners to be compensated by a fortuitous circumstance that developed throughout fish markets across the globe: in 1991-93, these markets were flooded with unsold inventories of processed and unprocessed fish catches of the bankrupt fishing fleets of the former Soviet Union, as literally hundreds of vessels from what had been the world's largest ocean-going fleet were constrained from returning to Russia until outstanding port fees were paid. The inventories were unloaded at distress prices, and the leading fishing corporations from Atlantic Canada, which had been great merchandising operations in the U.S. and certain world markets for decades before they had acquired fishing fleets, were quick in snapping them up. While 40,000 fishermen in the Atlantic region immediately lost their livelihood with the declaration of the moratorium, and hundreds of fishing communities basically went on welfare, the two largest companies responsible for more than 90 per cent of the vertically-integrated sector continued to accrue profits entirely on a mercantile basis of buying and selling the catches of others, without fishing themselves or operating their own trawling fleet.

In Chapters 2 and 3, a critique was developed to deal with the absence of any consideration of the role or significance of intangible components in economic affairs. The separation-rejection method of economic model-building which has been isolated here holds out serious consequences for elaborating and applying an economic theory that can account for what actually happens in the tangible realm. Accordingly, and retaining the eastern Canadian energy-food nexus as the main data-source and reference-point / reality-check, this chapter now proceeds to consider three directions from which, as a result of separation-rejection, the theoretical standing and importance of Nature as mother of all wealth was raped, leaving Labour as father of all wealth homeless and unprotected.

4.4. THE INTANGIBLE VALUE OF COASTAL FISHERMEN'S LIVES AND LABOUR IS PRICELESS – BUT ITS TANGIBLE VALUE TO BIG OIL IS NOWHERE DECLARED

With the imposition of the groundfish moratorium, there was an increasing evacuation of fishing vessels from the 200-mile limit. This opened the way for the oil and gas drilling and exploration rigs to occupy and command more and more of the economic space, using ever-larger-scale integration to carve new economic space. This has continued to date on a basis according to which only selected competitors will be able to give rise to actual production even though the field remained formally open to any operator to explore. Within the real-world economy of Canadian coastal fishing communities strung along the northwest Atlantic littoral, an erosion of the traditional fishing communities and their uprooting or replacement by the new order based on working in offshore industries formed the leading trend. Only this erosion, however, seems to have made any dent in the literature (House 1985, 1986).

For a certain period time, at the level of the Canada-Newfoundland Offshore Petroleum Board and the Canada-Nova Scotia Offshore Petroleum Board (which were established by the Canadian federal government to supervise sector-wide issues affecting employer-employee relations and company-province relations), certain trade union representatives occasionally hinted at the valued-added that the oil rig operators were appropriating without payment by compensating the workers only with the going wage for apprentices in this particular sector. Otherwise, however, the conventional line of analysis found in the literature has ignored the priceless intangible value of these communities' collective experience labouring in these dangerous waters.

Oil-gas exploration and production offshore appeared as the successor regime to that of the pre-moratorium fishery. The fishery of the preceding 30 years had waxed and then waned as a cockpit of contention between two superpowers, the United States and the Soviet Union, over which would retain absolute or veto control of the northwest Atlantic approaches to the North American continent. Within this collusion and contention among the Big Powers, Nature and Labour were exhausted in the pushing and shoving that enveloped the communities, governments and monopolies caught up defending their turf. Meanwhile, beneath the surface, Big Oil prepared a *coup*.

Recomputed on the basis of Statistics Canada data corrected from annual estimates for the provinces and the entire country, the figures in Table 4-7 reflect the growing role of Big oil in the Atlantic regional economy. The $4-billion net increase in the GDP of Newfoundland and Labrador alone – a greater than 25 per cent increase, incorporating a $6.5-billion increase in gross expenditures linked to offshore oil development – accounted for half the increase in the GDP of the entire region between 2001 and 2004; while the nearly $2-billion increase in the GDP for Nova Scotia incorporates an estimated $2.3-billion increase in gross expenditures linked to offshore gas development.

Of particular interest, however, is the fact that the regional GDP stood at 78.2 percent of the national GDP in 2001 and had barely moved, to 80.6 per cent, by 2004; thirty years earlier in 1974, when offshore oil and gas did not account for even one per cent of the regional GDP and fisheries occupied the position enjoyed by oil and gas today, the regional GDP stood at about 75 per cent of the national GDP. This snail's pace of change sharply refutes the claims of major progress of the region's share of national income attributable to getting rid of "old" allegedly backward technologies of raping fish stocks for "advanced" higher-level industrial technologies to plunder more "valuable" energy resources. Big Oil used its connections to the executive branch of the U.S. government on the one hand, and its easy dominance of relatively small and weak provincial governments in eastern Canada accounting for only 7.3 per cent of the national population, on the other, for the purpose of presenting the Canadian federal government with a *fait accompli*. The presence of Big Oil is premised less on a speculation about the rising world price of oil or the productive potential of the region than upon an increasing annexation by the United States of economically valuable parcels of Canadian-administered territory offshore, including a 200-mile limit in the northwest Atlantic which incorporates the largest single section of Continental Shelf of any such economic zone anywhere on earth.

Table 4-7. Evidence that Enormous Strides by Big Oil in Atlantic Canada Have Not Kept Pace With the Overall Expansion of the Canadian Economy as a Whole

	Gross Domestic Product – 2001		Gross Domestic Product – 2004	
	$ '000,000	*$ Per Capita*	*$ '000,000*	*$ Per Capita*
Nfld and Labrador	15,542		19,433	
Prince Edw'd Is.	3,665		4,023	
Nova Scotia	27,969		29,879	
New Brunswick	21,160		22,976	
Atlantic Region	*68,246*	*29,103*	*76,311*	*32,542*
Canada	*1,189,655*	*37,206*	*1,290,185*	*40,351*

The full significance of Big Oil's presence cannot be properly grasped without an understanding of the origins of the Canadian east coast fisheries, and the relative positions of Nature and Labour prior to the transformation of competitive capitalism of the colonial period into the oligopolistic capitalism of quasi-monopolies and cartels emerging after the First World War.

Although commonly examined in terms of the isolation, and marginalisation, of individual outports and sub-regions of the four Atlantic provinces, the east coast fisheries' actual historical development witnessed the formation from the outset of definite, distinct social classes – one class grouping together the interests of outport and city merchants, local politicians and buyers connected to final market destinations abroad, the other class grouping all those performing the productive labour of fishing but also dividing them into communities isolated in rural fishing ports and lacking convenient means of communication, transport or other social intercourse. The former maintained and advanced their positions by crushing the latter and grinding them down. How this was carried out, and resisted, shaped the resulting fishery of the northwest Atlantic littoral, including its current marginalisation in Canada's Atlantic region by the "black gold rush" – the frenzy to develop offshore oil and gas. This completely hidden, intangible consequence of such high-level development of a valued and extremely tangible resource serves as yet another important lesson about proceeding with the development of economic tangibles without any concern about their intangible element.

4.4.1. The Case of Newfoundland – Stripping the People of Rights

This process was extremely pronounced in Newfoundland, where – from 1583 to 1750 – year-round settlement of fishermen in coastal communities was forcibly banned by the Royal Navy. In the mid-18th century, when continued enforcement became more trouble than it was worth, in those communities where merchants resided this system was replaced with a single-level court system, *i.e.*, no recourse to appeals. A magistrate on his own could bring an action, or any person of property could lay a complaint: such was the daily state-terrorist method of colonial rule wherever the working people attained any freedom of movement beyond working for some master. In the fishing outports, there was no need for these forces of law and order: these locales wallowed in enforced isolation, without roads and without independent means of transport. The small open boats that individuals could afford to build or maintain were far too risky to take out in ocean waters most of the year. The rhythms of life were dictated entirely by a merchant (or his "factor") in St John's (or one of the handful of other larger centres around Conception or Trinity Bay), purchasing once a year the entire landed and dried salt cod for the season for transshipment to foreign markets. At considerable profit to the merchants of Bristol, England who controlled the transatlantic traffic in African slaves, the island's millions of quintals of dried salt fish were eventually delivered to the cotton, sugar and other agricultural plantations of the southern united States, British West Indies and Brazil to feed the work force. (Prowse 1896)

The Canadian government has left no stone unturned to enhance its reputation as a pursuer of war criminals and promoter of international-level tribunals to deal with war crimes. Mme Louise Arbour, today a member of the Supreme Court of Canada, prepared much of the formal case presented against Slobodan Milosevic at the special International Criminal Court convened to try him for war crimes. However, while NATO was bombing former Yugoslavia in the mid-to-late 1990s, the groundfish crisis of the east coast fishery was carving its deepest scars in the life and society of the people of Newfoundland – starting with laying off 40,000 fishermen from any further right to a livelihood in the fishery. This suggests the Canadian judicial system needs to unfolds a further new category of justice – that of "peace crimes" – to address social liability and responsibility for what the Canadian government and those mobilized in its service did, or allowed to be done, to the east coast fishery after the closure of the groundfish sector in July 1992 while otherwise occupied with making the world safe from war criminals. There is no shortage of individuals deserving of indictment. This closure ended almost 500 years of continuous fishing on the Grand Banks of Newfoundland, one of the richest natural food warehouses on the planet, at the stroke of a pen – while doing nothing whatsoever for the groundfish stocks.

From the end of the 18th to almost the end of the 20th century, the population of what became Canada rose 120 times from about one-quarter of a million to about 30 million, that of what became the United States 100 times from about 3 to about 300 million – and that of Newfoundland about seven times, from about 80,000 to about 560,000. But in fact the number of persons of Newfoundland descent in North America rose from almost nothing to 4 million. This is one of the largest internal diasporas of any North American ethnos. In these statistics of dispersal mark not only the price Newfoundlanders paid for their homeland being maintained as a staple food provider of the transatlantic slave trade of the British colonial system. These data also indicate, and indict, a certain hypocrisy on the part of Canadian governments that present themselves on the world's stage as the most persistent advocates of greater openness to the rights and needs of the world's immigrants and refugees.

The vast numbers of Newfoundlanders displaced across Canada in the dirtiest and most dangerous occupations might as well be Native Indians for all the concern that successive governments have shown in Ottawa or St. John's. Since joining the Canadian Confederation in 1949, the people of Newfoundland have reached the stage where there is not one family that does not have at least one member living in some other province or some American state because there was no employment available back home. The rise in per capita GDP in Newfoundland and Labrador since 1992 is attributed in the media and the scholarly literature to the rise in spending by Big Oil more than replacing the decline of the fishing industry. However, the true secret lies at least as much, if not more, in the greatly accelerated out-migration of tens of thousands who lost not only jobs in the fishery but the part-time off-season jobs they also used to fill within the province's forestry and mining sectors. The GDP per capita must rise that much more dramatically if, atop everything else, the number of heads to be counted also goes down. In the decennial Canadian census, Newfoundland remains the only province to have lost population from 1971 to 1981, from 1981 to 1991, and from 1991 to 2001. This open wound, rather than the statistics of the oil patch's expansion on The Rock, remains far more telling about the underlying reality.

4.4.2. Origins of the Permanently Temporary Groundfish Moratorium – Stealing the Fruits of People's Labour

What happened to the Canadian northwest Atlantic fisheries in 1992 and since is unprecedented only in its scale, and even then not in the scale of the crisis of the fish stocks nut in the ferocity of the contention of monopoly groups with divergent interests aided and abetted by tens of billions of dollars in private capital and sometimes entire governments in their service. The scale of the devastation inflicted on the lives and livelihoods of Newfoundlanders was particularly unprecedented, but the vulnerability of that society to such an assault had been historically conditioned over the preceding half-millennium. After a little more than 50 years as a province in the Canadian Confederation, it can hardly come as a surprise to find Newfoundlanders resuming serious discussion about some kind of future that would be truly independent of outside control. The Newfoundland economy's widely-touted "salvation through oil and gas" is storing up considerable troubles and conflicts down the road both within Newfoundland and Labrador as well as within Canada as a whole.

Historically, the Newfoundland people were placed repeatedly on the rack by the British colonial system and its agents in the colony, enduring a number of stages in the development of foreign dictate, marked by moments in which methods of exploitation and subjugation were further refined. Newfoundland was supposed to become a "plantation" of the first British Empire. "Plantations" were commercial concessions deeded by the monarch to syndicates of colonial adventurers. Many were encouraged under the Stuart dynasty (James I and Charles I) and vested with a royal monopoly over all the material wealth they might plunder in the colonial territory on the promise of encouraging settlement. The syndicates of Bristol merchants involved in the slave trade, however, wanted Newfoundland only for its fish. Seeing settlers as a source of competition, they withdrew sponsorship of settlement. The plantations which had been established were liquidated and Newfoundland came under the sway of the so-called "fishing admirals." This was a system for fastening an absolute dictatorship over all life and activity along the Newfoundland coast, aimed at enforcing the ban on settlement. It was exercised by the first fishing captain to reach the colony at the start of the fishing season, and bolstered by a parliamentary statute declaring settlement in Newfoundland a capital offense against the Crown. (Prowse: *ibid.*)

Establishing the means to exercise long-distance control was the earliest priority of the British Crown and Royal Navy in the colony. In 1660 the English Parliament passed the first of the so-called Navigation Acts. These converted Newfoundland into a fisheries appendage of the British empire for the next nearly 200 years (until the repeal of the Corn Laws in 1846).

The effect of these laws in Newfoundland was to prohibit development of any economic activity outside the fisheries on pain of heavy fines, lengthy prison terms and even death. In 1750, following its seizure of Louisbourg and establishment of Halifax as the North American base for its navy, the British replaced the "fishing admirals" with offshore patrols by the Royal Navy throughout Newfoundland waters along with appointing local magistrates in selected districts. This was part of a plan to use the control it had obtained in 1713 over the entrances to the St. Lawrence through the Maritimes and Newfoundland as a base from which to seize Quebec from France. In 1818, however, following the settlement of the Anglo-American War of 1812 and the collapse of the last French challenge, by Napoleon, to British marine supremacy, the Royal Navy was largely removed from Newfoundland waters.

The British Crown and commercial shipping interests had by now developed a symbiotic relationship in which the commercial shipping networks of English trade provided the support infrastructure and trained labour force for the Royal Navy. Thus with the ending of the system of fishing admirals, the Crown immediately proceeded to fasten another imperial yoke on Newfoundland, based this time on the control to be exercised by English seapower over all shipping throughout the Atlantic basin. Under this British hegemony, which would not be significantly adjusted until challenged by the U.S. and Canada during the 1870s, Newfoundland developed a world monopoly over the production of salted codfish, becoming the principal supplier of fish products to definite markets of particular importance to the British crown and overseas interests dependent on its protection, especially in the slave trade.

With superstructures and framework of control established and functioning, the economics of the fishery within the colony itself could be placed on a basis that secured the mercantile interest at minimal political or administrative cost to the British government. Until the middle of the nineteenth century, settlement was to be encouraged. A large labour force was enticed to remain fishing by instituting a payment system based on the principle of co-adventure. Fishermen would be paid according to their shares of the catch. On a steadily rising world market, fishermen and merchants developed extensive relations based on credit. In the inevitable crash which struck in 1837, all credit collapsed. Initially the recovery was so sharp that the merchants re-instituted the wages system in order to keep fishermen fishing for them, but the next slump hit in 1848 at the same moment that England inaugurated Free Trade and eliminated further colonial protection. The merchants shifted the new burdens and risks onto the fishermen in the form of the truck system. Fishermen bartered their catch for means of consumption, without cash changing hands. However, special areas of Newfoundland had been opened to the French and Americans under treaties arranged by the British a century before. When fishermen subverted the truck system by trading catches with the foreign vessels in those areas, the merchants at first demanded greater legislative autonomy from the British in order to forge other shackles onto the fishermen. They ended up striking a bargain with the British and Canadian railway syndicates, turning over enormous resource concessions as well as the keys to the colony's treasury in exchange for continued financing of their mercantile dictate over the fishermen.

Increasing Canadian involvements in Newfoundlanders' affairs emerged as an accidental and contradictory byproduct of 19th century transcontinental railway project finance withint the British Empire. In 1891 the Newfoundland colonial premier Robert Bond directly negotiated a reciprocity agreement with the American Secretary of State James Blaine. The Canadian government successfully intervened to nullify it. The merchants, now desperately squeezed for credit, joined with the foreign-financed railway and mining syndicates in 1892 to seek Confederation terms from the Canadian government. This fell apart when Ottawa refused to accept responsibility for the massive debts run up by the railway syndicate. Nevertheless, it was to mark the beginning of the end of the de facto political hegemony of the merchant clique. From 1894, when both of the colony's banks collapsed, until the end of the First World War, Anglo-Canadian finance seized Newfoundland by the throat. Economically the island became its vassal. Irrespective of the semi-autonomous political status which the colonial merchants had carved out for Newfoundland within the British empire, as a self-governing state enjoying so-called "responsible government", the island in economic terms became the vassal of modern monopoly capital from that time forward.

Local government was a shell, education and other public services non-existent, and thus the people of Newfoundland were bereft of any of the elementary means to look after their own affairs and put an end to outside interference. As a result, all the schemes and platforms implemented by the Newfoundland ruling cliques since that time further shifted these burdens onto the working people. For example, in 1933-34, at the depths of the Great Depression when the Newfoundland people rose up, their colonial masters smashed them. Direct rule from London was instituted by a committee advised by the syndicate of British banks that held the colony's debt. This so-called "Commission of Government" subsequently became notorious for setting unemployment relief at six cents a day.

As the British Empire breathed its last throughout the Atlantic basin during the Second World War, the structure of this yoke would again be modified as Canadian business and American military interests took over the island's economy. In 1949, with the dismantling of Commission of Government and erection of NATO and ICNAF, Newfoundland itself was folded into Confederation. Its economy ever since has been held hostage by a succession of fisheries and regional development programs of the Canadian federal government.

In the end result, Newfoundlanders have been saddled with a triple exploitation – at the hands of Newfoundland big business, Canadian government and high finance, and the requirements and demands of the American empire. The context and legacy under which the colonial merchants of the last century enslaved people to the truck system differs only in form, not in content, from the present, in which modern fish monopolies secured their position in the offshore fisheries by fastening the new fetters of "quotas" and "enterprise allocation" onto the fishery workers. The content of the quota system and of the truck system has been the same: unfettered freedom to exploit everyone else to the limit. Out of the narrowness of their outlook and in the blindness of their pursuit of self-interest, the ruling clique descended from these colonial merchants, doing exactly as they were bound, delivered Newfoundland over to the tender mercies of international finance. Hand in hand with plunderers domestic and foreign, they pillaged Newfoundland to the point where it became unfit for any existence other than as a semi-permanent impoverished ward of Canadian finance capital under American "protection" – to the point where "even the caplin swam away", as one long-time fishermen put it.

Once again, at the close of the twentieth century, life posed a burning question for the Newfoundlanders: was there some way out? The old answer always came back: go West young man – and indeed entire regions of the oil patch in northern Alberta are chock-a-block with displaced Newfoundlanders. The town of Fort MacMurray, in the heart of the Athabasca oil sands, is filled overwhelmingly with Newfoundlanders. But in addition, Big Oil came East, to the Newfoundland offshore, and this was painted as the wave of the future for Newfoundlanders who stay. Although the fishery is far from ended – the northern shrimp catching and processing sectors have become as industrialised in scale and operation as the groundfish sector ever was – its role and that of the men and women who work in it have been further marginalised.

4.4.3. Consequences of U.S. External Pressure and Interference for the East Coast Fishery

How such a disaster could have been visited on a small people who set out to harm no one seems truly incomprehensible without some introduction to the Canadian political system. Like any federal political system, Canada's governing structures assign different powers and competences to provinces and to the central government. The oldest political parties have also long divided themselves into national and provincial wings. The party system of government ends up placing tremendous discretionary authority in the hands of regional kingpins who are always assigned a place at the federal Cabinet table.[*] That part of the story might best be described as a tragedy of industrial feudalism in two acts: Act One – Plundering the Fish and Act Two – Sucking the Oil. What has made the buildup of intangible factors especially threatening in the present case, however, is the role of U.S. pressure to annex entire regions of Canada piecemeal.

In Newfoundland, the British Crown and shipping interests in the transatlantic slave trade at the start of the the 17th century developed a commercial fishery that also gave rise to European settlement. In the other three Atlantic provinces, it was the overthrow of the British Crown in the American colonies at the end of the 18th century that gave rise to a wave of British settlement that would also be compelled to engage in commercial fishing, only with the additional prospect of external U.S. pressure and interference from the outset.

What actually acted increasingly during the 19th century to unite the isolated fishing communities throughout colonial New Brunswick, Nova Scotia, Prince Edward Island and Newfoundland was their encounter with the persistent interference by the much larger-scale fishing interests of the "codfish aristocracy" of the New England states. Based in Gloucester, Massachusetts, these commercial interests meddled incessantly in the fisheries of the adjacent British colonies, seeking allies and positions against the British-connected merchants of these colonies, usually on the basis of interfering directly in the fishing grounds, especially off Nova Scotia, New Brunswick and Newfoundland, and thereby making the local fishermen pay for this mercantile competition with their livelihoods.

The question of Canadian sovereignty is extremely fraught these days, as there is much discussion of what it means relative to U.S. policies in Iraq and Afghanistan. However, the

---

[*] At the time the groundfish moratorium was imposed, the Newfoundland regional kingpin in the federal Cabinet, also serving in the portfolio of Minister of Fisheries and Oceans, was John Crosbie. Now retired from politics for slightly more than a decade, and professionally also semi-retired from legal practice, John Crosbie continues to be involved in current Newfoundland commercial affairs. He is a senior board member of the major fish processor in [*continued from the bottom of the previous page*] the province, Fisheries Products International. Crosbie also remains active on the board of the Atlantic Institute of Market Studies, a right-wing policy think tank based in Halifax, Nova Scotia that emulates the work of the Fraser Institute, an older longer-established right-wing policy think tank based on the other side of the country in British Columbia (Traynor and Seed 1999). A review of John Crosbie's political career and outlook goes a long way to explaining how and why an activity as strategically important for the human family as the cod fishery of the Grand Banks came to be destroyed entirely for the profit of those with capital vested in it and simultaneously entirely at the expense of its workforce and the surrounding society. See (Bains 1982) for fuller details.

aspects of the matter which are of concern here are those that help further elaborate the role within tangible economic development of an intangible element, *viz.*, the maintenance by successive Canadian governments since 1867 of an indeterminate, post-colonial character federal system that does not actually assert sovereignty until some established material interest becomes threatened. The emergence of the United States posed from the outset a major challenge to the existence of either an independent Canadian east coast fishery or an independent path of economic development in general fro what became "Canada". In this the notion of Canada as a pastiche of regions and sectors has played an especially dangerous role.

Historically, the east coast fisheries developed in four distinct settings:

a) fishing operations launched from Nova Scotian ports onto the "fishing banks" (offshore fishing grounds) in the open northwest Atlantic;
b) fishing operations launched from Newfoundland ports onto the Grand Banks;
c) the fisheries of the Gulf of St. Lawrence, prosecuted from the Gulf ports and fishing communities of New Brunswick, Nova Scotia, Prince Edward Island, Newfoundland and the Gaspe Peninsula (Quebec); and
d) near-shore banks fishing in the Bay of Fundy, Brown's Bank and George's Bank, prosecuted from southwestern New Brunswick and southwestern Nova Scotia.

Following the Second World War, fisheries prosecuted in the open Atlantic from eastern Canada came under increasingly centralised control. After 1949 Newfoundland was incorporated into Canada, rendering this centralisation especially and rapidly more pronounced. A relatively small handful of companies operated fishing fleets and processing plants in both Newfoundland and Nova Scotia. Confederation of Newfoundland with Canada fused the Atlantic coastal fisheries of the two provinces into one offshore fishery.

Historically, there were certain differences that developed in the relations of production between the different geographical bases of east coast fisheries. For example, in some areas, fisheries began with standing nets known as weirs. Fishermen continue to use weirs in these areas, especially in the fast-moving currents of tidal estuaries at the mouth and on the northeastern side of the Bay of Fundy. In such fisheries, as a consequence, the use of fishing vessels became confined to that of transshipping the catch to a landing point on shore, relatively near by. In other areas, such as along the Atlantic shores of Newfoundland and Nova Scotia, fisheries began near shore, prosecuted by individuals in small vessels, but moved further and further offshore into the open Atlantic. Such fisheries were carried on using larger and larger vessels with a single harvesting period extended from a day's trip to an expedition of 10 days to two weeks. In yet other areas, fisheries similarly extended from nearer shore to further away from shore, but remained within the confines of an inland sea such as the Gulf of St. Lawrence. The resulting line of development restricted the growth in the degree to which concentration of the means of harvesting became concentrated to those vessels with relatively limited crews and fishing expeditions to not more than four days round trip from home port.

These differences grew out of more fundamental differences bestowed originally by Nature. The range and genera of species available to be fished from each of these areas vary widely. They include bottom-feeding groundfish, pelagic fish (moving and feeding above the bottom but beneath the surface), anadromous species (species such as salmon that must come up freshwater streams of the continental margin to spawn, but otherwise travel and feed in the oceans in midwater schools), and crustaceans (shrimp, lobster).

Neither Nature nor geography, separately or jointly, however, entrenched or could have entrenched these differences. It was the demands of market capitalism and the processes of exploitation engendered in its service that served to transform these differences into a permanent and active factor. These demands continue to evolve in accordance with whatever commercial, industrial or financial combination of interests call the tune. This has been the case within particular fisheries and within particular regions of the east coast fisheries. For example, trawler fleets operating as the harvesting arm of a vertically integrated fish-processing enterprise dictated the pace and development of the fisheries along the Atlantic coast of Nova Scotia and Newfoundland. Other commercial interests managed to restrict the operation of trawler fleets so as to keep them out of the Gulf of St. Lawrence. Nevertheless, it has been the power of these monopoly combines, both in themselves and especially within the federal government machinery, which has prevailed.

The general sociological approach to the living outports of Atlantic Canada, in both their contemporary and historical aspect, has paid considerable attention to documenting in some detail the variety and character of the different forms and layers of social and working life in these communities. Their rural setting, their isolation from one another and from the services and facilities available only in a larger urban centre, and the apparently less pronounced differences in material conditions among outport residents compared to persons of comparable differentials in income living in cities have all been intensively and extensively studied. From this evidence – a fragment of the whole, with its peculiar features as well as features it shares in common with any other social cross-section one might examine – the conclusion was adduced that the underlying class structure of the fishing outport differed historically and fundamentally from that of the surrounding society (Brym and Sacouman 1979). This seriously overestimates the role of the peculiar features while failing to assign proper weight to the universal and common features, and derives from a failure to assess whether the peculiar features are vestigial, established or new. When one abstracts the general from the particular, features that are vestigial (passing away) cannot be considered part of what is general; they have to be explained separately in a different context. Similarly, features that are new have to be examined as to their enduring or persistent quality.

The reality of rural Canada is its intensive industrialization, in the form of literally hundreds of single-industry towns (Bains: *ibid.*). Rural populated regions of Canada have become industrialised, including fishing outports. As a result, the features common to industrial society throughout Canada are found there and dominate what happens. In the same way, Native peoples are forcibly marginalised throughout rural as well as urban Canada. Not as forcibly as Native people, but according to the same principle, immigrants and other newcomers are marginalised overlong, for varying lengths of time almost entirely in the cities, and are hardly to be found among the working population of the rural areas. Among the working people of town and country throughout Canada, some are fully transformed into people possessing no means of production or means of putting others to work. Most possess some inconsequential amount of equipment, or money set aside, that could be hired out or otherwise used to garner a living off the labour of others, including or not including oneself. There is a broad middle stratum straddling the middle classes at the upper-status end and this at the lower-status end, possessing more such monetary means. These differences in "physical" stratification affect the political response and consciousness of the members of these strata, but people's actual class position and role, their class interest, is objective. The class interest of people who are not large-scale owners of means of production employing other people, or who do not enjoy the privileged positions of being their managers or trusted servants, are generally the same; these interests are also generally by and large opposite to those of people who do own large-scale means of production employing other people, or enjoy the privileged positions of being their managers or trusted servants. These interests operate and exist independently of the subjective factor of individual consciousness, which is fragmentary.

By becoming entrenched, the localised and regionalised differences among the various outport segments of eastern Canada became part of the psychology and outlook of the various sections of the fishery. In other words, the processes of differentiation have developed to the point where they directly affect political perception and government policy in the fisheries. The government itself refers to these fisheries according to "sectors." These "sectors" are themselves defined partly according to geographical region and partly according to the range and genera of fish catches, which are themselves implicitly connected to the geographical part of the definition. However, the "experts' " perspective that the *sectoral differences among the various fisheries are more important than what they share in common* is something asserted beyond any available supporting evidence. The underlying logic of this perspective, that either the features unique to some sector of the fishery override the features that are common to the entire east coast fishery, or else these peculiar sectoral features more truly represent and characterise the fishery than those features that all sectors throughout the fishery share in common, is precisely what the historical line of development of the fishery and these fishing communities refutes in practice.

There is a profounder aspect to the question of sectors and sectoral differences in the fishery. It has everything to do with how readily corporate interests from the United States have been able to take over the industrialisation of rural Canada. Grouping and treating Canadian fishermen and their communities by sector has had a particularly devastating effect on the capacities either of government or the people to defend Canada's national sovereignty along the Atlantic coast. For example, the boundary waters in the Bay of Fundy-Gulf of Maine between the U.S. state of Maine and the Canadian provinces of New Brunswick and Nova Scotia is still not defined in proper form under a treaty binding both countries as sovereign entities in their own respective territories. There is a ruling by the International Court at The Hague rendered in 1984, which drew a line giving Canada not only the richest scallop bed in George's Bank, but also one of the zones in which the offshore oil and gas cartel attempted to obtain exploration drilling permits since the 1970s. There is a Joint Enforcement Agreement initialed 26 September 1990 by the two national governments. There is a protocol established in March 1992 spelling out that the coast guard authorities of both countries must detain and charge citizens of their own countries with infractions for which the other country has provided material evidence. However, there is no treaty. In this case, by not approving a treaty embodying these arrangements, the U.S. continues not to recognise that a country called Canada – created and expanded since 1867 on the northern and northeastern borders of the United States – enjoys full sovereign authority in its own territory. It continues thereby not only not to recognise Canada's sovereign authority in these particular boundary waters, but also continues not to recognise that the Gulf of St Lawrence is a Canadian inland sea, and not to recognise that the waters around the islands in Canada's Arctic are Canadian and no longer international waters. The existing arrangements enjoy legal force in the two countries not as matters of international law, but only as extensions of the principle of "reciprocity".

The doctrine and approach of sectors enables the Canadian government to contain the resistance of fishing communities to unjust acts of U.S. citizens on the Canadian side of these particular boundary waters. Every contentious issue is deflected, defused or trivialised into one of a dispute among "scallop fishermen", or "lobster fishermen", over a "shared resource". If a U.S. citizen, however, can operate in a Canadian sphere, safe in the knowledge that any Canadian protest about its sovereign rights being violated enjoys no standing at any level in the U.S. legal system, this invests the U.S. citizen at least potentially with the arrogance of those who commit crimes with impunity. What then are the rights of the Canadian worth when operating in the same sphere? After literally hundreds of "incidents" in these waters since the 1820s, the vast majority precipitated by actions of U.S citizens, no compensation for this known and evident inequality and inequity has been offered or provided Canadians by either their own or the U.S. government. For any given incident, this "impunity factor" may seem quite minor. Accumulated over centuries, it is bound to become considerable.

This U.S. intrusion grows especially readily when it encounters no resistance from Canadian governments. It has been arranged since the days of British colonial rule, and maintained with the compliance of Canadian governments since Confederation in 1867, that Canadians enjoy no government protection of their sovereign rights vis-à-vis the United States. This has profound consequences for issues that have any impact on the development either of the protein resources or the energy resources of the 200-mile limit off the east coast. The existence of the Atlantic provinces – before 1867 for New Brunswick and Nova Scotia, before 1873 for Prince Edward Island, and before 1949 for Newfoundland – was dominated by a colonial relationship with Britain as the Mother Country. The rights of the governments of these jurisdictions, and especially their communities and people, were defined according to arrangements struck between the United States and Great Britain. The most disturbing of these was established according to the terms of the Anglo-American Convention of 1818, which provided extraterritorial rights for citizens of the United States to catch and take fish in waters off the Atlantic provinces.

With the signing of the Joint Enforcement Agreement on 26 September 1990, the U.S. government was enabled for the first time to enforce a foreign fishery jurisdiction within Canadian waters. According to the joint communiqué of the two Canadian government departments Foreign Affairs and Fisheries and Oceans, that were parties to the deal, it would "become an offence under both Canadian and American law for any person to fish without authorisation, to have fishing gear on vessels readily able to be used to fish, and to resist efforts to enforce these laws in the other country's waters." This extended the Canadian government's jurisdiction over Canadian fishermen inside the Americans' 200-mile zone. At the same time, the U.S. would uphold the fishery regulations of the Canadian government tin the U.S. zone, such as fines of up to $100,000 upon conviction for "obstructing a fisheries officer". However, this did not and still does not exist as an offence under U.S. federal or state laws. Americans are not subject to fines on this scale for breaking fishing rules. The communiqué quoted the Canadian foreign affairs minister of the day saying that this agreement would "commit each country to use its legal authority to enforce the fisheries law of the other country when the offence occurs on the other side of the border." This effectively extended the already extremely unjust and unequal extraterritorial rights that the U.S. already enjoyed under the Anglo-American Convention of 1818, well beyond the realm of catching and taking fish.

There is constitutional law in Canada and Britain whereby Canada assumed powers formerly exercised by Britain. However, Canada has never repudiated the Anglo-American Convention, nor has the U.S. has renounced its extraterritorial rights under this law. In effect, every agreement reached between Canadian and U.S. governments regarding U.S. use or presence in these waters is ultimately subject to Washington deciding how far or whether to insist upon its rights under the Anglo-American Convention. As a result, Canada's 200-mile offshore exclusive economic zone is backed by no affirmations whatsoever of Canadian sovereign national rights. Canadian governments can negotiate reciprocal arrangements with U.S. oil companies and other foreign entities using this zone or extracting its resources. It can garner advantages for Canadian corporations ahead of others wherever economic circumstances favour such arrangements. However, it can assert no national rights nor defend Canadian national rights from being trampled. Indeed it enjoys less authority than the government of the humblest or weakest Arab emirate, whose borders, rights and competences under international law are completely defined.

Offshore oil and gas development matters in eastern Canada do not go between and are not discussed among the President of the United States (or someone from his cabinet) and the Prime Minister of Canada (or someone from the Canadian cabinet). This is not simply the expression of administrative convenience or "commonness of outlook and interests". The reason almost everything to do with these matters goes routinely, and secretively, between the oil companies and the Canada-Nova Scotia Offshore Petroleum Board or the Canada-Newfoundland Offshore Petroleum Board, *i.e.*, the agencies established to develop and implement government regulations in the companies' interests, is because the Canadian government possesses only the power to say: "Yes". Not being sovereign in its own territory, it lacks the power to say: "No".

Regardless of how intangible the role that it continues to play, this "sovereignty-deficiency" factor – we might designate it S^- ("big-S minus") – is thus clearly measurable, at least in terms of consequences of the kind just mentioned. This deficiency is actually visibly manifested in Map 4-1, reproduced earlier in this chapter at section 4.2.2, which was issued by the Canadian federal Department of Energy and Resources: although the pipeline routes are shown, the different provincial and state jurisdictions are delineated, and the jurisdictions that are Canadian provinces are distinguished by colour from those that are American states, The Hague Line drawn in 1984 by the International Court through George's Bank – a prime zone of pending and future interest to the offshore oil and gas lobby – is nowhere to be seen. Clearly, then, no serious "economics of intangibles" is complete or even conceivable without S^-. It implicitly challenges many assumptions about the sovereign power that formally independent countries are supposed to enjoy over what happens to their currencies, to the depletion of their resources through "development", etc. This extends even to valuations and assessments of a country's present and future economic prospects, undertaken and published by outside "independent" agencies (such as the *Economist Intelligence Unit* and others) sometimes even commissioned by the government in question.

The deficiency of Canadian sovereignty is the flipside of the excessive influence and domination exercised by the United States commercially and financially in the Canadian economy as a whole, including how its food production arrangements proceed and what interests it serves. It has become literally a life or death question for fishermen and the communities who depend on the scallop beds of George's Bank for their livelihood. With underused vessels retired from the groundfish sector and some refitting, the monopoly interests involved in scallop-dragging from the Canadian side stepped up their activity, striving to remain competitive against the Americans' scallop fisheries in George's Bank. Less than seven months after the imposition of the groundfish moratorium, on the night of 31 January 1993, this competition produced a disastrous sinking at sea, *en route* to George's Bank, of a Lunenburg-based scallop dragger, the *Cape Aspy*, and the loss of five members of the 12-man crew. Although fishermen for years have pressed the dragger fleet not to send them out at this time of year, because of the danger of freezing spray icing a ship's rigging enough to capsize it, the economic insecurities created by the groundfish moratorium left many crewmen feeling they had no choice but to accept any crew positions on offer, regardless of the danger.

This U.S. influence has other unexpected impacts. Although most of those who would point repeatedly through the 1980s to declining east coast groundfish catches as a sign of stress on the entire marine ecology of the region meriting urgent study and the attention of responsible policy-making bodies, the actual commercial collapse of the sector in the end had less than nothing to do with the actual state of the commercial stocks. It had far more to do with the state of monopolisation and cartelisation of the fishing industry domestically, with which U.S. influence and interests were intimately involved. It also had a great deal to do with the state of commercial corporate competition internationally, on the other, in which the vertically integrated sector of Canadian fish processing found itself as the Soviet Union disappeared. Ironically, the intangible role of the U.S. domination of the Canadian economy is the real secret of why it turned out to be the Canadian east coast fishing industry that took such a hit after the single greatest foreign fishing predator of coastal fishermen's livelihoods was removed is. As already discussed earlier in this chapter, this is a political crisis of genuine sovereignty and independence that became inextricably bound up with the chronic crisis endemic to the east coast fisheries.

4.4.4. The Development and Shutdown of Canada's Northwest Atlantic Offshore Fisheries in the Shadow of U.S. Expansion

The entire *context* of post-moratorium east coast fisheries discussed earlier landed an unprecedented opportunity in the lap of vertically-integrated Canadian fish processors most favourably positioned to intervene in world protein markets. It now become more remunerative to destroy an entire mass of productive forces, *i.e.*, take their own trawling fleets out of service regardless of the costs and burdens this would impose on affected fishing communities, rather than continue employing these forces in a "law of diminishing returns" race to the bottom, harvesting declining quantities of the commercially most valuable species per unit effort. As a condition of Canada's participation in the Free Trade Agreement and the North American Free Trade Agreement both struck in the 1980s, which banned government subsidies to industry as unfair competition, Canadian governments by the 1990s were entirely out of the business of subsidising new vessel construction for the vertically-integrated fish processors' fleets. The processors' existing aging fleets could therefore not be replaced on the basis of making the Canadian public pay 80 per cent of the cost, as had occurred when most of that fleet was being built in the late 1960s and early 1970s.

Finally there is the most serious crisis looming for the fisheries of the George's Bank – both scallop and lobster fisheries – which will break out in 2010. At that time, the 30-year-long moratorium on selling development licences for exploring offshore oil and gas in George's Bank will be lifted by the U.S. federal government. Neither the fishing interests in the provinces of Nova Scotia and New Brunswick or from the American states of Maine and Massachusetts, nor the Canadian government have any say in this. Worse: as a result of its lack of sovereign authority in the George's Bank, the Canadian government could be readily maneuvered into facilitating the will of the offshore energy cartel.

Fisheries production in the offshore sector is based principally on catches taken within 200 nautical miles of the open Atlantic coastline of Canada and more than a day's trip from home port. This includes fishing grounds off Nova Scotia's Eastern Shore, as well as the south, east and northeast coasts of Newfoundland (the Grand Banks). Fish catches are also purchased from inshore fishermen in certain species at certain times of the year for the fish processing plants of this sector, depending on market conditions.

This was the key sector dominated by National Sea Products and Fishery Products International until the groundfish moratorium of 1992. Monopoly domination did not end with the moratorium, however; it changed form once again. In 1994, National Sea Products had sold off much of its trawler fleet and restructured itself as High Liner Foods. On May 1, 2001, a single corporate entity emerged at the top of the heap: a cartel led by Clearwater Fine Foods of Bedford, NS, with major partners from Iceland and New Zealand, controlling Fishery Products International and the buying of catches of non-groundfish species throughout the region. In 2003, the Clearwater group of directors within Fishery Products International attempted to seize total control.

In the ensuing struggle, the reason Clearwater had striven so assiduously to take over FPI, a much larger outfit, two years before finally emerged in the light of day: FPI revenues were steadily exceeding half-a-billion dollars per year, while Clearwater had corporate debts exceeding $200-million and rising. Suspicious of a possible carpetbagging operation, the rest of FPI fought back, mobilising the provincial government on their side by invoking its responsibility under the province's "FPI Act" to prevent any share exchange that would dilute the provincial government's 15-per-cent ownership share in the company.[23]

Integration and concentrated ownership of both harvesting and processing means of production remains the norm, and the principal production cycle is still year-round, with seasonal plants playing a secondary role. Instead of taking groundfish, however, since the moratorium, the boats operating in winter are taking mainly shellfish species – shrimp and crab, in addition to lobster and scallop. Many plants are sustained by contracts to process catches of foreign fleets seeking an entrée for their products in the U.S. market. Before the moratorium, the principal harvesting means in this sector of the fishery were trawler fleets operating from several ports but coordinated from a central command, but the moratorium has greatly contracted its scale of operations. The principal processing means were large plants on

---

[23] The Newfoundland government's position prevailed for three years, but in the spring of 2006, Fishery Products International took yet another run at getting the legislation rewritten. The Clearwater directors, without selling off, lost interest in proceeding further with any of their plans for FPI, tackling their debt-repayment obligation by converting the company into an income trust. In terms of the model terminology already developed above, the S factor that would have to be computed as be fractionating or reductive in its effect on the livelihoods of Canadian fishermen taking scallops on George's Bank ceased in this case to be fractionating or reductive and operated to strengthen the benefits accruing to the province from maintaining its FPI stake intact.

ice-free oceanfront (on the Atlantic coast of Nova Scotia and south coast of Newfoundland). Today, much of their productive capacity has become redundant, but the narrowness of focus of corporate management on the shortest of short terms has meant that reserve unused production capacity is treated as a burdensome waste, threatening to empty entire communities such as Harbour Breton where a plant that used to employ the entire town directly and indirectly, on Newfoundland's south coast, was to be shut down. The remaining human productive forces of this sector of the fishery are fishermen who were converted into contract workers by the device of the so-called "individual transferable quotas" (ITQs), and plant workers under the direct and joint employ of the leading vertically integrated corporation or its surrogate. The main geographic and demographic base of this fishery used to be a collection of fishing ports enjoying year-round ice-free ocean access, each dominated by a single fishing corporation operating the trawler fleet and fish plant; many of these are now in bankruptcy, unable to maintain basic services like drinking water and losing education facilities such as schools as the young generation leave to find work elsewhere.

Depending on the market demand for products and bottlenecks arising in the production cycle in the primary part of the system, inshore fishermen and seasonal plant workers are employed as a reserve, in a secondary role. Since the moratorium, large reductions took place in the workforce that used to be directly employed in company fleets. The companies increased their reach and control through contract arrangements such as the ITQ. Before the moratorium, most of the struggles that broke out in this sector surfaced in the form of labour-management struggles and were waged more or less openly in this form. The companies' subsequent conversion of many of these workers under the ITQ system into contracted and subcontracted individuals, deeply cutting their family incomes, enabled the companies to continue to monopolise the outport economic space without having to keep it productive, instead shifting all the burdens of slow markets onto the contractors and sub-contractors.

The linchpin of Canadian fishing operations offshore since 1977 has been the government's claim of "sovereignty" in the 200-mile limit, in the form of management jurisdiction over fishery and other resource developments beyond the 12-mile limit of actual Canadian territory out to a distance of 200 (nautical) miles. Essentially, this has been carried out under the direction of the U.S. State Department. The actual content of this sovereignty has amounted to little more than a "power of sale". Before its proclaiming the new "exclusive economic zone" on 1 March 1977 (simultaneously with the United States and Mexico, as a gesture to the world from "Fortress North America"), Ottawa negotiated a bilateral fisheries treaty in 1975-76 with the Soviet Ministry Fisheries, operator of what was then the largest foreign fleet operating within 200 miles of Canada's east coast. This reserved Canadian fish processors' claims to the commercially most valuable stocks of groundfish, scallops and lobster. It also assigned rights over the remaining 88.4 per cent of the fish stocks in the zone to the Soviet fleet, as being "surplus to Canadian needs". Until the United Nations Third Law of the Sea Conference Convention came into effect during 1993-94, the Canadian government's claim enjoyed no form of protection whatsoever under any international treaty. During that time, its assertion of authority in the 200-mile limit had no formal standing outside of a handful of bilateral agreements. Either party to such an agreement could abrogate it in whole or in part at any time after giving the requisite notice. This is further evidence for the thesis that Canada can dispose of the resources of the 200-mile limit only as the servant of others, principally the U.S.

Before the groundfish moratorium, the offshore fishery had become the setting for contradictions both between Canadian and foreign vertically-integrated corporate entities over access to fish stocks, and within the then-Canadian groundfish cartel over access to (as well as control over) the most lucrative fishery resources inside the 200-mile limit. With the chaos in the global economy throughout the 1990s, and the moratorium, however, Canadian and foreign groundfish fleets were dispersed from the Grand Banks, and opportunities for Canadian processors to partner their processing facilities with foreign fleets became all the rage. Meanwhile, however, in the offshore zone, contention shifted away from issues of international disputes about fleet access to fish stocks to an increasingly open contradiction between shore-based fishing and harvesting operations on the east coast and incoming and expanding oil and gas exploration and production in the offshore. This has been the context in which mostly U.S.-owned oil and gas production and drilling interests have come to occupy the area on the basis of permanently excluding any return of fishing fleets from Canada or other countries.

Throughout the 1980s, the trawler fleets of the vertically integrated offshore sector were absent from the Gulf of St Lawrence. Formally, since December 1979, they were banned. In practice, however, what kept their fleets outside was not fear of the consequences of enforcement of this ban, but the rising cost of fuel to operate such fleets. As fuel prices rose in the 1970s and 1980s, it became increasingly costly, and decreasingly profitable, for the trawler fleets to put to sea longer and longer for catches of decreasing revenue potential. By concentrating harvesting efforts instead on groundfish stocks outside the Gulf, the trawler fleets reaped all the benefits of economies of scale, at a time when prices for groundfish as a high-protein food source were on the rise. The offshore companies dominated access to the market for the products of the Gulf of St. Lawrence and treated the resource of the Gulf of St. Lawrence as a reserve source of raw material.

The increasing intrusion of trawler fleets, Canadian as well as foreign, intensified the struggle of inshore fishermen inside and outside the Gulf of St Lawrence to catch enough fish in enough species to maintain a livelihood. This triggered a process that would end by hurling the livelihoods of scores of inshore fishermen and coastal fishing communities out of fishing and into bankruptcy. From the time the 200-mile limit was formalised until the groundfish moratorium, the provincial governments' fisheries loan boards advised and-or enabled these fishermen to invest in bigger more efficient vessels to "stay in the game", while the federal government carried on its practice of assigning foreign fleets the inshore fishermen's quotas in species that would be insufficiently profitable for the Canadian groundfish cartel. This entrenched the foreign fleets inside the Canadian 200-mile limit, with a permit to operate inside the 200-mile limit at the cost of the livelihoods of the scores of coastal communities in which the inshore fishermen were based. As witnessed in the gang-fishing techniques for which the Soviet-bloc fleets became particularly notorious, one critical side effect was that parts of the fishery were converted effectively into zones of foreign occupation. The cartel was prepared to bargain with Canada's formal sovereignty in this way because, and to the extent that, the inshore fishermen would continue fishing for (and thus also catching) those species that were of greatest interest to, and most profitable for, its members. This burdened the Canadian public with a devalued sovereignty, and the inshore fishermen with having to fish for two masters in order to continue garnering the livelihood they used to eke out when they were fishing just for one. The latter development affected all inshore fishermen from coastal communities not only outside but especially inside the Gulf of St Lawrence. The tangible measure of this intangible degradation is the burden of debt (in the form of vessel mortgages) exceeding the ability to repay, held by many of these fishermen within Canada's chartered banking system *via* government fisheries loan boards in the four Atlantic provinces.[24]

The most devastating blow coupled with this development came as, emboldened by U.S. non-recognition of a Canadian inland sea, some of the leading global fishing fleets of the 1980s from certain members of the then-Soviet bloc eventually plundered the small coastal fishermen's livelihoods inside the Gulf of St Lawrence. The Canadian government as stalking horse for the Canadian offshore fisheries cartel regulated this entire line of development, at the expense of local processors who had operated independently of the cartel.

Fisheries production of the Gulf of St Lawrence historically has engaged fishermen from all provinces with coastlines in the Gulf of St. Lawrence – the Atlantic provinces plus the Gaspé region of Quebec – but only on a seasonal basis, not the year round. The presence of pack ice and extensive ice fields limits this fishery to between six and eight months of the year. Monopolised corporate concentration of ownership of harvesting, as well as of processing, means of production were long present in this sector, although their weight and role were different from the offshore sector.

Although no other countries outside North America formally challenged Canada's drawing of "closing lines" at the entrances of the Gulf of St Lawrence (across the Cabot Strait between Newfoundland and Nova Scotia and between the island of Newfoundland and the Quebec-Labrador boundary), the State Department of the United States officially declared the waters inside the Gulf – beyond 12 miles of the coasts of the Quebec North Shore, the eastern coast of New Brunswick, the coastline of Prince Edward Island and the western coast of the island of Newfoundland – to be international waters. This exception created a loophole that various global fishing fleets active in the northwest Atlantic – from France and especially from the Soviet bloc – found useful to exploit.

In addition to owning and operating most of the seasonal processing plants of this sector, the Canadian offshore groundfish cartel controlled the marketing of the bulk of the products from this sector. They did not maintain their own trawler fleets in this sector, however, and depended for raw material mainly on purchasing the catches of the independent fishermen of this zone. Furthermore, some processing capacity and some marketing of fish products from this zone was controlled by fishermen's cooperatives in northeastern New Brunswick and Quebec. The situation was very different from the offshore fishery as regards the mix of species as well as how and where they are landed (and hence processed). There was a large Gulf cod fishery off western Newfoundland and Cape Breton, a redfish fishery in the Cabot Strait, and a major lobster fishery in the Northumberland Strait (northern Nova Scotia, southeastern New Brunswick and western Prince Edward Island). There also were (and still

---

[24] Large numbers of these fishermen were wiped out by the interest-rates spike in 1981. Even more were ruined as a by-blow of the 1987 stock market crash which demolished the Canadian brokerage house of Osler. As a result of the arrangements established by a senior Osler partner, the central credit union in the region – which had become one of the most trusted financial institutions in the fishing communities of eastern New Brunswick (inside the Gulf) and eastern Nova Scotia (outside the Gulf) since the Great Depression of the 1930s – relied on Osler's management of its financial market investments portfolio to finance its continued retention of the inshore fishermen's "paper". After Osler defaulted massively on its clients' accounts, including the credit union, it would eventually be established by an Ontario Securities Commission inquiry that "a sum exceeding $25-million" in fishing vessel mortgages was lost.

are) midwater fleets seeking herring catches and informal fleets of multi-purpose vessels capable of ranging throughout the Gulf in search of different species.

At one time, foreign fleets from all the non-Soviet-bloc member states of the International Commission for the Northwest Atlantic Fisheries (ICNAF) fished inside the Gulf. The Canadian processors operating trawler fleets plundered various fish stocks inside the Gulf on an irregular basis until the late 1970s. The Canadian government, as part of implementing a twelve-mile territorial sea, drew closing lines across the entrances to the Gulf in 1970-71. In effect, Canada declared the Gulf an "inland sea." Five of the fishing fleets from ICNAF member states that were also NATO members agreed to quit fishing inside the Gulf. The ban on these fleets entering (or re-entering) the Gulf was formally set at the same time that the Canadian government signed bilateral treaties with the Soviet-bloc fleets permitting them to continue fishing inside the limit.

Two years later, under political pressures mounted by a movement in the coastal fishing communities seeking to defend them from further predations by the Canadian monopoly fleets, although the word was spread everywhere that this was pro-actively undertaken to protect the fisheries ecology, environment, etc., the government reactively banned the Canadian trawler fleets from fishing inside the Gulf as well. At this point, however, the Canadian offshore companies did not see their long-term interest as lying with upholding sovereignty, and they persisted instead in treating the resource of the Gulf of St. Lawrence to be a reserve of raw material. By thus failing to shift to an operating principle based on the notion that doing good – in this case upholding Canada's fisheries sovereignty in its internal waters – was good business, they missed the last opportunity to save any future for that fishery or the communities depending upon it for livelihood in five provinces. Facing thre new pressures from the communities, the federal Department of Fisheries and Oceans proceeded to "manage" this sector in a manner that accelerated the elimination of independent fishermen's independence from external corporate dictate. First, they financed every producers' association in this area either directly or in the form of setting up special, so-called "over-the-side" fish sales between newly-organised groups and particular foreign fleets — especially the Polish, Bulgarian and Russian fleets. Then the government bestowed negotiating authority on those associations, pointing repeatedly to this "democracy of the producers" as proof that it was on the side of the "little people" against "the interests" while in fact pitting one section in one part of the region against another and driving independent local processors to the wall.

4.4.5. "True-costs" Modelling *versus* Separation-rejection Variant of Immediate-cost Models

The true costs, tangible and intangible, of how production of protein in the northwest Atlantic as the first food production system ever developed explicitly for world markets was displaced by the production of energy as a pretext for annexing half a continent, has not been modeled within conventional economic theory. In our view, it cannot be modeled by such theory. In the form of its leading "separation-rejection" variant identified earlier in this chapter, the conventional theory excises as "externalities" any mention – and thereafter censors any consideration – of long-term costs. The present work advances the case for developing and applying a different approach in which true costs of all kinds – as distinct from only "immediate" and, even then, only tangibly measurable costs – are modeled as far as possible. Ranging far afield from the case of the Canadian east coast, the general approach of arriving at a replacement cost for that which was extracted or violated but never replaced or justly compensated could be applied to everything from reparations payments for the consequences of the transcontinental slave trade – an actual preoccupation of a United Nations committee before 9-11 – to totting up the final bill that should be handed to the agents of the British colonial system that engineered the Great Bengali Famine of 1943, in which the British stockpiled the population's food supplies for its own troops allegedly with the aim of saving India from a possible Japanese invasion through Bengal that never got off the ground.

The examples elaborated at length so far in this chapter, unfolding how the two lines of attack develop in tandem against Nature and against Labour, have been deliberately selected because they raise profound issues concerning the *sustainability* of tangible economic processes. Implicit in the separation-rejection process is an effort to reject any notion that Labour could be the father of wealth and especially the notion that it should retain on that basis any claim on what becomes of its product after it has been produced. This takes place on the basis of rejecting any role for Nature as the mother of all wealth.

The kind of calculation required by a true-costs model for our "economics of intangibles" might look something like the following for pricing the true cost of energy production. Consider, for example,

- a wage rate ω, representing the per-hour rate for purchasing any some socially necessary amount of labour-time (determined as an average over all energy production-related activity);
- the number of hours η, representing the socially necessary average number of hours of labour required for a cycle of production;
- the quantity of raw material Q, representing the amount (in millions of tones) of raw material being consumed without being physically replaced;
- the amount of time τ, in billions of years, that it would take for natural processes to replace Q; and
- $\frac{\partial Q}{\partial \tau}$, the rate at which Q is replaced/deposited by natural processes

Then we could determine υ, the actual value of the raw material extracted in a typical production cycle, according to the following formula:

$$\upsilon = \omega \eta \frac{\partial Q}{\partial \tau} \tau$$

Similar recasting of the actual cost of extracting other materials that must be replaced by a natural process for such uses to be considered truly sustainable can also be developed. This would make it possible to recalculate the sustainable level at which dammed watercourses such as those created for producing hydroelectric power should actually be used – incorporating considerations of the actual costs of the human community displacement which such projects entail, the extent to which evaporation and other natural processes affect the supplies of diverted water over time, and the timespan over which a natural supply becomes affected by a weather disturbance such as episodic drought and excess precipitation or an excessive period of rain or sequence of especially arid dry seasons, etc.

4.5. Devil Theories of History and the Cultivation of Ignorance

Imposition of the separation-rejection process on economic model-building often follows the apparently fortuitous revelation of some hitherto undetected gap, inequality, mismatch or "disequation". Announcement of such a "discovery" frequently takes the form of "everything was going along tickety-boo when out of the blue – a catastrophe". Simultaneously within this, an enormous campaign of disinformation was purveyed everywhere – first during the 1970s concerning the role of Soviet Russia's roles and capacities as the world's premier fish harvester and processor operating beyond the dictates of the world capitalist system, and today again in the 2000s of post-Soviet Russia's roles and capacities as the world's premier non-OPEC energy exporter.

This is a key and enduring part of a global struggle among imperial Big Power blocs over spheres of influence. *Before* the Soviet Union's disappearance, part of this struggle took the form of a struggle between "socialism" on the one hand and "capitalism" on the other – ideologically manipulated sometime by and sometimes by the other superpower. Today, what remains of that contradiction persists as a struggle between a gigantic Russian-government-backed (but privately-run) syndicate/cartel of energy producers on the one hand and a variety of large, sometimes competing and sometimes colluding oil and gas giants based in Europe and America on the other.

With regard to the world's food supply: only in the 1980s, after the fishing fleets of the Soviet Union surpassed those of Japan and other large longer-term global plunderers, "overfishing" was suddenly discovered in 15 of the world's 18 leading commercial fishing basins. Not only was this deemed a "crisis", but coastal fishermen in Canada and many other countries as the catchers, desperately building and launching more and more small fishing vessels, were condemned as equal in guilt and responsibility for the "depletion of fish stocks" as the multinational vertically-integrated fish processing companies that capitalised vast fleets of stern trawlers, draggers, factory-freezer trawlers and fully-outfitted floating fish factories which vacuumed the oceans of the fish that used to supply coastal fishermen's livelihoods.[25] These fleets consumed the vast bulk of the extensive silver hake resource. The habitat of this species spanned a line running roughly parallel to, and almost the entire length of, the Atlantic coast of Nova Scotia approximately 100-110 miles offshore. With the disappearance of this silver hake stock, there coincided by the mid-1980s the unexpected disappearance of the extensive schools of herring that formerly migrated northward on the Gulf Stream to

---

[25] At the height of the Soviet fleet's activities off the Canadian east coast, from 1968 most intensively until 1987-88, a flotilla of more than 500 vessels of varying scale and productive capacity were rotated, on a schedule, through various sectors of the region's fisheries. This does not take into account the several score of vessels deployed by the fleets of Poland, Bulgaria, the then-"German Democratic Republic", Latvia, Lithuania and even Rumania as adjuncts of the overall COMECON fish-harvesting effort in the region. The full extent remains buried in the annals maintained by ВНИРО (*VNIRO* – the All-Russian Scientific Ichthyology and Fisheries Organisation), the arm of the former Soviet Ministry of Fisheries. Their records from that period remain unavailable.

feeding grounds off the southwest tip of Nova Scotia. There were a number of other ecological anomalies, including unexpected disappearance and reappearance of the capelin roll off the south coast of Newfoundland, that appear also to have been triggered by the scale and shifting focus of the COMECON fleets' harvesting efforts.

During the period of Soviet-American détente, Canadian fisheries science persistently refused to study or correlate the scale or shift of this harvesting effort with any changes in the levels of commercially valuable or other fish stocks in the area. With the emergence during the 1980s of the Reagan administration's restoration of a confrontational stance vis-à-vis the Soviet Union, there were endless reams of studies produced about the dark and hidden military-naval aims of "Soviet 'fisheries'", as the defence and military journals would invariably call it – but nothing whatever dispassionate or remotely scientific about the consequences for the fishery. By the 1990s, any further significance of the disappearance of Russia's global fishing fleet and its role was being denied. In Canada's east coast fishery, this only served to fuel the mystery of how it came to pass that, whereas coastal fishermen were ruined allegedly by "disappearance of the fish stocks", the fish processing monopolies of the capitalist world reaped unprecedented profits by snapping up dumped inventories of Soviet catches at distress prices for resale. The upshot thus remained: whatever went wrong in the fishery had been the fault of the Soviet Union, but, the Devil having died, the case was thereafter forever closed.

4.5.1. The Fetishism of Independent Global Rivals and the Secret Thereof: "Peak Oil" Fantasies and Cold War Reruns

Similar to the situation in ocean fisheries, with regard to the world's energy supply: today, once again when it comes to sustainability, no approach to supplying Humanity's energy needs is to be countenanced, or treated with anything but the greatest contempt, that does not genuflect in full obedience before those who insist that fossil fuels shall rule the supply picture forever. Here once again the question, not of the *relative* sustainability of this process *versus* that process, but rather of the *inherent* sustainability of the approach itself, poses itself extremely sharply. Instead of proceeding on the basis of escaping that path, conventional energy economics treats all plans or proposals for large-scale long-term replacement of oil with natural gas, or long-term replacement of oil- or gas-fired power generation with solar or wind sources, or using renewable energy sources directly rather than first converting them to electricity, with the greatest contempt. An enormous disinformation accompanies the promotion of short-term solutions, taking the form of a diet of what seem like the poorest-quality Grade-B movies, paralyzing fantasies about a "peak oil" dystopia interspersed with Cold War reruns.

In connection with notions of sustainability, there is much discussion currently of the "theory" of "peak oil". It is more correct to call it a projection into the future of empirical data about oil and gas reserves that had been collected and collated since the 1950s within the continental United States, but that was still incomplete when it came to world totals in the early 1970s. That was the time of the first attempt to project this timeseries sequence of observations into a theoretical prediction. This followed the tripling of the world oil price from about US$3 to about US$10 per barrel by members of the Organisation of Petroleum Exporting Countries (OPEC). The Shah of Iran, a major U.S. ally, sided with and enabled this price increase following the lifting of the oil embargo led by the Arab member-states of OPEC directed against allies of the State of Israel. (That U.S. ally had provoked a serious military conflict with Syria and Egypt in October 1973 which it "won" only after the U.S. declared a world-wide nuclear war alert, pushing the Soviet Union to press its Arab allies to pull back.)

The most evident limitation of the "peak oil" projection was that conditions of production that existed in the 1960s and early 1970s regarding U.S. oil majors' activities in the Middle East – and the technologies then available for extraction and processing – were extrapolated as a more-or-less constant factor. Graphically, the observations compiled originally by King Hubbert and coworkers from the U.S. Geological Service in 1974, and updated by Campbell and Laherrere in 1995, looked like this:

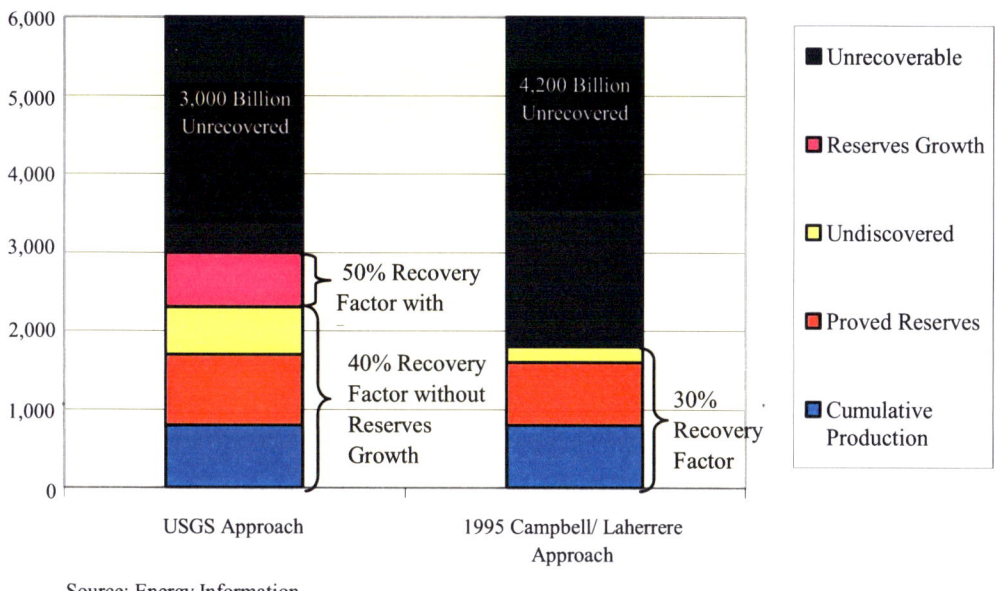

Different Interpretations of Hypothetical 6,000 Billion Barrel World Original Oil-inPlace Resource Base

Figure 4-5. "Peak Oil" Model of World Oil Supplies – The principal schema, before the Energy Information Administration of the U.S. Department of Energy undertook a revision and updating of the poeak-oil prediction in 2003-04, were based on a guesstimate of recoverability of unexploited reserves. As a consequence of assuming as static a late-1960s-era structure for petroleum extraction and processing technologies, so-called "non-conventional" reserves such as oil sands were excluded.

The predictions of possible "peaks" were tabulated as follows:

Table 4-5. Production-Peak Data Predictions

Probability Estimate	Ultimate Recovery BBbls	Annual Demand Growth, %	Peak year	Peak Rate, MMBbls/ yr	Peak Rate, MMBbls/ day
Low (95%)	2,248	0.0	2045	24,580	67
	2,248	1.0	2033	34,820	95
	2,248	2.0	2026	42,794	117
	2,248	3.0	2021	48,511	133
Mean (expected value)	3,003	0.0	2075	24,580	67
	3,003	1.0	2050	41,238	113
	3,003	2.0	2037	53,209	146
	3,003	3.0	2030	63,296	173
High (5%)	3,896	0.0	2112	24,580	67
	3,896	1.0	2067	48,838	134
	3,896	2.0	2047	64,862	178
	3,896	3.0	2037	77,846	213

Source: Energy Information Administration

The model developed by M. King Hubbert and co-workers at the U.S. Geological Survey, published in 1974, projected three possible scenarios for crude oil production peak-decline in the periods 2021-2045, 2030-2075 and 2037-2112, based on three different estimates of recoverability.

This has not been the only prediction of "peak oil". A great deal has been made of Hubbert's lonely isolation as a "voice in the wilderness" during the 1950s, sounding Cassandra-like warnings of the fate awaiting U.S. domestic oil production, only for events seeming to coincide in 1971, when U.S. domestic production was exceeded by domestic demand for the first time. However, in 1982, the journal Oil and Gas Science and Technology-*Revue de l'IFP*, produced by the Institut Français des Pétroles, published a serious projecting of global declines in fossil fuel production starting in 1990:

> Proven reserves of conventional hydrocarbons in the world amount to 90 billion tons of oil and 78 000 billion cubic meters of gas, respectively representing 30 and 50 years of supply at the present rate of production. Further reserves and resources yet to be discovered may be considered to be 2.3 to 2.4 times greater, but there is a high degree of uncertainty in these figures. Extensive resources of unconventional hydrocarbons exist, but they are costly to implement and, above all, require considerable investments. World petroleum production can be predicted to reach its maximum around 1990. (Bois 1982)

The reality was, and is, that all such predictions of some "maximum" extrapolate in terms of unchanging technology – a clearly unreasonable assumption no longer justifiable in any strategically important arena of production. However, can it be maintained that the tendency to look for some finite maximum arises mainly or only from lack of appropriate or sufficient data?

In 1798 Thomas Malthus published his *Essay on Population*. This asserted that population must always and everywhere expand to outstrip the capacity of societies to feed themselves. This has been repeatedly disproved everywhere – in developing countries as well as developed countries. Nevertheless in 1968, Paul R. Ehrlich published his work *The Population Bomb*, reiterating the same thesis with fancier computer projections. The first country that his model predicted would collapse calamitously was the People's Republic of China, the second was India. Today much of the steady rise in the world oil price since 2004 is being "blamed" on China and India raising their level of consumption to the level of more developed countries of Europe and the Americas. There is however no longer any serious talk or threat of their population growth – which is still large in both absolute and relative (percentage) terms relative to any other part of the planet – overwhelming the ability of their economies to feed their population.

These doom-laden predictions lack any foundation anywhere in engineering practice or scientific discourse. As far as any notions about raw materials in general being in finite supply, technological breakthroughs have continually been finding new ways to make or do more per unit output of products or finished goods using less energy and-or less raw material per unit input. The reality of these technological revolutions has repeatedly refuted all previous claims in every other field that there are "limits to growth" beyond which human existence or social or progress cannot be sustained. In the last twenty years, the elaboration of cost-effective and profitable means for exploiting the extensive so-called "unconventional reserves" of oil — like the oil sands of western Canada — has completely turned upside down the notion that the world's lights must go out when the last barrel of oil has been pumped in Saudi Arabia, Libya, Iraq or Iran. Where Malthus imprudently asserted that population must grow exponentially while food production could at best be increased only arithmetically, the work of Lord Boyd-Orr's team at the UN Food and Agricultural Organisation in the decade following the end of the Second World War, carrying on from his own classic pre-war investigations, as a professional nutritionist, of Scottish (Boyd-Orr, 1937) and English (Boyd-Orr, 1943) diet among the working classes, decisively refuted all notions that there was anything like a finite capacity for food production relative to any actual rate of population increase recorded anywhere on the planet.

Hence, such repeated predicting followed by the failure of reality to meet the prediction suggests that the activity of such prediction itself lacks any rational basis. It is a prejudice feeding the formation of yet another "devil theory of history": guess-who will be blamed as things fail to go so well for countries that presently think they are "on top" in world rankings…

"Peak oil" can thus only be understood as the latest attempt to prepare yet another devil theory of history. People will be blamed for consuming too much: governments were ignorant, corporations became excessively greedy, people became desperate… and the world went to hell. Apparently delivering another set of Cassandra-like warnings of impending doom, the proponents of the theory of peak oil and its purported consequences are also messing with people's ability to sort anything out rationally or scientifically. That is, they are turning prejudice into disinformation. Petroleum being the basis of plastics and much else, this dissemination of disinformation is exercising the most paralysing effect on developing and researching appropriate solutions to contemporary problems in all aspects of life. The following extracts from a 2004 article by James Howard Kunstler in the U.S. general-interest magazine *Rolling Stone*, with a wide readership in the 18-35 age group (the demographic that becomes socially crucial for the next 25-30 years), serve to illustrate the need for an "economics of intangibles" that breaks resolutely with such reasoning.

Many commentaries in the media and in academic discourse, pointing to the singular contemporary role of the United States, refer to this period as that of a unipolar world. The modeling of a useful "economics of intangibles", however, proceeds from an alternate premise: that we are in a post-bipolar world. It has become unipolar because one of the poles has disappeared. Just as modern cosmological theory posits the enormous gravitational pull of black holes in space to account for bending and curving space, this new theory proposes that the pathway as well as the fact of the Soviet bloc's disappearance has unleashed a tremendous disequilibrium in which many unforeseen opportunities and unprecedented possibilities as well as great potential disasters loom. One such dangerous pathway is the new kind of trade war emerging in the wake of the collapse of the Soviet bloc. It has become focused particularly on access to energy supplies as the ultimate backing for systems of currency and networks of trading relationships dependent on a secured and uninterrupted supply of credit. The issue is neither that the sky is falling nor that energy is disappearing, but simply that struggles between members of the oil cartel and governments have intensified, as they each seek to disentangle themselves from massive contradictions. These are the conflicts arising from the increasing paralysis and breakdown in the arrangements that were supposed to continue governing – well into this century – the allotment of marketing territories for various refined petroleum products, the refineries assigned throughout the North American continent to process crude oil imported from exporting countries located in designated regions of the globe, and the maintenance of investment capital flows sufficient to guarantee that declining production of crude oil in North American reservoirs would be replaced with natural gas (among other considerations). The fact of these contradictions and their sources remain very much obscured. There are literally layers of opacity that, in recent years, have enveloped the entire question of the sustainability of economies dependent on fossil fuels as their principal energy source – be it for transportation, for domestic uses such as heating, cooking etc., or for the provision of electrical power for industrial or domestic markets.

By demonstrating the long-term unsustainability of such dependence as a function of the purely arithmetic drawdown of purportedly finite supplies of these resources, a progressive-sounding case appears to be made for pursuing renewable alternative energy sources and redesigning the economic engine of modern life to require a far lower threshold of energy use. In both public and academic discourse, this position has been contending with the "Right"-wing case which also asserts limits to growth imposed by the finite availability of resources are a fact but insists, in contrast to this "progressive" wing, that these limits to growth are fixed, real and immutable, and messing with them is therefore irresponsible and extremist.

The absence of technical jargon in this article means the arguments are not condensed and telegraphed in technical terms freighted with special meanings for specialists. For this reason, it is necessary to quote the article at some length to grasp the overall argument. Popular journalism on matters of such importance is always a double-edged sword. On the one hand, the accessibility of the argument, which is what recommends such material to non-specialist general readers, would be dismissed as too unprofessional and unspecialized to attract or concern decision-makers. On the other hand, to the extent that it ensures someone somewhere will indeed be influenced perhaps to the extent of being able to repeat or elaborate the argument to others, the popular and accessible style is precisely the most subversive weapon. Surely it is not always a bad thing to swoop under the decision-makers' radar to generate serious discussion of serious matters. The problem in Kunstler's argument is neither its popularity or accessibility of its style and presentation, but the content of its argument.

Kunstler sets out the notion of the end of cheap energy (not only for oil, but, as will be seen, for gas as well) as follows:

Most immediately we face the end of the cheap-fossil-fuel era. It is no exaggeration to state that reliable supplies of cheap oil and natural gas underlie everything we identify as the necessities of modern life – not to mention all of its comforts and luxuries: central heating, air conditioning, cars, airplanes, electric lights, inexpensive clothing, recorded music, movies, hip-replacement surgery, national defense – you name it (Kunstler 2004).

In the next paragraph he points to the theory of peak oil but in a way that, without actually presenting that theory, suggests that he criticizes it "from the Left" so to speak, from the standpoint of arguing that reality need not be painted in the alarmist terms of the standard presentation of the theory to arrive at the same cataclysmic consequences:

The few Americans who are even aware that there is a gathering global-energy predicament usually misunderstand the core of the argument. That argument states that we don't have to run out of oil to start having severe problems with industrial civilization and its dependent systems. We only have to slip over the all-time production peak and begin a slide down the arc of steady depletion (Kunstler *ibid.*).

The trick in the argument is that the notion of the "end of cheap energy" has been conflated into the notion of "the theory of peak oil". The discovery of the theory of peak oil — an academically-advanced and debatable theory with a respectable peerage — is used to account for the assertion of the "end of cheap oil." This is the source of two distinct forms of disinformation: first, a Malthus-like notion that the relatively unstoppable increase in overall demand for energy must surely outstrip the comparatively fixed quantity of energy available to supply the demand; and second, the very claim that the recent period was an era of "cheap oil".

Was it "cheap" for those from whose territory and hide the wealth was extracted, and legally or illegally stolen? This is no small point. Nor is its significance confined to issues of justice and other non-economic categories.

Plunder of energy sources on terms dictated by — and thus most favorable to — the interests of the plunderers arose as a response to a crisis of overproduction that became chronic throughout the industrialized and vertically-integrated economies of North America and Europe following the First World War. The details are discussed later in this chapter, but at this point it suffices to summarise by saying that relative cheapness of petroleum products for consumers within the economies of North America and Europe was not and could not be anything but a symptom reflecting precisely the chronic nature of this crisis. The monopolised sectors of the economy could only be stimulated to remain productive by suppressing or eliminating any tendency or possibility for the real, *i.e.*, constant-dollar, cost of energy inputs actually to rise. If the relative cost of this input were to rise like any other input cost, the possibility to extract maximum profit in minimum time at the expense of all other competitors in a market would be undercut. Without that incentive, investment capital in a monopolized sector starts to search for other sectors in which to invest.

In the countries that were to become specialised in producing oil for export, keeping the relatively low costs of oil and gas production stationary in constant-dollar terms maintained the attractiveness of the sector for foreign investment, to the extent of discouraging any investment in any other sector of the economies of these countries. Thus all their needs came to be imported. No possibilities emerged to develop modern multi-branched economies capable of self-reliantly feeding the local population. Participation in the world economy consisted of exporting a single valuable raw material and importing everything else. Although the constant-dollar cost of production of the single valuable economic output of such economies remained low, these economies captured none of the added value produced downstream in the form of refined petroleum products, especially gasoline for transport, which remains the final destination of more than 60 percent of all petroleum refining and gas processing (Fleay, 1998). Gasoline taxes, along with other taxes collected on consumption including the consumption of the myriad of goods produced in whole or in part from petroleum refining byproducts such as plastics, are a major revenue generator for both governments and other industries throughout the main consuming countries of North America and Europe. These taxes also add a huge additional margin to the price of refined petroleum and its byproducts, no part of which can never be recaptured by the oil-exporting countries, even though they were the source of the raw material from which this additional wealth was generated. Meanwhile, as they were cut off from sharing in any of this additional wealth but costs continued to rise including the costs of maintaining their arrangements with consuming countries, a disproportionate share of the increased cost fell on the oil-exporting raw material producing country. However, in what amounts a "one-crop economy", the only way to capture sufficient revenues to cover these increasing costs has been to pump more oil faster. This has sped up the production of revenues from the associated consumption taxes collected by governments in the consuming countries in a process that is thus inherently inflationary and therefore tended over time also to cheapen the future value of dollar revenues from oil sales. So dramatic had this process become during the 1970s and 1980s that, instead of waiting for these inflationary effects to hit future oil export revenue, many oil-exporting countries borrowed fabulous sums from the banking systems of the consuming countries to use for current consumption needs in their own countries. Thus Saudi Arabia, the country that garners the greatest revenue of any oil producing state from its crude oil exports, has ended up with more than US$160 billions owing in debts to Western banks. What was never anticipated was the extent to which the burden of interest payments on such debts, extended as they are over lengthy terms of 10, 15, 20 and even 30 years, would eat into budgeting the current needs of their own growing population for goods and services that must be paid for at current prices and not at prices as they stood when these debts were initially contracted.

Such is the view on the edge of the precipice to which the oil exporting countries have been brought as a result of their participation in the era of (allegedly) "cheap" oil. The political vulnerability of economies that have been reduced to such a fragile condition is self-evident. Because the consuming countries are as dependent on these exporting countries for oil as the exporting countries are on these consuming countries as customers, anything threatening the economy of the exporter could spread considerable chaos in the economy of the consuming countries as well. It is to this threat that the world oil price mechanism has been responding and — in recent months — increasingly failing to respond in ways that had been heretofore predictable. Most fatefully of all, the OPEC price band for oil has disappeared since the 2004 re-election of the Bush administration (Islam and Zatzman 2005b) and events such as the annual hurricane season in the Gulf Stream and Gulf of Mexico which up to now almost never had more than the briefest blip effect on prices are playing a role in taking the price of oil to US$70 a barrel and climbing. The real story is not the "end of cheap oil" but rather the collapse of the producer-consumer nexus between the OPEC states and the leading consuming countries, and the knock-on effects of this collapse on the world oil price-setting mechanism.

Kunstler's approach buries all this reality from view. Instead, he ties certain elements from the theory of peak oil together in a manner that lumps together in one heap the serious proponents of researched innovation, the crank advocates of unproven theories, and the skeptics detecting the neo-Malthusian odour seeping from the bottom of this compost-pile of argumentation. Kunstler's first step is to assert that there is some "all-time total endowment" of a certain resource potential. First of all, just on this point, the writer is blithely ignoring the fact that knowledge of such a thing exists only at a given point in time. Secondly, the possibility is also being ignored (later it is outrightly dismissed) that the time it would take to exhaust that resource might be more than enough either to develop and spread a better technology — hydrogen, for example — that is cheaper and safer and more comprehensive, or to innovate more efficient technologies greatly to stretch the effective useful lifetime of that same endowment and efficient:

> The term "global oil-production peak" means yearly production will inexorably decline. It is usually represented graphically in a bell curve. The peak is the top of the curve, the halfway point of the world's all-time total endowment, meaning half the world's oil will be left. It's the half that is much more difficult to extract, far more costly to get, of much poorer quality and located mostly in places where the people hate us. A substantial amount of it will never be extracted.
> The United States passed its own oil peak – about 11 million barrels a day – in 1970… [Its own oil production in] 2004 … ran just above 5 million barrels a day [yet] we consume roughly 20 million barrels and the ratio will continue to worsen (Kunstler *ibid.*).

The argument then introduces another notion: that scarcity rewrote longstanding relations of power among western powers and between the western bloc and the OPEC producers' cartel. The specific content of what are presented as changes in the balance of power are actually first and foremost changes in patterns of capital investment in those parts of the oil and gas sector outside OPEC, aimed at lessening OPEC's leverage as a producers' cartel. About this, however, the author is silent. Nothing in the actual balance of power, however, either among the western powers or between the western bloc and OPEC, changed: on this point, the author is simply wrong.

It did indeed redivide shares in, and hence present and future profits to be garnered from, an already divided world market. These were redivisions of a kind that, earlier in the 20th century, provoked the First and Second World Wars. There was a bloody conflict attending this redivision. It was waged so successfully by the Arab neighbors of the State of Israel that the State of Israel's main prop, the United States at that time under the presidency of Richard Nixon, put the entire globe on nuclear war alert — DEFCON 3. Further spread of this conflict was only avoided by the refusal of the then-Soviet Union to continue bankrolling and arming non-oil-exporting Arab states standing on the front lines. Like many other proponents of the notion of peak oil, Kunstler mixes up the what the oil barons wanted, what the U.S. government wanted, and what the actual global conditions permitted the U.S. to undertake as an empire such that the story becomes all about how the United States maneuvered as best it could in the new conditions, but Nature just wasn't cooperating:

> The U.S. peak in 1970 brought on a portentous change in geoeconomic power. Within a few years, foreign producers, chiefly OPEC, were setting the price of oil, and this in turn led to the oil crises of the 1970s. In response, frantic development of non-OPEC oil, especially the

North Sea fields of England and Norway, essentially saved the West's ass for about two decades. Since 1999, these fields have entered depletion. Meanwhile, worldwide discovery of new oil has steadily declined to insignificant levels in 2003 and 2004 (Kunstler *ibid.*).

Then comes the attack on junk science and crank theories, in which the author strikes a Cassandra-like pose and pontificates as though no other alternative explanation was on offer anywhere to otherwise account for what has developed:

> Some "cornucopians" claim that the Earth has something like a creamy nougat center of "abiotic" oil that will naturally replenish the great oil fields of the world. The facts speak differently. There has been no replacement whatsoever of oil already extracted from the fields of America or any other place.
> Now we are faced with the global oil-production peak. The best estimates of when this will actually happen have been somewhere between now and 2010. In 2004, however, after demand from burgeoning China and India shot up, and revelations that Shell Oil wildly misstated its reserves, and Saudi Arabia proved incapable of goosing up its production despite promises to do so, the most knowledgeable experts revised their predictions and now concur that 2005 is apt to be the year of all-time global peak production (Kunstler *ibid.*).

Finally the prospects of developing natural gas as a substitute energy source are assessed, but from the angle of considering all its immediate inadequacies and downsides. In this part, he inadvertently and implicitly acknowledges that the forces behind Big Oil have a guiding whip hand over this process of substitution. However, instead of assessing the implications of that realisation, he tails behind the current propaganda from the so-called "war on terrorism" as though to say: there's nothing to be done.

> To aggravate matters, American natural-gas production is also declining, at five percent a year, despite frenetic new drilling, and with the potential of much steeper declines ahead. Because of the oil crises of the 1970s, the nuclear-plant disasters at Three Mile Island and Chernobyl and the acid-rain problem, the U.S. chose to make gas its first choice for electric-power generation. The result was that just about every power plant built after 1980 has to run on gas. Half the homes in America are heated with gas. To further complicate matters, gas isn't easy to import. Here in North America, it is distributed through a vast pipeline network. Gas imported from overseas would have to be compressed at minus-260 degrees Fahrenheit in pressurized tanker ships and unloaded (re-gasified) at special terminals, of which few exist in America. Moreover, the first attempts to site new terminals have met furious opposition because they are such ripe targets for terrorism (Kunstler *ibid.*).

What about the rest of the planet? Kunstler's tone seems to suggest that, presumably, those who are already starving will just have to eat less. What the proponents of the theory of peak oil and its assumptions concerning conventional or accessible energy reserves fail in general to grasp, however, is that the post-bipolar world is a big place, some corners of which do not share or participate in American ambitions. This in itself becomes a starting-point for yet more "devil" theories – this time about the intentions of Russia, a favourite U.S. target during the bipolar "Cold War" division of the world .

When it comes to assessing the credibility of such predictions of imminent disappearance of fossil fuel reserves, the systematic policy of excluding from consideration any approach to energy supply that is not currently favoured or managed by Big Oil has been a factor of inestimable importance. On this basis, for example, for decades the oil and gas reserves of the Soviet Union were of no interest and never counted in Western countries' estimates of global oil and gas reserves because they were commercially unavailable. Being commercially unavailable to Anglo-American interests and beyond Anglo-American control, they were deemed not to exist. Arrangements, however, between the Russian Gazprom conglomerate and its suppliers in Russia and central Asia have developed throughout the 1990s making Russia the premier supplier of the industrial and residential needs of Germany, the leading member of the European Union, for natural gas and refined petroleum products. The intimacy of this particular connexion is seen in the assumption of a senior executive position in Gazprom by the former German Chancellor Gerhard Schröder the moment he left office in November 2005. Post-Soviet Russia's effort, as Europe's premier natural-gas supplier, to raise the export price of natural gas in the winter of 2005-06 from US$50 to US$230 per thousand cu m, *i.e.*, from 3.8¢ per million BTU – about 1/250th the current US average price – to 17.95¢ per million BTU or about 1/50th the US average price, met with hysteria and frenzy throughout the European media. According to the EIA Natural Gas Weekly Update, the current Henry Hub average price of natural gas during December 2005 stood at US$10 per million BTU. These differentials serve to clarify the attractiveness of exporting LNG to US markets from Europe and North Africa, as well as show the Russian price increase undercuts various schemes in Europe to resell and deliver Russian gas into the US market as LNG from Europe and North Africa. As mentioned earlier in this chapter (at section 4.2.2), the Russians already have their own plans to deliver gas from the Shtokman field as LNG into the US market, via an LNG receiving port proposed for Gros Cacouna on the St Lawrence River in Quebec (Canada). With the prospect of occasional cold-season extreme fluctuations in the US price up to US$20, the prospects of reaping superprofits must seem irresistible.

This change in little more than 15 years in the status of Russia as an energy supplier, from almost not existing to being accused of highway robbery, underscores the necessity to dismiss all approaches to predicting energy supply on the basis of projecting future demand 30 years ahead in markets either currently controlled by Big Oil or which they hope to capture. Russia is also an interesting example because very little of its presently acknowledged reserves were delineated in this recent 15-year period. They have been known and under development for a much longer period. Since the 1990s, their gas supplies have become especially important for the future of most of the members of the European Union, in which natural gas is coveted as an industrial fuel as well as a heating and cooking source.

Another factor further transforming the picture stems from the absence of the corporate as well as government-owned sectors of the oil and gas industries of post-Soviet Russia from any of the existing U.S. or U.S.-European production or marketing cartels. The territories of the former Soviet Union (including the separate republics of Central Asia which emerged since 1991) possess the largest conventional oil reserves outside OPEC and the second-largest proven reserves of natural gas anywhere on earth. Its emergence as a major world-market "player" in its own right in the production and sale of crude and refined petroleum for markets in Europe, and especially for the fastest-growing markets in China and the Asian subcontinent, challenges both the demand-management model used by OPEC and backed by the U.S. oil majors to set and maintain a world oil price. As for natural gas, Russia provides the geographic linch-pin for delivering to markets anywhere in the Eurasian land mass. For the more than 4 billion people living on that land mass, this fact must over time erode any notion of any purely local market for natural gas. The global distribution of commercial natural gas and its production are described below.

Particularly of interst are the data on proven reserves — those that could be economically produced with the current technology. The former Soviet Union holds the world's largest natural gas reserves, 38 percent of the world's total. Together with the Middle East, which holds 35 percent of total reserves, they account for 73 percent of world natural gas reserves. In 2000 total world reserves were 150.19 trillion cubic meters. Global reserves more than doubled in the last twenty years. The world's ratio of proven natural gas reserves to production at current levels is between 60 and 70 years. This represents the time that remaining reserves would last if the present levels of production were maintained.

The world's main natural gas producing countries in 2000 were United States (22.9 percent of world production) and the Russian Federation (22.5 percent of total production). Other major producing countries are Canada, United Kingdom, Algeria, Indonesia, Iran, Netherlands, Norway and Uzbekistan. These ten countries alone accounted for more than 86 percent of total natural gas production in 2000. North America and the Former Soviet Union together accounted for 59 percent of global production. Total world production in 2000 was 2422.3 billion cubic meters. Production growth in 2000 was 4.3 percent, a significantly higher growth that the 1990-2000 annual average. Although production increased in all regions, the faster growth was recorded in the Middle East and Africa. During the nineties production rose in all regions but the Former Soviet Union.

Natural gas accounts for almost a quarter of world's energy consumption. Consumption of natural gas has increased considerably in the last 30 years. The world's main consuming countries in 2000 were United States, accounting for 27.2 percent of total consumption, and the Russian Federation, with 15.7 percent of total consumption. North America and the Former Soviet Union together consumed 55 percent of total natural gas. The share of Europe in total natural gas consumption was 19.1 percent. These three areas account for three quarters of global consumption. Consumption growth was 4.8 percent in 2000, with the highest rates of growth registered in Africa (12.8 percent) and Asia (7.8 percent). Total world consumption was 2404.6 billion cubic meters.

Post-Soviet Russia's situation represents one of the foremost features of the world picture of commercial production of natural gas. Russia's natural gas industry, a monopoly run by Gazprom which controls more than 95 percent of production, is the second major source of the world's commercial production of natural gas and the world's leading exporter of natural gas. Furthermore, within Russia, natural gas is the predominant industrial fuel, accounting for nearly half of the country's domestic energy consumption.

The gas industry in Europe consists mainly of downstream activities undertaken by transmission and distribution companies. More than 30 percent of gas consumption is met by pipeline imports from Former Soviet Union and Algeria as well as liquefied natural gas (LNG) imports from North Africa. The nearest and best source of supply is, logically, Russia. But as Figure 4-6 clarifies, the pipeline connections needed to feed that thirst are less than inadequate when actual population concentrations and their locations are taken into account.

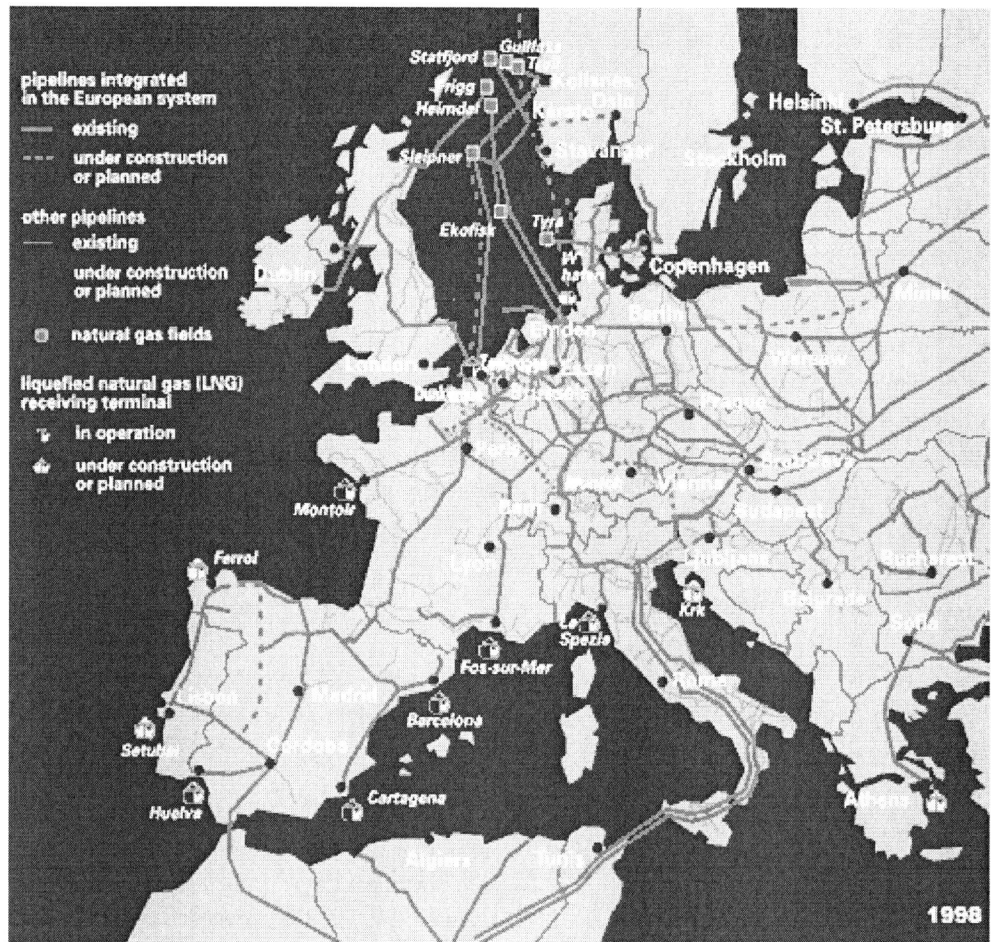

Source: Eurogas Consortium

Figure 4-6. Natural gas pipelines in Western and Eastern Europe.

Chapter 5

THE APHENOMENAL MODEL

ABSTRACT

In this chapter, the focus of concern shifts away from matters purely or mainly of theory, or even the engineered applications of theory, to the interface where knowledge of the truth encounters the policy-making machinery of government, industry, universities, etc. These are the points at which ideas are turned into products, research into technologies, and policy objectives into government programs.

Since conventional economics as social science plays major role in formulating policy options and objectives in all fields, addressing this active feature of the Aphenomenal Model becomes a matter of the highest priority. Along this line, the connection between the Aphenomenal Model and intentions is examined, some of the ways that the Aphenomenal Model is deployed to finesse any clear differentiation of truth from falsehood are identified, and the development of an entire theory and practice of "Consumption Without Production" is elaborated as the fullest expression of the Aphenomenal Model in economic theory and practice. The most fundamental version of the Aphenomenal Model which has become visible to the whole world in recent years is the Palestine model, and a recent discussion on a publicly-accessible website serves to illuminate how, when the maintenance of a huge injustice is at stake, truth and falsehood fight it out most intensely on the terrain of such normally self-evident matters as how to count heads. Recent diplomatic developments in the wake of the victory of Hamas, the Islamic Resistance Movement, in the 25 January 2006 elections to the Palestinian Legislative Council further serve to disclose how no truth is permitted to be stated no matter how many damning facts come to light about the activities of the Palestinians' oppressors. The response of the Bush Administration to the events of "9-11" have also served to trigger some other features that were long latent in the Aphenomenal Model but reactivated on a large scale only recently.

A variety and range of examples are summoned in evidence in order to bring home a key point, viz., that it is not enough to fight individual symptoms and manifestations of the Aphenomenal Model. Rather what is required is the development of multiple, diverse solutions to the problems actually presented in Nature and Humanity. A true political economy of intangibles is premised on the understanding that there is no one model, that one size cannot possibly fit all, and that the short-term pragmatic attractiveness of solutions that homogenise by curtailing or eliminating diversity may seriously damage

Humanity's long-term prospects, including matters as fundamental as the sustainability of life on this planet. This is a new starting-point for Chapter 6, in which a new synthesis is elaborated.

INTRODUCTION

In Chapters 2, 3 and 4, the most serious and profound failures and limitations in the theory and practice of economic development were presented as neither entirely accidental nor the product of conspiracy. Rather, the elaboration of an economic theory that denied any role for intention, coupled to practical implementations in industry, commerce and finance that were utterly obsessed with short-term aims – and thus inherently debarred from harnessing intangible components in the service of long-term aims – created and unleashed an accident waiting to happen.

The argument of the present work is that the characteristics which these failures share in common suggest the emergence and entrenchment of a model, marked by definite, identifiable features. Elsewhere this model has already been identified and discussed as something called the "aphenomenal model" (Khan, Zatzman and Islam 2005b). The outstanding feature of the aphenomenal model is how it facilitates pursuit of an objective put forward without any researched basis as to its actual necessity or feasibility by reducing and subdividing steps of the pathway to the goal down to the most immediate short-term, proclaiming the achievement of the latest such step as the justification for all the preceding steps as well as a green-light ticket to proceed with further such steps until "mission accomplished", as George W Bush declared on the flight deck of the *USS Abraham Lincoln* in May 2003.

Research aimed at establishing the truth, and a socially positive intention that takes into account the long-term, are the necessary and sufficient conditions for mastering, *i.e.*, comprehending and applying, the economics of intangibles. Fulfilling these two conditions is necessary as well as sufficient for detecting, deconstructing and preparing an effective intervention to defeat the operation of the aphenomenal model and reverse its effects. By zeroing in on how the policy machinery of the institutional sector – government departments, universities and the media – actually works to marginalise and stifle any approach that has not already been approved internally by this machinery, this chapter develops, and-or points the path on which to undertake development of, all the tools necessary and sufficient for such detection, deconstruction and intervention.

5.1. THE DECISION-MAKING PROCESS

The knowledge-based model shown in Figure 5-2 discloses how policy-making can turn theory into effective practice. Sound theory, theory based on useful and meaningful observations sifted and analysed properly, will lead to sound practice. A not very good theory will lead to not very good practice, and poor or weak theory will produce poor or weak practice. Regardless, however: wherever and whenever this model is actually implemented, it is always possible to model where failures occur, *i.e.*, to trace back where things went wrong, and correct one's course. It is not a unique pathway. There are other more elaborate versions of the same idea in any number of books on management organisation and administration.

However, there are and have been numerous instances in which sound, or otherwise unrefuted, theory is one thing, but the practices and implementations that emerge from it are another, often bearing little or no relationship to the knowledge and theory. This is frequently the result of an aphenomenal decision-making process being interposed.[26] This chapter is concerned with how the problem of "aphenomenality" poses itself whenever it comes to turning ideas into products, research into technologies, policy objectives into government programs, etc. The Aphenomenal Model subverts Knowledge-based model(s), from several directions. In the present work, the particular concern is with the general manner in which pathways to properly-researched theoretical understanding and any of its practical implementations are blocked and obscured by the imposition of utterly fictional phenomena that are invariably linear and intended to reduce complexity – and the accompanying likelihood of a multiplicity of solutions – to a single, "one-size-fits-all" solution. This has many consequences for economic theory and practice. The term "aphenomenality" has been coined and ascribed to this condition, whose essence is not only that of falsehood or error, but of asserting "phenomenality" where it never existed in the first place.

The Aphenomenal Model of decision-making is illustrated by Figure 5-1. It is the opposite of the knowledge-based decision-making model. It is a top-down model designed to produce decisions based on self-interest and short-term gains, entailing an inevitable resort to planted stories, cover-ups, and justification.

This serves to keep the general public unaware and uneducated about the decision-making process – an accomplishment that could not be but by intention. The need to discuss the Aphenomenal Model in the present work arises from the fact that economics as social science plays such major role in formulating policy options and objectives in all fields, and this model perches at the real-world interface where economic science and policy meet. Detecting the Aphenomenal Model and the intentions underlying its deployment are part and parcel of detecting the *modus operandi* of an anti-Knowledge intangible. In the natural

---

[26] One of the authors had rich direct personal experience of this back in 1977, while working as a newspaper journalist. He was commissioned at one point to produce a series of articles on the rural and Native housing program for "non-status Indians", *i.e.*, aboriginal persons lacking membership status in a federal-government-recognised native band, in the Canadian province of New Brunswick. The series reviewed the origin and development of the program, the successes and problems, and concluded that the program filled a gap left open by the peculiar Canadian constitutional circumstances whereby on the one hand, such native persons enjoyed none of the special entitlements of members of recognised native bands, and on the other hand provincial governments' hands were not tied in such cases (they were not permitted to have anything to do with the needs of members of recognised native bands). The last installment of the series ran the same day as the newspaper's editorial about the entire issue. The editorial opened with the somewhat startling observation that, "as readers following our series [on rural and Native housing] will be aware, this program has failed so abysmally that there is a basis to demand its review and the suspension for the time being of any further funding…" In other words: the writer had been expected to produce a series that would support this conclusion, and it had never occurred to anyone from the editorial board to mention that a preconceived conclusion was desired on this occasion, not honest or serious reportage. Years later, the author learned that the corporate interests controlling the newspaper, who owned most of the lumber sawmills in the province, wanted this program not reformed but eliminated. Why? Persons qualifying for assistance to build their own home were apparently not required, or under any other pressure, to purchase milled lumber. This circumstance had made it possible recipients of assistance under this program to build their own homes for less than 30 per cent of what it would have cost them using milled lumber purchased from any sawmill in the province but the provincial government could not obtain federal matching funds to maintain the program if conditions were attached to how qualified individuals using this assistance as intended went about spending it.

sciences and engineering, this anti-Knowledge intangible takes the form of declaring or assuming that Nature is broken and needs to be "fixed". Similarly, in social science, the same anti-Knowledge intangible operates behind the assumption that Humanity is broken and needs to be "fixed".

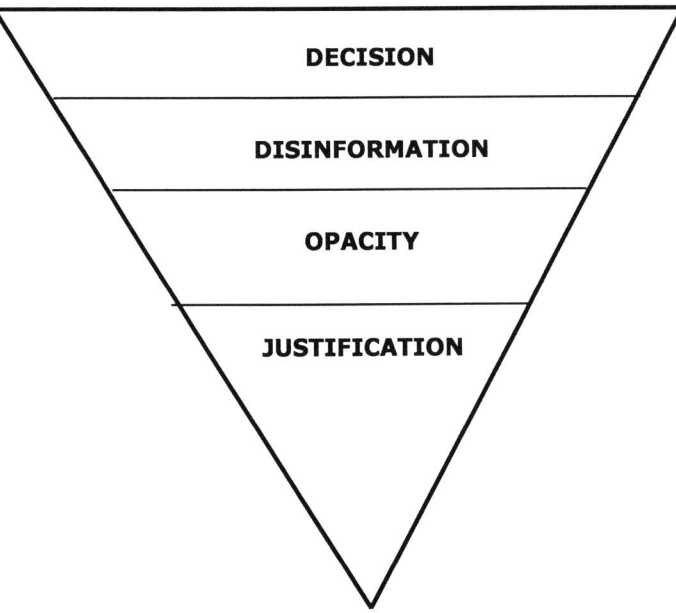

Figure 5-1. The Aphenomenal Model of Decision-Making – Beginning with a justification of the status-quo, as opposed to observations of current reality, layers of opacity are imposed, disinformation is generated that insulates and absolutises the decision-making authority, and then and only then is the policy decided.

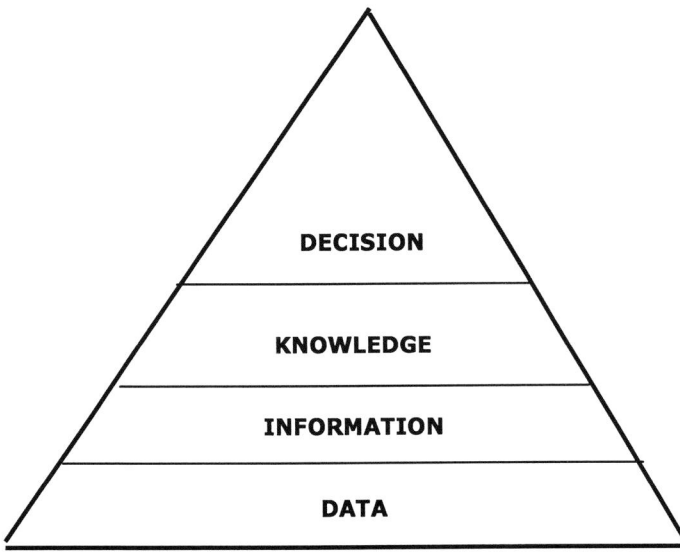

Figure 5-2. The Knowledge-Based Decision-Making Model – Decisions as to policy are rendered only *after* a process in which observations have been collected and refined into meaningful knowledge.

5.2. DECISIONS AND INTENTIONS

Deeds are but by intention; and every deed has two components: a motivator or driver, and a desired effect. A good deed (which is to say: a well-intended one) is driven by some rational choice, and it has as one of its aims the enhancement of the individual's sense of responsibility to surrounding society – to family, and-or to workmates, and-or to some other larger collective within which the individual carries out his/her deed. The intentions of those who do not accept the political mandate laid down by US President George W. Bush since "9-11", however are severely stigmatised. This mandate is summarised in his oft-quoted phrase: "you are either with us, or you are with the terrorists." To people still possessed of historical memory – something that the media and the entertainment industry of the United States seem largely to have obliterated in the U.S. – this phrase resonates with the tones of darkest reaction in Nazi Germany preceding the outbreak of the Second World War. *Der Führer* – "the Leader", as Hitler styled himself – would incessantly rant about how "the Jews" were the German people's historic burden – "unser Unglück" ["our misfortune"], he called them – and how anything and everything that had gone badly in the past, or that might still not go as desired in the present and future, could and should be ascribed to "the Jews". Notwithstanding President Bush's addition of sets of three-sided "Axes of Evil" (itself an unprecedented geometrical figure never before seen, since an axis is normally defined as a straight line joining two points at opposite ends of a solid), the list of bad things attributed to "Islamic terrorists" and "terrorism" by George W. Bush since 9-11 is remarkably similar to the litany of crimes laid at the door of "the Jews" by Adolf Hitler as well as at the door of "anti-Semites" by the State of Israel.[27]

The point of these ascriptions – of freedom fighters as "Islamic terrorists", of resistance to occupation as "terrorism" and of criticism or repudiation of the roles and policies of the State of Israel *vis-à-vis* the Arab world and Muslim *ummah* as "anti-semitism" – is not simply the fact that they are arrant nonsense. The real point is their method as a form of disinformation: anyone who does not share your intention is your enemy, but ... you need your leaders to advise you as to who these enemies are, because just looking at what

---

[27] To grasp this, substitute the words "Islamic terrorists" or "anti-semites" for the word "Jews" in the acidly satirical poem below. Written in 1934 by Bertholt Brecht, to protest the lethal implications of the Hitler régime's official anti-semitic policy, it is entitled "The Jew – A Misfortune for the People" (Brecht 1947):

As the loudspeaker of the Regime declares the Jew responsible for our misfortunes, this increasingly critical condition must, since the leadership is quite wise, be entirely the fault of the ever-diminishing numbers of Jews.

Only the Jews could be to blame for the hunger that reigns among the people, since even the great landowners are working themselves to death on their estates, and even the captains of industry are eating only the crumbs that fall from the workers' table.

And it can only be the Jew behind it if there is a shortage of wheat for bread after the military took so much land for their maneuvers and barracks that it equals the territory of an entire province.

Since the Jew is a misfortune for the people, this makes it very easy for the people to recognize one.

For this neither a birth certificate nor other external characteristics are necessary — all these can be deceptive — it is only necessary to ask: is that person a misfortune for us? Then he must be a Jew.

A misfortune is recognized not by its nose but by the fact that we are injured by it: deeds, not noses, are misfortunes.

No particular nose is necessary to rob the people, it is only necessary to be a part of the Regime!

Everyone knows that the Regime is a misfortune for the people and since all misfortunes are produced by Jews, it must be that the Regime is a product of the Jews.

Seems clear enough... (new translation from German original by G.M Zatzman)

motivated someone's deed and comparing that to whatever the deed achieved might fool any ordinary observer into trusting an enemy unless they had been properly so pre-advised.

These disinforming methods strip each one of us of any agency to produce a truly well-intended deed. By superimposing naked but inarticulate fear as the motivator or driver, rational choices are thrown out the window. By summoning powerful emotions of guilt and loathing as people second-guess and censor themselves before making further public utterance, the aim of enhancing social responsibility of each of us towards everyone else is overwhelmed. With the recent (January 2006) disclosure of systematic resort by the Bush Administration to widespread warrantless secret surveillance, private thought and discourse are now also under attack.

These most alarming developments, which have enveloped entire societies almost without warning, are actually the result of a lengthy gestation whose historical origins remain largely unknown and generally unappreciated in any depth. The immediate reason to outline this dimension of the subject of the chapter from such current material, however, is precisely because it forms part of the living thoughts in readers' minds. No knowledge of deeper historical origins is necessary to sense that, with the examples of the events just cited, an enormous falsification is being imposed. Nor, however, unlike what took place under the conditions of the Nazi era, has public compliance been obtained only at gunpoint. Rather, a definite technique has been deployed to block widescale dissemination of the facts surrounding any of these matters, while simultaneously obscuring what the truth looks like.

5.3. HALF-TRUTHS AND WHOLE LIES

As a function of the general pathway of the Aphenomenal Model in Figure 5-2 – proceeding "upwards" from Justification, through the addition of layers of Opacity, to Disinformation and finally Decision – the advisor or maker of policy who follows this model is most seriously incapacitated when it comes to any reliable method for eliminating from consideration that which is false. As a decision-making model, it threatens to entrench, and frequently does entrench, that which is false as a "fact on the ground", *i.e.*, as The Truth. In reality, the point at which True and False become differentiated is a non-linear branch-point, forming a cusp that is neither part of whatever may have been the continuum preceding it, nor part of whatever may comprise the continuum following it. That is why people say that 100 lies, i.e., partial truths, cannot approach the Truth.

All aphenomenal models fail to eliminate falsehood, but not all models that fail to eliminate falsehood are aphenomenal. The difference lies in the nature of the modeler's intention. If that intention is short-term and self-serving, application of the model will actually *entrench* as True that which is False, thus demonstrating aphenomenality. ("Entrenchment" means all the conclusions, or all the significant or fundamental conclusions, are false, not just some or a few.) The problem posed by falsehood is not merely its utterance, but its displacement of whatever is true. Such displacement becomes entrenched whenever the intention of the individual turning theory into practice is short-term and self-serving. Therefore, although *necessary* for finding the path back towards wherever or whatever the truth is, neither mere identification of the falsehood nor even its immediate purveyor is, or are, *sufficient* for this purpose. Here is where knowledge of intention becomes crucial. The present Information Age has opened unprecedented prospects for vastly increasing both opacity and transparency of information about all manner of things, including intentions. In effect, in our day, we can "Google" that anonymous Cretan who reportedly declared: "all Cretans are liars", divine his intentions, and therebyy remove one of the most famous of the allegedly irremovable paradoxes of classical Greek philosophy. Only along this path, for which knowledge of intention as well as knowledge of what the truth looks like together furnish the necessary and sufficient conditions to recapture the truth, can the aphenomenal model itself be combatted and displaced.

Because aphenomenal models serve a short-term and self-interested agenda, they confront a standing threat from knowledge-based research that gets to the truth, the seeking of truth from facts, and understanding based on conscious participation of the individual in acts of finding out. These latter approaches, all consistent with a scientific view of the world, attempt to establish what is true by eliminating what is false. This has the often useful side-effect of also isolating the sources, agents and purveyors of the falsehood. Aphenomenal models require, by contrast, the preservation of falsehood by insisting that truth itself (as distinct from the completeness of our knowledge of it) is a relative quantity to be located somewhere on a continuum. This has as its side-effect that sources, agents and purveyors of falsehoods cannot be established objectively from factual evidence, opening the door for asserting some Absolute Authority as the final arbiter. This defines the modern version of the Royal Prerogative exercised as the divine right of modern corporate-type kingship, including the leadership of corporate-style governments like that of the contemporary United States.

5.4. DETECTING FALSEHOOD *vs* CRUSHING ITS AGENTS

Several years ago, in the wake of the hysterical anti-Muslim scares unleashed following the terrorist assault on the World Trade Centre, one of the authors was involved in preparing and submitting a serious proposal to revisit the technology of lie detection with a development proposal that would apply contemporary scientific methods to detect any individual in the act of lying, without resorting to mass dragnetting of people deemed probable suspects on the basis of their ethnicity, physical appearance or religious belief. Entitled "An Accurate And Remotely Accessible Lie-Detection Machine" (Islam *et al.* 2002), the project's Summary noted:

> A recent survey ... conducted by the *Al-Hayat* Society reveals that there is a need for a mechanism of establishing the truth in an objective fashion in order to restore public confidence... Without such confidence, no amount of security measures can combat the feeling of insecurity among the public... [Company A and Company B have been involved before now] in developing a "fool-proof" lie detection machine for use by [the province's] Justice department. The [need exists] for ... a device that can be accurate and can eliminate the shortcomings of the existing polygraph tests... Because all shortcomings (including ethical and government control issues) of existing technologies hover around lack of objectivity, [Company A and Company B] led a concept development project on improving the accuracy of the lie detection machine to 99.99% – something that would be acceptable in court. However, it must be emphasised that the intention of this device is not to prove the guilt

of a person... [It] is rather proving the innocence of a suspect and also clearing investigative teams of bias and prejudice.

The proposed method involves the use of a new method for detecting truthfulness of a subject by measuring brain response as well as blood flow into the brain. In order to improve accuracy, three approaches are proposed. First, a new technique for signal ... and secondly, the combination of "brain response" with heart and skin response... further enhanced by observing retinal movement when responding to a [a scene of a crime]... Retinal *movement* is not to be confused with [the iris-retina pictures] currently being [taken and compiled] as a means of [unique personal identification]. Here, movement is the key, not the distribution of the blood vessels that can only serve as baseline... The method can be used to eliminate false accusations and minimize bias against a "suspect community"... [and to] ensure that illegal or unethical activities were not conducted by the investigation team ... [thus avoiding] future legal problems involved...

About the project's objectives, the proponents inserted the following salient remarks:

> In the current atmosphere of tension being felt in North America as a result of September 11, it is necessary to confirm certain facts in order to take preventive measures against further [such] events. A fool-proof lie detector test would confirm one's guilt without doubt and allow for more direct action to be taken to bring that person to justice. Money would be saved from various dragnet hunts that could be spent on more precisely targeted operations once the list of culprits has been narrowed down. Rather than relying on such deficient indications of guilt such as heartbeat and skin, a more accurate and certain method [than the polygraph for] determining it ... is to examine ... brain response. This project will look at the connection between the brain's blood flow, electronic response and lying, as well as the effect of lying on one's blood flow to the brain. It would provide a system of entrapment for those who know how to evade such tests.

Noting the well-known problem that conventional polygraphy has a high likelihood of producing false negatives, *i.e.*, guilty persons can fool it, it was also pointed out that:

> Even if the method is not accepted in court, it can be used to eliminate falsely accused ones or to ensure that illegal activities were not conducted by the investigation team

and that polygraphy means

> intimidation by state power, a degradation of employee and citizen rights. This defeats the purpose of national security in the minds and hearts of an honest population. Under the threat of loss of livelihood, each employee is to be coerced into a procedure in which their bodies are used against them, and during which they cannot have the personal witness of a legal representative – this is torture.

It is important to note that, in this proposal, the isolating of falsehood is not only completely separated from matters of guilt or innocence but is also to be applied to those charged with the investigative function that could produce a suspect or suspects for trial. Furthermore the best that can be hoped for, according to the premises of this proposal, is catching a person in the act of telling a specific lie. There are no physiological criteria or so-called "brain signatures" that can establish reliably, and without error, whether a subject tends generally to lie. Of course, establishing such a thing with the confidence level demanded in the courts – greater than 99 per cent – would also entail establishing the pattern or patterns of an individual's intention(s), and a machine capable of perpetual motion will likely be built before any mechanical means is designed to accomplish such a task.

5.5, EFFORTS TO DETECT "LIARS WITH NOTHING TO LOSE IF THEY'RE DETECTED, THE TRUE BELIEVERS WILLING TO DIE FOR THE CAUSE": EXPOSING THE DECADENCE OF THE APHENOMENAL MODEL

Modern industry modifies or completely renovates some technology or process according to a standardised pattern: feasibility of a proposal to make fixes or wholesale changes is established; the modification is developed, tested and implemented; and techniques to sample randomly for defective products are refined. Since those commissioning changes to the system place the system itself beyond question from the outset, failures are treated always as isolated aberrations, never systemic. In the case of industrial technologies entailing the processing and refining of natural source-materials, Nature can be blamed, but – almost as a matter of principle – processing and refining and their necessity cannot be questioned.

This divine right of corporate kings cannot be imposed in the absolutist manner of feudal monarchies, since profits in the hundreds of billions of dollars depend not only on enslaving tens of millions of employees and on hoodwinking consumers, but – even more important – on eliciting the more or less enthusiastic co-operation of millions of managerial-level personnel. Aphenomenal models bridge the chasms of irrationality and opacity routinely encountered by those whose job is to be able to defend and rationalise whatever is False as being True. This renders the development and elaboration of such models particularly crucial for securing the compliance of this stratum.

According to U.S. President George W. Bush, the Department of Homeland Security in Washington, DC and many others, the maintenance of beliefs by any individual that counter officially accepted views is a personality disorder of such toxicity as to mandate deployment of an entire system for attacking the psyche of such individuals until they "crack" or are destroyed. As a recent article in the *Sunday New York Times Magazine* discloses, this is being carefully prepared in a manner strikingly similar to the above-described norms of modern industry in modifying or completely renovating some technology or process. On this basis, with no interest whatsoever in establishing the truth of whatever anyone might actually be lying about, and with even less regard for social or political rights, what amounts to an entire regime of randomised psychological "torture-testing" of people is being justified as an effort to catch lies and liars in general on the basis of refining and overcoming the defects of polygraph technology in particular.

To grasp the decadence implicit in this proposition, consider the underlying logic of the Bush Administration on this matter:

- Either you are with us or you are with the terrorists (*Major Premise*)
- Those who are with us never lie (*Minor Premise*)
- Hence: all liars must be terrorists and all terrorists must be liars (*Conclusion*)

Two fraudulent premises have generated a false conclusion. This is a clear sign of "stage two" decay from what was discussed back in Chapter 2 as one of the signposts of the Aphenomenal Model's logic at work in the realms of science and research:

- All Americans speak French (*Major Premise*)
- Jacques Chirac is an American (*Minor Premise*)
- Therefore: Jacques Chirac speaks French (*Conclusion*)

As discussed back in Chapter 2, this model, which we might call "stage one" aphenomenality, illustrates how retrofitting and guesswork could be combined to provide a plausible explanation of observable reality (*e.g.*, that "Jacques Chirac speaks French"). It was implemented widely in many scientific fields during the 19th and 20th centuries. Often this served to make it possible to retain and maintain without question the eternal validity of certain shibboleths that were taken to be fundamental "laws of motion." The fallaciousness of the premises derived frequently from their being inferences from other observations, or someone's interpretation of others' data, rather than actual direct observations in themselves. Once this kind of aphenomenality is isolated, new observations can be taken and the earlier analysis and conclusions corrected; the problem that remains is mainly one of scale, *i.e.*, of the large burden of such fallacious "science" that has accumulated over the decades.

On the other hand, the reasoning that officials put forward to the public for the new initiatives in "improved polygraphy" merits scrutiny for other reasons. Not only does such scrutiny illuminate the dark and obscured pathway of this decay, but it also shows that the relatively simple corrective action that could address and reverse "stage one" aphenomenality cannot rescue the situation in this case:

> Most people think they're good at spotting liars, but studies show otherwise. A very small minority of people, probably fewer than 5 percent, seem to have some innate ability to sniff out deception with accuracy. But in general, even professional lie-catchers, like judges and customs officials, perform, when tested, at a level not much better than chance. In other words, even the experts would have been right almost as often if they had just flipped a coin.
>
> In the middle of the war on terrorism, the federal government is not willing to settle for 50-50 odds. "Credibility assessment" is the new catch phrase, which emerged at about the same time as "red-level alert" and "homeland security." Unfortunately, most of the devices now available, like the polygraph, detect not the lie but anxiety about the lie. The polygraph measures physiological responses to stress, like increases in blood pressure, respiration rate and electrodermal skin response. So it can miss the most dangerous liars: the ones who don't care that they're lying, don't know that they're lying or have been trained to lie. It can also miss liars with nothing to lose if they're detected, the true believers willing to die for the cause. (Henig 2006)

No concern whatsoever is expressed that this approach also scoops up, as suspects, those who, whether they are lying or not, are sufficiently stressed by the experience to generate truthful responses that can also be interpreted nevertheless as lies. Furthermore, the "false negatives" deficiency of polygraphy makes it impossible to distinguish terrorist liars from non-terrorist ones. That is why the justificatory logic of the first extremely decayed, syllogism becomes so essential.

Lying as a process is entirely intangible:

The English language has 112 words for deception, according to one count, each with a different shade of meaning: collusion, fakery, malingering, self-deception, confabulation, prevarication, exaggeration, denial. Lies can be verbal or nonverbal, kindhearted or self-serving, devious or baldfaced; they can be lies of omission or lies of commission; they can be lies that undermine national security or lies that make a child feel better. And each type might involve a unique neural pathway. (Henig *ibid.*)

Does it not therefore seem very much a fool's errand to propose or seek "mechanical" means of detecting such a thing? Mechanical (or electromechanical, or electromagnetic) detection of a characteristic indicator or set of indicators must be calibrated to search within a plausible or probable range, interval or spectrum. Differences of intention, however, do not fall within any finite range, interval or spectrum for which anyone could know or for which they could program in advance. Such an exercise seems as absurd on its face as the example introduced at the start of Chapter 4, of generating large quantities of data about rates of free-fall for all manner of objects in order to compare and rank these speeds according to an object's mass. Comparing things on a basis that does not and cannot relate them – because scientific investigation has previously established that no such basis can exist for relating them – can only carry on in the service of some ulterior motive. Rational people eventually had to give up trying to turn lead into gold – even Sir Isaac Newton was caught up in this madness – after it became manifestly apparent, following publication in 1869 and further filling-in during the 1870s of Russian chemist Dmitri Mendeleyev's periodic table of the elements, that the aim itself was the sheerest absurdity given the realities of the natural physical world: gold, element #79, is a Group Ib metal; lead, element #82, is a Group IVa one, and key properties of the member-elements from each of these groups are largely mutually exclusive. Unlike the situation encountered with "stage one" aphenomenality, the kind of opacity furthered by "stage two" aphenomenality renders impossible the recovery of the truth by backing up the pathway. The pathway itself is the problem.

As discussed earlier in Chapter 2, intangible features in social and economic matters have been ignored or dismissed for a long time precisely because no one could come up with some way to measure them or their impacts, while the best candidate methods for attempting such measurement also bring to light many limitations and outright nonsense infusing existing theories that were supposed to account for tangible features of society and economy. Truths and lies each contain both tangible and intangible components. However, the intangible component of a lie is aphenomenal. Aphenomenal elements likely work just fine for someone's self-interest in the short term. Hence the truth by itself, while necessary in and of itself, becomes insufficient to free Humanity from falsehoods and lies. Before the truth can emerge standing on its own, that which is false must first be exposed and repudiated.

However, in response to the U.S. federal government initiatives launched by the Bush Administration since "9-11",

> a handful of scientists are building a cognitive theory of deception to show what lying looks like — on a liar's face, in a liar's demeanor and, most important, in a liar's brain. The ultimate goal is a foolproof technology for deception detection: a brain signature of lying, something as visible and unambiguous as Pinocchio's nose. (Henig *ibid.*)

Here, both two principal desiderata, *viz.*, "foolproof technology" and the "brain signature...as visible and as unambiguous as Pinocchio's nose", are themselves utterly aphenomenal. Technology here means some bonanza for a gang of private shareholders. The notion that *such* technology could be "foolproof" is itself utterly aphenomenal. To render the detection of lies and liars dependent on the short-term self-interest of some corporation and its shareholders controlling a patented technology and concerned entirely with their own bottom line means placing the reduction of aphenomenality in the hands of those whose very existence is premised on the operation of the Aphenomenal Model. This is the modern-day version of the Greek Sophist's famous conundrum of relying on the Cretan to identify fellow liars. It is parallel to hiring the same company from which electronic voting machines were leased to count votes more accurately than humans for the purpose of not maintaining any paper audit trail of actual votes counted. It is equivalent to that irremovable contradiction of formal set theory, the set of all sets excluding itself.[28]

When it comes to the "brain signature…as visible and as unambiguous as Pinocchio's nose," as investigator Stephen Kosslyn has been pointing out to anyone who would listen, the assumptions of the research approves so far into a modernised polygraphy suited to this age of "wars on terrorism" are rife with aphenomenality:

> Over at Harvard, Stephen Kosslyn, a psychologist, was looking at the map [that research psychiatrist Daniel Langleben at the University of Pennsylvania] was starting to build and found himself troubled by the connection between deception and the anterior cingulate cortex. "Yes, it lights up during spontaneous lying," Kosslyn said, but it also lights up during other tasks, like the Stroop task, that have nothing to do with deception. "So it couldn't be the lie zone." Deception "is a huge, multidimensional space," he said, "in which every combination of things matters." Kosslyn began by thinking about the different dimensions, the various ways that lies differ from one another in terms of how they are produced. Is the lie about you, or about someone else? Is it about something you did yesterday or something your friend plans to do tomorrow? Do you feel strongly about the lie? Are there serious consequences to getting caught? Each type of lie might lead to activation of particular parts of the brain, since each type involves its own set of neural processes.

> He decided to compare the brain tracings for lies that are spontaneous, like those in Langleben's study, with those that are rehearsed. A spontaneous lie comes when a mother asks her teenage son, "Did you do your math homework?" A rehearsed lie comes when she asks him, "Why are you coming home an hour past your curfew?" The question about the homework probably surprises him, and he has to lie on the fly. The question about the curfew was probably one he had been anticipating, and concocting an answer to, for most of the previous hour.

---

[28] In addition to swindling people and compounding errors already committed, however, aphenomenality of this order and on this scale can actually kill people. Nobel theoretical physicist Dr Richard Feynman, the sole dissenting member of the commission of inquiry into the *Challenger* shuttle explosion of 1986, brought this out starkly in public when the commission delivered its report. Using a standard "O"-ring from the project's regular supplier, a cigarette lighter and a glass of water cooled near freezing, he demonstrated the real problem quickly and simply: the gasket had not been engineered to withstand anything approaching the extremely steep temperature gradient between the inside and outside of a fuel tank attached to an object accelerating towards escape velocity moving away from the Earth's surface. Not to re-engineer the gasket in order to finish within budget was a conscious decision. Fudging discussion between the shuttle project contractor, Martin-Marietta, and NASA of some of the potential consequences was another conscious decision. A large number of people within the project involved with production engineering were aware of the possible problem but, fearing for their jobs, dared not talk outside and therefore no one in mission control, or Challenger launch management, or the crew had any idea. Thus, while an impressively exhaustive number of mission items including all flight control details were checklisted, and indeed probably seemed "foolproof", something going wrong because of the "O"-ring seals was a condition that could be managed or anticipated neither from Houston Control nor aboard the shuttle craft (Feynman 1988).

As he predicted, Kosslyn found that as far as the brain was concerned, spontaneous and rehearsed lies were two different things. They both involved memory processing, but of different kinds of memories, which in turn activated different regions of the cortex: one part of the frontal lobe (involved in working memory) for the spontaneous lie; a different part in the right anterior frontal cortex (involved in retrieving episodic memory) for the lie that was rehearsed. That's not much of a map yet, but it is a cumulative movement toward a theory of deception: that lying involves different cognitive work than truth-telling and that it activates several regions in the cerebral cortex that are also activated during certain memory and thinking tasks.

Even as these small bits of data emerge through functional-M.R.I. imagery, however, Kosslyn remains skeptical about the brain-mapping enterprise as a whole. "If I'm right, and deception turns out to be not just one thing, we need to start pulling the bird apart by its joints and looking at the underlying systems involved," he said. A true understanding of deception requires a fuller knowledge of functions like memory, perception and visual imagery, he said, aspects of neuroscience investigations not directly related to deception at all.

In Kosslyn's view, brain mapping and lie detection are two different things. The first is an academic exercise that might reveal some basic information about how the brain works, not only during lying but also during other high-level tasks; it uses whatever technology is available in the sophisticated neurophysiology lab. The second is a real-world enterprise, best accomplished not necessarily by using elaborate instruments but by encouraging people "to use their two eyes and brains." Searching for a "lie zone" of the brain as a counterterrorism strategy, he said, is like trying to get to the moon by climbing a tree. It feels as if you're getting somewhere because you're moving higher and higher. But then you get to the top of the tree, and there's nowhere else to go, and the moon is still hundreds of thousands of miles away. Better to have stayed on the ground and really figured out the problem before setting off on a path that looks like progress but is really nothing more than motion. (Henig *ibid.*)

The conventional research technique and approach might be defined thus:

> To develop a theory of deception requires parsing the subject into its most basic components so it can be studied one element at a time. (Henig *ibid.*)

However, this is utterly inadequate for penetrating deeply the problem that Stephen Kosslyn has defined. No matter in how many distinct parts of the elephant individual researchers become specialists, it matters not at all until the existence of the elephant itself, as the sum of all those parts, is acknowledged, and a theory explicitly advanced in light of the fact that the parts must work together so that the original integrity of the elephant is fully restored.

5.6. CONSUMPTION WITHOUT PRODUCTION

Back in Chapter 2, the theory of "monopoly capital" advanced by Paul A. Baran and Paul M. Sweezy in the early 1960s was discussed with respect to its distortion of the role of the historical passage of time and its consequences for, and impacts on, fundamental economic transformations. It was mentioned that the Baran-Sweezy school's substitution of a basic tendency denies the existence of, or role for, any intention and especially intention in the form of a class aim. According to their approach, whatever takes place is to be accounted for mainly by the countless number of decisions about production and marketing at the level of individual corporate entities. In fact, this approach also serves to obscure from view the systemic mechanism that ensures that both Waste and the Surplus both continue to grow.

That mechanism, which is known as "state monopoly capitalism" but whose existence Baran and Sweezy explicitly deny, is actually evidence of the Aphenomenal Model at work. Its guiding principle and highest aim is the achievement of "consumption without production." The basic idea is that profits are maximised in minimum time by realising revenue through sale (both to capture surplus and to recover variable capital and replace wear-and-tear on constant capital). This undertaken on a basis rearranged so that the risks to Capital of investing more variable capital, *e.g.*, money for wages and salaries, and replacing or renewing constant capital, *e.g.*, money for machinery and equipment as well as raw material consumed in production, are or have been displaced elsewhere as much and as far as possible. A most salient and typical example of this is in war preparations and the parasitism of a great deal of so-called "defence spending."

Surpluses in Nature are, essentially unheard of – indeed, it can be said that physical or environmental surpluses are anti-Nature. It is hardly rocket science to notice that the handling and accumulating of surpluses in economies based on the production of commodities by means of the commodity of labour-time have also not gone well. Nevertheless, leading powers in the economy persisting in their pursuit and production of these surpluses even as they have clearly become similarly anti-societal. The question is: why?

The first-level approximation of a correct answer to this question was supplied by Karl Marx in the 1850s. His analysis is especially remarkable given both that free competition predominated in that era among the producers of commodities by means of the commodity of labour-time, and that there remained a wide range of goods and services that had not yet been commodified on the industrial model. Pointing to the contradictory condition of an irremovable tendency, despite the tendency for the surplus to rise, for the rate of profit to fall as a result of the accelerated replacement of living labour, *i.e.*, workers, with dead labour, *i.e.*, machines, Marx saw people as living beings whose existence was tolerated by Capital only as sources of labouring power that could be bought and sold as so many units of labour-time. Accordingly, while fully cognizant of the incessant tendency of the surplus to rise, he proposed rather the falling rate of profit as the "basic tendency" of the system overall. It followed that if workers defended their working conditions from further erosion and fought to raise their wages, Capital would have to respond in order to expand its profits and thereby withstand the trend of the basic tendency, and this struggle would have to be resolved. Baran and Sweezy, on the other hand, saw people as consumers who have capitulated and who do not live or struggle within a contradiction whose dynamic, because they are trapped inside it, remains intangible to them. According to their doctrine of "monopoly capital", infinite growth of the Surplus is the basic tendency, while any struggles are mere accidents or aberrations, in which there is no discernible tendency.

The intangibility of a contradiction, however, like the intangibility of anything else, does not render it inoperative, any more than the fact that we cannot measure gravity waves directly proves that the gravitational field cannot exist. For Baran and Sweezy's economic theory, unfortunately, this intangibility leads them to deny the existence of any class aim or intention. They see arrangements among monopolies to minimise competition, especially over product pricing, and declare the death of competition as the essence of monopoly. This fails to account, however, for how corporate monopolies and near-monopolies, by striving to maximise profits in minimum time, *i.e.*, in the $t =$ 'right now' timeframe, operate to displace or sublimate the continuing and irrepressible effects of their ruthlessly and mutually destructive competition especially over future market share and access to new markets. This intangible time component, rather than Baran and Sweezy's notion of each monopoly striving to avoid competition that would be ruinous to itself in the short term, proves in fact to be the critical element.

Baran and Sweezy accompany their characterisation of "monopoly capitalism" – as a system without class intentions but manifesting a basic tendency in which surpluses rise without limit – with what they consider the main side-effects and consequences flowing from this condition. The first such side-effect they detect is that of temporary economic crises that break out because of "underconsumption": the using-up of the social product cannot keep pace with the monopolies' hunger for profits. This challenges the classical explanation for the outbreak of periodic crises, which was: overproduction of goods. The underconsumption thesis thus begs an obviously embarrassing question: according to this theoretical perspective, what has happened to production? And, even more curiously, if underconsumption causes crises to break out, why is the exit from crisis most frequently accompanied either by the appearance of excess capacity in entire sectors of the economy, or no change in capacity utilisation rates before the outbreak of crisis? Only a rise in consumption can extricate an economy from a crisis of underconsumption, and such a rise means capacity utilisation rates must increase. Obviously, the appearance of excess unused capacity means the rate of capacity utilisation cannot possibly be increasing.

The problem cannot be resolved without tossing aside the thesis of underconsumption as a cause of crisis in monopolised economic systems, and bringing production back into the bigger picture. The fundamental feature of such an economy is neither the tendency for the surplus to rise without limit nor for its crises to be triggered by insufficient consumption. Rather, those economic forces that wield power within the State use political power alongside economic clout to maximise profits in minimum time by shifting all the costs and burdens of maintaining and supervising production onto others. For themselves they seek consumption without production.

5.6.1. Consumption without Production and "Market Uncertainty"

There are examples of Aphenomenal Model responses on display in many real-world economic contexts. Focusing specifically on some effects of the outlook that accommodates the notion of "consumption without production", there is the stock market. In this locale, claims on present or future production are exchanged. These exchanges take either the form of contracts on actual commodity production or, more commonly in the case of shares trading, an ownership claim on the capital of a going concern.

The first question to settle is: what constitutes "a claim on present or future production"? The actual answer to this seemingly simple and obvious query is rife with metaphysical subtleties that would tax the skill of St Thomas Aquinas or St Augustine. Future production does not yet exist. Present production is only partially complete. Neither has yet been distributed. What takes place in the market is an auctioning of claims the result of which will enable the producer to arrange distribution of what has been produced and when to complete the production run and its final distribution in the manner that will garner the most profit.

The claims themselves represent a promise to deliver to its holder some allotment of the profits finally collected from eventual sale of the producer's goods or services. These claims themselves, however, are neither promissory notes nor promises to pay and they cannot be said to extend the money supply by their issuance, as Treasury bills do, for example. Instead, the claimant, in exchange for a cut of the profits, helps finance some current and future production and distribution without any power to mandate decisions about production or distribution. All that can be distributed, therefore, is producer's risk. That which has not been produced, meanwhile cannot be distributed; at this stage, that is a factor that operates in effect to equalise, roughly speaking, the risks being assumed by the shareholder and the producer respectively.

Like any other contract, deed or other instrument by which private property is exchanged for a sum of money, these claims themselves are also exchangeable private property. The exchange of these claims for money spreads the original producer's risk more widely, reducing the risk assumed by any individual claimholder reduces by increasing the numbers of such claimants. The burden shared among claimant shareholders is the same in total but diminished with each extension of the number of shareholders, but the burden of risk carried on the producer's shoulders has remained the same. Now the fact that what has not been produced cannot be distributed becomes a powerful stimulus spurring production that will fulfill the outstanding obligations to shareholders. If the producer has reason to believe that he can continue distributing production after his shareholders have cashed out and taken their profits, in many cases this may also spur overproduction, because the producer senses an opportunity to keep all the profits from product distributed over and above what shareholders invested in. If overproduction becomes general and the excess product fails to sell, some producers will be ruined and others will accept a severe discounting of their shares in the market in order to retain investor interest in financing the producer's return to a restabilised marketplace. Producers who do not try to outsmart the market, on the other hand, and distributed what they produced as promised the shareholders will retain investor interest in their shares even as the price of their shares rises in recognition of their effective value.

As discussed earlier in Chapter 3, electronic trading in shares and related investment vehicles has spread worldwide. This has produced the phenomenon of programmed trading, whereby more than 90 percent of the volume of shares on stock exchanges are bought and sold according to signals given by computer programs operated by the biggest brokerage houses operating in markets around the world; some of the biggest producers are themselves major players as well in buying and selling stocks that are program-traded. What guarantees profit in this scenario is no longer actual production or distribution but simply the rate – both the absolute number of shares traded and the total number of trading transactions – at which stocks are bought and sold. This situation imposes the highest burden of risk on the shoulders of the smallest investors holding the least amount of security for their investments: for them, any hitch in producing what was promised or in distributing what was produced is fatal. If panic selling is triggered, an even wider swath of investors with some small amount of security will then be affected. If the so-called "circuit-breakers" cannot be invoked in time, the losses of paper value rise orders of magnitude more, and most investors other than are not likely to be able to recover even their original investment. The fact that what has not been produced cannot be distributed will be of little or no account, however, as far as institutional traders and brokers trading on their own account are concerned, as they are likely to possess the widest connections for moving and securing their investment capital in long-term bonds and other instruments that are similarly insulated from such volatility.

It is widely expected the US dollar will be clobbered during 2006 by the cumulative effects of the war in Iraq on US budget deficits and the inflationary buildup of increased military spending, as well as the opening of the Iranian oil bourse, which could shift a great deal of oil trades into Euros and out of the dollar. Meanwhile, their vision blindered by excessive focus on the effects of key indicators like the price of oil on consumer spending, conventional analysts observing the domestic US economy continue to produce utterly meaningless prognostications. A typical recent example:

> NEW YORK — The stock market hates uncertainty. Unfortunately, there's too much for it for Wall Street to bear right now.
>
> The economy is sending mixed signals, with job growth that could be characterized as either decent or mediocre, inflation gauges that show rising prices in some sectors and steady prices elsewhere, and economic growth that could either be healthy or anemic, depending on the metric du jour.
>
> Add to the mix energy prices that, while having fallen last week, are still around $65 per barrel — during a usually low-cost time of year — and corporate profits that are showing hints of a coming slowdown.
>
> Finally, the one hoped-for certainty that investors had clung to earlier this month — that the Federal Reserve would call a halt to its program of regular interest rate hikes — suffered a blow last week when the Fed apparently wouldn't rule out future rate hikes, depending on the economic and inflation data that comes in.
>
> And, of course, that data is mixed, contradictory and inconclusive.
>
> Investors can generally make money in any kind of environment, so long as they have a good idea of what's coming, even if it means hardship for the average person. But when uncertainty reigns and investors can't figure out what to do, sitting on stocks becomes risky — and you get a selloff.
>
> That's what happened last week, after the Fed's announcement and disappointing profits from Google Inc. and Amazon.com Inc. For the week, the Dow Jones industrial average lost 1.04 percent, the Standard and Poor's 500 fell 1.53 percent and the Nasdaq composite index dropped 1.81 percent.
>
> There's little in the week ahead that promises to provide any clarity. Barring some very positive earnings reports or steep drops in oil prices, the market could be in for more of the same.
>
> ECONOMIC DATA
>
> The economic number that has a chance of moving stocks this week is the Commerce Department's report on the nation's trade deficit, due Friday. The trade deficit is expected to have risen to $64.5 billion in December from $64.2 billion in November.
>
> Given the high cost of oil this winter, it's unlikely there's much room here for a positive surprise. However, as long as the deficit hasn't worsened considerably, investors could take it as a sign of stronger U.S. exports, which can only help corporate profits down the road. ..
> (From: Michael J. Martinez, "Mixed Data Could Keep Stock Market Murky", filed Sunday, 5 Feb 2006 at 1701 ET on the *Associated Press* Business Wire)

As to the role of programmed trading – not a word. The main problem from the stockbroker's standpoint of this article is the liquidity of shares in the market. There is no clearly emerging trend of anything that appears particularly attractive or repulsive, particularly attractive to buy or urgent to unload. Most interesting of all, however, is the almost passing mention of the U.S. trade deficit. This deficit is permanent. Nothing has been done since the decoupling of the dollar from gold on 15 August 1971 to cause the trade deficit to reverse. Most probably, this is because its net effect of cheapening the U.S. dollar also spreads purchasing power ever more widely within the U.S. – in which there is no market in any high-profit good or service that is not fully or excessively supplied – without having to print more currency and stimulate inflationary risks. However, the other aspect of the expanding trade deficit is that its financing, which has become increasingly dependent on Asian central banks, rearranges – globally and highly unevenly – the risk inherent in the warning about "that which has not been produced cannot be distributed". This is one of the fronts on which the aphenomenality of the doctrine of consumption without production poses the gravest threat to the future of many peoples around the world.

5.6.2. The U.S. Trade Deficit

There is the record $725.75-billion 2005 U.S. trade deficit – 17.5 per cent higher than 2004 – as a fact in the world, and there is the discussion of this fact and its significance, in which the Aphenomenal Model asserts itself with a vengeance, essentially justifying the missions of "consumption without production" and of living off the rest of the world without the slightest intention of taking any measures that would move any of their trading accounts back towards a balanced position. Of course, when it comes to dealing with the U.S. trade deficit as a fact in the world, it is a fact that many other countries, lacking ownership over a press of their own to print and distribute enormous tranches of the world's leading reserve currency whenever desired, also have either overall trade deficits, or overall trade surpluses, or oscillate between periods of each. Some have deficits persisting in certain departments of trade and surpluses in other departments, *e.g.*, Canada is always a net importer of machinery and equipment and always a net exporter of bread grains and forest products, while it oscillates between being sometimes a net importer and sometimes a net exporter of "energy". Furthermore, exports have remained at around 10 per cent of the U.S. GDP for several decades, while more than 90 per cent of the deficit in trade is accounted for by U.S. imports of automobiles and other consumer manufactured goods. When it comes to capital goods, overall the U.S. trade account is more or less in balance and in certain strategic areas such as aerospace it is the world's leading exporter. However, as the data compiled in Figure 5-3 may help to remind the reader, the U.S. trade deficit is the one that has become increasingly significant. As a result of the dramatic and permanent shifts in global energy markets since the disappearance of the former Soviet Union, and the rapid expansion in China of all forms of manufacturing, including the repositioning of U.S. and European goods manufacturers there since the 1980s, the trade deficit as a percentage of U.S. GDP crept up from about 3.8 per cent in the early 1980s to more than 5.0 per cent at the end of 2003, and is projected, at current (2005) rates of growth, to enter a range between 6.0 and 8.0 per cent of U.S. GDP by 2010. The effects have been shifted away from consumers in the U.S. economy by the Federal Reserve maintaining low interest rates, making it very cheap for U.S. sources to borrow in order to finance the deficit and profitable for foreign purchasers of U.S. debt obligations only if they are operating at the level of a central bank, prepared to finance very large volumes of the debt for 20-30 years into the future. To penetrate how the discussion around the U.S. trade deficit, understood in this light, is modulated is to begin to grasp how the Aphenomenal Model of "consumption of production" is sustained.

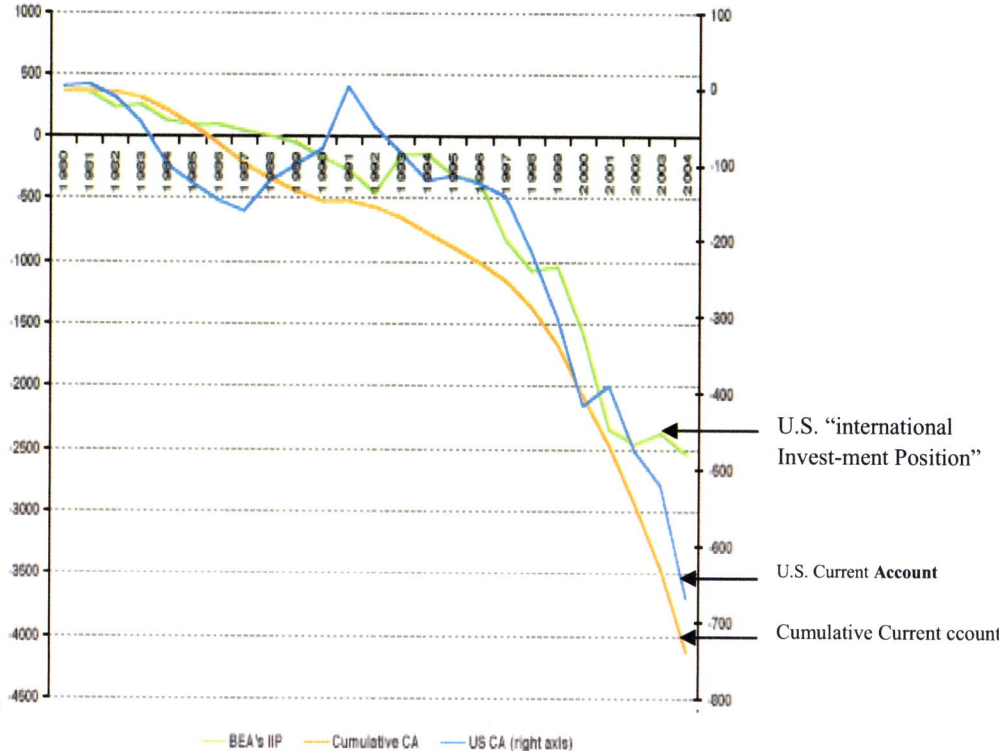

Figure 5-3. The International Investment Position (IIP) and Current Account (CA) of the United States 1900-2004, in US$ Billions – The U.S. trade balance (formally referred to as the Current Account) ran nearly a half-a-trillion-dollar surplus until the Soviet Union disappeared. Throughout the 1980s, while research, development and exports of computers and computer software waxed particularly strong in the United States, the trade deficit ran more than a half-a-trillion-dollar deficit, reaching its nadir during the stock-market crash of 1987 and its aftermath, before bouncing back. This reversal reflected the effect on the trade account of exports of the products being researched and developed while the trade deficit was trending downward. After the so-called "tech wreck" of March 2000, non-military hi-tech R and D collapsed across the U.S. economy, reflected in the steepening downward trend in all three curves. (Source: *Bureau of Economic Analysis, U.S. Department of Commerce – Washington DC*, from Haussmann and Sturzenegger [2005]).

In the context of what had long been – due to its massive domestic manufacturing base and plentiful domestic supplies of energy – the economic engine and workhorse of the global trading system, and subsequently its principal financier, the emergence of both the level of dependence on imported energy sources dislosed in Table 5-1, and the increasing role of imported manufactured goods disclosed in Figure 5-4 represent the hallmarks of an economy implementing the Aphenomenal Model of "consumption without production". They point to a quantum shift rather than the continuation of oscillations within a long-standing trend.

Table 5-1. Relative Trade Surpluses with the United States of Key Countries and Blocs

	Surplus with U.S	
	2005 (in billions)	**% Increase from 2004**
China	$201.63	25%
Europe	144.07	12
OPEC	92.73	29
Japan	82.68	9
Canada	76.52	15
Mexico	50.15	11

The table discloses that the fastest-rising component in the trade deficit is no longer due to cheap manufactured goods from China but to the ongoing U.S. dependence on imports to supply its energy demands. (Source: U.S. Department of Commerce, Washington DC)

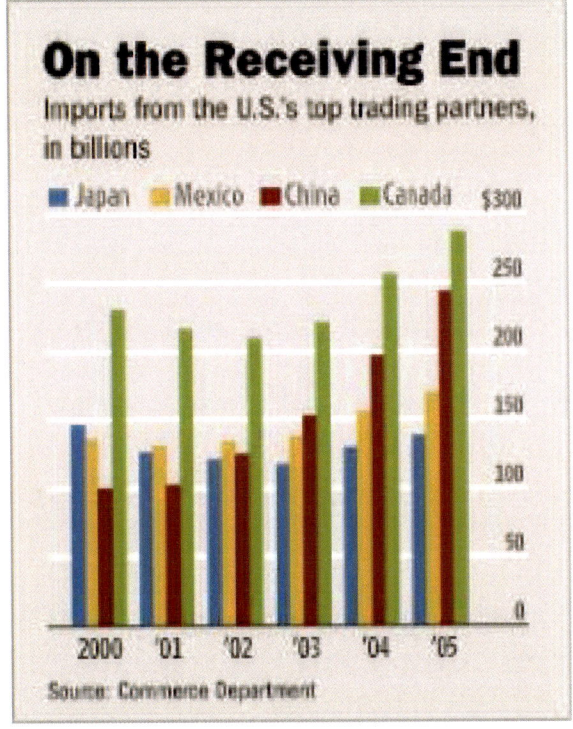

Figure 5-4. Leading exporters into U.S. markets – China's share rose 2.5 times in five years, now second only to Canada.

The entire concern instead, however, is whether the U.S. can continue to "pay its way" and finance these deficits. The logic is that so long as this financing can continue, there is nothing to worry about. Underlying this logic is what economists refer to as the theory of the "financial balance of terror" – the phrase coined by economist Larry Summers, and what was described in Chapter 3 as a powerful disinclination among the trade and financial partners of the United States, especially since the 1987 stock-market crash, to permit its economy to fail. As the rather dramatic data for 2005 were being compiled, however, among professional economists and other serious students of these questions, the "debate" and concern, which had been increasing since 2000, about whether foreign central banks, especially in Japan and South Korea, would continue indefinitely to loan the money necessary to finance these deficits, now elicited a truly bizarre response.

On the political side, President George W. Bush emphasised in his State of the Union Address of 31 January 2006 that the U.S. had become "addicted to foreign oil" and that its future depended on expanding domestic exploration and production of new sources of oil and gas as well as vigorous further efforts in developing "alternative" sources – but just how emphasis on the latter would overcome dependence on the former was nowhere indicated.

On the economists' battlefield, meanwhile, an entire alternative theory was being propagated to justify endless expansion of the U.S. trade deficit, under currrent conditions, as a kind of intangible economic power that the leading proponents of this theory label "dark matter". According to a *Wall Street Journal* article:

> Physicists for decades have used "dark matter" as Spackle to fill pesky anomalies that seem to defy theories about gravity, the Big Bang and more. Recently, economists have proposed a similar fix for apparent anomalies in U.S. economic data. Unlike dark matter in space, dark matter in economics is a concept that has been mostly derided by other economists. ...
>
> If you want to immerse yourself in the wonk-fest that is dark matter, feel free to read the recent paper, by Harvard economists Ricardo Hausmann and Frederico Sturzenegger ...
>
> [Economists] have long warned that this affront to the natural order can't be sustained, that the U.S. must pay off its debts ... But that day of reckoning hasn't come, and Messrs. Hausmann and Sturzenegger think they know why: The U.S. has a vast, imaginary asset – dark matter – that not only wipes out its debt but provides a surplus that generates that $30 billion a year in investment income.
>
> Working backward from the $30 billion, Messrs. Hausmann and Sturzenegger tried to put a value on that dark-matter generated surplus. By using what they thought was a reasonable rate of return on an investment – 5% a year – they decided that surplus must then be $600 billion. Thus the U.S. since 1980 has accumulated $3.1 trillion that, if accounted for, erases that $2.5 trillion in debt and then some.

Clearly: the first unstated problem is that this so-called "investment surplus" appears as a surplus because of the accounting techniques followed by the Bureau of Economic Analysis, which prepares and maintains both the data and format of these accounts. There is, however no evidence anywhere that there is $30-billion a year utilised annually as the seed money of further investments that are continuously rolled over as Hasusman and Sturzenegger have assumed.

> And, what is this dark matter? Mostly, the Harvard researchers say, it is simply a deep well of good old American know-how – the consistent ability to export, say, Kentucky Fried Chicken restaurants to Moscow that are more appealing and profitable than Rasputin's House of Chicken and Waffles. ...
>
> If this is true, then those economic storm clouds on the horizon are just a mirage, and a lot of U.S. assets – including stocks, bonds and the dollar – will continue to stay strong...

Here is the hint as to what is actually going on: disinformation is being cooked! If it is logical or acceptable to argue that a debt-obligation is purely the result of double-entry accounting and not otherwise real or owing, the possibilities become truly endless, and endlessly absurd:

> To many economists and investors, this smacks of a desperate effort to ignore a dangerous mountain of debt. The U.S. ability to export Euro Disneys and KFCs already turns up in international trade and profit data, they say, and is still not enough to make up for America's reliance on cheaply made foreign goods. "Think about what a fabulous excuse that is for anything," said Barry Ritholtz, chief investment officer at Ritholtz Capital Partners. " 'I wasn't doing 80, officer, I was doing 55. It's the dark matter that was doing 25.' "

The most astonishing element in the defence offered by the leading champion of the "dark matter" theory is that he and his colleague are "inferring" the existence of "dark matter"; they have no idea whether it exists. Because of what something "does to the balance sheet", it must exist – anything else is mere "haggling over…details"! Here is the declaration that whatever the truth is, and regardless of whether he and his colleague have actually captured it, it is and must be aphenomenal:

> … Goldman Sachs's Ed McKelvey and other economists have questioned several aspects of the dark-matter theory, including the assumptions Messrs. Hausmann and Sturzenegger used to "discover" dark matter and their guesstimates about its accumulation from year to year.
> Hausmann asserts that haggling over such details is missing the point. "We're putting the accent on something that is a longer-term phenomenon," he said in an interview. "There is probably a lot of noise in our measurement. In fact, it's not measurement; we're inferring dark matter's existence. But the important thing is what it does to the balance sheet."

One of the leading critics of the Hausmann-Sturzenegger approach pinpoints that actual trade and investment data do not generate a sufficient return on investment to justify the rosy view of America's future generated by the notion of "dark matter". Astonishingly, it also implies that "the world, rather than wasting its time investing in the U.S., should just lend money to U.S. companies and let them exploit dark matter." The fact no one has done this suggests that it is probably not really there to be done, and that Hausmann and Sturzenegger may have simply captured something exceptional in the data, connected to the current low-interest-rate environment, rather than something general or fundamental:

> Assuming Mr. Hausmann is correct, says Brad Setser, a former Treasury economist and head of global research for the Roubini Global Economics Monitor Web site, the U.S. still isn't accumulating enough dark matter to keep up with the growing trade deficit. Messrs. Hausmann and Sturzenegger estimate that dark matter grew by $559 billion a year between 2000 and 2004 – its fastest pace in the past 25 years. On average, annual dark-matter growth has been about $124 billion in the past quarter-century, according to the Hausmann-Sturzenegger study. Meanwhile, the U.S. is on track to accumulate nearly $1 trillion in debt in 2005. At such rates, America's tank of dark matter will be drained quickly.
> … "If the dark-matter thesis is true, then the world, rather than wasting its time investing in the U.S., should just lend money to U.S. companies and let them exploit dark matter," Mr. Setser said.
> Critics also note that the boom in dark-matter creation between 2000 and 2004 happened to coincide with the lowest interest rates in a generation. …

The apparent intangibility of "dark matter", meanwhile, seems like so much smoke and mirrors:

> The Bureau of Economic Analysis, keeper of the international-trade data questioned by Messrs. Hausmann and Sturzenegger, has no plans to even try to measure dark matter. "I'm really uncomfortable about trying to take implicit differences and label them as having a certain cause and then putting them into our accounts," said BEA Director Steven Landefeld. He says he has been hearing dark-matter-like theories since he joined the BEA in 1991.
>
> The BEA does have plans, though, to measure the deep thinking that creates the iPods and Happy Meals for which the rest of the world is willing to pay a premium. By the end of the decade, they may even include such research and development in gross domestic product measures.
>
> But the impact will be much smaller than suggested in [a recent article in *BusinessWeek* magazine], which speculated that some $1 trillion in intellectual-capital creation – a vast store of future cool products sitting in the ether waiting to be discovered – goes unmeasured every year. The BEA says it won't include spending on worker training or brand marketing, and it will adjust R and D for all the spending that goes nowhere – or, worse, flops, such as Coca-Cola's New Coke.
>
> "If a pharmaceutical firm puts $1 billion into Drug XYZ and it's a bust, what is that?" asked Mr. Ritholtz. "Dark anti-matter?"
>
> (from: Mark Gongloff, "Is 'Dark Matter' in the Deficit? Spackle for Economic Anomalies Looks to Explain How U.S. Operates With Massive Debt", published 10 Feb 2006 in *The Wall Street Journal Online*)

What, indeed, is "consumption without production" but ... "dark anti-matter"?!

5.6.3. Neoliberal Bankruptcy – The Stelco Case

The absurdities proposed to explain and even to celebrate the ever burgeoning U.S. trade deficit, one of the great economic global cancers of our time, exemplify the aphenomenality of economic theorising based on reproducing some effect or sequence of effects without any knowledge of their real-world causes. As already noted, this meshes perfectly with economic practice that is premised upon *consumption without production*. What has made the problem especially serious, however, is that, while the trade deficit imbalance of the United States in particular is permitted to expand practically without limit, large masses of human and material productive forces are routinely destroyed through wars and bankruptcies.

The steel industry is one of the main economic fields globally in which there has been extensive resort to mergers and bankruptcies throughout the 1990s to date. The steelmaking industry remains one of the main foundations of industrial production as a system. Notwithstanding the broad development of all manner of alternative materials of equivalent or even superior strength and other useful properties, without the smelting of iron into steel there would have arisen no industry or industrial system as societies have come to know them since the 1700s. The state of the steel industry worldwide is one of the least deceptive indexes as to the true economic health of the economic system. After almost 25 years of contraction, the global steel industry resumed expanding in the late 1990s almost entirely in response to the huge demand occasioned by the growth of heavy industry in China and India.

Without containing or restraining the powerful tendencies within the global economy that continue to threaten an extremely profound financial collapse, the enormous expansion of manufacturing industry throughout Asia since the early 1990s has nevertheless fended off the long-anticipated "day of reckoning" to the point where a number of central banks in capital-overripe countries, critically-positioned energy-exporting countries and even newly-risen manufacturing powers have been planning and preparing the substitution of Euros for their US dollar reserves so as to insulate their economies from the long-anticipated "hard landing" of the US economy. A major "event" of this kind is expected and believed inevitable because the U.S. economy is seen to be hugely over-extended in terms of the hundreds of billions of US dollars that continue to grow in quantity while persisting in circulating entirely and apparently permanently outside US territory.

In Japan, in the leading economies of western Europe and in Canada and the United States, wide swaths of basic industry, such as steelmaking, had literally been rusting since the 1970s – when along came the powerful increase in demand from the Chinese and Indian economic expansion, which their own basic industry was not sufficient to fully supply. The other side of the coin of this decay of basic industry in these economies is an enormous superfluity of capital and credit redirected into more profitable lines. Some of this capital has increasingly come to be redirected into "industrial restructuring" schemes being applied in those parts of basic industry that enjoy secure market positions but which are normally of little interest to those seeking the fastest return on their investment. One of the areas in which such restructurings can be rendered particularly profitable is the field of corporate bankruptcy.

In the case of older basic industries with secure markets that have been turned into public corporations, with shares held by members of the general public, such restructurings under bankruptcy become an exercise in which a small group of what the financial markets call venture capitalists (and the employees whose jobs are on the line call "vulture capitalists") swoop in, swapping newly-created equity for accumulated corporate debt but eventually declaring worthless a large portion of the stock widely held publicly before the company entered into bankruptcy. This was precisely the case with the Steel Company of Canada, known as Stelco and based in Hamilton, a steel-making centre about 30 miles southwest of Toronto, which filed for bankruptcy under the Canadian *Corporate Creditors Arrangements Act* in 2004 and emerged, "restructured", in February 2006.

Stelco's process is an example of what might be called "neo-liberal bankruptcy." It is appropriate to call it neoliberal because, in outline, at the level of a basic industry of indispensable importance to the broader economy, it may be said to have been carried out according to the same logic and principle that the World Bank and International Monetary Fund apply to developing countries with large debts to repay, *viz.*, the neoliberal doctrine that the debtor restructure as a condition of retaining access to future financing of its needs. Here is what has happened:

The forces pushing the process have drained the productive entity of over $100 million in costs paid to the restructuring agents. Stelco's manufacturing plants and mini-mills have been sold-off, weakening the base of active workers supplying added-value and new pensioners to the pension plans. The owners of Stelco equity have had their property rights declared void and taken by new owners. The original and new owners of debt have enhanced their monopoly right to profit from Stelco's social assets. The owners of Stelco debt forced government of the province of Ontario and federal government of Canada to give them $180 million in return for 3 per cent of the new shares. Of course, these new shares cost nothing, as they are simply the old shares under new ownership. By accepting the right to new shares, the Ontario government became an active partner in the devaluation of the old shares, not simply a passive observer. The government money is essentially the only new injection of funds into the company, as the rest is mainly a turning over of old debt. A revolving loan of $375 million, supplied by Tricap – the leading group of financiers managing the process on behalf of the really powerful financial groups behind the entire maneuver – will only be sparsely touched, depending mainly on steel market prices, although the loan still requires expensive servicing. The main day-to-day funds will continue to come from the asset-based loan of $600 million until receipts overtake expenditures, which may be quite soon once the drain of restructuring costs is put to a merciful end. The main "action" will be with the "new" shares and the marketing of them around the world, but that "action" and any rise in their market value means nothing to the Stelco productive entity as any gain will be pocketed by the new owners – mainly Tricap, which captures a 35 per cent share.

This neo-liberal bankruptcy began with what appeared to be an imminent liquidity crisis. The main argument or proof of the crisis was an actuarial report that the pension plans were underfunded by around $1.3 billion. Actuarial reports can be manipulated to say whatever a client wishes them to say but that is not the main problem. Until pension plans are discontinued, or wound up, they rely on a constant flow of new added-value or revenue and new pensioners replacing those who pass away. Both new added-value and new pensioners are essential for pensions to flourish and survive. Stelco's pension plans were still receiving both essential factors in January 2004 even though executive management was diverting some added-value to the Ontario government's Pension Benefits Guarantee Fund in lieu of putting added-value into the plans (a policy decision that could be changed at any time).

Diverting funds to the government fund and deliberately underfunding pension plans are part of the preparations for a neo-liberal bankruptcy. Underfunded pension plans, as described in actuarial reports, become a concocted bogus issue serving a secret agenda. The real issue and concern for active and retired employees is the stopping of the creation of new added-value available for pensions and the elimination of a supply of new pensioners. In Stelco's case that could only mean a secret agenda to crater Hilton Works and stop the production of steel and the supply of new added-value and pensioners into the main pension plans.

Everything else at Stelco in January 2004 was status quo. Steelworkers were producing steel. All debt was being serviced. Gambling of Stelco shares was still underway on the Toronto Stock Exchange. No dividends had been paid for some time but similar to the diversion of added-value from the pension plans to the Ontario government, the stopping of dividend payments is a policy decision of executive management and directors to weaken the stock, which becomes another aspect of a secret agenda. There was a problem of suitable market prices for steel but that has been the case for decades. Those forces that monopolise and concentrate ownership and-or control over sectors of the economy want to control prices themselves and will not even discuss government intervention to stabilize steel prices at or near prices of production.

In a neo-liberal bankruptcy such as Stelco, repeated at Air Canada and Algoma Steel, the winners in the end may or may not be the original players, and the secret agenda can undergo changes as the battle progresses. Neo-liberal bankruptcies are now so common a cottage industry of plotters exists that is freely lurking behind the scenes ready to pounce at a moments notice. The New York billionaire David Tepper, who in concert with

Tricap/Brookfield managed to come up with a large slice of Stelco, has been deeply involved in the Chapter 11 bankruptcies of the U.S. steel industry along with Wilbur Ross of ISG and Mittal. Tepper also boasts of his newfound interest in the auto industry and the possibilities of a big score. He recently purchased $20 million of Delphi debt, giving him an active role in the Chapter 11 process of that offspring of General Motors. Tricap of course is well established in neo-liberal bankruptcy and seems to have brought on board as junior partners a section of the official trade union movement. Tricap has emerged as the main winner at Stelco acquiring more than enough new shares to make a killing, gaining four members of the new nine member Stelco Board of Directors, winning a "break-fee" payoff of $11.3 million for changing its own restructuring plan, and acquiring ownership of guaranteed Stelco debt with substantial fees and interest. Tricap's ruling partnership at Brookfield will be happy indeed, as this has all been accomplished with virtually no risk to any of their private money. This is evidence of a veritable *coup* proving to themselves at least that consumption can even be increased without producing anything. Does the fact that Tricap emerges as the main winner at the end mean that it was in on the plotting at the beginning? Maybe an insider will leak some information in due course but when all is said and done, the monopoly capitalist community in Canada is not that big. Members communicate and conspire with and against one another socially and in business gatherings all the time. Courtney Pratt, the CEO of Stelco as it went into CCAA bankruptcy restructuring and stepping down only now as it emerges from CCAA, was an executive with a Brookfield subsidiary (formerly Brascan) for the better part of his management career.

Neo-liberal bankruptcies are hazardous to the health of any economy. Nothing can be taken for granted when the rulers of the economy believe that consumption can occur without production, when the rulers of the economy believe that circulation, trading and theft of already produced wealth are more important and profitable than renewing and properly managing existing sources of production and building new productive sources of wealth as part of nation-building.

5.7. APHENOMENAL MODEL AND COMMODIFICATION

Up to now, the focus was on the Aphenomenal Model's entrenching of a general economic line of "consumption without production". Here we encounter the corollary: the promotion and development of new forms of production to accommodate and commodify the consequences of excessive consumption. As the following extracts from a recent newspaper article serve to document, a socially negative, downward trend is being converted into modifications of existing products. Notification of the public comes not from an economics or health expert but the newspaper's "social trends reporter". In other words: at the scientific level, it's just part of the where things are trending; at the economic level it's just another way to make money; at the policy level, it's something to be accommodated. The words "accommodation" and "commodity" share a common root. Here lies the intangible connection in the following little-known and largely unremarked tale of economic progress through the already well-known and widely-remarked obesity disaster. Would such developments even be in the running if anyone was thinking past the immediate short-term?

First a great tragedy is recounted, but from the standpoint of presenting a great new entrepreneurial opportunity:

> Their pheasant-hunting trip on Ontario's secluded Pelee Island had come to an end. It was supposed to be a quick flight home for the eight friends.
>
> But shortly after takeoff, the small plane nosedived into icy Lake Erie, killing the hunters, the pilot, and his girlfriend.
>
> As investigators probed the 2004 crash, they pointed in an unusual direction: weight. The aircraft's occupants, including their carry-on baggage, each weighed an average of about 240 pounds (108 kilograms) – 30 per cent more than regulations allowed.

The scale of the opportunity is then delineated – planes, trains, automobiles, even hospitals:

> Canadians' growing girth – six in 10 adults are considered obese or overweight – is triggering myriad safety and policy concerns. As waistlines expand, regulatory bodies, public agencies and health organizations are being pressed to develop new rules and equipment.
>
> And for private companies, the extra bulk means new business opportunities, everything from oversized chairs and stretchers to cars and coffins.
>
> "There's been a big shift in the demographics to people that are well above 250 pounds," said Ed Breen, executive vice-president of Nightingale, a company based in Mississauga, Ont., that is the country's second-largest office chair manufacturer.
>
> "The market, quite frankly, is just not getting thinner. They're getting bigger."
>
> Sales of Nightingale's two largest chairs – the Husky and 247, which have 180-kilogram capacities – have grown 124 per cent over the past three years.
>
> And while the models represent a fraction of the firm's overall business, the niche is so promising that the company has developed two more prototypes.
>
> At the country's biggest casket maker, Canadians' increasing dimensions have also led to new products. Like others in the industry, the Victoriaville Group, based in Victoriaville, Que., makes "oversized" coffins that are 68, and even 76, centimetres wide. A standard unit is about 61 centimetres across. Since 2002, sales of the large models have increased more than fourfold.
>
> But in the public arena, seat size – whether in airplanes, buses, stadiums or parks – has been slow to catch up to widening derrières. Take Howard Moscoe, the imposing councillor and chairman of the Toronto Transit Commission, who finds the city's subway seats, which measure 43 centimetres across, far too narrow.
>
> "I have a wide *tuchas* – *tuchas* in Yiddish means rear end," says Mr. Moscoe, who is 6 foot 1 (1.8 metres) and weighs 275 pounds (124 kilograms). "Notwithstanding the fact that Canadians are getting bigger, I'm at the broad end of the range when it comes to my rear end."
>
> Mr. Moscoe also pays more for goods, including made-to-measure suits. And he recently bought a new car – a Chrysler 300 – that cost more than he planned, but which won him over with its wide seats and roomy interior.
>
> Auto manufacturers are clambering to adapt to society's changing figure, which, along with more sedentary lifestyles, is also due to the glut of aging, widening baby boomers.
>
> Perhaps not surprisingly, car makers' modifications simultaneously suit the big and the old. Along with more legroom and ample seats, cars often feature steering wheels with radio controls to save drivers the effort of reaching. Pedals and seat springs are sometimes adjustable. Door openings are wider and higher.
>
> "The overall approach is . . . let's make this easy to do," said Jeffrey Pike, a senior technical specialist at Ford. "Someone shouldn't even have to be thinking about it."

For staff in hospitals or for paramedics, working with heavy patients, especially lifting them, is "very much a safety issue," said Emile Therien, president of the Canada Safety Council.

This year, after tracking staff injuries, the Ottawa Paramedic Service reconfigured an ambulance and bought a "large body surface attachment" to transform a standard 60-centimetre, 135-kilogram-capacity stretcher into one that is 91 centimetres wide and can carry up to 292 kilograms.

It is also considering buying a winch and ramp system similar to one Montreal paramedics use.

Such paraphernalia is costly. Since demand began to rise less than three years ago, the non-profit agency that buys equipment for several Toronto hospitals has acquired many items for the very obese: two critical-care beds, two portable lifts, five stretcher chairs, two wheelchairs with scales, 10 shower chairs and three commodes. The cost was $162,000; the same standard gear would have cost less than $90,000.

"[Hospitals] don't have a lot of money to spend on capital and when they have to spend it on special needs . . . it does take away from the general pool," said Sandy May, director of contract management for Shared Healthcare Supply Services.

At Oversize Medical Rental and Sales, which sells everything from 225-kilogram capacity crutches to 495-kilogram capacity beds, business has increased almost 100 per cent a year since the company was founded in Mississauga in 2000.

"No matter how you say it," vice-president Ted Clark said, "it sounds like a pun: big business, growing business, growth opportunity."

Then comes the "argument" of the article, which is that people who would stand in the way of such potential economic progress – like doctors and other health specialists – just don't "get it":

On average, adult Canadians are 10-per-cent heavier than 25 years ago, despite being just slightly taller. Men weigh an average of 182 pounds (82 kilograms), according to Statistics Canada, compared with 167 pounds in the late 1970s. Women's average is 153 pounds (69 kilograms), up from 138 pounds. In 2004, according to the national statistics agency, 23 per cent of Canadians were classed as obese and an additional 36 per cent as overweight.

Business aside, physicians are increasingly frustrated that the public is paying little heed to the health hazards of obesity, which include diabetes, heart disease and premature death.

"At the same time we're adapting to the larger body sizes that are out there, we really need to, I think, do a better job of informing the public of the health risks," said Peter Katzmarzyk, a Queen's University professor of epidemiology who specializes in obesity.

"It is a huge public-health issue, we can't detract from that."

Referring to the boom in oversized caskets, he said: "Not only are they going to have to make larger ones, they're going to have to make more."

As the crash of the plane, a Georgian Express Cessna Caravan 208B, off Pelee Island illustrates, weight can also be a life-or-death public-safety issue. The case was not the first of its kind in Canada: Higher-than-allowed passenger weights have been a factor in at least four other fatal air accidents in which 24 people died.

Finally – just "get with the program", there's fortunes to be made out there:

The Transportation Safety Board of Canada, which is still investigating the Jan. 17, 2004, crash and suspects ice on the wings may also have been a factor, has already recommended that actual weights – not assumptions – be used for flights with nine or fewer passengers.

It also advocated that weight values be adjusted to "reflect the current realities." Transport Canada acted on both suggestions; Maximum allowable averages are now 200 pounds for men and 165 pounds for women.

"What we're faced with is the changing demographics," said Denis Rivard, the TSB's investigator in charge of the file.

"That's why from time to time the regulations need to be revisited to see if they're still accurate."

But outdated presumptions are currently part of the North American elevator code. Capacity is based on an average weight of 160 pounds – 22 pounds lighter than the average Canadian man, although seven pounds heavier than the typical woman. (However, officials note the code says elevators must be able to stop with 25 per cent more people than the posted capacity.)

And when was the 160-pound average set?

1975.

(from: Jill Mahoney, Social Trends Reporter, "Canada's added girth a growing concern", *The Globe and Mail* [Toronto], Sat. 10 Dec 2005

5.8. APHENOMENAL MODEL IN SOCIAL SCIENCE: "WELL-INTENDED" AND "ILL-INTENDED" METHODS OF COUNTING

The entire proceeding that follows turns on what might better be described as "well-intended" versus "ill-intended" methods of counting Arabs, Jews and Muslims. In what is supposed to be an internal discussion reviewing a new book about Iraqi Jewish life, a fight breaks out over how to define, and distinguish, sets of religious belief from subsets of religious belief. The real fight going on is between those who retain allegiance to Eurocentric (and, especially, Zionist) definitions of collective identifiers on the one hand, and those who challenge the racist and supremacist assumptions implicit in these definitions on the other. A recent work on *The Last Jews in Baghdad* has re-sparked this discussion

It emerges that how the counting is arranged has everything with the intention of those doing the counting. At the same time, ill-intended methods of counting are occasionally defended not on the basis of their intention but because someone has so-many "years experience" doing things a certain way.

A substantive discussion of *The Last Jews in Baghdad*[29] has been reproduced here from material appearing on the World Wide Web and published by then director of the Institute of Near Eastern and African Studies (Website 4). Some minor narrative continuity and sequential referencing of the documents have been added to assist readers. It contains a number of startling moments in which intentions reveal themselves damningly.

In this case, where one cannot tell the players without a program, it is also necessary to identify from the outset who the main participants are in this correspondence:

---

[29] This material can be examined, and later developments followed further, on the blogspot, at http://zennobia.blogspot.com/2006/01/last-jews-in-baghdad.html. The blog is associated with the Institute of Near Eastern and African Studies, founded in 1994 by Iraqi scholar Wafaa' Al-Natheema. The Institute of Near Eastern and African Studies can be reached at P.O. Box 425125, Cambridge, MA 02142 USA. The website is http://www.ineas.org and the e-mail address is INEAS@mail.INEAS.org

1. *Wafaa' Al-Natheema* – She maintains the website, the blog and the Institute all mentioned below. She initiates a correspondence with
2. *Naseem Rejwan*, author of *The Last Jews in Baghdad*, which incorporated characterisations of Iraqi Jews as a phenomenon existing outside the history of the Arab world;
3. *Pete Sluglett*, a scholar-expert entering into the discussion in support of Naseem Rejwan's discussion of Iraqi Jews as something distinct from and not partaking in the Arab personality of Iraq;
4. *Joachim Martillo*, an independent scholar taking issue with any tendency to confuse the category "Jew", as a purely religious category devoid of any uniquely identifying ethnic content, and the categories "Arab" or "Iraqi", both of which are national and ethnic categories and each neither of which uniquely identifies any single religious content in particular; and
5. *Sheila Musaji*, from the "American Muslim" website, which publishes summaries and digests of mainstream academic essays and journal articles about trends in, and affairs of, the ummah in the United States

Document No. 1 – Introducing the Series

"The Last Jews in Baghdad"
Letter Writing Series
Wafaa' Al-Natheema

January 30, 2006

Dear Naseem/Nassim:

This is part III of my letter writing series.

Since the middle of October when I sent you the first letter regarding the subject matter of your book, "The Last Jews in Baghdad," I've been on several short and long trips. So, this letter series has been delayed.

I also felt that maybe I was wasting my time and energy when Joel Beinin didn't care to respond, and when I received three insignificant emails from you! Instead I received an email from Peter Sluglett discussing the issue of Jewish Arabs in the typical manner the so-called scholars of the industrial west argue it and referring to Joel Beinin as a scholar! With all do respect to Beinin, had he been truly a scholar, he wouldn't have made many errors and misconceptions in the writing of your book's forward and, as the definition of a scholar states, he would have at least responded to give feedback and equally learn!

In this letter, I intend to bring your attention to the various errors and misconceptions in your book's chapter one as well as to some of the wonderfully described objects and anecdotes. I hope you take the liberty of correcting the errors or rewriting the misconceptions and other viewpoints in a way that makes them less-or-non-debatable in the second edition with wishes to you for continued health to see it published.

The objective and intelligent writer, reporter and/or historian, must not get involved in biases and negative thoughts and should report or document with clear vision, compare and contrast without sectarianism, sexism or soap-opera-like stories. Unfortunately some of the documentation provided in your book's forward by Joel Beinin and in chapter one fit in with these categories.

This brings me to the following points in chapter one of your book, "The Last Jews in Baghdad":

1. In the first paragraph of page 1, you lamented about the Jews in the Babylonian diaspora, the number of synagogues left, about prayers and Prophet Jeremiah and gave a religious tone to your documentation and feelings. I hope that you are not one of the Israeli Jewish vast majority that though does not believe in God, still believe that God gave the land (of Palestine) to the "promised people"!!

2. In the same paragraph, you stated, "For those who, like myself, were born, grew up, and lived in Baghdad in the years preceding the mass exodus of Jews from Iraq in 1950-51, this state of affairs is extremely hard to imagine." In this entire chapter, you failed to mention why the mass exodus has happened. You probably mentioned about it in later chapters, but providing few lines briefly explaining why it happened or referring to it being mentioned in chapter 'so and so' would have been appropriate. This way, the readers would not be left with question marks and exclamations as they read chapter one.

3. In paragraph two, you provided some of the most disputed and highly debated statistics about Baghdad's population and its majority and minorities: "In October 1921, a British publication quoted these population figures for the city as given in the last official yearbook of vilayet: Total number of inhabitants 202,000, of whom 80,000 were Jews; 12,000 Christians; 8,000 Kurds; 800 Persians; and 101,400 Arabs, Turks and other Muslims." This is indeed a stunning work by IRAQ's occupiers; the Anglo Saxon "uncles" as Iraqis sometime refer to them sarcastically. These statistics are worm cans opener hinting the "Divide to Rule" fragrance of occupation. Here is why: Kurds and Iranians (not Persians as indicated in the statistics) are mostly Moslems, why were they not included with the "Arabs, Turks and other Moslems"? And who are the "other Moslems" included in the so-called 101,400 figure? Moslems of IRAQ are Arabs, Kurds, Iranians and Turkmen (who are Iraq's Turks). So who are the others? Knowing the fact that several ethnic groups (not just Persians) came from Iran to Iraq, and knowing that the statistics were taken at the beginning of the 20th century during which it was called Iran and not Persia, it is wrong to refer to them as Persians.

The "Divide and Rule" of the current American occupiers has gone farther by neglecting the notion and term of 'Moslems' all together. Now they refer to Moslems as Shiites and Sunnis just like Joel Beinin did in your book's forward. Imagine eliminating the word 'Jews' and constantly referring to them as Orthodox and Reformers. I don't think Jews would like that.

It was equally disturbing, if not funny, to separate (in the statistics above) Jews and Christians from Arabs when Jews are near entirely Arabs (with very few Kurdish and Turkmen exceptions) and the vast majority of Christians are Arabs as well!!

4. Thank you for making me laugh at the British proclamation that states, "A proclamation issued by the British military governor early in 1919 fixed the number of sheep to be slaughtered daily in Baghdad East (al-Risafa, the more populous half of the city) at 220 for Jewish butchers and 160 for Moslems and other butchers." It is interesting to read again the British so-called accuracy by using the term "Other"; even butchers have others. And what about Christians? Shame on them they don't have butchers? J They just buy and eat? What was the significance of this piece of statistics? To present Jews as richer, more spoiled and ate more lamb, and were unfriendly slayers of sheep or to prove that their number in east Baghdad was higher? To include the sheep figures in your book immediately after the paragraph on population figures without commenting on them indicates that the number of killed sheep is used to prove the high number of Jews in Baghdad, which is irrelevant. And what made the British and you, for quoting them, rule out the possibility that Jewish butchers may sell sheep to non-Jews, and the same for Moslem butchers. Another issue of concern is the fact that the sheep figures were only provided for the east part of Baghdad. What about the west side (al-Karkh)?

5. In Hebrew language, the R is pronounced like the French R and like the Arabic sound of the letter 'ghayn'. Therefore your transliteration of the Arabic-Hebrew word for 'water well' in page 4 should have been el-Beer and NOT el-Bigh.

6. I loved your description of hib on page 5, last paragraph: "The hib was a many-faceted device. Apart from keeping the water clean and fit for drinking it also served as a kind of primitive refrigerator. The water was always cool thanks to the breeze, which no matter how burning hot it was itself, always managed to cool the outside of the hib by contact with its damp walls. Moreover the hib, which was rounded and with a narrow base, was placed on a steady wooden "cage" with small holes that, while permitting the draught to circulate inside out, kept the place out of reach of scorpions, cockroaches, snakes, and other intruders from land. It was in this "cage," qafas, that some of the most valuable necessities were tucked away. Besides the special jug that was placed right under the hib's base to gather the water dripping therefrom, there was ample space in it to accommodate pots, bottles, and plates containing cooked meals, milk, yogurt, liquid medications, fruits and vegetables, which were preserved in reasonable coolness through the sweltering heat of summer and kept out of harm's reach. The qafas also prevented the cats from reaching the meats and the milk products."

I wished your paragraphs about Iraq's majority and minorities, the Jews' exodus and other topics mentioned in chapter one were described in the eloquence and extent of details as those awarded to the hib.

7. I also loved the anecdotes you provided about the snakes and how Iraqis dealt with them in paragraph two on page 6, which reads, "It was rare in those days for a house in Baghdad to be free of scorpions and snakes, and in many households it was customary for the head of the family to go to bed only after he had inspected the holes in the walls for snakes. Although destroying scorpions was a duty, killing or harming a snake was strictly forbidden. Usually ground dry leaves of the nice-smelling butnaj were spread on the floor in the belief that snakes cannot stand the smell and consequently refrain from intruding any further. In certain households, again, the mistress of the house left a plate of milk around so that a snake drinking it

would become pacified and friendly to members of the household. In such cases the mother chants, "O snake of the house, do not do us harm and we won't harm you! "

A variety of issues came to mind as I read the paragraph about the snakes: One- you did not specify whether the killing of snakes was forbidden due to practice by all Iraqis or only by Jews! Two- it shows that Iraqi households were friendlier to other beings than after the 1960s, as it has been around the world, by living more with machinery and in crowded cities and due to the reduction of green landscape for the sake of construction. Three- it even indicates that Iraqis (like people worldwide) were more understanding of and tolerant with animals than (again) after the 1960s! Four- In English, Butnaj means "Betony". If you click on this link http://ar.wikipedia.org/wiki/%D8%A8%D8%B7%D9%86%D8%AC%AC, you will find a detailed and interesting description of butnaj in Arabic.

8. In paragraph three on page 6, you wrote, "One day when I was about four years of age, the head of some little snake somehow came out of one of the holes in a wall in the inner house. Panic reigned; no one dared either to push the snake inside or bring it out. In the end, a certain "professional," a Muslim living in the neighborhood, was brought to the scene...." Why did you need to indicate that the "professional" was a Moslem?

9. On page 6, last paragraph, you wrote, "The work of clearing the drains and the toilets was considered – and in fact was – the most menial of all menial jobs. It was undertaken almost exclusively by Christians from a certain small town in north of Iraq called Talkeif, but there were also Jews who engaged in the work; but never, never a Muslim. As small children, we used to dub every Christian nazzah, the name Baghdadis gave a man who cleaned drains and toilets. And Iraq's immortal popular poet and versifier Mulla 'Abbud al-Karkhi had an unforgettable poem in which he asks, among scores of other rhetorical questions: "Yimkin Mislim yisir nazzah? Yimkin yehudi yisir tcharkhatchi?" (Is it possible for a Muslim to be a latrine cleaner? A Jew to be a night watchman?)"

This paragraph is one vivid example of the non-scholarly writing that you have done in your book so far. It is racist, soap-opera type of writing. You failed to analyze it objectively. It showed that your bad-meaning-malice side is live and kicking. Why was such a paragraph necessary to document? Here are some of the errors and points you failed to mention and analyze in this paragraph: Not all Iraqis dubbed Christians as nazzah (or sewage cleaner), not even the majority of Iraqis! They did not dub Christians in general; they dubbed the few who lived in Talkeif. By dubbing every Christian nazzah, as you wrote, you and your Jewish community were racist and disrespectful as well, not just the Moslems especially when, as you indicated, some Jews were working in this menial job! Shouldn't you dub Jews as well? And where else in the world that such unfair and racist dubbing does not take place? Isn't this happening in every society? Do you want me to remind you about how non-Jewish Arabs (Christians and especially Moslems) have been dubbed and working in all kinds of odd jobs in their own homeland since the European Jews established the racist and Zionist state of Israel? You are documenting this gossip and soap-opera-like stories while living in Israel. Do you want to document valuable information and provide objective analysis for the readers to appreciate your Jewish community and its accomplishments or do you want to use a writing style that antagonizes others in order to show how victimized you, Jews, have been? If the first was your purpose behind writing this book, this entire paragraph should be deleted with an apology!

10. You are dead wrong about paragraph three, page 7, which reads, "It is interesting to note here, in parentheses, that in Iraq – and presumably in other parts of the Arabic-speaking world – in those days the appellation Arab was never used to define a person's identity, and the Jew-Arab opposition we constantly encounter today was never used either in writing or in daily discourse. A Baghdadian was usually said to be a Jew, a Muslim, a Kurd, a Christian, Armenian, Turk, Persian." This paragraph is worth deleting. I guess living in the Zionist state of Israel for a long time somehow affected your memory and style of documentation! The information in this short distortion of facts is contradictory to the British statistics you thought worth providing in the first page of this chapter (one). How would they include so many Arabs in the figures of Baghdad's population if people didn't identify themselves as Arabs? You are right about the absence of Jew-Arab opposition in writing or in daily discourse at that time, but wrong about the Arab identity in Iraq and in some other Arab countries and about the list you provided showing how a Baghdadi (not Baghdadian) identified him/herself. Additionally, it is important to enlist either only ethnic or only religious groups together in order to be accurate and avoid replication. Enlisting Christian and Armenian means you are repeating yourself since all Armenians are Christians and partially repeating yourself since among Christians are the Armenians. The same is true about your inclusion of Moslems, Kurds and Turks together in one list. Remember and never forget the fact that IRAQ is a majority Arab country including Baghdad whether the Americans, British and Israelis like to admit it or not.

Thank you for taking the time to read this (second) letter. I hope you and the publisher of your book take these comments and corrections seriously for the betterment of your wonderful book!

Wishing You Continued Health,
Wafaa' Al-Natheema, Founder
Institute of Near Eastern and African Studies (INEAS)

Document No. 2

Saturday, October 22, 2005
To Naseem Rejwan on Jews, Sunnis and Shiites

Dear Naseem:

I hope this note finds you well and in good health.

I am so grateful to Oded Halahmy (in NY) for introducing me to your book, "The Last Jews in Baghdad." Since I finished reading the introduction and chapter one of this book, I have been meaning to write you a letter with commentary about certain issues mentioned in the forward. Finally in a train ride with two hours to go, I decided to write you a letter and to eventually publish it on the Internet as well as emailing it to our Institute's very large list of recipients worldwide.

I also decided that I make my letter writing to you as a series in which I comment on other chapters in your book, which coincides well with the editing of my documentary, "The Other Arabs" about the life and accomplishments of Jewish Arabs with the hope to produce part II and III on the Mandaeans and Druze.

As I opened your book and read the very first quote by Louise Gluck, "Because you were foolish enough to love one place, now you are homeless," I paused for long with my thoughts and torturing nostalgia thinking how true was this saying! Luckily I woke up from my ghafwa (sleep) telling myself if I've loved another place, it means I've become promiscuous! How can I commit such mischief? Let us assume that I didn't think promiscuousness is a bad thing. Still I couldn't love another place besides Iraq. Nature, people and fate know well I've tried so hard. I have visited cities all over Europe, North America, the Middle East, North Africa and as far as South Korea! They all had their beauty with great nature sometimes and/or had nice cities, people and food, BUT lacked that ancient beauty, unique richness and spiritual intoxication IRAQ had and still has despite the wars and the destruction. One of the reasons why I wish to visit China and India is the desire to finally become promiscuous and hopefully rise in love with one or both of these countries!

Then I flipped the pages to read the forward written by Joel Beinin. It provided interesting information and was written in a way that made me read it all with pleasure. It mentions on the first page of the forward that Jews constituted 53,000 of the 150,000 inhabitants of Baghdad in 1908. Although it later provides footnotes indicating that such statistics was taken from Hanna Batatu's book, "The Old Social Classes and The Revolutionary Movements of Iraq: A Study of Iraq's Old Landed and Commercial Classes and of Its Communists, Ba'thists, and Free Officers." I am wondering based on which source Hanna Batatu provided these statistics and how reliable such a source knowing that these statistics were published during the Ottoman domination!

On page xvi, Joel Beinin writes, "The first modern Arabic play in Mesopotamia was written in 1888 by a Christian." In 1888, it was not called Mesopotamia.

It is a source of pride to read that just before WWI Khadduri Shahrabani organized a Jewish company that performed theater pieces in Arabic in Basra and India. It is actually a source of pride to Iraqis and Arabs alike knowing these productions were written and performed in Arabic language.

On page xvii, the family name of the leading maqaam singer of the 20th century was misspelled. His correct name is Mohammed Al-Qubbanchi or Al-Qubbanji (but not Al-Qubbanshi). It also mentions that "Hesqel Mu'allim accompanied the Egyptian diva, Umm Kalthoum, when she performed in Iraq in the 1930s." But it didn't indicate how he accompanied her whether as an instrumentalist, vocalist or part of a chorus!

There were very serious errors on page xviii about Jewish Arabs and the Sunni Arab so-called minority. They were so wrong that I don't know from where to begin. The lines read, "Many Jews were eager to be Iraqi Arabs. But like most Arabic-speaking minorities, they were suspicious of the romantic and racialist aspect of pan-Arabism. Moreover, in Iraq pan-Arabism was associated with the continuing dominance of the Sunni Arab minority."

1. Joel's sentence, "But like most Arabic-speaking minorities" surprised me. Iraqi Jews are near entirely Arabs. They are nothing, but Arabs. Writing that Jews are Arabic speaking means that they speak Arabic, but not necessarily Arabs! Then she made another grave error by considering Arabic-speaking in IRAQ as a minority or several minorities when nearly 90% of the society spoke (and still speaks) Arabic regardless of whether they are Arabs or not. The suspicion by Iraqi Jews of pan-Arab nationalism was not due to being part of an Arabic-speaking so-called minority, but because the vast majority of Arabs were Moslems. The element of religion was what brought Iraqi Jews closer to communism than both Zionism and pan-Arab nationalism. Please make sure that Joel Beinin read this letter with hopes that you make corrections of this paragraph should you print a new edition. After all, pan-Arab ethnicity/nationalism is in no way as romantic and racialist as Zionism and in fact easier to accomplish than the latter.
2. This brings me to the part in which Joel wrote that Sunni Arabs are a minority, which was one of the main reasons why I decided to write you this letter. As soon as I read this line, I flipped the book pages backward to see when it was published. I had a bet with myself that your book was published recently and I was right. Knowing it was published in 2004, neither you nor Joel seemed to investigate the truth behind the claim that the Sunnis are a minority in IRAQ. In fact, it has been surprising to me that no one Iraqi, Arab, Moslem or knowledgeable American has analyzed or challenged this claim.

Here are the reasons why this aspect of Sunni minority is untrue:

1. Since at least the 1940s, all census conducted in IRAQ including those under the Baath party were not providing questionnaire about any religion's sects (Orthodox, Catholic, Sunni, Shiite, etc.) The forms requested individuals to fill in whether they were Moslems, Christians, Jews or Sabeans. So how did the industrial west come to the conclusion that Sunnis are the minority in Iraq when this matter has not been documented?
2. Knowing Arabs are the majority in Iraq (whether the industrial west, Iran and the Kurds like to admit it or not) and the largest two minorities are the Kurds and Turkmans, let us then conduct some calculations. There is indeed a large Shiite Arab community in Iraq, but there is no documentation whatsoever as to whether they are more than Sunni Arabs or not. Now one must remember that Arabs are not only Moslems. They are Christians, Jews (until the early 1970s) and Sabeans. Putting all that in mind how can Shiites be the majority amongst Arabs? It is also a known fact that the vast majority of Kurds and Turkmans are Sunnis. Now you and I know that with the use of a calculator and the facts above, even a teenage kid would come to the realization that Sunnis do not constitute a minority in IRAQ.
3. Here is another reason why Sunnis are not a minority: Regionally, Shiites (mostly Arabs) are only a majority in the South of Iraq, but they are not a majority in the middle or the north. In fact, Shiites are a minority in the middle and a minute

minority in the North. Additionally, the population density in the South of Iraq is the least in comparison to the population density in the middle and the north. If the Shiites are the majority in only one-third, least populated IRAQ, how can they constitute a majority when two-thirds of Iraq are comprised of a Sunni majority? So even if we made grave approximations and exaggerations, the end result will not make the Sunnis a minority!

It put me in great discomfort to discuss the subject from a sectarian standpoint. It is indeed primitive. However, in light of the shocking propaganda for years about nearly every aspect with regard to IRAQ leaves us with no choice sometimes, but to get in this vicious cycle with the hope to at least slows it down or relatively correct some of its myths and errors! To keep repeating an error or a myth without enough challenge and constructive arguments, such an error or a myth eventually becomes the norm. By documenting the myth or the error, we will be misleading the world and the next generations as well.

It will be like the myth of the "Red Indians". There were (and are) no such people or race existed in our history. Yet the powerful European white created this race and the terminology and has been using them in school curriculum all over North America and beyond. The term, "Red Indians" was even translated to nearly all earth's languages despite the fact that they were and are known as and want to be called Native Americans, but the white Europeans who took the name (Americans) and the entire continent by force and terrorism are getting away with everything including the terminology of "Red Indians". Christopher Columbus was heading to India not to America. He got lost and ended up in America thinking that he reached India, so he called the Natives "Red Indians". This example and many others make me very worried about Iraq's history and that of the Arab and Islamic worlds being decided upon by the white Europeans and Euro-Americans AGAIN!

PLEASE, PLEASE make the necessary corrections about the Jewish Arabs of IRAQ and about the Sunni and Shiite Moslems in your book's forward with appreciation.

Thank you so much for writing, "The Last Jews in Baghdad". In part II of this series of letter writing to you, I will comment on Chapter one of your book.

Cordially,

Wafaa' Al-Natheema

[Following the above letter to Naseem Rejwan, author of *The Last Jews in Baghdad*, which was emailed to him and to Joel Beinin (who wrote the book's Foreword) at the end of October, we did not receive any reply from Joel Beinin, but received three insignificant and brief replies from Naseem Rejwan – *Note from Wafaa' Al-Natheema*]

Document No. 3

Saturday, January 28, 2006

Peter Sluglett on IRAQI Jews

Dear Wafaa' Al-Natheema,

Someone has shown me your letter to Nissim Rejwan. I think the record has to be set straight. I have been working on 19th and 29th century Iraqi history for the last 30 years.

In the Iraqi context, it's nonsense to talk about 'Jewish Arabs'. The correct terminology is 'Arabic-speaking Jews.' It's like this. Arabs originate in the Arabian Peninsula. They begin to migrate out in the 4th and 5th centuries AD, and then do so in a big way in the 7th century, with the Arab conquests. Long before the Arab conquests, there were Jews in what is now Iraq. We cannot call them Arab Jews (unless we mean 'Arabic-speaking Jews') because their ancestors were there many centuries before the Arabs.

The Jewish population of Baghdad: this is the figure which everyone in the field accepts. The Ottoman salnames and censuses are the most reliable sources we have (because the Ottomans based jizya and other tax collection on them). Batatu's book (1978) is the most reliable account that we have: it is impossible to write anything serious on Iraq without reading it. Batatu (d.2002) taught Political Science first at AUB and then at Georgetown.

Joel's sentence, "But like most Arabic-speaking minorities" shocked me. Iraqi Jews are near entirely Arabs. They are nothing, but Arabs. Writing that Jews are Arabic speaking means that they speak Arabic, but not necessarily Arabs! Then she made another grave error by considering Arabic-speaking in IRAQ as a minority or several minorities when nearly 90% of the society spoke (and still speaks) Arabic regardless of whether they are Arabs or not.

This is based on a misunderstanding of English. 'Arabic speaking minorities' = 'Arabic-speaking non-Muslim minorities'; (For instance, Maronites and Orthodox Christians and Druzes in Lebanon, Chaldeans, Suriani, Ashuri, Jews etc in Iraq). I have already explained that the Iraqi Jews are not and cannot be Arabs. Joel Beinin is a man (i.e. not 'she'); he is a highly respected historian of the labor movement in Egypt and Palestine, a Professor of History at Stanford.

[On page xvi, Joel Beinin writes, "The first modern Arabic play in Mesopotamia was written in 1888 by a Christian." Please note that in 1888 it was not called Mesopotamia.]

This is silly: it wasn't called Iraq either!! Iraq referred only to the provinces of Baghdad and Basra.

Pan-Arab nationalism is a load of a-historical nonsense invented by Sati' al-Husri in the 1920s and has no relation whatever to the realities of Arab history. There was never a time, except perhaps between 700 and 850, when it would have been possible to talk about a united Arab world – after 850-900 the Arab world was ruled by different dynasties of Turkish (or Persian) origin. Furthermore, very few Arabs were attracted to Arab nationalism before WW1, since the Ottoman Empire was the only thing standing between them and European colonisation, a fact of which even Arab Christians were aware. When the Ottomans fell, sure enough, the Arab provinces were taken over by France and Britain.

Zionism is equally fallacious in historical terms; two wrongs do not make a right!

Finally, your remarks about the Sunnis: All the people whose names I've quoted have been writing about Iraq or the Middle East since the 1970s. You will not find any reputable scholar who thinks that the Sunnis Arabs are a majority, although, as you say, the terms 'Sunni' and 'Shi'i' do not occur in the censuses. I assure you that this is not an invention by the Americans since 2003, it's what anyone writing on Iraq has been saying for the past 70 years.

The picture is roughly this, in percentages:

Kurds	24
Turcomen	6
Other non-Arabs (Armenians, Assyrians etc)	3
Arabs	67
Of which Arab Sunni provinces and Arab Sunni parts of Baghdad	27
Arab Shi'is and Shi'i parts of Baghdad	40

Of course this can't be absolutely accurate, but if you take half the population of Baghdad, and add all the obviously Shi'i areas south of Baghdad (find me the Sunnis between Baghdad and Basra) that's more or less what you end up with.

If you want to see what I, or Beinin, or Batatu have published, look us up on the Harvard University Catalog: http://www.harvard.edu/ (Hollis catalog). We all have doctorates, we're all professionals, and have been in the field for many years.

Peter Sluglett
History Department, University of Utah

[Sluglett's reply provoked the following response from Joachim Martillo, an independent scholar of the origins of peoples that have become associated with Jewish religion. Martillo was not previously party to any of the foregoing discussion. His intervention is nevertheless important as he gtackles the confusions created by misunderstanding the difference between "Jew" as a religious category, lacking any single unique ethnic content or identification, and categorties such as "Arab", "Iraqi" etc. which can contain any nuymber of religious groupings but are themselves national-ethnic identifiers, not religious ones. – *GZ.*]

Document No. 4

Subject: RE Jewish Arabs
Date: 10/26/2005 1:57:54 AM Eastern Standard Time
From: Joachim Martillo
To: Sluglett
CC: president@utah.edu

In a message dated 10/25/2005 11:55:45 PM Eastern Daylight Time, Professor Sluglett writes:

"In the Iraqi context, it's nonsense to talk about 'Jewish Arabs'. The correct terminology is 'Arabic-speaking Jews.' It's like this. Arabs originate in the Arabian Peninsula. They begin to migrate out in the 4th and 5th centuries AD, and then do so in a big way in the 7th century, with the Arab conquests. Long before the Arab conquests, there were Jews in what is now Iraq. We cannot call them Arab Jews (unless we mean 'Arabic-speaking Jews') because their ancestors were there many centuries before the Arabs."

Dear Professor Sluglett:

Some friends of mine passed your email to me because I am an expert in the period that you address in the above paragraph.

I am completely astounded that anyone with any sort of training in history would try to equate ancient Arabs of 4th-7th century Arabia with the modern Arabic population.

It is a combination of primordialism and essentialism that went out of style with the defeat of the German Nazis, who tried to equate modern Germans with ancient Germanic and Teutonic tribes.

All the populations of the Middle East that spoke some form of Semitic or Egyptian language were Arabicized with the development of the early Islamic empires, and those populations included all the Aramaic-speaking populations that practiced some form of Judean religion. All these populations together evolved into the ethno-linguistic groups that are commonly called Arab today.

It is a major error to describe any populations before the 10th century as Jewish. Modern Rabbinic and Karaite Judaism do not crystallize until the time of Saadya Gaon. There are several cumbersome terminologies to describe various categories of Judean or earlier Judahite populations, but one point is clear as Shaye Cohen of Harvard University has carefully pointed out. "Judean" lost all ethnic or territorial sense by the 3rd century CE. I would argue that his time frame is several centuries too late, but any attempt to trace modern Eastern European Yiddish-speaking populations to ancient Greek and Aramaic-speaking populations of the Roman Empire that practiced some form of 2nd Temple Judaism belongs more to the realm of essentialist and primordialist propaganda than it does to genuine scholarship.

Because you pretend to be a scholar in Middle East Languages and Area Studies, I have appended a very simple introduction to the terminology necessary to discussing Judaica coherently since the development of Zionist ideology.

Patrick Geary has written a basic history book entitled The Myth of Nations. You should read it, for the very elementary points that he makes applies as much to the Middle East and North Africa as it does to Europe.

Joachim Martillo

Document No. 5

Sluglett-Al-Natheema-Martillo Correspondence:

a. Wafaa Al-Natheema to Joachim Martillo (after he forwarded her the above commentary by Peter Sluglett)

In a message dated 10/27/2005 1:06:49 AM Eastern Daylight Time, Sluglett@aol.com writes:

"I accept, and am grateful for, your criticism and detailed information on the 'Jewish Arabs', a subject I should not have raised since what I know about is the 19th and 20th century, and I defer to your evidently greater knowledge of the earlier period.

"However, while I know that Iraqi Jews always thought of themselves as Iraqis, I am not sure that they thought of themselves as Arabs (who just happened to be Jewish) – unlike, for example, the Greek Orthodox population of Syria who are quite unambiguously Arab in their own self-identification. Under the Ottoman Empire, of course, people thought in sectarian and religious terms (Muslims, Christians and Jews), but while it's clear that Iraqi Jewish novelists, poets and so on between 1920 and 1950 felt that they were participants in Arab culture (since they spoke Arabic – and only Arabic) I wonder whether - after the foundation of the state in 1920 - they thought of themselves as Arabs. Frankly, I rather doubt it, but I'm ready to be proved wrong !

"Peter Sluglett"
[end of email]

Most Iraqi Jews considered themselves Arabs, but the Industrial west and western Ashkenazi Jews didn't care or paid attention to this reality. They always made their own assumptions, distorted facts and worse yet invented their own "facts" and terminology to fit their agenda about various matters related to the East.

When Jewish Arabs lived in IRAQ, until they had to flee to Israel (a country that treated them horribly), they considered themselves Arabs. Many continued to consider themselves Arabs and even spoke Arabic or Arabized Hebrew even while living in Israel at least until the defeat of neighboring Arab countries in confronting Israel. Peter Sluglett or any of the western so-called scholars did not live in IRAQ in that era to witness that reality. They copy each other's findings, writings and statements often without listening to far better sources; the people themselves and their stories, concepts and behaviors.

Peter Sluglett should listen to the commentary by Iraqi Jews in Samir's documentary, "Forget Baghdad", should read the scholarly writings of Naeem Giladi who currently lives in NY and should also read the writing of the great Iraqi Jew, Ahmed Soussa, who never left IRAQ and converted to Islam later in his life, not because he wanted to stay in Iraq. He also should read the carefully written and well analyzed writings on the subject by Prof. Ella Shohat who also lives in NY. Jewish Arabs like the late Sameer An-Naqqash (Iraq) and David Shasha (Iraq/Syria) would have given Sluglett and other such history teachers a good piece of their mind. So it was not just a matter of speaking Arabic as mentioned in Sluglett's response and Joel Beinin's forward in Nissim Rejwan's book.

When Arabs began to lose in confronting Israel and when they began to be more divided and in trouble with each other politically, many began to disassociate themselves from Arab nationalism or from the Arab community and ceased telling publicly that they were Arabs for obvious reasons.

Jewish Arabs in the industrial west began to associate themselves with the Jews rather than Arabs because their causes get better funded with the Jewish and/or Zionist communities/organizations than with those of the Arabs! Additionally, the Jewish Arabs, whether living in the industrial west or Israel, have not been recognized and treated well, and with the terrible treatment of foreigners especially Arabs in general for decades and the privileges and power Jews have in the industrial west, it is understood why Jewish Arabs disassociate themselves from Arabs.

However, all of the above mentioned scenarios did not and will not change the fact that they were/are as nothing but ethnically Arabs whether they like to admit it or not.

Regards,
Wafaa' Al-Natheema

b. Pete Sluglett to Wafaa' Al-Natheema

Subject: Re: Jewish Arabs
Date: 10/27/2005 2:36:12 PM Eastern Standard Time
To: Wafaa' Al-Natheema
From: Sluglett

I have written the foreword to Abbas Shiblak, Iraqi Jews: a History of Mass Exodus (London, Saqi Books, 2005), so I am not entirely unaware of the points that you make.

However, I am still not sure that, their own self-perception, Iraqi Jews fall into quite the same category as, say, Syrian or Iraqi Christians who, (unless they are of Armenian or Assyrian origin) are clearly Arab in their own self-identification. Thus, while Arab Christians certainly regard themselves as Arabs who happen to be Christians, I wonder (since this is a question of self-perception, not necessarily of 'reality') whether Jews from Arab countries regard themselves as Arabs who just happen to be Jews. That they regard themselves as Iraqis or Egyptians I have no doubt.

Incidentally, you all seem to put a lot of stress on Israel and the various nonsenses which the Zionists may or may not have concocted. This is not part of my concern. If you read anything I have written – and if you are at all interested in 19th and 20th century Iraqi history you will see that I have written quite a lot on Iraq, both with my late wife Marion Farouk-Sluglett before her death in 1996 and by myself subsequently, you will see that it is all solidly grounded in empirical evidence.

Peter Sluglett

c. Wafaa' Al-Natheema to Peter Sluglett:

Subject: Re: Jewish Arabs
Date: 10/27/2005
To: Sluglett

In a message dated 10/27/2005 2:36:12 PM Eastern Standard Time, Sluglett writes:
"However, I am still not sure that, their own self-perception, Iraqi Jews fall into quite the same category as, say, Syrian or Iraqi Christians who, (unless they are of Armenian or Assyrian origin) are clearly Arab in their own self-identification. Thus, while Arab Christians certainly regard themselves as Arabs who happen to be Christians, I wonder (since this is a question of self-perception, not necessarily of 'reality') whether Jews from Arab countries regard themselves as Arabs who just happen to be Jews. That they regard themselves as Iraqis or Egyptians I have no doubt."

Yes, as I indicated earlier, they are Arabs and they consider themselves Arabs and part of Arab history, definitely.

Below are sources emailed to us after I sent my commentary this morning [Document No. 6, below]. The sender asked that we forward it to you.

Regards,
Wafaa' Al-Natheema

Document No. 6

Subject: Re: Jewish Arabs
Date: 10/27/2005 2:43:57 PM Eastern Standard Time
From: Sheilamusaji

Salaam,

We have had a number of articles on The American Muslim website on the subject of Jewish Arabs (by a Jewish Arab, David Shasha)
A Jewish Voice Left Silent: Trying to Articulate 'The Levantine Option', David Shasha http://www.theamericanmuslim.org/2003jan_comments.php?id=253_0_17_0_C
A Portrait of the Artist as a Young Arab - The Last Jews of Baghdad, David Shasha http://www.theamericanmuslim.org/2005jan_comments.php?id=553_0_31_0_C
Eclipse of SUFFEH, David Shasha http://theamericanmuslim.org/2005jan_comments.php?id=552_0_31_0_C
Masking Identity: Sephardim as Ashkenazim, David Shasha http://www.theamericanmuslim.org/2005august_comments.php?id=948_0_44_30_C
On the Use of the Term Arab Jew, David Shasha http://www.theamericanmuslim.org/2005august_comments.php?id=947_0_44_30_C
Restoring the Andalusian-Arabic Tradition in Western Civilization, David Shasha http://theamericanmuslim.org/2004oct_comments.php?id=499_0_37_0_C and we have an article coming up in the November issue "Rediscovering the Arab-Jewish Past"
It would seem clear that there are at least some who consider themselves Arab-Jews.
You are welcome to share this information.'

God bless,
Sheila Musaji

The above exchange illustrates how insistence on re-imposing – in the name of science – an entirely falsified historical narrative structure, one that can be readily demonstrated to stand utterly at variance with basic demographic facts, ends up converting what ought to have been a perfectly resolvable academic difference into a dialogue of the deaf. In the next section, we propose "Palestinisation" as a term to describe all forms of the Aphenomenal Model generated from such tamperings with fundamental narrative structures.

5.9. APHENOMENAL MODEL: "PALESTINISATION" OF SOLUTIONS PREVENTING PEOPLE TACKLING PROBLEMS AT THEIR ROOT

5.9.1. The Aphenomenal Model and the Secret of Why the Palestinian Question has Remained Unresolved

Since the imposition in 1948 of the State of Israel on their land by an international arrangement through the United Nations in which the native population was never consulted, Palestine and the Palestinians have not strayed far or long from world news headlines. At certain particularly dire moments, such as October 1973, the United States even put its forces on world-wide nuclear alert, "DEFCON 3", threatening the Arab world with nuclear annihilation unless it capitulated to before the illegal military occupation of Palestinian-resident territories of the West Bank and the Gaza Strip imposed by the State of Israel by means of an earlier aggression in June 1967. In 1947-48, more than three-quarters of a million Palestinians were uprooted from their homes and lands by armed forces assembled by the international Zionist movement supported principally from the United States and, in violation of longstanding international law, forbidden and otherwise continually blocked from returning or from obtaining compensation. Neither was the portion of the international agreement that promised the Palestinians a state alongside the State of Israel ever implemented, nor the United Nations' condition that it would expel the State of Israel unless it enabled and permitted the Palestinians' "right of return" ever to be acted upon.

Since those crucial moments in the Middle East in 1948 and 1967, one of the principal axes of world politics, around which many vital issues of the day have revolved, has been the prevention of the Palestinians' exercising their right to self-determination in the name of preserving a "right to exist" for the State of Israel. The deliberate flouting of international law by the State of Israel on many of its most cherished tenets has come to symbolise everything reactionary and unacceptable about rule by exception and everything necessary about ensuring the rule of law according to historic standards set by the world community. Among those standards, the methods of genocide and the use of military occupation rule to displace and dispossess conquered peoples, generalised during the Second World War by the Nazi German empire, were particularly stigmatised in the world-historic Fourth Geneva Convention, adopted in 1949. Although the State of Israel is a signatory, it remains unique among the world's governments in having violated every single one of its provisions. For these reasons, within the global polity, this nexus between the Palestinians and the State of Israel has come to define and represent the fullest manifestation of the Aphenomenal Model. Its aphenomenality is that its very exceptionalism is declared normal on the basis of questioning the readiness, viability, etc. of the Palestinians to get back what was theirs in the first place.

So ruthlessly effective has this implementation become that most of the facts from the Palestinian reality are hardly known beyond Palestine, whereas the distortions developed by the world Zionist movement, the State of Israel and the government of the United States, especially since the installation of the illegal military occupation of the West Bank and Gaza Strip in 1967, have spread literally worldwide. For quite disastrous reasons of its own at a moment highly critical for its own future after more than three years into the fruitless bloodletting of the First World War, the British Empire decided to offer European Jews, in numbers it hoped to control, a protected status on Palestinian Arab territory. Otherwise, however, the non-Palestinian five million or so residents of the present State of Israel have no historic connection whatsoever to that part of the world. Nevertheless, a muddled and nonsensical narrative has spread widely instead that "Israel" is the "ancient homeland" of the "Jewish people" which the Zionist movement simply came along to "redeem." To point out that any of their asserted "facts" are actually otherwise is to run the risk of being damned as worse than a child molester: an "anti-Semite". This suppression of the other narrative is also conducted worldwide.

On 19 October 2004, a Canadian freelance broadcast journalist with a reputation for "controversy", Michael Coren, invited four individuals, among them the National President of the Canadian Islamic Congress, Dr M.I. Elmasry, and Adam Aptowitzer, a spokesman from the Bnai Brith organisation, onto his show to "discuss the Israel-Palestine conflict". The programs segment degenerated into an entrapment and metaphorical lynching of Dr. Elmasry as some kind of supporter and advocate of suicide bombing. In the course of springing this trap, however, Bnai Brith representative Aptowitzer, who offered the bait with the not very subtle encouragement of Coren playing "neutral" emcee, blatantly defended the "state terrorism" (his phrase) of the Israeli military occupation as necessary and justified no matter how many innocent Palestinian civilian lives were sacrificed in the name of "combatting terrorism". This provocative tag-team line-up exposed itself clearly in the full transcript of the program (Website 5). However, although there would follow much pressure against Dr Elmasry before he was exonerated, fully, both by his academic superiors at the University of Waterloo and within the board of the Canadian Islamic Congress, it was in the end the Bnai Brith representative who was fired – never to be heard from again in any public capacity speaking or acting on behalf of any section of Jewish community organisations in Ontario or Quebec. While the full transcript referenced above shows how and by whom the trap was set and sprung, the host and his producers released at first only a partial transcript of Dr Elmasry's remarks. Aptowitzer's provocations were "redacted" such that the remaining text slanderously implied Dr Elmasry was some raving anti-semitic bigot with an Arab accent. In the week following the show, this "evidence" from the partial, *i.e.*, "redacted", transcript was widely cited on the CBC, in the *Toronto Star* and *The Globe and Mail*, building the hysteria that led to demands that Dr Elmasry resign his university position and the presidency of the CIC. The entire affair seriously backfired on those who had engineered it, with a wide swath of public opinion from all sections of Canadian society and all religious backgrounds coming forward in support of Dr Elmasry, in opposition to the lynching in the corporate media, or both.

This case exemplifies how, in thrashing out real contradictions within the polity, the inherent instability of the Aphenomenal Model (recall the triangle of Figure 5-1, balanced on its tip) makes it unsustainable beyond the very short-term. This feature has been manifesting itself on the international plane since the Palestinian populace, with 78 per cent of them participating in their Legislative Council elections on 25 January 2006, voted for candidates from the Islamic Resistance Movement (Hamas) to represent them in 76 of the Council's 132 seats. The State of Israel, the United States and not a few others have all but predicted the imminent end of the world as we know it is about to descend because allegedly the "party of suicide bombers" has taken power.

As remarked earlier near the beginning of the chapter, one of the great paradoxes of the Information Age remains that it can provide an orders of magnitude increase either in transparency or opacity. Increasingly, around the world – in Cuba, in Venezuela, in Haiti, in Bolivia, in Iran – there have emerged other attempts similarly to "Palestinise" the discourse of peoples who were victims of long-standing repression and marginalisation by Great-Power politics when they dared to hold their heads up and speak and act for themselves in concert with the rest of Humanity. Whether it is at work in the economy trying to fasten the theory and practice of consumption withoutn production onto people's lives, or in the global polity subverting the struggles for self-determination and rights, the long-term, and sometimes just exposure to the light of day, is the kiss of death for the Aphenomenal Model. In Chapter 6, some new syntheses are elaborated of "ways forward" for Humanity that escape the Aphenomenal Model once and for all.

5.9.2. More "Palestinisation": The Interest-rate / Gross Domestic Product "scissors" and Developing Countries' Economic Prospects

The deeply perverse reality facing developing countries' economic development in the face of the international interest-rate mechanism represents another "Palestinised" global economic problem of crisis proportions. Relative to the value placed on capital-intensive industry still owned in the main by corporate interests headquartered in the leading metropolises of the developed world, the labour-intensive productive activity of people working in countries whose economies are dominated by primary resource extraction is severely and systematically devalued. The key factor operating to devalue the latter relative to the former is the interest-rate mechanism by which tribute is levied and exacted on the governments of these countries by creditors from banking syndicates headquartered as well in the metropolises of the developed world. This lies at the heart of the uneven economic development directly afflicting a population totalling more than 4 billion people over the entire face of the planet but concentrated in Africa, South and central Asia and Latin America. The fact that a "prime" interest rate developed between the World Bank, the International Monetary Fund and the U.S. Federal Reserve – all headquartered in Washington DC – sets in stone the fate of entire countries, rather than the actual productive activity of a people, means there is no way out for these countries and peoples relying purely and solely on conventional economic solutions based on tangible economic factors and products.

5.9.3. Yet More "Palestinisation": Why Savings Can only Promote Waste

Regardless of whether they are reinvested or hoarded, some *intention* of one kind or another always attaches to "savings". Savings may be "unexpected" in the sense that their magnitude exceeds or falls short of expectations. However, for an economics of intangibles, the two key things about savings are:

1. whether they are the result of reducing waste or a basis for increasing it, and
2. whether the savings themselves are then re-applied to further reducing waste or to further increasing it.

"Savings" emerge as the result of restraining or reducing consumption. In conventional economic theory, total "instantaneous" demand for all goods and services produced by an economy at some given point is defined as the total of savings and investment in the economy at that given point (Keynes 1936). Unfortunately, this approach renders two things immaterial:

a) whether the source of the aforementioned restraint or reduction was a planned result of more careful budgeting by the individual or more efficient deployment of factors of production by a firm, or happened fortuitously; and
b) how and whether the savings are re-used, *i.e.*, to some social purpose, or to a purely individual one.

Can we say that "savings" from fortuitous sources, *e.g.*, savings arising from one-off events ranging from lottery winnings to profitable selloff of shares at the top of the market, play any role in the "savings plus investment" definitions of the aggregate demand functions of Keynesian economics? These are classic examples of superprofits, a short-term blip of excess in the social surplus that is intentionally distributed to unintended individuals or enterprises. That is to say: the payout is intentional – in the sense of legally mandated – but the identity of the beneficial recipient is arbitrary. Unless such windfalls are invested in creating new economic demand that did not exist before, they can only go otherwise to wasteful forms of consumption.

In general, therefore, such windfalls cannot be considered as forming any part of the "Savings + Investment" source of the economy's Total Demand function. Unnecessary confusion is created by attaching in this way the "savings" label to any source of previously unaccounted spending power. The sources of previously unaccounted spending power are thus not at all immaterial; the fact that they are all previously unaccounted does not mean they can all function as "savings" in the same defined sense.

According to conventional economic theory, the expenditure of savings as a resumption of the circulation of goods, services and-or capital, whether reinvested in the social economy or used to buy consumption goods for personal use or expended on interest-bearing instruments, is automatically positive. Again, this view is so broad as to wipe out any meaningful content to a definition of what constitutes "savings". According to the economics of intangibles, only reinvested saving can be considered *ipso facto* positive for the social economy. In general, it is unnaturally anti-social to withhold savings from the social economy for any extended period of time, or for individuals entirely to reserve them for wasteful non-productive forms of consumption. Savings should be considered the object of a "waste conversion" program, subjected to taxation regime that would discourage hoarding and encourage social reinvestment of savings for long-term benefit of the entire society.

Since the end of World War II, the extent and nature of the growth of oligopoly, quasi-monopoly and cartelisation in the economic life of the entire globe suggest that the notions advanced by J.M. Keynes (*ibid.*) concerning the nature of what was called "aggregate demand" are far too incomplete in their naïve assumption that governments could continue to operate independently of private corporate will when it came to ensuring full employment, to assuring the provisioning of all essential demands of the population, or even to making sure that the system supposed to supply these demands was up to the mark and that the government as representative of the popular will was setting the priorities, not the private corporate sector.

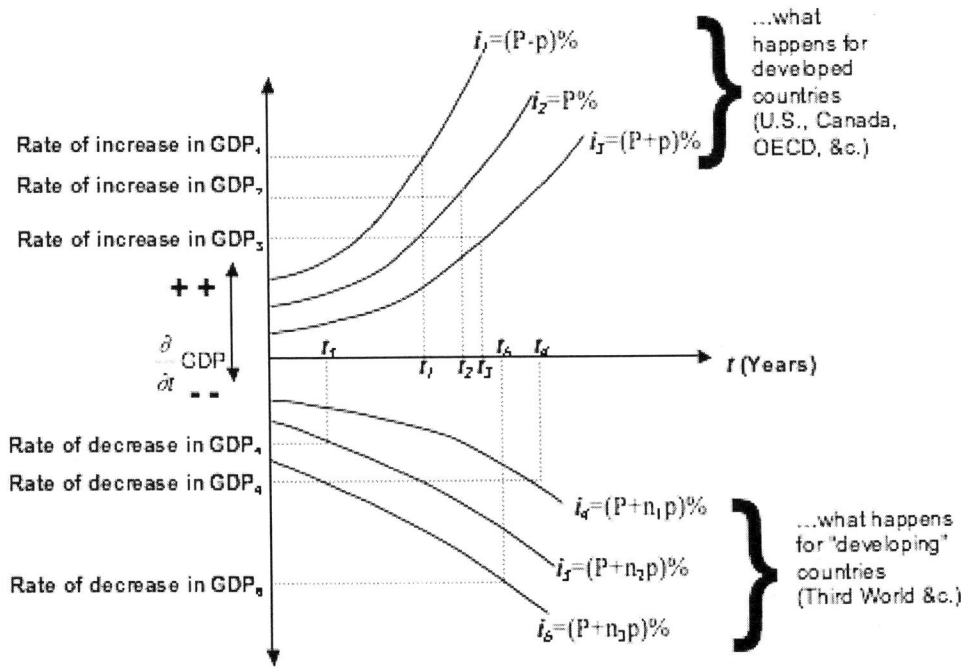

Figure 5-5. For the developed countries (from the OECD bloc, for example), assuming a given standard or "prime" rate of interest as P per cent per annum, such as I_2, another lower rate such as i_1 secures a higher rate of increase in GDP whereas a high rate of interest such as i_3 secures a lower rate of increase in GDP. For developing countries from the Third World, on the other hand, the higher the interest rate "above prime," the more rapidly GDP will contract.

In modern economic life, savings have increasingly come to represent that part of aggregate demand which is most likely to form a seeding ground for wasteful consumption, *i.e.*, for consumption that does not give rise to new production of necessary goods or services. This was not always the case. When free competition reigned generally throughout much of the economy – before the economic space was overtaken by oligopolies, quasi-monopolies and cartels – savings by individuals largely did reflect "economising" on household or business expenditure. Today they promote waste and as savings grow so does waste. This decay has become particularly evident in many departments of socially necessary expenditures, where saving has led to the generation of large "slush funds" in the tens and hundreds of billions of dollars being set aside. What are the results?

Education→Training, *i.e.*, "1/Education"

Health/Wellness→Maintenance, *i.e.*, "1/Health"

Cures→Symptom-delaying pharmaceuticals, *i.e.*, "1/Cures"

Investment→Bankruptcy, *i.e.*, "1/Investment"

Science→Technology, *i.e.*, "1/Science"

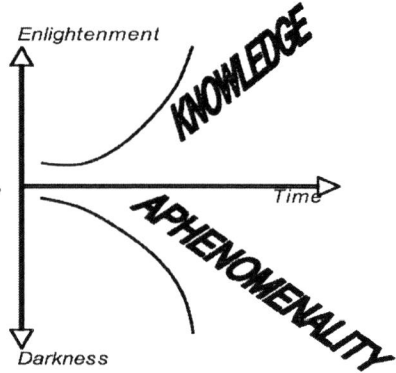

Figure 5-6. The savings cycle under prevailing conditions of the Aphenomenal Model fuels the growth of waste throughout the economy, especially in the provisioning of socially essential goods and services.

5.9.4. "Palestinisation" of Information Itself: With Enough Data…

A sound and grounded theory of the economics of intangibles is needed in order to resolve important questions of what constitutes supersufficiency, as opposed to insufficiency, of information, and how to distinguish one condition from the other. With enough data, one can "find" any pattern desired. As the following article illustrates, the question becomes one of intention in the aphenomenal sense of "what would you like?":

> Security is so passé, so last year. What businesses want in their software today is the capability to turn reams of data into strategic intelligence, says the man behind one of the largest private software companies in the world.
> "Right now this whole area of business intelligence is the No. 1 thing that's on the IT managers' minds," said James Goodnight, co-founder and chief executive officer of SAS Institute Inc. …
> The advances can give customers powerful new capabilities. For example, a bank developing a rewards program will want to determine who are its most loyal and reliable customers. To do so, it will need to scour large databases of transactions.
> Even for a small bank, the task is enormous, often involving an analysis of at least one billion transactions. In the past, such a project has required a company to crunch numbers in long batch runs overnights. But today, using the latest computer technology, a bank can mine that data in an hour, said Mr. Goodnight, who holds a doctorate in statistics from North Carolina State University.
> "Companies get so much data today, and they are realizing this data can be a strategic asset if they use analytics to find out the patterns inside," he said.
> SAS's analytics software helps companies analyze their data to spot unseen trends and predict outcomes based on historical patterns. It helps managers forecast demand, assess staffing and other resource needs, and predict customer and market behaviour. … (from Simon Avery, "Data mining: Deeper, smarter and way, way faster; SAS boss says hardware developments are driving advances in business intelligence", *The Globe and Mail Report on Business* [Toronto] 4 May 2006)

Here is an example of the supersufficiency of data being used to cook results. The same data mining techniques are at the heart of the entire Terrorism Information Awareness project at the Pentagon, unfolded as part of the Bush Administration's "global war on terrorism" and widely held responsible for netting as "suspects", or enabling the intentional or unintentional smearing of personal reputations, of untold numbers of persons from Muslim countries with names that that are identical by Anglo-American standards but who are otherwise utterly unrelated to one another. Electrical and electronic engineers are familiar with the principle of this phenomenon of information transmission, sometimes described as the substitution of the noise for the signal – but here it is occurring in the service of an aphenomenal intention.

Data insufficiency, created by an aphenomenally-based process of editing by which apparently extraneous information – such as the history of what gave rise in the first place to the phenomenon of interest, or under study – is simply eliminated. The example to be elaborated here comes from is the body of formal theorizing about what is called "development economics", which purports to account for what happens in the economies of developing countries in Africa, Asia and Latin America.

The real-life history of these societies since the middle of the 20th century has been a process of moving away from foreign domination by colonial powers, a global process that has affected the economies of developed countries no less than these countries. If that nexus is pictured or envisioned, it emerges that the economies of developing countries have been set up to approach a point of either implosion or explosion, rather than "takeoff" or development as the formal theory expounds. As a result of how formal economic theory cuts out this moving historical dimension as extraneous and unnecessary, the actual movement in the direction of implosive-explosive points of bifurcation is completely masked.

If in the *super*sufficient case just described, noise was substituted for information, in the following case, an *in*sufficiency is imposed to justify aphenomenal conclusions.

5.10. THE APHENOMENAL MODEL AND THE CONSEQUENCES OF "9-11"

A number of elements that were already latent in the Aphenomenal Model have become far more openly expressed in the context of waging the so-called "global war on terrorism" (GWOT). This "war" and its necessity have been discussed as though directed only against those committing actual acts of terrorism. In fact, it has come to include a rapidly broadening spectrum of pre-emptive actions. These run the gamut from warrantless surveillance by the National Security Agency to planning a military strike against the Islamic Republic of Iran over its alleged "potential" nuclear weapons ambitions. This latest war planning proceeds in the teeth of repeated exonerations of the Iranian govenrment's conduct of nuclear energy research, by the United Nations' International Atomic Energy Authority (IAEA), of all accusations of violating the 1968 Nuclear non-Proliferation Treaty. These tendencies taken together suggest the GWOT is about neither stopping nor punishing actual terrorist acts or their perpetrators. Rather it is a pretext for conducting a long-term, unilateral campaign, including military actions, targeting whomever supports anything principled, or whomever acts on the basis of conscience, or whomever acts other than on the orders of the United States. As far as the aim of justifying the *status quo* is concerned, the Aphenomenal Model since 11 September 2001 is the same model that existed on Septermber 10. Its methods, however, have been refined to a far more "advanced" level. Most significantly, the techniques of polling and professional "public relations", known as "PR 'spin'", have become merged with modern techniques of mass disinformation wielded through the corporate media.

The starting point of this pathway goes back to the years preceding the First World War. Such techniques as repetition as reinforcement, and conditioned stimulus-conditioned response have become well-known and extensively understood as tools for establishing a particular understanding of some phenomenon of real-life experience. Development of psychological theory and practice based on these orientations, which have burgeoned especially in the United States since the early 20th century, had their launch in the grounding by U.S.-based researchers of the entire field of cognitive psychology on the work opened up by the work of I.P. Pavlov, the Russian physiologist who was one of the earliest Nobel Prize laureates (in 1904, for medicine). Taken in the direction of what became known as "behavioural psychology" by the work of Edward L. Thorndike (1911) and John B. Watson (1913) during in the 1910s, this would be simultaneously applied to converting the field of advertising from a sales sideline before the First World War into an industry in its own right by the 1920s. Modern advertising was refined into a conscious practice on the basis of applying the vast array of tools that this work supplied for the purpose of manipulating people to buy products according to impulses having little or nothing to do with actual needs.

These tools themselves were very much refined by the practical experience in government-directed "opinion formation", including the earliest efforts in mass public opinion polling. The U.S. entered the First World War declaring war on Imperial Germany on 6 April 1917 with little public support. On 9 April, President Wilson's "Committee on Public Information" (CPI) was set up under the public relations lobbyist George Creel to whip up support for the entry of the United States into the war on the basis of demonising everything "German" and central-European as inimical to "true Americanism". The Committee became the first propaganda ministry in the history of the United States (Creel 1920). Although dismantled after the war, its practices and lessons would be re-used to build U.S. public opinion in favour of entering the Second World War following the 7 December 1941 attack on Pearl Harbour by the air and naval forces of Imperial Japan.

For the purposes of waging the GWOT, for the first time since Creel's CPI was dismantled, the Bush Administration reverted to assigning sensitive propaganda functions its own office. Had this been spelled out at the time to the U.S. public, it would very likely have been rejected. Accordingly, the "Office of Special Plans", previously known as the "Office of Strategic Influence" was set up under U.S. Defence Secretary Donald Rumsfeld denying it any importance, then claiming it was important only for influencing opinion outside the United States, and at one point claiming it had been closed down even though it was simply continued under a new name. The OSI/OSP has taken all the experience of Creel's CPI plus the experience of the Cold War even further to create public opinion in favour of pre-emptive military intervention based on a totally fabricated narrative about the Saddam Hussein government in Iraq having stockpiled "weapons of mass destruction" (WMD) and maintained "development programs" for a wide variety of WMD. In the first two years of its existence, Secretary Rumsfeld denied this office was involved in any way in planting false stories about the existence of Iraqi WMD, even as it was uncovered that this office was financing a high-level U.S.-Israeli-Iranian operative, at the rate of $340,000 per month, to plant such stories in the world press.[30]

Combined with modern opinion polling techniques, such deliberate lying quickly locks in a pre-determined course of government policy before any opposition can form and express itself within the normally available institutional order of either the legislature or the media. Based on the idea that individuals' political and social opinions can be classified and quantified by a random selection process that assumes all possible opinion expressions to be equally likely, these techniques provide the justification for extrapolating and assigning specific opinion choices to tens of millions of individuals, without actual verification, from a pre-arranged set of opinoiins surveyed among among some relatively extremely tiny sample of usually less than 1,100 persons. Polling results are bought and paid for mainly – indeed, almost entirely – by elite groups from the ruloing circles who control or represent the corporate media that will publish and circulate the polling results. In the United States in particular, where "public opinion" has acquired a kind of cult status according to the ancient Roman maxim *Vox populi vox Dei*, i.e., "the voice of the People is the voice of God", these results are a major instrument in the hands of political and corporate elites for inventing the public's opinion about something where the opinion did not exist and for marginalising trends among the public opposed to the elite wherever some issue has become contentious. Polls themselves are completely aphenomenal, creating as they do a "reality" that did not previously exist. The key thing about them is not their content but rather their function: to reinforce the narrative imposed by the poll buyer or the propaganda of the government, and thus assure that the lies being mediatised in newspapers, magazines, television, cyberspace and wherever people gather to discuss anything are taking hold in the collective and individual perceptorium of the polity.

Contrary to the judicial standard widely popularised in the movies and on television about "the whole truth and nothing but the truth", the aphenomenal notion that "Value depends upon Utility" (Jevons 1870), making every individual Consumer into a King of the Economy, is locked in by the advertisers' standard of truth, which is that whatever ratchets up sales fastest and highest must be true. In the post-911 environment, it should not come as any shock to observe the merger of the techniques of government-directed disinformation within commercial advertising of various kinds. But if this fact comes as no surprise in itself, the degree to which it has extended is another matter. At the core stands the interlock of corporate media and government elites, but no longer only for the well-established role of maintaining "good press" for the government of the day. Also, and increasingly, whether in the form of providing news or entertainment or advertising, these media play the role of ideological leaders as well as censors for the interests of an empire operating on a global scale, regardless of the party occupying posts in government at any given time. Because of the global reach of these media, this mission has had far greater impact, in the relatively condensed time-period of the last 50 years, than the preceding four centuries of Eurocentric religious missions outside Europe or even the century and a half of post-religious "civilising models" undertaken by the British and French colonial systems and based on selecting, raising and educating generations of local servants for their interests. Displaced onto the stage of global empire, the

---

[30] A subsequent independent study by the Knight-Ridder newspaper chain published in 2004 established this operative and his political front as the source of 108 such stories planted in *The* [London UK] *Guardian*, *The New York Times*, *The Washington Post* and other prominent media without any further attempt on the part of these organisations to verify the reports.

Congressional-military-industrial complex chaired by the U.S. government, in league with modern corporate media from that country, have recapitulated the same colonising mission undertaken in an earlier time by the pioneering wing of United States capital, as it expanded westward with the railway across the North American continent back in middle third of the 19th century. In that era, the leading cattleman or rancher, directly or through agents in his pay, was frequently judge, jury and executioner combined into one when it came to asserting the Rule of Law on any question. In our era, the American imperial complex speaking through these media, lay down law on the most distant continents, much of it disguised in and preceded by what are put forward as apolitical norms of "American culture and society". It thus becomes impossible to identify or distinguish where mere commercial advertising ends and disinformation in the service of imperial aims begins.

A particularly rich example of this last point is provided by the travel magazine *Bradmans*. This outfit produces a series of travel guides annually about the main cities in various regions of the globe – Europe, the Middle East / Africa, North America, etc. The material is presented in thre form of what is called "service journalism": a collection of current, immediately useful information and historical facts informing the reader about how people of the target region live now, framing a view of how they have come to be what they are, and helping the outsider come to terms with, and function without undue problems in, an unfamiliar environment. Bradmans annual for the Middle East / Africa 2005 (Bradmans 2005), aimed at the business traveler based in Europe or North America and compelled to visit major business centres in the Middle East, is especially interesting, depending entirely as it does for its impact on the post 9-11 shift within the Aphenomenal Model.

The contemporary travel book/guide/journal emerges from an extensive literature of the adventurer's memoir from the 19th and early 20th centuries. This literature, which in its original form modeled or chronicled individual's conduct, usually in the service of the British Empire somewhere on the globe, continues today in the service of a U.S.-led global imperial effort, but in a revised form in which ideological message-making is disguised between the lines of conveying useful information about the unfamiliar customs of the local population. The leaders of the British colonial system periodically worried aloud about its own representatives becoming sufficiently disgusted with the brutality and exploitation they were supposed to be fronting in its far-flung colonies as to abandon the British side and "go Native", *i.e.*, start to support the local exploited population against the coloniser. The revived version of this literary form which Bradmans Middle East / Africa 2005 exemplifies strives especially hard to finesse that possibility among its market of modern-day business colonisers by cocooning any of the hard edges of reality in the smoothest wrappings of corporate media cotton wool.

The prime audience for this particular *Bradmans* annual includes British or British-connected business executives involved largely in marketing and finance in the global oil business in general, and the command, control and other arrangements needed to generate and sustain investment and other related activity in the principal fossil fuel resource basins of the Middle East in particular. Demonstrating the British tilt is the *Bradmans* annual's inclusion of Lebanon, Syria, each of the Emirates, and Iran. Just as remarkable as further evidence of this British tilt is its exclusion of Saudi Arabia – a region whose oil business, until the Kingdom started very recently entertaining major new business partnerships with the People's Republic of China, was colonised almost exclusively by U.S. oil companies as well as its exclusion of Iraq, where whatever oil business there now is has also been reserved entirely for U.S.-based

Halliburton Corp., where the United States' vice-president, Richard W. Cheney, served as CEO before joining the Bush Administration, and its nominees. The central disinformation of this *Bradmans* annual is that the various forms of social strife in the Middle East, whatever their causes and insofar as they are even noted inside its covers, appear to have nothing, absolutely nothing to do either with the insertion into the region of the State of Israel since 1948 or the suppression of Palestinian rights and its ripple effects.[31] That conflict appears nowhere – not even indirectly, by reference – between the covers of *Bradmans* Middle East / Africa 2005.

For some time, the implementation of top-down policy-making models of the aphenomenal type has been detected inducing an indefinitely-extended period of instability, comparable to riding the roller-coaster in an amusement park – a phenomenon that has been covered, or more precisely uncovered, elsewhere with respect to the education system (Islam 2003[32]). Unlike the amusement-park ride whence passengers suffering various stages of near nausea could normally disembark and go on their way, however, this roller-coaster is incapable of returning to its starting-point and becomes instead something we experience as a sense of feeling overwhelmed by events. In the circumstances that have overtaken world events since 9-11, the opening of every new "front in the global war on terrorism" is not only an aphenomenal event in itself but is attended by another specialised but undetected vehicle that strives to control the volatilities inherent in all forms and instances of the Aphenomenal Model so that the interests of those in this vehicle remain intact and unimpacted.

Fossil-fuel resource development and marketing is one of those arenas of the global economy where Herculean efforts are mounted continually in an attempt to assert control, only to provoke developments that take matters even further outside anyone's control. What the global energy situation looks like can be likened to the situation of a certain group of people traveling through this world as though aboard a sealed train which shuts out any of the effects of the external environment and travels largely unobserved among the chaos of the lives being experienced by the vast majority of people outside its windows (Islam *et al.* 2006).

This invisibility is not unlike what happens with certain patterns of wave interference, such as polarisation, which operate to effectively filter out large portions of spectrum by the simple device of intersecting at a more or less mutually orthogonal angle all other wave phenomena of the surrounding or ambient reality. The effect of such phase cancellations includes both complete disappearance from view of the sealed train where the radian measure of the angle of intersection is exactly "$2k\pi + (\pi/4)$" (over all integer values of k), alongside partial and episodic appearances of incoherent, disconnected bits and pieces of the sealed train wherever the cancellation effects of the interference are less than complete. We are indeed more than likely to dismiss such appearances as "noise" forming no part of "signal". In this way the direction, although not the magnitude, of most of the dislocating impacts

---

[31] This seems also typically highly British, almost to the point of caricature, recalling to mind the episode of the world-renowned *Fawlty Towers* television comedy series in which the Fawlty Towers hotel receives a group of tourists from Germany, and the manager – after making a very big deal of reminding the entire staff: "Don't talk about The War!", meaning the Second World War – then subverts himself, unable to resist mentioning "the War" every moment that he is in his guests' presence. *Bradmans*' editors not only don't mention Palestine, but have excluded "Israel" from this annual (and placed it instead in their Europe annual), going to the extent of advising one researcher that they wanted to avoid antagonising potential customers both in the State of Israel as well as throughout the Arab world (Shapiro 2006).

[32] Chapter Two of that work is entitled: "The Roller-Coaster Ride of the Modern Age"

arising from of the general aphenomenality throughout the economy may be "regulated". The inverted commas are required in order to acknowledge that what is being regulated is neither the aphenomenality nor its oscillation but only that, regardless of what happens to any other interests, those of the richest and most powerful are kept safe from harm.

For those more comfortable with the realm of the concrete rather than the realm of the abstract, the foregoing exposition may seem abstruse, so for a concrete example it may help to consider what has happened over recent years in the real world of economic and fiscal policy-setting for the U.S. economy – and hence for many other parts as well of the world economy. Throughout the entire period of Alan Greenspan's multiple terms at head of the U.S. Federal Reserve, and more crucially than ever after the events of 9-11, that body became preoccupied tgo the point of obsession with what was called the "soft landing" of the economy. At issue was never whether there might be costly shifts in economic circumstances especially for society's weakest members, but only that the unstoppable dislocations unleashed throughout the economy as a result of hewing to the Aphenomenal Model would not dislodge the interests of the richest or most powerful. The costs of this roller coaster are to be borne entirely outside their ranks, and anyone whose sense of fairness or justice is outraged or even ruffled at the very thought let alone the fact must be handled as a potential terrorist threat.

Chapter 6

THE NEW SYNTHESIS

INTRODUCTION

There are three central concerns that the elaboration – including the processes of scientific research and proper application – of human social solutions to human social problems must address. These are:

1. overcoming the "interest trap" and resisting in general all other pressures to mortgage the Future in the name of indefinitely extending the Present;
2. going with Nature rather than against it; and
3. confronting pressures to expand or intensify the scale of political-economic integration and homogenisation with the counter-demand that the matter of "who decides?" be settled first, before anything else.

There are already many alternatives to the "interest trap". These range from conceptions of Islamic banking in which interest and any of its equivalents are truly eliminated as drivers, to variations on that theme, such as Grameen Bank microcredit schemes, that rely on socially distributing and sharing collective risks as opposed to submitting to corporate management of risk. At bottom all these ideas share the same basic notion of looking after the future *not* by mortgaging it so as to indefinitely extend the present, but rather by working and-or arranging matters in the present so as to take care of the long-term and thereby also ensure the short-term as well. It is especially crucial that knowledge-gathering activities, such as research, be reordered on such a basis in all fields of science and engineering. By its advocacy of tackling today's problems today without unduly burdening future generations, this outlook overcomes serious limitations inherent in the long-standing mantra of "Reduce, Reuse and Recycle", associated with the agenda of "environmental protection", and substitutes, in the place of the pragmatic stance of these so-called "three Rs", a natural act of personal stewardship and taking responsibility for the fate of Humanity, based on the aim of truly sustainable development with appropriate criteria.

Reorganising scientific and engineering research, and all other activities in life and work, to go with Nature rather than against it is the single most crucial item on any such sustainability agenda. To reduce the environmental protection agenda to whether this or that isolated and individually-considered process is sustainable is to dodge fundamental questions about whether an overall approach is inherently sustainable or bound instead to "come up short" (so to speak) in the long term. Reorienting outlook in this more general sense of seeking solutions that go with Nature rather than against provides some check against these limiting tendencies. This thereby puts in place a long-term solution to the problem of restoring and maintaining respect for Nature as the mother of all wealth. In this regard, there are positive developments emerging on the front of research into energy pricing and how it may be transformed by reorganising the supply, processing, refining or management of energy sources on a pro-Nature basis. Prototypes of many examples of these approaches, currently in development at the EEC Research Group, provide material illustrations of what is already possible right now.

The matter of "who decides?", a political question, cannot be separated from economics. Conventional economics of tangibles, incapable of responding to the question, simply ignores or suppresses it. A proper of economics of intangibles, on the other hand, offers an approach that makes possible a more efficient, more "economical" end-result across the board, in every activity, from information and high technology to oil and gas development. The biggest piece of the Big Picture, requiring the fullest public societal input is the determination of the scale of integration. This defines the essence of the obstacle placed in people's path by the Aphenomenal Model and its economic doctrine of "consumption without production" elaborated in Chapter 5. Solving this problem on the basis of enhancing the role of socially positive intentions for the long-term will itself restore a proper appreciation of the fundamental truth that nature is the mother as Labour is the father of all wealth.

6.0. CAN ECONOMICS GO *WITH* NATURE?

Table 6-1, outlining a comparison of some of the better-known properties of natural, engineered and economic processes, discloses how much closer to engineered ones the processes of conventional economics stand than to natural ones:

This indicates the terrain our proposed economics of intangibles needs to traverse to approach a state of affairs that does not place Humanity at war with Nature. On each of just these 13 characteristic properties, theorising and modelling an economics of intangibles useful to Humanity entails taking definite decisions about how actual subject matter is to be approached as well as handled.

For example, to forego statistical modeling, which is the clear implication emerging from the comparison of properties [1] and [2], entails finding ways to assemble, maintain and use items of data in their individuality and uniqueness, and not only when and-or where data items can be grouped in the same class, or in those aspects that these data share in common with other items of data.

Giving Property [3] its due consideration means that, for an economics of intangibles, all quantitative comparisons must be accompanied with, and cannot be used in the absence of, a qualitative comparison.

Giving Property [4] its proper weight entails the researching and disclosure of the historical evolution of any aspect of a process deemed to be an extension of "human nature" in order to establish the relevant features of its originating era and attendant social and economic conditions.

Table 6-1. Natural, engineered and economic processes compared

Nature	Engineering	Economics
1. Multiple/flexible	1. Exact/rigid	1. Stochastic
2. Non-linear	2. Linear	2. Linear-regressive (statistics-based)
3. Heterogeneous	3. Homogenous/uniform	3. Reducible to money-value
4. All-natural processes	4. Artificially-imposed processes	4. Artificial, ascribed to "human nature"
5. Characteristic life-cycles	5. Disposable (one-time use)	5. Periodic
6. Infinite	6. Finite	6. Finite
7. Non-symmetric	7. Symmetric	7. Complementary
8. Productive design	8. Reproductive design	8. Extended reproductive design
9. Reversible	9. Irreversible	9. Threshold
10. Knowledge	10. Ignorance (anti-knowledge)	10. Differential "knowledge"
11. Sustainable	11. Unsustainable (aphenomenal)	11. Demand-driven or supply-driven
12. Dynamic/chaotic	12. Static	12. Astable
13. No boundary	12. Based on boundary conditions	13. Path-dependent and bounded

As for Property [5], when intangibles are taken into account [as was painstakingly attempted in Chapter 2], many economic relations and processes turn out to be aperiodic, even chaotic.

Regarding Property [6], the tangible as well as the intangible return on an investment alters dramatically when its term is no longer bound by the spans – thirty years and less, all well within the average individual's lifetime – that are routinely applied in conventional economics.

Properties [7] and [9], taken together, point to a habit of thinking deeply ingrained in conventional economics, greatly reinforced by the requirements of commercial accounting practice, by which, at the end of any process, everything is in or returns to a state of balance. The complementarities of debit and credit, for example, are not unlike aphenomenal notions in natural science about equilibrium as a steady, rather than a transient, state. The associated notion that any given economic condition can be either imposed or maintained indefinitely or altered at will depending on the presence or absence of some threshold or other is at the very least an illusion, if not a delusion.

Property [8] in conventional economics poses a problem insofar as it considers reproduction entirely in its quantitative aspect, without regard to qualitative impacts or characteristics: to be able to produce, reproduce and sell plastic widgets in increasing amounts may represent something in quantitative terms but the plastic imposes a huge waste and likely health-care burden on Humanity over time.

With regard to Property [10], adjusting for the different knowledge of buyer and seller in the market – as discussed in Chapter 3 – may attenuate an inequality that might otherwise induce some undesirable disequilibrium in the market over time, but the fullest transparency from the outset would forestall the outbreak of the inequality to begin with.

Property [11] points to a similar source of ongoing disequilibrium that appears to be somewhat self-correcting in the short term, and is therefore not examined much in depth over the long term, but as with Property [10], if perceived supply and demand of some product were replaced with actual knowledge of all the relevant resources available, the source of the disequilibrium itself would be removed.

Again, for Property [12], knowledge and transparency similarly obviate the deleterious consequences arising from the astable character of economic transitions.

Finally, Property [13] is very much an outgrowth of the intangible components at work in any economic process. Knowledge and consciousness of these components, however, empowers people with an appropriate sense of what is actually possible.

Definite social, political and economic forms have evolved historically since the middle of the 17th century to accommodate and enable utilization of the discovery that Nature is the mother and Labour the father of societal wealth. In the first stage of this movement, as part of "bourgeois revolution" in England, the Man of Capital emerged to bring the factors of Nature and Labour together, giving rise to Industrial Revolution. As this evolved into oligopoly, monopoly and cartels displacing free competition and the economic space became completely occupied, a second phase of counter-movement emerged, punctuated by the Bolshevik Revolution and subsequent uprisings, in which Labour asserted itself *in the place of* the Man of Capital, wielding its authority through a new kind of State that retained certain forms of compulsion against the return of the Man of Capital but which was no longer a weapon in the hands of Capital to be wielded over Labour's head. In the next, third stage, this motion gave rise to its counter-movement of attempts to suppress new forms of social organisation with superior technological means. Eventually, with the emergence of Information Age, a fourth stage was embarked in which all the processes that were displacing the role-in-general of the Man of Capital with the collectively organized labour of humanity stood in increasingly antagonistic contradiction with the increasingly key role assigned to science, technology and those wielding technical knowledge as power (*e.g.*, technocratic elites). Today, as the character of this technocratic power, based on a aphenomenalised "science" corrupted by the power of money, has increasingly compromised itself in people's eyes, a fifth stage of the process has begun. Now, it is knowledge itself and those who actually undertake the labour of producing it – individuals developing their understanding of real phenomena based on the participation in acts of finding out – that has become positioned increasingly to take command. Another world is become possible in which there can be an economics that goes with, instead of against, Nature.

6.1. Escaping the "Interest Trap"

Ignorance has emerged as the single greatest obstacle to innovation and change in the Information Age. The ignorance referenced here is not reducible simply to lack of knowledge; rather, it is rooted in rabid and rockribbed hostility to acquiring any knowledge that would disturb current arrangements. The response of the current economic and political structures is that since the future is unknown, and the past cannot be changed, the best course is to extend and continue the Present – indefinitely. This aspect has rendered the Aphenomenal Model a particularly daunting opponent of solutions that are truly innovative, economically attractive, environmentally appealing and socially responsible.

Finance dictates everything in the modern world. However, while conventional finance routinely mortgages the future in the name of indefinitely extending the present, there are other models that not. These models, appropriately adapted, open prospects for making an economic and social space for introducing useful innovations that enhance the life choices of social collectives.

At all the United Nations agencies, village life in the developing world has long been a byword for the most elemental type of social collective. From the villages and teeming cities of that developing world, society in the countries of the allegedly "advanced" Western world seems awash in its own decadence. Nevertheless, when it comes to economics and technology, Westernised countries are universally deemed to represent some kind of paragon towards which all others should strive, whereas the widespread backwardness which persists undisguised in village life of developing countries such settings is held up as evidence an almost unbridgeable gap between purportedly outmoded tradition and the modern world.

6.1.1. Islamic Banking

What are some of these traditions that the modernising trend – or the "global war on terrorism" – have presumably ditched forever by the side of Humanity's road? In this chapter, two outstanding examples serve to illustrate the issues involved and their relevance for a sustainability agenda that can hold its own against the degenerative pressures of the Aphenomenal Model. At the macroscopic level, there is the phenomenon of "Islamic banking", which has become a factor to contend with on a growing scale within the global economy.

As media and various personages from the United States and parts of Europe have persisted in demonising Islamic belief and equating it with "terrorism", the Islamic Bank of Britain (IBB) opened its doors 22 September 2004, as the first bank in that country to operate on Islamic principles, including interest-free loans. In the summer of 1978, the British government hosted a conference that discarded any notion of Islamic banking as "absurd", in which it was even forecast that a similar system promoted in Pakistan would collapse in a matter of months. Perhaps the sky was falling? What could be going on?

As headlined at *Al-Jazeera* (from which the information and quotes in the following report are taken) as it remained unmentioned throughout North American media, news reports highlighted:

1. how *Shari'a* law imposes a series of restrictions on banks, including a ban on charging interest for loans and prohibiting clients' money from being invested in activities linked to alcohol, tobacco and pornography; and
2. the redefinition of "interest" as a fixed price, segmented into payment installments that also incorporate the profit to be collected for providing the service.

"We charge a profit for the services which we provide," according to the Bank's director of operations, Michael Hanlon, "we do not charge interest." And he stressed the 'No money for money' policy: "We do not trade money for money. We are actually involved in the physical supply of goods and services to customers."

At issue is actually the matter of *compound* interest, which is actually the making of money from money, as distinct from simple interest, which can be seen simply as a fee charged for the service of looking after someone else's property With compounding, relative to the original principal, and as a result of the fact that the amount of interest accumulates more rapidly since interest is applied to the entire amount (*i.e.*, on the original principal plus interest due so far), the effective interest rate itself appears to increase. On the other hand, if profit is collected in installments, along with payments of the actual principal amount, it becomes equivalent to what is known as simple interest – a fixed percentage applied only on the original principal, and assessed as though it were charged over, and collected at the end of, one entire period. Of course, for the person whose viewpoint has been previously framed to consider each of these to be forms of interest, this looks like quibbling over words to justify collecting an interest payment, albeit a non-compounded one. But the intentions of the two schema are obviously quite different, regardless of the framing of the argument that these are variants of the same category called "interest".

Although savings accounts are the only service currently on offer, mortgages are due to be available soon. Online banking will be offered from next year. The bank has posted Arabic-language details of its products in the windows to attract potential customers. Opening hours are identical to a conventional bank, with the exception of Fridays, when the bank closes between 1 p.m. and 3 p.m. to allow its employees to attend prayers at the mosque. "The biggest issue obviously is the interest rate," a Moroccan customer told a British reporter. "We've always been waiting for these opportunities to have an account in a bank where you can get profits which are allowed in our religion." About 150 Islamic financial institutions operate in 40 countries, but are still far and few between in western countries. The IBB was granted formal approval to operate by the Financial Services Authority last month, and is the first bank in Europe to specifically address the needs of Muslims, of whom there are 1.8 million in Britain alone. It is starting out with a capital of £14 million ($25.2 million) and plans to raise another £40 million via a stock market float. "The capital that we have and the capital that we'll be raising is more than sufficient to establish the bank," said Hanlon. The IBB is being supported by a group of investors based both in the Middle East and Britain, including some major financial institutions. Bank president Abd Al-Rahman Abd Al-Malik formerly headed the Abu Dhabi Islamic Bank, while other top managers come from institutions including Jordan International Bank and British-based Barclays.

This much of the story of Islamic banking already discloses the possibility of a system of financial management that escapes and avoids one of the most aphenomenal aspects of the contemporary scene. One of the forms in which the aphenomenality of "consumption without production" expresses itself increasingly these days is the widespread practice of floating new companies not as actual "going concerns" with real employees producing actual goods or services, but only as shells legally empowered to own and exchange property or other elements to which a monetary value may be attached. The holding or exchange of valuable property is an act of either potential or actual consumption entailing absolutely no increase or decrease whatsoever in productive activity. Even though, by an act of exchange, a surplus revenue is collected by the seller from the buyer, no new value or source of value has necessarily been produced.

The argument that such shell companies are potentially productive and therefore should be classed as utterly parasitic does not withstand scrutiny when the real world of new company flotations is examined. A recent article in *The Wall Street Journal*[33] disclosed that the U.S. government has become involved in finding ways to catch those cases where such new corporations "have become popular tools for facilitating criminal activity," according to a report published by the Government Accounting Office on 26 April 2006:

> Last year, Russian and Ukrainian prosecutors filed more than 100 requests with the U.S. Justice Department for help investigating U.S. shell companies. The Federal Bureau of Investigation told the GAO that a majority of its 100-plus cases of market manipulation involve the use of U.S. shell companies. U.S. officials believe shell companies are being used to launder as much as $36 billion from the former Soviet Union alone.
>
> Of the 50 U.S. states, the GAO found, 42 impose no extra requirements on foreign individuals seeking to set up a U.S. corporation. In states including Delaware, Kentucky and Nevada, numerous local firms sell so-called limited-liability *corporations* [*Emphasis added – Ed.*] to foreign buyers with few questions asked. Law-enforcement officials complained to the GAO that many firms submit fake names for directors and officers. The report found that not a single U.S. state seeks to verify the names of officers and directors submitted on new company registrations. (Simpson 2006b)

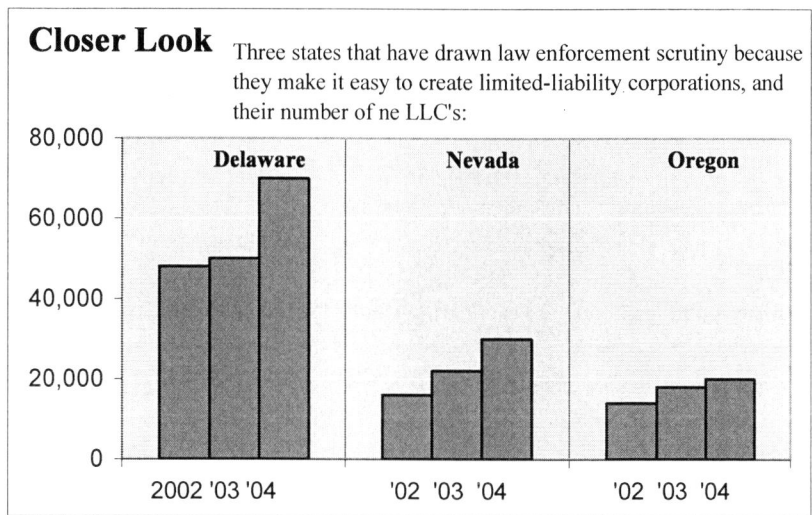

Figure 6-1. The chart demonstrates the dramatic increase in the formation of such shells in those U.S. state jurisdictions with the easiest reporting requirements for newly-incorporating business entities (Simpson *ibid.*).

These shell corporations are a step further advanced than the well-established earlier notion of the limited liability *company*. Corporations enjoy far greater impunity and freedom from accountability to government agencies than mere companies; a corporate official has far greater latitude than a mere company officer to commit criminal fraud without any risk of going to jail even if convicted.

---

[33] Glenn R Simpson, "Proliferation☐Of 'Shell' Companies☐Arouses Scrutiny", *The Wall Street Journal*, 25 Apr 2006, p. A4

The article points out:

> ... U.S. corporate agents operate much like counterparts in offshore tax havens, "using nominee officers to keep the foreign beneficial owner anonymous." But the big advantage of U.S.-based companies is their address, which confers instant legitimacy in international commerce as well as easier access to U.S. bank accounts and dollars.
>
> Shell companies generally have no employees, products or physical assets. In the U.S., most shells are limited-liability corporations, a legal entity designed for small businesses that requires very little paperwork to set up. Now, 300,000 more of them are formed annually than are traditional corporations, and their total numbers nearly doubled between 2001 and 2004.
>
> A hybrid of a partnership and a corporation, they were first endorsed by Wyoming in 1977 to let owners of small firms enjoy the liability protections of big companies without bearing the paperwork and tax burdens. ... [Their] simplicity and legal protections also make LLCs ideal shell companies for laundering money to hide its origins. In many states, they can be registered by foreign citizens via the Internet in just minutes without any ownership information being supplied. ...
>
> In one case reported to the GAO by the Immigration and Customs Enforcement agency, a Nevada LLC received 3,774 wire transfers for $81 million in just two years from locales such as Russia, Latvia and the British Virgin Islands, but agents were unable to even come up with a suspect because the company's true owner was never identified in any records.
>
> ...[It is well-known among finance industry insiders that] identifying the real owners behind would-be corporate customers "absorbs time and resources, because institutions must sometimes peel back layers of corporations or hire private investigators."
>
> As foreign police officials seek information on owners of U.S.-based LLCs, often the Justice Department turns them away empted-handed, the GAO says. Many states never ask who the true foreign owners are, so even a federal subpoena won't produce data that isn't collected in the first place. (Simpson *ibid.*)

What is really at issue is what might be called the parasitism of modern economics. As in early Christianity, the strictures of the Qu'ran against "usury" – the exaction of tribute, of money charged for the mere use of, or access to, money, without reference to adding anything to the world's supply of useful goods or services – express a rejection of parasitism as a basis for relations among human beings, according to a viewpoint that sees Nature and its bounty as gifts over which no human or gang of humans has a right to assert any proprietary privilege at the expense of their fellow humans. Various passages in the Qu'ran encapsulate an obligation on human beings to treat money or any other object as a trust, *e.g.*, "And let not those who covetously withhold of the gifts which Allah hath given them of His Grace, think that is good for them: Nay, it will be the worse for them: soon it will be tied to their necks like a twisted collar, on the Day of Judgment. To Allah belongs the heritage of the heavens and the earth; and Allah is well-acquainted with all that ye do." (3.180). This trust principle explicitly rejects the conversion of economic relations into parasitic master-slave arrangements, and it includes any other "belonging", including heritage.

Treating everything as a trust is a time-honored principle, even if only a few peoples acknowledge abiding by it (*e.g.*, the Native American community and their treatment of Nature). If this principle were adhered to consistently, there would be neither need nor room to hoard wealth; greed ("Greed is good!" proclaims Gordon Gekko, the Machiavellian hero of the movie *Wall Street*) would become homeless. This notion of trust has one further extremely profound corollary. Regardless of what arrangements may develop as to *use or enjoyment* of property, *ownership* of property may not be vested in any fixed or eternal manner in individuals. Vesting may be allowed in institutions, or groups with some social, long-term or otherwise non-self-seeking purpose – perhaps; but a right of private property ownership as something supreme and unconditional: No.

All Eurocentric economic notions address ownership of property as the central issue – with everything else (use, enjoyment, lease, etc.) deriving from the arrangements set down in law to define or to buttress definitions of ownership. Here lies a very deep problem.

Economic "existence" differs from social existence or physical existence insofar as only that is said to exist which has an owner. In much of conventional economic theory, the owner or element designated by the owner appears in the market as owner of a commodity which is to be supplied, through a market transaction, to meet a demand from another party seeking to own the said commodity. That is, in the conventional presentation of economic theory, the owner appears merely as the agency of economic relations taking place between things that are owned. In real life, this ownership is the main preoccupation, whereas the economic relations taking place between things that are owned are considered merely a theoretical formulation. There has developed an entire legal system buttressing the claims of owners.

What is applied to inanimate objects by this economic theory formulated since the 18th century was applied for millennia before that time to slaves, wives and children: they also existed only if they were owned, and many traditions in the legal system retain or express vestiges of these notions. Far from being – and conventional theory strongly implies this is the case, albeit without outrightly saying so – a general phenomenon of all human societies, however, this is in fact an ethnoculturally determined one. What gives this fact away is the phenomenon of the changing of a wife's surname to that of her husband. In Europe and North America, this has long been the norm; in Islamic societies it is unheard of. (Interestingly in Spanish-speaking countries of Spain and Latin America, the Moorish influence still survives in that the wife keeps her surname after her husband's and the surnames of children of the union follow the same pattern.)

Ownership of property as an enslaving act has thus emerged as something fundamental to an economics of tangibles; use of property as a trust, on the other hand, is a major feature of an economics of intangibles.

Eurocentric notions of trust confine themselves to assigning certain managerial privileges and prerogatives quite explicitly to non-owners of valuable property. This idea of trust explicitly presupposes an existing regime defining and defending quite separately the private ownership of property. Here precisely is where there arises great confusion and profound conflict. On the one hand: the fundament of capitalism in the Eurocentric world, and worldview, is that property can always be alienated privately. Backstopping this idea stands an entire legal system and state order available to defend private property ownership, not merely as some customary arrangement but as an indefeasible right to which all other claims are subordinate and from which all other rights under law may be said to flow.

The fact of the matter remains, however, that the Islamic principle of trust which, on the one hand, treats non-personal property mainly as a usufruct, and treats ownership on the other hand as neither private nor a right, is sufficient in itself for rendering the entire direction of modern economic policy obsolete. This principle is inherently subversive to the interests of modern, large-scale, monopoly-based, international financial capitalism. Beneath and behind the deafening cacophony aimed at impressing on one and all how unprepared the Islamic world is for "modern civilisation", a titanic struggle has broken out over how to square this circle. So, we have to ask: what stands at the center and core of modern economic policy?

The conventional answer is widely assumed to be: "growth." Of course, cancers are an example of a kind of "growth" as well. In economics, this is reflected in the absurdity that vast quantities of waste and expenditure on management and disposal of waste (without any re-conversion into something useful) is routinely incorporated as part of the reported "growth" in gross domestic product. However, an even more widespread phenomenon just as falsely identified with growth is parasitism. The modern view on the high road of civilisation is to humanise the natural environment; the conventional Eurocentric view is to privatise it, and the view propounded in the Qu'ran stands profoundly at odds with the Eurocentric convention.

Parasitism in our time has come to embrace a bewildering variety of forms – chief among which is the phenomenon of international finance and economics known as "interest rates." Interest rates are both the Achilles' heel of, and principal instrument of diktat for, the leading factions within international capitalism. Thus it is no accident that various circles from the United States see in Islamic doctrines an attempt to sidestep the authority of their power over interest rates and have therefore unleashed the most rabid attacks on Islamic belief in general.

Thus although such coverage as there has been of the latest developments in Islamic banking have the singular merit of providing some objective data about a phenomenon normally mired in a great deal of mystification and sectarian ranting and raving against "financing Islamic terrorism", there are some elements of the broader picture that need to be elaborated in order correctly to position and illustrate the overall significance of the development itself.

First, what is not happening needs to be pointed out: "Islamic banking" is not becoming British (or, more generally, European). It is British only by an accident of geographic location. The City is an international financial octopus. In that famous square mile recognized worldwide by its with the telltale postal code of "EC4", there is no serious financial force or scheme or undertaking that is not represented, seeking representation, lining up membership in an investment syndicate, etc. In comparison with New York, the City has far more connections with European continental financial institutions and with entire regions of the globe such as the Indian subcontinent. There, until extremely recently, American finance (as distinct from industrial combines and conglomerates like Union Carbide and the whole range of Tata- or Birla-fronted companies which spring like dandelions after the rain throughout the economies of India, Pakistan and Bangladesh) was largely absent or without deep-going links among already-established economic forces of the region. At this level, the Islamic banking trend represents a bid for a position within a portion of the international financial constellation that possesses or has developed various means for keeping direct U.S. domination and-or dictate at bay.

Second: sections of the international financial community have evidently begun to sense that interest-rate-based economic and financial regimes and ways-of-doing-business, by which the U.S. financial system keeps all its clients on a chain yoked to the Federal Reserve in Washington, can be overcome or subverted or circumvented by organising one's banking systems and processes *not* to make money off money, but instead without interest rates. The mechanism is simple: redesign banking as a service for re-circulating goods and services produced and exchanged earlier between some producer and consumer.

This is a "post-bipolar" condition, a state of affairs that emerged with the demise of the Soviet superpower and of the global competition between two superpowers. It is post-bipolar not only because powerful international financial groups based or centered in the U.S. want to seize control of the vacuum that has opened up as a result of the Soviet Union's demise, but in this case (support emerging in the City for Islamic banking) it is also post-bipolar in the sense that those whose positions are threatened by this hegemonic drive being led from the U.S.-based sections of international finance have been compelled to look at other paradigms of banking activity in order to stand a chance of surviving the U.S.-based invasion.

In earlier times, one faction or group of factions organised wars to contend for re-division of the spoils against rival factions. This has now become far more dangerous than anyone anticipated. It has become dangerous not only (and not mainly) because of thermonuclear weapons and all that sort of thing, but rather, and mainly, because the military balance is so extremely asymmetric, *e.g.*, the *increase* in U.S. military spending from 2002 to 2003 was more than the entire national budget of the U.K., that the ability of the losing side to rebuild as part of the capitalist system would probably be thoroughly compromised, and their own peoples might well rise up and seize the initiative and get rid of the entire system of exploitation of persons by persons. Thus, for the international financial groups contending against the further expansion of the interests of U.S.-based groups, "Islamic banking" offers a lifeline, or the promise of a lifeline, for retaining within the existing international system of financial enslavement the possibility for these giant groups to contend and collude even when one side cannot muster anything approaching the military means of its rival.

6.1.2. Defining a Natural Economics

Many representations "explain" Islamic banking – and therefore Islamic economics – as synonymous with the "no-interest" feature, in much the same manner that Islamic *Shari'a* law is rendered synonymous with criminal codes. In the case of the first misleading or deficient equation, the issue of the purpose of economic relations to begin with, as viewed from the standpoint of the *Qu'ran*, is not even addressed – the "no money for money" principle of Islamic banking is a symptom but not the driving force – just as, in discussions of *Shari'a*, the concepts of law and justice backed by a State are assumed to be the same as the concepts of law and justice adumbrated to serve the needs of a voluntary union of believers as a voluntary union and not as a State.

The table (above, Table 6-1), delineating the leading features of natural, engineered and economic processes, suggests a definition for a "natural" science of economics. By natural, we mean that which corresponds to fundamental characteristic features of human social existence, taking into account both what has changed in a people's history and what has remained consistent or relatively invariant. From that standpoint, the following definition of a "natural" scientific approach to economics is proposed:

> "the study and propagation of methods and arrangements favouring the most rational acquisition and consumption of the energetic and material requirements needed to sustain human social existence in any given period and conditions"

Consideration of the "most rational acquisition and consumption of energetic and material requirements" means taking intangibles into account, as does the consideration of whatever is "needed to sustain human social existence in any given period and conditions". Whatever the law of development that ought to follow upon "the study and propagation of such methods...", it must provide for securing the maximum satisfaction of the constantly rising material and cultural requirements of the whole of society through continuous expansion and perfection of production on the basis of higher techniques. Although certain aspects of how to get there from here, coming from the realm of knowledge-gathering and applications for novel pathways in technological development, are broached in section 3, entitled "Who Decides?", the broader question of what kind of social and political systems will favour or block realisation of such a law of development must be set aside as a matter for separate consideration in a different book.

If the divergence between Eurocentric and Islamic conceptions on these fundamental aspects is not made conscious, there are only two possibilities. We are left either with a total focus on externals, on appearances – a focus that does not and cannot inform; or we are left with dogmatic renderings. Dogmatic renderings are fatal to arriving at a researched understanding, based on conscious participation of the individual in acts of finding out.

The key to an human approach to economics is to acquire a grasp of intangibles – what they are, and how they affect matters. In economics, the essential intangibles are concentrated in the form of relations between persons. In this regard, the modern Information Age has the potential to deepen a furrow that the Bolshevik Revolution only just started to plough, *viz.,* the *subordination* of the relations that human beings impose upon the physical environment in pursuit of livelihood to the requirements of the relations of production, that is – those relations between persons in which significant new intangibles come into play, such as the possession of information, or how research is conducted and its results made available. A significant limitation within conventional economics remains its insistence upon continuing to subordinate the relations between persons to the narrowest possible focus on ownership of the forces of production and the concentration of those forces of production as well as of their ownership.

Current economic models do not include intangible costs and benefits. As a result they are rife with short-sighted forecasts focusing entirely on money. Consider for example the following: the tangible economic benefit to the U.S. economy of the Monica Lewinsky scandal six years ago was estimated to be US$1.2 billion, but the intangible cost of trust between the ruled and their rulers that was squandered and unknown effects of the moral degradation imposed as a consequence on the future generation might be in the trillions. Another example: the Iraqi invasion of Kuwait and the unleashing of the First Gulf War. Indeed all U.S. interventions since the disappearance of the Soviet bloc have proven as profitable in their material destruction and subsequent reconstruction activities as they have proven profoundly destabilising both for the entire system of rule in the United States as well as in the extremely wide swath cut by the tentacles of U.S. power throughout the international community.

Some may consider it impudent, challenging, or even heretical, to propose an approach that cites very definite starting-points from the *Qu'ran*, of all places, among others – all while explicity eschewing dogmatic renderings. But, standing more than a decade and a half after the collapse of the bipolar division of the globe, it seems more than clear that a major source of many of our current problems lay precisely with the dogmatic renderings and false certainties propounded by the systems of exploitation of persons by persons defended fervently by both the American and Soviet superpowers as they proceeded with subjugating entire peoples and regions to their plundering and rivalry. These dogmatic renderings, however, attacked and in some cases even crushed the human tendency to imagine, to dream and to aspire. Meanwhile, the peoples are not going to wait to be saved by others, nor go back to sleep trusting in others' promises of salvation.[34] Such is the "cunning of history" that this has become the content of human conscience everywhere throughout the contemporary world. The assault on Islamic faith and belief today aims precisely at extinguishing that conscience among all peoples, Muslim and non-Muslim, along with any form of outlook that defends or creates space for conscience.

Consider here, for example, the widespread notion that Islamic economic principle is closer to capitalism than it is to communism. This is being revived more vigorously than ever, alongside the international expansion of Islamic banking, more than a decade after the disappearance of the Soviet bloc. This dogma is not supported by Qura'nic principle, which would in fact require that people spend more money for others than for self, while minimising waste.[35] Indeed, for many Muslims, spending is maximised when it comes to charity – as the longest-term investment one can make.

If money is treated as a trust, many self-indulgent pursuits fall by the wayside. On the other hand, the individual as proprietor, which stands front and centre in the Eurocentric ethos at the core of capitalist social practice and outlook, is expected to determine priorities of expenditure entirely around what expands his/her interests both as an individual and as someone possessing property. Thus, spending on personal indulgences – including such obsessions as making more money, procuring more sex, and attaining or being in a position to display the accoutrements of higher social status – is deemed inherently no more nor less worthwhile than laying money aside for actual objective needs or social responsibilities. If the proprietary Eurocentric self were not part of this competition, placing itself at the centre, spending for others could become instead the foundation of a prosperous economic infrastructure for all.[36]

The long-term investment concept envisioned here is illustrated by Figure 6-2. The outstanding feature of this figure is that endowments and charitable giving in which there is no return to the investor – not even an "incentivised" kickback in the form of a deduction on the investor's income tax liability – generate the highest rate of return for the longest investment term. In effect, the more social and less self-centred the intention of the investor, the higher the return. What is most natural about the economics of intangibles is this restoration of an explicit role for intention. In today's world, in the field of actual economic practice, the power of The Monied has reached the point where the greater the investment-attracting interest rate, the greater the amount of foreign direct investment – and the greater the long-term indebtedness of the receiving economy, both in the amount of the debt as well as the speed at which it is wracked up, as well as the greater the denial that this was in any

---

[34] The ongoing and utterly total failure of aggression by the armed might of the State of Israel to "teach" the Palestinians to be "reasonable" and give up pursuing their right of self-determination comes to mind.

[35] The Qu'ran states: "…They ask thee how much they are to spend; Say: 'What is beyond your needs.'"…2.219.

[36] This points to another truism of which sight has been lost, viz., that Islamic economics cannot be implemented without an Islamic system – otherwise it cannot maintain coherence or integrity. In the absence of such coherence and integrity, an "Islamic economy" might start to look much like the Saudi judicial system: Islamic in its outward appearance, while standing for everything Islam once stood against.

way intentional (Perkins 2004). It is inherently unreasonable believe this crisis could not be removed, or not have been averted in the first place, if the intentions of interested investors towards these countries and peoples, and not just their resource riches, had been screened in the first place. In the field of economic theory, within the Eurocentric tradition, this has reached the point where the academic discipline itself is no longer called "political economy": the University of Toronto made a big deal out of renaming its Department of Political Economy the Department of Economics a few years ago, and only what are deemed the fringes – on the Left, the Marxists, or on the Right, the followers of Friedrich A. Hayek or Ludwig von Mises – have retained the perfectly clear notion that anything and everything connected to economics comes with an intention. Thus, for example, as illustrated in Figure 6-3, it is inherently reasonable to anticipate improved revenue performance for the enterprise that can bank on employer-employee trust.

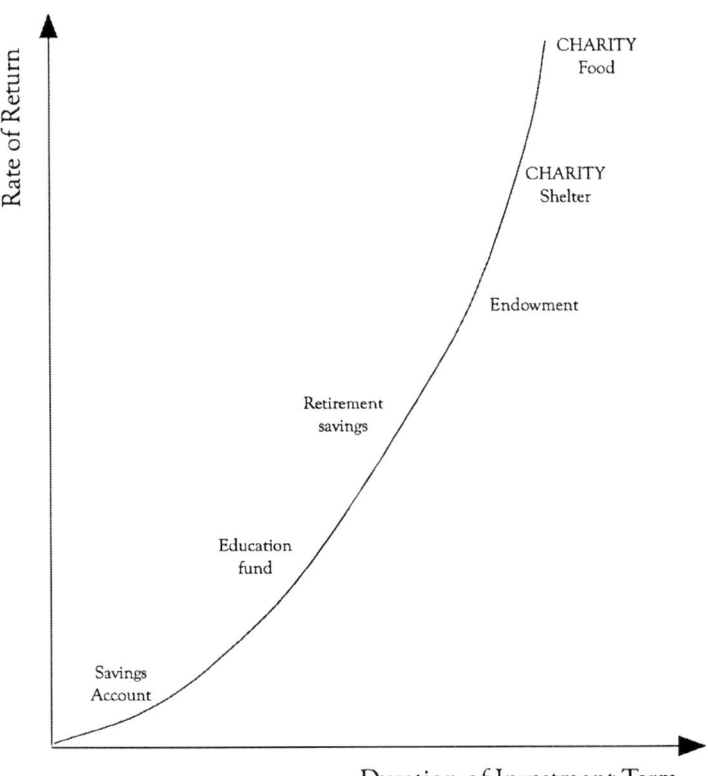

Figure 6-2. Maximising the Rate of Return on Investments for Others – This figure illustrates one prospect that becomes practically possible if intangible benefits are calculated into, and as part of, a well-known conventional treatment of investment capital that was developed initially to deal purely with tangible aspects of the process and on the assumption that money would normally be invested only to generate a financial return to its investor.

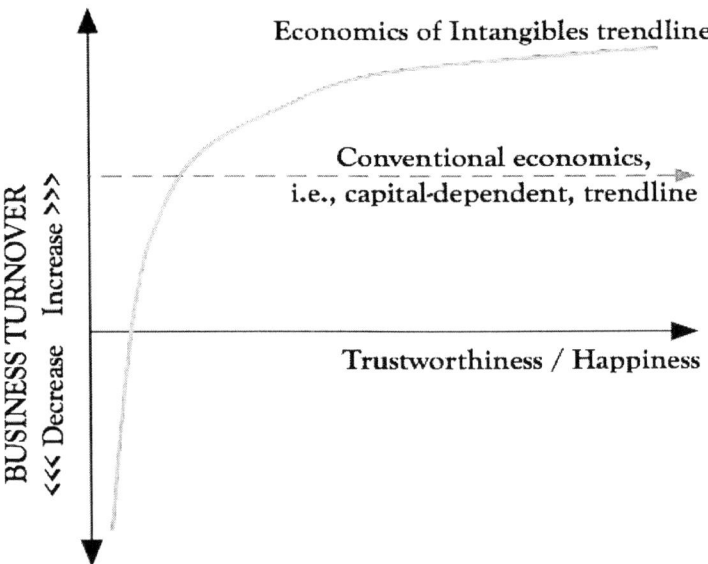

Figure 6-3. Sensitivity of business turnover to employer-employee trust – Under a regime guided by the norms of capital-dependent conventional economics, trustworthiness counts for nothing. Under an economic approach that takes intangibles into account, on the other hand, revenue growth in an enterprise should be enhanced.

6.1.3. Grameen Microlending

Often it assists to understand the presentation of matters in the "big picture" by looking at the same principles in application on a more immediately comprehensible, human scale. In recent years, an economic development model known as "microlending," developed within the context of the village life of Bangladesh, has taken the entire world, and especially the field of what economists call "community economic development," by storm. The Grameen model attempts to implement many of the principles and considerations just discussed, transferable to a wide range of other situations beyond the villages of South Asia.

Far from remaining confined to Third World countries, an international conference is being held in Halifax, Canada in November 2006 investigating possible applications of the Grameen Bank model in developed countries of the West:

> If the microcredit Summit Campaign stays on track, Halifax next year will witness a Neil Armstrong moment in a great endeavour – the reduction of poverty.
> Eight years ago, the international microcredit campaign set out to alleviate poverty by making small self-employment loans to 100 million of the world's poorest people.
> The goal was to hit the target next year, and a Halifax summit of the 3,164 lenders now involved will do the final tally, Nov. 12-15, 2006.
> The borrowers' needs were tiny. Typically, enough to buy seeds, craft materials, a rickshaw will start their businesses. But the campaign itself was "a bit like putting a man on the moon by the end of the decade," says its director, Washington-based Sam Daley-Harris, who was in Halifax last week. At first, it didn't have the tools to measure progress on its lofty goal. UN development agencies were skeptical that lending could be viable to the very poorest

people – which the campaign defines as those living on a dollar a day or less, or the poorest half of people below any country's poverty line.

But participants "wanted a dramatic reduction in poverty" and believed microlending does this, when done well. They had seen it done well by Bangladesh's pioneering Grameen Bank and others in Asia and Latin America since the 1970s.

Today, they are close to their goal and have already proven that great leaps can come from small loans. The annual progress report released at the UN last Wednesday says 92 million poor clients had received microloans from participants at the end of 2004 and 66.6 million of these were in the very poor category (below a dollar a day or in the poorest half of their nation's poor). Mr. Daley-Harris says the campaign should reach 100 million total borrowers next year, but will probably take another year or two to bring the very poor group to 100 million. In the world of development goals, however, actually achieving a target, even a bit behind schedule, is a rare success.

Mr. Daley-Harris says microlending has avoided two common constraints of development programs – lack of funds and difficulty reaching the poorest people. Microlenders commonly need donor funds to begin, but as loans are paid back they sustain the growing business. As for reaching the poorest, microlending is all about experimentation in finding ways to cut overhead and lend cheaply, beginning with Grameen's invention of group lending circles of clients who review and guarantee each other's loans.

Mr. Daley-Harris is convinced that, while no panacea, microlending is a powerful tool for reducing poverty. He cites a 14-year study by World Bank researcher Shahidur Khandar of the three largest Bangladeshi microlenders. It concluded their lending programs accounted for 40 per cent of poverty reduction in rural areas.

As a recent survey in The Economist newsmagazine reports, microcredit is proliferating and evolving into many different models, from non-profits to those aiming to attract investors, and from banking-only to those offering health, education and human rights services along with the finance. A year from now, Halifax will be at the centre of this fascinating phenomenon as the moon landing makes its final descent. (Editorial 2005)[37]

When it comes to credit unions and similar cooperative enterprises, which stand in between fully private and fully socialised enterprise, the devil, as they say, is in the details, and Grameen has proven no less immune to abuse than credit unions and producers' cooperatives in western capitalist countries. Accordingly, nevertheless, the details of the Grameen idea, from the most recent data supplied by the Grameen Bank (updated as of 26 January 2006) follow for the next several pages:

1.0 Owned by the Poor
- Grameen Bank Project was born in the village of Jobra, Bangladesh, in 1976. In 1983 it was transformed into a formal bank under a special law passed for its creation. It is owned by the poor borrowers of the bank who are mostly women. It works exclusively for them. Borrowers of Grameen Bank at present own 94

---

[37] The Grameen example intersects the life experience of both the authors from entirely different directions. One, born and raised in East Pakistan which later became Bangladesh, has observed its development as someone acutely conscious of its implications for challenging some of the plagues of underdevelopment arising from foreign dictation of export and development credit. The other, introduced at a very early age to the concepts of community of economic development by a close family relative who was an early post-World War I pioneer of credit unions in eastern Canada, undertook his own study of the Mondragón phenomenon in the Basque country of northern Spain in the early 1970s and of the Antigonish Cooperative Movement in the Canadian province of Nova Scotia in the mid-1970s

per cent of the total equity of the bank. Remaining 6 percent is owned by the government.

2.0 No Collateral, No Legal Instrument, No Group-Guarantee or Joint Liability
   – Grameen Bank does not require any collateral against its micro-loans. Since the bank does not wish to take any borrower to the court of law in case of non-repayment, it does not require the borrowers to sign any legal instrument.
   – Although each borrower must belong to a five-member group, the group is not required to give any guarantee for a loan to its member. Repayment responsibility solely rests on the individual borrower, while the group and the centre oversee that everyone behaves in a responsible way and none gets into repayment problem. There is no form of joint liability, i.e. group members are not responsible to pay on behalf of a defaulting member.

3.0 96 per cent Women
   – Total number of borrowers is 5.58 million, 96 per cent of them are women.

4.0 Branches
   – Grameen Bank has 1,735 branches. It works in 59,912 villages. Total staff is 16,142.

5.0 Over Tk 257 billion Disbursed
   – Total amount of loan disbursed by Grameen Bank, since inception, is Tk 256.50 billion (US$ 5.23 billion). Out of this, Tk 228.53 billion (US$ 4.64 billion) has been repaid. Current amount of outstanding loans stands at TK 27.97 billion (US$ 425.15 million). During the past 12 months (from January to December, 2005) Grameen Bank disbursed Tk. 39.19 billion (US $ 611.74 million). Monthly average loan disbursement over the past 12 month was Tk 3.27 billion (US $ 50.98 million).
   Projected disbursement for 2006 is Tk 54.00 billion (US $ 821 million), i.e. monthly disbursement of Tk 4.50 billion (US $ 68.40 million). End of the year outstanding loan is projected to be at Tk 38.50 billion (US $ 585 million).

6.0 Recovery Rate 99 per cent
   – Loan recovery rate is 99.01 per cent.

7.0 100 per cent Loans Financed From Bank's Deposits
   – Grameen Bank finances 100 per cent of its outstanding loan from its deposits. Over 64 per cent of its deposits come from bank's own borrowers. Deposits amount to 113 per cent of the outstanding loans. If we combine both deposits and own resources it becomes 135 per cent of loans outstanding.

8.0 No Donor Money, No Loans
   – In 1995, GB decided not to receive any more donor funds. Since then, it has not requested any fresh funds from donors. Last installment of donor fund, which was in the pipeline, was received in 1998. GB does not see any need to take any donor money or even take loans from local or external sources in future. GB's growing amount of deposits will be more than enough to run and expand its credit programme and repay its existing loans.

9.0 Earns Profit
   – Ever since Grameen Bank came into being, it has made profit every year except in 1983, 1991, and 1992. It has published its audited balance-sheet every year,

audited by two internationally reputed audit firms of the country. All these reports are available on CD, and some on our web-site : www.grameen.com.

10.0 Revenue and Expenditure
- Total revenue generated by Grameen Bank in 2004 was Tk 4.69 billion (US $ 79.00 million). Total expenditure was Tk 4.27 billion (US $ 71.84 million). Interest payment on deposits of Tk 1.58 billion (US $ 26.58 million) was the largest component of expenditure (37 per cent). Expenditure on salary, allowances, pension benefits amounted to Tk 1.25 billion (US $ 21.00 million), which was the second largest component of the total expenditure (29 per cent). Grameen Bank made a profit of Tk 422 million (US $ 7.16 million) in 2004. Entire profit is transferred to a Rehabilitation Fund created to cope with disaster situations. This is done in fulfillment of a condition imposed by the government for exempting Grameen Bank from paying corporate income tax.

11.0 Low Interest Rates
- Government of Bangladesh has fixed interest rate for government-run microcredit programmes at 11 per cent at flat rate. It amounts to about 22 per cent at declining basis. Grameen Bank's interest rate is lower than government rate.

There are four interest rates for loans from Grameen Bank : 20% (declining basis) for income generating loans, 8% for housing loans, 5% for student loans, and 0% (interest-free) loans for Struggling Members (beggars). All interests are simple interest, calculated on declining balance method. This means, if a borrower takes an income-generating loan of say, Tk 1,000, and pays back the entire amount within a year in weekly instalments, she'll pay a total amount of Tk 1,100, i.e. Tk 1,000 as principal, plus Tk 100 as interest for the year, equivalent to 10% flat rate.

12.0 Deposit Rates
- Grameen Bank offers very attractive rates for deposits. Minimum interest offered is 8.5 per cent. Maximum rate is 12 per cent.

13.0 Beggars As Members
- Begging is the last resort for survival for a poor person, unless he/she turns into crime or other forms of illegal activities. Among the beggars there are disabled, blind, and retarded people, as well as old people with ill health. Grameen Bank has taken up a special programme, called Struggling Members Programme, to reach out to the beggars. About 63,000 beggars have already joined the programme. Total amount disbursed stands at Tk. 45.92 million. Of that amount of Tk. 23.69 million has already been paid off.

Basic features of the programme are :
1) All loans are interest-free. Loans can be for very long term, to make repayment instalments very small. For example, for a loan to buy a quilt or a mosquito-net, or an umbrella, many borrowers are paying Tk 2.00 (3.4 cents US) per week.
2) Beggar members are covered under life insurance and loan insurance programmes without paying any cost.

3) Groups and centres are encouraged to become patrons of the beggar members.
4) Each member receives an identity badge with Grameen Bank logo. She can display this as she goes about her daily life, to let everybody know that she is a Grameen Bank member and this national institution stands behind her.
5) Members are not required to give up begging, but are encouraged to take up an additional income-generating activity like selling popular consumer items door to door, or at the place of begging. Objective of the programme is to provide financial services to the beggars to help them find a dignified livelihood, send their children to school and graduate into becoming regular Grameen Bank members. We wish to make sure that no one in the Grameen Bank villages has to beg for survival.

14.0 Housing For the Poor
- Grameen Bank introduced housing loan in 1984. It became a very attractive programme for the borrowers. This programme was awarded Aga Khan International Award for Architecture in 1989. Maximum amount given for housing loan is Tk 15,000 (US $ 249) to be repaid over a period of 5 years in weekly instalments. Interest rate is 8 per cent. 627,058 houses have been constructed with the housing loans averaging Tk 13,291 (US $ 202). A total amount of Tk 8.33 billion (US $ 127 million) has been disbursed for housing loans. During the past 12 months (from January to December, 2005) 19,643 houses have been built with housing loans amounting to Tk 187.07 million (US $ 2.94 million).

15.0 Micro-enterprise Loans
- Many borrowers are moving ahead in businesses faster than others for many favourable reasons, such as, proximity to the market, presence of experienced male members in the family, etc. Grameen Bank provides larger loans, called micro-enterprise loans, for these fast moving members. There is no restriction on the loan size. So far 668,389 members took micro-enterprise loans. A total of Tk 14.50 billion (US $ 235.00 million) has been disbursed under this category of loans. Average loan size is Tk 21,695 (US $ 330), maximum loan taken so far is Tk 1.2 million (US $ 19,897). This was used in purchasing a truck which is operated by the husband of the borrower. Power-tiller, irrigation pump, transport vehicle, and river-craft for transportation and fishing are popular items for micro-enterprise loans.

16.0 Scholarships
- Scholarships are given, every year, to the children of Grameen members, with priority on girl children, to encourage them to get better grades in schools. Each year, about 9,000 children, at various levels of school education, receive these scholarships.

17.0 Education Loans
- Students who succeed in reaching the tertiary level of education are given higher education loans, covering tuition, maintenance, and other school expenses. By December 2005, 8,926 students received higher education loans, of them 8,294 students are studying at various universities; 99 are studying in medical schools,

211 are studying to become engineers, 322 are studying in other professional institutions.

18.0 Grameen Network
- Grameen Bank does not own any share of the following companies in the Grameen network. Nor has it given any loan or received any loan from any of these companies. They are all independent companies, registered under Companies Act of Bangladesh, with obligation to pay all taxes and duties, just like any other company in the country.

  1) Grameen Phone Ltd. 2) Grameen Telecom 3) Grameen Communications 4) Grameen Cybernet Ltd. 5) Grameen Software Ltd. 6) Grameen IT Park 7) Grameen Information Highways Ltd. 8) Grameen Star Education Ltd. 9) Grameen Bitek Ltd. 10) Grameen Uddog (Enterprise) 11) Grameen Shamogree (Products) 12) Grameen Knitwear Ltd. 13) Gonoshasthaya Grameen Textile Mills Ltd. 14) Grameen Shikkha (Education) 15) Grameen Capital Management Ltd. 16) Grameen Byabosa Bikash (Business Promotion) 17) Grameen Trust

19.0 Grameen Bank-Created Companies
- The following companies in the Grameen network were created by Grameen Bank, as separate legal entities, to spin off some projects within Grameen Bank funded by donors. Donor funds transferred to Grameen Fund were given as a loan from Grameen Bank. These companies have the following loan liability to Grameen Bank :

  Grameen Fund : Tk 373.2 million (US $ 6.38 million) Grameen Krishi Foundation : Tk 19 million (US $ .33 million) Grameen Motsho (Fisheries) Foundation : Tk 15 million (US $ .26 million)

Grameen Bank provided guarantees in favour of the following organizations while they were receiving loans from the government and the financial organizations. These guarantees are still in effect.

Grameen Shakti : Tk 17 million (US $ 0.29 million)

Grameen Motsho (Fisheries) Foundation : Tk 10 million (US $ .17 million)

Grameen Kalyan

Grameen Kalyan (well-being) is a spin off company created by Grameen Bank. Grameen Bank created an internal fund called Social Advancement Fund (SAF) by imputing interest on all the grant money it received from various donors. SAF has been converted into a separate company to carry out its mandate to undertake social advance activities among the Grameen borrowers, such as, education, health, technology, etc.

20.0 Loans Paid Off At Death
- In case of death of a borrower, all outstanding loans are paid off under Loan Insurance Programme. Under this programme, an insurance fund is created by the interest generated in a savings account created by deposits of the borrowers made for loan insurance purpose, at the time of receiving loans. Each time an amount equal to 3 per cent of the loan amount is deposited in this account. This amount is transferred from the Special Savings account. If the current balance in the insurance savings account is equal or more than the 3 per cent of the loan

amount, the borrower does not need to add any more money in this account. If it is less than 3 per cent of the loan amount, she has to deposit enough money to make it equal.

Coverage of the loan insurance programme has also been extended to the husbands with additional deposits in the loan insurance deposit account. A borrower can get the outstanding amount of loan paid off by insurance if her husband dies. She can continue to borrow as if she has paid off the loan.

Total deposits in the loan insurance savings account stood at Tk 1990.54 million (US$ 30.26 million) as on December 31, 2005. Up to that date 40,338 insured borrowers and insured husbands died and a total outstanding loans and interest of Tk 308.97 million (US $ 5.04 million) left behind was paid off by the bank under the programme. The families of the deceased borrowers are not be required to pay off their debt burden any more, because the insured borrowers or their insured husbands do not leave behind any debt burden to take care of.

21.0 Life Insurance
- Each year families of deceased borrowers of Grameen Bank receive a total of Tk 8 to 10 million (US $ 0.14 million to 0.17 million) in life insurance benefits. Each family receives Tk 1,500. A total of 81,750 borrowers died so far in Grameen Bank. Their families collectively received a total amount of Tk 158.97 million (US$ 3.55 million). Borrowers are not required to pay any premium for this life insurance. Borrowers come under this insurance coverage by being a shareholder of the bank.

22.0 Deposits
- By the end of December, 2005 total deposit in Grameen Bank stood at Tk. 31.66 billion (US$ 481.22 million). Member deposit constituted 64 per cent of the total deposits. Balance of member deposits has increased at a monthly average rate of 3.83 per cent during the last 12 months.

23.0 Pension Fund for Borrowers
- As borrowers grow older they worry about what will happen to them when they cannot work and earn any more. Grameen Bank addressed that issue by introducing the programme of creating a Pension Fund for old age. It immediately became a very popular programme.

  Under this programme a borrower is required to save a small amount, such as Tk 50 (US $ 0.86), each month over a period of 10 years. The depositor gets almost twice the amount of money she saved, at the end of the period. The borrowers find it very attractive. By the end of December 2005 the balance under this account comes to a total of Tk 8.99 billion (US $ 147.66 million). Tk 3.19 billion (US $ 47.82 million) was added during the past 12 months (January-December, 2005). We expect the balance in this account to grow by Tk 4.98 billion (US $ 75.70 million) in 2006 making the balance to reach Tk 13.97 billion (US $ 212.34 million).

24.0 Loan Loss Reserve
- Grameen Bank has a very rigourous policy on bad debt provisioning. If a loan does not get paid back on time it is converted into a special type of loan called "Flexible Loan", and 50 per cent provisioning is done at the first annual closing.

Hundred per cent provisioning is done when flexible loan completes the second year. At its third year, the outstanding amount is completely written off even if the loan repayment still continues.

Balance in the loan loss reserve stood at Tk 2.98 billion (US $ 50.13 million) at the end of 2004 after writing off an amount of Tk 1.59 billion (US $ 26.75 million) during 2004. Out of the total amount written off in the past an amount of Tk 0.15 billion (US $ 2.52 million) has been recovered during 2004.

25.0 Retirement Benefits Paid Out
- Grameen Bank has an attractive retirement policy. Any staff can retire after completing ten years or more of service. At the time of retirement he receives a retirement benefit in cash. It is usually paid out within a month after retirement. Since this benefit was introduced 5,589 staff members retired and received a total amount of Tk 2.85 billion (US $ 53.19 million) in cash. This amounts to Tk 0.51 million (US $ 9,617) per retiring staff. During the past 12 months 350 staff went on retirement collecting a retirement benefit of Tk 296.30 million (US $ 4.64 million). Average retirement benefit per staff was Tk 0.85 million (US $ 13,257).

26.0 Telephone-Ladies
- To-date Grameen Bank has provided loans to 187,187 borrowers to buy mobile phones and offer telecommunication services in nearly half of the villages of Bangladesh where this service never existed before. Telephone-ladies run a very profitable business with these phones.

Telephone-ladies play an important role in the telecommunication sector of the country, and also in generating revenue for Grameen Phone, the largest telephone company in the country. Telephone ladies use 16 per cent of the total air-time of the company, while their number is only 4 per cent of the total number of telephone subscribers of the company.

27.0 Getting Elected in Local Bodies
- Grameen system makes the borrowers familiar with election process. They routinely go through electing group chairmen and secretaries, centre-chiefs and deputy centre-chiefs every year. They elect board members for running Grameen Bank every three years. This experience has prepared them to run for public offices. They are contesting and getting elected in the local governments. In 2003 local government (Union Porishad) election 7,442 Grameen members contested in the reserved seats for women, 3,059 members got elected. They constitute 24 per cent of the total members elected in the seats reserved for women members in the Union Porishad local government. During 1997 local government election 1,753 members got elected to these reserved seats.

28.0 Computerised MIS and Accounting System
- Accounting and information management of nearly all the branches (1,455, out of 1,735) has been computerised. This has freed the branch staff to devote more time to the borrowers rather than spend it in paper-work. Branch staff are provided with pre-printed repayment figures for each weekly meeting. If every borrower pays according to the repayment schedule, the staff has nothing to

write on the document except for putting the signature. Only the deviations are recorded. Paper work that remains to be done at the village level is to enter figures in the borrowers' passbooks.

Fifteen zones, out of 21, are connected with the head office, and with each other, through intra-net. This has made data transfer and communications very easy.

29.0 Policy For Opening New Branches
- New branches are required to fund themselves entirely with the deposits they moblise. No fund from head office or any other office is lent to them. A new branch is expected to break-even within the first year of its operation.

30.0 Crossing the Poverty-Line
- According to a recent internal survey, 55 per cent of Grameen borrowers' families of Grameen borrowers have crossed the poverty line. The remaining families are moving steadily towards the poverty line from below.

31.0 'Stars' for Achievements

Grameen Bank provides colour-coded stars to branches and staff for 100 percent achievement of a specific task. A branch (or a staff) having five-stars indicate the highest level of performance. At the end of June 2005 branches showed the following result.

989 branches, out of the total of 1,537 branches, received stars (green) for maintaining 100 per cent repayment record.

1072 branches received stars (blue) for earning profit. (Grameen Bank as a whole earns profit because the total profit of the profit-earning branches exceeds the total loss of the loss-incurring branches.)

805 branches earned stars (violet) by meeting all their financing out of their earned income and deposits. These branches not only carry out their business with their own funds, but also contribute their surpluses to meet the fund requirement of deficit branches.

243 branches have applied for stars (brown) for ensuring education for 100% of the children of Grameen families. After the completion of the verification processes their stars will be confirmed. 39 branches have applied for stars (red) indicating branches those have succeeded in taking all its borrowers' families (usually 3,000 families per branch) over the poverty line.

The star will be confirmed only after the verification procedure is completed. Each month branches are coming closer to achieving new stars. Grameen staff look forward to transforming all the branches of Grameen Bank into five star branches. (Website 3)

This discloses a number of interesting features. The bank is a category of institution that everyone conventionally expects to collect interest. But what Grameen calls "interest" is actually an accumulating share of entrepreneurial risk in the lender's venture. Since the price of the loan called "interest" is not compounded, it actually is not "usury", *i.e.*, making money from money, in the conventionally understood sense of Western banking. Depositors – and it is clear in the Grameen case that the depositor base does not comprise wealthy people – get a return on the savings that they park in an account at the bank. The bank, however, uses that money to stake entrepreneurial ventures, not to enrich shareholders. If the intention does not remain that of helping from the bootom up, of course, this becomes a terrible weapon for dismantling any kind of economic future, and evidence has accumulated of landlords and people with government connections converting into their debt slaves individual village entrepreneurs who initiated enterprises through micro-borrowing that became self-sustaining. When discussing this model, it is important to keep in mind how vulnerable it remains to powerful private interests doing such "end runs" around it.

The perspective elaborated here is focused not on microlending as a general solution to rural underemployment and social decay in developing countries but on development models that attempt to look after the future not by mortgaging it so as to indefinitely extend the present, but rather by working and-or arranging matters in the present so as to take care of the long-term and thereby also ensure the short-term as well. It is especially crucial that knowledge-gathering activities, such as research, be reordered on such a basis in all fields of science and engineering.

As always, in a social system that not only places pursuit of self-interest in the short term ahead of any consideration of a larger societal interest in the long-term as well as the short term but reserves the greatest rewards for those who accomplish this on the greatest scale, accumulating the most wealth, there are many tricks and traps in "community economic development" that dog micro-lending, credit unions, consumer and producer cooperatives or any of the other well-known community-based institutional props of such approaches. Section 6.3 *infra*, entitled "Who Decides?" discusses some correctives that can assist in maintaining support for, as well as participation in, approaches to and practical implementations of the new synthesis that fulfill meaningful sustainability criteria.

6.2. GOING WITH NATURE

Contrary to the portentous tone of its title, this book has not followed the arc of, and indeed was never intended as, a conventional economics text. Nor is it, however, simply a counter-text concerned only to pose disturbing questions about the prevailing orthodoxies in economics and technological development. Its appearance is inspired by actual ongoing research into and development of, applications intended to meet actual human social needs. What these applications happen to share in common is their design was modeled in whole or in part on how certain processes in Nature actually work. This effort is responsible for "opening a vein", so to speak, that raised all the profound questions with which the authors wrestled in the preceding chapters.

It was contemplation of the necessary and sufficient conditions for realising the fullest potential of these R and D applications that helped uncover the tangible-intangible nexus, that led to uncovering the very different pathways and destinies of key intangible and tangible elements of the contemporary economy, and that framed the basis for isolating the Aphenomenal Model as probably the single biggest obstacle to realising the fullest potential of not only these particular projects, but of any, and many, others that could come to fruition in future.

The conventional route has been to reconcile the principles discovered and innovations produced by such an effort with the demands and requirements identified earlier with the Aphenomenal Model. While this certainly remains open and available, there is an alternative.

It consists in reformulating the deeper problem to be solved as that of "humanisation of the environment". This solution has infinite pathways, but all pathways to a solution must meet a single guideline. That guideline may be outlined by defining what "change" looks like, so that people are not fooled by claims based purely on external appearances of "change" alone. The essential point to distinguish is that, while the basis of change is internal, the conditions of change are external. Here, in this context, the basis is determined by Structure, Function and Intention, whereas conditions are prepared historically through time. Furthermore, by this definition, the relevant criteria of necessity and sufficiency are that, without preparations of the conditions of change, none of the internal structures, functions and intentions can guarantee or sustain the changes for which they provide the basis.

It is especially crucial that knowledge-gathering activities, such as research, be re-ordered in all fields of science and engineering on the basis of looking after the future not by mortgaging it so as to indefinitely extend the present, but rather by working and-or arranging matters in the present so as to take care of the long-term and thereby also ensure the short-term as well. By its advocacy of tackling today's problems today without unduly burdening future generations, this outlook overcomes serious limitations inherent in the long-standing mantra of "Reduce, Reuse and Recycle", associated (falsely, in the authors' view) with the agenda of "environmental protection", and substitutes, in the place of the pragmatic stance of these so-called "three Rs", a natural act of personal stewardship and taking responsibility for the fate of Humanity, based on the aim of truly sustainable development with appropriate criteria.

What is here being labeled a "new synthesis" includes both new elements alongside existing phenomena, and new ways of arranging both new and existing elements. As a general society-wide process, "humanisation of the environment" appears as something external to the individual, and thus as part of the conditions of change. Its role is nothing less than to elevate Conscience to its place as the driver of everything, unfolding a social and economic order that is needs-based rather than greed-based. The detail of the systematic workings of what we are calling the "economics of intangibles" will be provided by what comes out of the struggle to introduce these innovations, and not before.

With Conscience as driver, this much can be sketched. The following key intangibles can assume their proper roles when redefined as follows:

1. *time* for the long-term or the characteristic term, rather than $t = $ 'right now'
2. *knowledge* of things-in-themselves *and* in-relation, rather than only the perception of things in their external appearance; and
3. *intention* redefined to include the effects of our actions on others, based on recognising that deeds are but by the intention of individuals.

Although the deeds are external to the individual, intention is internal and thus forms part of the basis of change. When modelling anything for the new synthesis based on these key intangible criteria, intentions should become transparent, on both the social as well as the individual scale, in order that, among other things, the meaning of certain conventional economic actions is transformed:

a) Investment can be viewed as something undertaken for the long-term. Under the new temporal criteria of Δt → not-zero, investments that amount to little more than hoarding disguised as "saving" are not considered worthy of the name.
b) Whatever has not been produced cannot be distributed. Hence, any treatment of production, distribution and exchange as objects of speculation is superseded.
c) Beyond what is required to purchase whatever is needed by one's dependents, money must be treated as a trust, and no longer as a source of usury or any other form of enslavement. This is rife with consequences. For example, charity becomes possible only *without* strings.[38]

What is meant by "a social and economic order that is needs-based rather than greed-based"? First and foremost, it means self-interest cannot be the final arbiter and that, where they conflict, the interests of the individual and of the society must be consciously, and conscientiously, reconciled. This in turn is part of a larger picture in which nothing in the natural-physical environment can be treated with any less care than one would treat any other human. This means putting an end to the subordination to human whims of everything in the natural-physical environment, as well as to the subordination of the social to the individual. In sum: "a social and economic order that is needs-based rather than greed-based" means putting an end to separation of Humanity from the natural-physical environment, and separation of the individual from the social environment of all Humanity.[39]

From the standpoint of the economics of everyday living, the most important aspect of "a social and economic order that is needs-based rather than greed-based" is that it demonstrates in practice how doing good can be good business, *i.e.*, that by organising with a view to ensuring the long term, material success in the short term may not only actually be as high or better than what would be achieved by conventional approaches but it would also acquires a future based on maintaining a sustainable set of practices from the outset.

Is an entire social order premised on such a basis mere wishful thinking? Tsarist Russia was a society that consciously set out in 1917 to change the course of the preceding 16 or 17 centuries, as it undertook the world's first revolution aimed explicitly at achieving precisely such a transformation from a greed-based to a needs-based society and economy. The system built there survived a titanic global conflict before, during and following the Second World

---

[38] Compare this with the following revealing, and blunt, declarations from a recent major U.S. newspaper editorial: Neither President Bush nor acting Israeli Prime Minister Ehud Olmert have made any secret of their intention to isolate Hamas and deprive the Palestinian Authority of funds once Hamas assumes the reins of government. Nor is there any shame in doing so: *Donors have the right to impose conditions on their beneficiaries...*" (Emphasis added - Ed.) [from: "Review and Outlook: Friends of Hamas", The Wall Street Journal, 15 Feb 2006, p. A16]
On the other hand there is charity that begins at home, disclosed in this headline about Barbara Bush: "Former First Lady's Donation Aids Son", by Cynthia Leonora Garza, in *The Houston Chronicle*, 23 Mar '06

[39] These separations are of course not real – if they were, we could exist neither as individuals nor in society. The notion of such separation is effected at the level of outlook, as the individual, from earliest consciousness, is guided to interpret and internalise the notion that Humanity stands at the top of the food chain. From this, it may be readily – but falsely – inferred that Humanity collectively and individually must enjoys some entitlement ahead and even at the expense of other natural phenomena. This has consequences when it comes to grasping crucial distinctions affecting the interrelationship between the tangible and intangible. For example, does living matter or dead matter degrade faster? Rigid focus on tangibles guarantees the conclusion that dead matter must degrade faster. Clearly this is nonsense, as the processes of organic existence itself include the continual shedding of dead cells and their replacement, so obviously, over the same period of time, the total amount of dead matter returned to the environment from living organisms must be orders of magnitude greater than the amount by which already dead matter further degrades.

War, in which its new social system was deliberately targeted for destruction by its allies, aided by corrupted, self-seeking forces inside the country as well as its open enemies outside. In 1953, the leading defenders of the system were poisoned or otherwise eliminated by foreign agents within the leadership, who spent the next 48 years turning the powerful industrial base erected by the heroism and sacrifice of their people into their private property, until the entire edifice imploded in 1991. The entire saga of its rise and fall provided the most sobering lesson yet in world history of the necessity for all those who commit to such revolutionary transformations to update one's knowledge continually in light of the latest developments of practice in any field, never conceding to complacency or letting oneself become rusty or allowing the sharp edge honed in the struggle to establish the truth to become blunted. The only reliable path to understanding and the achievement of reliable knowledge of the truth is participation of the individual continuously throughout life in acts of "finding out". In the early stages of the 20th century this was mandatory for social and political revolutionaries; today it is mandatory for all those who are serious about pushing back any part of the frontiers of knowledge.

Today there is no corner of the globe in which technological innovation is not undertaken. One of the lessons is that we have an enormous amount yet to learn all over again from a vast array of traditional methods and technologies that were developed over centuries and millennia in the traditional village life of Asia, Africa and Latin America but spurned as backward and excessively labour-intensive by all those who premise economic development

1. on a prior infusion of money capital,
2. on market-based standards of commodity production, and
3. on a notion that associates economic efficiency with diminishing and minimising the application of creative human labouring power.

The first of these premises says intention is worthless and is to be totally discounted: "show me the money!" The second says in effect that even if Nature was at some point the mother of all wealth, we're all grown up these days and once you're all grown up, who needs their mother? The third says that even if Labour at some point was the father of all wealth, there comes a time when the upcoming generation has to give the fathers' generation the old heave-ho. Those hewing to these principles pride themselves on their hard-headed realism. But is the essential message of these principles that dreams are one thing but reality is another, or is the real message that doing good is one thing but good business must be another?

The next several subsections propose answers to that question that affirm exactly how and under what conditions doing good can indeed be good business, *i.e.*, that it is possible to take care of the short term quite well by looking out for the long-term. Some technologies and innovations are discussed which have been researched and-or brought to various stages of practical implementation in the last several years and that meet this challenge by providing solutions that are innovative, economically attractive, environmentally appealing and socially responsible. A very wide range of possibilities emerge, from systems of "zero-waste" living to *naturally-based* binding agents, toxic-waste adsorbents, cleaning agents, polishing agents, insulation materials, construction materials, renewable fuel energy sources and liquid filtration technologies. There's even an oil spill recovery technology being developed based on nothing but Archimedes Principle – and no chemical surfactants (MI Khan and Islam

2006). Six especially intriguing examples are outlined below, all of which share the characteristic of "going with Nature" – indeed the key to their sustainability, to their innovative quality, to their econmic attractiveness and environmental appeal, even to their socially responsible approach – all stem from this key characteristic.

6.2.1. Zero-waste Living

As discussed earlier, the current economic system based exclusively on tangibles has reached pf producing ever vaster amounts of what is deemed to be waste: production of surplus on the scale demanded by a system monopolised by cartels and oligarchies is inseparable from producing waste in vast and growing amounts. Recently reported research into the design of residential systems that produce zero-net-waste, however, discloses previously little-considered possibilities in the realm of waste conversion, raising *en route* not a few questions as to the necessity or sufficiency of the present allegedly most cost-effective design of mass residential units.

Zero-waste energy and mass utilisation as concepts are as old as human civilization itself, yet these notions remain at the concept level – more so at the dawn of the information age than ever before. Although it is well known that energy or mass cannot be created or destroyed, all modern engineered schemes operate on the basis of positive entropy for energy production, with little or no emphasis on waste minimisation for mass utilisation. Most existing processes are energy-inefficient and mass-wasteful. Even when solar energy is utilised, the mere fact that the most common usage is the use of photovoltaic, the maximum efficiency can be only around 20%. The process efficiency can be increased very significantly by utilising solar energy directly. Only recently, such a scheme has been included to develop comprehensive energy solutions (MI Khan *et al.* 2005). In terms of mass, the problem is reduced to developing closed loops that would utilize all produced waste. The process can be made equivalent to negative entropy by adding microbial activities to the overall scheme.

Nature does not produce any waste, only transforming material from one phase to another.Its highest efficiencies correspond to maintaining a generally healthy environment for all living beings. This suggests why we should expect imitation of nature to take us on the path of a truly sustainable lifestyle. The model of interest here, which has been researched and reported, incorporates a number of novel designs, including biomass energy, solar energy (refrigeration and other applications) and a novel desalination process.

Throughout the industrial revolution and since, civilisation has become synonymous with a wasting habit, and the energy and mass consumption options in widest use are among the most inefficient ever experienced by Humanity. If the pathway itself is re-thought, starting with the notion of expanding production and consumption for our own needs but on the basis of a net-zero waste of mass or energy, either at the input or output of any process, it becomes feasible to propose approaches to zero-waste (mass) living in an urban setting, including processing and regeneration of solid, liquid and gas. This particular process is illustrated in Figure 6-4.

In this research, an integrated loop system was investigated for an apartment building of one hundred two-bedroom units for an approximate total population of three hundred people. The initial energy input source is free sunlight. The system includes an anaerobic digester (Figure 6-5), which is the key unit of the integrated process. Anaerobic bio-digestion is the mechanism of converting waste into value added materials such as bio-gas, ammonia and manure. This produces a sufficient amount of methane gas to use as fuel for applications ranging from cooking to solar-absorption-based refrigeration in the absence of sunlight. The purification of the gas can also find suitable applications in fuel cells, which convert chemical energy to electricity.

The guiding principle of this research was the mass balance equation, well-known to engineers, which was used to estimate methane production in biogas and ammonia production in the effluent. The ammonia-enriched effluent along with CO_2 (exhaust) from the digester can be used for desalination plants. This ammonia can also be used to run absorption refrigeration units. Besides, free solar energy has a wide range of household applications, including heating or cooling of water, apartments and running the absorption refrigerators. These not only reduce the energy requirements supplied from fossil fuel but also contribute to a substantial cost-savings leading to a cleaner and more economical zero-net-waste living.

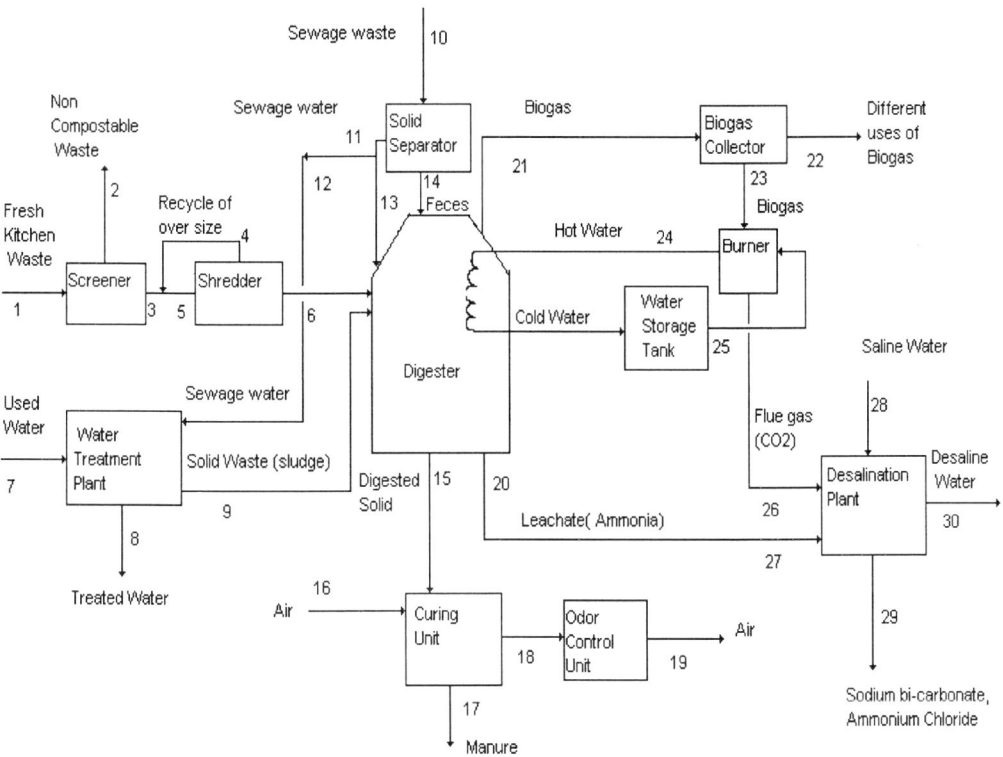

Figure 6-4. Zero-waste mass utilization scheme (MM Khan *et al.* 2005).

The principal value-added output of the bio-digester is biogas, containing about 65% methane gas; the rest is carbon dioxide. Biogas can be used directly for cooking, heating and all other applications using methane. Trace amounts of other gases in the biogas mixture, such as hydrogen sulfide and ammonia, which can be removed by means of environmentally-friendly technologies (Basu *et al.* 2005).

When desalination and fuel cell technology are integrated, the economics of bio-digester operation increase, approaching the threshold of zero-net-waste living. Zero-waste living with efficient and maximum utilization of solar heating is highly attractive. This scheme is socially responsible and environmentally appealing as well as economically attractive. The input – sunlight – is sustainable subject only to the constraint of the sun burning out, something extremely unlikely in anyone's lifetime for some time to come, as is the output, which – not being chemically processed – adds no toxic load to the environment.

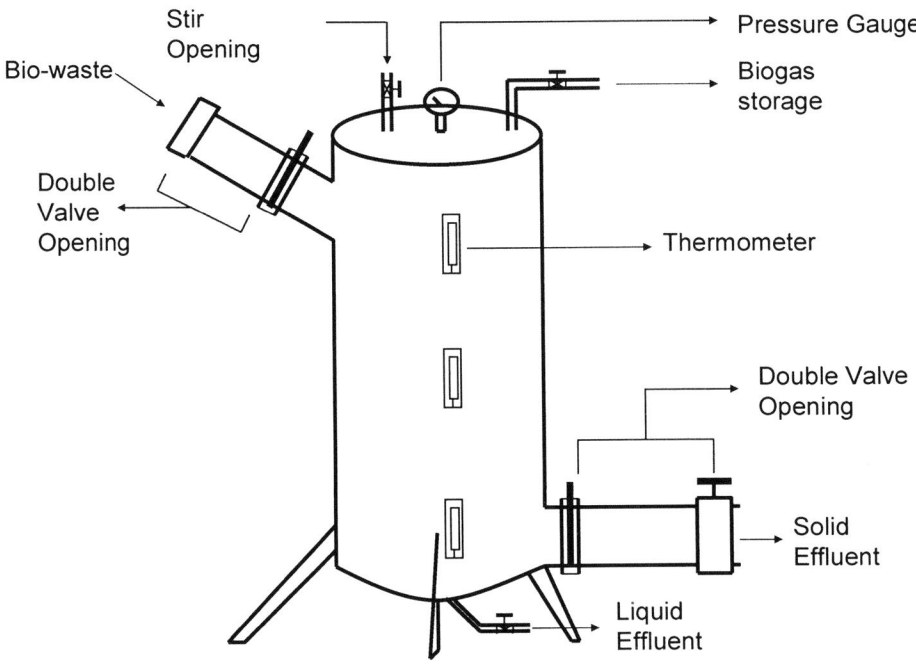

Figure 6-5. Schematic diagram of a bio-digester.

What is truly innovative about this solution is its starting-point: none of the inputs are commodities, i.e., things processed by others, and none of the outputs are processed as commodities. The philosophic essence of every revolutionary process, defined as "the throwing of the Form, the transformation of the Content" (Hegel 1833), is fulfilled in this example by the throwing off of the "form" of commodity-supplied inputs and substitution of the everyday activities of the residents of the apartment units for the processing stages that would normally be engineered and applied to those commodity-supplied inputs, so that the energy content of the input could be harnessed to generate a useful and valuable output that is every bit as environmentally benign as its input source. The science is that of mass balance and energy balance. The moment the selection of possible inputs to the mass- or energy-balance formulation of a problem is broadened to include the so-called waste output from another process effected for some other purpose that was already bought and paid for, this scientific approach discloses its latent, inherently revolutionary potential for "the throwing off of the Form, the transformation of the Content". Once the notion is taken up that a good business result for the long term and the short term is achieved not by seeking to make money in the short term but by choosing to do good – in this case, choosing not to harm the environment – in the first place, on a basis that can be sustained for the long term, it follows that precisely such revolutionary transformations can also form the basis no longer of dreamy-eyed blue-sky research but of extremely practical solutions demanded in the short-term that, by virtue of their environmentally benign or neutral character, are also sustainable for the long term.

6.2.2. Binding – Natural Cement from Biomaterials

Plaster of Paris, long found very useful for its binding properties, has been used for the construction of plaster board, insulation board, slabs, mold, and tiles. Plaster of Paris itself – chemical formula $CaSO_4 \cdot \frac{1}{2} H_2O$ – is derived from gypsum ($CaSO_4, 2 H_2O$), a sedimentary rock. Employing biomaterials as a calcium source, however, opens up the prospect of a sustainable way to make similarly functional binding agents. Sea shell, the hard outer shell of a mollusk, is actually calcium carbonate which is grown by a biological process. Calcination of the sea shell produces quicklime (CaO); this can be accomplished at atmospheric temperature and pressure simply by igniting the shell. Mixed with sugar or honey and water, this quicklime demonstrates different types of binding properties, suitable for cementing wood, leather, and glassware (MM Khan 2006).

Slaked Lime with Sugar

If quick lime is mixed with water, it forms calcium hydroxide ($Ca(OH)_2$) known as slaked lime. When the slaked lime is mixed with sugar in different ratio (commonly 1:2) it shows binding properties similar to that of Plaster of Paris. Upon mixing with sugar the semi-liquid pastes quickly dries (two or three minutes), hardens, and binds the surfaces of interest. Because sugar itself is a product of an unsustainable technology, further investigation had to be conducted with 100% natural products. For this, honey was the product of choice and was used to replace sugar. Because, honey have a far more complex chemical structure, this is substitution was expected to create further bonding than that with sugar.

Quicklime with Honey

When quicklime is mixed with honey, in a ratio of 2:3, it exhibits an excellent gluing property which is good enough to join wood surfaces. It takes longer time to become hard but shows stronger binding properties. It is also good for gluing ceramic and glass wares.

Slaked Lime with Honey

When honey is added with slack lime, it reacts so vigorously that it creates smoke, burns and turns the mixture to a brown-black color lump. Slowly this lump solidified and work as adhesive to attach to wood or glassware. This newly-made glue has been tested for attaching different media. It is proved to be a good binder. The lump is harder and it can be used as a binding material before it hardens.

Other Possibilities

Numerous other application ca be cited for this product. At present, investigations are underway to use this product to develop composite material, such as fiberglass, and fifer reinforced plastic (both synthetic and natural fiber and plastic). Also the same product can be used as an environment- friendly coating and pint and many other applications.

The single most astonishing fact about this entire approach: none of the initial knowledge was "new". Rather, its sustainable use was all largely forgotten, dismissed as something rural people unfamiliar with the demands of modern industry did in the villages of Asia, worth not even a footnote in the historical record. Neem and many other seemingly magical substances have been appropriated by industry in the Western world on the basis, discussed earlier back in Chapter 4, of the "sampling without replacement" approach to plundering natural resources. In fact: their real value is disclosed only in the context of being used within some sustainable application. This is yet another case of doing good being good business, in the sense of good for the short term as well as the long.

6.2.3. Adsorbing – Using Non-toxic Natural Wastes to Remove Heavy Metal Toxic Wastes

Zero-waste sustainable technology, as the best solution for all environmental pollution, has stimulated extensive study around d the world of natural alternatives to existing industrial systems and approaches. Traditional chemical engineering practices led to the generation of extremely high volumes of waste, posing serious long-term problems when heavy metals are present. The use of waste and naturally-occurring elements as potentially valuable assets converts waste material to highly-specialised uses that are often suitable replacements for far more expensive, allegedly purer-concentrated, but unfortunately synthetically-produced chemicals that could prove more toxic than the original toxic waste. By devising solutions that converge over long periods of time, irreversible damage to the earth from the temporary presence of wastes that have not yet been thoroughly neutralised is averted.

Mango Pits for Heavy Metals Removal

In this project, a novel bio-adsorbent was studied by M.M. Khan *et al.* (2005b). Kernels from mango stones, that are usually considered as a waste, show very high efficiency (as high as 90%) when used to remove lead contaminants. More importantly, they show delayed breakthrough, indicating high adsorptive capacity. The numbers are more impressive than conventional adsorbents, such as activated carbon or resins. The observed effect of pH on metal uptake by this material disclosed that, for the same initial concentration, no appreciable changes in equilibrium concentration occurred, suggesting that kernels from mango stones can be used as a new adsorbent for the removal of lead. After use, the substrate can finally be converted into non-toxic composts, consistent with maintaining zero net waste.

Use of Fish Scale for the Purification of Metal Enriched Effluents

The use of fish scale waste has been found suitable for purifying metal-enriched aqueous streams. One study showed more than 80% of lead contaminant could be removed using Atlantic Cod scale, while Shouairi fish-scale waste successfully removed metal contaminants such as cobalt, zinc, lead, strontium (Mustafiz *et al.* 2002). Mathematical modelling of this process was daunting: adsorption is nonlinear and not readily amenable to conventional modeling techniques (Basu *et al.* 2006).

Tea-Waste as a Natural Alternative for Remediating Pollution from "Produced Water"...

Mehedi *et al.* (2006) verified an hypothesis about the possibility of using tea waste as an adsorbent for removing lead from contaminated water, such as the "produced water" commonly outputted in oil and gas production. Typically loaded with heavy metals, waters thus contaminated disrupt ecosystem integrity and threaten irreversible environmental damage.

...And as a Commercial Fertiliser

An analysis of the chemical composition of tea-waste incidental to investigatiung its capabilitires as an adsorbent showed the presence of micro-nutrients such as iron and aluminum, elements that play important roles in agricultural productivity. It thus appears tea-waste can also be used as a fertiliser source of micro-nutrients.

Wood Sawdust and Wood Ash as Natural Adsorbents of Heavy Metals

Research by S. Rahman (2006) and M.H. Rahman *et al.* (2004) has established the effectiveness of this low-cost approach for removing Arsenic III and Arsenic V species. Although the process is slow – in one series of experiments the adsorbency took 20 days to achieve equilibrium – its efficiency in removing extremely low concentrations in the 5 ppb [parts per billion] range was as good or better than any "chemical" approach, far cheaper and much less toxic. Furthermore in some developing countries with serious arsenic problems in the water supply, such as Bangladesh, wood ash is plentifully at hand in the same areas as these contamination problems are found.

6.2.4. A Naturally-renewable Fuel Energy Source

The production of biodiesel has received considerable attention throughout the world in the past few years. As an alternative to petrodiesel, biodiesel is a renewable fuel that is derived from vegetable oils and animal fats. However, existing biodiesel production process is neither completely "green" nor renewable because it utilizes fossil fuels, mainly natural gas as an input for methanol production. Also the catalysts currently in use are highly caustic and toxic. Work to develop green biodiesel proposes a new concept that uses waste vegetable oil and non edible plant oils as biodiesel feedstock and non-toxic, inexpensive and natural catalysts that overcome the limitation of the existing process (Chhetri and Islam 2006a).

The proposed new approach is based on the use of alcohol produced from renewable sources. Methanol is produced by utilizing microbes to convert methane to methanol. Methane produced from anaerobic digestion, is acted upon by methanotrophs that convert methane into methanol (Figure 6-6). Methanotrophs – aerobic bacteria which utilize methane as their sole carbon and energy source – are physically versatile and can be effectively utilised to produce methanol from wide variety of wastes.

Use of ethyl alcohol fermented from grain-bascd biomass such as corn or swcct sorghum and molasses from sugar for alcoholysis of vegetable oils or fats is also a sustainable option (Figure 6-7). Both of these alternatives eliminate the consumption of huge amount of natural gas to make methanol. No expensive and toxic chemicals are involved in these processes. MI

Khan *et al.* (2006a) have analysed the sustainability for biodiesel based on economic, environment and social criteria, demonstrating a truly green biodiesel is a sustainable technology.

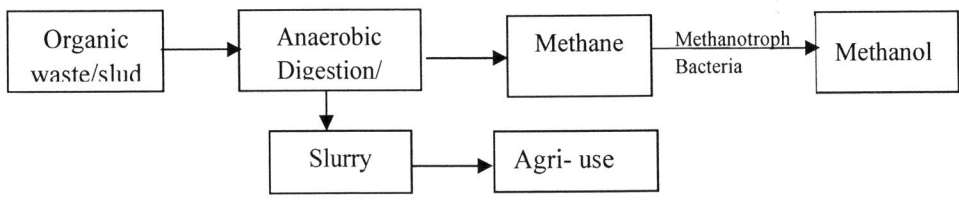

Figure 6-6. Production of methanol from methane by microbial conversion.

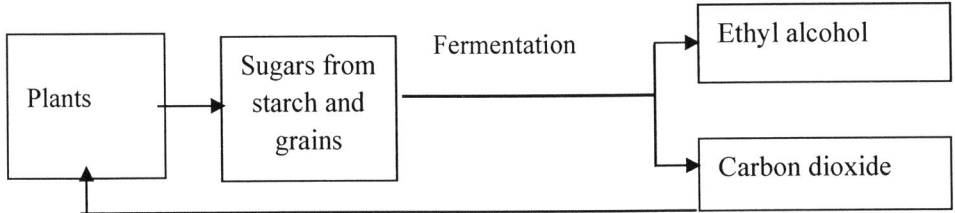

Figure 6-7. Flow process for production of ethyl alcohol.

Identification problem with current practices in biodiesel production and proposed a new technique to render the Biodiesel truly green by using natural catalysts and non toxic chemicals. A flow chart is shown below as process for biodiesel production. Sodium hydroxide and potassium hydroxide is proposed to be extracted from wood ash and alcohol for alcoholysis is to be prepared from renewable based corn or similar byproducts which make the process truly green. Potash from natural ores or sodium from the sea salt is also proposed to use as catalysts.

This schematic diagrams the proposed new concept of biodiesel production, in which potassium hydroxide derived from wood ash or sodium hydroxide derived from sea salt is used as catalyst along with bio-based methanol or ethyl alcohol. The biodiesel produced from this process is a non-toxic product because all the chemicals and catalysts are non-toxic. The CO_2 produced is 'new' CO_2 with lighter isotopes and it is not contaminated by any chemicals because the biological sources produce new CO_2 (Islam, 2005).

Plants will synthesize this 'fresh' CO_2 and complete the carbon cycle. Similarly, the NOx and CO produced during combustion of non toxic biodiesel is not harmful compared to the petrodiesel and conventional biodiesel. Formaldehyde and other emissions from biodiesel combustion are different from those emitted from petrodiesel or conventional biodiesel.

This new concept of biodiesel production from waste vegetable oils and fats, using inexpensive and natural catalysts that are free of any toxic chemicals, proves this fuel to be economical in long run as this process has little or no negative impact on environment and public health. Extraction of sodium hydroxide from sea salt is neither expensive not has negative environmental impact. Billions of people are using wood for their cooking and wood ash is abundantly available in many parts of the world. Wood ash is a good and cheap source of potassium and sodium hydroxide. These are non-toxic catalysts. The direct application of solar energy for biodiesel convention should make the process economically promising. Oil heated by direct solar energy can be effectively utilized to with higher efficiency (MM Khan *et al.* 2005d), which should help reduce the energy costs of biodiesel production.

6.2.5. Filtering – Natural Desalination and Related Filtration Processes

This discovery process began as an examination of whether natural or chemically-treated goat-skin and sheep skin could be used as membranes to filter water. The focus was on desalinating water, and on removing oil from aqueous streams – a huge issue for the oil and gas industry, where synthetic polymeric membranes are currently used for liquid-liquid separation with results that are acceptable but at a considerable cost in monetary investment and expenditure of energy (Basu *et al.*: *ibid.*). A further concern was the inherent unsustainability of synthetic polymers. Were there useful membranes that exist naturally? A series of screening tests determined goat-skin and sheepskin could be substituted in certain separation processes for polymeric membranes, and there were some initial findings suggesting their effectiveness both for desalination and for separating oil emulsified in water. Goatskin membranes were easily rendered ineffective by microbial growth on the surface, but application of olive oil, a natural source, could arrest microbial growth and render the membrane impermeable to water – a property very useful for separating oil emulsified in water. This separation process is now being optimised in the process of further experiments aimed at exploiting features of the membrane's microstructure (MM Khan and Islam 2004).

Once again: doing good is good business. The conventional route, on the other hand, premised on the commodified approach of employing chemically-treated membranes, piles up an environmental crisis in the short term and the long term, and only makes money in the short term for those who can afford the entrance fee – the cost of these specially-treated membranes – which is high to begin with.

6.2.6. A Novel Oil-spill Cleanup Barge

Oil spills have received worldwide attention in recent years. Although a common phenomenon in the past, disasters such as the *Exxon Valdez*, collapse of Enron and the implosion of corporate culture has led to renewed interest in developing inexpensive techniques for cleaning up a man-made environmental mess. The most vulnerable situation is that of the spill in the ocean. Existing techniques are so expensive as to be practically unusable in most instances. In addition, none of the existing techniques can be used to recover the spilled oil. Now a new technology is emerging that would collect spilled oil from large volume water surface, while keeping out nearly 99% of the water. Its secret is more than 2000 years old: Archimedes Principle.

This research was carried out by combining this technology with a National Research Council of Canada-funded technology that manufactured the world's first barge from recycled plastic (Prior *et al.* 2005). This offered a unique combination for creating a line of low-cost multi-purpose boats usable for oil spill recovery on demand. Overall, as one environmentalist put it: "it is an example of how two environmentally disruptive products such as oil and plastic can be recycled and reused to reclaim the environment." The overall impact of the proposed technology is phenomenal.

Prior et al. (2005) reported both architectural and engineering design aspects of the new barge with the structural gains made due to the usage of the new material. They also made a comparison will be made with currently used technologies along with economic considerations as well as long-term sustainability features.

A simple and effective technique has been successfully demonstrated in a laboratory of the University of the United Arab Emirates at Al-Ain. A team led by O. Chaalal proved with a scaled model the feasibility, by means of a relatively simple modification of conventional hull design, of skimming the surface of an oil spill and, as the hull passes over the spill, taking the oil up a chamber in which it displaces water. Such separation *via* Archimedes' Principle leapfrogs, at an opportunity cost of 0, all the complex and extravagant attempts until now to effect oil-water separation by chemical methods. The last remaining obstacle is the design of a practical vessel that implements the technique.

There now are hull design technologies using recycled plastic that have emerged and are being demonstrated in the aquaculture sector. These use barges at least 13 m. in overall length. Such a vessel can carry loads exceeding 30 tonnes with little or no stability problems, either in coastal or open ocean waters further offshore.

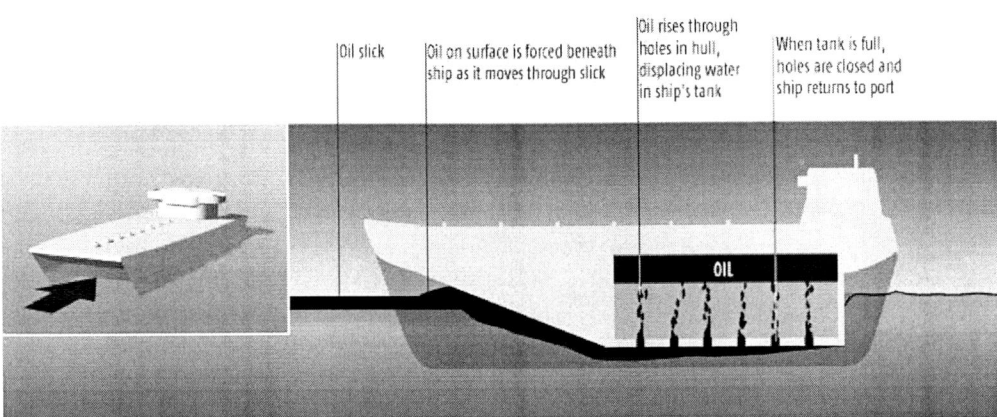

Figure 6-8. The Chaalal tanker uses the simple Archimedes' principle to preferentially recover oil – a technology that allows complete recovery of the spilled oil (Editorial, 2003).

Figure 6-8 shows the schematic of the oilspill barge as envisioned by Chaalal. The proposed design uses the similar concept and completes the concept with an engineering design that would be based on the proposed research results.

Figure 6-9. This barge made out of recycled plastic (equivalent to some 150,000 pop bottles) was manufactured by SSBW and was sold to United States for $350,000.

Proposed Design of the Oil Spilled Barge

Prior *et al.* (2005) proposed an oil spill clean-up vessel 10 m x 2.1m (Figure 6-10) with recycled plastic lumber using techniques recently developed by David Prior in conjunction with the NRC. It will be equipped with a wheelhouse and diesel engine. To provide flotation, a conventional barge built this way utilizes custom-cut foam blocks placed between the transverse frames (usually spaced 60 cm apart).

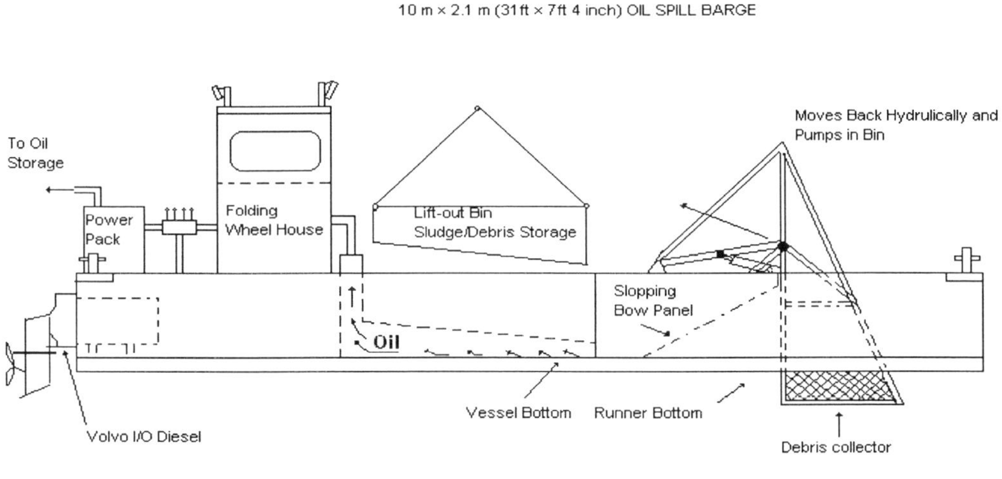

Figure 6-10. Side view of oil spilled clean up barge (Prior *et al.* 2005).

This oil-recovery barge will substitute some of the blocks with a welded polypropylene tank (Prior *et al.* 2005). This tank will be open in the bottom to allow the ingress of oil. Recovered oil will be pumped aft to a floating bag towed behind the vessel. The tank will incorporate a translucent viewing "well" to check the oil level. This tank will be primed by a Venturi vacuum pump that will lift a column of water upward to the top of the tank. As the oil passes beneath and floats upward through this water column, it accumulates at the top and displaces the water downward. Periodically, this accumulated oil is pumped aft to the floating storage bag.

Even if we assume that we will come to our senses and not produce plastic waste, this technology offers the beginning of a revolution in the areas of converting waste into value-added material, applied in environmental clean-up and recovery of products. Future tasks would include the amalgamation of bioplastic with the proposed technology, which in itself can be characterized as a revolution in material science. One of the most prominent features of this barge is its multifunctionality. Besides spill oil cleanups, this barge can be used as vessels for ferrying food, lubricants, general supplies, personnel, etc. to anchored ships. They also need floating platforms for wharf maintenance, and others. Being able to land on a beach is also an asset around a harbor. The oil spill recovery barge we envision could perform all these tasks economically and effectively. It is an example of how two environmentally disruptive products such as oil and plastic can be recycled, and reused to reclaim the environment.

6.3. WHO DECIDES?

"We do not say that a man who takes no interest in politics is a man who minds his own business. We say he has no business here at all." – Pericles' funeral oration, Athens, 431 BCE

A peculiar epigraph – the stuff of street mobs, perhaps, or ancient city states – but surely hardly of any relevance, many would think (and some would say), to complex modern societies with multi-branched economies, high technology industry and services?

In fact, no economic model that allots the proper place to the main intangibles discussed in this work – time, intentions and knowledge based on research to distinguish what is true from what is not – can offer any hope *without* ensuring and arranging the fullest participation "from below", so to speak, from all those affected by, or participating in, the unfolding development and not just policy-makers, engineers, scientists or corporate honchos.

"Who decides?" is the question of political power. In the present work, that refers to the power, in the sense of sovereign authority, that any collective of humans may exercise when they take up dealing with the common concerns of all members of the collective. The collective is always a polity, regardless of whatever other condition or conditions brought people together in one place. It possesses and may find ways to exercise a power of decision in the name of all its members. Institutions and apparatuses of government, representation etc. are all derivative from this more fundamental idea of any and every collective as a polity, latent or immediate.

6.3.1. The Stakeholder Model of a "Community" Comprising Both Hunters and the Hunted

Those positioned to turn technologies and processes into, or retain control over them as, private property have no reason to let the rest of the world in on their "action" unless pressed.

Since the 1990s, in the wake of increasing hazards to public health posed by the proliferation of illegal toxic waste dumps, accompanied by increasingly lax regulation of oil spills and especially of oil spill cleanup on land and at sea, such pressures have proliferated. These pressures have given rise to the "stakeholder model," often involving community representatives in consultation with corporate polluters and government officials. Although "pressure" implicitly suggests giving rise to expediency rather than well-thought-out solutions, the picture is not entirely black. To the extent that it energises the community involved with using technologies to seek answers and elicit responsible behaviour from corporate resource developers, this model has a certain usefulness wherever such communities and corporate resource developers have established some common ground, for putting sustainable technologies on the agenda (Khan, Chhetri and Islam 2005).

In more general form, this model currently also predominates discussions everywhere about "community economic development." The precepts and assumptions of this version of the model provide the baling-wire of almost every "development" or "civil society" NGO (non-governmental organisation) – of which there are now about 50,000 – ever given a budget or a mandate by any agency of the United Nations (Veltmeyer and Petras 2001). The object of such exercises in stakeholder consultation is not, however, to establish the stake of the community, but to protect the financial stake of the polluter. The divergence of these intentions, along with the asymmetries of power of the main players in the given situation – especially the relatively overwhelming strength of the corporate side (often aided and abetted by the government) – ensure that such exercises usually sink without trace.

The stakeholder model is not referenced here, therefore, where intentions have already clearly diverged, as a solution, or even as a failed solution, to the problem of "who decides?". Rather, how the model itself came into existence and proliferated in recent years provides an index of the acuteness of the contradictions that have emerged between those with a stake in protecting some self-interest in the short term and those proposing anything at any time that would innovate in the best interests of all for the long term.

Once a divergence of intentions becomes clear, the expediency defence for retaining the stakeholder model fails. The reason for this is to be found in the pervasiveness of the Aphenomenal Model. The economics of intangibles developed in the present work, and the technologies and processes discussed in the previous section, serve to demonstrate

1. that Humanity is not fated to be consumed by the Aphenomenal Model, and
2. that the struggle to surmount the Aphenomenal Model with new content encounters the especially tenacious resistance from the existing forms, traditions and habits received and retained from the past into the present. This is sometimes described by the phrase well known in English constitutional doctrine as "The King is dead! Long live the King!" and in the annals of the doctrine of absolute monarchy developed in pre-Revolutionary France by the phrase *"le mort saisit le vif"* (literally: "the Dead seize the Living").

The technologies and processes discussed above in connection with the notion of a "new synthesis" meet crucial sustainability criteria. Inherent in these criteria – very much in the same vein that the analysis of classical economics uncovered an undeclared civil war between Labour and Capital raging beneath the physical surface of goods produced and marketed as commodities – is a struggle against the foreshortening of Humanity's prospects by placing the self-interest of a few in the immediate present ahead of the best interests of all for the long term. Recognition of these realities in connection with sustainability is in itself necessary, but by itself such recognition is still insufficient. The New needs defending from the ravages of the Old, by those who share a positive good intention in common, and the science of how to organise such a bulwark is very much still a work in progress.

At the same time, skill and success in organising the correct, *i.e.*, most effective, relation of forces at the appropriate moment is as much an art as it is a science, and everything is at stake:

> There is a tide in the affairs of men
> Which, taken at the flood, leads on to fortune;
> Omitted, all the voyage of their life
> Is bound in shallows and in miseries.
> On such a full sea are we now afloat;
> And we must take the current when it serves,
> Or lose our ventures.
>
> *Brutus, addressing Cassius, in Act* IV *Sc* III *of* Julius Caesar, *at ll.* 218-24,
> *by William Shakespeare*

The necessity of truly sustainable development has been on Humanity's agenda for some time. The Grameen micro-lending approach cited in detail at the start of this chapter is one of the byproducts of wrestling with such practical necessity. Another product of this struggle is the "Necessity for Change" analysis, put forward formally at an historic conference convened in London, U.K. during 1-15 August 1967, which promulgated the fundamental insight that "understanding requires the conscious participation of the individual, an act of 'finding out'" and issued the call to "Smash the 'Triple-I' of Ignorance, Impotence and Indifference!" (Bains 1967).

This points to something often ignored in discussions of "sustainable development": the discussion itself arose out of a deep-going ideological, social and political struggle over Humanity's future that spread around the world during the 1960s. This is a major historical turning point which the structural and functional descriptions of sustainability in the literature have all failed to take into account or properly appreciate.

The profound societal struggle of the 1960s was spearheaded by youth, especially students, in massive rebellion against the *status-quo* of Western society led by the U.S. and Britain – and it included within it another profound rebellion symbolized by the enormous wave of support for China and Chairman Mao Zedong, against the social and ideological *status-quo* in the Soviet camp (Bains 2005). A common source of these superficially very different rebellions lay in the discovery, and sense of deep betrayal at this discovery, that progress in science and technology would not be sufficient to bring justice where injustice was rampant, or equity where inequities stalked society. The peoples of the developing world were ordered to toe the line and rein in population growth because they were otherwise saddling the world with a "population bomb" in which their numbers would outstrip the capacity of the planet to feed itself. The youth rising up in rebellion in the Western countries, attacked from all directions by the forces of "law and order", were offered the ruinous cocktail of revolutionary outlook provided they accepted being shackled to a lifestyle aimed at serving self ahead of anything and anyone else. The sentiments of peoples inside the Soviet bloc were to be met by not just Soviet but actually Warsaw Pact troops, guns and tanks. Those fighting for national liberation in southeast Asia or elsewhere were to be napalmed into submission. At a time when daily life everywhere was registering one and the same message, *viz.*, that people were no longer prepared to go on living in the existing ways, the answer coming back loud and clear from all the forces of the *status-quo* was unanimous: authentic changes initiated from below were to be smashed with the utmost ruthlessness.

What moved the situation forward, at the same time avoiding a bloodbath in which the undefended and unprepared populace would have been mowed down by even more widespread displays of military might, was that those forces leading the rebellion among the youth and students with a long-term social aim were successful in shifting the energies of the real movement into asking deep questions and seeking their own answers. This was the force that challenged all the mainstream theories of "population bomb", of so-called "limits to growth" put forward by the Club of Rome, of why the donor countries and companies did far better out of "foreign aid" than any recipient country, etc. This force took up reinvestigating all the actual political and economic arrangements of the contemporary world rather than repeating the ideologically-filtered, predigested mantras of the orthodox capitalist or "socialist" theoreticians strutting the world stage at that time.

By the late 1980s, an entire generation of people moving into the policy-making apparatuses had been exposed to quite a number of the penetrating questions raised by, or as an outgrowth of, this movement. The *status-quo* flexed its ideological muscles in response – and produced the Brundtland Commission report, which popularised the terms and concepts of "sustainable development" around the globe (WCED 1987). Considering needs as principally the needs of the world's poor, and taking into account as limitations mainly the limits imposed by the state of technology and social organization on the environments ability to meet present and future needs, this report famously defined "sustainable development" as *"development that meets the needs of the present without compromising the needs of future generations to meet their own needs"* (Emphasis added – Ed.).

This approach ignores and thereby finesses the unavoidable facts that:

1. the principal barrier to meeting the needs of the present has been that those in greatest need hold no political power, thus
2. the only "needs of the present" that can be met are those of the elites and privileged strata holding political power, and
3. these elites and privileged strata, while struggling for advantages with respect to one another, retain political power precisely for the purpose of sustaining the present indefinitely into the future, hence
4. in order to achieve the desired "sustainable development," some things would have to be sacrificed. Inherent in this notion of sustainability, in effect, were all the discredited arguments about "limits to growth", only translated now into the new discourse of "sustainable development".

Contrary to the rose-tinted view of the matter that would emerge later after the 1992 Rio Summit and the 1995 targets on greenhouse gas reductions that emanated from Kyoto, the actual thesis of the Brundtland Commission was not about what is sustainable in terms of what can be done without harming the prospects of society or Nature in the long term. Rather, sustainability was to be defined according to limits determined and-or set in advance by some "authority" or "experts" using criteria to which only that authority or those experts enjoyed access. There is serious amnesia today about this originating and inherently elitist bias in favour of preserving the status quo. Anything standing in the way of those whose interests commanded the economic destinies of everyone else was thereby declared "unsustainable". Public opinion was henceforth to be corralled, browbeaten or otherwise disinformed to accept as sustainable, and necessary, only that which these interests approved or demanded.

The stock-market crash of October 1987 was the key, most resonant political-economic event of the time that was to supply the greatest reinforcement for the thrust of the Commission's argument and logic. That such an opinion forms no part of the ruling orthodoxy in the scholarly-academic literature and discussion of development theory is most likely because many have accepted the professed humanitarian intentions of the Commission at face value. For those who do not share such an assumption, however, the connection between this particular dogma about sustainable development, on the one hand, and the manner in which key levers of the world economy were adjusted following this crash, on the other, is very clear.

On paper, the 1987 crash event proved many times more destructive than the Crash of 1929 which triggered the Great Depression of the 1930s. Demands were raised in its wake that world trade should now be reorganised to avoid a repeat of the tariff wars of the Great Depression. This led to the final Uruguay Round of the U.S.-organised and U.N.-endorsed General Agreement on Tariffs and Trade (GATT). Its mandate was to lay the foundations of the World Trade Organisation (WTO). The WTO would enable countries from the socialist bloc to apply for admission on equal terms with capitalist member countries. However, the delivery of socially necessary services in the socialist countries – health care, education, etc. – all achieved without any private Western corporate investment would now be counted as an "unsustainable" liability to be eliminated by the candidate member in order to gain entry. As this was clearly an impossible and unacceptable ransom demand, a compromise was proposed and arranged. The compromise was the large-scale takeover of a great deal of these countries' foreign trade by the Western banking system. In this way, these countries became rapidly and deeply enmeshed in Western-controlled banking and credit. This amounted in effect to an extension of the IMF-World Bank's undeclared "Washington Consensus" of 1980 regarding "structural adjustment" conditions to be demanded of client-borrowers particularly in Latin American develolping countries, and it prepared the conditions for the plug to be pulled on the economic and social systems of the COMECON-bloc countries – where private ownership of means of production had been largely eliminated – whenever it suited the creditors to declare "unsustainable" their clients' behaviour as debtors. Whereas the Reagan Administrations tried and failed by diplomatic means and political and strategic threats to destroy the wall preserving the independence of the Soviet bloc from Western corporate control, it would be the first Bush Administration (1988-92) that would deploy this economically corrupting strategy with unanticipated but devastating success. These regimes accordingly having been destroyed between 1989 and 1991, many writers on these topics subsequently expunged any memory or record of these rather ruthless deployments of "sustainability" criteria by the international financial oligarchy.

The Reagan Administration's political-diplomatic assault had run up against geopolitical reality – and stalled. There is widespread historical amnesia about it today, but the startling fact is that no one in Europe at the time was interested to permit the reunification, pro-capitalist or pro-socialist, of Germany. They wanted the growing power of the Deutschmark contained. What was then the Federal Republic of Germany, commonly known then as West Germany, was already overpowering all its capitalist European neighbours. Reunification with the eastern part of Germany, then a separate country known as the German Democratic Republic (GDR) or East Germany, offered West Germany's competitors the following dismal prospect: a reunified Germany would increase its population by one-third and become the single biggest national market within the European Economic Community, poised to impose its standards on all the others.

Following the 1987 crash, however, the leading central banks and financial powers in the rest of Europe, still uninterested in German reunification, did become interested to align themselves with the U.S.-led policy of rendering as liquid as possible the credit and trade links to the eastern bloc. The result of this policy direction, however, was the overextension of the Deutschmark – the currency of West Germany. This was the end-result of the interplay of a number of factors. Chief among them was the fact that the Deutschmark had come to play a role not only as the unofficial reserve currency for the entire European Economic Community, but also a substitute "hard currency" where U.S. dollars were in short supply, such as Poland, Hungary, Czechoslovakia, Rumania, Yugoslavia and Albania.

These accumulating pressures on the Deutschmark provided the backdrop to the 1987 crash. It had been the German central bankers' call to "short-sell" currency holdings of U.S. dollars, in order to relieve the short-term – but very high – pressures on the Deutschmark, which triggered the massive worldwide unloading of U.S. dollars that culminated in crashing stock markets around the world. The crash itself then delivered the shock that would trigger an outcome whose conditions had been in preparation for the preceding two decades – since the Warsaw Pact invasion of Czechoslovakia of 20 August 1968 – but for which no one was prepared when it came. With the crash, the same dynamic that had tied the east European members of COMECON to the Soviet Union reversed itself 180 degrees. Now these governments wanted to be free of the Deutschmark at any price.

In the result, the GDR was increasingly set adrift from the east and pulled closer to West Germany. The GDR's currency had been at par with the Deutschmark. It had developed an extensive trade and commerce in relatively cheap industrial goods. From the 1960s through the 1980s, this served to anchor and provide financial backing for much of the rest of the COMECON bloc trade of its east European neighbours. When the Berlin Wall was torn down in November 1989 by the populace in defiance of warnings from both the West German and East German authorities, however, the long-feared East-West military clash between the American and Soviet superpowers never materialised. Instead of the GDR becoming a cockpit of superpower contention, the extensive ties of the entire eastern bloc were sundered. All the COMECON economies affected were placed at the mercy of Western financial creditors. This ensured the destruction of the entire social economy of the Soviet bloc. Regardless of anyone's preferences for capitalist or socialist economic theories, the consequences for such indices as life expectancy, public health, extremes of wealth and poverty, etc. in each of these countries have proven utterly shattering.

Paradoxically, as their financing of COMECON-bloc trade became so liquid, the corporate and banking interests of the leading capitalist countries could no longer look to the "East-West divide" as a source of maximum profits in minimum time. The leading lights of world finance accordingly adjusted their sights and pursued more profitable prospects in the developing world. This new direction was embodied in what was officially called the Washington Consensus after 1990. The silence in the literature about the connection of the sustainable development agenda to wrecking the economies of the Soviet bloc is overmatched by the deafening volume of articles and books about sustainable development and the Washington Consensus. Developing countries were told by the International Monetary Fund and the World Bank that the demands of the new era required them to submit to "structural adjustment" mandates to cut their spending on social programs support. The discussion in the literature implies that the source of the difficulty in meeting targets for sustainable development lay with the developing countries, but the historical record refutes such an inference. The Reagan Administration in Washington, having spent like drunken sailors on new weapons systems converted the U.S. economy in less than six years from the world's richest creditor state into its biggest debtor state: that was why George H.W. Bush as Reagan's vice-president hung the contemptuous label of "voodoo economics" on the administration's policy.

Succeeding Ronald Reagan in office, that Bush Administration now compelled the rest of the world to undertake "structural adjustment" of their economies and economic plans to conform to the reality of yet another generation upcoming of ever-increasing budgetary and current account deficits. Stripping away the rhetorical flourishes in all their palaver about "sustainable development", the forces occupying the commanding heights of the U.S. economy were dictating the terms on which the rest of the world would now be expected to sustain the continued development of U.S. overlordship of the global economy.

The Bush Administration set out to capture China – hardly an accident, given that George Bush had served as US Ambassador there as well as focused heavily on Chinese affairs as head of the Central Intelligence Agency. They stoked the movement that led to the confrontation on Tienanmen Square in June 1989 with the aim of engineering a pro-U.S. coup. When the Chinese government and party rounded up all the U.S. intelligence assets and rolled up the coup plot, uncounted numbers of Chinese had been killed – but the levers of the Chinese government and economy remained beyond U.S. or other Western control. China paid the price of continued exclusion from access to Western trade and finance, but it quickly mastered the necessities of economic self-reliance in an unprecedented post-bipolar era, becoming an independent factor in world politics.

In the years of the Reagan and first Bush administrations, Washington maintained all the anti-communist positions of the Cold War era and rewarded elites that openly rejected non-U.S. models but formulated no stance towards those who had not yet joined. The Clinton administration attempted to convert this free trade approach into neoliberal protected zones where anything and everything was available for the regimes that acceded to U.S. conditions of trade and investment, while for those who rejected these conditions, hell could freeze over before they could hope to receive the slightest consideration. This was the conundrum confronting the Republic of Cuba as its chief economic support, the Soviet bloc, disappeared but U.S. hostility to the Castro regime and determination to put an end to its independence from the United States remained intact. Similarly, the Islamic Republic of Iran was kept in the doghouse as punishment for the Iranian people's decision to eliminate the corrupt and murderous regime of the Shah whom the U.S. had created and imposed on the Iranian people literally for a generation, from 1954 to 1979.

Thus it turned out that first victim of the new sustainability agenda would be the Soviet bloc and the COMECON economies, whereas the embargo and isolation inflicted on China by post-Tienanmen Europe and America insulated it from any of these impacts, just as the cold shoulder towards, and deliberate subversion attempted against, Cuba and Iran taught them the single most valuable and crucial lesson in modern day self-reliance, which is that real life and a future may exist for the long term only outside the orbit of the American Empire. The underlying principle of U.S.-directed sustainability, reinforced by the neoliberal doctrines of Clintonomics, was "my way... or the highway".

The other victims of this agenda were the non-corporate general publics of the developing countries and the developed countries. As a result of the 1992 "Earth Summit" in Rio de Janeiro and the Kyoto Accords of 1995, their countries became saddled with the "environmental agenda" of the leading financial powers' ruthless version of "sustainable development". This saw huge cuts in social services spending in all the developed countries. This was the context in which there eventually emerged the so-called "stakeholder model" of "participation from below" – based directly on the principles of the shareholder model of governance followed in every corporation. The guiding principle of the model has been described accurately if somewhat cynically as the "golden rule": no matter how many individuals or "constituencies" get to "have their say," he who has the most gold makes all the rules. In effect, the stakeholder model of "community" comprises both hunters and their prey. While there is nothing wrong with this for the animal kingdom in general, when it comes to Humanity the end of this story is always the same and depressingly familiar: good for some and bad for others means bad for everyone. The reason for elaborating the foregoing historical context was to clarify that the officially-fostered stakeholder model has to date been no more about sharing-in-general than the officially-supported sustainability agenda has been about sustainability-in-general. The nub of the problem all along has been, and remains to date: sharing for whom and sustainability for whom, and in what timeframe?

6.3.2. Reorganising Relations of Primary, Secondary and Tertiary Industry to Serve the Long Term, and not Just Recirculate Capital

The solutions that contribute to a new synthesis share a number of important identifiable characteristics. Stemming from the conscious choice of modeling as closely as possible from Nature, rather than from existing engineered or pre-processed "solutions", the needs-based approach advanced in the examples of the present work breaks, or offers the option to break, any rigid link between meeting the needs of an individual or community on the one hand and the operation or existence of any industrial base outside the community and not controlled by the community on the other. It breaks the link because the resort to and deliberate preference for natural materials ahead of processed materials opens up the prospect that a large concentrated capital, at some central factory or similar processing facility, for example, may no longer furnish the *sine qua non* for the possibility of socially useful production with the most cost-effective economies of scale.

The conventional argument against such approaches has centred around the notion of "saving labour". Labour – meaning the expenditure of socially necessary labour-time – is considered to be "saved" when and if the same amount of labour-time normally dedicated to primary production, *e.g.*, agriculture, or mining, is redirected into secondary manufacturing, to generating far more finished goods. The gathering of natural materials has been traditionally associated with assembling the raw material that must eventually be processed into finished products. According to the conventional explanation, economies based on mainly primary extraction develop a multi-branched apparatus of production only with the greatest difficulty. In the contemporary world, the argument goes, such economies are compelled to import large quantities of finished goods which they are in no position to produce themselves, because the society's labour resources are otherwise engaged in primary production. Thus for example Iceland, whose resources are overwhelmingly given over to fish harvesting, sells its primary products (and some finished fish products) to buy everything else it needs. However, the per capita debt obligation on its less than 250,000 citizens is low in all its various segments – from merchantable trade in finished goods to capital equipment to any of the services that are essential for a modern economy. It is dependent on international trade in order to maintain an Iceland-standard of existence, and it operates within world capital markets to finance its existence, which ties it to the European Union. However, it is not a political or economic dependency of any other single country.

How does the conventional explanation account, then, for economies like that of Canada? The Canadian economy does not lack either for raw materials or the capability to build its own machines to make all manner of finished goods. It can transport goods overland to any part of the North American continent and is well-supplied with ocean seaports fully fitted out to handle the largest cargo vessels from anywhere on earth. Yet it is the most foreign-dependent industrial economy on the planet, its people carry a large per capita debt burden, and the heights of its economy are commanded from the leading financial and industrial centres of the United States, a foreign country.

The explanations of "saving labour" and the related arguments about "comparative advantage" assign labels that rationalise a condition after the fact. Canada did not become a hewer of wood, drawer of water and passer of gas to and for the United States because there were comparative advantages available to its entrepreneurs or workers for so doing. The other side of "saving labour" is simply "growing a surplus". The other side of the "comparative advantage" coin is that others are made to pay. Ultimately, underlying such conceptions is a notion that *Nature* conferred advantages on one group and deprivations on others. This unscientific view provides the thin tissue of justification after-the-fact for racist or other discriminatory treatment. For the last two centuries the United States solemnly explained why all peoples and countries lying to the south of it in the Western Hemisphere would require U.S. intervention to save them from utter destitution: the "Latin races" were "naturally incapable" of hard work, and were bequeathed "habits of indolence" by "Nature." It has become quite fascinating during the first decade of the 21st century to watch one after another of these purportedly "hopelessly indolent" peoples and countries – Venezuela, Brazil, Argentina, Ecuador, Chile, Bolivia – seeking various ways and means to throw off the yoke of U.S. domination and dependence.

Far more labour is saved – in the sense of being neither wasted, nor excessively exploited – if the knowledge-based discoveries and their applications (in terms of naturally available materials) are made available throughout communities as they need them, and harnessed to a plan that uses the entire collective labour resource of the community to gather the necessary natural materials, fabricate the devices required, install them, keep up-to-date accounts of the time expended and actual costs incurred for materials and other related expenses, and work out a plan to compensate all those who should be compensated. It is not that the community needs are met, only without capturing a surplus – as though this lack of surplus-capture were a limitation or downside. It is rather that the community's needs were met precisely and mainly because no stake in any surplus was permitted from the outset.

Saving labour thus becomes important, but not for the reasons conventionally presented by advocates of ordinary industrial production and extended reproduction. The best reason to save labour is not for the sake of achieving higher efficiencies in production, but to ensure the social collective can enjoy the future that its labours in the present are intended to secure. This is what it means to take care of the human factor-social consciousness, truly to humanise the environment and ensure both that Nature remains the mother of all wealth and that Labour can meet its obligations as the father of all wealth. Labour will become ground down if it does not go beyond merely meeting these obligations and takes up directly, by and for itself in an organised way, all aspects including researching and gathering knowledge, establishing what is the truth and providing for new and emerging social and individual needs "without waiting". The interests of those who have the greatest stake in these reasons for saving labour will necessarily and inevitably diverge from those whose interest to save labour is solely to achieve higher efficiencies in production within the present forms of industrial and commercial organisation. In our era, agreement as to objectives is necessary but insufficient: intentions must also be in alignment. What is at stake here is the reorganisation of the relations of primary, secondary and tertiary industry to serve the long term, and not just recirculate capital. This is a very critical part of the answer to the question of "who decides?"

6.3.2.1. Truly Sustainable Development: Some Implications for Society's Current Legal and Collective Social Superstructures

For the entire history of the Industrial Revolution – beginning in Britain in the middle of the 18th century – one constant theme has been the ever-increasing scale on which production carries on. The drive towards more cost-effective energy systems powering industry – from coal to petroleum to electricity to natural gas – has encouraged ever greater levels of concentration of production, while the ruinous consequences of periodic crises of overproduction led stronger capital formations to absorb weaker formations, thereby – over time – increasingly concentrating ownership of the productive forces as well. The combined concentration of production itself with concentration of its ownership has accelerated tendencies towards integration of primary, secondary and tertiary phases of production and distribution under a single corporate umbrella, in a process generally labelled "vertical integration." The notion of "transmission belt" provides a unifying common metaphor defining the interrelationships of the various structures and functions under such an umbrella. According to this metaphor, demand for products on the one hand and their supply on the other hand can be balanced overall, even though certain markets and portions of the corporate space may experience temporary surpluses or shortages of supply or demand. This apparently elegant unity of structure, function and purpose at the level of very large-scale monopolies and cartels is one side of the coin. The other side is seen in the actual fate of the millions of much smaller enterprises. For these entities, partial integration down to outright hard-scrabble competitive scramble-for-position is the rule, and they remain always much more vulnerable to mismatching of and swings in demand and supply. The conventional accounting for these phenomena assumes that the vertically-integrated "upstream-downstream" model is the most desirable and the fate of the small enterprise is some throwback that "economic evolution" will dispose of in the same way that entire species disappear from the natural world of the plant and animal kingdom. What the conventional account fails to explain, however, is the utterly unsustainable scale of resource rape and plunder that the assertedly superior vertically-integrated "upstream-downstream" enterprise seems to require in order to maintain its superiority.

From de Quesnay's *Tableau économique* in the 1760s to the work of 1973 Nobel Economics laureate and Harvard University professor Wassily Leontieff *et al.* in the 1930s, 1940s and 1950s (Leontieff 1973), transmission-belt theories of productive organisation, along with all the "input-output" models of economic processes spawned from its premises, have focused entirely, and actually very narrowly, on accounting for the circulation of capital – and nothing else. Whatever this position has been based on, it is not science. During the 19th century Karl Marx's work on the circulation of capital (Marx 1883), and in the 20th century the works produced by the neo-Ricardian school of classical economics developed by Piero Sraffa *et al.*, starting in the 1920s and culminating in his *Production of Commodities By Means of Commodities* (Sraffa 1960), all demonstrated that the rich getting richer and the poor getting poorer was inherent and inevitable in any system that buys and expends the special commodity known as labour-time in order to produce whatever society needs in the form of commodities. Their research established that the circulation of variable capital (wages spent to buy consumer goods) runs counter and actually opposite to the circulation of constant capital (money spent on raw materials used in production and for replacing, repairing or maintaining machine and equipment used up or partially "consumed" in the processes of production). In effect: merely redistributing the output of such a system more equitably cannot overcome inherent tendencies of such systems towards either crises of overproduction or a cumulative unevenness of development with wealth accumulating rapidly at one pole and poverty at the other. These tendencies can only be overcome in conditions where people's work is no longer treated as a commodity. How is labour-time to be decommodified?

There are various pathways to decommodifying labour-time. For an economics of intangibles, time is considered as the quantity of labour-time needed to produce / reproduce society's needs on a self-sustaining basis. Supply is planned on the basis of researched knowledge. Its provision is planned according to the expressed needs and decision of collectives. Meanwhile, production is organised to maximise inputs from natural sources on a sustainable basis. Primary producers organise through their collectives. Industrial workers and managers organise their participation in production through their collectives. Those involved in wholesale or retail distribution organise their participation through their collectives. The common intention is not the maximum capture of surplus by this or that part of the production-distribution transmission-belt, but rather to meet the overall social need. Setting and meeting this intention is the acid test-criterion for all the socialist social-economic experiments past, present and future, as well as for community economic development mechanisms like micro-lending. The economics of intangibles fills a huge theoretical gap in this respect. Its emphasis on intention, however, also challenges many essentially Eurocentric notions that tend to discount its role. Considerable resistance can be anticipated from all those who are convinced that no advance in civilisation can possibly come in a package not labelled "Western".

One of the greatest obstacles to achieving sustainable development on these lines is the pressure to produce on the largest possible scale. Although such a production scheme is nominally intended to realise the greatest so-called "economies" and "savings of labour", it also comes into sharp contradiction with the competitive drive by individual enterprises to maximise returns on investment in the short term. Modern society grants all intentions full freedom to diverge, without prioritising the provisioning of social needs. This means, however, that every individual, group or enterprise considers its cycle and social responsibility completed and discharged when the short-term objective, whatever it may be, is achieved. The only way to engender and spread truly sustainable development, on the other hand, is to engage all individuals and their collectives for, and according to, common long-term intentions and, on that basis, harmonise the differing interests in the short-term of the individual and the collective.

Although the execution of any plan, however well-designed, requires hierarchy, order and sequence, it does not follow at all that plans in themselves must also be produced in a top-down manner. This top-down approach to drawing up economic plans was one of the gravest weaknesses of the eastern-bloc economies that disappeared with the Soviet Union. Starved of the flow of externally-supplied credit, the bureaucratised centre on which everything depended became brain-dead. Nowhere else in their systems could economic initiative be restored "from below."

The Republic of Cuba learned this lesson the hard way when Soviet support disappeared and their economic output shrank by more than one-third. It was not just the extreme and government-enforced rationing measures of the subsequent Special Period, however, that saved the day. It was that these measures were drawn up from, and at, the base. They included the extremely sage decision not to close a single clinic or medical facility or school or educational facility, whatever else might be sacrificed in the short term. That notion was considered anathema and crazy by many of the experts, but they swallowed hard and accepted the collective wisdom. This collective wisdom turned out to be vastly wiser than that of the experts. Cuba today is the world's most advanced exporter of health and education services – including a wide range of specialised emergency hospital and clinic setups, effective but non-commercial drugs and medicines, and even 90-day crash literacy courses in Spanish and some other languages.

Cuba is not the model for all, but it is one model of how the new synthesis of true sustainability can be consciously piloted in particular circumstances. This merits attention.

The destructiveness of the U.S. prejudices about Cuba, meanwhile, has started taking its toll of American lives. In the summer of 2005, the world watched with astonishment as a season of severe hurricanes lashed the entire Gulf of Mexico, including the Gulf Coast of the United States, the island of Cuba, the Yucatan Peninsula in Mexico, etc. Two of the most destructive hurricanes to hit Cuba directly (one of them, Rita, went on to lash the US Gulf Coast as well) forced the temporary evacuation of more than 2.5 million residents, but not a single person lost their life nor was there any report of looting of personal property. This was not surprising news around the Caribbean, where Cuba has acquired an international reputation in the field of hurricane emergency response. Meanwhile, however, the situation unfolding on the U.S. Gulf Coast must rank as one of the great tragedies of an already severely ravaged 21st century. Hurricanes Rita and, earlier, Katrina, created a huge disaster in the city of New Orleans, rendering much of it uninhabitable after the long-neglected levee system gave way. With the publication (on 1 March 2006) of the evidence of a video conference call involving President George W Bush and senior federal and state emergency management officials the day before Katrina struck, it has become established as fact that the highest levels of the U.S. government took no serious preventive action in advance of the expected levee breach. At the same time, only days after Katrina, the U.S. government rejected a sincere offer by Cuba of more than 1,500 emergency doctors and other trained medical personnel. Meanwhile (as of March 2006), there were still no reliable estimate of the final death toll or total of the numbers of New Orleans residents displaced by and since the hurricane. It is becoming complicated to sort out which is the greater crime against humanity: the U.S. government leaving one of its cities to drown in its own sewage, or a prejudice so reactionary that tens of thousands of Gulf Coast residents were left without any medical assistance at a most critical moment?

Could the Cubans' notion of saving, preserving and enhancing human capital as a fundamental requirement for truly sustainable development be implemented in such directions if they had relied exclusively on top-down methods? The answer must be: No. Having decided to facilitate the fullest possible expression of a humanitarian intention, they proceeded to accomplish the aim as expeditiously as possible. This lesson is being applied repeatedly in all other areas of Cuban life. For example, as a result of the continuing U.S. trade embargo combined with the loss of food imports from the former Soviet bloc, Havana today is the only city on the planet that is approaching self-sufficiency in the provision, from rooftop gardens and plots on vacant land around that city, of fresh and entirely organic fruits and vegetables for its nearly two million residents – something unthinkable without extensive planning developed from the base.

Truly sustainable development encounters another serious hurdle from the prevailing legal systems of North America. In this arena, the greatest obstacle arises from the law's prioritising of protection for property that can be used to make money or exploit others over protection of people's individual and collective rights as individuals born to society. One of the forms in which this finds expression is the definition and treatment of corporate entities as legal persons, who unlike physical persons are exempt from imprisonment upon prosecution and conviction for the commission of criminal acts. The prioritising bias of the existing legal system, expressed most rigidly in its unconditional defence of the sanctity of contract, has many implications as well for the manner in which money and credit may be offered or withdrawn in conventional business dealings among business entities, corporate or individual: the shifting needs of real human collectives affected by such changes take second place to the actual wording of a contract, regardless of the conditions in which it was drawn up. This gives wide latitude for any individual or group that would seek to wreck the interests of any well-intended collective, while affording the victims of sharp practice almost no remedy.

6.3.3. Toward a New Science of Human Social Organisation

The sustainability of the new synthesis is also a function of whether the required new science of human social organisation is developed and implemented alongside development and implementation of technologies and processes that are truly innovative, economically attractive, environmentally appealing and socially responsible. One of the profoundest problems of human society to date has been that while people spontaneously organise the livelihood and sustenance of their family, or possibly their village (where the village is actually a form of extended kinship group), the organisation of livelihood and sustenance on a social basis has only begun to be undertaken in the 20th century, and even then beginning with the available expedients of top-down, government-led organising.

During the 20th century and to date, many social experiments in this line broadened the activating group to include militants of voluntary formations beyond those of the State. However, it was only with difficulty and after years of trial-and-error effort that ways have developed in particular cases to broaden considerably the common ground on which to raise such voluntary formations. Like anything truly new, these experiments most often emerged from baptism by fire, or more precisely from baptism under fire – usually in the cauldron of guerrilla wars that peoples were forced to wage in order to defend their right to exist against a marauding and pitiless invader. The great mistake, frequently committed after the pressure of war or general adversity was finally lifted, takes the form of a decision that the modalities developed under extreme conditions can and should be dispensed with once those extreme conditions no longer apply. It is one thing to remove unnecessary stringencies imposed under emergency conditions. It is however quite another to throw out new methods and lessons learned in dealing with those exceptional conditions. It was in the process of learning those new methods and lessons that people were and are themselves transformed, and if for no other reason that is why those new methods and lessons are essential to retain.

It has been sagely remarked that the greatest danger threatens from the obstacle against which struggle has ceased to be waged. This is very similar to the great mistake committed when perfectly functional and appropriate technologies are challenged by the emergence of new technologies that do all the same things only slightly faster or allegedly more "efficiently" – but usually at some considerable cost to the natural environment, because their pathway involves something, or several things which are fundamentally anti-Nature. Dealing with the matter at hand, *viz.*, the practical content of an economics of intangibles: the objective must be to find ways that go with social needs and not against them of adapting sustainable technologies that go with Nature rather than against it.

6.3.4. Saving for Whom?

When intangible elements are taken into account and included with tangibles, it becomes possible to position the "savings" mania correctly, especially its logic of "saving for a rainy day." Albert Einstein provides the most pointed retort to this idea, where he writes: "the thinking that got you into trouble will not get you out." If you do not rethink what is new – positive and negative – in the overall picture when adversity strikes, "savings as a hedge against future adversity" will be useless and meaningless, although doubtless of great value to the financial powers that were "looking after your nest egg" while you waited for disaster to strike. As thousands of employees of Enron Corp. learned the hard way when the company imploded in 2001-2002, if a predator has been looking after your nest, nothing whatsoever will be available as a retirement fund or even as severance. The greatest fraud lies in the notion that such savings represent the individual's power over the future, or to shape the future. The news flash that seems to have passed many by is that the future arrives because it has already been shaped. Hence this so-called "power" is a false, aphenomenal power, not an intangible power. Those who stay ignorant stay powerless, and no amount of saving can save them. Only gathering one's own knowledge and applying it to serve one's long-term interest can accomplish anything.

Human behaviour can be driven by any number of obsessions – for more money, more sex or more status – but the notion that equates the acquisition and display of money, sex and-or status with the acquisition and display of power by the individual is mired in deepest ignorance. Consider the following analogy: energy exists in two fundamental states, potential or kinetic (speaking generally), and yet every kinetic energy-state was "potential energy" at some prior point. A very limited number of forms of potential energy are tangible: the vast majority are entirely intangible. Whereas all tangible forms of energy take an immediate, external usually kinetic form, purely kinetic tangible energy cannot be delivered continuously – even though all Nature is perpetually in motion – and the "perpetual motion" machine is impossible. There is no tangible energy without its intangible potential state. Similarly, without knowledge, no matter the number or variety of tangible obsessions and drivers they may have accumulated, people who remain ignorant remain truly vulnerable and powerless. It is not quite true that "knowledge is power", but it cannot be doubted that ignorance always and everywhere is a state of utter powerlessness. Truly economic drivers should increase our ability truly to "economise", to do more with less. Any other driver that increases only the ability to waste – and that defines exactly the purpose of acquiring more sex, more money and more status – is aphenomenal as far as economics is concerned: it increases consumption without giving the slightest care to increasing production or especially improving the relations or conditions of production.

Looking at the "money = power" equation from yet another vantage point, it becomes clearer just what kind of power and what kind of money are involved here. The intention of this kind of money is to exercise power over others by withholding expenditure or lavishing expenditure, *i.e.*, wasting; the intention is not to provision the actual needs of the individual, or the individual's family, or any wider social collective in which the individual participates. Similarly, the intention of the kind of power mentioned in this equation is to compel and subordinate others, not to defend one's sovereign right-to-be or any other rights connected to such sovereign expression by the individual, or the individual's family, or any wider social collective in which the individual participates. In each case, for money or for power, the latter-mentioned intangible intention has its tangible representation which can be sustained only by continuing to use money and power for positive good to serve actual need.

6.3.5. Knowledge for Whom?

Conventional economic theory correlates stable, and relatively low, interest rates with higher well-being as expressed in a large per-capita Gross Domestic Product. By such measures, the United States, Canada and the leading economies of western Europe routinely "come out on top" in the international rankings. Conversely, by the same ranking process, the most impoverished societies from the Third World have the lowest per-capita GDP and quite high interest rates – seemingly "clinching the argument".

The moment one looks beyond the relatively narrow band of highly tangible evidence available to support these claims and correlations, however, the larger picture suggests how partial and limited this correlation is. The veritable jungle of channels and pathways facilitated by an entirely corporate-dominated system of money supply (in which "money" includes credit and other forms of term indebtedness) is the structural underpinning of intangible relationships that stimulate an intense competition to issue debt and therefore competition to keep interest rates within a narrow band. In societies lacking such extensive corporation-generated networks or the accompanying web of relationships, the nature and extent of the risks a lender undertakes cannot be fully accommodated in local markets or not accommodated in a sufficiently timely fashion that interest rates can remain low for any extended period. These gaps are bridged in practice by a welter of private, temporary, family-

or clan-based and definitely non-corporate relationships enabling certain classes of customer to repay large portions of the debt they have contracted in various non-cash forms. Those with more means will repay more in cash. The really wealthy borrow from, and do business with, Western banking institutions or their commercial correspondents in these countries. The hard-currency sectors of the economy, largely in the hands of government officials and foreign corporations and their local agents, are transferring out of the country a large portion of profits garnered from commerce conducted inside the country. The upshot is that the GDP total for such countries starts at a much lower level and looks far poorer in per capita terms compared to any "developed" country. What happens as Western corporations and financial networks penetrate these societies further? More money and credit circulate longer inside the country before completing their circuit and exiting the economy as hard currency in foreign bank accounts and payments on government loans, so per capita GDP appears to go up. And as these networks spread internally and compete to attract borrowers, interest rates decline and increasingly occupy a more stable and narrowing band. This is what is then described as the underdeveloped "catching up" to the developing countries.

That claim, however, represents the end-point of a completely aphenomenal chain. The correlation of interest rates and GDP per capita is a chimaera. Neither is actually the reason for the inverse behaviour of the other. The corporatisation that has overtaken society and become the effective source of the supply of money and credit has generated a competition to attract borrowers, such that the interest rate, which is supposed to be the cost of money at the point where the supply of money and credit and its supply, operating under conditions of relatively free competition, are at equilibrium, is only the temporary equilibrium price produced by that corporatised, *i.e.*, monopolistic, competition. The extension of credit on a mass scale under such conditions unleashes inevitably all manner of new and unpredictable centrifugal forces. These operate to distort many inherent internal contradictions and even liquidate many internal organic social links. There are a number of consequences that follow in developed economies. For example, the social solidarity of working people who possess no capital of their own starts to fray as those at the upper income band can increasingly afford to live "like" those at the lower end of the next higher income band, among the middle professional classes. Since stable employment is the actual premise of the extension of personal credit, those sectors whose employment is least stable have no access to such credit and they sink lower and lower, and these strata are already the least organised to defend themselves and hence become the most marginalised. The youth entering the workforce pay the heaviest toll, followed by women and ethnic minorities. In developing, *i.e.*, underdeveloped, economies, the same easing of credit very sharply either undermines the population of the countryside relative to urban dwellers, or fosters increasing stratification in the rural villages according to income and access to credit. These structural realities suggest how absurd it is to undertake social engineering premised simple-mindedly either on raising the GDP in the name of lowering and-or stabilising interest rates, or lowering interest rates in order to boost GDP. The short-term intention and the long-term aim of any course of action must first be clearly ascertained. The most crucial intangible of all, *viz.*, the knowledge of the overall picture, must then be researched and assembled.

The destructiveness of the dictate exercised by the interest rate on the world scale is incomprehensible without some appreciation of how its role has been transformed by the sharp ascent since the end of the Second World War of the highly centralised powers of finance in the United States economy over the older, more decentralised forms of power that were exercised by leading sectors of industrial manufacturing. The interest rate itself has become a mechanism entrenching the structure of this centralisation, as client banks borrow from the US Federal Reserve system at a lower rate than they charge their customers. This is a portion of the surplus utterly disconnected from anything that happens in production – increase or decrease. This difference is retained not as a transaction cost covering some additional part of production, distribution or exchange of goods and services in the economy, but purely as the bank's "cut", as a middleman, for servicing customer demand for some portion of the entire accumulated capital resources in the economy.

There is more to the interest rate than the quantity of money it can earn the lender atop what has been loaned out. For example, the International Monetary Fund and the World Bank, both headquartered in Washington DC, between them imposed policies of what is known as "structural adjustment" on developing countries, particularly in south and east Asia, west, central and east Africa and Latin America since 1980 as a condition of even permitting them to become financially enslaved to these powers, much less repay the loans at the current prime rate-plus. In Asian countries, structural adjustment demands of 'the Bank' and 'the Fund' have include requirements for governments to eliminate crucial subsidies on food staples like rice and to open their markets to US wheat exports at the going world-market price. Official data portray the effects of such loans as relatively neutral only because exogenous consequences are considered as "externalities" and not accounted – the effective boost such arrangements give to the revenue of US grain exporters, who enjoy hefty US government subsidies on the evidence of delivery contracts filed with the US Department of Agriculture; the effective losses in export income suffered by exporters in the aid-receiving country as a result of the high tariff walls maintained in the US against raw material imports from these countries; and the consequent tendency for the aid-receiving countries' terms of trade with the developed countries to erode further over the duration of these loan arrangements. As a result, the effective rate of exchange of the aid-receiving country's currency against the US dollar, compared to the officially published rate, weakens over time, such that when these economies are enjoying a growth spurt their currencies become extremely vulnerable to large-scale short-selling organised outside the jurisdiction of their central banks.[40] Prior to the outbreak of the Asian currency crisis of 1997-98, the academic discourse surrounding structural adjustment policies and their impact was suffused with a dangerous naïvete concerning the benefits of the open-market posture these economies were compelled by their lenders – 'the Fund' and 'the Bank' – towards the richest and most excessively capitalised economies on the planet (Eggleston 1997; Hill 1997; Sankaran 1991).

Following the collapse of the Soviet bloc and the bipolar division of the world economy, the United States, leading countries of Europe plus Japan and South Korea vastly expanded their export of capital in various forms. The U.S. Federal Reserve became the clearing house

---

[40] Such was the havoc wrought by the widely-hailed global "philanthropist" George Soros, a modern day vulture capitalist when it comes to foreign exchange trading, on a number of the so-called "newly-industrialising economies" of east Asia in 1997-8 (Mahathir 1997). Direct evidence collected by the Malaysian government pointed to Soros' hedge-fund manipulations of the national currency (the ringgit) The academic case exonerating Soros and his hedge fund speculations of any responsibility was possible only by elaborating an abstract model possessing – its authors admitted – no direct evidence to support their exonerating inferences because… there were no legal requirements to report data used by hedge funds to take crucial decisions moving billions of dollars out of one or more instruments into one or more other instruments! Hence, they built their model instead from indirect evidence, lacking any concrete information whatsoever about investors' actual intentions (Goetzmann, Brown and Park 1998).

of the entire world financial system. London became the global clearing house for large scale trading in commodities – spot sales of crude oil and large contracts in raw foodstuffs and other raw materials from Asia and Africa. Banks in Tokyo and *chaebols* in Seoul became large investors in U.S. government debt. During this period, the economies of Russia and parts of eastern Europe, the former Soviet Union and Cuba which had become most dependent on it for trade links spiraled into chaos – Russian life expectancy contracted from 73 years to 58, the Cuban economy contracted by 35 per cent in two years, etc. China planned around the upcoming 1997 absorption of Hongkong, so it became uniquely positioned as the world's premier exporter of secondary manufactured goods, rather than capital, directed most of all to those economies that were expanding their export of capital at the expense of domestic manufacturing. Accordingly, all China's newest industries would build a special economic zone adjacent and use the former colony's global trading connections, while its existing railway and port infrastructure along with light manufacturing would be modernised to penetrate the U.S. market with irresistibly cheap manufactured goods. The upshot was booming prosperity in China, which basically ended its reliance on foreign loans to prime any pump anywhere in its economy. In Cuba the upshot was to reorganise their entire economy not only without giving up a single one of the social gains in health and education but deliberately enhancing these sectors as source of human capital for their own economy and the rest of the world. The Russians, by contrast, took almost a decade to recover, making their economy in the process even more top-heavily monopolistic and dependent on hard currency earnings in the foreign market to purchase needed manufactured goods for the domestic market. Some 93 per cent of its hard currency earnings in 2002 came from exports of oil and gas. So severe is the Russian devastation of agriculture and domestic manufacturing that its population, which stood at nearly 300 million in 1989 and fell to about 160 million in the reorganisation of the so-called Commonwealth of Independent States after 1991, is predicted to fall below 100 million by 2020 (Smith 2006). The Chinese and Cuban responses were knowledge-based and oriented to boosting intangible alongside tangible elements; the Russian response was entirely in the realm of reordering one set of tangible arrangements into another – and now they risk losing both major intangible along with more tangible assets.

In the hands of those richest in capital, the interest-rate can operate – with or without explicit policy direction – as a weapon, or be sprung as a trap, to subjugate countries that are richest in the human resource, by compelling such countries to cede control of many key economic intangibles along with tangible opportunities like valuable raw materials. Additionally, two other well-known major economic indices associated with overall economic well-being – the inflation rate and the unemployment rate – produce an entirely different yet related set of obstacles to grasping the essence of actual problems of economic development. These indices are seen as being much more subject to explicit policy direction under all circumstances. However, solving – in the direction of sustaining the long-term interests of societies and all their individual members – the problems that follow in the train of either their opposite movement or the failure of their movement altogether turns out to be no less intractable, as – once again, just as with interest rates – it is the intangible aspects and consequences that are stripped out.

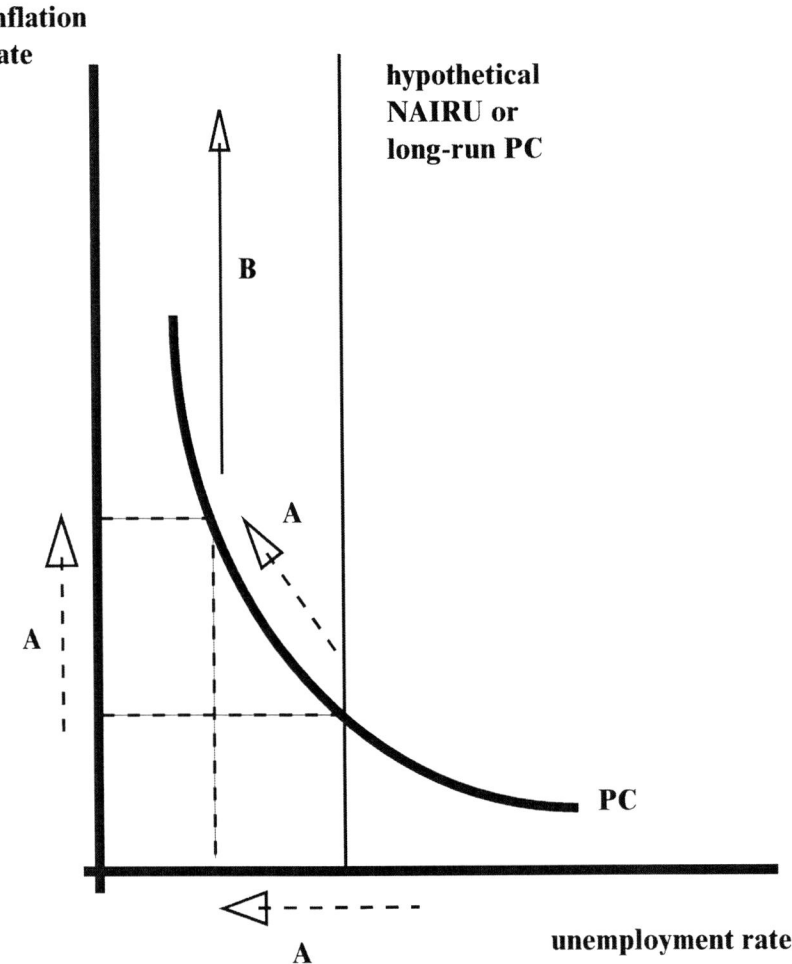

Figure 6-11. The "Phillips curve" or PC above, as elaborated in (Phillips 1958), purported to explain how relatively full employment might be possible for periods of relatively high inflation of money-prices, suggesting monetary or fiscal policy intervention by governments and-or central banks could counter increases in unemployment in the short-term by increasing the money supply in the short-term, e.g., moving policy targets from condition "A" to condition "B". Stagflation in the US economy, which followed extrication of US military forces from wars in Southeast Asia and consequent reductions in spending by the Department of Defence, demonstrated just how baseless this optimistic scenario turned out to be.

The modern understanding of the relationship between the unemployment rate and rate of inflation was elaborated in the 1950s and 1960s, in what was known as the "Phillips curve" (Figure 6-11). What is there that is not aphenomenal about the very notion that the two trends could move together at all, let alone inversely? In order to elaborate such a relationship, it is necessary in the first place to elaborate some additional conceptions such as the "non-accelerating inflation rate of unemployment" (NAIRU). Inflation, meanwhile, is never defined in terms of employment or underemployment of production factors even in general, let alone in terms of the workforce: there is no such animal as a "non-accelerating unemployment rate of inflation". It refers purely and only to the phenomenon of the amount of money circulating in the economy (including debt and credit) exceeding on an accumulating basis the sales-value of the supply of goods and services normally being consumed. Furthermore, the unemployment rate itself is calculated on a basis that excludes, from the potential total number of workers in any given period of time, all those who have left the workforce for that period of time – even though the vast majority of such individuals indeed form, over the years, part of the workforce. The range in which the rate of inflation can move, therefore, is far broader and less bounded than the range in which that total can move. Therefore, also, it follows that the comparability of movement in the unemployment rate and the rate of inflation is purely notional.

6.3.6. The Knowledge Dimension and How Disinformation is Distilled

A great deal of what passes for social science consists of data whose actual trend-line comes not from the actual development of events as they are observed and unfolded, but rather from the intentions of the researcher compiling the information. This has been the source of much mischief, including the correlations discussed in the previous section. Although such distillations of information are presented ads a contribution to knowledge, it is actually difficult to determine the truth of such an assertion in any given case when only selected data points are provided. The following sets of graphs comprising Figure 6-12 demonstrate how data extracted from the knowledge dimension in such selective ways can obscure understanding of the larger picture in profound ways. The overarching development since the late 1950s in the developing countries has been a struggle to broaden independence from the political to the economic sphere. This process has been impelled by historical factors continuing to work themselves out in the present. More recent developments have accelerated or decelerated the cycle but the overall path is similar to any Julia or Mandelbrot set, i.e., classical mathematical chaos, only expressed over the passage of historical time and therefore appearing as an ongoing cycle of self-similar but aperiodic helices.

The commentaries down the right-hand side of each of the three pages elaborates each of three well-known distortions that can be distilled in the bottom-left graph from the "big picture" top-left graph.

In each case, the disinformation perpetrated by the second graph from each pair can only take hold when one is not paying attention to what is actually decisive in social and economic matters. The moment any preconceived notion is placed ahead of what is being discovered by one's own act of finding out, the disinformation can threaten to overwhelm knowledge of the bigger picture.

It has become something of a fad in recent decades to dub just about any apparent recycling, in the present, of something established from the past with the prefix "neo-". What actually links these phenomena is their historical context. They all developed in response to the emergence of political independence from old European colonial powers in various parts of Africa and from the post-Soviet Russia in central Asia.

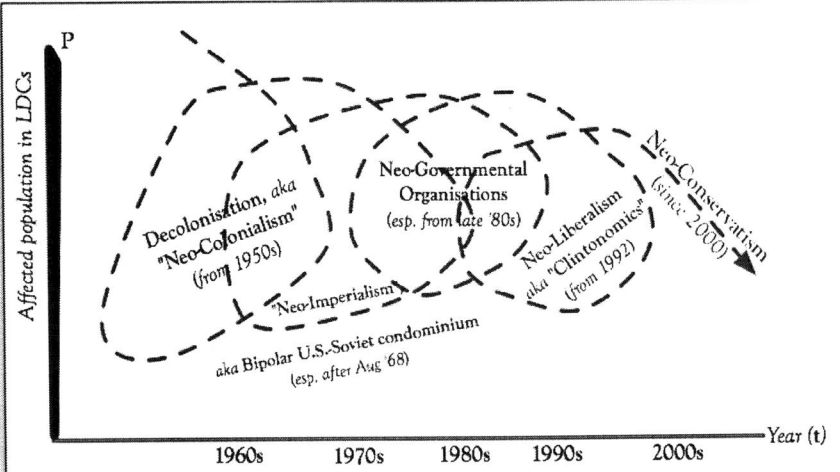

NOTE: *Each helix identifies a specific "neo-" spiral in the order of its historical appearance. In general, as time moves forward, these helices appear "tighter", i.e., the average individual radius diminishes. Depending on the phase space selected as the frame of reference, one might see the complete picture (this graphic, in the Knowledge dimension). Depending on which effects of other dependent parameters are discounted or included, one might alternatively see mainly a rising trend (graphic 'b'), a falling trend (graphic 'c') or a steady state (graphic 'd').*

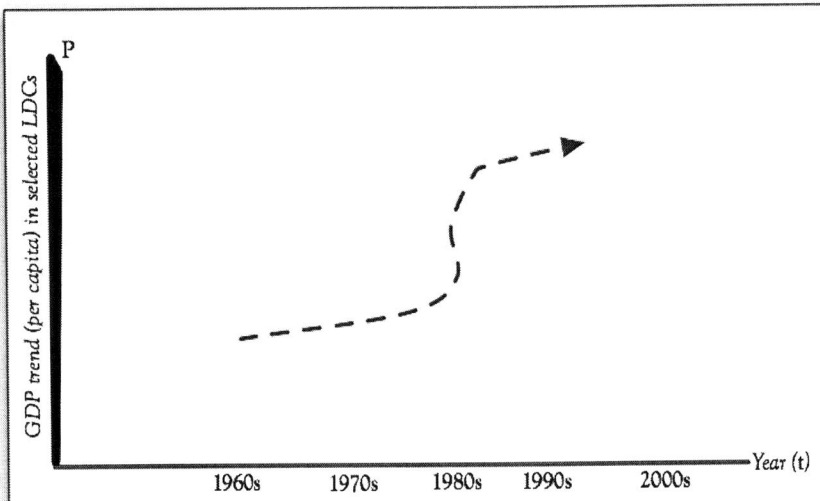

GRAPHIC 'b': *For selected less-developed countries, the GDP per capita demonstrates a clearly rising trend that has continues from the 1960s into the 21st century. In this collection of points, sequenced identically from a subset of points in the Knowledge phase-space of the neo-spiral graphic, a large amount of information that would have served to disclose the actual historical course of development of the global political economy in this timespan - providing the actual context of this GDP increase - has been lost.*

Figure 6-12-(i).a and b. Full historical view of increasingly implosive trend of neo-colonial decay in "developing" countries compared to trend of GDP per capita in selected LDCs.

The processes of "decolonisation" in former British, French, Portuguese, Spanish and Belgian territories of Africa was correctly dubbed "neo-colonialism" by Patrice Lumumba, the Congolese independence leader widely believed to have been murdered by the US Central Intelligence Agency acting on behalf of the Kingdom of Belgium. This term let the cat out of the bag by stressing the continuity of foreign economic domination of these countries, usually by their former colonial occupiers, for some indefinite but considerable period following formal political independence.

Certain other processes then developed in the wake of these unfolding neo-colonial relations.

The top panel on each of these three pages illustrates how the neocolonial process fed into the emergence of a neo-imperialist system. In this rearrangement, sometimes called the "bipolar division of the globe," the then-Soviet Union dropped any pretence of defending its "socialist camp" from actual or threatened attack by the US or its NATO bloc and resorted to definite arrangements with the US bloc to divide the globe into spheres of influence consisting of countries not necessarily sharing the same social or economic system as their Big Brother, nevertheless depending on one or the other superpower for security from external attack.

As this encountered growing resistance in these countries "from below", both superpowers and especially the United Nations spawned large numbers of what were called "non-governmental organisations" (NGOs). These were really neo-governmental organisations, supposedly supplementing inadequate local services but also gathering intelligence on incipient protest movements. With the disappearance of the USSR, the pretence of social service for society's sake was dumped and a ruthless neoliberal doctrine declared only the "fittest" developing countries could survive.

This was followed by the expounding of a neo-conservative doctrine, justifying the unilateral resort to armed force by the strongest power to extract whatever resources or other privileges it wants or needs. Behind a pretext of concern to stop terrorism, a sole superpower decides whether entire nations and peoples will live or die and whether their resources are to be exclusively looted under "production sharing agreements" or divided among any of those joining them in their aggression.

As the tightening sequence of helical spirals indicates, this process is increasingly implosive with time. However, as graphs 'b', 'c' and 'd' illustrate, by "slicing" this view of the overall data trend from the Knowledge dimension so as to *exclude* the actual progression of historical time, one can extract many a rosy scenario about what is happening to social and economic conditions in the weakest and most vulnerable parts of the world, known euphemistically as either the "less-developed" or "least-developed" countries (LDCs), as the noose tightens around the necks of the neocolonies of this world system.

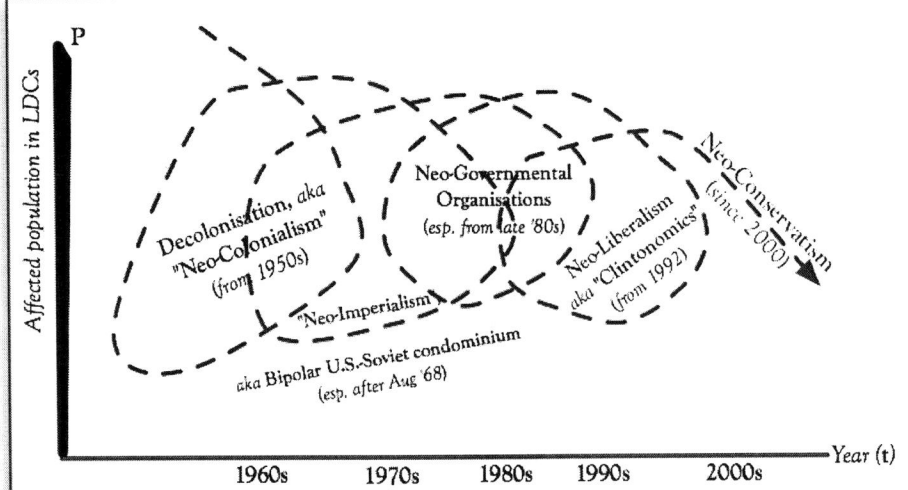

NOTE: Each helix identifies a specific "neo-" spiral in the order of its historical appearance. In general, as time moves forward, these helices appear "tighter", i.e., the average individual radius diminishes. Depending on the phase space selected as the frame of reference, one might see the complete picture (this graphic, in the Knowledge dimension). Depending on which effects of other dependent parameters are discounted or included, one might alternatively see mainly a rising trend (graphic 'b'), a falling trend (graphic 'c') or a steady state (graphic 'd').

GRAPH 'c': The falling trend in the proportion of GDP due to primary production in the fastest growing economies among the less-developed countries can be readily reconstituted from yet another subset of identically-sequenced points abstracted from the fuller picture of the Knowledge-dimension phase-space illustrated in the first graph. As in Graph 'b', everything historically specific has been stripped out, so that the direction suggested by the trendline is actually... meaningless

Figure 6-12-(ii).a and c. Full historical view of increasingly implosive trend of neo-colonial decay in "developing" countries compared to primary-production share of GDP per cap in selected LDCs.

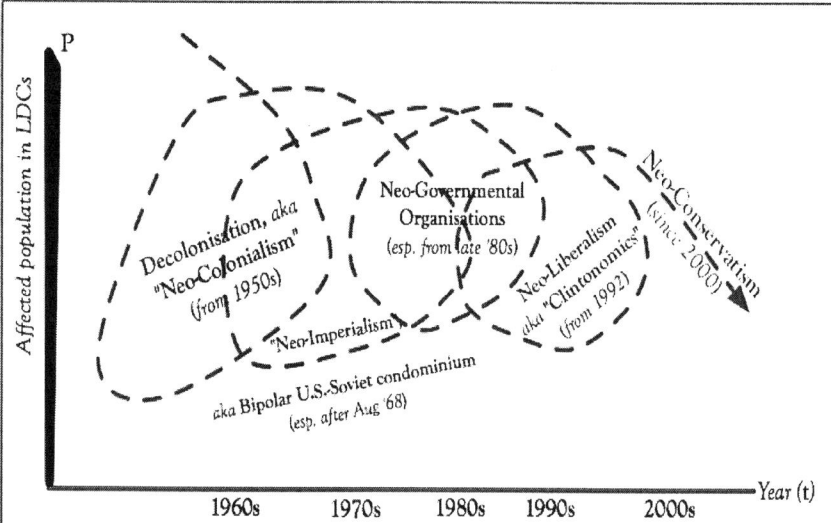

NOTE: *Each helix identifies a specific "neo-" spiral in the order of its historical appearance. In general, as time moves forward, these helices appear "tighter", i.e., the average individual radius diminishes. Depending on the phase space selected as the frame of reference, one might see the complete picture (this graphic, in the Knowledge dimension). Depending on which effects of other dependent parameters are discounted or included, one might alternatively see mainly a rising trend (graphic 'b'), a falling trend (graphic 'c') or a steady state (graphic 'd').*

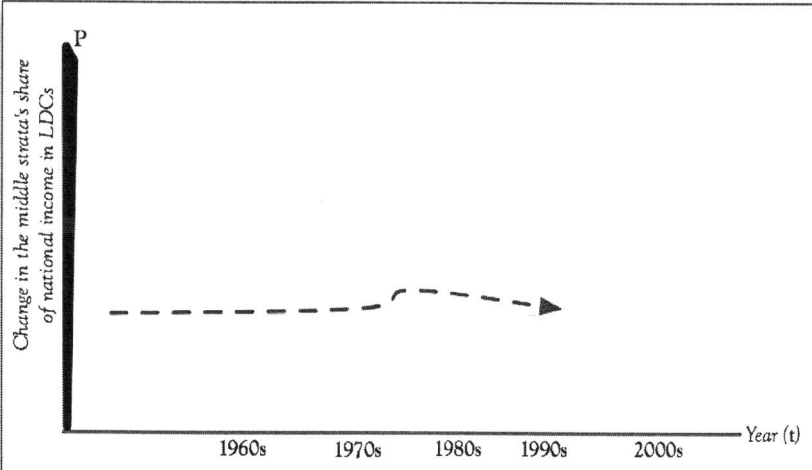

GRAPH 'd': *The data points in the above graph depict the steady-state trend in the share of national income enjoyed up to the early 1990s by the small middle stratum found in most LDCs. As in Graphs 'b' & 'c', the data points are sequenced exactly as they were located in the original "neo"-spiral graph, and all historically specific information removed.*

Figure 6-12-(iii).a and d. Full historical view of increasingly implosive trend of neo-colonial decay in "developing" countries compared to middle classes' share of national income in selected LDCs.

6.3.7. "Zones of Optimality" *versus* Complete Sets of Multiple Solutions

A standard logical syllogism goes: All A is B, some B is C, therefore some A is C. Logically this will always hold; factually, matters may be otherwise if it is either not the case that all A is B, or that any B is C, or that both are false. Then the conclusion that some A is C will no longer stand in fact. In economics, the analysis of multiple supply and demand functions relating to the production and sale of some inter-related set of goods and services can appear to generate multiple solutions for the best or most likely equilibrium price – a desirable and seemingly sophisticated outcome, tending to give some confidence that the analysis has not been cooked to produce a single preconceived answer. Such analyses produce optimal rather than unique solutions, but if the independence from one another of each of the component supply and demand functions cannot be assured, the region in which such an analysis may locate the optimum range of solutions, on the one hand, and the region in which the actual equilibrium price possibilities are found, on the other, may not bear any relationship to one another:

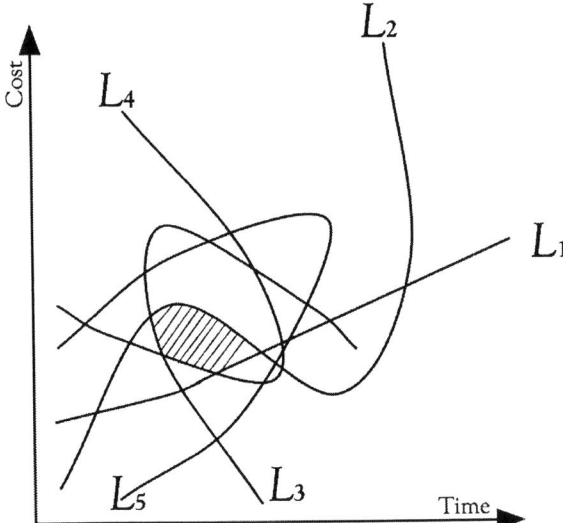

According to the conventional presentation of economics, supply and demand functions L_1 through L_5 should produce an optimum equilibrium price in the shaded region shown above. The premise underlying the above presentation's so-called "simplex" model, however, is that supply and demand functions L_1 through L_5 are independent of one another. The more oligopolies and quasi-monopolies occupy the available economic space, the more dependencies are created between smaller outfits dependent in a number of ways on larger outfits, hence the less likely such a condition of independence can be guaranteed. Thus, even though optimality analysis provides a region of multiple solutions, its fundamental premise may not be true in the real-world conditions being modelled, reducing the promise of optimality to merely groundless optimism.

Figure 6-13. While all non-linear systems should produce zones of multiple solutions, the existence of such zones is insufficient to assert existence of any of the interdependencies characteristic of many non-linear systems.

Non-linear systems, in which not all functions may be independent over the entirety of their common domain, are certain to produce multiple solutions. However, these may occur in different non-contiguous intervals. That is: it may be that they do not occur necessarily in a single space bounded by a single common subset of the points of intersection of all the functions. Here is another source of disinformation that can overwhelm sound decision-taking. In general: "zones of optimality" are a linearisation, a "fudge"-factoring type of exercise; complete sets of multiple solutions are actually and ultimately non-linear.

6.3.8. Is Consumption → "Happiness" Humanity's Ultimate Destiny?

In North America north of Mexico, as spring finally takes hold after the dead hand of winter has been released by the passage of the seasons, the corporate media invariably run "upbeat" stories. These centre around topics on the general theme of what makes people happy, and this year once again in these media, the usual spate of such material has emerged. This "journalism" exploits a well-studied and established psychological predisposition of people to buy more if they feel better about their prospects. This year's crop of feel-good bumpf even includes discussions of "the economics of happiness".

Pitching the "buy more, now" message in this manner itself points to a growing counter-trend implicit in the social psychology of modern-day marketing campaigns. The more educated and better-off sections of the consuming marketplace can no longer be taken for granted: sections of consumers in these strata have started looking for quality. This development has come at a time when the ruthless competition in retail – exemplified by the acute crisis that has broken out since 2002-03 around the future of Wal-Mart in the U.S., Canada and Europe as well as in so called "emerging markets" such as China – can only be settled by maximising the overall volume and quantity of sales, as competition has intensified the tendency to shave profit margins razor-thin and even to "dump", *i.e.*, to sell below actual costs of production, certain classes of goods in certain markets. The bottom line is that those strata with greater disposable income also tend to discriminate more among the quality of goods on offer than strata possessing less disposable income. Therefore it has become a matter of urgent necessity for giant retailers to provide such people with a rationale to maximise the overall quantity of their purchasing and put considerations of quality in second place.

These considerations provide the contemporary actual material foundation for the notion that happiness can only be sustained by increased consumption. The notion itself has become central to Eurocentric outlook since the time Jeremy Bentham proclaimed his Utilitarian doctrine of the best society in the increasingly industrialising world economy of the late 18th century being that which provides "the greatest good for the greatest number". Bentham's philosophy was explicitly converted into economic form by William Stanley Jevons (discussed extensively back in Chapter One). What Jevons elaborated – which took matters further than, and down a path not anticipated by, Bentham – was to link individual happiness generated by material consumption to the ultimate destiny of individuals as economic actors. That linkage of happiness and destiny of entire societies through successive and endless acts of material consumption by its individual members was implicit in, and undergirded, Jevons' most celebrated dictum that "Value depends entirely upon Utility" (Jevons 1870), *i.e.*, that the individual seeking to satisfy some need determines the value of objects brought for sale in the market by whatever amount s/he is prepared to pay to acquire the good or service that fulfills the need.

Word	Arabic	Root	Meaning
Happiness	Sa'ada	Sa'd	Destiny

Figure 6-14. Origins of the Arabic word for "happiness" – a non-Eurocentric view.

Miring itself since the days of Jevons, Walras, Menger and Marshall in neo-classical notions of "consumer sovereignty" and similar related notions tying happiness to consumption as Humanity's destiny, conventional economics has erased any other prospect or possibility for happiness not tied to a vast engine of material consumption. Human needs, examined in the large, loom as something massive – as the totality of what billions of humans need. However, what humans need as individual or individual family units (no matter how extended) – in other words: what per capita requirement the material productive apparatus needs to supply – is a vastly different matter. As Figure 6-14 serves to illustrate, in much of the world not informed by the Eurocentric standpoint, "happiness" really stands for an end-point, a destination, rather than some all-consuming appetite to be fed continually regardless of actual need, the driver for building and maintaining the "economy" as an engine for producing ever-mounting piles of waste.

Chapter 7

CONCLUSION

Nature, which is to say: all that which is inherent in, or otherwise characteristic of, any actual phenomenon, is the ultimate source of all authentic, fundamental knowledge. Regardless of human interventions and any of their impacts, the world – which is to say: all natural contents and their forms in the physical as well as the social environment – reveals itself. By a careful and painstaking process of cataloguing the sense-data of one's own observations, directly and-or instrumentally, and comparing and assessing what they disclose against existing knowledge, the individual can in fact find out what the world has revealed. Such is the essence of the process of research aimed at establishing the truth. Whatever one's intention, so long as it is not merely self-serving, the individual proceeding along these lines and employing ordinary powers of ratiocination can arrive at knowledge that may be harnessed in the service and best interests of others. This knowledge, even though not complete, may be further refined by applying scientific methods to weed falsehoods out.

Engineering and social sciences like economics – the broad fields of study from which the authors come – strive to harness knowledge to practical ends. It is undeniable that many practical solutions have emerged that were never anticipated even by the most elaborate developments in the field of theory. Does such a thing provide evidence for the notion that there exist inherent limitations in elaborating theory as the basis and guide for practice, or only that practice can sometimes be ahead of what theory has comprehended? Much of the discussion of such gaps between Theory and Practice has been the source of "noise" of the sort that practical people tend to tune out as they get on with seeking solutions to actual problems. In the case of economics, this work argues:

1. an entire realm of what has been described, defined and discussed here as "intangibles", lies buried in the warp of that "noise";
2. what has brought about the deep discrediting of a great deal of the the field of economic theory can be corrected and-or junked, and the entire field of economic theory itself renewed, if intangible components of economic reality and their role in shaping that reality are explicitly identified alongside the readily-observable tangible components; and
3. the principal obstacles on this path to renewal have become entrenched as a result not of a lack or insufficiency of information or knowledge, but precisely as the result of an enormously burdensome ideological and cultural legacy of Eurocentric biases and prejudice which have become encrusted over centuries of use and abuse.

In the alternative, a "natural economics" suggests itself as the body of theory and practice to be developed, in which the key intangibles of time, intention and contextual knowledge play a dual role providing both analytical as well as practical guidelines. Evidences of the prospects for a "new synthesis" based on such an economics can be seen already in the elaboration of a growing catalogue of technologies that provide solutions which are innovative, economically attractive, environmentally appealing and socially responsible. Everything top-down having demonstrated nothing but thoroughgoing aphenomenality, there remains nothing for it but to proceed with such a natural economics from the bottom up. The thinking that got us into present problems cannot get us out, and no one should expect cures from the Gods of Plague.

REFERENCES AND BIBLIOGRAPHY

Abbott, Edwin Abbott. 1884. *Flatland – A Romance in Many Dimensions* London: Macmillan.

Allen, David W., Richard B. Allen, Robert E. Black *et al*.1979. *Effects on Commercial Fishing of Petroleum Development off the Northeastern United States.* Woods Hole MA: Woods Hole Oceanographic Institute.

Amin, Samir.1972. *Accumulation on a World Scale*. New York:Monthly Review Press.

Amoroso, Bruno 2003. *Global Apartheid* Roskilde [Denmark]: Roskilde UP.

Anders, George. 2005. "As Oil Prices Swing, Gas-Station Owners Try Futures Market", *The Wall Street Journal* [New York] Jun 21 p.A1.

Anderson, Eric L. and Malcolm L. Spaulding.1981. "Application of an Oil Spill Fates Model to Environmental Management on Georges Bank" *The Environmental Professional,* 3:131-32.

Armstrong, Jane. 2006a. "Revival On The Rock- Williams Seeks A Piece Of The Action [Part 1 Of 3]" *The Globe And Mail Report On Business* [Toronto] Mar 15 p.1.

——— . 2006b. "Black Stuff Puts Nfld In The Black", *The Globe And Mail Report On Business* [Toronto] Mar 31 p.1.

Augier, M. 1842. *Du Crédit Public*. Paris.

Aumann, Robert J. 2005. "War and Peace – Nobel Lecture 8 December", in Torsten Persson, *Nobel Lectures in Economic Sciences*. Singapore: World Scientific Publishing [in press].

Avery, Simon. 2006. "Data mining: Deeper, smarter and way, way faster; SAS boss says hardware developments are driving advances in business intelligence", *The Globe and Mail Report on Business* [Toronto] May 04, p.8.

Bahree, Bhushan and Jeffrey Ball. 2005a. "Oil Giants Face New Competition For Future Supply; Big Players Focus on Returns As Rivals Undercut Them; Limping Away From Libya" *Wall Street Journal* [NewYork] Apr 19 p.A1.

——— . 2005b. "Saudis Vow Action on Oil Demand, Doubling Spending On Energy Development to US$50-Billion, Will Ignore Output Caps" *Wall Street Journal* [New York] Apr 22 p.A2.

——— and Thaddeus Herrick. 2005c. "Oil Industry's Refining Squeeze Limits Prospects of Price Relief" *Wall Street Journal* [New York] May 24 p.A1.

———. 2005d. "Big Thirst for Oil Is Unslaked", *Wall Street Journal* [New York] Jun 21 p.A2.

―― and Russell Gold. 2005e. "Pursuit of New Oil Supplies Runs Into a Bottleneck", *Wall Street Journal* [New York] Jun 28 p.A1.

―― and Thaddeus Herrick.2005f_ "Exxon, Aramco Join Sinopec In Refinery Venture in China", *Wall Street Journal* [New York] Jul 11 p.A2.

――. 2006a. "OPEC Ministers Agree To Keep Oil Output Steady", *Wall Street Journal* [New York] Jan 31 p.A2.

―― and Chip Cummins. 2006b. "Thwarted Attack At Saudi Facility Stirs Energy Fears", *Wall Street Journal* [New York] Feb 25 p.A1.

――. 2006d. "OPEC Will Keep Oil Output Steady As US Stores Rise", *Wall Street Journal* [New York] Mar 09 p.A2.

――. 2006e. "Venezuela Seizes Total, ENI Oil Fields", *Wall Street Journal* [New York] Apr 04 pA2.

―― and Ann Davis. 2006f. "Oil Settles Above $70 a Barrel, Despite Inventories at 8-Year High", *Wall Street Journal* [New York] Apr 18 p.A1.

――, Carla Anne Robbins and Chip Cummins. 2006g. "Oil Minister Iran Won't Cut Exports Despite Nuclear Standoff", *The Wall Street Journal* [New York] Apr 26 p.A1.

Bains, H.S. 1967. *Necessity for Change*. London: The Internationalists.

――. 1982. *The Necessity for Revolution*. Toronto: MELS Institute.

――. 2005. *Thinking of the Sixties*. Toronto: National Publications Centre.

Ball, Jeffrey and Chip Cummins. 2005a. "Exxon and Shell Profits Surge Even as Oil Production Declines", *Wall Street Journal* [New York] Apr 29 p.A2.

――. 2005b. "Exxon Chief Makes A Cold Calculation On Global Warming", *Wall Street Journal* [New York] Jun 14 p.A1.

――. 2005c. "Texas Truckers Turn To Newfangled Fuel- A Willie Nelson Brand", *Wall Street Journal* [New York] Jul 05 p.A1.

―― and Benoît Faucon. 2005d_ "Exxon, Shell Profits Climb Sharply", *Wall Street Journal* [New York] Jul 29 p.A3.

――, John J. Fialka and Russell Gold. 2005e. "Texas Backlash Spreads As Profits Surge At Oil Companies", *Wall Street Journal* [New York] Oct 28 p.A1.

――, John J. Fialka and Russell Gold. 2005f. "Oil Patch Faces Rough Patch", *Wall Street Journal* [New York] Nov 04 p.A4.

――. 2005g. "US Oil Firms Reach Deal With Libya", *Wall Street Journal* [New York] Dec 30 p.A3.

――. 2006a. "As Exxon Pursues African Oil, Charity Becomes Political Issue", *Wall Street Journal* [New York] Jan 10 p.A1.

――. 2006b. "The New Act at Exxon- Diplomacy of Controlling Future Oil and Gas Reserves", *Wall Street Journal* [New York] Mar 08 p.B1.

――. 2006c. "Energy- Mixed Messages from Big Oil", *Wall Street Journal* [New York] Mar 11 p.A2.

――. 2006d. "With a Big Nuclear Push, France Transforms Its Energy Equation", *Wall Street Journal* [New York] Mar 28 p.A1.

――. 2006e. "As the Price of Gasoline Takes Off, Oil and Auto Firms Trade Barbs", *Wall Street Journal* [New York] Apr 12 p.A1.

――. 2006f. "Exxon's $8.4 Billion Net Faces Fire on All Fronts", *Wall Street Journal* [New York] Apr 28 p.A2.

—— . 2006g. "As Gasoline Prices Soar, Americans Resist Major Cuts in Consumption", *Wall Street Journal* [New York] May 01 p.A1.

Baran, Paul A. 1957. *The Political Economy of Growth*. New York: Monthly Review.

—— . and Paul M. Sweezy. 1965. *Monopoly Capital* New York: Monthly Review.

Barta, Patrick and Matt Pottinger. 2005a. "Why Cnooc May Not Be Such a Big Threat", *The Wall Street Journal* [New York] Jun 03 p.A1.

—— and Sarah Nassauer .2005b. "Turkey in the Tank- High Price of Gasoline Is a Boon for Biofuels", *The Wall Street Journal* [New York] Oct 28 p.A1.

Basu, A., J. Akhter, M.H. Rahman, and M.R. Islam. 2005. "A review of separation of gases using membranes", *Journal of Petroleum Science and Technology* [in press].

——, Mustafiz, S., N. Bjorndalen, S. Rahaman and M.R. Islam. 2006. "A Comprehensive Approach for Modeling Sorption of Lead and Cobalt Ions through Fish-Scales as an Adsorbent", *Chem. Eng. Comm.*, Vol. 193: 580-605.

Begg, H. M. And S. McDowell.1981. *Industrial Performance and Prospects in Areas Affected by Oil Development,* Edinburgh: Scottish Economic Planning Department, ESU Research Paper No. 3.

Berkeley, George. 1734. "The Analyst", in George Sampson ed., *The Works of George Berkeley* London: G. Bell and Sons, 1898.

Berman, Dennis K. 2005a. "US Seems Wary Of Giving Cnooc Fast Review of Bid", *The Wall Street Journal*[New York] Jun 28 p.A2.

—— and Russell Gold. 2005c. "As Rancor Mounts, Cnooc Needs to Push Its Offer for Unocal", *The Wall Street Journal*[New York] Jul 05 p.C1.

—— and Mark Heinzl. 2005d. "Canada Welcomes China's Cash", *The Wall Street Journal* [New York] Jul 15 p. C1.

—— and Russell Gold. 2005e. "Chevron Raises Its Bid for Unocal", *The Wall Street Journal*[New York] Jul 20 p.A3.

Bilby, Kenneth 1986. *The General: David Sarnoff and the rise of the communications industry* New York:Harper and Row.

Bilmes, Linda and Joseph E. Stiglitz. 2006. "The Economic Costs of the Iraq War: An Appraisal Three Years After the Beginning of the Conflict" Boston MA: American Economics Association Meeting, 8 January.

Blair, Tony. (1998). *The Third Way: New Politics for the New Century*. London: Fabian Society, ISBN 0716305887.

Böhm-Bawerk, Eugen. 1898. *Karl Marx and the Close of His System*. Translated by Alice McDonald. London: T. Fisher Unwin. Reprinted in *Karl Marx and the Close of His System*. New York: Augustus M. Kelley, 1949.

Boyd-Orr, John.1937. *Food, Nutrition and Income*. London: Macmillan.

—— and David Lubbock. 1940. *Feeding the People in Wartime*. London: Macmillan.

—— . 1943. *Food and the People*. London: Macmillan.

Bois, C. 1982. "World Hydrocarbon Reserves, Resources and Availabilities", *Revue de l'IFP* Vol 37 No 2. 135:148.

Boyer, Richard O. and Herbert M. Morais 1973. *Labor's Untold Story* New York, NY: UE.

Braverman, Harry 1974. *Labor and Monopoly Capital: The Degradation of Work in the Twentieth Century* New York: Monthly Review Press.

Bradley, Susan and Steve Proctor. 2005. "Goldboro To Get LNG Plant; Eastern Shore To Get $5-Billion Petrochemical Refinery, Says Keltic President", *The Chronicle-Herald* [Halifax] Dec 20 p.A1.

Bradmans. 2005. *Middle East/Africa 2005*. London: Bradmans [periodical; CIP catalogued at British Library].

Brattain, Walter H. 1956. "Surface Properties of Semiconductors – Nobel Lecture 11 December", in *Nobel Lectures, Physics 1942-1962*. Amsterdam: Elsevier [1964].

Brecht, B. and Kurt Weill. 1928. *Der Dreigroschenoper* [The Threepenny Opera].Berlin: Theater am Schiffbauerdamm.

———. 1947. *Selected Poems*. New York: Harcourt-Brace. Translations by H.R. Hays.

Brethour, Patrick R. 2005a. "Following the boom, a bitter divide", *The Globe and Mail Report on Business* [Toronto] Apr 06 pp. 8-9.

———. 2005b. "How to grind the oil sands into a 'sausage factory'", *The Globe and Mail Report on Business* [Toronto] May 21 p.3.

———. 2005c. "North-South energy links grow ever tighter", *The Globe and Mail Report on Business* [Toronto] May 21 p.18.

———. 2005d. "Canadian oil could be headed to China under latest deal", *The Globe and Mail Report on Business* [Toronto] Jun 01p1.

———. 2005e. "Oil soars to record high after terrorist threat, refinery woes", *The Globe and Mail Report on Business* [Toronto] Jun 18 p.5.

———. 2005f. "Petrocan results", *The Globe and Mail Report on Business* [Toronto] Jul 27 p.1.

———. 2005g. "Rig costs cap profits in oil patch", *The Globe and Mail Report on Business* [Toronto] Jul 29 p.1.

——— and Dave Ebner.2005h. "Bidding war may erupt in Alberta oil sands", *The Globe and Mail Report on Business* [Toronto] Aug 04 p.14.

———. 2005i. "Shell doubles oil sands expansion budget", *The Globe and Mail Report on Business* [Toronto] Aug 10 p.1.

———. 2005j. "Why Canada's feeling the pain at the pumps", *The Globe and Mail Report on Business* [Toronto] Sep 02 p.1.

———. 2005k. "Pump prices in Nfld to jump", *The Globe and Mail Report on Business* [Toronto] Sep 03 p.24.

———. 2005l. "Alberta boosts oil exports to aid US", *The Globe and Mail Report on Business* [Toronto] Sep 05 p.1.

———. 2005m. "Oil patch unions seize initiative in tackling labour shortage", *The Globe and Mail Report on Business* [Toronto] Sep 09 p.3.

———. 2005n. "Nexen, OPTI plan $10-billion expansion for oil sands venture", *The Globe and Mail Report on Business* [Toronto] Sep 15 p.1.

———. 2005o. "Fox lends support to Canada over NAFTA", *The Globe and Mail* [Toronto] Sep 30 p.A8.

———. 2005p. "There's still lots of oil – at a price- IEA", *The Globe and Mail Report on Business* [Toronto] Nov 08 p.11.

———. 2005q. "Shell spending to rocket 60% next year", *The Globe and Mail Report on Business* [Toronto] Nov 18 p.3.

———. 2005r. "Pembina Institute for Sustainable Development urges slowdown on oil sands", *The Globe and Mail Report on Business* [Toronto] Nov 24 p.6.

———. 2005s. "Petro-Canada wants stake in Syrian asset sold by year's end", *The Globe and Mail Report on Business* [Toronto] Nov 26 p.3.

———, Bill Curry and Jane Armstrong. 2005t. "Newfoundland takes aim at oil firms", *The Globe and Mail Report on Business* [Toronto] Nov 30 p.10.

———. 2005u. "Oil- A new continental divide", *The Globe and Mail Report on Business* [Toronto] Dec 20 p.1.

———. 2006a. "Husky aims for third offshore project", *The Globe and Mail Report on Business* [Toronto] Jan 17 p.3.

———. 2006b. "How a Tory win could open door to Petrocan sale", *The Globe and Mail Report on Business* [Toronto] Jan 19 p.1.

———. 2006c. "Petrocan to build oil sands upgrader near Edmonton", *The Globe and Mail Report on Business* [Toronto] Jan 27 p.7.

——— and Dave Ebner. 2006d. "Petrocan gets LNG link with Gazprom", *The Globe and Mail Report on Business* [Toronto] Mar 15 p.1.

——— and Sinclair Stewart. 2006e. "How the oil patch is cashing in" *The Globe and Mail Report on Business* [Toronto] Apr 08 p.4.

———. 2006f. "Williams wants expropriation tools", *The Globe and Mail Report on Business* [Toronto] Apr 11 p.1.

——— and Steven Chase. 2006g. "Chevron rushes to disband", *The Globe and Mail Report on Business* [Toronto] Apr 12 p.1.

Brym, Robert J. and R. James Sacouman, edd. 1979. *Underdevelopment and Social Movements in Atlantic Canada* Toronto: University of Toronto – New Hogtown.

Buchanan, Susan. 2006. "Raw-Sugar Futures Fall Off High As Brazil Ethanol Rumors Swirl", *The Wall Street Journal* [New York] Jan 04 p.C2.

Butterfield, Herbert. 1931. *The Whig Interpretation of History*. London: Bell.

———. 1968. *The Origins of Modern Science 1300-1800* Toronto: Clarke, Irwin,.

Byron, R.1986. *Sea Change A Shetland Society, 1970-1979*. St. John's NL: Institute of Social and Economic Research, Memorial University of Newfoundland.

Calmes, Jackie and Guy Chazan. 2005. "Evans Declines Putin's Job Offer At State Oil Firm", *The Wall Street Journal* [New York] Dec 20 p.B11.

Canada. 1976. *Community and Employment Implications of Restructuring the Atlantic Groundfisheries*. Ottawa: Department of Regional Economic Expansion.

———. 1983. *Venture Development Project: Report of the Sable Island Environmental Assessment Panel* Ottawa.

———. 1999. *Interdepartmental Review of the Canadian Patrol Frigate Project: Report on the Contract Management Framework*. Ottawa: Departments of National Defence, and Public Works and Government Services, 26 March.

———. 2004. *Canadian Natural Gas - Review of 2003 and Outlook to 2020*. Ottawa: Department of Natural Resources Energy Policy Sector, Petroleum Resources Branch - Natural Gas Division [December].

Canadian Association of Petroleum Producers [CAPP]. 2006. "Canada's Upstream Oil And Gas Industry Energized- Climate Change Report", *The Globe and Mail Special Report* [Toronto] Feb 23 p.F2.

Campbell, Murray. 2005. "The smokestacks are going cold", *The Globe and Mail* [Toronto] Jul 05 p.A7.

Canning, Stratford G. and C. M. Campbell.1982. "Prospects for Co-Existence: An Analysis of Potential Interactions between Onshore Petroleum Development and the Established Fishery in Southeastern Newfoundland" NORDCO Ltd. – Paper presented to International Conference on Oil and the Environment, Halifax.

Carey, Alex. 1995. *Taking the Risk out of Democracy: Propaganda in the U.S. and Australia*. Sydney: University of New South Wales Press.

Carlton, Jim.2006. "BP Finds New Pipeline Rupture Caused By Corrosion In Alaska", *The Wall Street Journal* [New York] Apr 17 p.A3.

Carlyle, Tamsin. 2005a. "Boom in Alberta Oil Sands Fuels Pipeline Dreams to West Coast, China Markets", *The Wall Street Journal* [New York] May 31 p.A2.

——. 2005b. "Nexen Targets Canada Oil Sands, To Sell Some Conventional Fields", *The Wall Street Journal* [New York] Jul 06 p.B10.

——. 2005c."Ontario Nuclear Power Plant Units to Be Restarted", *The Wall Street Journal* [New York] Oct 18 p.A11.

——. 2006a. "Alberta's Draw- Oil Sands, and Technology", *The Wall Street Journal* [New York] Feb 14 p.A17.

——. 2006b. "EnCana Slashes Capital Budget; Profit Falls 8.3%" *The Wall Street Journal* [New York] Feb 16 pA2.

Catton, William R. Jr. 1980. *Overshoot: The Ecological Basis of Revolutionary Change* Chicago: University of Illinois Press.

Champion, Marc. 2006. "Oil-Price Shock Tops List Of Global Economic Risks Amid Supply, Geopolitical Worries", *The Wall Street Journal* [New York] Jan 30 p.A2.

Chase, Steven and Simon Tuck. 2005a. "'National security' bill not aimed at energy takeovers- David Emerson", *The Globe and Mail Report on Business* [Toronto] Jul 15 p.1.

—— and Simon Tuck. 2005b. "EnCana's 'field of dreams' has Colorado locals crying the blues", *The Globe and Mail Report on Business* [Toronto] Jul 15 p.4.

——. 2005c. "Ottawa strikes oil and gas bonanza", *The Globe and Mail* [Toronto] Sep 24 p.A11.

—— and Dave Ebner. 2006a. "Plug pulled on Hebron offshore project", *The Globe and Mail Report on Business* [Toronto] Apr 04 p.1.

—— 2006b. "Eastern businesses seek slice of booming Alberta's oil wealth", *The Globe and Mail Report on Business* [Toronto] Apr 10 p.1.

Chassany, Anne-Sylvaine. 2006. "Total's Net Profit Declines 37% Despite Jump In Energy Prices", *The Wall Street Journal* [New York] Feb 16 p.A2.

Chazan, Guy. 2006. "Russia Says It Plans To Loosen State Monopoly On Gas Exports", *The Wall Street Journal* [New York] Feb 13 p.A4.

Chernenko, K.U. and M S Smirtyukov, edd.1967. Решения партий и правительства по хозяиственным вопросам [*Resheniya partii i pravitel'stva po khozyaystvennym voprosam* – Resolutions of the Party and the Government on Economic Questions], Vol. 1: 1917 – 1928. Moscow.

Chester, Lewis, Stephen Fay and Hugo Young. 1967. *The Zinoviev Letter*. London: Heinemann.

Chhetri, A.B and Islam, M.R. 2006a. "Towards producing a true green biodiesel", *Energy Sources, submitted*.

Chown, Marcus. 2001. "*Principia Mathematica* III – Opinion/Interview with Stephen Wolfram", in *New Scientist* 25 August 2001.

Cohen, A.1980. "A Sense of Time, a Sense of Place: The Meaning of Close Social Association in Whalsay, Shetland", in A. Cohen ed., *Belonging: Identity and Social Organization in British Rural Cultures.* Manchester UK: Manchester University Press and St. John's NL: Institute of Social and Economic Research, Memorial University of Newfoundland.

Cohen, Adam. 2005. "Spain Wins Final Antitrust Say On Energy Deal", *The Wall Street Journal* [New York] Nov 15 p, A20.

Cole, G.D.H. 1944. *A Century of Co-operation*. London: G. Allen and Unwin Ltd.

——— . 1956. *A History of Socialist Thought*. London: Macmillan.

Comte, Auguste. 1848. *A General View Of Positivism.* Paris.

Cook, Fred J. 1962. *The Warfare State.* New York: Macmillan.

Cordahi, James and Will Kennedy. 2006. "Saudi Arabia Looks To Eastern Markets", *The Globe And Mail Report On Business* [Toronto] Jan 23 p.7.

Corey, Lewis 1930. *The House of Morgan* New York: Grosset and Dunlap.

Creel, George.1920. *How We Advertised America*. New York: Harper and Brothers.

Cummins, Chip and Thaddeus Herrick. 2005a. "An Oil Giant Faces Questions About a Deadly Blast in Texas", *The Wall Street Journal* [New York] Jul 27 p.A1.

——— . 2005b. "Istanbul Moment- Sir, There's a Ship In Your Bedroom", *The Wall Street Journal* [New York] Jul 28 p.A1.

———, Bhushan Bahree and Jeffrey Ball. 2005c. "Why the World Is One Storm Away From Energy Crisis", *The Wall Street Journal* [New York] Sep 24 p.A1.

——— and Bhushan Bahree, Shai Oster and John Fialka. 2005d. "Five Who Laid the Groundwork For Historic Spike in Oil Market", *The Wall Street Journal* [New York] Dec 20 p.A1.

——— . 2006. "As Oil Supplies Are Stretched, Rebels, Terrorists Get New Clout", *The Wall Street Journal* [New York] Apr 10 p.A1.

Dales, H. Garth and W. Hugh Woodin.1996. *Super-Real Fields.* Clarendon Press.

Darwin, Charles. 1859. *The Origin of Species.* London.

——— . 1871. *The Descent of Man and Selection in Relation to Sex*. London: John Murray.

Darwin, Francis, ed. 1892. *The Autobiography of Charles Darwin and Selected Letters* New York: Dover.

Decloet, Derek.2006. "Oil", *The Globe and Mail* [Toronto] Apr 20 p.A1.

de Córdoba, José. 2005. "Bolivia Election Portends Foreign-Investor Clash", *The Wall Street Journal* [New York] Dec 20 p.A13.

——— . 2006. "In Bolivia, A New Sheriff's In Town", *The Wall Street Journal* [New York] Feb 03 p.A10.

de Pian, Louis 1962. *Linear Active Network Theory* Englewood Cliffs, N.J:. Prentice-Hall.

Deveau, Scott. 2005. "US threatens Pakistan over Iran pipeline plan", *The Globe and Mail* [Toronto] Jun 17 p.S3.

Dowlee, Andrew and Beth Heinsohn. 2005. "More Outages Hit US Oil Refineries", *The Wall Street Journal* [New York] Aug 09 p.A5.

Dummett, Ben. 2005. "Chinese Firms to Pay $1.42 Billion For EnCana Oil Assets in Ecuador", *The Wall Street Journal* [New York] Sep 14 p.A3.

Durkheim, Emil.1897. *Suicide* Paris.

Eagle, Lyon, Pope Associates.1981. "Shetland Offshore Hazard Risk Assessment" Prepared for the Shetland Islands Council.

Easterbrook, W.T. and Hugh G.J. Aitken 1956 *Canadian Economic History* Toronto: Macmillan.

Easterbrook, W.T. and M.H. Watkins, edd. 1967. *Approaches to Canadian Economic History* Toronto:McClelland and Stewart.

Ebner, Dave. 2005a. "High oil prices revive shelved Nfld Project", *The Globe and Mail Report on Business* [Toronto] Apr 06 p.3.

——— . 2005b. "The Pembina deposit, Highpine Oil and Gas, the Stollery clan", *The Globe and Mail Report on Business* [Toronto] Apr 07 p.1.

——— . 2005c. "Kazakh courts seize Turgai", *The Globe and Mail Report on Business* [Toronto] Apr 16 p.5.

——— . 2005d. "Imperial, Exxon pumping up to $6.5-billion more into oil sands", *The Globe and Mail Report on Business* [Toronto] Jun 13 p.1.

——— . 2005e. "EnCana unveils plans to sell Alberta hub for gas storage" *The Globe and Mail Report on Business* [Toronto] Jun 21 p.1.

——— . 2005f. "How's this for contrarian- World now facing oil glut", *The Globe and Mail Report on Business* [Toronto] Jun 22 p.1.

——— . 2005g. "Imperial Oil gets 3rd chief for Mackenzie Valley pipeline project", *The Globe and Mail Report on Business* [Toronto] Jun 25 p.6.

——— . 2005h. "PetroKaz soars as company considers sale offers from India, China", *The Globe and Mail Report on Business* [Toronto] Jun 28 p.1.

——— . 2005i. "More US oil exploration urged", *The Globe and Mail Report on Business* [Toronto] Jun 29 p.8.

——— . 2005j. "Moving fuel -- history of Canadian long-distance pipeline construction", *The Globe and Mail* [Toronto] Jun 30 p.A13.

——— . 2005k. "Following China's interest, Snow visits oil sands [!]", *The Globe and Mail Report on Business* [Toronto] Jul 08 p.5.

——— . 2005l. "Ottawa, Deh Cho reach pipeline deal", *The Globe and Mail* [Toronto] *Report on Business* Jul 12 p1).

———, Dawn Walton and Deborah Yedlin. 2005m. "Oil-field success leads to Stampede excess", *The Globe and Mail* [Toronto] Jul 13 p.A1.

——— . 2005n. "Behind EnCana's swagger, it remains steady as she goes", *The Globe and Mail Report on Business* [Toronto] Jul 14 p.4.

——— . 2005o. "Upstart firm gets regulatory nod for plan to sell raw bitumen in oil sands for others to upgrade", *The Globe and Mail Report on Business* [Toronto] Jul 21 p.6.

——— . 2005p. "Shell profit gushes 85% to a record on high prices", *The Globe and Mail Report on Business* [Toronto] Jul 22 p.3.

——— . 2005q. "EnCana to drill new offshore well near Deep Panuke", *The Globe and Mail Report on Business* [Toronto] Jul 23 p.8.

——— . 2005r. "French firm snags oil sands project", *The Globe and Mail Report on Business* [Toronto] Aug 03 p.1.

——— . 2005s. "If $65-a-barrel oil doesn't curb demand, future price shocks will, analyst says", *The Globe and Mail Report on Business* [Toronto]Aug 11 p.2.

——— . 2005t. "Enbridge inks deals on oil sands pipeline", *The Globe and Mail Report on Business* [Toronto] Sep 10 p.7.

——— . 2005u. "Shell prepared to spend billions on oil sands in Peace River area", *The Globe and Mail Report on Business* [Toronto] Sep 14 p.3.

——— . 2005v. "Oil sands trigger race for diluent supply", *The Globe and Mail Report on Business* [Toronto] Sep 21 p.3.

——— . 2005w. "Oil sands worth $1.4-trillion, study finds", *The Globe and Mail Report on Business* [Toronto] Sep 30 p.1.

——— . 2005x. "Morgan hands over reins, signals EnCana not for sale", *The Globe and Mail Report on Business* [Toronto] Oct 26 p.1.

——— . 2005y. "Day after Morgan announces step-down, hedge contracts blast EnCana profit", *The Globe and Mail Report on Business* [Toronto] Oct 27 p.1.

——— . 2005z. "Elite club of Alberta oil barons sits on billions in paper riches", *The Globe and Mail Report on Business* [Toronto] Oct 28 p.1.

——— . 2005aa. "CNQ bets $25-billion on oil sands", *The Globe and Mail Report on Business* [Toronto] Nov 03 p.1.

——— . 2005bb. "EnCana outlines bold expansion in the oil sands", *The Globe and Mail Report on Business* [Toronto] Nov 08 p.1.

——— . 2005cc. "Saudi oil- Ample or apocalyptically low?", *The Globe and Mail Report on Business* [Toronto] Nov 15 p.9.

——— and Simon Tuck. 2005dd. "Ottawa set to give Imperial concessions", *The Globe and Mail Report on Business* [Toronto] Nov 18 p.1.

——— . 2005ee. "Imperial Oil to reveal Mackenzie plans" *The Globe and Mail Report on Business* [Toronto] Nov 23 p.7.

——— . 2005ff. "Deep Panuke probably will be a go, Hamm says", *The Globe and Mail Report on Business* [Toronto] Nov 24 p.2.

——— . 2005gg. "Imperial's pipeline plan back on track", *The Globe and Mail Report on Business* [Toronto] Nov 24 .p3.

——— . 2005hh. "Alberta poised for huge drilling rights sale", *The Globe and Mail Report on Business* [Toronto] Dec 12 p.1.

——— . 2006a. "Exploration licenses expire offshore Nova Scotia", *The Globe and Mail Report on Business* [Toronto] Jan 04 p.8.

——— and Dawn Walton. 2006b. "Alberta rejects sour gas wells request", *The Globe and Mail Report on Business* [Toronto] Jan 05 p.1.

——— . 2006c. "EnCana to pay $250,000 for environmental offence", *The Globe and Mail Report on Business* [Toronto] Jan 12 p.18.

——— . 2006d. "New government won't scrap pipeline fund, Imperial says" *The Globe and Mail Report on Business* [Toronto] Jan 16 p.3.

——— . 2006e. "Mackenzie Valley Where Pipe Dreams, Fears Collide", *The Globe and Mail Report on Business* [Toronto] Jan 23 p.1.

——— . 2006f. "India not eyeing oil sands, analyst says", *The Globe and Mail Report on Business* [Toronto] Jan 31 p.7.

——— . 2006g. "TransCanada's Keystone line to ship oil sands crude", *The Globe and Mail Report on Business* [Toronto] Feb 01 p.5.

——— . 2006h. "New battle of Alberta- pipelines", *The Globe and Mail Report on Business* [Toronto] Feb 03 p.3.

———. 2006i. "Natural gas price crunch seen", *The Globe and Mail Report on Business* [Toronto] Mar 28 p1.

———. 2006j. "Penn West nabs Petrofund for $3.1-billion", *The Globe and Mail Report on Business* [Toronto] Apr 18 p.1.

———. 2006k. "Focus Trust buys Profico for $1.1-billion", *The Globe and Mail Report on Business* [Toronto] Apr 25 p.1.

———. 2006l. "EnCana CEO may spin out oil sands unit", *The Globe and Mail Report on Business* [Toronto] Apr 27 p.1.

EDITORIAL. 2005. "Anti-poverty's moon landing", *The Sunday Herald* [Halifax], Dec 11 p.A16.

El-Rashidi, Yasmine. 2005. "In Kuwait, Gush Of Oil Wealth Dulls Economic Change", *The Wall Street Journal* [New York] Nov 04 p.A1.

Engels, Frederick. 189x. *The Origin of the Family, Private Property, and the State* New York, NY: Pathfinder - 1983 ed.

Faucon, Benoît. 2005. "SEC Asks Oil Firms - Especially Major Non-US Competitors - to Disclose Any Commissions Paid in Iran", *The Wall Street Journal* [New York] May 05 p.A2.

"Feed The Goat", *The Globe and Mail Report on Business*, 13 July 2004, p2.

Feynman, Richard P. 1985. *Surely You're Joking, Mr. Feynman!Adventures of a Curious Character* New York, London: W.W. Norton and Company.

———. 1988. *What Do You Care What Other People Think?* New York: London, W.W. Norton and Company.

Fialka, John J. 2005a. "Oil, Coal Lobbyists Mount Attack On Senate Plan To Curb Emissions", *The Wall Street Journal* [New York] Jun 21 p.A4.

———, Russell Gold and Rafael Gerena-Morales. 2005b. "US Releases Oil From Stockpile To Ease Crunch", *The Wall Street Journal* [New York] Sep 01p.A3.

——— and Bhushan Bahree. 2005c. "Congress Weighs Oil-Patch Aid, Military's Role", *The Wall Street Journal* [New York] Sep 27 p.A3.

———. 2005d. "Deal Is Near On Offshore Drilling", *The Wall Street Journal* [New York] Oct 06 p.A3.

———. 2005e. "Oil Executives Could Face Probe Of Their Testimony To Congress", *The Wall Street Journal* [New York] Nov 17 p.A10.

———. 2005f. "New England Braces For Energy Squeeze", *The Wall Street Journal* [New York] Dec 21 p.A4.

———. 2006a. "Coalition Turns On To 'Plug-In Hybrids' ", *The Wall Street Journal* [New York] Jan 25 p.A4.

———. 2006c. "Interior Department Seeks New Offshore Leasing", *The Wall Street Journal* [New York] Feb 09 p.A4.

——— and Jeffrey Ball. 2006b. "Bush's Latest Energy Solution, Like Its Forebears, Faces Hurdles", *The Wall Street Journal* [New York] Feb 02 p.A1.

———. 2006d. "Senators Push For Drilling In Gulf Of Mexico", *The Wall Street Journal* [New York] Feb 17 p.A6.

——— and Chip Cummins. 2006e. "Oil-Firm Merger, Tactic Controls Appear To Advance In The Senate", *The Wall Street Journal* [New York] Mar 15 p.A8.

———. 2006f. "Wildcat Producer Sparks Oil Boom On Montana Plains", *The Wall Street Journal* [New York] Apr 05 p.A1.

——, Russell Gold and Laura Meckler. 2006g. "Bush to Seek Overhaul Of Cars' Fuel-Economy Levels", *The Wall Street Journal* [New York] Apr 28 p.A2.

—— and Laura Meckler. 2006h. "Republicans Plan Series of Votes To Gain Control of Energy Issue", *The Wall Street Journal* [New York] May 11 p.A6.

Fisheries And Offshore Oil Consultative Group FOOCG.1983. "Abandonment of Disused Pipelines" Paper presented at a meeting of the FOOCG subgroup on Pipelines at Aberdeen, October.

Fleay, B.J. 1998. "Climaxing oil: How will transport adapt?", *Chartered Institute of Transport in Australia National Symposium - Proceedings* (Launceston).

Frazer, Sir James George. 1890. *The New Golden Bough* Updated ed. by Theodor H.Gaster published 1964 at NY: Mentor Books.

Freeman, Alan. 2005. "Chrétien uses PMO number for business", *The Globe and Mail* [Toronto] Oct 26 p.A7.

Friedman, Milton J. 1948. "A Monetary and Fiscal Framework for Economic Stability", *American Economic Review*, Vol. 38 3., p.245-64. Reprinted in Friedman, 1953.

——. 1951a. "Some Comments on the Significance of Labor Unions for Economic Policy", in D. McC. Wright, ed., *The Impact of the Union* New York: Harcourt Brace.

——. 1951b. "Commodity-Reserve Currency", *Journal of Political Economy*, Vol. 59, p.203-32. Reprinted in Friedman, 1953.

——. 1953. *Essays in Positive Economics*. Chicago: University of Chicago Press.

——. 1956. "The Quantity Theory of Money: A restatement", in M. Friedman, editor, *Studies in the Quantity Theory of Money*. Chicago: University of Chicago Press. Reprinted in Friedman, 1969.

——. 1957. *A Theory of the Consumption Function*. Princeton, NJ: Princeton University Press.

——. 1958. "The Supply of Money and Changes in Prices and Output", in *The Relationship of Prices to Economic Stability and Growth*. Washington, DC: U.S. Congress, Joint Economic Committee. Reprinted in Friedman, 1969.

——. 1959a. *A Program for Monetary Stability*. New York: Fordham University Press.

——. 1959b. "The Demand for Money: Some theoretical and empirical results", *Journal of Political Economy*, Vol. 67 4., p.327-51.

——. 1961. "The Lag in the Effect of Monetary Policy", *Journal of Political Economy*, Vol. 69, p.447-66. Reprinted in Friedman, 1969.

——. 1962a. *Capitalism and Freedom*. 1977 edition, Chicago: University of Chicago Press.

——. 1962b. "Should There be an Independent Monetary Authority?", in L.B. Yeager, editor, *In Search of a Monetary Constitution*. Cambridge, Mass: Harvard University Press.

——. 1963. *Inflation: Causes and consequences*. New York: Asia Publishing House.

——. 1966a. "Interest Rates and the Demand for Money", *Journal of Law and Economics*, Vol. 9, p.71-85. Reprinted in Friedman, 1969.

——. 1966b. "What Price Guideposts?", in G.P. Schultz, R.Z. Aliber, editors, *Guildelines: Informal controls and the market place*. Chicago: University of Chicago Press.

——. 1968a. "The Role of Monetary Policy", *American Economic Review*, Vol. 58, p.1-17. Reprinted in Friedman, 1969.

——. 1968b. "Money: the Quantity Theory", *International Encyclopedia of the Social Sciences*, p.432-37. Reprinted in Friedman, 1969.

———. 1969. *The Optimum Quantity of Money and Other Essays*. London: Macmillan.

———. 1970a. "Comment on Tobin", *Quarterly Journal of Economics*, Vol. 74, p.318-27.

———. 1970b. "A Theoretical Framework for Monetary Analysis", *Journal of Political Economy*, Vol. 78 2., p.193-238.

———. 1970c. *The Counter-Revolution in Monetary Theory*. London: Institute of Economic Affairs.

———. 1971. "A Monetary Theory of National Income", *Journal of Political Economy*, Vol. 79, p.323-37.

———. 1974a. "Comments on the Critics", in Gordon, 1974.

———. 1974b. *Monetary Correction: A proposal for escalation clauses to reduce the cost of ending inflation*. London: Institute of Economic Affairs.

———. 1976a. "Comments on Tobin and Buiter", in J. Stein, editor, *Monetarism*, Amstedam: North-Holland.

———. 1976b. "Inflation and Unemployment – The Nobel Prize Lecture" 13 December., in Assar Lindbeck, ed., *Nobel Lectures in Economic Sciences 1969-1980* (Stockholm: Stockholm University, 1981.

———. 1977. "Inflation and Unemployment", *Journal of Political Economy*, Vol. 85 3., p.451-72.

———. 1984. "Monetary Policy: Tactics versus strategy", in Moore, editor, *To Promote Prosperity*. Stanford, Calif: Hoover Institute.

———. 1985. "The Case for Overhauling the Federal Reserve", *Challenge*, July/August, p.4-12.

———. 1987. "Quantity Theory of Money", in J. Eatwell, M. Milgate, P. Newman, editors, *The New Palgrave: A dictionary of economics*. London: Macmillan.

——— and R. Friedman. 1980. *Free to Choose: A personal statement*. New York: Harcourt Brace Jovanovich.

——— and D. Meiselman. 1963. "The Relative Stability of Monetary Velocity and the Investment Multiplier in the United States, 1898-1958", in Commission on Money and Credit, *Stabilization Policies*. Englewood Cliffs, NJ: Prentice-Hall.

——— and A.J. Schwartz. 1963. *A Monetary History of the United States, 1867-1960*. 1971 edition, Princeton: Princeton University Press.

——— and A.J. Schwartz. 1963. "Money and Business Cycle", *Review of Economics and Statistics*, Vol. 30, p.32-64.

——— and A.J. Schwartz. 1970. *Monetary Statistics of the United States: Sources, methods*. New York: Columbia University Press.

——— and A.J. Schwartz. 1982. *Monetary Trends in the United States and the United Kingdom: Their relations to income, prices and interest rates, 1876-1975*. Chicago: University of Chicago Press.

——— and A.J. Schwartz. 1986. "Has Government Any Role in Money?", *Journal of Monetary Economics*, Vol. 17 1., pp. 37-62.

Fukuyama, Francis. 1992. *The End of History and the Last Man*. New York: Free Press.

Galbraith, John Kenneth.1967. *The New Industrial State* Boston: Houghton-Mifflin.

Galina, Andrea, ed. 2003. *Globalization and Meso-Regions* Denmark: Roskilde University.

Gallegos, Raul. 2005. "Venezuela's Oil Moves Signal a New Policy", *The Wall Street Journal* [New York] Jun 14 p.A12.

Gaskin, M. ed. 1978. *The Economic Impact of North Sea Oil on Scotland* London UK: Her Majesty's Stationary Office.

George, Susan 1979. *How the Other Half Dies: The Reasons for World Hunger* England:Penguin.

Gever, J., Kaufmann, R., D. Skole, and C. Vorosmarty. 1991. *Beyond Oil*. Boulder: University Press of Colorado.

Gillman, L. and M. Jerison. 1960. *Rings of Continuous Functions* Van Nostrand.

Glazebrook, G.P. deT. 1966. *A History of Canadian External Relations* Toronto: McClelland and Stewart. 2 vols.

Godfrey, David and Douglas Parkhill eds. 1980. *Gutenberg Two: The New Electronics and Social Change* Toronto: Press Porcépic.

Gold, Russell. 2005a. "Boom Town – Drilling for Natural Gas Faces A Sizable Hurdle As Fort Worth, The US's Largest Field, Lies Under 1.6 Million People And Not Everyone - Especially Those Holding No Subsurface Rights - Can Benefit", *The Wall Street Journal* [New York] Apr 29 p.A1.

─────, Matt Pottinger and Dennis K. Berman. 2005b. "China's CNOOC Lobs In Rival $18.5-Billion Bid To Acquire Unocal, Stop Chevron", *The Wall Street Journal* [New York] Jun 23 p.A1.

───── and Greg Hitt. 2005c. "Chevron Labors to Derail Rival's Unocal Bid", *The Wall Street Journal* [New York] Jun 30 p.A4.

─────. 2005d. "In Deal for Unocal, Chevron Gambles On High Oil Prices", *The Wall Street Journal* [New York] Aug 10 p.A1.

───── and Thaddeus L. Herrick. 2005e. "Damage to Oil and Gas Facilities Pushes U.S. Closer to Energy Crisis", *The Wall Street Journal* [New York] Sep 02 p.A1.

───── 2005f. "Big Oil Firms Join Hunt For Natural Gas in US", *The Wall Street Journal* [New York] Nov 29 p.A1.

─────. 2005g. "Bidding War Chills U.S. Plan To Import Gas", *The Wall Street Journal* [New York] Dec 19 p.C1.

─────. 2006. "As Prices Surge, Oil Giants Turn Sludge Into Gold", *The Wall Street Journal* [New York] Mar 27 p.A1.

Goldblatt, Robert. 1998. *Lectures on the hyperreals : an introduction to nonstandard analysis* Springer.

Gongloff, Mark. 2006. "Is 'Dark Matter' in the Deficit? Spackle for Economic Anomalies Looks to Explain How U.S. Operates With Massive Debt", *The Wall Street Journal Online* [New York] Feb 10.

Goulden, Joseph, C. 1968. *Monopoly* New York:Putnam.

Grant, John P. 1978. "The Conflict Between the Fishing and the Oil Industries in the North Sea; A Case Study", *Ocean Management,* 4:137-49. Glasgow: Department of Public International Law, University of Glasgow.

Grare, Frederic and Georges Perkovich. 2006. "Baluchistan", *The Wall Street Journal* [New York] Jan 16 p.A15.

Graveland, Bill. 2005. "Shell seeks to double Athabasca oil sands production" *The Globe and Mail Report on Business* [Toronto] Apr 30 p.2.

Grinnell, H. Rae. 1981. *The Implications of Offshore Petroleum Development for Offshore Atlantic Fisheries: A Social-Economic Overview* Ottawa: Department of Fisheries and Oceans, Economic Research Division.

Gromyko, A.A. et al. 1973. *Soviet Peace Efforts on the Eve of World War II* Moscow: Novosti. 2 vols.

Gunder Frank, Andre. 1969. *Capitalism and Underdevelopment in Latin America: Historical studies of Chile and Brazil* New York, London: Monthly Review Press.

——— . 2000. "Immanuel and Me With-Out Hyphen", in *Journal of World Systems Research*, vol XI, no 2 [Summer/Fall Special Issue: Festchrift for Immanuel Wallerstein – Part I] pp. 216-231.

Hackett, Robert A., Richard Gruneau et al. 2000. *The Missing News:Filters and Blind Spots in Canada's Press* Ontario:Garamond Press.

Hardy, G.H. 1940. *Ramanujan: Twelve Twelve Lectures on Subjects Suggested by His Life and Work* Cambridge UP.

Harris, Michael. 1998. *Lament for an Ocean: The Collapse of the Atlantic Cod Fishery- A True Crime Story*. Toronto: McClelland and Stewart.

Hasbrouck, Joel, George Sofianos and Deborah Sosebee. 1993. "New York Stock Exchange Systems and Trading Procedures", *New York Stock Exchange Working Paper #93-01*. New York: New York University Stern School of Business.

Hausmann, R. and Federico Sturzenegger.2005. "U.S. and global imbalances: Can 'dark matter' prevent a Big Bang?" in Centre for International Development, *Report* Cambridge MA: Harvard University, 30 November.

Hayashi, Yuka. 2005. "China Studies Japan's Mistakes As the Pursuit for Oil Continues", *The Wall Street Journal* [New York] Aug 03 p.A2.

Hayes, Dennis. 1989. *Behind the Silicon Curtain: The Seductions of Work in a Lonely Era* Boston: South End Press.

Heber, Robert W. 1981. "Social Environmental Impacts of Offshore Petroleum Development in Nova Scotia" M.A. Thesis, Institute for Resource and Environmental Studies, Dalhousie University, Halifax.

Hegel, Georg Wilhelm Friedrich. 1833. *The Philosophy of Right*. Berlin.

Heen, Knut. 1984. *Labour Market Behaviour of Fishermen* Tromso NO; Institute of Fisheries, University of Tromso.

Henig, Robin Marantz. 2006. "Looking for the Lie", in *The Sunday New York Times Magazine* New York: The Times Publishing Co., 5 February.

Henwood, Douglas. 2005. "The long strange career of Jeffrey D. Sachs", *Left Business Observer* (Number 111, August).

Herrick, Thaddeus L. 2005a. "As Oil Tops $60, What's Next", *The Wall Street Journal* [New York] Jun 28 p.C1.

——— . 2005b. "Refiners Upgrade Oil Processing, Not the Capacity", *The Wall Street Journal* [New York] Aug 04 p.A2.

——— , Bhushan Bhahree and Keith Johnson. 2005c. "US Resists Building Refineries As Overseas Firms Move Ahead", *The Wall Street Journal* [New York] Dec 28 p.A2.

Hickman T. Alex 1984. *Royal Commsion Report on the Ocean Ranger Marine Disaster.*
Ottawa: Canada Supply and Services.Hobson, John A. 1902. *Imperialism* London.

Higgins, Andrew. 2005a. "Democracy Project In Bahrain Falters; Gulf Kingdom Reverses Course", *The Wall Street Journal* [New York] May 11 p.A1.

——— . 2005b. "As Oil Riches Gush, a Sheik Loosens His Grip on Economy", *The Wall Street Journal* [New York] Oct 21 p.A1.

———. 2005c. "Oil-Rich Norway Hires Philosopher As Moral Compass", *The Wall Street Journal* [New York] Dec 01 p.A1.

Higham, Charles 1983. *Trading With The Enemy: The Nazi-American Money Plot 1933-1949.* New York: Delacorte.

Hilferding, Rudolf. 1910. *Das Finanzkapital – Eine Studie über die jüngste Entwicklung des Kapitalismus* [Finance Capital: A study in the latest development of capitalism]. Vienna.

Hill, Robert H.1983. *The Social Context of Work and the Reality of Unemployment in Newfoundland Society.* St. John's NL: Community Services Council of Newfoundland and Labrador.

Hilsenrath, Jon E. 2005a. "Energy Network Is Further Strained", *The Wall Street Journal* [New York] Aug 31 p.A5.

———. 2005b. "Novel Way to Assess School Competition Stirs Academic Row", *The Wall Street Journal* [New York] Oct 24 p.A1.

Hobbes, Thomas. 1651. *The Leviathan* London, 1st ed.

Holland, W. J. 2000. *The Navy.* Washington DC: Naval Historical Foundation.

House, J. D.1985. *The Challenge of Oil: Newfoundland's Quest for Controlled Development.* St. John's NL: Institute of Social and Economic Research, Memorial University of Newfoundland.

———, ed. 1986. *Fish vs Oil: Resources and Rural Development in North Atlantic Societies* St. John's NL: Institute of Social and Economic Research, Social and Economic Papers Series No. 16, Memorial University of Newfoundland.

Howlett Karen. 2005a. "New Brunswick Premier seeks national nuclear plan", *The Globe and Mail* [Toronto] Aug 10 p.A4.

———. 2005b. "Energy rebates withheld- Regulator keeps $570-million it owes electricity users, but money will cushion coming rate" *The Globe and Mail* [Toronto] Nov 17 p.A9.

Hunt, Michael H. 1983. *The Making of a Special Relationship: The United States and China to 1914.* New York: Columbia UP.

Hunter, G. L.1976. "Fisheries and Oil", in John Button ed., *The Shetland Way of Oil* Sandwick, Shetland: Thuleprint Limited.

Immen, Wallace. 2005. "Oil patch turnaround uncorks a gusher of jobs", *The Globe and Mail Report on Business* [Toronto] May 21 p.9.

Inhaber, H., and Saunders, H. 1994. "Road to Nowhere", *The Sciences*, Vol. 34, No. 6, November/December 1994.

Innis, Harold A. 1962. *Essays in Canadian Economic History* Toronto: University of Toronto Press.

———. 1954. *The Cod Fishery* Toronto: U of T Press.

———. 1930. *The Fur Trade in Canada* Toronto: U of T Press.

Ip, Greg. 2005. "Will Katrina Cause The Fed to Pause", *The Wall Street Journal* [New York] Sep 01 p.A2.

Irvine, W. 1955. *Apes, Angels, and Victorians: The Story of Darwin, Huxley, and Evolution.* McGraw-Hill, New York.

Islam, M.R., S. Sevgur and T. Lay. 2002. "An Accurate And Remotely Accessible Lie-Detection Machine" [Draft Research Proposal – from M.R. Islam's files].

Islam, M.R. 2003. *Revolution in Education.* Halifax [Canada]: EEC Research Group.

——— . 2005. "Unraveling The Mysteries Of Chaos And Change: The Knowledge-Based Technology Development", *Proceeding of the First International Conference on Modeling, Simulation and Applied Optimization.* Sharjah, U.A.E.: 1-3 February.

Islam, M.R., 2005b. "Knowledge-Based Technologies For The Information Age", JICEC05-Keynote speech, *Jordan International Chemical Engineering Conference V.* Amman, Jordan: JICEC'05, Sep 12-15.

——— and G.M. Zatzman. 2004a. "A New Energy Pricing Model", *MPC 2004* Tripoli [Libya]: International Energy Foundation, February.

——— and G.M. Zatzman. 2005a. "A New Energy Pricing Model: The escalating failure of neoclassical economic models and some possible implications for future relations between the Dollar and the Euro", *CSCE 2005* Toronto: Canadian Society of Civil Engineers 33rd Annual Meeting, June.

——— and G.M. Zatzman. 2005b. "A New Energy Pricing Model: Exploring the evolving relationship between international reserve currencies and global shifts in access to and control over strategic energy resources", *ICERD-3.* Kuwait: 3rd International Conference on Energy Research and Development, November.

——— and G.M. Zatzman. 2006. "Natural Gas Pricing", in S. Mokhatab, J.G. Speight and and W.A. Poe, edd., *Handbook of Natural Gas Transmission and Processing* (Elsevier).

——— , G.M. Zatzman and R. Shapiro. 2006. "The Energy Crunch: What More Lies Ahead", in M. Masood, *Global Dialogue on Energy.* No. 2 in a series, convened 3-4 April in Washington DC at the Centre for Strategic and International Studies.

Iverson, Noel and D. Ralph Mathews 1968. *Communities in Decline: An Examination of Household Resettlement in Newfoundland* St. John's: Newfoundland Institute of Social and Economic Research.

Jenkins, Holman W., Jr. 2005. "The Real 'Oil Crisis' ", *The Wall Street Journal* [New York] Dec 28 p. A15.

——— . 2006. " 'Le Gazprom' " *The Wall Street Journal* [New York] Mar 15 p.A23.

Jevons, W. Stanley. 1865. *The Coal Question* London.

——— . 1870. *Theory of Political Economy* London.

Johnson, Avery. 2005. "Hotel Industry Awakening To Bedbug Problem; With Pesticides Out of Favor, Critters Show Up More; A 1920s Cure = Gasoline", *The Wall Street Journal* [New York] Apr 21 p.A1.

Johnson, H.G. 1971. "The Keynesian Revolution and the Monetarist Counter-Revolution", *American Economic Review*, Vol 2, pp.1-14.

Johnson, Keith.2006. "Spain Looks Set To Clear Gas Natural-Endesa Deal", *The Wall Street Journal* [New York] Feb 02 p.A6.

Johnson, Mark. 2005. "Ethanol burns more than it saves- study", *The Globe and Mail Report on Business* [Toronto] Jul 18 p.6.

Jones, Jeffrey. 2006. "India To Invest $1-Billion In Oil Sands", *The Globe And Mail Report On Business* [Toronto] Feb 01 p.5.

Kaldor, N. 1982. *The Scourge of Monetarism* Oxford: Oxford University Press.

Kato, Hiromi. 2005. "Effects of the Oil Price Upsurge on the World Economy", *Journal of the Institute of Energy Economics Japan* [December].

Keisler, H Jerome.1976. *Elementary Calculus* Boston MA: Prindle, Weber and Schmidt.

Kennedy, Peter. 2005. "Ottawa to review US takeover of Terasen", *The Globe and Mail* [Toronto] Oct 21 p.S1.

Kermisch, Ron and Paul Smith. 2005. "Telecom's Other 'Merger'", *The Wall Street Journal* [New York] May 17 p.C1.

Keynes, J.M. Lord. 1936.The General Theory of Employment, Interest and Money. London: Macmillan Cambridge UP.

Khan, M.I., A.B. Chhetri and M.R. Islam. 2005a. Community-Based Energy Model: A Novel Approach in Developing Sustainable Energy [in press].

―――, G.M. Zatzman and M.R. Islam. 2005b. "A Novel Sustainability Criterion as Applied in Developing Technologies and Management Tools", *Jordan International Chemical Engineering Conference V.* Amman, Jordan: JICEC'05, Sep 12-15.

―――, A.B. Chhetri and M.R. Islam. 2006. "Analyzing sustainability of community-based energy development technologies", *Energy Sources*: in press.

――― and M.R. Islam. 2006. *Achieving True Sustainability in Technological Development and Natural Resources Management.* New York: Nova Science Publishers [in press].

Khan, M.M. and M.R. Islam. 2004. "Down-hole separation of petroleum fluids", *J. Petroleum Science and Technology* [in press].

―――, D. Prior, and M. R. Islam. 2005a. "Zero-waste living with inherently sustainable technologies", *Jordan International Chemical Engineering Conference V.* Amman, Jordan: JICEC'05, Sep 12-15.

―――, A. R. Mills, M.Y. Mehedi, O. Chaalal and M.R. Islam. 2005b. "Bioabsorbents for the removal of heavy metals from aqueous streams", *Jordan International Chemical Engineering Conference V.* Amman, Jordan: JICEC'05, Sep 12-15.

―――, D. Prior, and M. R. Islam. 2005d. "Direct-usage solar refrigeration: from irreversible thermodynamics to sustainable engineering", *Jordan International Chemical Engineering Conference V.* Amman, Jordan: JICEC'05, Sep 12-15.

―――, 2006. Personal communication, Department of Civil and Resource Engineering, Dalhousie University, Halifax, Feb 10.

Khazanie, Ramakant 1976. *Basic Probability Theory and Applications* Pacific Palisades: California, Goodyear, Pacific Palisades, California.

Kilby, Jack. 2000. "Turning Potential Into Realities: The Invention of the Integrated Circuit - The Nobel Lecture" (8 December), in Ekspong, Gösta, ed. 2003. *Nobel Lectures in Physics 1996-2000.* Singapore: World Scientific Publishers. pp.474-485.

King, Neil Jr., Greg Hitt and Jeffrey Ball. 2005. "Oil Battle Sets Showdown Over China", *The Wall Street Journal* [New York] Jun 24 p.A1.

Kirby, Michael J. 1982. *Navigating Troubled Waters: Report of the Task Force on Atlantic Fisheries*, Chairman. Ottawa: Supply and Services Canada.

Klein, Naomi. 2002. *No Logo.*

Kline, Morris 1972. *Mathematical Thought from Ancient to Modern Times* New York: Oxford University Press.

Kondratieff, N. 1935. "The Long Waves in Economic Life", *Review of Economic Statistics* Vol XVII, No 6 - November.

Koring, Paul. 2006. "US 'Addicted To Oil,' Bush Concedes", *The Globe And Mail* [Toronto] Feb 01 p.A1.

Kranhold, Kathryn And John M Biers. 2005. "GE In Talks to Buy Technology For Offshore Oil, Gas Production", *The Wall Street Journal* [New York] Aug 01 p.A2.

Kumar, Himendra. 2005. "India Rejects Plan To Buy Stake In Nigeria Oil Field", *The Wall Street Journal* [New York] Dec 19 p.A15Larkin, John. 2005. "Oil-Well Fire in

'Bombay High' Oil Field Complicates Indian Energy Picture", *The Wall Street Journal* [New York] Jul 28 p.A9.

Kunstler, James Howard. 2004. "The Long Emergency: What's going to happen as we start running out of cheap gas to guzzle?", in *Rolling Stone* [New York], Mar 24.

Kuznets, Simon. 1971. "Modern Economic Growth: Findings and Reflections – The Nobel Prize Lecture" 11 December., in Assar Lindbeck, ed., *Nobel Lectures in Economic Sciences 1969-1980* Stockholm: Stockholm University, 1981.

Lipson, Michael. 1999. "The Reincarnation Of Cocom: Explaining Post-Cold War Export Controls", *The Nonproliferation Review* [Winter] pp. 33-51. Monterey CA: Monterey Institute of International Studies.

Lange, Oskar. 1938. *On the Economic Theory of Socialism*. Minneapolis: University of Minnesota.

Leontieff, W. 1973. "Structure of the World Economy: Outline of a Simple Input-Output Formulation Reflections – The Nobel Prize Lecture" 11 December. in Assar Lindbeck, ed., *Nobel Lectures in Economic Sciences 1969-1980* Stockholm: Stockholm University, 1981.

Lenin, V.I. 1916. *Imperialism, The Highest Stage of Capitalism* Peking: Foreign Language Press – 1975 ed.

Levine, Steve, Christopher Cooper and Michael Corkery. 2005. "Katrina's Oily Wake", *The Wall Street Journal* [New York] Sep 12 p.B1.

——— and Jeffrey Ball. 2006. "Exxon's Reliance On Qatar Field Raises Concerns", *The Wall Street Journal* [New York] Feb 16 p.A2.

Lewis, T.M. And I.H. Mcnicoll. 1978. *North Sea Oil and Scotland's Economic Prospects* London: Croon Helm.

Lienhard, John H. 2000. *The Engines of Our Ingenuity: An Engineer Looks at Technology and Culture* Oxford UP.

Lindbeck, Assar, ed. 1981. *Nobel Lectures in Economic Sciences 1969-1980* Stockholm: Stockholm University.

Linebaugh, Kate, Matt Pottinger, Greg Hitt and Jason Singer. 2005. "After Earlier Fumbles, Cnooc Uses Wall Street Tactics in Unocal Bid", *The Wall Street Journal* [New York] Jun 27 p.A1.

Luhnow, David and Geraldo Samor. 2006a. "As Brazil Fills Up on Ethanol, It Weans Off Energy Imports", *The Wall Street Journal* [New York] Jan 09 pA1.

———. 2006b. "How Brazil Broke Its Oil Habit", *The Wall Street Journal* [New York] Feb 06 pA9.

———. 2006c. "Mexico's Oil Output May Decline Sharply", *The Wall Street Journal* [New York] Feb 09 pA4.

——— and Peter Millard. 2006d. "Chávez Plans to Take More Control Of Oil Away From Foreign Firms", *The Wall Street Journal* [New York] Apr 24 pA1.

——— and José De Córdoba. 2006e. "Bolivia Seizes Natural-Gas Fields In a Show of Energy Nationalism", *The Wall Street Journal* [New York] May 02 pA1.

Lyons, John. 2006. "Panama Takes Step Toward Expanding The Canal", *The Wall Street Journal* [New York] Apr 24 p.A8.

Macgillivray, Don and Brian Tennyson 1981. *Cape Breton Historical Essays* Nova Scotia: College of Cape Breton Press.

Mackay, R.A. 1971. *Canadian Foreign Policy 1945-1954: Selected Speeches and Documents* Toronto:McClelland and Stewart.

Macpherson, C.Brough. 1967. *The Real World of Democracy* Toronto: CBC.

———. 1964. *The Political Theory of Possessive Individualism* Oxford: Oxford UP.

Maher, Kris. 2005. "Making Out Like Bandits As Oil Price Hikes Push Coal from $30 to $50 a Ton", *The Wall Street Journal* [New York] May 05 p.A2.

Mahoney, Jill. 2005. "Canada's added girth a growing concern", *The Globe and Mail* [Toronto], Dec 10.

Malthus, Thomas. 1798. *Essay on Population* London.

Marshall, Alfred. 1890. *Principles of Economics* London: Macmillan.

Martinez, Michael J. 2006. "Mixed Data Could Keep Stock Market Murky", *Associated Press* Business Wire, filed Sunday, Feb 05 at 17:01 ET.

Marx, K. 1892. *Capital: A Critique of Political Economy Vol. III* London, Edited by Frederick Engels.

———. 1883. *Capital: A Critique of Political Economy Vol. II* London, Edited by Frederick Engels.

———. 1867. *Capital: A Critique of Political Economy Vol. I* London, English ed translated from the German by Samuel Aveling.

———. 1859. *A Contribution to the Critique of Political Economy.* English ed. Chicago: Charles H. Kerr, 1918.

Massachusetts Institute Of Technology MIT.1973. *The Georges Bank Petroleum Study* Cambridge MA: Offshore Oil Task Group - Vol.1.

McCarthy, Shawn. 2005a. "Oil price seen sparking alternatives", *The Globe and Mail Report on Business* [Toronto] May 21 p.4.

———. 2005b. "IEA turns on the oil reserves taps", *The Globe and Mail Report on Business* [Toronto] Sep 03 p.24.

———. 2006. "Exxon Plays Hardball – And Hebron One Example", *The Globe And Mail Report On Business* [Toronto] Apr 17 p.1.

McChesney, Robert W. 2004. *The Problem of the Media: U.S Communication Politics in the 21st Century* New York: Monthly Review Press.

McCloy, John J., Nathan W. Pearson and Beverley Matthews. 1976. *The Great Oil Spill.* New York: Chelsea House.

McDonald, Joe. 2005. "The man at the heart of CNOOC's quest", *The Globe and Mail Report on Business* [Toronto] Jun 30 p.15.

McKenna, Barrie and Patrick Brethour. 2005a. "Katrina hits refineries; strategic reserves tapped", *The Globe and Mail Report on Business* [Toronto] Sep 01 p.1.

———. 2005b. "Race for Arctic pipeline heats up for Canada, US", *The Globe and Mail Report on Business* [Toronto] Oct 08 p.6.

———. 2005c. "Canada- Energy Nation", *The Globe and Mail Report on Business* [Toronto] Dec 15 p.1.

McKinnon, John D, John J Fialka and Jeffrey Ball.2006??. "Bush Takes Steps To Expand Oil Supplies", *The Wall Street Journal* [New York] Apr 26 p.A4.

McKinnon, Mark. 2005. "The great Caspian Sea adventure-bubble", *The Globe and Mail Report on Business* [Toronto] May 24 p.6.

McLean, Catherine. 2005. "Kinder Morgan enters oil sands with $3-billion Terasen purchase", *The Globe and Mail Report on Business* [Toronto] Aug 02 p.1.

McLuhan, H. Marshall. 1964. *Understanding Media: the Extensions of Man* New York: Signet, New American Library.

———. 1969. *The Gutenberg Galaxy* New York: Signet - New American Library.

Mcnicoll, I.H. 1980 "The Impact of Oil on the Shetland Economy" *Managerial and Decision Economics,* 12.

———. 1982 "Ex-Post Appraisal of an Input-Output Forecast" *Urban Studies,* 19:397-404.

——— and G. Walter.1971. *The Shetland Economy 1976-1977* Lerwick: Shetland Islands Council.

McQuaig, Linda. 2004. *It's the Crude, Dude: War, Big Oil, and the Fight for the Planet.* Toronto-New York: Doubleday.

Melzak, Z.A. 1983. *Bypasses: A Simple Approach to Complexity* Toronto:Wiley,.

Menger, Carl. 1871. *Principles of Economics* Vienna.

Mikesell, R.F., William H. Bartsch *et al.*1971. *Foreign Investment in the Petroleum and Mineral Industries* Baltimore MD: John Hopkins Press for Resources for the Future.

Millard, Peter. 2005. "Exxon Resists Venezuelan Contract Overhaul", *The Wall Street Journal* [New York] Dec 20 p.A12.

———. 2006. "Venezuela To Raise Tax On Foreign Firms In Orinoco Oil Field", *The Wall Street Journal* [New York] Mar 15 p.A8.

Mills, C. Wright. 1951. *White Collar: The American Middle Classes.* New York: Oxford UP.

———. 1956. *The Power Elite.* New York: Oxford UP.

Mittelstaedt, Martin. 2005. "Pollution Debate Born Of Chemical Valley's Girl-Baby Boom", *The Globe And Mail* [Toronto] Nov 15 p.A3.

Mobil Oil Canada Limited. 1983. *Venture Development Project Environmental Impact Statement* Halifax. Submitted to the Government of Canada and Province of Nova Scotia.

Moore, Barrington, Jr. 1967. *Social Origins of Dictatorship and Democracy: Lord and Peasant in the Making of the Modern World* Boston: Beacon Press.

Moore, Oliver. 2005. "US House Drops Plans To Drill In Arctic Refuge", *The Globe And Mail* [Toronto] Nov 10 p.A1.

Morgan, Bernice. 1992. *Random Passage.* St. John's: Breakwater Books.

Morgan, Dan, 1980. *Merchants of Grain* New York:Penguin.

Mosselmans, Bert.1999. "Reproduction and Scarcity: the Population Mechanism in Classicism and in the 'Jevonian Revolution'", *The European Journal of the History of Economic Thought* Vol. 6, No. 1 Spring 1999.

Mufson, Steven and Shailagh Murray. 2006. "Profits, Prices Spur Oil Outrage", Washington Post [Washington DC] Apr 28 p.A01.

Mullens, Brody. 2005a. "Senate Overwhelmingly Passes Energy Bill Long Sought by Bush", *The Wall Street Journal* [New York] Jun 29 p.A2.

———. 2005b. "White House Backs Oil Firms' Attempt To Avoid New Tax", *The Wall Street Journal* [New York] Nov 18 p.A6.

Mustafiz, S., A. Basu, A. Dewaidar, O. Chaalal, and M.R. Islam. 2002. "A Novel Method for Heavy Metal Removal from Aqueous Streams", from: S. Mustafiz, MASc thesis, Dalhousie University, Canada.

Myers, Ransom A. and Boris Worm. 2003. "Rapid worldwide depletion of predatory fish communities", *Nature* v.423: 280-283 [May 15].

Myrden, Judy. 2006a. "Marauder to hunt for natural gas off coast", *The Chronicle Herald*, [Halifax] Oct 04 p.C1.

———. 2006b. "Will Sable still be able? Dalhousie professor says time is running out for natural gas project", *The Chronicle-Herald*, [Halifax] Jan 09 p.C1.

———. 2006c. "Offshore may see delays; Industry study suggests LNG supplies could hinder projects", *The Chronicle-Herald*, [Halifax] Feb 09 pC1.

———. 2006d. "Goldboro project gets a lift", *TheChronicleHerald* [Halifax] Mar 21p.C1.

———. 2006e. "More than just pipe dreams; Region has LNG advantages, but must adapt to needs of rapidly changing industry", *The Chronicle-Herald* [Halifax] Apr 10 p.C1.

Nadesan, S. 1993. *A History of the Up-Country Tamil People in Sri Lanka* Sri Lanka: Ranko Printers and Publishers.

Naylor, Tom. 1975a. *The History of Canadian Business 1867 -1914-Vol I: the Banks and Finance Capital* Totonto: Lorimer.

———. 1975b. *The History of Canadian Business 1867-1914-Vol II: Industrial Development* Toronto: Lorimer.

Neidorf, Robert 1967. *Deductive Forms : An Elementary Logic* New York: Harper and Row.

New England River Basin Commission Reports NERBC/RALI. 1976. *Onshore Facilities Related to Offshore Oil and Gas Development: Estimates for New England* Boston MA.

Newton, Sir Isaac.1687. *Mathematical Principles of Natural Philosophy* [1729 translation of *Principia Mathematica* from Latin original, by Andrew Motte] London.

Nicolson, J.R. 1975. *Shetland and Oil* London: William Luscombe.

NORDCO. 1981a. *"It Were Well to Live Mainly Off Fish": The Place of the Northern.*
Cod in Newfoundland's Development. St. John's NL.

———. 1981b. *A Study of the Potential Social-Economic Effects on the Newfoundland Fishing Industry from Offshore Petroleum Development* Prepared for the East Coast Petroleum Operators Association IEPOA, St. John's, NL.

———.1981c. "Fisheries Utilization in Eastern and Southern Newfoundland: An Assessment of the Impact of the Hibemia Development in the Period 1980-1990" *Report of the Fisheries Component - Environmental Impact Statement* Prepared for Mobil Oil Canada Ltd., St. John's NL.

———.1983. *A Study of the Potential Socio-Economic Effects Upon the Nova Scotia Fishery from Offshore Petroleum Development* St. John's NL.

———.1984 "The Newfoundland Fishery and an Assessment of Possible Impacts Associated with the Hibernia Development" *Background Report for the Hibernia EIS* St. John's NL.

Odum, H.T. 1971. *Environment, Power, and Society.* New York: Wiley-Interscience.

——— and E.C. 1981. *Energy Basis for Man and Nature.* New York: McGraw Hill. and Co.

O'Grady, Mary Anastasia. 2005 "Bolivarian Revolution = 'Cubanization' of Latin America", *The Wall Street Journal* [New York] Apr 29 p.A17.

Ohtsuki, H. C. Hauert, E. Lieberman and M. A. Nowak. 2006. "A simple rule for the evolution of cooperation on graphs and social networks", in *Nature* 441: 502-505 (25 May).

Okun, Arthur M. 1981. *Prices and Quantities: A macroeconomic analysis* Washington, DC: Brookings Institution.

Parenti, Michael 1996. *Dirty Truths: Reflections on Politics, Media, Ideology, Conspiracy, Ethnic Life and Class Power* San Francisco: City Lights.

Parkinson, Dave. 2005. "Road to 10,000 on TSX index greased with oil", *The Globe and Mail Report on Business* [Toronto] Jun 23 p.1.

Partridge, John. 2005a. "Fairbank wells in Ontario still pumping after all these years", *The Globe and Mail* [Toronto] May 21 pA1.

———. 2005b. "Sustained high prices redraw Canada's regional economic map", *The Globe and Mail Report on Business* [Toronto] May 21 p.18.

———. 2005c. "Loonie's rise greased as world is lured to new petro-currency", *The Globe and Mail Report on Business* [Toronto] Aug 12 p.1.

Patinkin, Don. 1956. *Money, Interest and Prices: An integration of monetary and value theory* New York: Harper and Row - 1965 edition.

———. 1969. "The Chicago Tradition, the Quantity Theory and Friedman", *Journal of Money, Credit and Banking*, Vol. 1, pp.46-70.

———. 1972. "Friedman on the Quantity Theory and Keynesian Economics", *Journal of Political Economy*, Vol. 80, pp. 883-905.

———. 1981. *Essays On and In the Chicago Tradition*. Durham, NC: Duke University Press.

Pearson, Karl W.1892. *The Grammar of Science*. London: Walter Scott.

Perkins, John. 2004. *Confessions of an Economic Hit-Man*. San Francisco: Berrett-Koehler.

Petras, James and Henry Veltmeyer. 2001. *Globalization Unmasked: Imperialism ikn the 21st Century* Halifax [Canada]: Fernwood.

Petty, William. 1678. *Politicall Arithmetick* London.

———. 1662. *A Treatise of Taxes and Contributions* London.

Phillips, A.W. 1958. "The Relation between Unemployment and the Rate of Change of Money Wage Rates in the United Kingdom, 1861-1957", *Economica*, Vol. 25, pp. 283-99.

Pigou, A.C. 1933. *The Theory of Unemployment* London: Macmillan.

Pittman, Todd. 2005. "US turns an eye to oil-rich Gulf of Guinea", *The Globe and Mail Report on Business* [Toronto] Aug 08 p.5.

Pitts, Gordon.2006. "Taking A Stand- How One CEO Gained Respect", *The Globe And Mail Report On Business* [Toronto] Jan 31 p.8.

Pocock, J.G.A. 1957. *The Ancient Constitution and the Feudal Law: A Study of English Historical Thought in the Seventeenth Century*. Cambridge UK: Cambridge University Press.

Polya, George 1981. *Mathematical Discovery: On Understanding, Learning, and Teaching Problem Solving* Toronto: Wiley.

Pottinger, Matt. 2005a. "Cnooc's Fu Shows Complex Trends In Chinese Firms", *The Wall Street Journal* [New York] Jun 24 p.C4.

———. 2005b. "Aramco Discusses A Second Project Based in China", *The Wall Street Journal* [New York] Jul 12 p.A2.

Prior, D., M.M. Khan, M.R. Islam and F. Taheri. 2005. "A novel oil-spill cleanup barge", *Jordan International Chemical Engineering Conference V.* Amman, Jordan: JICEC'05, Sep 12-15.

Prowse, D.W. 1896. *A History of Newfoundland*. London: Eyre and Spottiswoode.

Quesnay, François. 1766. "Analyse de la formule arithmétique du Tableau Economique de la distribution des dépenses annuelles d'une Nation agricole", *Journal de l'agriculture, du commerce et des finances* Paris.

Radowitz, Bernd. 2006. "Brazil, Argentina and Venezuela Set $9.2 Million Plan For Study Of Gas Line", *The Wall Street Journal* [New York] Mar 13 p.A8.

Rahman, M.H, M.N.Wasiuddin and M.R. Islam. 2004. "Experimental and Numerical Modeling Studies of Arsenic Removal with Wood Ash from Aqueous Streams", Vol. 82: 968-977.

Rahman, S., 2006. Personal communication, Dalhousie University, Halifax, Mar 02.

Rampton, Sheldon and John Stauber. 2002. *Trust Us, We're Experts*. New York: Tarcher [Penguin USA].

——— . 2003. *Weapons of Mass Deception*. New York: Tarcher [Penguin USA].

Ricardo, David.1817. *On the Principles of Political Economy and Taxation*. London: John Murray,.

Richer, Shawna. 2005. "Cape Bretoners look forward to return of smaller King Coal at Donkin Mine", *The Globe and Mail Report on Business* [Toronto] Jul 06 p.1.

Riesman, David. 1950. *The Lonely Crowd: A Study of the Changing American Character*. London and New Haven: Yale UP.

Robinson, Abraham.1966. *Nonstandard Analysis* Princeton UP.

Robbins, Carla Anne. 2006. "West Talks Tough With Iran, Treads Lightly", *The Wall Street Journal* [New York] Jan 23 p.A4.

Rogers, Raymond A. 1995. *The Oceans Are Emptying: Fish Wars and Sustainability* Montreal: Black Rose Books.

Rosie, G. 1975. *The Scramble for Oil* Edinburgh: Canongate.

Rostow, W.W. 1960. *The Stages of Economic Growth: A Non-Communist Manifesto*. Cambridge UP.

Samor, Geraldo. 2006a. "Brazil's Petrobras- Self-Reliant Or Pliant", *The Wall Street Journal* [New York] Apr 21 p.A7.

——— . 2006b. "Brazil's Petrobras Halts Investment Planned In Bolivia", *The Wall Street Journal* [New York] May 04 p.A4.

Sampson, Anthony. 1976. *The Seven Sisters: The Great Oil Companies and the World They Shaped* New York:Viking/Bantam.

——— . 1978. *The Arms Bazaar: The Companies, The Dealers, the Bribes: from Vickers to Lockheed* Great Britain: Hodder and Stoughton.

——— . 1981. *The Money Lenders: Bankers in a Dangerous World* Great Britain: Hodder and Stoughton.

Samuelson, Paul A. 1970. "Maximum Principles in Analytical Economics – The Nobel Prize Lecture" 11 December 1970., in Assar Lindbeck, ed., *Nobel Lectures in Economic Sciences 1969-1980* Stockholm: Stockholm University, 1981.

——— and Robert M. Solow. 1960. "Analytical Aspects of Anti-Inflation Policy", *American Economic Review*, Vol. 50 2., pp.177-94.

Sayers, Michael and Albert E. Kahn. 1947. *The Great Conspiracy*. New York: Boni and Gaer.

Scheer, Robert. 1982. *With Enough Shovels: Reagan, Bush and Nuclear War* New York: Random House.

Schierow, Linda-Jo. 2001. *The Role of Risk Analysis and Risk Management in Environmental Protection* (Congressional Research Service - Resources, Science, and Industry Division, Sep 6 - B94036).

Schumpeter, Joseph. 1939. *Business Cycles: A Theoretical, Historical and Statistical Analysis of the Capitalist Process* New York: McGraw-Hill.

Schwartzkopff, Frances and Benoît Faucon. 2005. "Kerr-McGee to Sell North Sea Assets", *The Wall Street Journal* [New York] Aug 09 p.C4.

Scoffield, Heather, Gordon Pitts and Greg Keenan. 2006. "Manufacturing Change: At The Crossroads, Adapt Or Perish", *The Globe And Mail Report On Business* [Toronto] Apr 27 p.8.

Shahed, Kalam 2002. *Ethnic Movements and Hegemony in South Asia* Bangladesh: Hakkani Publishers.

Shapiro, Rhoda. 2006. Personal communication about e-mail correspondence with Bradmans editor Michael Keating.

Shockley, William J. 1956. "Transistor technology evokes new physics – Nobel Lecture 11 December", in in *Nobel Lectures, Physics 1942-1962*. Amsterdam: Elsevier [1964].

Silver, Sara, Shawn Young and Leila Abboud. 2006. "Alcatel's Merger With Lucent Stirs Culture Questions; Paris-Based Giant Will Get American CEO, but French May Exert Greater Influence", *The Wall Street Journal* [New York] Apr 03 p.A1.

Simons, Geoff. 1994. *Iraq: From Sumer to Saddam* (London: St. Martins Press).

Simpson, Glenn R and David Crawford. 2006a. "US Investigates Critical Supplier Of Russian Gas", *The Wall Street Journal* [New York] Apr 2 p.A6.

———. 2006b. "Proliferation☐Of 'Shell' Companies☐Arouses Scrutiny", *The Wall Street Journal* Apr 25 p.A4.

Smith, Adam. 1776. *An Inquiry into the Nature and Causes of the Wealth of Nations* (Edinburgh).

Smith, Graeme. 2006. "Ottawa To Push For Gas Deal Between Petrocan, Gazprom", *The Globe and Mail Report on Business* [Toronto] Feb 13 p.1.

Smith, Rebecca. 2005. "California Takes Steps To Prevent Utility Shutoffs", *The Wall Street Journal* [New York] Oct 28 p.C4.

Solomon, Jay and Neil King Jr. 2005. "Iran Pipeline Complicates South Asia Policy", *The Wall Street Journal* [New York] Jun 24 p.A4.

Solow, Robert M. 1978. "Summary and Evalution", in *After the Phillips Curve: Persistence of high inflation and high unemployment* Boston: Federal Reserve.

Seed, T. 2006. "A Media of Progress, Enlightenment and Freedom is Possible", in Seed, T. et al. *Media and Disinformation – The Last Ten Years*. Halifax: New Media [in press].

Spencer, Herbert. 1857. "Progess: Its Law and Causes", *The Westminster Review*, Vol 67 (April), pp 445-447, 451, 454-456, 464-65.

Sraffa, P. 1960. *Production of Commodities by Means of Commodities*. Cambridge: Cambridge University Press.

Stackhouse, John. 2005 "The new energy shock", *The Globe and Mail Report on Business* [Toronto] May 21 p.3.

Stalin, Joseph V. 1952. *Economic Problems of Socialism in the USSR*. Moscow: International Publishers.

Stecklow, Steve. 2006. "Did A Group Financed By Exxon Prompt IRS To Audit Greenpeace", *The Wall Street Journal* [New York] Mar 21 p.A1.

Stevenson, James. 2006. "Hebron Partners Suspend Project As Talks With Newfoundland 'Stall'", *The Chronicle-Herald* [Halifax], Apr 04 p.E6.

Stiglitz, Joseph E., "Information and the Change in the Paradigm in Economics" [Prize Lecture 8 December 2001], in Frängsmyr, Tore, ed. 2002. *Les prix Nobel – The Nobel Prizes* Stockholm, Nobel Foundation. 472:540.

Stockdale, Scott 2003. *History's Greatest Fraud: German External Loan 1924* Light Years Communications Brantford Ontario ISBN 0-9732118-0-6.

Stonehouse, David. 2005. "Fears of supertankers plowing through the vista", *The Globe and Mail* [Toronto]Oct 11 p.A1.

Stueck, Wendy. 2005. "Soaring coal prices energise western Canadian output, shipments", *The Globe and Mail Report on Business* [Toronto] Apr 06 p.1.

Subrahmaniyan, Nesa. 2005. "China plans $3-billion refinery expansion", *The Globe and Mail Report on Business* [Toronto] Jun 20 p.8.

Sumerlin, Marc. 2006. "The Upside Of The Oil Curse", *The Wall Street Journal* [New York] Jan 10 p.A14.

Taber, Jane. 2005. "PM scolds Harper, Klein on US trade spat", *The Globe and Mail* [Toronto] Oct 13 p.A6.

Talley, Ian. 2006. "Oil Lubricates Oslo Bourse" *The Wall Street Journal* [New York] Jan 16 p.C8.

Tarbell, Ida M. 1904. *History of the Standard Oil Company* (New York: McClure Phillips and Co., 2 vols.).

Taylor, A.J.P. 1961. *The Origins of the Second World War* New York: Fawcett.

———. 1974. *Beaverbrook* Middlesex, England: Penguin Books,.

Taylor, Roger.2006. "Exact fate of Deep Panuke still a mystery", *The Chronicle-Herald* [Halifax] Jan 04 p.C1.

Texas Instruments Corp. 1974. *TTL Handbook*. Lubbock TX: Texas Instruments.

Thorndike, E. L. 1911. *Animal Intelligence*. New York: Macmillan.

Thucydides, 1954. *The Peloponnesian War* England:Penguin.

Tobin, James. 1963. "Commercial Banks as Creators of Money", in D. Carson, ed., *Banking and Monetary Studies* Homewood, Ill.: Irwin.

———. 1965. "The Monetary Interpretation of History", *American Economic Review*, Vol. 55 3., pp.645-84.

———. 1970a. "Money and Income: Post Hoc Ergo Propter Hoc?", *Quarterly Journal of Economics*, Vol. 84 2., pp. 301-17.

———. 1970b. "Rejoinder to Friedman", *Quarterly Journal of Economics*, Vol. 84, p.327.

———. 1972a. "Friedman's Theoretical Framework", *Journal of Political Economy*, Vol. 78 6., pp. 853-63.

———. 1972b. "Inflation and Unemployment", *American Economic Review*, Vol. 62, pp.1-18.

———. 1980. *Asset Accumulation and Economic Activity: Reflections on contemporary macroeconomic activity* Chicago: University of Chicago Press.

———. 1981. "The Monetarist Counter-Revolution Today: An appraisal", *Economic Journal*, Vol. 91 1. pp.29-42.

———. 1982. "Money and Finance in the Macroeconomic Process", *Journal of Money, Credit and Banking*, Vol. 14 2., pp. 171-204.

Traynor, Fiona and Tony Seed. 1999. "AIMS – A Fish Story…", *shunpiking 26* [Halifax, Canada].

Tuchman, Barbara W. 1962. *The Guns of August* New York: Random House.

Tuck, Simon. 2005. "Energy plan to include gas-price monitor", *The Globe and Mail* [Toronto] Sep 30 p.A1.

Turner, James S., ed. 1970. *The Nader Report: The Chemical Feast* New York, NY:Grossman.

Udall, Randy and Steve Andrews. 2001. *Methane Madness: A Natural Gas Primer* (Denver CO: Community Office for Resource Efficiency).

United Nations. 2004. *Statistical Review of World Energy*. New York: UNCTAD.

United States. 1999. "An overview and history of gas deregulation". Washington DC: Low-Income Home Energy Assistance Program [LIHEAP] Clearinghouse – Department of Health and Human Services.

———. 2004. *Annual Energy Review*. Washington DC: Department of Energy.

———. 2005. *Canada – Country Analysis Brief*. Washington DC: Department of Energy – Energy Information Administration [February].

Ushakov, Yuri V. 2006. "Don't Blame Russia", *The Wall Street Journal* [New York] Feb 13 p.A17.

Vallely, Paul . 2006. "Joseph Stiglitz: 'Politicians like Blair and Brown have given global poverty new prominence' - The Monday Interview: Former chief economist, World Bank", *The Independent* [London], Feb 20.

Vardanis, Christina. 2005. "A bitter wind blows into cottage country over wind-farm alt-energy scheme", *The Globe and Mail* [Toronto] May 21 p.M1.

Veblen, Thorstein J. 1909. "The Limitations of Marginal Utility", *Journal of Political Economy* Vol 17.

Veltmeyer, H and J. Petras. 2001. *Globalization Unmasked*. Halifax: Fernwood.

Vajda, S. 1981. *Linear Programming: Algorithms and Applications* London: Chapman and Hall.

Wadel, Cato. 1969. *Marginal Adaptations and Modernization in Newfoundland* St. John's: Newfoundland Institute of Social and Economic Research.

———. 1973. "Capitalization and Ownership: The Persistence of Fishermen-Ownership in the Norwegian Herring Fishery", in R. Andersen and C. Wadel edd., *North Atlantic Fishermen: Anthropological Essays on Modern Fishing* St. John's NL: Institute of Social and Economic Research, Memorial University of Newfoundland.

Wallace, David Foster. 2003. *Everything and More: A Compact History of* ∞ New York: Norton.

Wallerstein, Immanuel.1974. *The modern world-system: Capitalist agriculture and the origins of the European world-economy in the sixteenth century*. New York: Academic Press.

Walras, Leon. 1874. *Éléments d'économie politique pure, ou théorie de la richesse sociale* [Elements of Pure Economics, or the theory of social wealth] Lausanne.

Wang, Michael, Sarah Spikes and Simeon Kerr. 2005. "Middle East Oil-Cash Gusher Lures Foreign Investment Banks", *The Wall Street Journal* [New York] Oct 14 p.C6.

Warren, Susan and Jeffrey Ball. 2005. "A Change of Leadership For Big Oil Companies", *The Wall Street Journal* [New York] Aug 05 p.A3.

Watson, John B. 1913. "Psychology as the behaviorist views it", in *Psychological Review* [20]:158-177.

Webb, Sydney and Beatrice. 1920. *A Constitution for the Socialist Commonwealth of Britain*. London: Longmans and Green.

Website 1: United States Department of Energy – Energy Information Administration, http://tonto.eia.doe.gov/dnav/ng/ng_sum_lsum_dcu_nus_m.htm, last accessed 11 May 2006.

Website 2: Anadarko Petroleum, http://www.anadarko.com/, last accessed 11 May 2006.

Website 3: Grameen Bank, http://www.grameen-info.org/bank/GBGlance.htm, last accessed 13 May 2006.

Website 4: Institute of Near Eastern and African Studies discussion-blog, http://zennobia.blogspot.com/2006/01/last-jews-in-baghdad.html, last accessed 14 May 2006.

Website 5: Montreal Muslim News (transcript of television panel discussion) http://www.montrealmuslimnews.net/fulltranscript.htm, last accessed 14 May 2006.

Website 6: Petersen, Kim. 2005. "Disinformation: A Crime Against Humanity and a Crime Against Peace", *Shunpiking Online* Vol. 2 No. 6. Halifax [Canada]: New Media Publications, April. See http://www.shunpiking.com/ol0206/0206-mc-kp-miinfo-crime.htm, last accessed 22 May 2006.

Welton, Michael R. 2001. *Little Mosie from the Margaree: A Biography of Michael Moses Coady* Toronto: Thompson Educational Publishing.

Wessel, David, 2005. "Unlike Other Big Storms, This One Could Have Longer-Term Impact", *The Wall Street Journal* [New York] Sep 01 p.A1.

White, Gregory L. and Chip Cummins. 2005a. "Moscow's Plans In Energy Sector Rattle Foreigners; Ownership Limits Proposed For All Non-Russian Firms; BP Chief Lord Browne Meets Putin" *The Wall Street Journal* [New York] Apr 22 pA11.

──── . 2005b. "Yukos Ex-Chief Sentenced to 9 Years", *The Wall Street Journal* [New York] Jun 01 p.A3.

──── . 2005c. "Russia Turns Up Gas Pressure", *The Wall Street Journal* [New York] Dec 19 p.A15.

──── . 2006a. "Flush With Oil, Kremlin Explores Biggest-Ever IPO", *The Wall Street Journal* [New York] Apr 18 p.A1.

Wicksteed, Philip H. 1910. *The Common Sense of Political Economy*. London: Macmillan.

Willis, Andrew and Patrick Brethour. 2006. "Oil Patch Expects Richer Shell HQ Buyout Offer", *The Globe And Mail Report On Business* [Toronto] Jan 03 p.1.

Wolfram, Stephen. 2002. *A New Kind of Science* Wolfram Media.

Wood, John H.; Gary R. Long and David F. Morehouse Energy Information Administration. 2003. "Long-Term World Oil Supply Scenarios – The Future Is Neither as Bleak or Rosy as Some Assert" United States. Department of Energy.

World Commission on Environment Development. 1987. *Our Common Future* ["The Brundtland Report"]. New York: United Nations, Doc. A/42/427.

Wysocki, Bernard Jr and Jacob M Schlesinger. 2005. "For US, China A Replay of Japan", *The Wall Street Journal* [New York] Jun 27 p.A2.

Yates, Frances A. 1978. *The Art of Memory* UK: Penguin Books.

Yergin, Daniel. 2006. "How Much Oil Is Really Down There", *The Wall Street Journal* [New York] Apr 27 p.A18.

York, Geoffrey. 2005a. "Demand China's unquenchable thirst", *The Globe and Mail Report on Business* [Toronto] May 21 p.19.

—— and Dave Ebner. 2005b. "Oil thirst from China adds fuel to trade tussle", *The Globe and Mail* [Toronto] Jan 14 p.A1.

——. 2005c. "Saskatchewan says China itching to acquire oil, uranium assets", *The Globe and Mail Report on Business* [Toronto] Jan 26 p.4.

——. 2006d. "Blowout In Bangladesh- Niko Resources' tale of woes", *The Globe and Mail Report on Business* [Toronto] Apr 01 p.1.

Young, Marilyn. 1968. *The Rhetoric of Empire: American China Policy, 1895-1901* (Cambridge, MA: Harvard UP).

Zatzman, G.M., I. Saney and M.R. Islam. 2003. "The Bush Doctrine: Hegemonism and 'Free-Market' Solutions", *Proceedings of the 6th International Conference of Economists and Accountants on Globalization, 9-13 Feb 2004*. Havana.

——. 1975. "American destroyer visit a 'first' since the end of WW2", *Evening Telegram* [St. John's NL] Aug 12.

INDEX

A

Abraham Lincoln, 236
academics, 77
acceptance, 51, 60, 76, 118, 174
access, 25, 38, 90, 114, 130, 134, 163, 172, 175, 178, 185, 189, 216, 217, 226, 249, 258, 298, 332, 334, 343, 372
accommodation, 134, 260
accountability, 18, 75, 140, 297
accounting, 3, 5, 6, 24, 29, 31, 79, 91, 117, 165, 202, 232, 255, 256, 293, 337, 338
accumulation, 19, 26, 73, 74, 75, 79, 82, 83, 84, 92, 93, 99, 256
accuracy, 86, 138, 166, 241, 242, 244, 266
achievement, 42, 48, 49, 75, 121, 150, 152, 236, 248, 313, 317
acid, 230, 338
activated carbon, 322
activation, 246
adjustment, 165, 186, 344
adsorption, 322
adult literacy, 154
adults, 154, 261
advertisements, 106
advertising, 10, 103, 139, 285, 286
advocacy, 291, 315
aerobic bacteria, 323
aerospace, 252
affect, 12, 118, 173, 195, 210, 211, 220, 302
Afghanistan, 6, 39, 107, 208
Africa, 16, 17, 21, 22, 80, 135, 144, 148, 166, 180, 231, 232, 280, 284, 287, 288, 317, 344, 345, 347, 349, 360
African Americans, 16
age, 8, 24, 90, 104, 106, 113, 115, 144, 225, 246, 267, 306, 318
agent, 37, 91
aggregate demand, 167, 281, 282
aggregation, 34
aggression, 6, 104, 106, 111, 112, 114, 278, 303, 349
aging, 142, 191, 214, 261
agriculture, 17, 87, 88, 134, 335, 345, 382
Albania, 333
alcohol, 138, 173, 295, 323, 324
alcohol consumption, 173
alcoholism, 134
Algeria, 232
algorithm, 37
alternative, 8, 9, 10, 16, 55, 56, 82, 87, 111, 118, 119, 120, 133, 135, 162, 176, 195, 197, 226, 230, 255, 257, 314, 323, 356
alternative energy, 226
alternatives, 8, 38, 55, 109, 291, 322, 323, 375
alters, 293
aluminum, 323
amalgam, 21
amendments, 41
American culture, 287
ammonia, 142, 319
amnesia, 6, 332
amortization, 179
anatomy, 36
anger, 22
animal husbandry, 166
animals, 122, 131, 134, 150, 267
annihilation, 278
antagonism, 33
anterior cingulate cortex, 246
anterior frontal cortex, 247
anxiety, 154, 183, 244
appetite, 115, 133, 354
applied mathematics, 43, 47
Arab countries, 268, 275, 276
Arab world, 105, 106, 160, 187, 239, 264, 272, 278, 288
Argentina, 110, 134, 336, 379

argument, 10, 26, 29, 31, 40, 47, 48, 51, 56, 82, 83, 84, 91, 98, 124, 127, 226, 227, 229, 236, 259, 262, 296, 297, 332, 335, 342
Aristotle, 33, 166
arithmetic, 29, 226
armed forces, 81, 278
Armenians, 268, 273
arrest, 325
arsenic, 323
arthritis, 142
articulation, 86, 115, 176
ASEAN, 134
ash, 323, 324
Ashkenazi Jews, 275
Asia, 16, 21, 22, 80, 128, 130, 131, 134, 135, 144, 148, 180, 231, 232, 258, 280, 284, 306, 317, 322, 331, 344, 345, 347, 367
Asian countries, 344
aspiration, 130
assassination, 56, 179
assault, 12, 40, 63, 73, 167, 205, 241, 303, 332
assessment, 193, 244
assets, 17, 128, 172, 255, 258, 298, 322, 334, 345, 384
assignment, 127
association, 55, 174, 219
assumptions, 25, 31, 36, 37, 43, 47, 51, 67, 69, 76, 86, 102, 119, 125, 190, 200, 213, 230, 246, 256, 262, 263, 275, 329
asthma, 142
asymmetry, 125
attachment, 262
attacker, 135
attacks, 10, 12, 39, 40, 62, 135, 146, 161, 300
attention, 3, 31, 65, 99, 118, 128, 136, 155, 210, 214, 264, 275, 323, 325, 339, 347
attitudes, 118
attractiveness, 227, 231, 235, 318
Australia, 362, 367
authority, 18, 22, 34, 41, 42, 48, 50, 56, 62, 63, 75, 76, 96, 128, 132, 150, 166, 172, 174, 179, 189, 194, 208, 211, 212, 213, 215, 216, 219, 238, 294, 300, 328, 332
automata, 120
automation, 85
automobiles, 252, 261
autonomy, 206
availability, 17, 23, 24, 26, 123, 125, 185, 226
average variable cost, 184
averaging, 5, 162, 309
awareness, 149, 154

B

baby boomers, 167, 261
bad day, 121
baggage, 31, 84, 118, 261
Bahrain, 370
balance sheet, 256
Bangladesh, 144, 163, 300, 305, 306, 308, 310, 312, 323, 380, 384
Bank of England, 22
banking, viii, 21, 22, 24, 30, 106, 125, 128, 160, 164, 218, 228, 280, 291, 295, 296, 300, 301, 303, 306, 313, 332, 333, 343
bankruptcy, 24, 216, 217, 258, 259
banks, 17, 24, 27, 156, 207, 209, 228, 295, 344
barriers, 38
barter, 14, 18
basic needs, 6
basic services, 216
Bayesian methods, 61
BEA, 257
beer, 191
behavior, 122, 125
bending, 226
beneficial effect, 136
benign, 320
bias, 62, 77, 130, 152, 174, 177, 242, 332, 340
Big Bang, 59, 255, 370
binding, 211, 317, 321
biodiesel, 323, 324, 362
biomass, 138, 318, 323
biomaterials, 321
birth, 89, 137, 138, 239
birth control, 137, 138
black hole, 31, 226
blame, 3, 60, 181, 239
blindness, 207
blocks, 28, 197, 327
blog, 263, 264, 383
blood, 20, 22, 37, 242, 244
blood flow, 242
blood vessels, 242
board members, 312
body, 1, 2, 8, 11, 18, 28, 36, 59, 65, 103, 110, 120, 130, 131, 132, 138, 142, 155, 192, 262, 284, 289, 356
body size, 262
Bolivia, 110, 134, 160, 188, 280, 336, 363, 374, 379
Bolshevik Revolution, viii, 82, 131, 133, 294, 302
bonding, 321
bonds, 3, 251, 255
borrowers, 306, 307, 308, 309, 310, 311, 312, 313, 332, 343

borrowing, 107, 108, 314
brain, 6, 142, 242, 245, 246, 247, 339
Brazil, 55, 110, 134, 204, 336, 361, 370, 374, 379
breakdown, 157, 226
break-even, 313
breathing, viii
Britain, 38, 56, 77, 80, 85, 132, 189, 212, 213, 272, 295, 296, 330, 337, 383
brutality, 287
budget deficit, 105, 107, 251
buildings, 135, 151
Bulgaria, 221
bureaucracy, 82, 135
burning, 27, 135, 182, 207, 266, 320
business cycle, 19, 29
business management, 104

C

cabinets, 16
calcium, 321
calcium carbonate, 321
calculus, 32, 41, 43, 44, 45, 47, 53, 74, 145
Cambodia, 105
campaigns, 353
Canada, ix, 6, 13, 31, 39, 54, 63, 64, 65, 67, 87, 89, 90, 94, 95, 108, 137, 152, 161, 174, 188, 189, 190, 192, 193, 194, 195, 196, 197, 198, 199, 201, 202, 203, 204, 205, 206, 208, 209, 210, 211, 213, 215, 216, 217, 219, 221, 225, 231, 232, 252, 254, 258, 259, 262, 263, 305, 306, 325, 336, 342, 353, 359, 360, 361, 362, 370, 371, 373, 375, 376, 377, 378, 382, 383
cancer, 142
candidates, 279
capital accumulation, 79, 84
capital flows, 128
capital goods, 19, 184, 185, 252
capital markets, 336
capitalism, 28, 73, 76, 77, 79, 80, 83, 84, 85, 89, 92, 94, 95, 96, 97, 98, 99, 109, 118, 131, 203, 210, 221, 248, 249, 299, 300, 303, 371
carbohydrate, 138
carbon, 319, 323, 324
Caribbean, 339
cartel, 178, 181, 184, 211, 215, 217, 218, 221, 226, 229
Caspian Sea, 375
cast, 26, 33, 54, 118
catalyst, 324
Catholic Church, 34, 41, 42, 130
causal relationship, 60, 175
causation, 63

celestial bodies, 41
cell, 92, 95, 319
Central Asia, 231
central bank, 22, 24, 106, 252, 255, 258, 333, 344, 346
central planning, 127
centralisation, 209, 344
ceramic, 149, 321
cerebral cortex, 247
certificate, 239
chaebols, 345
channels, 128, 342
chaos, 53, 145, 146, 156, 217, 228, 288, 345, 347
chicken, 99
Chief Justice, 2
childhood, 28
children, 62, 105, 153, 167, 267, 299, 309, 313
Chile, 134, 336, 370
China, 21, 22, 81, 88, 97, 110, 127, 130, 134, 162, 169, 173, 180, 197, 225, 230, 231, 252, 254, 257, 269, 287, 330, 334, 345, 353, 358, 359, 360, 362, 364, 369, 370, 371, 373, 378, 381, 383, 384
chopping, 33, 35, 83
Christianity, 130, 298
CIA, 11, 106
circulation, 19, 22, 24, 33, 88, 89, 99, 105, 106, 110, 133, 260, 281, 338
citizenship, 132, 173
civil society, 329
civil war, 93, 139, 329
classes, 22, 90, 96, 210, 225, 343, 353
classical economics, 160, 329, 338
classification, 36, 176
clean air, 55, 135
cleaning, 136, 317, 325
clients, 300, 306
climate change, 54
closure, 204
CO_2, 54, 103, 319, 324
coal, 4, 9, 27, 28, 29, 32, 90, 176, 181, 190, 337, 381
coastal communities, 65, 67, 90, 161, 198, 203, 217
cobalt, 322
cognition, 12, 39, 40
cognitive psychology, 285
coherence, 77, 303
Cold War, 39, 77, 82, 116, 154, 161, 189, 222, 230, 285, 334, 374
collaboration, 144, 194
collateral, 307
collusion, 202, 245
colonial rule, 86, 204, 212
colonisation, 8, 68, 80, 272
combustion, 48, 136, 150, 324

commercial bank, 24
commitment, 70, 72, 83
commodity, vii, 4, 5, 6, 13, 14, 15, 18, 19, 22, 23, 26, 31, 32, 33, 37, 57, 88, 91, 92, 93, 94, 95, 99, 104, 113, 134, 139, 169, 170, 190, 248, 249, 260, 299, 317, 320, 338
Commonwealth of Independent States, 345
communication, 203, 373, 379, 380
communism, 127, 270, 303
Communist Party, 79, 133
community, 82, 89, 140, 189, 200, 220, 242, 260, 267, 270, 275, 278, 279, 298, 300, 302, 305, 306, 314, 329, 335, 336, 338, 373
comparative advantage, 184, 336
compensation, 189, 212, 278
competition, 5, 28, 29, 30, 31, 57, 62, 63, 76, 83, 86, 98, 111, 116, 119, 125, 127, 129, 162, 165, 174, 175, 176, 177, 179, 181, 190, 205, 208, 214, 248, 282, 294, 303, 342, 343, 353
complementarity, 70
complexity, 237
compliance, 212, 240, 243
components, 9, 13, 15, 101, 112, 113, 120, 121, 150, 164, 201, 236, 239, 245, 247, 294, 355
composition, 323
comprehension, 34, 35, 40
compulsion, 2, 93, 123, 294
computation, 52, 83
computer software, 108, 253
computer technology, 283
computing, 45, 47, 85, 110, 111, 114
concentration, 18, 113, 169, 176, 185, 209, 218, 302, 322, 337
conception, 10, 32, 49, 53, 58, 67, 80, 86, 104, 113, 120, 127
concrete, 119, 120, 172, 289, 344
conditioned response, 285
conditioned stimulus, 285
conditioning, 178, 227
conduct, 69, 106, 141, 173, 189, 270, 284, 287
conductor, 111
confidence, 103, 154, 166, 242, 352
confidentiality, 3
confinement, 102
conflict, 12, 70, 98, 102, 141, 223, 229, 279, 288, 299, 316
confrontation, 334
confusion, viii, 13, 68, 71, 73, 81, 164, 174, 281, 299
consciousness, vii, viii, 8, 12, 39, 40, 55, 56, 65, 67, 71, 79, 85, 95, 101, 121, 130, 149, 150, 151, 197, 210, 294, 316, 337
consensus, 118, 181
conservation, 28, 29, 36

consolidation, 31
conspiracy, 2, 15, 99, 236
constitution, 189
constitutional law, 189, 213
construction, 6, 80, 91, 108, 214, 267, 317, 321, 364
consumer goods, 185, 338
consumer price index, 184
consumer sovereignty, 4, 354
consumers, 18, 105, 115, 137, 148, 161, 176, 184, 185, 187, 227, 243, 248, 252, 353
consumption, 5, 18, 19, 23, 27, 28, 29, 30, 32, 34, 81, 84, 93, 94, 99, 122, 152, 153, 158, 159, 161, 165, 167, 176, 179, 181, 190, 191, 194, 206, 225, 228, 232, 248, 249, 252, 253, 257, 260, 280, 281, 282, 292, 296, 301, 302, 318, 323, 342, 353, 354
consumption function, 34
contaminant, 322
contamination, 323
continuity, 42, 43, 45, 77, 78, 263, 349
control, 1, 8, 16, 17, 19, 22, 42, 63, 65, 68, 89, 96, 97, 101, 105, 106, 107, 108, 109, 110, 114, 115, 123, 127, 128, 130, 135, 137, 166, 168, 174, 175, 176, 178, 189, 200, 202, 205, 206, 209, 215, 216, 217, 231, 241, 246, 259, 279, 286, 287, 288, 301, 328, 332, 334, 345, 372
convergence, 83, 169
conversion, 111, 128, 216, 281, 298, 300, 318, 324
conviction, 212, 340
cooking, 142, 176, 226, 231, 319, 324
cooling, 319
corn, 323, 324
corporate governance, 128
corporate sector, 1, 3, 65, 90, 174, 201, 282
corporations, 17, 18, 71, 72, 87, 90, 96, 97, 115, 132, 134, 152, 161, 168, 172, 173, 180, 200, 201, 213, 225, 297, 298, 343
correlation, 60, 61, 342, 343
correlation coefficient, 60
corrosion, 191
corruption, 17, 172
cortex, 247
costs, 1, 3, 13, 19, 29, 139, 158, 172, 175, 177, 179, 180, 182, 184, 191, 198, 214, 219, 220, 227, 249, 258, 289, 302, 325, 336, 353, 360
costs of production, 13, 29, 182, 184, 353
cotton, 138, 204, 287
counterterrorism strategy, 247
coverage, 97, 198, 300, 311
covering, 108, 137, 142, 159, 174, 197, 309, 344
crack, 243
creativity, 163
credibility, 197, 230

credit, 5, 14, 23, 24, 88, 106, 107, 108, 148, 164, 167, 206, 218, 226, 258, 293, 306, 307, 314, 332, 333, 339, 340, 342, 343, 346
creditors, 109, 148, 153, 184, 280, 332, 333
crime, 23, 56, 242, 308, 340, 383
criminal activity, 297
criminal acts, 340
criminal justice system, 141
criminals, 204
criticism, 123, 163, 239, 274
crops, 161, 198
crude oil, 120, 169, 170, 174, 180, 182, 184, 185, 195, 198, 224, 226, 228, 345
crying, 362
CSCE, 372
Cuba, 75, 85, 110, 134, 151, 280, 334, 339, 345
cultivation, 200
culture, 118, 131, 133, 135, 137, 141, 143, 160, 187, 275, 325
currency, 22, 23, 24, 35, 105, 107, 108, 110, 131, 171, 226, 252, 333, 343, 344, 345, 378
current account, 334
current account deficit, 334
current balance, 310
current prices, 182, 228
curriculum, 145, 271
customers, 91, 97, 125, 154, 178, 197, 228, 283, 288, 296, 298, 344
cyberspace, 286
cycles, 27, 45, 48, 53, 74, 75, 84, 136, 293

D

daily living, 50
damage, 27, 133, 169, 235, 322, 323
danger, ix, 26, 214, 341
dark matter, 31, 167, 255, 256, 257, 370
Darwinism, 15, 16
data mining, 284
database, 103, 106
death, 17, 25, 27, 30, 42, 75, 103, 131, 132, 206, 213, 239, 248, 262, 276, 280, 310, 340
debt, 23, 27, 31, 79, 108, 148, 153, 181, 207, 215, 218, 252, 255, 256, 258, 259, 260, 303, 311, 314, 336, 342, 345, 346
debtors, 332
debts, 11, 22, 24, 185, 207, 215, 228, 255, 258
decay, 125, 126, 134, 244, 258, 282, 314, 348, 350, 351
decentralization, 112
decision-making process, 237
decisions, 3, 18, 19, 141, 149, 152, 172, 237, 248, 250, 292, 344

deconstruction, 72, 73, 104, 158, 236
decoupling, 252
deduction, 61, 303
defects, 8, 54, 92, 117, 243
defense, 181, 227
deficiency, 213, 244
deficit, 26, 153, 167, 251, 252, 253, 257, 313
definition, vii, 7, 11, 14, 41, 52, 83, 94, 95, 175, 211, 264, 281, 301, 315, 340
degenerate, 61
degradation, 74, 91, 218, 242, 302
delivery, 15, 174, 177, 190, 192, 197, 332, 344
demand, 5, 9, 13, 18, 19, 25, 34, 36, 57, 108, 111, 124, 125, 131, 165, 167, 178, 181, 182, 183, 184, 185, 190, 191, 195, 216, 227, 230, 231, 237, 257, 258, 262, 281, 283, 291, 294, 299, 325, 332, 337, 344, 352, 364
demand curve, 19
democracy, 49, 130, 219
demographics, 61, 261, 263
denial, 39, 50, 245, 303
Denmark, 357, 368
density, 271
Department of Agriculture, 344
Department of Energy, 169, 183, 194, 213, 223, 382, 383
Department of Health and Human Services, 382
Department of Homeland Security, 156, 243
deposits, 21, 200, 307, 308, 310, 311, 313
depression, 85, 142
deregulation, 175, 176, 177, 178, 179, 190, 382
derivatives, 42, 43, 46
desire, 25, 33, 42, 96, 269
destruction, 2, 8, 16, 31, 109, 128, 156, 200, 269, 302, 317, 333
detachment, 143
detection, 67, 236, 241, 245, 246, 247
devaluation, 105, 259
developed countries, 54, 83, 114, 117, 144, 181, 182, 184, 187, 224, 282, 284, 305, 335, 344
developing countries, 11, 19, 54, 75, 77, 83, 114, 115, 117, 144, 224, 258, 280, 282, 284, 295, 314, 323, 334, 335, 343, 344, 347, 349
devolution, 131
diet, 163, 166, 222, 225
differential equations, 42
differentiation, 41, 42, 54, 211, 235
digestion, 318, 323
dignity, 174
dimensionality, 33
diminishing returns, 214
dioxin, 142
direct action, 242

direct observation, 33, 77
disaster, 2, 64, 138, 148, 191, 208, 260, 308, 339, 341
disbursement, 307
discipline, 66, 115, 304
disclosure, 128, 129, 240, 292
discomfort, 271
discontinuity, 43, 52
discounting, 250
discourse, 10, 40, 71, 75, 161, 162, 225, 226, 240, 268, 280, 331, 344
disequilibrium, 226, 294
displacement, 20, 30, 84, 86, 220, 240
disposable income, 353
disposition, 133, 174
distortions, 12, 118, 127, 278, 347
distress, 91, 201, 222
distribution, 18, 37, 60, 99, 125, 126, 127, 133, 139, 150, 158, 169, 176, 184, 185, 186, 190, 192, 195, 232, 242, 249, 250, 316, 337, 338, 344, 379
divergence, 167, 170, 180, 302, 329
diversity, 136, 235
division, 7, 22, 23, 29, 88, 92, 114, 230, 301, 302, 344, 349
DNA, 139
doctors, 262, 339
domain, 25, 42, 44, 53, 144, 353
domestic demand, 224
domestic markets, 195, 226
dominance, 88, 202, 270
donors, 307, 310
doors, 295
downsizing, 94
dream, 303
drinking water, 216
drought, 167, 221
drugs, 339
drying, 88
duopoly, 171
durability, 142
duration, 74, 102, 145, 179, 344

E

early retirement, 167
earnings, 152, 251, 345
earth, vii, 34, 49, 102, 134, 135, 146, 166, 203, 231, 298, 322, 336
East Asia, 128
Eastern Europe, 233, 274
eating, 28, 115, 164, 239
ecology, 214, 219

economic activity, vii, viii, 35, 67, 70, 152, 162, 163, 206
economic behaviour, 6, 25, 165
economic crisis, 104, 112
economic development, 8, 26, 74, 81, 82, 83, 110, 114, 126, 133, 152, 209, 236, 280, 305, 306, 314, 317, 329, 338, 345
economic development model, 305
economic efficiency, 29, 317
economic growth, 79, 85, 153, 164, 184, 251
economic indicator, 106
economic institutions, 116, 129
economic integration, 110, 291
economic performance, 117
economic policy, 97, 299
economic problem, 20, 120, 280
economic systems, 64, 82, 86, 249
economic theory, 6, 8, 9, 23, 26, 27, 28, 32, 39, 57, 65, 72, 83, 117, 118, 120, 123, 127, 128, 151, 158, 164, 165, 167, 188, 201, 219, 235, 236, 237, 248, 281, 284, 299, 304, 342, 355
economic transformation, 150, 247
economic welfare, 144
economics, vii, 1, 2, 4, 6, 7, 8, 9, 10, 13, 19, 20, 24, 25, 27, 35, 36, 38, 49, 50, 55, 61, 62, 63, 64, 66, 68, 69, 70, 76, 79, 80, 84, 91, 101, 102, 104, 117, 118, 120, 121, 123, 124, 126, 127, 129, 130, 144, 146, 150, 158, 159, 162, 164, 165, 188, 190, 198, 200, 206, 213, 220, 222, 225, 235, 236, 237, 255, 260, 280, 281, 283, 284, 292, 293, 294, 295, 298, 299, 300, 301, 302, 303, 305, 314, 315, 316, 319, 329, 338, 341, 342, 352, 353, 354, 355, 356, 368
economies of scale, 113, 180, 217, 335
ecosystem, 64, 103, 142, 200, 323
Ecuador, 110, 134, 336, 363
educational process, 103
educational system, 155
efficient resource allocation, 126
effluent, 319
egg, 99, 137, 341
Egypt, 21, 130, 223, 272
elaboration, 7, 15, 40, 57, 58, 225, 236, 243, 291, 356
election, 140, 187, 228, 312
electric field, 112
electricity, 27, 136, 162, 177, 185, 190, 191, 198, 222, 319, 337, 371
electromagnetic, 245
electronic systems, 116
email, 264, 274
embargo, 29, 105, 107, 179, 223, 334, 340
emergence, 14, 15, 20, 21, 22, 26, 51, 59, 63, 71, 73, 74, 75, 76, 78, 84, 97, 112, 115, 125, 127, 130,

132, 150, 156, 162, 166, 177, 209, 222, 231, 236, 253, 294, 341, 347, 349
emergency management, 339
emergency response, 339
emerging markets, 353
emigration, 89
emission, 54
emotions, 240
employees, 121, 122, 132, 243, 258, 259, 296, 298, 341
employment, 5, 23, 27, 167, 204, 343, 346
empowerment, 50
encouragement, 80, 279
energy, 4, 8, 9, 13, 23, 27, 28, 29, 30, 31, 40, 48, 50, 82, 103, 110, 111, 112, 133, 136, 137, 157, 158, 159, 160, 162, 168, 169, 171, 175, 176, 177, 180, 181, 184, 185, 190, 191, 193, 195, 197, 198, 201, 202, 212, 215, 219, 220, 221, 222, 225, 226, 227, 230, 231, 232, 251, 252, 253, 254, 258, 264, 284, 288, 292, 317, 318, 319, 320, 323, 324, 325, 337, 341, 360, 362, 372, 373, 380, 382
energy consumption, 28, 30, 181, 184, 232
energy supply, 23, 28, 162, 169, 177, 185, 222, 230, 231
England, 10, 22, 25, 27, 28, 35, 41, 42, 88, 89, 90, 91, 189, 191, 192, 204, 206, 208, 230, 294, 366, 369, 377, 381
enslavement, 81, 164, 301, 316
enthusiasm, 85
entrepreneurs, 314, 336
entropy, 318
environment, viii, 8, 11, 27, 35, 48, 51, 55, 68, 77, 115, 117, 120, 121, 126, 136, 154, 175, 219, 251, 256, 286, 287, 300, 315, 316, 318, 320, 321, 322, 324, 325, 328, 337, 341
environmental crisis, 40, 325
environmental impact, 193, 324
environmental protection, 291, 315
epidemic, 142
epidemiology, 262
episodic memory, 247
equality, 80, 120, 123, 168
equating, 198, 295
equilibrium, 34, 36, 43, 47, 48, 49, 50, 51, 54, 77, 80, 101, 102, 119, 121, 122, 124, 125, 126, 176, 180, 181, 293, 322, 323, 343, 352
equilibrium price, 34, 101, 343, 352
equipment, 84, 90, 127, 164, 166, 185, 210, 248, 252, 261, 262, 336, 338
equity, 136, 258, 307, 330
erosion, 202, 248
estimating, 191
ethnic groups, 265

ethnicity, 241, 270
ethyl alcohol, 323, 324
etiology, 120
eugenics, 16
Euro, 24, 110, 256, 271, 372
Europe, 21, 27, 41, 47, 49, 77, 84, 88, 106, 107, 110, 115, 131, 132, 133, 134, 141, 162, 163, 169, 199, 221, 225, 227, 228, 231, 232, 254, 258, 269, 274, 286, 287, 288, 295, 296, 299, 332, 333, 334, 342, 344, 353
European Commission, 110
European Union, 110, 197, 231, 336
evacuation, 201, 339
evaporation, 220
evidence, 16, 24, 27, 54, 59, 60, 61, 62, 63, 64, 67, 70, 72, 74, 79, 97, 98, 101, 124, 129, 146, 174, 178, 194, 199, 200, 210, 211, 216, 235, 241, 248, 255, 260, 276, 279, 287, 295, 314, 339, 342, 344, 355
evil, 135, 141, 142
evolution, viii, 8, 15, 31, 43, 51, 59, 76, 83, 86, 98, 113, 114, 126, 129, 166, 167, 197, 292, 337, 377
exaggeration, 227, 245
excess demand, 182
exchange rate, 22
exclusion, 75, 287, 334
excuse, 256
execution, 339
exercise, 8, 40, 82, 87, 96, 118, 155, 166, 174, 176, 205, 245, 247, 258, 328, 342, 353
expectation, 47
expenditures, 6, 202, 259, 282
expertise, 72, 171
experts, 72, 191, 230, 244, 332, 339
exploitation, 8, 16, 17, 18, 66, 67, 85, 94, 98, 128, 169, 174, 177, 205, 207, 210, 287, 301, 303
exports, 108, 184, 185, 187, 195, 228, 251, 252, 253, 344, 345, 360
exposure, 59, 76, 135, 177, 280
expression, 15, 21, 84, 125, 213, 235, 340, 342
external environment, 288
externalities, 1, 2, 6, 127, 219, 344
extraction, 53, 87, 98, 132, 160, 161, 163, 172, 174, 177, 191, 196, 197, 198, 223, 280, 335
extrapolation, 59
extrinsic rewards, 118

F

fabric, 138
failure, 2, 8, 27, 31, 59, 66, 68, 101, 117, 122, 126, 127, 128, 149, 151, 157, 174, 200, 210, 225, 303, 345, 372

fairness, 289
faith, 60, 102, 132, 152, 303
false negative, 242, 244
family, 5, 21, 46, 96, 131, 132, 143, 167, 201, 204, 208, 216, 239, 266, 269, 306, 309, 311, 340, 342, 354
family planning, 143
family system, 167
family units, 354
famine, 89
farmers, 161, 177, 198
fear, 3, 105, 146, 217, 240
federal government initiatives, 245
feedback, 112, 264
feelings, 133, 265
feet, 190, 191, 193, 195
fertilizers, 144
filtration, 317
finance, 23, 27, 30, 31, 71, 96, 105, 116, 117, 127, 128, 129, 133, 167, 171, 206, 207, 218, 236, 250, 252, 254, 287, 295, 298, 300, 301, 333, 336, 343
financial capital, 189, 299
financial crisis, 128
financial institutions, 118, 218, 296, 300
financial markets, 258
financial sector, 167
Financial Services Authority, 296
financial system, 109, 300, 345
financing, 171, 206, 250, 252, 254, 258, 285, 300, 313, 333
fires, 29, 162
firms, 124, 177, 297, 308, 361
first generation, 111
First World, viii, 15, 31, 76, 90, 125, 168, 169, 171, 180, 203, 207, 227, 278, 285
fiscal policy, 289, 346
fish, 8, 31, 40, 64, 65, 67, 70, 72, 88, 90, 91, 159, 161, 189, 198, 199, 200, 201, 202, 204, 205, 206, 207, 208, 209, 210, 211, 212, 214, 215, 216, 217, 218, 219, 221, 222, 322, 336, 376
fisheries, 8, 31, 40, 63, 64, 66, 67, 68, 70, 71, 73, 75, 87, 89, 90, 91, 189, 202, 203, 205, 207, 208, 209, 210, 211, 212, 214, 215, 216, 217, 218, 219, 221, 222
fishing, 40, 64, 66, 68, 70, 72, 86, 87, 88, 89, 90, 91, 95, 159, 161, 200, 201, 203, 204, 205, 206, 208, 209, 210, 211, 212, 214, 215, 216, 217, 218, 219, 221, 222, 309
flatness, 34
flexibility, 136, 181
flight, 236, 246, 261
float, 31, 296
flood, 157, 330

flora, 15, 103
flora and fauna, 15, 103
flotation, 2, 327
fluctuations, 231
focusing, viii, 51, 136, 199, 302
food, 14, 40, 59, 70, 88, 90, 91, 131, 151, 152, 158, 161, 163, 166, 185, 188, 200, 201, 204, 213, 217, 219, 221, 225, 269, 316, 328, 340, 344
food production, 59, 213, 219, 225
Ford, 171, 179, 261
foreign aid, 81, 331
foreign direct investment, 134, 303
foreign exchange, 344
foreign investment, 227
foreign policy, 189
forests, 54
forgetting, 155
formaldehyde, 138, 142
fossil, 23, 76, 162, 170, 187, 189, 191, 222, 224, 226, 227, 230, 287, 319, 323
framing, 28, 59, 138, 287, 296
France, 25, 35, 49, 80, 81, 131, 132, 137, 160, 162, 171, 184, 206, 218, 272, 329, 358
Franklin Delano Roosevelt, 171
fraud, 297, 341
free trade, 334
freedom, 1, 22, 26, 49, 72, 75, 78, 90, 119, 123, 125, 127, 130, 134, 139, 146, 151, 181, 204, 207, 239, 297, 338
freezing, 53, 214, 246
freshwater, 210
friends, 12, 17, 261, 274
frontal lobe, 247
fruits, 30, 93, 151, 266, 340
fuel, 23, 27, 28, 29, 48, 135, 170, 181, 185, 187, 191, 195, 217, 222, 224, 227, 230, 231, 232, 246, 287, 288, 317, 319, 323, 324, 364, 384
fulfillment, 308
full employment, 281, 346
funding, 131, 237

G

Galaxy, 376
gasoline, 197, 228
GATT, 109, 332
GDP, 128, 153, 185, 202, 204, 252, 282, 342, 343, 348, 350
GDP per capita, 205, 343, 348
General Agreement on Tariffs and Trade, 91, 332
General Motors, 260

generation, 19, 27, 56, 60, 79, 85, 90, 116, 132, 152, 162, 167, 175, 176, 177, 190, 191, 197, 216, 222, 230, 256, 282, 302, 317, 322, 331, 334
Geneva Convention, 278
genocide, 131, 278
geography, 95, 210
George Berkeley, 42, 359
Georgia, 2
Germany, 171, 231, 285, 288, 332, 333
gestation, 240
global competition, 301
global economy, 110, 167, 217, 258, 288, 295, 334
globalization, 109, 110
glucose, 103
goals, 159, 306
God, 41, 58, 150, 172, 265, 277, 286
gold, 21, 22, 23, 105, 106, 110, 203, 245, 252, 335
goods and services, 10, 18, 19, 21, 27, 33, 57, 101, 150, 158, 161, 184, 185, 228, 248, 281, 283, 296, 300, 344, 347, 352
gossip, 267
governance, 128, 129, 140, 335
government, 2, 3, 13, 16, 17, 18, 22, 23, 26, 36, 40, 49, 55, 64, 65, 66, 68, 74, 80, 91, 94, 97, 98, 105, 106, 107, 108, 115, 116, 117, 126, 127, 129, 131, 134, 140, 152, 153, 160, 161, 163, 167, 172, 173, 174, 176, 179, 187, 190, 195, 198, 200, 201, 202, 204, 206, 207, 208, 210, 211, 212, 213, 214, 215, 217, 218, 219, 229, 235, 236, 237, 241, 244, 258, 259, 278, 282, 285, 286, 295, 297, 308, 310, 312, 314, 329, 334, 339, 343, 344, 345, 365
government intervention, 97, 126, 127, 167, 259
government policy, 94, 108, 126, 211, 286
grades, 309
grading, 181
grains, 252
grants, 162, 338
graph, 44, 45, 58, 145, 347
gravitation, 57, 188
gravitational effect, 31
gravitational field, 248
gravitational pull, 226
gravity, 41, 154, 248, 255
Great Britain, viii, 27, 32, 49, 105, 162, 171, 173, 212, 379
Great Depression, 19, 26, 77, 108, 167, 176, 207, 218, 332
Greece, 21
greed, 26, 138, 143, 148, 149, 150, 185, 298, 315, 316
green land, 267
greenhouse gases, 182
gross domestic product, 257, 300

grounding, 285
grouping, 57, 60, 81, 122, 166, 203
groups, 15, 36, 68, 80, 96, 97, 111, 115, 176, 205, 219, 245, 259, 268, 274, 286, 299, 301
growth, 10, 24, 28, 59, 83, 126, 153, 158, 159, 169, 181, 186, 190, 209, 225, 226, 232, 248, 251, 252, 256, 257, 262, 281, 283, 300, 305, 325, 331, 344
growth spurt, 344
guidelines, 356
guilt, 161, 221, 240, 241, 242
guilty, 135, 141, 242
Guinea, 54, 166, 378
Gulf Coast, 190, 191, 339
Gulf of Mexico, 2, 156, 170, 228, 339

H

habitat, 221
hands, 4, 15, 23, 67, 91, 93, 112, 117, 131, 151, 158, 187, 189, 206, 207, 208, 237, 246, 286, 294, 343, 345, 365
happiness, 353, 354
hard currency, 333, 343, 345
harm, 150, 208, 267, 289, 320
harvesting, 65, 67, 161, 190, 198, 200, 201, 209, 210, 214, 215, 217, 218, 221, 222, 336
hate, 229
hazards, 262, 329
health, 16, 60, 119, 131, 138, 143, 144, 153, 257, 260, 261, 262, 264, 268, 293, 306, 308, 310, 332, 339, 345
health care, 16
heart attack, 136
heart disease, 262
heat, 112, 266
heating, 176, 184, 190, 191, 226, 227, 231, 319, 320
heavy metals, 322, 323, 373
hedging, 52
height, 32, 39, 122, 221
helical conformation, 139
hemisphere, 184
Henry Ford, 171
heroism, 317
heterogeneity, 136
higher education, 309
highways, 6
hip, 227
hiring, 88, 246
hole argument, 63
homework, 246
homogeneity, 136
homosexuals, 16
hormone, 137

host, 174, 279
hostility, 294, 334
House, 130, 140, 160, 187, 202, 255, 363, 367, 371, 375, 376, 379, 382
housing, 190, 237, 308, 309
hub, 169, 190, 197, 364
human actions, 25
human agency, 40
human animal, 96
human brain, 102, 103, 136, 141
human capital, 164, 340, 345
human development, 21
human resources, 158
human rights, 306
humility, 53, 77
hunting, 166, 261
Hurricane Katrina, 2, 156, 169
hurricanes, 339
husband, 299, 309, 311
hybrid, 298
hydrocarbons, 224
hydroelectric power, 220
hydrogen, 229, 319
hydroxide, 321, 324
hypocrisy, 204
hypothesis, 62, 70, 121, 146, 323

I

idealism, 58, 87
ideas, 10, 11, 28, 76, 114, 117, 235, 237, 291
identification, 82, 111, 240, 242, 273, 275, 276
identity, 7, 268, 281, 309
ideology, 72, 77, 116, 274
illusion, 52, 77, 148, 293
imagery, 247
images, 52
imagination, 159
imbalances, 370
IMF, 128, 144, 332
imitation, 318
immigrants, 204, 210
immigration, 90
immortality, 132
immune system, 144
immunity, 135
imperialism, 95, 98
implementation, 3, 117, 236, 237, 278, 288, 314, 317, 340
imports, 152, 232, 252, 254, 340, 344
impotence, 136, 159
imprisonment, 340
incentives, 36, 54, 122, 123, 127, 129, 152, 178

inclusion, 117, 268, 287
income, 67, 90, 127, 146, 147, 152, 153, 161, 167, 179, 198, 210, 215, 255, 303, 308, 309, 313, 343, 344, 353, 368
income support, 161, 198
income tax, 179, 303, 308
independence, 52, 89, 109, 184, 214, 219, 332, 334, 347, 349, 352
independent variable, 73, 74, 145, 146, 147
India, 88, 97, 110, 134, 142, 162, 169, 220, 225, 230, 257, 269, 271, 300, 364, 365, 372, 373
Indians, 204, 237, 271
indicators, 54, 75, 182, 245, 251
indices, 128, 134, 163, 164, 333, 345
indigenous, 131
individual differences, 164
individuality, 292
Indonesia, 79, 80, 232
induction, 16
inductor, 112
industrial restructuring, 258
industrial revolution, viii, 56, 318
industrial sectors, 115
industrialisation, 4, 211
industry, viii, 13, 14, 15, 17, 28, 40, 56, 66, 68, 69, 81, 82, 87, 89, 90, 91, 94, 110, 111, 113, 114, 134, 137, 159, 164, 167, 171, 175, 176, 177, 178, 180, 182, 185, 190, 191, 192, 193, 196, 205, 210, 214, 232, 235, 236, 239, 243, 257, 258, 259, 261, 280, 285, 298, 322, 325, 328, 337, 359, 377
inefficiency, 118, 198
inelastic, 182
inequality, 32, 80, 82, 161, 212, 221, 293
inequity, 212
inertia, 48
infant mortality, 134
inferences, 69, 122, 244, 344
inferiority, 17
infinite, 35, 41, 42, 48, 99, 102, 104, 106, 123, 124, 148, 248, 315
inflation, 20, 24, 27, 36, 105, 108, 165, 171, 251, 345, 346, 368, 380
influence, 19, 41, 79, 96, 107, 123, 131, 171, 213, 214, 221, 299, 349
information technology, vii, 106
infrastructure, 4, 55, 116, 175, 190, 191, 197, 206, 303, 345
ingestion, 144
inheritance, 132
inmates, 17
innocence, 242
innovation, viii, 124, 172, 173, 229, 294, 317

input, 18, 63, 77, 111, 112, 152, 185, 225, 227, 292, 318, 320, 323, 338
insecurity, 184, 241
insertion, 288
insight, 20, 27, 108, 146, 167, 330
inspectors, 14
inspiration, 141
instability, 279, 288
instinct, 25, 54, 150
institutions, vii, 22, 24, 62, 63, 109, 117, 125, 128, 129, 136, 144, 296, 298, 299, 310, 343
instruction, 52
instruments, 70, 135, 159, 247, 251, 281, 344
insulation, 317, 321
insurance, 119, 121, 122, 124, 308, 310, 311
integrated circuits, 111
integration, 160, 185, 188, 190, 197, 199, 201, 292, 337, 378
integrity, 48, 53, 60, 61, 63, 69, 77, 247, 303, 323
intellectual property, 108
intelligence, 56, 112, 115, 136, 163, 283, 334, 349, 357
intensity, 60, 67, 136
intent, vii
intentions, 2, 7, 15, 21, 33, 34, 35, 36, 37, 57, 68, 70, 71, 74, 79, 103, 104, 120, 122, 129, 130, 135, 136, 141, 142, 144, 149, 152, 165, 188, 230, 235, 237, 239, 241, 249, 263, 292, 296, 304, 315, 328, 329, 332, 337, 338, 344, 347
interaction, 68
interactions, 135, 174
interest, vii, 11, 16, 18, 21, 22, 23, 24, 26, 27, 32, 43, 50, 52, 53, 55, 56, 67, 72, 74, 79, 81, 83, 85, 90, 93, 94, 96, 97, 102, 107, 108, 141, 144, 150, 154, 165, 180, 181, 191, 192, 197, 202, 206, 207, 209, 211, 213, 215, 217, 218, 219, 225, 228, 231, 243, 250, 251, 252, 256, 258, 260, 280, 281, 282, 284, 291, 295, 296, 300, 301, 303, 308, 310, 311, 313, 314, 318, 321, 325, 328, 337, 341, 342, 343, 344, 345, 364, 368
interest groups, 96, 97
interest rates, 21, 107, 256, 300, 308, 342, 343, 345
interface, 114, 235, 237
interference, 68, 115, 172, 174, 207, 208, 288
international law, 108, 173, 212, 213, 278
International Monetary Fund, 109, 116, 117, 258, 280, 334, 344
international trade, 25, 184, 256, 336
interpretation, 15, 51, 64, 68, 130, 145, 244
interrelations, 43
interrelationships, 31, 64, 337
interval, 7, 44, 46, 67, 74, 145, 245

intervention, 56, 57, 80, 82, 98, 121, 127, 128, 129, 150, 155, 159, 162, 165, 167, 176, 188, 236, 273, 285, 336, 346
interview, 54, 256
intimacy, 231
intimidation, 242
intoxication, 269
intrinsic value, 22
invariants, 67
investment, 1, 3, 26, 53, 74, 75, 87, 94, 113, 144, 152, 153, 163, 167, 175, 177, 179, 180, 186, 192, 195, 201, 226, 227, 229, 250, 255, 256, 258, 281, 287, 293, 300, 303, 304, 325, 332, 334, 338
investment capital, 226, 227, 251, 304
investors, 3, 90, 250, 251, 256, 296, 304, 306, 345
invisible hand, 26, 56, 57, 58, 68, 126, 165
Iran, 2, 105, 106, 107, 160, 162, 169, 171, 187, 197, 222, 225, 232, 265, 270, 280, 284, 287, 334, 358, 363, 366, 379, 380
Iraq, 6, 49, 55, 80, 107, 134, 160, 163, 171, 172, 183, 187, 208, 225, 251, 264, 265, 267, 268, 269, 270, 272, 273, 275, 276, 285, 287, 359, 380
Iraq War, 359
iris, 242
iron, 28, 110, 257, 323
Islam, 4, 53, 61, 72, 102, 103, 183, 228, 236, 241, 275, 288, 303, 318, 323, 325, 329, 378
Islamic world, 271, 300
isolation, 37, 52, 166, 203, 204, 210, 224, 334
Israel, 80, 105, 106, 223, 229, 239, 267, 268, 275, 276, 278, 279, 288, 303

J

Japan, 27, 105, 130, 161, 173, 176, 187, 197, 221, 254, 255, 258, 285, 344, 372, 383
job skills, 136
jobs, 27, 55, 205, 246, 258, 267, 371
joints, 247
joint-stock companies, 31
Jordan, 2, 296, 372, 373, 378
journalism, 137, 226, 287, 353
judges, 244
judgment, 13, 63, 71
jurisdiction, 2, 115, 160, 173, 188, 189, 212, 216, 344
justice, 82, 136, 137, 204, 227, 242, 289, 301, 330
justification, 18, 51, 56, 70, 74, 81, 133, 142, 153, 166, 167, 236, 237, 238, 286, 336

K

Kenneth Galbraith, 1
Keynes, 26, 51, 153, 167, 281, 373
Keynesian, 27, 62, 153, 167, 281, 372, 378
kidnapping, 88
knees, 151
knowledge, 3, 6, 7, 8, 9, 10, 11, 12, 20, 24, 35, 40, 42, 50, 60, 63, 75, 76, 79, 83, 102, 103, 118, 121, 130, 133, 136, 137, 139, 140, 144, 151, 152, 153, 154, 155, 163, 164, 165, 168, 200, 212, 229, 235, 236, 237, 238, 240, 241, 247, 257, 274, 291, 293, 294, 302, 314, 315, 317, 322, 328, 336, 337, 338, 341, 342, 343, 345, 347, 355, 356
Korea, 134
Kurds, 160, 187, 265, 268, 270, 273
Kuwait, 302, 366, 372

L

labeling, 6
labor, 131, 272
labour, 2, 4, 5, 6, 14, 17, 20, 21, 22, 23, 24, 26, 29, 33, 35, 39, 41, 64, 66, 68, 70, 85, 88, 90, 91, 92, 93, 94, 95, 114, 127, 160, 164, 167, 200, 203, 206, 210, 216, 220, 248, 280, 294, 317, 335, 336, 337, 338, 360
labour force, 66, 206
labour market, 167
Lake Pontchartrain, 156
land, 29, 34, 91, 95, 97, 123, 131, 132, 162, 172, 174, 177, 179, 189, 231, 239, 265, 266, 278, 328, 329, 340
language, 10, 245, 266, 269, 274, 296
laptop, 104, 110
Latin America, 16, 79, 80, 81, 134, 144, 148, 180, 280, 284, 299, 306, 317, 332, 344, 370, 377
Latvia, 221, 298
laughing, 58
laws, 21, 40, 41, 42, 52, 53, 57, 58, 71, 87, 98, 125, 126, 129, 131, 134, 151, 173, 178, 206, 212, 244
layering, 120
layoffs, 94
LDCs, 348, 349, 350, 351
lead, 6, 63, 64, 94, 95, 125, 126, 128, 131, 138, 148, 150, 155, 165, 166, 178, 188, 236, 245, 246, 322, 323
leadership, 18, 79, 133, 239, 241, 317
learning, 18, 153, 341
Lebanon, 80, 272, 287
legal protection, 173, 298
legality, 189
legislation, 215
lending, 21, 105, 305, 306, 314, 330, 338
levees, 156
liability, 2, 18, 179, 204, 297, 298, 303, 307, 310, 332
liberation, 8, 176, 331
licenses, 365
life expectancy, 109, 138, 333, 345
lifespan, 53
lifestyle, 166, 318, 330
lifetime, 31, 47, 77, 79, 229, 293, 320
likelihood, 61, 237, 242
limitation, 223, 302, 323, 336
limited liability, 297
linear model, 52, 137
linear systems, 352, 353
linkage, 27, 30, 127, 185, 353
links, 4, 7, 11, 13, 66, 104, 188, 300, 333, 343, 345, 347, 360
liquefied natural gas, 192, 232
liquidate, 343
liquidity, 167, 251, 259
listening, 50, 275
literacy, 154, 339
Lithuania, 221
living conditions, 14, 67
loans, 128, 295, 305, 306, 307, 308, 309, 310, 311, 312, 343, 344, 345
lobbyists, 178
local authorities, 174, 192
local government, 312
location, 61, 86, 96, 300
logical reasoning, 58
long run, 51, 184, 324
long-term indebtedness, 303
Louisiana, 156, 169
love, 269
loyalty, 132
lubricants, 328
lung cancer, 142
lying, 7, 35, 45, 60, 65, 73, 137, 156, 219, 241, 242, 243, 244, 245, 246, 247, 286, 336
Lyndon Johnson, 179

M

machinery, 5, 20, 98, 107, 210, 235, 236, 248, 252, 267
macroeconomic policy, 116, 117
magazines, 106, 286
magnetic field, 110, 112
malingering, 245
malnutrition, 163

management, 17, 22, 23, 96, 110, 121, 174, 181, 216, 218, 231, 237, 246, 259, 260, 262, 291, 292, 296, 300, 312
mandates, 176, 334
mania, 341
manipulation, 73, 148, 297
mantle, 69
manufactured goods, 252, 253, 254, 345
manufacturing, 4, 89, 163, 252, 253, 258, 335, 344, 345
manure, 319
mapping, 5, 7, 247
marches, 55
marginal utility, 4, 5, 24, 25, 27, 28, 33, 36, 86, 119
marginalization, 65
market, 5, 14, 15, 18, 19, 20, 30, 34, 35, 36, 37, 54, 55, 62, 67, 77, 88, 89, 90, 97, 101, 103, 108, 109, 111, 112, 116, 118, 119, 121, 122, 123, 124, 125, 126, 127, 128, 133, 134, 139, 167, 169, 174, 175, 176, 177, 178, 181, 182, 183, 184, 186, 187, 189, 190, 196, 197, 199, 203, 206, 210, 215, 216, 217, 218, 227, 229, 231, 249, 250, 251, 253, 254, 258, 259, 261, 281, 283, 287, 293, 296, 297, 299, 309, 317, 332, 333, 344, 345, 354, 367
market economy, 118, 119, 126, 127
market failure, 124, 127
market position, 258
market share, 112, 176, 249
marketing, 38, 114, 117, 133, 137, 169, 180, 181, 182, 184, 185, 190, 196, 197, 218, 226, 231, 248, 257, 259, 287, 288, 353
markets, viii, 4, 26, 31, 34, 67, 81, 86, 90, 91, 101, 102, 108, 111, 114, 117, 118, 119, 122, 124, 125, 126, 127, 135, 139, 169, 170, 174, 180, 184, 189, 190, 191, 194, 197, 201, 204, 206, 214, 216, 219, 231, 249, 250, 252, 254, 258, 337, 342, 344, 353
marriage, 20
Marx, viii, 14, 15, 16, 22, 26, 30, 36, 49, 55, 58, 71, 73, 75, 76, 85, 88, 89, 92, 98, 248, 338, 359, 375
masking, 161
mass, 19, 29, 65, 73, 81, 94, 95, 103, 112, 137, 141, 146, 159, 189, 200, 214, 231, 241, 245, 265, 285, 318, 319, 320, 343
materialism, 87
mathematical methods, 155
mathematics, 7, 41, 42, 43, 45, 47, 51, 83, 145, 155, 158
matrix, 12, 13
meals, 266
meanings, 68, 226
measurement, 33, 188, 245, 256
measures, 2, 38, 52, 76, 172, 241, 242, 244, 252, 257, 339, 342

meat, 63, 151, 164
media, 10, 12, 18, 21, 27, 174, 204, 225, 231, 236, 239, 279, 285, 286, 287, 295, 321, 353
mediation, 12
medium of exchange, 22
membership, 7, 54, 74, 237, 300
membranes, 325, 359
memory, 12, 110, 239, 247, 268, 332
men, 23, 42, 71, 105, 107, 131, 142, 208, 263, 330
menstruation, 137
mentor, 47
mergers, 97, 257
metals, 21, 23
metaphor, 2, 6, 56, 337
methanol, 323, 324
methodology, 51, 63
Mexico, 190, 191, 195, 216, 254, 339, 353, 366
microeconomic theory, 4, 120
microstructure, 325
Middle East, 21, 130, 170, 171, 172, 173, 174, 177, 179, 180, 223, 232, 269, 272, 274, 278, 287, 296, 360, 382
migration, 205
military, 6, 10, 36, 39, 80, 81, 86, 105, 108, 111, 114, 115, 116, 130, 133, 160, 165, 188, 207, 222, 223, 239, 251, 253, 266, 278, 279, 284, 285, 287, 301, 331, 333, 346
military spending, 6, 36, 108, 165, 251, 301
milk, 266
Milton Friedman, 62
mining, 63, 90, 205, 206, 283, 335, 357
minorities, 265, 266, 269, 270, 272, 343
minority, 140, 244, 269, 270, 272
misconceptions, 264
missions, 134, 252, 286
Mississippi River, 156
misunderstanding, 59, 92, 138, 272, 273
mixing, 321
mobile phone, 312
mode, 5, 12, 14, 24, 25, 40, 48, 59, 70, 84, 88, 92, 93, 94, 96, 98, 105, 155, 185
modeling, 2, 8, 45, 47, 52, 75, 78, 79, 120, 121, 122, 190, 198, 200, 225, 292, 322, 335
models, 35, 47, 51, 52, 53, 54, 75, 77, 102, 118, 119, 120, 121, 123, 133, 137, 139, 150, 165, 181, 190, 240, 241, 243, 261, 286, 288, 295, 302, 306, 314, 334, 338, 372
modern capitalism, 74
modern society, 95, 131
modernisation, viii
modernity, 133
modernization, 115
modus operandi, 5, 135, 237

molasses, 323
mold, 321
momentum, 42
money, 4, 5, 14, 15, 16, 17, 18, 19, 20, 21, 22, 23, 24, 54, 57, 89, 91, 93, 94, 105, 108, 123, 129, 131, 132, 133, 134, 135, 136, 139, 144, 162, 168, 179, 210, 248, 250, 251, 255, 256, 259, 260, 262, 293, 294, 295, 296, 298, 300, 301, 302, 303, 304, 307, 310, 311, 313, 316, 317, 320, 325, 338, 340, 341, 342, 343, 344, 346, 371
money laundering, 129
money supply, 108, 250, 342, 346
monomers, 120
monopolistic competition, 112, 127
monopoly, 10, 24, 30, 39, 76, 86, 91, 95, 96, 97, 98, 99, 115, 116, 125, 127, 128, 160, 172, 174, 175, 176, 177, 178, 205, 206, 207, 210, 214, 219, 232, 247, 248, 249, 258, 260, 281, 294, 299
Moon, 166
morale, 118
moratorium, 64, 90, 91, 200, 201, 202, 208, 214, 215, 216, 217
morning, 14, 108, 277
Moscow, 65, 77, 161, 255, 362, 370, 380
mothers, 137
motion, 27, 36, 40, 41, 42, 48, 50, 52, 57, 58, 69, 71, 80, 87, 88, 94, 98, 102, 126, 131, 151, 165, 243, 244, 247, 294, 342
motivation, 20
mountains, 8, 181
movement, 16, 39, 72, 74, 95, 127, 129, 131, 171, 177, 204, 219, 242, 247, 260, 272, 278, 284, 294, 331, 334, 345, 347
multidimensional, 246
multiplication, 6, 33
muscles, 331
music, 17, 227
Muslims, 263, 265, 275, 296, 303
myopia, 129

N

NAFTA, 195, 360
narratives, 57
national income, 202, 351
National Research Council, 325
national security, 115, 179, 242, 245
nationalism, 270, 272, 275
nation-building, 260
Native Americans, 21, 271
native population, 278
NATO, 6, 81, 108, 204, 207, 219, 349
natural evolution, 104, 115

natural gas, 162, 169, 170, 174, 175, 176, 177, 178, 179, 180, 181, 182, 190, 191, 194, 195, 196, 197, 198, 222, 226, 227, 230, 231, 232, 323, 337, 377
natural laws, 42, 58
natural resources, 22, 81, 114, 132, 158, 322
natural sciences, 43, 51, 55, 63, 76, 156, 175, 238
natural selection, 76
nausea, 137, 288
Nazi Germany, 105, 239
needs, 2, 5, 10, 14, 28, 38, 50, 59, 75, 81, 96, 99, 117, 123, 134, 136, 139, 162, 169, 172, 190, 197, 198, 204, 222, 227, 231, 237, 238, 262, 292, 296, 300, 301, 303, 305, 317, 318, 330, 331, 335, 336, 337, 338, 340, 341, 342, 354, 377
negative consequences, 18, 60, 71, 131, 176
neglect, 156
negotiating, 219
Netherlands, 232
network, 14, 49, 107, 116, 169, 180, 184, 230, 310
neurophysiology, 247
neuroscience, 247
New South Wales, 362
New Zealand, 63, 215
newspapers, 286
next generation, 136, 271
NGOs, 349
niche market, 175
Nigeria, 373
Nobel Prize, 62, 104, 116, 117, 123, 144, 285, 368, 374, 379, 381
noise, 256, 284, 288, 355
normal development, 135
normal distribution, 164
North Africa, 231, 232, 269, 274
North America, 11, 16, 66, 81, 89, 95, 115, 135, 166, 169, 195, 196, 202, 204, 206, 214, 216, 218, 226, 227, 228, 230, 232, 242, 263, 269, 271, 287, 295, 299, 336, 340, 353
North American Free Trade Agreement, 195, 214
Norway, 230, 232, 371
novelty, 163
nuclear weapons, 284
nudity, 137
nutrients, 103, 142, 323
nutrition, 142, 163

O

obedience, 162, 222
obesity, 142, 260, 262
objectivity, 70, 241
obligation, 215, 255, 298, 310, 336

observations, 45, 70, 104, 136, 138, 139, 155, 156, 222, 223, 236, 238, 244, 355
Oceania, 21
oceans, viii, 210, 221
octopus, 300
OECD, 129, 182, 183, 184, 185, 282
oil, 2, 13, 28, 29, 92, 105, 106, 107, 127, 150, 159, 160, 162, 168, 169, 170, 171, 172, 173, 174, 175, 176, 177, 178, 179, 180, 181, 182, 183, 184, 185, 186, 187, 188, 189, 190, 191, 193, 195, 197, 198, 200, 201, 202, 203, 205, 207, 211, 213, 215, 217, 221, 222, 223, 224, 225, 226, 227, 228, 229, 230, 231, 251, 255, 287, 292, 317, 323, 325, 326, 327, 328, 329, 345, 360, 361, 362, 364, 365, 366, 367, 369, 375, 378, 384
oil production, 107, 160, 176, 177, 184, 187, 224, 229
oil sands, 196, 207, 223, 225, 360, 361, 364, 365, 366, 369, 375
oil spill, 317, 325, 326, 327, 328, 329
oils, 323
old age, 311
oligopolies, 30, 125, 126, 177, 282
oligopoly, 30, 125, 127, 281, 294
omission, 245
openness, 204
operator, 7, 19, 43, 45, 114, 154, 193, 202, 216
opinion polls, 49
opposition parties, 140
oppression, 91
optimism, 1, 2
orbit, 48, 145, 335
ores, 19, 324
organism, 18, 103
organization, 94, 331
organizations, 261, 275, 310
orientation, 198
oscillation, 289
outline, 36, 240, 258
output, 2, 18, 26, 45, 66, 67, 77, 111, 112, 138, 183, 225, 228, 318, 319, 320, 338, 339, 381
overpopulation, 59
overproduction, 26, 31, 74, 94, 99, 227, 249, 250, 337, 338
overweight, 261, 262
ownership, 17, 26, 30, 67, 92, 96, 113, 114, 128, 172, 174, 215, 218, 249, 252, 259, 260, 298, 299, 302, 337

P

Pacific, 193, 373
pain, 25, 32, 33, 136, 142, 206, 360
Pakistan, 2, 295, 300, 306, 363
Panama, 374
paralysis, 226
parameter, 102
parents, 62, 167
Pareto, 101, 102, 124, 126
Paris Club, 148, 184
partnership, 114, 260, 298
passive, 75, 259
pasteurization, 138
patents, 97
pathways, 1, 3, 54, 77, 117, 124, 135, 145, 146, 159, 237, 302, 314, 315, 338, 342
peers, 51
pension plans, 258, 259
pensioners, 258, 259
pensions, 259
Pentagon, 107, 112, 115, 116, 284
permit, 45, 53, 155, 217, 254, 332
personal responsibility, 18
personality, 79, 132, 243, 264
personality disorder, 243
perspective, 14, 25, 67, 69, 98, 133, 211, 249, 314
persuasion, 10
pessimism, 2
pesticide, 142
pH, 322
Phillips curve, 346
philosophers, 12
physical environment, 120, 121, 302, 316
physical sciences, 47
physics, 58, 81, 145, 380
pitch, 3
planets, 41
planning, 2, 72, 82, 117, 129, 176, 190, 258, 284, 340
plants, 90, 103, 122, 134, 178, 191, 209, 215, 218, 258, 319
plastic surgery, 138
plastics, 136, 138, 225, 228
pleasure, 25, 32, 33, 269
PM, 273, 276, 277, 381
poison, 172
Poland, 17, 221, 333
police, 107, 174, 298
political crisis, 214
political parties, 208
politics, 15, 48, 55, 63, 64, 66, 68, 70, 79, 80, 82, 129, 148, 189, 208, 278, 280, 328, 334
polling, 285, 286
polluters, 329
pollution, 1, 127, 134, 181, 322
polymeric membranes, 325

polymers, 120
polypropylene, 327
pools, 90
poor, 16, 53, 59, 62, 81, 116, 236, 306, 308, 331, 338
poor performance, 62
population, 22, 59, 60, 61, 66, 74, 89, 131, 133, 138, 143, 160, 163, 172, 188, 190, 194, 197, 202, 204, 205, 224, 225, 227, 232, 242, 265, 266, 268, 271, 272, 273, 274, 275, 280, 281, 287, 318, 330, 331, 333, 343, 345
population density, 271
population growth, 59, 143, 225, 330
porosity, 125, 126
portfolio, 208, 218
ports, 174, 193, 197, 203, 209, 215
posture, 42, 144, 344
potassium, 324
poverty, 82, 83, 128, 305, 306, 313, 333, 338, 382
poverty line, 306, 313
power, 4, 5, 12, 14, 15, 20, 21, 22, 23, 27, 29, 32, 57, 68, 77, 79, 81, 83, 92, 93, 96, 97, 98, 105, 110, 112, 115, 117, 123, 127, 131, 132, 133, 135, 140, 152, 154, 158, 159, 160, 162, 174, 177, 178, 182, 186, 187, 190, 191, 197, 200, 210, 213, 216, 222, 226, 229, 230, 242, 248, 249, 250, 255, 275, 279, 281, 294, 300, 302, 303, 317, 328, 329, 331, 332, 341, 342, 343, 349
power plants, 177, 178, 191
power sharing, 131
pragmatism, 40, 87, 116
precipitation, 221
prediction, 76, 85, 102, 222, 223, 224, 225
preference, 24, 70, 335
pregnancy, 137
prejudice, 14, 47, 51, 60, 139, 225, 242, 340, 355
premature death, 134, 262
preparation, 333
preparedness, 55
presidency, 17, 55, 179, 229, 279
President Clinton, 10
pressure, 13, 50, 51, 107, 177, 181, 208, 237, 244, 279, 321, 329, 338, 341
prevention, 278
price band, 186, 187, 228
price index, 184
price mechanism, 228
prices, 13, 31, 91, 101, 125, 128, 169, 170, 175, 181, 182, 183, 184, 186, 187, 190, 191, 196, 201, 217, 222, 228, 251, 259, 346, 360, 364, 368, 378, 381
primacy, 77, 150
primary products, 336
prime rate, 344

principle, 5, 16, 19, 25, 36, 39, 53, 56, 57, 65, 70, 74, 78, 82, 99, 103, 112, 126, 132, 145, 152, 164, 173, 193, 198, 206, 210, 212, 219, 243, 248, 258, 284, 298, 299, 301, 303, 319, 326, 335
prisoners, 160, 188
prisons, 18
private investment, 81
private ownership, 16, 17, 76, 82, 299, 332
private sector, 16, 17, 19, 81, 117, 152, 153, 195
privatization, 10, 128
probability, 7, 52, 60, 63, 76, 122
probability distribution, 52, 60
processing stages, 320
producers, 33, 71, 87, 88, 89, 93, 95, 107, 161, 167, 176, 178, 180, 181, 184, 185, 186, 190, 192, 195, 219, 221, 229, 248, 250, 279, 338
production, vii, viii, ix, 4, 6, 13, 14, 15, 18, 19, 20, 23, 25, 26, 27, 28, 29, 30, 31, 33, 34, 37, 38, 53, 56, 57, 59, 67, 71, 74, 75, 76, 80, 82, 83, 84, 86, 88, 89, 92, 93, 94, 95, 96, 98, 99, 104, 105, 108, 110, 113, 114, 121, 122, 127, 132, 133, 139, 150, 151, 158, 159, 160, 161, 165, 168, 169, 170, 171, 177, 179, 181, 182, 184, 185, 186, 187, 189, 190, 191, 192, 195, 197, 200, 201, 202, 206, 209, 210, 215, 216, 217, 218, 219, 220, 223, 224, 225, 226, 227, 229, 230, 231, 232, 246, 248, 249, 250, 252, 253, 255, 257, 259, 260, 280, 281, 282, 292, 296, 302, 316, 317, 318, 319, 323, 324, 332, 335, 337, 338, 342, 344, 346, 349, 350, 352, 369
production function, 34, 71, 185
production quota, 186
productive capacity, 216, 221
productivity, 30, 67, 105, 323
profit margin, 139, 353
profitability, 197
profits, 1, 6, 26, 72, 84, 86, 94, 111, 115, 125, 132, 167, 179, 182, 185, 187, 201, 222, 229, 243, 248, 249, 250, 251, 296, 306, 333, 343, 360
program, 8, 108, 111, 112, 114, 135, 140, 153, 161, 178, 198, 237, 245, 250, 251, 262, 263, 279, 281, 283
programmability, 112
programming, 115
proliferation, 21, 329
promoter, 204
propaganda, 112, 143, 230, 271, 274, 285, 286
propagation, 301, 302
property rights, 258
proposition, 3, 30, 97, 127, 243
prosperity, 133, 345
protocol, 211
Prozac, 136, 142
psychiatrist, 246

psychology, 43, 166, 211, 285
public corporations, 258
public financing, 192
public health, 109, 324, 329, 333
public interest, 56, 128
public opinion, 16, 80, 279, 285, 286
public schools, 61, 62
public sector, 18, 19, 152
public service, 16, 207
public support, 285
pulse, 103, 106
pumps, 360
punishment, 334
purchasing power, 24, 252
purification, 319
PVC, 149

Q

qualifications, 55
qualitative differences, 95
quality of life, 144
Quantity Theory of Money, 367, 368
quantum mechanics, 52, 58, 76
query, 249
question mark, 265
questioning, 27, 278
quotas, 207, 216, 217

R

race, 15, 187, 214, 271, 365
racism, 16
radar, 159, 226
radio, 261
rain, 55, 221, 230, 300
rain forest, 55
range, 3, 5, 13, 20, 22, 37, 42, 48, 55, 64, 81, 83, 102, 111, 114, 130, 146, 151, 155, 184, 189, 209, 211, 235, 245, 248, 252, 261, 291, 300, 305, 317, 319, 323, 339, 347, 352
rape, 337
rate of return, 177, 255, 303
rationalisation, 94
rationality, 122
raw materials, 70, 81, 84, 189, 197, 225, 336, 338, 345
readership, 225
reading, 154, 171, 269, 272
real numbers, 7
real time, 68
realism, 317

reality, 7, 12, 18, 20, 25, 26, 37, 43, 45, 47, 48, 50, 52, 53, 59, 60, 66, 69, 70, 71, 81, 96, 98, 102, 103, 104, 109, 113, 115, 116, 117, 119, 131, 137, 145, 152, 156, 162, 164, 168, 181, 190, 193, 198, 200, 201, 205, 210, 224, 225, 227, 229, 238, 240, 244, 275, 278, 280, 286, 287, 288, 317, 332, 334, 355
reasoning, 60, 61, 71, 74, 82, 85, 135, 165, 225, 244
recall, 279
recalling, 288
reception, 139, 154
recession, 27, 107, 112
reciprocity, 206, 212
recognition, 31, 78, 128, 135, 144, 151, 162, 218, 250, 330
reconcile, 85, 122, 126, 314
reconciliation, 99
reconstruction, 68, 72, 171, 302
recovery, 206, 245, 307, 317, 325, 326, 327, 328
recovery technology, 317
recruiting, 96
recurrence, 74
recycling, 103, 347
reduction, 9, 77, 84, 86, 153, 246, 267, 281, 305, 306
reference frame, 76, 130, 161, 198
refining, 8, 54, 127, 161, 169, 180, 181, 182, 184, 185, 187, 188, 198, 228, 243, 292
reflection, 13, 197
reforms, 16, 127, 140
refugees, 204
regenerate, 99
regeneration, 318
regulation, 176, 177, 329
regulations, 2, 212, 213, 261, 263
regulatory bodies, 27, 261
regulatory oversight, 176
reinforcement, 285, 332
rejection, 32, 70, 161, 198, 201, 219, 220, 221, 298
relationship, 11, 30, 31, 36, 37, 53, 56, 60, 65, 124, 141, 150, 168, 198, 200, 206, 212, 237, 346, 352, 372
relationships, vii, 9, 21, 24, 30, 33, 53, 56, 70, 75, 89, 93, 135, 200, 226, 342
relative size, 37
relativity, 76
relevance, 35, 295, 328
reliability, 130
religion, 16, 22, 131, 270, 273, 274, 296
renewable energy, 162, 222
rent, 94, 179
repair, 16, 136, 188
repetitions, 23

replacement, 17, 29, 76, 85, 111, 115, 131, 152, 159, 162, 191, 202, 220, 222, 227, 230, 248, 316, 322
repression, 114, 280
reproduction, 19, 36, 92, 93, 293, 337
Republicans, 367
reputation, 62, 77, 129, 204, 279, 339
reserve currency, 23, 106, 252, 333
reserves, 28, 166, 170, 195, 222, 223, 224, 225, 230, 231, 232, 258, 314, 375
resistance, 16, 27, 38, 39, 48, 115, 166, 181, 187, 193, 200, 212, 239, 329, 338, 349
resolution, 78
resources, 4, 8, 10, 18, 26, 32, 38, 57, 62, 75, 91, 112, 126, 127, 159, 164, 171, 172, 174, 177, 181, 189, 194, 197, 198, 200, 202, 212, 213, 216, 217, 224, 226, 294, 298, 307, 336, 344, 349, 372
respiration, 244
responsibility, 1, 2, 18, 26, 32, 60, 72, 131, 135, 154, 161, 165, 204, 207, 215, 221, 239, 291, 307, 315, 344
restitution, 185
restructuring, 178, 258, 260
retail, 338, 353
retaliation, 30
retention, 218
retina, 242
retirement, 167, 179, 312, 341
retrieval, 12
returns, 293, 338
revenue, 19, 56, 91, 179, 185, 190, 197, 198, 217, 228, 248, 259, 296, 304, 305, 308, 312, 344
rewards, 54, 132, 283, 314
rice, 163, 344
Richard Nixon, 105, 229
rights, 17, 32, 89, 108, 131, 132, 134, 172, 173, 174, 175, 180, 189, 191, 204, 212, 213, 216, 242, 243, 280, 288, 299, 340, 342, 365
risk, 22, 119, 133, 150, 179, 184, 250, 252, 260, 279, 291, 297, 313, 345
Ronald Reagan, 10, 16, 38, 334
rule of law, 278
runoff, 134
rural people, 322
rural population, 59
Russia, viii, 17, 54, 76, 81, 110, 127, 154, 162, 166, 180, 184, 201, 230, 231, 232, 298, 316, 345, 347, 362, 382, 383

S

sacrifice, 317
Saddam Hussein, 49, 55, 107, 184, 285
safety, 2, 136, 167, 261, 262
sales, 3, 105, 139, 178, 179, 185, 186, 219, 228, 261, 285, 286, 345, 347, 353
salmon, 209
sample, 152, 164, 243, 286
sampling, 322
sanctions, 135, 183
satisfaction, 26, 86, 127, 302
saturated fat, 142
saturation, 177
Saudi Arabia, 107, 171, 173, 225, 228, 230, 287, 363
savings, 23, 153, 167, 168, 280, 281, 282, 283, 296, 310, 311, 313, 319, 338, 341
savings account, 296, 310, 311
scandal, 17, 140, 179, 190, 302
scarce resources, 26
scarcity, 28, 32, 229
schema, 42, 52, 118, 149, 223, 296
scholarship, 50, 274
school, 52, 61, 62, 92, 95, 118, 135, 154, 163, 210, 216, 221, 271, 309, 338, 339
schooling, 154, 164
scientific method, 16, 36, 69, 73, 75, 175
scientific theory, 59
scores, 2, 217, 267
search, 8, 23, 89, 170, 174, 191, 219, 227, 245
searches, 132
Second World, 8, 27, 105, 112, 114, 153, 167, 170, 171, 173, 184, 207, 209, 225, 229, 239, 278, 285, 288, 316, 343, 381
Secretary of the Treasury, 10
security, 56, 106, 167, 195, 241, 244, 250, 349
sedentary lifestyle, 261
seed, 255
seeding, 282
segregation, 16
seizure, 206
selecting, 47, 59, 114, 139, 145, 286
self, 5, 9, 17, 18, 20, 23, 25, 26, 28, 32, 48, 56, 70, 75, 90, 133, 137, 138, 140, 141, 142, 150, 151, 154, 173, 198, 207, 227, 228, 235, 237, 240, 241, 245, 246, 275, 276, 278, 280, 294, 299, 303, 305, 314, 316, 317, 329, 330, 334, 335, 338, 340, 347, 355
self-employment, 305
self-interest, 20, 25, 26, 32, 56, 133, 137, 138, 142, 151, 237, 245, 246, 314, 316, 329, 330
semiconductor, 112
Senate, 140, 366, 376
sensitivity, 53
separation, 48, 68, 70, 127, 134, 161, 178, 180, 198, 201, 219, 220, 221, 316, 325, 326, 359, 373
September 11, 242

series, 45, 75, 96, 97, 106, 111, 165, 237, 264, 269, 271, 287, 288, 295, 323, 325, 372
service provider, 97
services, 10, 15, 16, 17, 18, 19, 21, 24, 26, 33, 34, 38, 56, 82, 97, 114, 133, 143, 172, 178, 184, 190, 210, 250, 281, 282, 295, 296, 298, 306, 309, 312, 328, 332, 336, 339, 349
set theory, 246
sewage, 267, 340
sex, 137, 303, 341
sexism, 265
shade, 245
shame, 7, 316
shape, 177, 341
shaping, 355
shareholders, 18, 128, 132, 163, 246, 250, 313
shares, 36, 80, 88, 116, 206, 210, 229, 249, 250, 251, 258, 259, 260, 281
sharing, 131, 228, 291, 335, 349
sheep, 266, 325
shellfish, 215
shelter, 156, 167
Shiites, 265, 268, 270
shock, 105, 168, 286, 333, 380
shores, 209
shortage, 40, 182, 204, 239, 360
shoulders, 67, 250
shrimp, 207, 210, 215
sign, 21, 33, 51, 214, 244, 251, 307
signals, 250, 251, 365
Silicon Valley, 115
silver, 21, 221
similarity, 84
Singapore, 357, 373
single market, 110
skeleton, 36
skimming, 326
skin, 142, 242, 244, 325
skin cancer, 142
slavery, 91, 95, 117
slaves, 21, 22, 88, 131, 204, 299, 314
small firms, 298
smoke, 257, 321
snakes, 266, 267
social capital, 74
social change, 165
social class, 32, 83, 89, 96, 203
social control, 1
social development, 1, 14, 22, 49, 96, 137, 138, 148
social environment, 316, 355
social events, 52
social fabric, viii
social indicator, 128

social justice, 82
social life, 82
social movements, 80
social order, 26, 27, 49, 59, 75, 316
social participation, 150
social phenomena, 50
social problems, 1, 291
social psychology, 353
social relations, vii, 36, 37, 86, 94, 95, 96, 151, 161
social responsibility, 75, 154, 158, 159, 240, 339
social sciences, 51, 52, 55, 60, 63, 75, 76, 79, 138, 146, 156, 159, 163, 355
social services, 18, 81, 335
social standing, 132
social status, 303
social support, 167
social theory, 16
social welfare, 128
socialism, 77, 79, 80, 83, 221
sodium, 324
sodium hydroxide, 324
software, 108, 115, 120, 283
soil, 103, 142
solar system, 145
solidarity, 343
South Asia, 305, 380
South Korea, 255, 269, 344
Southeast Asia, 106, 111, 112, 346
sovereignty, 65, 89, 131, 174, 184, 208, 211, 213, 214, 216, 217, 219
Soviet Union, vii, 10, 19, 36, 39, 49, 65, 79, 80, 81, 82, 90, 106, 109, 119, 128, 133, 134, 161, 201, 202, 214, 221, 222, 223, 229, 231, 232, 252, 253, 297, 301, 333, 339, 345, 349
Spain, 68, 299, 306, 363, 372
specialisation, 29, 130, 154
species, ix, 15, 51, 59, 64, 65, 75, 102, 126, 161, 166, 198, 200, 209, 214, 215, 217, 218, 221, 323, 337
specific knowledge, 163
spectrum, 2, 13, 27, 110, 114, 127, 129, 154, 165, 245, 284, 288
speculation, 27, 169, 202, 316
speech, 139, 144, 372
speed, 41, 48, 106, 303
speed of light, 41
spelling, 211
sperm, 142
spin, 310, 366
spot market, 169
Sri Lanka, 377
stability, viii, 32, 53, 110, 326
stages, 57, 80, 115, 172, 205, 288, 317

stagflation, 36
standard error, 138
standard of living, 67
standards, 130, 134, 137, 160, 164, 188, 278, 284, 317, 333
stars, 313
starvation, 25
stasis, viii, 77
state intervention, 56, 82
state planning, 82
statistics, 52, 109, 128, 204, 205, 262, 265, 266, 268, 269, 283, 293
steel, 29, 190, 257, 258, 259, 260
steel industry, 257, 260
stimulus, 250
stock, 6, 29, 31, 90, 96, 108, 115, 118, 161, 163, 167, 198, 200, 218, 221, 249, 250, 251, 253, 254, 258, 259, 296, 332, 333
stock exchange, 108, 250
stock markets, 6, 31, 108, 115, 333
stock price, 163
storage, 21, 104, 175, 178, 192, 328, 364
store of value, 22
strategic planning, 106
strategies, 118
stratification, 210, 343
streams, 61, 62, 210, 322, 325, 373
strength, 37, 89, 126, 136, 160, 188, 257, 329
stress, 214, 244, 276
strictures, 298
stroke, 109, 204
strontium, 322
structural adjustment, 332, 334, 344
students, 154, 255, 309, 330, 331
subjective judgments, 165
subpoena, 298
subscribers, 312
subsidy, 13, 91
subsistence, 89, 163
substitutes, 127, 291, 315
substitution, 96, 230, 247, 258, 284, 320, 321
subtraction, 7
sugar, 138, 204, 321, 323
suicidal behavior, 142
suicide, 2, 279
sulfur, 181
summaries, 264
summer, 184, 266, 295, 339
Sun, 87, 132, 138, 145, 166
Sunnis, 265, 268, 270, 272, 273
superiority, 17, 49, 56, 338
suppliers, 101, 177, 178, 181, 231

supply, 5, 8, 9, 13, 17, 19, 25, 28, 34, 36, 48, 57, 59, 82, 90, 91, 101, 106, 124, 125, 159, 161, 162, 165, 175, 176, 177, 178, 181, 182, 183, 184, 195, 200, 221, 222, 224, 225, 226, 227, 232, 254, 258, 259, 281, 292, 293, 294, 296, 298, 323, 332, 333, 337, 343, 347, 352, 354, 365
suppression, 24, 76, 103, 184, 279, 288
Supreme Court, 2, 172, 173, 176, 204
surplus, 1, 5, 6, 14, 19, 49, 65, 84, 85, 86, 89, 90, 92, 93, 94, 95, 98, 99, 216, 248, 249, 253, 255, 281, 296, 318, 336, 338, 344
surprise, 205, 286
surveillance, 240, 284
survival, 15, 55, 115, 165, 175, 308, 309
suspects, 241, 242, 244, 262, 284
sustainability, 11, 103, 150, 161, 162, 220, 222, 226, 236, 291, 295, 314, 318, 324, 326, 329, 330, 331, 332, 334, 335, 339, 340, 373
sustainable development, 121, 291, 315, 330, 331, 332, 334, 335, 338, 340
Sweden, 129
switching, 112, 114
symmetry, 47, 137
symptom, 124, 227, 301
symptoms, 11, 116, 124, 125, 142, 235
syndrome, 10, 38, 39, 55, 56, 59, 69, 70, 72, 73
synthesis, 236, 314, 315, 329, 335, 339, 340, 356
synthetic fiber, 149
synthetic polymers, 325
systems, viii, 52, 71, 80, 82, 92, 106, 107, 108, 111, 112, 116, 130, 133, 163, 164, 172, 174, 176, 226, 227, 228, 247, 286, 300, 302, 303, 317, 318, 322, 332, 334, 337, 338, 339, 340, 352

T

takeover, 17, 94, 332, 372
talent, 82
tangible resources, 151
tanks, 331
Tanzania, 21
targets, 11, 12, 230, 331, 334, 346
tariff, 332, 344
tax collection, 272
tax incentive, 179
taxation, 152, 153, 185, 281
teachers, 275
teaching, 61, 63, 103
technological change, 28, 29
technological developments, 104
technological revolution, 110, 225
technology, 29, 52, 103, 104, 106, 110, 111, 112, 113, 114, 115, 116, 118, 125, 126, 127, 133, 136,

138, 142, 143, 148, 152, 181, 224, 229, 232, 241, 243, 245, 247, 292, 294, 295, 310, 319, 321, 322, 324, 325, 326, 328, 330, 331, 380
teeth, 284
telecommunications, 97
telephone, 97, 312
television, 97, 106, 286, 288, 383
temperature, 246, 321
tension, 242
terminals, 193, 194, 230
terrorism, 230, 271
terrorist acts, 284
test scores, 62
textbooks, 19, 178
Thailand, 129
theft, 260
theory, 4, 5, 6, 7, 8, 9, 11, 15, 16, 19, 20, 24, 25, 26, 27, 36, 41, 42, 43, 51, 54, 56, 59, 72, 76, 79, 80, 81, 82, 83, 84, 85, 86, 92, 95, 101, 103, 116, 117, 118, 119, 120, 121, 122, 124, 126, 145, 146, 151, 158, 161, 162, 165, 168, 174, 188, 189, 219, 225, 226, 227, 229, 230, 235, 236, 237, 240, 245, 247, 254, 255, 256, 280, 283, 284, 285, 299, 332, 355, 356, 378, 382
thermodynamics, 25, 373
thinking, viii, 50, 77, 79, 114, 118, 119, 121, 137, 141, 146, 151, 152, 156, 175, 246, 247, 257, 260, 261, 269, 271, 293, 316, 341, 356
Third World, 23, 54, 282, 305, 342
threat, 11, 21, 24, 26, 54, 107, 225, 228, 241, 242, 252, 289, 360
threats, 332
three-dimensional space, 34, 35
threshold, 186, 226, 293, 319
timber, 95
time, viii, 1, 2, 3, 4, 6, 7, 8, 9, 10, 11, 12, 13, 14, 19, 20, 21, 22, 23, 24, 25, 26, 27, 28, 29, 30, 31, 37, 38, 39, 40, 41, 43, 45, 47, 49, 50, 51, 52, 53, 55, 56, 58, 59, 60, 62, 63, 64, 65, 66, 67, 68, 69, 70, 71, 72, 73, 74, 75, 76, 77, 78, 79, 80, 81, 82, 83, 84, 85, 87, 90, 94, 95, 97, 98, 101, 102, 103, 104, 105, 106, 107, 108, 110, 111, 112, 113, 115, 117, 121, 125, 126, 127, 132, 134, 140, 144, 145, 146, 147, 151, 153, 154, 156, 158, 159, 161, 163, 165, 166, 167, 169, 170, 171, 172, 173, 174, 176, 179, 180, 183, 184, 187, 189, 191, 192, 198, 200, 201, 202, 205, 206, 207, 208, 210, 212, 214, 215, 216, 217, 219, 220, 221, 222, 224, 227, 228, 229, 230, 231, 232, 237, 244, 245, 247, 248, 249, 250, 251, 256, 257, 259, 260, 262, 263, 264, 268, 272, 274, 281, 285, 286, 288, 293, 294, 298, 299, 300, 310, 311, 312, 315, 316, 317, 320, 321, 322, 328, 329, 330, 331, 332, 333, 335, 336, 337, 338, 339, 344, 347, 349, 353, 356, 377
time factors, 102
time frame, 104, 274
timing, 179
tin, 212
tissue, 336
tobacco, 138, 295
Togo, 21
tornadoes, 157
torture, 107
total product, 232
toxicity, 243
toys, 29
tracking, 262
trade, viii, 8, 14, 21, 22, 23, 27, 54, 56, 90, 95, 107, 108, 169, 184, 195, 202, 204, 205, 206, 208, 220, 226, 251, 252, 253, 254, 255, 256, 257, 260, 296, 332, 333, 334, 336, 340, 344, 345, 381, 384
trade deficit, 251, 252, 253, 254, 255, 256, 257
trade union, 202, 260
trade war, 226
trading, 4, 22, 54, 55, 88, 108, 186, 206, 226, 249, 250, 251, 252, 253, 260, 344, 345
tradition, 54, 95, 295, 304
traffic, 68, 88, 107, 204
training, 85, 136, 152, 155, 257, 274
traits, 150
tranches, 252
transactions, 9, 37, 92, 94, 102, 106, 108, 250, 283
transformation, 23, 67, 68, 82, 83, 86, 88, 118, 126, 153, 203, 316, 320
transformations, ix, 68, 317, 321
transistor, 110, 111, 112
transition, 5, 90, 113, 114, 127, 148, 154
transitions, 75, 138, 149, 294
translation, 32, 239, 377
transmission, 24, 104, 141, 232, 284, 337, 338
transparency, 128, 129, 241, 280, 294
transport, 10, 16, 18, 38, 176, 177, 180, 181, 184, 203, 204, 228, 309, 336, 367
transportation, 131, 177, 178, 184, 226, 309
trauma, 167
Treasury bills, 250
treaties, 174, 206, 219
trend, 8, 15, 28, 49, 63, 68, 137, 141, 147, 150, 163, 181, 182, 197, 202, 248, 251, 253, 260, 295, 300, 347, 348, 349, 350, 351, 353
trial, 242, 340
tribes, 160, 166, 172, 187, 274
triggers, 112
trust, 24, 97, 152, 160, 298, 299, 302, 305
trustworthiness, 305

tuition, 309
turbulence, 52
Turkey, 2, 359
turnover, 305
two-dimensional space, 35

U

U.S. economy, 107, 191, 252, 253, 258, 289, 302, 334
U.S. Geological Survey, 224
U.S. Treasury, 105, 108
UK, 286, 363, 369, 378, 383
UN, 225, 305, 306
uncertainty, 52, 76, 167, 224, 251
unemployment, 19, 36, 94, 107, 124, 165, 207, 345, 346, 380
unemployment rate, 345, 346
uniform, 35, 74, 76, 137, 151, 293
Union Carbide, 300
unions, 62, 306, 314, 360
unit cost, 28, 29, 113
United Kingdom, 232, 368, 378
United Nations, 115, 163, 216, 220, 278, 284, 295, 329, 349, 382, 383
United States, 15, 16, 38, 49, 63, 80, 81, 83, 85, 89, 90, 105, 106, 107, 108, 109, 115, 117, 118, 128, 129, 133, 135, 137, 144, 146, 152, 156, 160, 171, 173, 176, 178, 180, 186, 187, 189, 190, 191, 193, 194, 195, 198, 201, 202, 204, 209, 211, 212, 213, 216, 218, 222, 225, 229, 232, 239, 241, 253, 254, 257, 258, 264, 278, 279, 284, 285, 286, 287, 288, 295, 300, 302, 327, 334, 336, 339, 342, 343, 344, 357, 368, 371, 382, 383
universality, 87
universe, 58, 70, 71, 76
universities, 77, 136, 235, 236, 309
updating, 223
uranium, 384
urban areas, 191
urban centers, 192
urban centres, 23
urine, 138
Uruguay, 91, 332
Uruguay Round, 91, 332
USSR, 122, 349, 380
Uzbekistan, 232

V

vacuum, 110, 301, 327
validity, 26, 120, 244

values, 7, 33, 42, 44, 45, 73, 75, 93, 108, 127, 145, 168, 190, 263, 288
variable, 74, 93, 155, 248, 338
variables, 25, 40, 155, 158
variance, 277
vector, 43
vegetable oil, 323, 324
vegetables, 151, 266, 340
vegetation, 120
vehicles, 33, 167, 250
vein, 165, 314, 329
velocity, 42, 246
Venezuela, 13, 110, 134, 160, 169, 188, 280, 336, 358, 376, 379
venture capital, 258
vertical integration, 31, 337
vessels, 14, 91, 107, 161, 174, 200, 201, 206, 209, 212, 214, 217, 219, 221, 328, 336
victims, 148, 280, 335, 340
Vietnam, 81, 105, 107, 111, 112
village, 166, 295, 305, 306, 313, 314, 317, 340
viruses, 150
vision, 83, 84, 91, 251, 265
voice, 140, 224, 286
volatility, 251
voodoo economics, 334
voting, 246
vouchers, 62
vulnerability, 24, 196, 205, 228

W

wage rate, 220
wages, 18, 84, 90, 127, 206, 248, 338
walking, 55
war, 6, 19, 55, 89, 96, 115, 116, 131, 163, 167, 171, 176, 184, 190, 192, 204, 223, 225, 229, 230, 244, 248, 251, 284, 285, 288, 292, 295, 341, 360
war crimes, 204
Warsaw Pact, 80, 331, 333
Washington Consensus, 116, 332, 333
water, 19, 35, 55, 61, 81, 132, 134, 142, 156, 196, 221, 246, 266, 319, 321, 323, 325, 326, 327, 336
watershed, 40
wealth, ix, 9, 20, 21, 22, 28, 39, 64, 68, 69, 74, 75, 82, 90, 92, 93, 96, 101, 102, 125, 128, 150, 152, 160, 161, 181, 185, 201, 205, 220, 227, 228, 260, 292, 294, 298, 314, 317, 333, 337, 338, 362, 382
weapons, 36, 106, 111, 114, 116, 133, 285, 301, 334
weapons of mass destruction, 285
wear, 84, 248
web, 308, 342
welfare, 26, 126, 201

welfare economics, 126
well-being, 310, 342, 345
wells, 184, 365, 378
West Indies, 88, 204
Western aid, 17
Western Civilization, 277
Western countries, 19, 231, 330
wetting, 138
wheat, 95, 239, 344
White House, 376
wholesale, 243, 338
wilderness, 91, 224
wildlife, 140
wind, 156, 162, 181, 222, 382
windows, 288, 296
winter, 157, 184, 191, 193, 215, 231, 251, 353
witnesses, 188
wives, 299
women, 105, 131, 137, 173, 208, 263, 306, 307, 312, 343
wood, 81, 138, 142, 194, 321, 323, 324, 336
wool, 287
words, 19, 29, 54, 58, 72, 79, 87, 88, 96, 126, 129, 211, 237, 239, 244, 245, 260, 296, 354
work, ix, 1, 2, 7, 9, 11, 14, 15, 18, 20, 35, 36, 38, 39, 40, 41, 42, 43, 45, 47, 49, 50, 51, 52, 59, 60, 61, 62, 64, 65, 67, 68, 69, 71, 72, 76, 77, 78, 79, 85, 86, 87, 89, 94, 98, 101, 102, 103, 104, 115, 116, 117, 118, 119, 120, 123, 126, 128, 132, 137, 138, 139, 144, 146, 150, 151, 152, 155, 168, 175, 178, 190, 199, 200, 204, 208, 210, 216, 219, 224, 225, 236, 237, 244, 245, 247, 248, 263, 265, 267, 280, 285, 288, 291, 294, 311, 312, 314, 321, 328, 329, 330, 335, 336, 338, 347, 355
workers, 2, 5, 17, 24, 30, 37, 52, 67, 81, 88, 93, 98, 110, 114, 119, 123, 124, 136, 202, 207, 216, 224, 248, 258, 336, 338, 347
workflow, 18
working conditions, 67, 248
working memory, 247
working population, 210
workplace, 115
World Bank, 109, 116, 117, 118, 144, 258, 280, 306, 332, 334, 344, 382
World Trade Organization (WTO), 109, 332
World War I, 86, 176, 281, 306, 370
World Wide Web, 8, 115, 263
worry, 167, 254, 311
writing, 11, 20, 21, 23, 30, 63, 130, 151, 174, 193, 264, 267, 268, 269, 271, 272, 275, 312

Y

Yemen, 171
yield, 42, 142
young men, 135
Yugoslavia, 204, 333

Z

zinc, 163, 322
zoology, 36
zooplankton, 103